REVISED EDITION

THE
POLITICS OF LAW

A PROGRESSIVE CRITIQUE

REVISED EDITION

THE
POLITICS OF LAW

A PROGRESSIVE CRITIQUE

EDITED BY DAVID KAIRYS

PANTHEON BOOKS  NEW YORK

"The History of Mainstream Legal Thought" Copyright © 1982, 1990 by Elizabeth Mensch • "Legal Education as Training for Hierarchy" Copyright © 1982 by Duncan Kennedy • "Critical Theory and Labor Relations Law" Copyright © 1982, 1990 by Karl E. Klare • "Social Duties and the Problem of Rights in the American Welfare State" (previously, in different form, as "Legal Entitlement and Welfare Benefits") Copyright © 1982, 1990 by Rand E. Rosenblatt • "Law and Race in Early America" Copyright © 1982 by W. Haywood Burns • "Antidiscrimination Law: The View from 1989" Copyright © 1990 by Alan Freeman • "Women's Subordination and the Role of Law" (previously, in different form, as "Perspectives on Women's Subordination and the Role of Law") Copyright © 1982, 1990 by Nadine Taub and Elizabeth M. Schneider • "A Crime Not Fit to Be Named: Sex, Lies, and the Constitution" Copyright © 1990 by Rhonda Copelon • "The Politics of Constitutional Law" Copyright © 1990 by Mark Tushnet • "Foreign Affairs and the Constitution" Copyright © 1990 by Jules Lobel • "Crime, Justice, and the Social Environment" Copyright © 1990 by Elliott Currie • "The Criminal Justice System and the Role of the Police" Copyright © 1982, 1990 by David Rudovsky • "Torts" Copyright © 1982, 1990 by Richard L. Abel • "The Doctrine of Objective Causation" Copyright © 1982 by Morton J. Horwitz • "Contract Law as Ideology" Copyright © 1982, 1990 by Jay M. Feinman and Peter Gabel • "Contract Versus Politics in Corporation Doctrine" Copyright © 1990 by William H. Simon • "New Developments in Legal Theory" Copyright © 1982, 1990 by Robert W. Gordon • "The Radical Tradition in the Law" Copyright © 1982 by Victor Rabinowitz • "A Critique of Conservative Legal Thought" Copyright © 1990 by Mark Kelman • "The Sex of Law" Copyright © 1990 by Frances Olsen • "The Role of Law in Progressive Politics" Copyright © 1990 by Cornel West

Grateful acknowledgment is made to the following for permission to reprint previously published material: *Stanford Law Review:* "Employer Abuse of Low-Status Workers: The Possibility of Uncommon Relief from the Common Law" by Regina Austin and Sharon Dietrich was originally published in different form as "Employer Abuse, Worker Resistance, and the Tort of Intentional Infliction of Emotional Distress" in the *Stanford Law Review*, vol. 41 (1988). Copyright © 1988 by the Board of Trustees of the Leland Stanford Junior University. *University of Chicago:* "A Black Feminist Critique of Antidiscrimination Law and Politics" by Kimberle Crenshaw was previously published as "Demarginalizing the Intersection of Race and Sex: A Black Feminist Critique of Antidiscrimination Doctrine, Feminist Theory and Antiracist Politics" in the 1989 *University of Chicago Legal Forum*. The University of Chicago retains all rights to this material. *University of Pennsylvania Law Review and Fred B. Rothman & Co.:* Excerpts from book review by David Kairys, *University of Pennsylvania Law Review*, vol. 126 (1978). Copyright © 1978 by University of Pennsylvania Law Review. Repritned by permission of University of Pennsylvania Law Review and Fred B. Rothman & Co.

Library of Congress Cataloging-in-Publication Data
The politics of law : a progressive critique / edited by David Kairys.
    p. cm.
    Includes bibliographical references.
    ISBN 0-679-73161-X
    1. Political questions and judicial power—United States,
    2. Justice, Administration of—United States. 3. Judicial process—
    United States. 4. Law and politics. I. Kairys, David.
    KF8700.P65 1990
    349.73—dc20
    [347.3]   90-52555

Book Design by Fearn Cutler
Manufactured in the United States of America
9876

CONTENTS

The Constitution

Crime

Personal Injury

Business

ACKNOWLEDGMENTS

Many people made important contributions to the first and second editions of this book. Drafts were generally circulated among the authors, and revisions benefitted from input by many of them. Helpful comments and suggestions were regularly provided by Jay Feinman, Duncan Kennedy, Karl Klare, Rand Rosenblatt, David Rudovsky, and Adam Thurschwell. Organizational bases for dialogue and support have been provided by the Conference on Critical Legal Studies and the National Lawyers Guild. The book has been greatly enhanced and effectively supported by our editors at Pantheon, Susan Rabiner (second edition), Philip Pochoda, and Don Guttenplan, and by André Schiffrin.

EDITOR'S DEDICATION
*To Antje Mattheus
and to our children,
Marah and Hannah*

PREFACE TO THE REVISED EDITION

Since the first edition was published in 1982, law, and the politics of law, have seen a changing of the guard. Judicial appointments by President Reagan, screened for their conservative credentials, have come to constitute over half of the federal judges, and the Supreme Court is now dominated by a Reagan-Rehnquist majority. The results are already evident: in a decade characterized by public celebration of individual freedom and hostility to government, the courts have increasingly favored government, corporations, and those at the top of the social ladder over middle-class and poor people, minorities, women, and individual and organized working people. The government's power to constrain individuals has been enhanced, and business enjoys more freedom to do as it pleases—regardless of the effects on workers, the community, or the environment—than at any time over the last several decades.

At the same time, mainstream legal thought has been shaken by criticism from the left and right. Law schools and law reviews are bubbling these days about conservative trends like law and economics and libertarianism and progressive trends like critical legal studies. There is now a large and growing body of critical legal studies scholarship and responses from a variety of perspectives, and recent writings by minority and feminist scholars have raised new challenges and possibilities. There is in the legal profession, the law schools, and a variety of academic disciplines more questioning and interest regarding the social role and functioning of the law than in any other period over the last fifty years. As law and justice are increasingly distinct and in conflict and there is renewed interest in legal theory, we thought it a good time to reevaluate and expand as well as to update.

Half of the chapters are completely new, while the core of the first edition has been maintained, with updating and revision throughout, by substantially increasing the total number of pages. We have broadened the legal fields and issues addressed, substantially expanded the range and depth of the presentations of alternative progressive approaches to law, and developed a new focus on the conservative shift in the law and society accomplished during the Reagan decade.

The new chapters cover a variety of topics, including corporations, constitutional law, foreign affairs and international law, crime, abuse of low-status workers, criminalization of gay sex, the legal and political marginalization of black women, and the major conservative approaches to law (libertarianism and law and economics). The book is still separated into three parts: Traditional Jurisprudence and Legal Education, Selected Fields of Law and Substantive Issues, and Progressive Approaches to the Law. However, with the additions, we now cover a sufficiently wide range of fields and issues to reorganize the substantive chapters into five broad categories: Class, Race, and Sex; The Constitution; Crime; Personal Injury; and Business.

The new authors include criminologist Elliott Currie; philosopher and social critic Cornel West; and law professors Regina Austin, Rhonda Copelon, Kimberle Crenshaw, Mark Kelman, Jules Lobel, Frances Olsen, William H. Simon, and Mark Tushnet. The core of authors from the first edition, who have updated and revised their chapters, include Richard Abel, W. Haywood Burns, Jay M. Feinman, Alan Freeman, Peter Gabel, Robert W. Gordon, Morton Horwitz, Duncan Kennedy, Karl Klare, Elizabeth Mensch, Victor Rabinowitz, Rand Rosenblatt, David Rudovsky, Elizabeth Schneider, and Nadine Taub.

David Kairys
Philadelphia
November 1989

REVISED EDITION

THE
POLITICS OF LAW

A PROGRESSIVE CRITIQUE

DAVID KAIRYS

INTRODUCTION

WE Americans turn over more of our society's disputes, decisions, and concerns to courts and lawyers than does any other nation. Yet, in a society that places considerable value on democracy, courts would seem to have a peculiarly difficult problem justifying their power and maintaining their legitimacy. The judiciary is a nonmajoritarian institution, whose guiding lights are neither popularly chosen nor even expected to express or implement the will of the people. Rather, its legitimacy rests on notions of honesty and fairness and, most importantly, on popular perceptions of the judicial process.

Basic to the popular perception of the judicial process is the notion of government by law, not people. Law is depicted as separate from—and "above"—politics, economics, culture, and the values or preferences of judges. This separation is supposedly accomplished and ensured by a number of perceived attributes of the decision-making process, including judicial subservience to a Constitution, statutes, and precedent; the quasi-scientific, objective nature of legal analysis; and the technical expertise of judges and lawyers.

Together, these attributes constitute an idealized decision-making process in which (1) the law on a particular issue is preexisting, clear, predictable, and available to anyone with reasonable legal skill; (2) the facts relevant to disposition of a case are ascertained by objective hearing and evidentiary rules that reasonably ensure that the truth will emerge; (3) the result in a particular case is determined by a rather routine application of the law to the facts; and (4) except for the occasional bad judge, any reasonably competent and fair judge will reach the "correct" decision.

Of course, there are significant segments of the bar and trends in legal scholarship, as well as popularly held beliefs, that repudiate this idealized model. The school of jurisprudence known as legal realism long ago exposed its falsity; and later jurisprudential developments, such as theories resting the legitimacy of law on the existence of widely shared values, at least implicitly recognize the social and political content of law. Moreover, concepts like public policy and social utility, while limited to certain notions of the public good, are generally acknowledged as appropriate considerations for judges, and it is commonly known that the particular judge assigned to a case has a significant bearing on the outcome.

But most of this thinking is either limited to law journals or compartmentalized, existing alongside and often presented as part of the idealized process. For example, "balancing tests," where judges decide which of two or more conflicting policies or interests will predominate, are presented and applied as if there were objective and neutral answers, as if it were possible to perform such a balance independent of political, social, and personal values that vary among our people and (to a lesser extent) among our judges.

Despite the various scholarly trends and the open consideration of social policy and utility, legal decisions are expressed and justified, and the courts as well as their decisions are depicted and discussed throughout society, in terms of the idealized process. The public perception—the crucial perception from the standpoint of legitimacy—is generally limited to the idealized model. One will often hear cynical views about the law, such as "the system is fixed" or "it's all politics," but even such observations are usually meant to describe departures from, rather than characteristics of, the legal process. While this perception is not monolithic or static (at various times substantial segments of society have come to question the idealized model), it has fairly consistently had more currency in the United States than in any other country.

Indeed, public debate over judicial decisions usually focuses on whether courts have deviated from the idealized model rather than on the substance of decisions or the nature and social significance of judicial power. Perceived deviations undermine the legitimacy and power of the courts, and are usually greeted with a variety of institutional and public challenges, including attacks by politicians and the press, proposals for statutory or constitutional change, and, occasionally, threats or attempts to impeach judges.

While there is presently considerable dissatisfaction with the courts and their decisions from a variety of political perspectives, it is usually expressed in terms of this notion of deviation from the idealized model. Thus, the conservative criticism that the courts have overstepped their bounds—going beyond or outside legal reasoning and the idealized process—is now commonplace, as is the accompanying plea for judicial restraint to allow our "democratic processes" to function.

The conservative critique of law, once thought to be outside the margins, has gained mainstream status over the last two decades. In the courts, as in society generally, social problems, such as the drug epidemic, homelessness, and AIDS, are regularly viewed as individual predicaments, the subjects of optional pity rather than social analysis or action; and the people suffering the most are routinely blamed. In this view of society and jurisprudence, the government is the people; democracy and freedom are fully defined and realized by available government processes, no matter how impenetrable, skewed, or corrupt. There is little or no room for popular participation or scrutiny, and appeals to privacy or individual autonomy are often greeted with contempt. Powerful, largely corporate, interests; the patriarchal, authoritarian family; and government officials are generally not to be interfered with, by the courts or by the people. This has become the judicial philosophy and politics of a majority of the Supreme Court. It is the political hallmark of our time that this view of law and society has been implemented by a regime that rose to power largely based on appeals to its opposite: government was to be taken off the backs of the people (translated into tax cuts for the rich and removal of environmental, safety, and other limits on their ability to get richer); government was to be reduced (translated into cuts in social programs more than offset by a military buildup); courts were to be restrained (translated into a growing judicial activism to achieve conservative goals); and waste and corruption were to be eliminated (translated into unprecedented levels of both).

There is a conservative hegemony in the law as in other areas of public life that renders criticism of conservative views and assumptions naive, "soft," and the subject of mockery. Thus, while we have been extremely "tough" on crime for over fifteen years—to the extent that our prison population has tripled (to over one million) and we imprison a higher proportion of our population than any other country except the Soviet Union and South Africa (see chapter 13)—when in 1989 the Bush administration announced another "get tough" war on drugs, the only visible "critics" demanded a bigger and more costly war. We seem unable to deal with major crises that threaten our stability and cohesiveness as a nation with any degree of understanding or social analysis. There is afoot, as E. L. Doctorow has recently said, "a gangsterism of the spirit."[1]

In this context, it is time to talk about basics, which is what the authors of this book have attempted to do in both editions. The law should not escape the attention of anyone wishing to understand or change American society, and we believe it is best understood by focusing on a range of substantive, socially important areas of law rather than addressing the law only abstractly. The twenty-five essays in this second edition, while they present differing and sometimes conflicting views, suggest a progressive critique of law with four basic elements.

First, we reject the idealized model and the notion that a distinctly legal mode of reasoning or analysis determines legal results or characterizes the legal process. The problem is not that courts deviate from legal reasoning. There is no legal reasoning in the sense of a legal methodology or process for reaching particular, correct results. There is a distinctly legal and quite elaborate system of discourse and body of knowledge, replete with its own language and conventions of argumentation, logic, and even manners. In some ways these aspects of the law are so distinct and all-embracing as to amount to a separate culture. For many lawyers the courthouse, the law firm, the language, the style, become a way of life, so much so that their behavior can be difficult for nonlawyer spouses and friends to understand or accept. But in terms of a method or process for decision making—for determining correct rules, facts, or results—the law provides only a wide and conflicting variety of stylized rationalizations from which courts pick and choose. Social and political judgments about the substance, parties, and context of a case guide such choices, even when they are not the explicit or conscious basis of decision.

This does not mean that the law lacks content or meaning or is unpredictable. To the contrary, some rules and results—though not legally required—seem more "sensible" and are relatively predictable in particular social contexts. This is not, however, based on any legal methodology or logic; rather, there is often in particular periods and contexts a prevalent set of social and political values and judgments regarding some issues or areas of law. For example, the courts will now generally protect a person handing out leaflets on a street corner from interference by local officials, but before the 1930s, although the same constitutional provisions were in effect, there was no such protection (see chapter 11).

Judges are the often unknowing objects, as well as among the staunchest supporters, of the myth of legal reasoning. Decisions are predicated upon a complex mixture of social, political, institutional, experiential, and personal factors; however, they are expressed and justified, and largely perceived by judges themselves, in terms of "facts" that have been objectively determined and "law" that has been objectively and rationally "found" and "applied." One result is a judicial schizophrenia that permeates decisions, arguments, and banter among lawyers.

Law students, trying to understand and master legal reasoning, are commonly puzzled by the array of majority and dissenting opinions and the pointed views of law professors regarding the cases presented to them. Differing judicial opinions each cite earlier cases and possess other apparent indicia of validity. The professor often has a theme and explanation for a string of decisions that is not found in any of the opinions. Everybody seems to have a claim to being right but the student, whose common reaction is laced with confusion, vulnerability, and insecurity. There is clear pressure to learn to "think like a lawyer," which often seems to involve abandoment of progressive values and the hope of social action (see chapter 2).

Second, we place fundamental importance on democracy, by which we mean popular participation in the decisions that shape our society and affect our lives. While there is a very real sense of powerlessness that pervades contemporary society, to blame this solely or even principally on the courts misses the point.

Those democratic processes that the courts are supposedly invading in the conservative view consist essentially of the right to vote and freedom of speech and association. These democratic processes, while certainly important, do not provide meaningful choices or constitute meaningful mechanisms for popular control or input, which is, perhaps, why half our people do not vote. Moreover, our society allows no democracy outside this "public" sphere of our lives. For example, the economic decisions that most crucially shape our society and affect our lives, on basic social issues like the use of our resources, investment, the environment, and the work of our people, are regarded as "private" and are not made democratically or by the government officials elected in the public sphere. The public/private split ideologically legitimizes private—mainly corporate—dominance, masks the lack of real participation or democracy, and personalizes the powerlessness it breeds.

The law plays a crucial role in this: the idealized model, the notion of technical expertise, and the notion of the law as neutral, objective, and quasi-scientific lend legitimacy to the judicial process, which in turn lends a broader legitimacy to the social and power relations and ideology that are reflected, articulated, and enforced by the courts. The law serves to depoliticize—removing crucial issues from the public agenda—and to cast the structure and distribution of things as they are as somehow achieved without the need for any human agency. Decisions and social structures that have been made by people—and can be unmade or remade—are depicted as neutral, objective, preordained, or even God-given, providing a false legitimacy to existing social and power relations.

The current and seemingly endless debate over judicial restraint or activism also misses the point. There is no coherent framework or principled resolution of this debate within the legal system, just as and because legal reasoning does not yield required rules or results. Rather, with very few exceptions, the pleas for judicial restraint and activism, sometimes unintentionally or unconsciously, mask a political direction and are wholly dependent on the historical and social contexts. If one favored Social Security and restriction of child labor over maximization of profits during the New Deal, one was for judicial restraint; if one favored racial equality and justice over maintenance of white privilege and the historical oppression of black people in the 1960s, one was for judicial activism; if one favored prohibition of abortions by choice prior to 1973, one was for judicial restraint, but achievement of that same goal in the 1990s requires a judicial activism that would not hesitate to overrule the pro-choice *Roe* v. *Wade* decision.

Third, we reject the common characterization of the law and the state as neutral, value-free arbiters, independent of and unaffected by social and economic relations, political forces, and cultural phenomena. Traditional jurisprudence largely ignores social and historical reality, and masks the existence of social conflict and oppression with ideological myths about objectivity and neutrality. The dominant system of values has been declared value free; it then follows that all others suffer from bias and can be thoughtlessly dismissed.

Progressive thinking about the law and the state has long recognized this political content and lack of neutrality. However, there has been a tendency to oversimplify with analyses that often seem to seek an almost mystical, linear, causal chain that translates economics into law. For example, a common orthodox Marxist explanation is that law is a "superstructural" phenomena that is mysteriously governed and determined by an underlying "base" of economic relations and/or instrumentally controlled by the ruling elite or class. But the law is not simply an armed receptacle for values and priorities determined elsewhere; it is part of a complex social totality in which it constitutes as well as is constituted, shapes as well as is shaped. Moreover, such analyses lose sight of the fact that the law consists of people-made decisions and doctrines, and the thought processes and modes of reconciling conflicting considerations of these people (judges) are not mystical, inevitable, or very different from the rest of ours. It is often difficult to resist dehumanization of one's opponents and a blanket rejection of all institutions and people that constitute and symbolize a system one deeply wishes to transform.

However, judges are not robots that are—or need to be—mysteriously or conspiratorily controlled. Rather, they, like the rest of us, form values and prioritize conflicting considerations based on their experience, socialization, political perspectives, self-perceptions, hopes, fears, and a variety of other factors. The results are not, however, random; their particular backgrounds, socialization, and experiences—in which law schools and the practice of law play an important role—result in a patterning, a consistency, in the ways they categorize, approach, and resolve social and political conflicts. This is the great source of the law's power: it enforces, reflects, constitutes, and legitimizes dominant social and power relations without a need for or the appearance of control from outside and by means of social actors who largely believe in their own neutrality and the myth of nonpolitical, legally determined results.

This complex process whereby participants are encouraged to see their roles and express themselves as neutral and objective social agents also pervades the realm of law practice. Lawyers are trained to communicate as if they have no self-interests or values and are merely promoting what the law requires, which just happens to coincide with their clients' interests. The most effective practitioners discover the art of simultaneously projecting both objectivity and principled belief in what they do, regardless of what they actually believe. The tendency or need to believe in what they do and the people and interests they represent is often overwhelming, and lawyers frequently adopt and express preposterous explanations and justifications for their clients and the positions they advocate.

This schizophrenia is compounded by the extreme aggressiveness of the legal world. A lawyer functions in the only profession where someone is hired and has as his or her specific responsibility to oppose and criticize everything you say or do. This all takes a heavy toll on lawyers, and burnout is common.

There is also strong pressure to take up the cause of the rich: the myth in the legal world is that, for example, finding tax breaks for people who are already sufficiently rich is somehow more interesting and personally as well as financially more rewarding than representing environmentalists, working people trying to make their workplaces safer or more fulfilling, or poor people whose legal problems bring out the lawyer's resourcefulness and ingenuity. Many lawyers devote their lives to making rich people richer even though their own values are more egalitarian and socially conscious. The reality is that the legal world provides—if one chooses it—the opportunity for quite interesting work that yields more than adequate financial rewards and offers the possibility of making the world around us a somewhat better place to live.

Fourth, while the law has many important functions, the legitimation function is crucial to an understanding of its doctrines, rationalizations, results, and social role. The law's ultimate mechanism for control and enforcement is institutional violence, but it protects the dominant system of social and power relations against political and ideological as well as physical challenges. The law is a major vehicle for the maintenance of existing social and power relations by the consent or acquiescence of the lower and middle classes. The law's perceived legitimacy confers a broader legitimacy on a social system and ideology that, despite their claims to kinship with nature, science, or God, are most fairly characterized by domination by a very small, mainly corporatized elite. This perceived legitimacy of the law is primarily based on notions of technical expertise and objectivity and the idealized model of the legal process—in short, as described above, on the distorted notion of government by law, not people. But it is also greatly enhanced by the reality that the law is, on some occasions, just and sometimes serves to restrain the exercise of power.

A realistic, understandable approach to the law that explains its operation and social role must acknowledge the fundamental conflicts in society; the class, race, and sex basis of these conflicts; and the dominance of an ideology that is not natural, scientifically determined, or objective. The discretionary nature of court decisions, the importance of social and political judgments, and the dominance of the ideology of advanced capitalism characterize our judicial process far better than any notions of justice, objectivity, expertise, or science.

Ours is a government by people, not law. Those robed people sitting behind ornate oversized desks are not controlled or bound by law; regardless of their honest self-appraisals or their pretensions, they are in the business of politics. But the politics they practice is mediated through law—theirs is not unfettered political choice—and their perceptions and values are socially formed and patterned. Usually judges find confirming legal rationalizations for their choices or adopt whatever seems easiest or least controversial, which often involves ignoring or distorting contrary arguments, authorities, facts, or social realities. They are most influenced by the culture that pervades their daily lives, their associations, their self-perceptions, and the world around them. They sometimes feel constraints, such as a moral hesitance to do what they think is expected of them, or as a fear that doing the right thing might be embarrassing to them or to the courts or other institutions. In such constraint situations, however, it is still a political choice; and it is made by a person, not by "the law" and not required by legal reasoning or by the dictates or logic of any underlying social or economic system.

This book is an attempt to present a progressive, critical analysis of the operation and social role of the law in contemporary American society. Our approach is interdisciplinary, including authors and methods based in sociology, economics, history, and political science as well as law, and draws upon the experience of law practitioners as well as teachers. We seek a theoretical and practical understanding of the law that places its institutions and individual actors in their social and historical contexts, and views the law as part of and intimately connected to a social totality.

It is our hope that this second edition will continue to provide insight, understanding, and an impetus and basis for further development to a wide variety of readers. These include, in addition to legal theorists, law teachers, and members of the legal profession generally, law students seeking an understanding of the bewildering world of law school and the discipline that is largely being mystified rather than revealed in their classes; law practitioners and legal workers seeking an understanding of the meaning of their work; students and teachers concerned with the social role and operation of the law and the state in legal studies, sociology, political science, economics, history, and other disciplines; progressive people and groups seeking a better understanding of their law-related goals and strategies; and anyone interested in the nature and role of the law and the state in contemporary society. We have attempted to minimize use of terms and references unfamiliar to non-law-trained readers, although due to space limitations it has not been possible to explain every legal term or concept used.

The book is divided into three parts. Part 1 considers traditional jurisprudence (chapter 1) and legal education (chapter 2). Part 2 consists of seventeen chapters that focus on selected substantive issues and fields of law. These are presented in five categories: class, race, and sex; the Constitution; crime; personal injury; and business. Part 3 presents five short essays that introduce and discuss a variety of progressive approaches to the law.

This book originated in 1979 as a project of the Theoretical Studies Committee of the National Lawyers Guild and proceeded, at first informally and later formally, as a joint project with the Conference on Critical Legal Studies. The guild, founded in 1937, is a national organization of progressive lawyers, law students, and legal workers with over seven thousand members and offices in most major cities. The conference, founded in 1977, is primarily composed of law teachers and holds periodic conferences.[2]

The reader will see reflected in this book a variety of political perspectives and methodologies, and some variance in the audiences to which the selections are addressed. While the book is intended to be more coherent as a whole than collections usually are, we have not attempted to harmonize the style or content of the contributions or to present a single, fully developed approach. Each author is responsible for the content of his or her selection.

A NOTE ON THE NOTES

The bibliographic style of the notes generally follows that specified for footnotes in *A Manual of Style*, by the University of Chicago Press. However, legal citations generally follow *A Uniform System of Citations*, published by the Harvard Law Review Association, except that many words usually abbreviated have been written out to aid the non-law-trained reader. The content of the notes has generally been limited to citations to authority, and, unlike most legal writing, authorities cited with reference to a paragraph or thought are often collected in one footnote.

NOTES

1. E. L. Doctorow, Commencement Address at Brandeis University, May 21, 1989, published in *The Nation*, October 2, 1989, p. 348.
2. The Conference on Critical Legal Studies can be contacted c/o Elizabeth Mensch and Alan Freeman, SUNY-Buffalo Law School, O'Brien Hall, Buffalo, N.Y. 14260; the National Lawyers Guild is at 55 Avenue of the Americas, New York, N.Y. 10013.

I
TRADITIONAL JURISPRUDENCE AND LEGAL EDUCATION

1 ELIZABETH MENSCH

THE HISTORY OF MAINSTREAM LEGAL THOUGHT

THE most corrosive message of legal history is the message of contingency.[1] Routinely, the justificatory language of law parades as the unquestionable embodiment of Reason and Universal Truth; yet even a brief romp through the history of American legal thought reveals how quickly the Obvious Logic of one period becomes superseded by the equally obvious, though contradictory, logic of subsequent orthodoxy. The account that follows is a short, and necessarily superficial, summary of the major changes that have taken place in American legal thought since the start of the nineteenth century. There will be no attempt to examine the complex causes of those changes, nor any effort to locate them in social or economic context. The goal is more limited: to describe the legal consciousness of distinct (although overlapping) periods of American legal thought. Since the effort is to reconstruct the worldview of those who have been most directly concerned with making, explaining, and applying legal doctrine, many theorists who have written on the fundamental questions of jurisprudence are not included. This is an account of conventional, and therefore often wholly unreflecting and unselfconscious, legal consciousness.[2]

PRECLASSICAL CONSCIOUSNESS (1776–1885)

During the disruptive and potentially radical period that immediately followed the Revolution, elite American jurists devoted themselves to reestablishing legal authority. As the embodiment of reason and continuity, law seemed to offer the only source of stability in a nation where republicanism, if conceived as mere participatory democracy, would quickly dissolve into the frenzied, leveling passions of the people who had now so rashly been declared sovereign.[3] The ultimate expression of this response was the Constitution itself, serving simultaneously as the declared expression of popular sovereignty ("We the people . . .") and as a distinctly *legal* text, to be interpreted authoritatively only by those learned in the profession.[4]

In a flowery vocabulary drawn largely from the natural-law tradition, late-eighteenth- and early-nineteenth-century legal speakers made extravagant claims about the role of law and lawyers. They described law as reflecting here on earth the universal principles of divine justice, which, in their purest form, reigned in the Celestial City. For example, the single most popular legal quotation, for rhetorical purposes, was taken from the Anglican theologian Hooker: "Of law no less can be acknowledged, than that her seat is the bosom of God; her voice harmony of the world.[5]

Similarly, lawyers portrayed their own professional character as the embodiment of republican virtue. Ideally, within each well-educated lawyer reason had subdued the unruly passions, and that triumph rendered the lawyer fit to consecrate himself to the service of law, as a "priest at the temple of justice." In this role the lawyer/priest was to act, not as an instrument of his client's unbridled will, but as a "trustee" for the interests of the whole community. As adviser and guardian, he would attempt to elicit elevated rather than base motives in his clients, guiding them to promote a social order consistent with those universal principles that were ordained by God and most clearly understood by lawyers.

This special trusteeship meant that lawyers played a vital political role in the new democracy, where principle and legal right continually faced the threat of mass assault. Leaders of the bar often described lawyers as sentinels, placed on the dangerous outposts of defense, preserving the virtue of the republic from the specifically democratic threats of irrational legislation and mob rule. Not surprisingly, many nineteenth-century jurists cited with satisfaction de Tocqueville's observation that the legal profession constituted a distinctively American aristocracy, providing order in an otherwise unstable democracy.

The universal principle that seemed to require the most zealous protection was the sanctity of private property. With something approaching paranoia, leading American jurists explained that the redistributive passions of the majority, if ever allowed to overrun the barrier of legal principle, would sweep away the nation's whole social and economic foundation. Thus Joseph Story, upon his inauguration as professor of law at Harvard, announced that the lawyer's most "glorious and not infrequently perilous" duty was to guard the "sacred rights of property" from the "rapacity" of the majority. Only the "solitary citadel" of justice stood between property and redistribution; it was the lawyer's noble task to man that citadel, whatever the personal cost. "What sacrifice could be more pure than in such a cause? What martyrdom more worthy to be canonized in our hearts?"[6]

The ornate legal rhetoric of the period obscured a number of dilemmas deep at the core of early American legal theory. First, despite the rhetorical appeal to natural law as a source of legitimacy, most jurists readily conceded that natural law alone was too indeterminate to guide judicial decision making in specific cases. Natural law provided divine sanction but yielded few concrete rules or results. Moreover, pure natural-law theory could lead in unwanted directions. The notion of natural reason upon which it rested, for example, could be translated to mean the natural reason of the sovereign people—Thomas Paine's common sense—rather than the reason of trained lawyers. That suggested precisely the unlimited popular will which most jurists feared. Furthermore, the moral content of natural-law theory often led in contradictory directions. One key example was the right to property: while a Lockean natural-law tradition asserted the sanctity of private property, an even older (and alarmingly popular) natural-law tradition questioned the morality of all social and economic inequality.[7]

Most early-nineteenth-century lawyers were thus ready to concede that the most immediate, practical source and definition of law was to be found in positive law—not statutes, which were feared because of their origin in unpredictable representative assemblies[8]—but the complex, ancient forms of the English common law. The legitimacy of those forms was said to derive not from universal moral principle but from custom and long usage. It was the extraordinary technicality of the common law that provided lawyers with their claim to expertise and served, by its very artificiality, to distinguish legal reasoning from the "common-sense" reason of the general populace.[9] Moreover, common-law rules, however quirky, seemed able to supply the certainty and formal predictability impossible to find in the vague morality of natural law.

The precise relation between natural-law and common-law forms was inevitably problematic. Occasionally, it was announced that the common law and natural law were simply identical, but that claim was inherently implausible. Many technical rules of the common law were purely whimsical, rooted exclusively in the English legal tradition and often derived from the history of feudal property relations which Americans had explicitly repudiated. Some rules had already been declared wholly inapplicable to the New World, where they had been modified, in quite various ways, in each of the colonies. Even in England there had been obvious changes within the supposed changelessness of the common law. Thus, it was hard to argue that each common-law rule was an expression of immutable, universal truth.

Early leading jurists like Hamilton and Marshall recognized that one could secure emerging property rights more coherently by locating them in the positive law of the constitutional text, thereby severing them from the debatable vagaries of both the natural-law and the common-law traditions. An important example is *Fletcher* v. *Peck*,[10] where in 1810 Marshall deftly blended natural law and selective analogy to common law to protect vested property rights from legislative redistribution, relying on the contract clause of the Constitution as the ultimate basis for decision.

Meanwhile, in private law, the potential conflict between natural-law conceptions and the common-law tradition, as well as between contradictory assertions within natural law, was obscured in the early-nineteenth century by a surprisingly self-confident assurance that one could always reach a just conclusion by employing two techniques of legal reasoning: liberality of interpretation and implication. By the first, judges and treatise writers meant a willingness to interpret technical common-law rules—which were still unquestioningly assumed to form the bulk of the law—with a flexible, progressive American spirit and, in particular, with concern for commercial utility. Lord Mansfield in England, who had often drawn on civil law to modify rigid common-law rules in the name of commercial good sense, was often cited as an example to be followed by enlightened American decision makers.

This notion of utility became a key mediating concept in liberal interpretation. It suggested that one did not have to choose *between* a strict, rigid adherence to common-law technicalities and the less certain demands of substantive justice, nor *between* commercial utility and the moralistic claims of traditional natural law. Instead, it was common to cite utility as a justification for departing from common-law rules, often on the claim that the common law itself, properly understood by liberal judges like Mansfield, had always allowed for utilitarian change; and then to further explain that in the form of commercial "reasonableness," utility was implicit in natural reason and therefore in the whole natural-law and civil-law tradition. Thus, modern departures from common-law rules could be seen as both consistent with the long "changing changelessness" of the common-law tradition[11] and also as evidence of the common law's link to natural reason and universal principle.

The technique of implied intent, also basic to early-nineteenth-century legal thought, performed a similar function. Often, judges appealed to the intent of the parties as a basis for decision making, which coincided with the increased use of contract imagery in judicial opinions. The emphasis on implied intent did not, however, necessarily evidence concern with the actual, subjective intent of individual parties. Instead, it represented a fusion of subjective intent with socially imposed duty. Legal thinkers confidently assumed that they could find the "law" within the obligations inherent in particular social and commercial relations, obligations which, it could be claimed, parties intended to assume when they entered the relationship.

For example, in his important treatise on contract law,[12] Parsons devoted over 90 percent of the pages to a description of various types of parties (e.g., agents, guardians, servants) and relational contexts (e.g., marriage, bailment, service contracts, sale of goods). Each category represented a social entity with its own implicit duties and reasonable expectations. A party entering into a particular relationship would be said to have intended to conform to the standards of reasonable behavior that inhered in such a relationship. Specific rules could then be defended or modified depending upon whether they promoted the principles and policies basic to that relationship (encouraged transactions in goods, promoted honorable dealing between merchants, etc.). Subjectivity and free will were thus combined with the potentially conflicting imposition of objective, judicially created obligations; and both notions were integrated into the amorphous blend of natural law, positive law, morality, and utility, which made up the justificatory language of early-nineteenth-century law.

Despite the confidence with which early-nineteenth-century judges invoked liberality and implied intent, the conceptual mush they made of legal theory posed serious problems for the emerging liberal conception, in constitutional law, of a sovereignty limited by private legal rights. Public-law thinking was dominated by the Lockean model of the individual rightholder confronting a potentially oppressive sovereign power. Within that worldview, there ideally existed a realm of pure private autonomy, free from state intrusion. It was a realm in which individuals owned property protected from the encroachment of others and made self-willed, freely bargained-for choices. Of course there was also a legitimate public realm, comprised of state and federal institutions entrusted with maintaining public order and serving clearly delineated public functions. Nevertheless, the public realm and the private were clearly and strictly bounded. They were conceived as wholly separate, in-or-out categories that could allow for no blurring or intermeshing. It was, in effect, the strict boundary between public and private that jurists of the early nineteenth century promised to guard with such everlasting zeal.

Yet, in order to justify protecting private rights from public power, it was necessary to conceive of the private as purely private. This demanded, in turn, a fully rationalized structure of private law, which, in theory, did no more than protect and facilitate the exercise of private will and which could also give concrete, objective content to the private rights supposedly protected by the Constitution. The loose hodgepodge of conflicting premises that made up early-nineteenth-century private law was woefully deficient for that purpose, and the great thrust of nineteenth-century legal thought was toward higher and higher levels of rationalization and generalization. Eventually, that process produced a grandly integrated conceptual scheme that seemed, for a fleeting moment in history, to bring coherence to the whole structure of American law, and to liberal political theory in general.

CLASSICAL LEGAL CONSCIOUSNESS (1885–1935)

The nineteenth century's process of legal rationalization resulted in the abstraction of law from both particularized social relations and substantive moral standards. By the "rule of law" classical jurists meant quite specifically a structure of positivised, objective, formally defined rights. They viewed the legal world not as a multitude of discrete, traditional relations but as a structure of protected spheres of rights and powers. Logically derivable boundaries defined for each individual her own sphere of pure private autonomy while simultaneously defining those spheres within which public power could be exercised freely and absolutely.

This conception of social action as the exercise of absolute rights and powers within bounded spheres extended to all possible relations: in a way inconceivable to the early nineteenth century, the relation of private parties to each other was seen as deeply analogous to the relation of private parties to states, of states to each other and to federal powers, etc. Through this process of analogic refinement run rampant, the boundary between public and private repeatedly reproduced itself. For example, quasi-contracts, which constituted the public sphere within contract law, were to be carefully distinguished from contracts based on intent; and contract law generally was to be kept wholly distinct from the more public realm of torts. Furthermore, within the private sphere, women were relegated to the utterly "private" realm of familial domesticity, leaving to men the more "public" sphere of economic activity.[13] Within this elaborate structure of spheres and analogies, the key legal question, in every instance of disputes, was whether the relevant actors had stayed within their own protected sphere of activity or had crossed over the boundary and invaded the sphere of another. To the classics, freedom *meant* the legal guarantee that rights and powers would be protected as absolute within their own sphere, but that no rightholder/powerholder would be allowed to invade the sphere of another.

In the classical scheme, the utterly crucial task of boundary definition was assigned to the judiciary. Necessarily, this task required objectivity and impartiality. Other actors were free, within their own spheres, to exercise unbridled will in pursuit of their particular (subjective) moral, political, or economic goals. In contrast, the judicial role of boundary finding required the exercise of reason—a reason now conceived, not as embodying universal moral principles and knowledge of the public good, but strictly as the application of objective methodology to the task of defining the scope of legal rights. Upon the supposed objectivity of that method hinged the liberal faith that the rule of law resolved the conflict between freedom as private, civil right and freedom as the republican ideal of public participation and civic virtue.

The supposed judicial objectivity upon which the classical structure depended was based in turn upon the intersection of constitutional language and an increasingly generalized, rationalized conception of private law. First, jurists pointed out that by enacting the Constitution, the sovereign American people had unequivocally (and wisely) adopted a government premised on private rights and strictly limited public powers. Thus, while it was certainly the exalted function of the judiciary to protect private rights from uncontrolled public passion, this function required merely the application of positive constitutional law—there was no painful choice to be made between positive law and natural rights.

Second, and of prime importance, the objective definition given to rights protected by the Constitution could be found within the common-law tradition, which had been wonderfully cleansed of both messy social particularity and natural-law morality. Classical jurists claimed that as a result of an enlightened, scientific process of rationalization, the common law could now properly be reconceived as based upon a few general and powerful—but clearly positivised—conceptual categories (like property and free contract), which had also been incorporated into the Constitution as protected rights. All of the specific rules of the common law (at least the "correct" rules) were said to be deduced from those general categories. For example, Williston's monumental treatise on contracts[14] assumed that from the general principle of free contract one could derive the few central doctrines around which the treatise was organized—offer and acceptance, consideration, excuse, etc.—and from the logic of those central doctrines one could derive all of the specific rules that made up the law of contracts. Those rules could then be applied, rigidly and formally, to *any* particular social context; in fact, failure to do so would be evidence of judicial irrationality and/or irresponsibility. Moreover, because every rule was based upon the principle of free contract, the logical coherence of contract doctrine, correctly applied, ensured that private contracting was always an expression of pure autonomy. With no small amount of self-congratulation, classical jurists contrasted their conceptualization of private autonomy to Parson's description of contract law as something to be found *within* numberless particular social relations. In retrospect, Parsons could be viewed as naive and unscientific.

The new rationalization of common law meant that the old conflict between formal "rules" and substantive "justice" seemed resolved. Common-law rules were no longer a quirky relic from the English feudal past. Instead, they were both an expression and a definition of rights, and of course the protection of rights constituted the highest form of justice. Furthermore, as integrated into the constitutional law structure, the rationalization of private law meant that the boundary between the realm of private autonomy and the realm of public power could be objectively determined by reference to specific common-law doctrine.

The notorious case of *Coppage* v. *Kansas*[15] provides a clear example of the classical approach. In that case the Kansas state legislature had passed a statute outlawing yellow-dog contracts (*i.e.*, contracts in which workers agreed not to engage in union activities). The question was whether this was a reasonable exercise of police power (*i.e.*, fell within the bounded sphere of public power) or whether it constituted an invasion of private contract right, a right considered implicit in the even more general category of liberty protected by the Fourteenth Amendment.

An earlier case, *Adair* v. *United States*,[16] had declared that a similar federal regulation was invalid. Through the Fourteenth Amendment the constitutional protection of liberty as against the federal government was made applicable to the states—evidence of the deep analogy now perceived in what were once conceived as quite different relationships. In response to the argument that *Adair* controlled, however, Kansas argued that its statute was designed specifically to outlaw contracts formed under coercion. Since workers had no realistic choice but to accept the terms obviously imposed by employers, the agreement to sign yellow-dog contracts was not an expression of freedom, and it was no violation of liberty to regulate a "choice" that was never freely made. The Court refused to accept that argument, *not* because it denied the obvious inequality between workers and employers, but because freedom of contract as a legal category had to be defined objectively, which meant according to common-law doctrine. Since the common law had excluded economic pressure from its definition of duress as a legal excuse for nonperformance of contracts, then *by definition* yellow-dog contracts were not formed under duress and were therefore freely entered. It then followed logically that the statute constituted an invasion of liberty protected by the Constitution.

Cases like *Coppage* are now commonly cited as representing a judiciary determined to impose its own economic biases on the country. This both trivializes the underlying power of the classical conceptual scheme and, more significantly, trivializes the importance of the realist assault that revealed its incoherence. In fact, courts during the classical period described a police power as absolute in its sphere as were private rights in theirs, and they by no means overruled all legislation designed to regulate corporate power. Their key claim was that they could objectively "find" the boundary that separated private from public, and it was that supposed objectivity that gave the appearance of coherence and reality to the legal (and social/political) model of bounded rights and powers. That basic model, although in bankrupt form, is with us still, despite the realist challenge that demolished its premises. The message the model conveys is that actual power relations in the real world are by definition legitimate and most go unchallenged.

THE REALIST CHALLENGE (1920—1939)

The realist movement was a part of the general twentieth-century revolt against formalism and conceptualism. As applied to law, that revolt was directed against the whole highly conceptualized classical legal structure. More specifically and politically, realism was also a reaction against Supreme Court decisions like *Coppage*, which had invalidated progressive regulatory legislation favored even by many business leaders.

The realist movement drew upon the earliest Progressive critique of property rights which had sought to blur the distinction between public and private so as to justify regulating and rendering accountable the vast accumulations of private power that had come to characterize the large-scale capitalist American economy by the close of the nineteenth century. That meant recognizing the growing importance of government—especially administrative agencies—in an advanced industrial economy. Thus the realists urged judges to eschew the rigid, abstract formalism of constitutionally protected property and contract rights in favor of increasing deference to the legislative adjustment of competing claims, enacted in the service of a larger "public interest."[17] Meanwhile, in private law, enlightened, progressive judges should be willing to sacrifice rigid adherence to the logic of doctrine for the sake of doing a more commonsense and overtly policy-oriented "justice" within the particular context of each case.[18]

At its most extreme, however, the realist critique cut so deeply into the premises of American thought that subsequent legal thinkers are still struggling to rebuild a convincingly coherent structure. Chiefly, the realists undermined all faith in the objective existence of "rights" by challenging the coherence of the key legal categories that gave content to the notion of bounded public and private spheres. Traditionally, legal discourse had justified decisions by making reference to rights. An opinion, for example, would set out as a reason for finding the defendant liable that she had invaded the property rights of the plaintiff—or, similarly, would justify declaring a statute unconstitutional by saying that it violated the right of property. Yet, as the realists pointed out, such justifications are inevitably circular. There will be a right if, and *only* if, the court finds for the plaintiff or declares the statute unconstitutional. Rights are not a preexisting fact of nature, to be found somewhere "out there," but are a function of legal decision making itself. What the court cites as the *reason* for the decision—the existence of a right—is, in fact, only the *result*.

Moreover, perfectly logical but contradictory arguments can always be generated about whether or not one has a particular right. As a matter of pure logic, nothing is excluded from the state's legitimate concern for the public welfare. Similarly, as between two conflicting private rights, logical arguments can always be made for either side. My private right to be secure from the invasion of a nuisance, like the chemicals a neighbor sprays on her lawn, conflicts with her right to use her property freely. My right to be secure from "unfair" competitition conflicts with her freedom to engage in unbridled freedom on the market. The legal system cannot simply protect rights, but must always choose between two perfectly logical but mutually exclusive rights.[19]

The realist attack upon the logic of rights theory was closely linked to an attack upon the logic of precedent. The realists pointed out that no two cases are ever exactly alike. There will always be some difference in the multitude of facts surrounding them. Thus, the "rule" of a former case can never simply be applied to a new case; rather, the judge must *choose* whether or not the ruling in the former case should be extended to include the new case. That choice is essentially a choice about the relevancy of facts, and those choices can never be logically compelled. Given shared social assumptions, some facts might seem obviously irrelevant (e.g., the color of socks worn by the offeree should not influence the enforceability of a contract), but decisions about the relevance of other distinguishing facts are more obviously value-laden and dependent on the historical context (e.g., the relative wealth of the parties).

That dilemma does not vanish when the "law" to be applied comes not from cases but from the language of statutory or constitutional provisions, or the language of a private contract. There was a time when words were thought to have a fixed, determinate content, a meaning partaking of objective Platonic forms. In the absence of a belief in Platonic intelligible essences, however, no interpretation or application of language can be logically required by the language itself. Words are created by people in history, and their definition inevitably varies with particular context and with the meaning brought to them by the judges who are asked to interpret them. That act of interpretation is, in every instance, an act of social choice.

Thus, the realists claimed that the effort of the nineteenth century to cleanse law of messy social particularity and moral choice was inevitably a failure. There was *no such thing* as an objective legal methodology behind which judges could hide in order to evade responsibility for the social consequences of legal decision making. Every decision they made was a moral and political choice.[20]

Furthermore, the realists understood, as had the classics, that the whole structure of the classical scheme depended upon the coherence of private law and the public/private distinction. Thus, the realists spent little time attacking the methodology of constitutional law and concentrated instead upon undermining the coherence of the key private-law categories that purported to define a sphere of pure autonomy. For example, Morris Cohen's essay "Property and Sovereignty"[21] pointed out that property is necessarily public, not private. Property *means* the legally granted power to withhold from others. As such, it is created by the state and given its only content by legal decisions that limit or extend the property owner's power over others. Thus, property is really an (always conditional) delegation of sovereignty, and property law is simply a form of public law. Whereas the classics (and liberal theorists generally) had drawn a bright line separating (private) property from (public) sovereignty, Cohen collapsed the two categories.

Hale made a similar point about the supposed private right of free contract: state enforcement of a contract right represents, like property, a delegation of sovereign power.[22] Moreover, he also pointed out that coercion, including legal coercion, lies at the heart of every "freely" chosen exchange. Coercion is inherent in each party's legally protected threat to withhold what is owned; that right to withhold creates the right to force submission to one's own terms. Since ownership is a function of legal entitlement, every bargain is a function of the legal order. Thus, there is no "inner" core of free, autonomous bargaining to be protected from "outside" state action. The inner and outer dissolve into each other.

The realist critique did not, by itself, mandate any particular form of social or economic organization. At the extremes, for example, neither centralized state economic planning nor radical deconcentration of industry was logically entailed by their arguments, nor was any particular arrangement that fell between those extremes. Instead, their goal was to clear the air of beguiling but misleading conceptual categories (termed by Felix Cohen's "transcendental nonsense") so that thought could be redirected to the two levels that required attention before sensible and responsible economic and political decisions could be made: first, to a close, contextual examination of social reality—to *facts*, rather than the nonexistent spheres of classicism; and second, to ethics, for if social decision making was inevitably moral choice, then policymakers needed some basis upon which to make their choices.[23]

Potentially, however, the realist collapse of spheres also carried with it the collapse of the whole structure of American legal thought. Realism had effectively undermined the fundamental premises of liberal legalism, particularly the crucial distinction between legislation (subjective exercise of will) and adjudication (objective exercise of reason). Inescapably, it had also suggested that the whole liberal worldview of (private) rights and (public) sovereignty mediated by the rule of law was only a mirage, a pretty fantasy that masked the reality of economic and political power.

Since the realists, American jurists have dedicated themselves to the task of reconstruction; indeed, the realist message was so corrosive that many of the most influential realists evaded the full implications of their own criticism and quickly sought instead to articulate a new justification for legal reasoning's old claim to objectivity and legitimacy. That effort seemed especially crucial after the rise of fascism in Europe: If the liberal model of legally protected private rights was mere illusion, then where could one look for protection against totalitarian statism?[24] Nevertheless, the modern search for a new legitimacy, however earnest, was destined always to have a slightly defensive tone. After realism, American legal theorists had, as it were, eaten of the tree of knowledge, and there could be no return to the naive confidence of the past.

ATTEMPTS AT MODERN RECONSTRUCTION (1940–PRESENT)

During the 1940s, Laswell and McDougal at Yale[25] followed out the implications of realism by announcing that since law students were destined to be the policymakers of the future, Yale should simply abandon the traditional law school curriculum and teach students how to make and implement policy decisions. Their simultaneously antidemocratic and antilegalist message was a bit jarring; most of the major postrealist reconstructors of American legal thought have been more rhetorically restrained. Indeed, much of the reconstruction has consisted of simply conceding a number of key realist insights and then attempting to incorporate those insights into an otherwise intact doctrinal structure. What were once perceived as deep and unsettling logical flaws have been translated into the strengths of a progressive legal system. For example, the indeterminancy of rules has become the *flexibility* required for sensible, policy-oriented decision making; and the collapse of rights into contradiction has been recast as "competing interests," which are inevitable in a complex world and which obviously require an enlightened judicial *balancing*. In other words, we justify as legal sophistication what the classics would have viewed as the obvious abandonment of legality.

The most elaborate attempt to resurrect the legitimacy of the whole American lawmaking structure can be found in the extraordinarily influential Hart and Sacks legal process materials of the 1950s.[26] Those materials were premised on a vision of American society which, it seemed for a time, offered a viable alternative to the classical worldview. Hart and Sacks started by explaining that the critical view of law as a "mask for force, providing a cover of legitimacy" for the exercise of political and economic power, was based on "the fallacy of the static pie." According to Hart and Sacks, the "pie" of both tangible and intangible goods was in fact everexpanding, and a primary, shared purpose of social life was to keep the pie growing.

Within the Hart and Sacks description of American society, the essentially private actors who shared the goal of expansion also shared a belief in the stability afforded by the institutional settlement (by law) of the few disputes that were likely to arise, and more specifically in the particular distribution of functions that was set out in the American Constitution. That distribution was itself designed to ensure both the maximization of valid human wants and a "fair" (although not necessarily equal) distribution of tangible and intangible goods.

The effect was to postulate not particular substantive rights but rather a shared social value in the *process* by which rights were defined—a shared value in distinct institutional competencies. That implied, in turn, a differentiation of the processes by which judges, in contrast to legislators and administrators, reached decisions. According to Hart and Sacks, judges had the competence to settle questions that lent themselves to a process of "reasoned elaboration"—that could, in other words, be justified by reference to general, articulated standards which could be applied in all like cases: that process was to be contrasted with the "unbuttoned discretion" enjoyed by legislators. Presumably, it was the judiciary who decided which questions lent themselves to this process of reasoned elaboration.

The shift from an emphasis on substance to an emphasis on process seemed for a time to satisfy the realist critique of substantive rights; but of course it still rested on the distinction between reasoned elaboration and discretion, which in turn rested on the availability of principled, objective, substantive categories to which judges could make reference. More generally, it also rested on the complacent, simplistic assumption that American society consisted of happy, private actors cheerfully maximizing their valid human wants while sharing their profound belief in institutional competencies. That may have reflected the mind-set of many in the 1950s, but by the end of the 1960s it seemed oddly out of touch with reality.

Another response to the collapse of clear conceptual categories has been less self-consciously articulated than Hart and Sacks's, but pervades modern case law. The prevailing pattern is to accept as inevitable and "in the nature of things" the absence of clear boundaries between categories. Instead, boundaries are portrayed as fluid, or blurred, meaning that many particular examples will occupy a mushy middle position, which includes attributes of two nonetheless distinct categories. Thus, the collapse of spheres is not total, and the goal is to deal comfortably with a world made up largely of middle positions.

This blurring of boundaries cuts across all doctrinal lines. For example, the traditional rule of jurisdiction was that a state court could exercise jurisdiction only over a defendant who was within the borders of the state; the line was as clear as the state's boundary marker. That straightforward "in or out" conception has now given way to a conception that recognizes "presence" as often a middle ground, sort-of-in sort-of-out notion, to be determined by standards of "fair play and substantial justice" and by a "balance" of the interests of the relevant parties and forums.[27] Similarly, whereas classical doctrine had drawn a clear line, at the moment of formation, between contract and no contract, modern reference to reliance breaks down that clarity by recognizing a sort-of contract prior to formation, based on one party's reasonable reliance on the other's precontract negotiating promises.[28] The same notion also breaks down the once sharp contract/tort distinction (i.e., obligations agreed to by the parties as distinct from obligations imposed by law), since reliance is the basis of neither a recognized tort nor a fully contractual cause of action.

In constitutional law, the line between public and private, once the mainstay of legal coherence, can now be located only by applying a puzzling array of increasingly refined and contextual "tests." For example, in the state action cases, to determine whether an ostensibly private actor is to be charged with state accountability under the Fourteenth Amendment, we must measure the degree of "state involvement" to see if it is sufficiently "significant," a process that can be accomplished only by "weighing facts and sifting circumstances" in a particular case.[29] Thus we learn that an actor performing a "public function" remains private unless the function in question is one "traditionally" and "exclusively" a public one (ownership of town, or voting, but not education or dispute resolution, e.g.), and that activities authorized by the state are not chargeable to the public if they are not "encouraged" but merely "approved" or "acquiesced in."[30] Similarly, in the space of eight short years, the Supreme Court treated large privately owned shopping centers as, first, functionally public, then, functionally public and formally private at the same time, and, finally, formally private for all purposes.[31] Notably, however, one formal line does remain intact—the one between capital and labor.[32]

Closely paralleling the emergence of blurred boundaries has been the breakdown of the deep sense of analogy and uniformity that once characterized classical thought. Private-law categories such as property or contract were then thought to have fixed meanings that did not vary with differences in context. That uniformity was conceived to be crucial to the ideal of rationality and formal equality. Now, however, it is common to concede that rights may vary depending upon status and relationship. As Justice Robert Jackson explained in *United States* v. *Willow River Power Company*,[33] simply because a particular water-flow level might constitute property as between two private parties, that did not necessarily mean that the same flow constituted property as between a private party and the federal government.

Despite the breakdown of boundaries and uniform, generally applicable categories, modern American legal thought continues to be premised on the distinction between private law and public law. Private law is still assumed to be *about* private actors with private rights, making private choices, even though sophisticated judges tend quite frankly to refer to public policy when justifying private-law decision making. Similarly, the major postrealist reconstructors of private-law theory, like Edward Levi and Karl Llewellyn, acknowledged the necessary role of policy choice in legal decision making but described judicial choices as still specifically "legal" because judges worked within a long-established judicial tradition, which exerted a steadying (if not precisely "logical") constraint. By training, judges acquire a "craft-consciousness," which leads them to respond to new situations through a "reworking of the heritage" rather than through unguided impulse. The result is neither unbridled choice nor inflexible formalism but "continuity with growth" and "vision with tradition."[34] The new private-law heroes were therefore not the rigorous Willistonians, who refused to acknowledge the role of social change in shaping law, but (once again) Mansfield in England, America's own preclassical nineteenth-century judges, and, in more recent times, Benjamin Cardozo.

As an example of enlightened decision making, Levi[35] described with admiration Cardozo's opinion in *McPherson* v. *Buick Motors Company*.[36] There, Cardozo had modified the classical privity of contract rule (according to which a manufacturer's liability for personal injuries due to a defective product extended only to those with whom he had directly entered a contract) in order to hold Buick liable for a "foreseeable" injury to a party not in privity. As justification, Cardozo had specifically referred to changes in automobile retailing practices, because of which only retailers, and rarely consumers, directly contracted with manufacturers. Under the privity rule, consumers would almost always be left unprotected when defective cars caused injuries, an "anomalous" result, Cardozo said, which he did not want to reach.

Cardozo also justified his decision by referring to the category of "abnormally dangerous" products, which had evolved as an exception to the privity rule, and to the standard of "foreseeability" upon which Cardozo claimed that exception was based. Using the notion of foreseeability, Cardozo masterfully suggested that his decision was a reasoned application of past doctrine, not simply a result-oriented exercise of judicial policy choice. Nevertheless, the skilled craft of the opinion obscured rather than solved the key realist point: for every rule there is bound to be a counterrule, *because* the choice to be made is always between the contradictory claims of freedom and security. In their extreme form here, that would mean freedom as complete absence of manufacturer liability versus consumer security as manufacturer liability for all injuries caused by use of his product. Cardozo used the tort doctrine of foreseeability to mediate those extremes, yet no jurist of his time knew better than Cardozo just how manipulable the doctrine of foreseeability could be. It was Cardozo's decision in *Palsgraf* which rendered a statistically foreseeable injury to a railroad passenger "unforeseeable" because of its odd mode of occurrence—at an utterly individualized level, there was too little closeness in the relationship between the risk undertaken (which was to the property interest of a different passenger) and the personal injury suffered by Mrs. Palsgraf.[37] At the most general, social level of statistical probability, of course, risk is always foreseeable; yet in their complete particularity individual injuries can never be "foreseen." Legal logic offers no reason for drawing the line at any single point between the general and the particular. Recasting the problem as one of a supposedly neutral public policy does not resolve the dilemma, for we have now learned that trite, conventional economic policy arguments can be made for *either* freedom or security.

As with policy, modern private-law thinking has both conceded and evaded the inevitability of value choice in legal decision making. The great postrealist treatise writers, Corbin on contracts and Prosser on torts, appeal at least as often to presumably neutral, shared standards of substantive "justice" and "reasonableness" as they do to fixed rules. But the vocabulary of modern treatises is still the vocabulary of classical doctrine—questions of justice emerge *within* discussions of offer and acceptance, the elements of a cause of action in negligence, etc. The message is that we can advance beyond the silly stage of formalism while still retaining the basic structure and premises of classical thought. Both Prosser and Corbin, however, leave unresolved the old conflict between formal rules and general standards of substantive justice; and neither explains where, within liberalism's supposed subjectivity of values, one is to find a source for objective standards of justice.

The most sophisticated version of private-law reconstruction can be found in the Sales Article of the Uniform Commercial Code—essentially Llewellyn's revamping of traditional contract law. Like Corbin and Prosser, Llewellyn relied on standard doctrine for most of his vocabulary, but he also sought to replace a formalistic application of rules with standards of good faith and reasonableness. Those standards were to be known not as the abstract universals of natural law but through a judicial understanding of actual intent and reasonable expectations within each specific fact situation and within the customs and usages of specific trades. This was Llewellyn's famous "situation-sense," which, he insisted, was distinctly "legal" because it drew on the legal tradition of craft, reason, and principle, and at the same time saw (universal) reason as embodied *within* the particularity of specific commercial practice.

Llewellyn's "singing reason," as he perhaps unfortunately termed it,[38] has already raised methodological problems. The facts of particular customs or situations tend to elude objective judicial determination so that some courts have simply refused to hear all of the conflicting testimony with which they are confronted. The choice as to relevancy, of course, remains a *choice*; and even if objectively "known," the precise role of custom and usage in relation to traditional rules is still problematic. It is commonly said, for example, that custom and usage can be used to interpret contracts but not to create them, yet it is unclear why the line should be drawn at that point, or whether the distinction is even an intelligible one. Equally problematic is the precise relation between reason and custom[39]—a problem as old as the coexistence of a natural-law and a (supposedly customary) common-law tradition. Without standards of reasonableness *outside* existing practice, singing reason is simply ratification of the status quo—the "is" automatically becomes the "ought." Yet absent a fully developed natural-law theory, the source of any external normative standard remains unavailable. Moreover, taking custom and usage as a source of legal standards does not really avoid the problem of self-referencing, which was inevitable in rights theory, since social practice and reasonable expectations are, like "free" bargains, in large measure a *function* of the legal order. The wholly spontaneous custom and usage is rare, if it exists at all. Thus, by reflecting "custom," the law in large measure reflects only itself, and the nagging problem of legitimacy reemerges.

The hodgepodge of policy, situation sense, and leftover doctrine that now makes up the indeterminate body of private law provides scant basis for a rationalization of constitutional rights. The search for some coherent foundation for rights analysis, particularly for judicial review, has been the preoccupation of modern constitutional law theorists. From the "legal process" school, which in its various forms dominated mainstream academic thought about constitutional law until the late 1960s, came two major responses to realism—the strategy of deference, and the strategy of craft. The deference approach focused on the relative "competence" of institutions, demanding extraordinary justification for judicial override of democratically elected legislatures. The emphasis on craft, however, sought to rescue legal reasoning from a realist assimilation into generalized "policy-making" by claiming for it a unique status as "reasoned elaboration," and demanding from judicial opinions a sufficient level of intellectual rigor, fit to be called "principled" decisionmaking. Typical of the call for deference was the influential work of Alexander Bickel; typical of the call for craft was the equally influential work of Herbert Wechsler.

During the New Deal, the Supreme Court virtually abandoned to the legislature the field of economic regulation, once subject to invalidation under the categories of property and free contract. Deference in that area, however, left unresolved the fate of other supposed constitutional rights. For some theorists, deference simply became the preferred model for all cases. Bickel[40] created a new category, somewhere between general principle and mere expediency, which he called prudence. A prudent Supreme Court would avoid judicial review by using procedural grounds (e.g., problems of ripeness or standing) to justify a refusal to reach the merits. The Court could thereby avoid both the criticism that it stood in the way of the democratic majority (the basic argument against judicial review) and the criticism that it legitimated, by finding constitutional, action that seemed to violate fundamental rights. One of Bickel's examples was the notorious *Korematsu* case,[41] where the Supreme Court upheld the detention of all Japanese-Americans living on the West Coast in holding camps during World War II. Bickel argued that the Court should have dodged the question rather than label the detention and its underlying statute constitutional. The exercise of such prudence would have gained the trust of the country and placed the Court in the position of "teacher" in the public discussion of values. Then, when a time of *real* crisis to the Constitution arose, the Court would have been in a position to act on principle, with the backing of the people.

Bickel's "passive virtues" inevitably represent something of a retreat from the juristic model of rights and sovereignty. The person in a concentration camp is presumably not comforted with the knowledge that her case has been prudently decided on procedural rather than constitutional grounds; and a Court unprepared to make hard decisions in such a case is in a weak position to then hold out legal rights as the ultimate protection against totalitarianism. Bickel maintained that the prudent Court could still act when the dictator's troops came marching down Massachusetts Avenue, but his claim rang a bit hollow.

Moreover, the Bickel approach of deference to the legislative process, while on the surface the most obvious answer to the claim that judicial review is undemocratic, evades questions about the nature of our particular form of representation. The American legislative model is not, under our constitutional structure, itself a model of pure, participatory consensualism; its particular form is not more unquestionably democratic or legitimate than is judicial review. *Both* are part of a total constitutional structure, as interpreted by past legal decision making. In fact, an attack on any single part of that structure inevitably calls into question the legitimacy of the whole structure. Also, Hale's critique of free choice in the market can be applied to the political process (the marketplace of ideas) as well. So-called free political choice takes place within a system of legally protected economic power, which is a function of past legal decision making and which profoundly affects outcomes in the political decision-making process. The Court, by suddenly avoiding judicial review, cannot escape responsibility for the social decisions that are made.

Alternatively, Wechsler[42] advocated a return to "general" and "neutral" principles as the only sound basis for judicial review. He complained, for example, that in the *Brown* case[43] the Court rested its decision on sociological fact rather than on constitutional principle. Yet he also acknowledged that the only available, general principle that seemed to cover the case was "freedom of association," which quickly confronts an equally neutral and general but contradictory principle barring forced association. As he conceded, at the level of pure, ahistorical generality there was no logical resolution; yet the necessary move to greater particularity raises the dilemma of necessarily illogical choice somewhere *between* abstract, transcendental generality and ad hoc, "unprincipled" case-by-case decision making. The choice is bound to appear arbitrary.

Even as the legal academics called for judicial restraint and more intellectually satisfying opinions, the federal judiciary, led by the Warren Court, was extending the scope and expanding the content of personal liberty and equality rights as had no other Supreme Court in U.S. history. During the Warren Court period the federal courts revolutionized criminal procedure law, created modern antidiscrimination law, recaptured the First Amendment from the shambles of McCarthyism, and restructured American politics through reapportionment. In response, the legal process school directed its criticism at the Warren Court's "activism," charging usurpation of power or, even when applauding the results, denouncing the Court's opinions for being ad hoc or unprincipled.

In reaction to that critical tradition, however, a new generation of liberal legal scholars was emerging. Many of these scholars celebrated the Warren Court, even believing, however naively, that determined litigators could persuade the Supreme Court to deploy constitutional interpretation to usher in a new era of substantive social justice. Such an era would see the realization of the failed promise of the New Deal—that Americans would be entitled as of right to minimum guarantees of education, housing, health care, and welfare assistance.[44] The big challenge for these emerging liberal constitutionalists was to square their substantive vision of social justice with their fervent belief in legalism and the rule of law, against the shaky backdrop of the corrosive realist tradition. Thus the *Harvard Law Review*, in a rare "editorial" in its February 1970 issue, expressed its "endorsement" of the "activism" of the Warren Court, yet remained troubled due to a "strong preference" for "principled as opposed to result-oriented adjudication," coupled with a "mistrust of interest balancing" (a legacy of realism), as "unprincipled" and leaving far too much to "the individual judge's predilections."[45]

In the 1970s, liberal legal scholars seemingly took up this call, seeking to justify, with appeals to "principle," substantive results inspired by or implicit in the most liberal of the Warren Court's activist decisions. Ironically, this enterprise was launched during the same period that the Supreme Court first became the "Burger Court," in 1969, and then, by 1972, contained four justices appointed by Richard Nixon. Yet, seemingly oblivious to the possibility that conservatives might come to dominate the federal judiciary once again, ultraliberal Judge J. Skelly Wright (of the D.C. Circuit) published in 1971 an article in the *Harvard Law Review* affirming the frank assertion of ethical values by federal judges, and in fact calling for a judicial form of existential moral choice.[46] Others sought harder to stay within the boundaries of "principled" legal decisionmaking, vacillating between a more or less veiled reliance on natural-law theory (David Richards, Kenneth Karst, Ronald Dworkin, Lawrence Tribe), and recourse to a model, somewhat more sophisticated than Hart and Sacks's, of shared American values (Harry Wellington, Michael Perry).[47] John Ely,[48] criticizing both approaches, has attempted to take a stand somewhere between the assertion of affirmative substantive rights and complete deference. He has postulated instead a supposedly value-neutral "participation-oriented, representation-reinforcing" standard for judicial review. Drawing on Justice Harlan Fiske Stone's suggestion,[49] Ely argues that the judiciary should actively scrutinize only that legislation (1) "which restricts those political processes which can ordinarily be expected to bring about repeal of undesirable legislation," or (2) which is based on "prejudice against discrete and insular minorities." Yet this approach too rests on a conception of substantive values—the value of participation within this particular form of representative structure and the "badness" of prejudice as opposed to all those other values which the legislature would be left free to implement.[50] As in the Hart and Sacks materials, the nagging problem of asserting objective, substantive values within a system premised on a pluralistic subjectivity of values inevitably reemerges.

One is hard pressed, as we enter the 1990s, to identify any perspective as "mainstream" legal thought, especially in constitutional law. Some scholars are, in fact, despairingly proclaiming the "death of law."[51] Others, wistfully seeking to perpetuate the spirit of the bygone era of the Warren Court, still attempt to fashion substantive moral content from the multiplicity inherent in the subjectivity of value. As in the monumental *A Theory of Justice*,[52] where John Rawls tried to transcend Kant himself by transforming procedure into moral principle, modern liberal scholars continue to pursue the alchemical goal of turning process into substance. Thus, in the 1980s, there was for a time an emphasis on "dialogic" values and "hermeneutic" traditions,[53] and, more recently, an attempt to revive, in constitutional law, the classical republican ideal of civic virtue through deliberative process.[54]

Others, however anachronistically, still believe in the seemingly quaint worldview of the Hart and Sacks legal process school.[55] These adherents persist in their views despite the relentless critiques produced by Critical Legal scholars, whose basic mission was to demolish the presumption and pretense of the legal process school by exposing the incoherence, contingency, and political character of their basic postulates: shared process values, progress, the objective reality of the public/private distinction, formal equality, legal neutrality, and the fetishism of expertise, especially the privileged autonomy of legal reasoning.

The key message of CLS has been that law is politics. Ironically, that point has been proved best by the political right, with Reagan's "litmus test" approach to judicial appointments demonstrating that explicit attention to particularized and detailed political agendas (e.g., opposition to affirmative action) can produce politically desirable judicial decisions. Thus, as academics continue to fuss about the best arguments to support a liberal moralistic vision of constitutional law, the Supreme Court has reverted to its traditional American role as protector of hierarchy and vested rights. Characteristic of its emerging jurisprudence of callous indifference are a renewed insistence on an almost classical formalism of property[56] and contract,[57] a vigorous judicial activism on behalf of property and power against democratic regulation or redistribution (in the guise, ironically, of liberty and equality rights),[58] and a refusal to acknowledge historical or social reality as having any relevance to judicial decision making.[59]

Nevertheless, the right does not speak with a single voice, as revealed by some of the most recent Supreme Court decisions.[60] Traditionally conservatives in America have tended toward libertarianism in economic theory and toward social control in matters of life-style and political dissent (whereas the left has done the opposite). The alliance of libertarianism and social conservatism is an uneasy one; and even within economic thought, libertarianism is ultimately at odds with the market utilitarianism of the law and economics movement, which now dominates much of conservative legal scholarship.[61]

Meanwhile, the most promising direction from left legal scholars has been to eschew the formulation of yet one more grand, integrative scheme of constitutional law jurisprudence. Instead, there is a new willingness to learn from those who have traditionally been marginalized and excluded by mainstream legal thought—especially women and persons of color. This "outsider" jurisprudence which is now emerging understands "rights" only in relation to moral practice and as situated in historical and experiential context.[62] It is the most hopeful sign of the future we now have.

NOTES

1. *See*, especially, Robert Gordon, "Historicism in Legal Scholarship," 90 *Yale Law Journal* 1017 (1981), and Comment, "The Historical Contingency of the Role of History," 90 *Yale Law Journal* 1057 (1981).
2. The best and most thorough account of these changes is to be found in Duncan Kennedy, "Toward an Historical Understanding of Legal Consciousness: The Case of Classical Legal Thought in America, 1850–1940," in *Research in Law and Sociology*, ed. S. Spitzer (Greenwich, Conn.: JAI Press, 1980), vol. 3.
3. *See generally* Gordon Wood, *The Creation of the American Republic, 1776–1787* (Chapel Hill: University of North Carolina Press, 1969).
4. *See* Elizabeth Mensch and Alan Freeman, "A Republican Agenda for Hobbesian America?" 41 *University of Florida Law Review* 581 (1989).
5. This assertion and some of the others that follow are based upon a reading of collected but unpublished nineteenth-century addresses, speeches, and other miscellaneous examples of legal discourse. The collection is to be found, uncataloged under a single title, in the Cornell Law School Library. Hooker's quotation is still inscribed, in large letters, on the wall of the Harvard Law School Library.
6. Joseph Story, Discourse upon the Inauguration of the Author as Dane Professor of Law, 1829 (Cornell Law School Collection). *See also* R. Kent Newmyer, "Harvard Law School, New England Legal Culture, and the Antebellum Origins of American Jurisprudence," 74 *Journal of American History* 814 (1987).
7. For a seventeenth-century version, *see* Christopher Hill, "The Religion of Gerrard Winstanley," in *The Collected Essays of Christopher Hill*, (Amherst: University of Massachusetts Press, 1986), 2: 185–252. *See also* Norman Cohn, *The Pursuit of the Millennium* (New York: Harper & Brothers, 1961).
8. *See* Morton Horwitz, *The Transformation of American Law, 1780–1860* (Cambridge, Mass.: Harvard University Press, 1977), p. 257.
9. The claim was as old as the confrontation between Sir Edward Coke and King James I, in which Coke explained that whereas others besides judges (including, especially, the king) had excellent natural reason, they did not have the "artificial reason" of the law, which "is an art which requires long study and experience, before that a man can attain to the cognizance of it." 12 Coke's Reports 63, 65, 77 English Reports 1342, 1343 (King's Bench, 1608).
10. 10 U.S. (6 Cranch) 87 (1810). For Marshall's debt to Hamilton, *see* C. Peter McGrath, *Yazoo: Law and Politics in the New Republic* (Providence, R.I.: Brown University Press, 1966), app. E.
11. Again, nineteenth-century jurists were able to draw on a long English tradition for such notions. *See* Matthew Hale, "Considerations Touching the Amendment and Alteration of Laws," *A Collection of Tracts Relative to the*

Law of England, ed. Francis Hargrave (Dublin: W. Colles, 1787), 1:249.

12. Theophilus Parsons, *Law of Contracts* (Boston: Little, Brown, 1855).

13. *See generally* Frances Olsen, "The Family and the Market: A Study of Ideology and Legal Reform," 96 *Harvard Law Review* 1497 (1983). For the rich history describing the sphere of domesticity as containment of the more radical assertion of female equality that followed the American Revolution, *see, e.g.*, Mary Beth Norton, *Liberty's Daughters: The Revolutionary Experience of American Women, 1750–1800* (Boston and Toronto: Little, Brown, 1980).

14. Samuel Williston, *The Law of Contracts*, 1st ed. (New York: Baker, Voorhis, 1920).

15. Coppage v. Kansas, 236 U.S. 1 (1915).

16. Adair v. United States, 208 U.S. 161 (1908).

17. *See* Frank Michelman, "Possession vs. Distribution in the Constitutional Idea of Property," 72 *Iowa Law Review* 1319, 1334–37 (1987). For a good judicial example, *see* Pennsylvania Coal Co. v. Mahon, 260 U.S. 393, 416–22 (1922) (Brandeis, J., dissenting).

18. As an early example of that approach, *see* Roscoe Pound, "Mechanical Jurisprudence," 8 *Columbia Law Review* 605 (1908).

19. See generally, Alan Freeman and Elizabeth Mensch, "The Public-Private Distinction in American Law and Life," 36 *Buffalo Law Review* 237 (1988).

20. For one of the best single examples of the realist assault upon the objectivity of rights theory and legal analysis in general, *see* Felix Cohen, "Transcendental Nonsense and the Functional Approach," 35 *Columbia Law Review* 809 (1935).

21. Morris Cohen, "Property and Sovereignty," 13 *Cornell Law Quarterly* 8 (1927).

22. Robert Hale, "Bargaining, Duress and Economic Liberty," 43 *Columbia Law Review* 603 (1943); Robert Hale, "Coercion and Distribution in a Supposedly Non-Coercive State," 38 *Political Science Quarterly* 470 (1923). See also Elizabeth Mensch, "Freedom of Contract as Ideology," 33 *Stanford Law Review* 753 (1981).

23. *See, e.g.*, F. Cohen, "The Ethical Basis of Legal Criticism," 41 *Yale Law Journal* 201 (1931).

24. For a discussion of this dilemma, and of American realism in general, *see* Edward Purcell, *The Crisis of Democratic Theory: Scientific Naturalism and the Problem of Value* (Lexington: University of Kentucky Press, 1973).

25. Howard Laswell and Myres McDougal, "Legal Education and Public Policy: Professional Training in the Public Interest," 52 *Yale Law Journal* 203 (1943).

26. Henry Hart and Albert Sacks, *The Legal Process: Basic Problems in the Making and Application of Law* (tent. ed. 1958).

27. International Shoe Co. v. State of Washington, 326 U.S. 310 (1945), the landmark modern case on personal jurisdiction.

28. Hoffman v. Red Owl Stores, Inc., 26 Wis. 2d 683 (1965).

29. *See* Burton v. Wilmington Parking Authority, 365 U.S. 715 (1961).

30. *See* Flagg Bros., Inc. v. Brooks, 436 U.S. 149 (1978).

31. Compare Amalgamated Food Employees Union v. Logan Valley Plaza, 391 U.S. 308 (1968), with Lloyd Corp. v. Tanner, 407 U.S. 551 (1972), with Hudgens v. NLRB, 424 U.S. 507 (1976).

32. *E.g.*, NLRB v. Yeshiva University, 444 U.S. 672 (1980). *See* Katherine Van Wezel Stone, "Labor and the Corporate Structure: Changing Conceptions and Emerging Possibilities," 55 *University of Chicago Law Review*, 73, 131–38 (1988).

33. United States v. Willow River Power Co., 324 U.S. 499 (1945).

34. Karl Llewellyn, *The Common Law Tradition, Deciding Appeals* (Boston: Little, Brown, 1960).

35. Edward Levi, *An Introduction to Legal Reasoning* (Chicago: University of Chicago Press, 1948).

36. McPherson v. Buick Motors Co. 217 N.Y. 382 (1916).

37. Palsgraf v. Long Island R.R., 248 N.Y. 339, 162 N.E. 99 (1928). *See also* John Noonan, Jr., *Persons and Masks of the Law* (New York: Farrar, Straus & Giroux, 1976), p. 111, for the contexual reality behind the case.

38. Llewellyn, *supra* note 34.

39. *See, e.g.*, Franklin Schultz, "The Firm Offer Puzzle: A Study of Business Practice in the Construction Industry," 19 *Chicago Law Review* 237 (1952).

40. Alexander Bickel, "The Passive Virtues," 75 *Harvard Law Review* 40 (1961).

41. Korematsu v. United States, 323 U.S. 214 (1944).

42. Herbert Wechsler, "Toward Neutral Principles of Constitutional Law," 73 *Harvard Law Review* 1 (1959). *See generally* Gary Peller, "Neutral Principles in the 1950's," 21 *University of Michigan Journal of Law Reform* 561 (1988).

43. Brown v. Board of Education, 347 U.S. 483 (1954).

44. The paradigmatic example of this effort is Frank Michelman, "On Protecting the Poor Through the Fourteenth Amendment," 83 *Harvard Law Review*. 7 (1969).

45. "With the Editors," 83 *Harvard Law Review* vii (1970). (Note: this section is usually omitted from the bound volumes found in libraries, but may be found in the individual paperbound issue as originally published.)

46. See J. Skelly Wright, "Professor Bickel, The Scholarly Tradition, and the Supreme Court," 84 *Harvard Law Review* 769 (1971), which is also an excellent review of Alexander Bickel's work, especially that directed critically at the Warren Court.

47. For a good overview, see Paul Brest, "The Fundamental Rights Controversy: The Essential Contradictions of Normative Constitutional Scholarship," 90 *Yale Law Journal* 1063 (1981).

48. John Ely, *Democracy and Distrust: A Theory of Judicial Review* (Cambridge, Mass.: Harvard University Press, 1980).

49. United States v. Carolene Products Company, 304 U.S. 144, 152, n. 4 (1938).

50. *See* Paul Brest, "The Substance of Process," 42 *Ohio State Law Journal* 131 (1981).
51. *E.g.*, Owen Fiss, "The Death of the Law?" 72 *Cornell Law Review* 1 (1986). For a thorough overview of the jurisprudential scene at the close of the eighties, *see* Gary Minda, "The Jurisprudential Movements of the 1980's," 50 *Ohio State Law Journal* 599 (1989).
52. John Rawls, A *Theory of Justice* (Cambridge, Mass.: Harvard University Press, 1971). For an excellent critique, *see* Robert Paul Wolff, *Understanding Rawls* (Princeton, N.J.: Princeton University Press, 1977).
53. *E.g.*, Robert·Cover, "Forewood: Nomos and Narrative," 97 *Harvard Law Review* 4 (1983); Martha Minow, "Interpreting Rights: An Essay for Robert Cover," 96 *Yale Law Journal* 1860 (1987). *See generally* Mark Tushnet, "Anti-Formalism in Recent Constitutional Theory," 83 *Michigan Law Review* 1502 (1985).
54. *See, e.g.*, "Symposium: The Republican Civic Tradition," 97 *Yale Law Journal* 1493–1723 (1988). For a critical response, *see* Mensch and Freeman, *supra* note 4.
55. *E.g.*, David Shapiro, "Courts, Legislatures, and Paternalism," 74 *Virginia Law Review* 519 (1988). *See also* Steven Burton, An *Introduction to Law and Legal Reasoning* (Boston and Toronto: Little, Brown, 1985).
56. *E.g.*, Nollan v. California Coastal Comm'n, 107 S.Ct. 3141 (1987).
57. *E.g.*, Patterson v. McLean Credit Union, 109 S. Ct. 2363 (1989).
58. Powerful examples are the Court's use of the First Amendment to insulate corporate power from public regulation, e.g., First Nat'l Bank v. Bellotti, 435 U.S. 765 (1978); Consolidated Edison Co. v. Public Service Comm'n, 447 U.S. 530 (1980), and the use of the Equal Protection Clause to prevent a democratically elected local legislature from redistributing contract access in order to redress a long-standing condition of racial inequality, City of Richmond v. J. A. Croson Co., 109 S. Ct. 706 (1989).
59. *E.g.*, Wards Cove Packing Co. v. Atonio, 109 S.Ct. 2115 (1989).
60. A powerful example is Texas v. Johnson, 109 S.Ct. 2533 (1989), where Justices Scalia and Kennedy followed the impulse of libertarian conservativism to the point of allying with liberals Brennan, Marshall, and Blackmun, to form a majority of five to overturn on First Amendment grounds a conviction for burning the American flag.
61. *See generally* Mark Kelman, "Conservative Legal Thought," in this volume.
62. *See, e.g.*, the chapters by Cornel West and Kimberle Crenshaw in this volume, and Mari Matsuda, "Public Response to Racist Speech: Considering the Victim's Story," 87 *Michigan Law Review* 2320 (1989).

2 DUNCAN KENNEDY

LEGAL EDUCATION AS TRAINING FOR HIERARCHY

LAW schools are intensely political places despite the fact that the modern law school seems intellectually unpretentious, barren of theoretical ambition or practical vision of what social life might be. The trade-school mentality, the endless attention to trees at the expense of forests, the alternating grimness and chumminess of focus on the limited task at hand, all these are only a part of what is going on. The other part is ideological training for willing service in the hierarchies of the corporate welfare state.

To say that law school is ideological is to say that what teachers teach along with basic skills is wrong, is nonsense about what law is and how it works; that the message about the nature of legal competence, and its distribution among students, is wrong, is nonsense; that the ideas about the possibilities of life as a lawyer that students pick up from legal education are wrong, are nonsense. But all this is nonsense with a tilt; it is biased and motivated rather than random error. What it says is that it is natural, efficient, and fair for law firms, the bar as a whole, and the society the bar services to be organized in their actual patterns of hierarchy and domination.

Because students believe what they are told, explicitly and implicitly, about the world they are entering, they behave in ways that fulfill the prophecies the system makes about them and about that world. This is the linkback that completes the system: students do more than accept the way things are, and ideology does more than damp opposition. Students act affirmatively within the channels cut for them, cutting them deeper, giving the whole a patina of consent, and weaving complicity into everyone's life story.

In this chapter, I take up in turn the initial first-year experience, the ideological content of the law school curriculum, and the noncurricular

An enlarged version of this chapter entitled *Legal Education and the Reproduction of Hierarchy* is available in pamphlet form from the author.

practices of law schools that train students to accept and participate in the hierarchical structure of life in the law.

THE FIRST-YEAR EXPERIENCE

A surprisingly large number of law students go to law school with the notion that being a lawyer means something more, something more socially constructive than just doing a highly respectable job. There is the idea of playing the role an earlier generation associated with Brandeis: the role of service through law, carried out with superb technical competence and also with a deep belief that in its essence law is a progressive force, however much it may be distorted by the actual arrangements of capitalism. There is a contrasting, more radical notion that law is a tool of established interests, that it is in essence superstructural, but that it is a tool that a coldly effective professional can sometimes turn against the dominators. Whereas in the first notion the student aspires to help the oppressed and transform society by bringing out the latent content of a valid ideal, in the second the student sees herself as part technician, part judo expert, able to turn the tables exactly because she never lets herself be mystified by the rhetoric that is so important to other students.

Then there are the conflicting motives, which are equally real for both types. People think of law school as extremely competitive, as a place where a tough, hardworking, smart style is cultivated and rewarded. Students enter law school with a sense that they will develop that side of themselves. Even if they disapprove, on principle, of that side of themselves, they have had other experiences in which it turned out that they wanted and liked aspects of themselves that on principle they disapproved of. How is one to know that one is not "really" looking to develop oneself in this way as much as one is motivated by the vocation of social transformation?

There is also the issue of social mobility. Almost everyone whose parents were not members of the professional/technical intelligentsia seems to feel that going to law school is an advance in terms of the family history. This is true even for children of high-level business managers, so long as their parents' positions were due to hard work and struggle rather than to birth into the upper echelons. It is rare for parents to actively *disapprove* of their children going to law school, whatever their origins. So taking this particular step has a social meaning, however much the student may reject it, and that social meaning is success. The success is bittersweet if one feels one should have gotten into a better school, but both the bitter and the sweet suggest that one's motives are impure.

The initial classroom experience sustains rather than dissipates ambivalence. The teachers are overwhelmingly white, male, and deadeningly straight and middle class in manner. The classroom is hierarchical with a vengeance, the teacher receiving a degree of deference and arousing fears that remind one of high school rather than college. The sense of autonomy one has in a lecture, with the rule that you must let teacher drone on without interruption balanced by the rule that teacher can't *do* anything to you, is gone. In its place is a demand for a pseudoparticipation in which one struggles desperately, in front of a large audience, to read a mind determined to elude you. It is almost never anything as bad as *The Paper Chase* or *One-L*, but it is still humiliating to be frightened and unsure of oneself, especially when what renders one unsure is a classroom arrangement that suggests at once the patriarchal family and a Kafkalike riddle state. The law school classroom at the beginning of the first year is culturally reactionary.

But it is also engaging. You are learning a new language, and it *is* possible to learn it. Pseudoparticipation makes one intensely aware of how everyone else is doing, providing endless bases for comparison. Information is coming in on all sides, and things that you knew were out there but you didn't understand are becoming intelligible. The teacher offers subtle encouragements as well as not-so-subtle reasons for alarm. Performance is on one's mind, adrenaline flows, success has a nightly and daily meaning in terms of the material assigned. After all, this is the next segment: one is moving from the vaguely sentimental world of college, or the frustrating world of office work or housework, into something that promises a dose of "reality," even if it's cold and scary reality.

It quickly emerges that neither the students nor the faculty are as homogeneous as they at first appeared. Some teachers are more authoritarian than others; some students other than oneself reacted with horror to the infantilization of the first days or weeks. There even seems to be a connection between classroom manner and substantive views, with the "softer" teachers also seeming to be more "liberal," perhaps more sympathetic to plaintiffs in the torts course, more willing to hear what are called policy arguments, as well as less intimidating in class discussion. But there is a disturbing aspect to this process of differentiation: in most law schools, it turns out that the tougher, less policy-oriented teachers are the more popular. The softies seem to get less matter across, they let things wander, and one begins to worry that their niceness is at the expense of a metaphysical quality called rigor, thought to be essential to success on bar exams and in the grown-up world of practice. Ambivalence reasserts itself. As between the conservatives and the mushy centrists, enemies who scare you but subtly reassure you may seem more attractive than allies no better anchored than yourself.

There is an intellectual experience that somewhat corresponds to the emotional one: the gradual revelation that there is no purchase for left or even for committed liberal thinking on any part of the smooth surface of legal education. The issue in the classroom is not left against right, but pedagogical conservatism against moderate, disintegrated liberalism. No teacher is likely to present a model of either left pedagogy or vital left theoretical enterprise, though some *are* likely to be vaguely sympathetic to progressive causes, and some may even be moonlighting as left lawyers. Students are struggling for cognitive mastery and against the sneaking depression of the preprofessional. The actual intellectual content of the law seems to consist of learning rules—what they are and why they have to be the way they are—while rooting for the occasional judge who seems willing to make them marginally more humane. The basic experience is of double surrender: to a passivizing classroom experience and to a passive attitude toward the content of the legal system.

The first step toward this sense of the irrelevance of liberal or left thinking is the opposition in the first-year curriculum between the technical, boring, difficult, obscure legal case and the occasional case with outrageous facts and a piggish judicial opinion endorsing or tolerating the outrage. The first kind of case—call it a cold case—is a challenge to interest, understanding, even to wakefulness. It can be on any subject, so long as it is of no political or moral or emotional significance. Just to understand what happened and what's being said about it, you have to learn a lot of new terms, a little potted legal history, and lots of rules, none of which is carefully explained by the casebook or the teacher. It is difficult to figure out why the case is there in the first place, difficult to figure out whether you have grasped it, and difficult to anticipate what the teacher will ask and what one should respond.

The other kind of case—call it a hot case—usually involves a sympathetic plaintiff—say, an Appalachian farm family—and an unsympathetic defendant—say, a coal company. On first reading, it appears that the coal company has screwed the farm family by renting their land for strip mining, with a promise to restore it to its original condition once the coal has been extracted, and then reneging on the promise. And the case should include a judicial opinion that does something like award a meaningless couple of hundred dollars to the farm family rather than making the coal company perform the restoration work. The point of the class discussion will be that your initial reaction of outrage is naive, nonlegal, irrelevant to what you're supposed to be learning, and maybe substantively wrong into the bargain. There are "good reasons" for the awful result, when you take a legal and logical "large" view, as opposed to the knee-jerk passionate view; and if you can't muster those reasons, maybe you aren't cut out to be a lawyer.

Most students can't fight this combination of a cold case and a hot case. The cold case is boring, but you have to do it if you want to become a lawyer. The hot case cries out for response, seems to say that if you can't respond you've already sold out; but the system tells you to put away childish things, and your reaction to the hot case is one of them. Without any intellectual resources, in the way of knowledge of the legal system and of the character of legal reasoning, it will appear that emoting will only isolate and incapacitate you. The choice is to develop some calluses and hit the books, or admit failure almost before you've begun.

THE IDEOLOGICAL CONTENT OF LEGAL EDUCATION

One can distinguish in a rough way between two aspects of legal education as a reproducer of hierarchy. A lot of what happens is the inculcation through a formal curriculum and the classroom experience of a set of political attitudes toward the economy and society in general, toward law, and toward the possibilities of life in the profession. These have a general ideological significance, and they have an impact on the lives even of law students who never practice law. Then there is a complicated set of institutional practices that orient students to willing participation in the specialized hierarchical roles of lawyers. Students begin to absorb the more general ideological message before they have much in the way of a conception of life after law school, so I will describe this formal aspect of the educational process before describing the ways in which the institutional practice of law schools bear on those realities.

Law students sometimes speak as though they learned *nothing* in school. In fact, they learn skills to do a list of simple but important things. They learn to retain large numbers of rules organized into categorical systems (requisites for a contract, rules about breach, etc.). They learn "issue spotting," which means identifying the ways in which the rules are ambiguous, in conflict, or have a gap when applied to particular fact situations. They learn elementary case analysis, meaning the art of generating broad holdings for cases so they will apply beyond their intuitive scope, and narrow holdings for cases so that they won't apply where it at first seemed they would. And they learn a list of balanced, formulaic, pro/con policy arguments that lawyers use in arguing that a given rule should apply to a situation despite a gap, conflict, or ambiguity, or that a given case should be extended or narrowed. These are arguments like "the need for certainty" and "the need for flexibility," "the need to promote competition" and the "need to encourage production by letting producers keep the rewards of their labor."

One should neither exalt these skills nor denigrate them. By comparison with the first-year students' tendency to flip-flop between formalism and mere equitable intuition, they represent a real intellectual advance. Lawyers actually do use them in practice; and when properly, consciously mastered, they have "critical" bite. They are a help in thinking about politics, public policy, ethical discourse in general, because they show the indeterminacy and manipulability of ideas and institutions that are central to liberalism.

On the other hand, law schools teach these rather rudimentary, essentially instrumental skills in a way that almost completely mystifies them for almost all law students. The mystification has three parts. First, the schools teach skills through class discussions of cases in which it is asserted that law emerges from a rigorous analytical procedure called legal reasoning, which is unintelligible to the layperson but somehow both explains and validates the great majority of the rules in force in our system. At the same time, the class context and the materials present every legal issue as distinct from every other—as a tub on its own bottom, so to speak—with no hope or even any reason to hope that from law study one might derive an integrating vision of what law is, how it works, or how it might be changed (other than in any incremental, case-by-case, reformist way).

Second, the teaching of skills in the mystified context of legal reasoning about utterly unconnected legal problems means that skills are taught badly, unself-consciously, to be absorbed by osmosis as one picks up the knack of "thinking like a lawyer." Bad or only randomly good teaching generates and then accentuates real differences and imagined differences in student capabilities. But it does so in such a way that students don't know when they are learning and when they aren't, and have no way of improving or even understanding their own learning processes. They experience skills training as the gradual emergence of differences among themselves, as a process of ranking that reflects something that is just "there" inside them.

Third, the schools teach skills in isolation from actual lawyering experience. "Legal reasoning" is sharply distinguished from law practice, and one learns nothing about practice. This procedure disables students from any future role but that of apprentice in a law firm organized in the same manner as a law school, with older lawyers controlling the content and pace of depoliticized craft training in a setting of intense competition and no feedback.

THE FORMAL CURRICULUM:
LEGAL RULES AND LEGAL REASONING

The intellectual core of the ideology is the distinction between law and policy. Teachers convince students that legal reasoning exists, and is different from policy analysis, by bullying them into accepting as valid in particular cases arguments about legal correctness that are circular, question-begging, incoherent, or so vague as to be meaningless. Sometimes these are just arguments from authority, with the validity of the authoritative premise put outside discussion by professorial fiat. Sometimes they are policy arguments (e.g., security of transaction, business certainty) that are treated in a particular

situation as though they were rules that everyone accepts but that will be
ignored in the next case when they would suggest that the decision was
wrong. Sometimes they are exercises in formal logic that wouldn't stand up
for a minute in a discussion between equals (e.g., the small print in a form
contract represents the "will of the parties").

Within a given subfield, the teacher is likely to treat cases in three different
ways. There are the cases that present and justify the basic rules and basic
ideas of the field. These are treated as cursory exercises in legal logic. Then
there are cases that are anomalous—"outdated" or "wrongly decided" because
they don't follow the supposed inner logic of the area. There won't be many
of these, but they are important because their treatment persuades students
that the technique of legal reasoning is at least minimally independent of
the results reached by particular judges and is therefore capable of criticizing
as well as legitimating. Finally, there will be an equally small number of
peripheral or "cutting-edge" cases the teacher sees as raising policy issues
about growth or change in the law. Whereas in discussing the first two kinds
of cases the teacher behaves in an authoritarian way supposedly based on
his objective knowledge of the technique of legal reasoning, here everything
is different. Because we are dealing with "value judgments" that have "political" overtones, the discussion will be much more freewheeling. Rather
than every student comment being right or wrong, all student comments get
pluralist acceptance, and the teacher will reveal himself to be either a liberal
or a conservative rather than merely a legal technician.

The curriculum as a whole has a rather similar structure. It is not really
a random assortment of tubs on their own bottoms, a forest of tubs. First,
there are contracts, torts, property, criminal law, and civil procedure. The
rules in these courses are the ground rules of late-nineteenth-century laissez-
faire capitalism. Teachers teach them as though they had an inner logic, as
an exercise in legal reasoning, with policy (e.g., commercial certainty in the
contracts course) playing a relatively minor role. Then there are second- and
third-year courses that expound the moderate reformist program of the New
Deal and the administrative structure of the modern regulatory state (with
passing reference to the racial egalitarianism of the Warren Court). These
courses are more policy oriented than first-year courses, and also much more
ad hoc. Teachers teach students that limited interference with the market
makes sense and is as authoritatively grounded in statutes as the ground rules
of laissez-faire are grounded in natural law. But each problem is discrete,
enormously complicated, and understood in a way that guarantees the practical impotence of the reform program. Finally, there are peripheral subjects,
like legal philosophy or legal history, legal process, clinical legal education.
These are presented as not truly relevant to the "hard" objective, serious,

rigorous analytic core of law; they are a kind of playground or finishing school for learning the social art of self-presentation as a lawyer.

This whole body of implicit messages is nonsense. Teachers teach nonsense when they persuade students that legal reasoning is distinct, *as a method for reaching correct results*, from ethical and political discourse in general (i.e., from policy analysis). It is true that there is a distinctive lawyers' body of knowledge of the rules in force. It is true that there are distinctive lawyers' argumentative techniques for spotting gaps, conflicts, and ambiguities in the rules, for arguing broad and narrow holdings of cases, and for generating pro and con policy arguments. But these are *only* argumentative techniques. There is never a "correct legal solution" that is other than the correct ethical and political solution to that legal problem. Put another way, everything taught, except the formal rules themselves and the argumentative techniques for manipulating them, is policy and nothing more. It follows that the classroom distinction between the unproblematic, legal case and the policy-oriented case is a mere artifact: each could as well be taught in the opposite way. And the curricular distinction between the "nature" of contract law as highly legal and technical by contrast, say, with environmental law is equally a mystification.

These errors have a bias in favor of the center liberal program of limited reform of the market economy and pro forma gestures toward racial and sexual equality. The bias arises because law school teaching makes the choice of hierarchy and domination, which is implicit in the adoption of the rules of property, contract, and tort, look as though it flows from and is required by legal reasoning rather than being a matter of politics and economics. The bias is reinforced when the center liberal reformist program of regulation is presented as equally authoritative but somehow more policy oriented, and therefore less fundamental. The message is that the system is basically OK, since we have patched up the few areas open to abuse, and that it has a limited but important place for value-oriented debate about further change and improvement. If there is to be more fundamental questioning, it is relegated to the periphery of history or philosophy. The real world is kept at bay by treating clinical legal education, which might bring in a lot of information threatening to the cozy liberal consensus, as free legal drudge work for the local bar or as mere skills training.

It would be an extraordinary first-year student who could, on his own, develop a theoretically critical attitude toward this system. Entering students just don't know enough to figure out where the teacher is fudging, misrepresenting, or otherwise distorting legal thinking and legal reality. To make matters worse, the two most common kinds of left thinking the student is likely to bring with her are likely to hinder rather than assist in the struggle to maintain some intellectual autonomy from the experience. Most liberal students believe that the left program can be reduced to guaranteeing people their rights and to bringing about the triumph of human rights over mere property rights. In this picture, the trouble with the legal system is that it fails to put the state behind the rights of the oppressed, or that the system fails to enforce the rights formally recognized. If one thinks about law this way, one is inescapably dependent on the very techniques of legal reasoning that are being marshalled in defense of the status quo.

This wouldn't be so bad if the problem with legal education were that the teachers *misused* rights reasoning to restrict the range of the rights of the oppressed. But the problem is much deeper than that. Rights discourse is internally inconsistent, vacuous, or circular. Legal thought can generate equally plausible rights justifications for almost any result. Moreover, the discourse of rights imposes constraints on those who use it that make it almost impossible for it to function effectively as a tool of radical transformation. Rights are by their nature "formal," meaning that they secure to individuals legal protection for as well as from arbitrariness—to speak of rights is precisely *not* to speak of justice between social classes, races, or sexes. Rights discourse, moreover, simply presupposes or takes for granted that the world is and should be divided between a state sector that enforces rights and a private world of "civil society" in which atomized individuals pursue their diverse goals. This framework is, *in itself*, a part of the problem rather than of the solution. It makes it difficult even to conceptualize radical proposals such as, for example, decentralized democratic worker control of factories.

Because it is logically incoherent and manipulable, traditionally individualist, and willfully blind to the realities of *substantive* inequality, rights discourse is a trap. As long as one stays within it, one can produce good pieces of argument about the occasional case on the periphery where everyone recognizes value judgments have to be made. But one is without guidance in deciding what to do about fundamental questions and fated to the gradual loss of confidence in the convincingness of what one has to say in favor of the very results one believes in most passionately.

The alternative left stance is to undertake the Procrustean task of reinterpreting every judicial action as the expression of class interest. One may adopt a conspiracy theory in which judges deliberately subordinate "justice" (usually just a left liberal rights theory) to the short-run financial interests of the ruling class, or a much more subtle thesis about the "logic" or "needs" or "structural prerequisites" of a particular "stage of monopoly capitalism." But however one sets out to do it, there are two difficulties. The first is that there is just too much dreck, too much raw matter of the legal system, and too little time to give everything you have to study a sinister significance. It would be a full-time job just to give instrumental Marxist accounts of the cases on consideration doctrine in first-year contracts. Just exactly why was it that late-nineteenth-century capitalism needed to render an uncle's promise to pay his nephew a handsome sum if he didn't smoke till age twenty-one, a legal nullity? Or was it the other way around: that capitalism *needed* such promises to be enforceable?

The second difficulty is that there is no "logic" to monopoly capitalism, and law cannot be usefully understood, by someone who has to deal with it in all its complexity, as "superstructural." Legal rules the state enforces and legal concepts that permeate all aspects of social thought constitute capitalism as well as responding to the interests that operate within it. Law is an aspect of the social totality, not just the tail of the dog. The rules in force are a factor in the power or impotence of all social actors (though they certainly do not determine outcomes in the way liberal legalists sometimes suggest they do). Because it is part of the equation of power rather than simply a function of it, people struggle for power through law, constrained by their limited understanding and limited ability to predict the consequences of their maneuvers. To understand law is to understand this struggle as an aspect of class struggle *and* as an aspect of the human struggle to grasp the conditions of social justice. The outcomes of struggle are not preordained by any aspect of the social totality, and the outcomes within law have no "inherent logic" that would allow one to predict outcomes "scientifically" or to reject in advance specific attempts by judges and lawyers to work limited transformations of the system.

Left liberal rights analysis submerges the student in legal rhetoric but, because of its inherent vacuousness, can provide no more than an emotional stance against the legal order. The instrumental Marxist approach is highly critical of law but also dismissive. It is no help in coming to grips with the particularity of rules and rhetoric because it treats them, a priori, as mere window dressing. These theories fail left students because they offer no base for the mastery of ambivalence. What is needed is to think about law in a way that will allow one to enter into it, to criticize it without utterly rejecting it, and to manipulate it without self-abandonment to *their* system of thinking and doing.

STUDENT EVALUATION

Law schools teach a small number of useful skills. But they teach them only obliquely. It would threaten the professional ideology and the academic pretensions of teachers to make their students as good as they can be at the relatively simple tasks that they will have to perform in practice. But it would also upset the process by which a hierarchical arrangement analogous to that of law school applicants, law schools, and law firms is established within a given student body.

To teach the repetitive skills of legal analysis effectively, one would have to isolate the general procedures that make them up, and then devise large numbers of factual and doctrinal hypotheticals where students could practice those skills, knowing what they were doing and learning in every single case whether their performance was good or bad. As legal education now works, on the other hand, students do exercises designed to discover what the "correct solution" to a legal problem might be, those exercises are treated as unrelated to one another, and students receive no feedback at all except a grade on a single examination at the end of the course. Students generally experience these grades as almost totally arbitrary—unrelated to how much you worked, how much you liked the subject, how much you thought you understood going into the exam, and what you thought about the class and the teacher.

This is silly, looked at as pedagogy. But it is more than silly when looked at as ideology. The system generates a rank ordering of students based on grades, and students learn that there is little or nothing they can do to change their place in that ordering, or to change the way the school generates it. Grading as practiced teaches the inevitability and also the justice of hierarchy, a hierarchy that is at once false and unnecessary.

It is unnecessary because it is largely irrelevant to what students will do as lawyers. Most of the process of differentiating students into bad, better, and good could simply be dispensed with without the slightest detriment to the quality of legal services. It is false, first, because insomuch as it does involve the measuring of the real and useful skills of potential lawyers, the differences between students could be "leveled up" at minimal cost, whereas the actual practice of legal education systematically accentuates differences in real capacities. If law schools invested some of the time and money they now put into Socratic classes in developing systematic skills training, and committed themselves to giving constant, detailed feedback on student progress in learning those skills, they could graduate the vast majority of all the law students in the country at the level of technical proficiency now achieved by a small minority in each institution.

Law schools convey their factual message to each student about his or her place in the ranking of students along with the implicit corollary that place is individually earned, and therefore deserved. The system tells you that you learned as much as you were capable of learning, and that if you feel incompetent or that you could have become better at what you do, it is your own fault. Opposition is sour grapes. Students internalize this message about themselves and about the world, and so prepare themselves for all the hierarchies to follow.

INCAPACITATION FOR ALTERNATIVE PRACTICE

Law schools channel their students into jobs in the hierarchy of the bar according to their own standing in the hierarchy of schools. Students confronted with the choice of what to do after they graduate experience themselves as largely helpless: they have no "real" alternative to taking a job in one of the conventional firms that hires from their school. Partly, faculties generate this sense of student helplessness by propagating myths about the character of the different kinds of practice. They extol the forms that are accessible to their students; they subtly denigrate or express envy about the jobs that will be beyond their students' reach; they dismiss as ethically and socially suspect the jobs their students won't have to take.

As for any form of work outside the established system—for example, legal services for the poor and neighborhood law practice—they convey to students that, although morally exalted, the work is hopelessly dull and unchallenging, and that the possibilities of reaching a standard of living appropriate to a lawyer are slim or nonexistent. These messages are just nonsense—the rationalizations of law teachers who long upward, fear status degradation, and above all hate the idea of risk. Legal services practice, for example, is far more intellectually stimulating and demanding, even with a high caseload, than most of what corporate lawyers do. It is also more fun.

Beyond this dimension of professional mythology, law schools act in more concrete ways to guarantee that their students will fit themselves into their appropriate niches in the existing system of practice. First, the actual content of what is taught in a given school will incapacitate students from any other form of practice than that allotted graduates of that institution. This looks superficially like a rational adaptation to the needs of the market, but it is in fact almost entirely unnecessary. Law schools teach so little, and that so incompetently, that they cannot, as now constituted, prepare students for more than one career at the bar. But the reason for this is that they embed skills training in mystificatory nonsense and devote most of their teaching time to transmitting masses of ill-digested rules. A more rational system would emphasize the way to learn law rather than rules, and skills rather than answers. Student capacities would be more equal as a result, but students would also be radically more flexible in what they could do in practice.

A second incapacitating device is the teaching of doctrine in isolation from practice skills. Students who have no practice skills tend to exaggerate how difficult it is to acquire them. There is a distinct lawyers' mystique of the irrelevance of the "theoretical" material learned in school, and of the crucial importance of abilities that cannot be known or developed until one is out in the "real world" and "in the trenches." Students have little alternative to getting training in this dimension of things after law school. It therefore seems hopelessly impractical to think about setting up your own law firm, and only a little less impractical to go to a small or political or unconventional firm rather than to one of those that offer the standard package of postgraduate education. Law schools are wholly responsible for this situation. They could quite easily revamp their curricula so that any student who wanted it would have a meaningful choice between independence and servility.

A third form of incapacitation is more subtle. Law school, as an extension of the educational system as a whole, teaches students that they are weak, lazy, incompetent, and insecure. And it also teaches them that if they are willing to accept dependency, large institutions will take care of them almost no matter what. The terms of the bargain are relatively clear. The institution will set limited, clearly defined tasks and specify minimum requirements in their performance. The student/associate has no other responsibilities than performance of those tasks. The institution takes care of all the contingencies of life, both within the law (supervision and backup from other firm members; firm resources and prestige to bail you out if you make a mistake) and in private life (firms offer money but also long-term job security and delicious benefits packages aimed to reduce risks of disaster). In exchange, you renounce any claim to control your work setting or the actual content of what you do, and agree to show the appropriate form of deference to those above and condescension to those below.

By comparison, the alternatives are risky. Law school does not train you to run a small law business, to realistically assess the outcome of a complex process involving many different actors, or to enjoy the feeling of independence and moral integrity that comes of creating your own job to serve your own goals. It tries to persuade you that you are barely competent to perform the much more limited roles it allows you, and strongly suggests that it is more prudent to kiss the lash than to strike out on your own.

THE MODELING OF HIERARCHICAL RELATIONSHIPS

Law teachers model for students how they are supposed to think, feel, and act in their future professional roles. Some of this is a matter of teaching by example, some of it a matter of more active learning from interactions that are a kind of clinical education for lawyerlike behavior. This training is a major factor in the hierarchical life of the bar. It encodes the message of the legitimacy of the whole system into the smallest details of personal style, daily routine, gesture, tone of voice, facial expression—a plethora of little p's and q's for everyone to mind. Partly, these will serve as a language—a way for the young lawyer to convey that she knows what the rules of the game are and intends to play by them. What's going on is partly a matter of ritual oaths and affirmations—by adopting the mannerisms, one pledges one's troth to inequality. And partly it is a substantive matter of value. Hierarchical behavior will come to express and realize the hierarchical selves of people who were initially only wearers of masks.

Law teachers enlist on the side of hierarchy all the vulnerabilities students feel as they begin to understand what lies ahead of them. In law school, students have to come to grips with implications of their social class and sex and race in a way that is different from (but not necessarily less important than) the experience of college. People discover that preserving their class status is extremely important to them, so important that no alternative to the best law job they can get seems possible to them. Or they discover that they want to rise, or that they are trapped in a way they hadn't anticipated. People change the way they dress and talk; they change their opinions and even their emotions. None of this is easy for anyone, but progressive and left students have the special set of humiliations involved in discovering the limits of their commitment and often the instability of attitudes they thought were basic to themselves.

Another kind of vulnerability has to do with one's own competence. Law school wields frightening instruments of judgment, including not only the grading system but also the more subtle systems of teacher approval in class, reputation among fellow students, and out-of-class faculty contact and respect. Left students sometimes begin law school with an apparently unshakable confidence in their own competence and with a related confidence in their own left analysis. But even these apparently self-assured students quickly find that adverse judgments—even judgments that are only imagined or projected onto others—count and hurt. They have to decide whether this responsiveness in themselves is something to accept, whether the judgments in question have validity and refer to things they care about, or whether they should reject them. They have to wonder whether they have embarked on a subtle course of accommodating themselves intellectually in order to be in the ball park where people win and lose teacher and peer approval. And they have, in most or at least many cases, to deal with actual failure to live up to their highest hopes of accomplishment within the conventional system of rewards.

A first lesson is that professors are intensely preoccupied with the status rankings of their schools, and show themselves willing to sacrifice to improve their status in the rankings and to prevent downward drift. They approach the appointment of colleagues in the spirit of trying to get people who are as high up as possible in a conventionally defined hierarchy of teaching applicants, and they are notoriously hostile to affirmative action in faculty hiring, even when they are quite willing to practice it for student admissions and in filling administrative posts. Assistant professors begin their careers as the little darlings of their older colleagues. They end up in tense competition for the prize of tenure, trying to accommodate themselves to standards and expectations that are, typically, too vague to master except by a commitment to please at any cost. In these respects, law schools are a good preview of what law firms will be like.

Law professors, like lawyers, have secretaries. Students deal with them off and on through law school, watch how their bosses treat them, how they treat their bosses, and how "a secretary" relates to "a professor" even when one does not work for the other. Students learn that it is acceptable, even if it's not always and everywhere the norm, for faculty to treat their secretaries petulantly, condescendingly, with a perfectionism that is a matter of the bosses' face rather than of the demands of the job itself, as though they were personal body servants, utterly impersonally, or as objects of sexual harassment. They learn that "a secretary" treats "a professor" with elaborate deference, as though her time and her dignity meant nothing and his everything, even when he is not her boss. In general, they learn that humane relations in the workplace are a matter of the superior's grace rather than of human need and social justice.

These lessons are repeated in the relationships of professors and secretaries with administrators and with maintenance and support staff. Teachers convey a sense of their own superiority and practice a social segregation sufficiently extreme so that there are no occasions on which the reality of that superiority might be tested. As a group, they accept and willingly support the division of labor that consigns everyone in the institution but them to boredom and stagnation. Friendly but deferential social relations reinforce everyone's sense that all's for the best, making hierarchy seem to disappear in the midst of cordiality when in fact any serious challenge to the regime would be met with outrage and retaliation.

All of this is teaching by example. In their relations with students, and in the student culture they foster, teachers get the message across more directly and more powerfully. The teacher/student relationship is the model for relations between junior associates and senior partners, and also for the relationship between lawyers and judges. The student/student relationship is the model for relations among lawyers as peers, for the age cohort within a law firm, and for the "fraternity" of the courthouse crowd.

In the classroom and out of it, students learn a particular style of deference. They learn to suffer with positive cheerfulness interruption in midsentence, mockery, ad hominem assault, inconsequent asides, questions that are so vague as to be unanswerable but can somehow be answered wrong all the same, abrupt dismissal, and stinginess of praise (even if these things are not always and everywhere the norm). They learn, if they have talent, that submission is most effective flavored with a pinch of rebellion, to bridle a little before they bend. They learn to savor crumbs, while picking from the air the indications of the master's mood that can mean the difference between a good day and misery. They learn to take it all in good sort, that there is often shyness, good intentions, some real commitment to your learning something behind the authoritarian facade. So it will be with many a robed curmudgeon in years to come.

Then there is affiliation. From among many possibilities, each student gets to choose a mentor, or several, to admire and depend on, to become sort of friends with if the mentor is a liberal, to sit at the feet of if the mentor is more "traditional." You learn how he or she is different from other teachers, and to be supportive of those differences, as the mentor learns something of your particular strengths and weaknesses, both of you trying to prevent the inevitability of letters of recommendation from corrupting the whole experience. This can be fruitful and satisfying, or degrading, or both at once. So it will be a few years later with your "father in the law."

There is a third, more subtle, and less conscious message conveyed in student/teacher relations. Teachers are overwhelmingly white, male, and middle class; and most (by no means all) black and women law teachers give the impression of thorough assimilation to that style, or of insecurity and unhappiness. Students who are women or black or working class find out something important about the professional universe from the first day of class: that it is not even nominally pluralist in cultural terms. The teacher sets the tone—a white, male, middle-class tone. Students adapt. They do so partly out of fear, partly out of hope of gain, partly out of genuine admiration for their role models. But the line between adaptation to the intellectual and skills content of legal education and adaptation to the white, male, middle-class cultural style is a fine one, easily lost sight of.

While students quickly understand that there is diversity among their fellow students and that the faculty is not really homogeneous in terms of character, background, or opinions, the classroom itself becomes more rather than less uniform as legal education progresses. You'll find Fred Astaire and Howard Cosell over and over again, but never Richard Pryor or Betty Friedan. It's not that the teacher punishes you if you use slang or wear clothes or give examples or voice opinions that identify you as different, though that *might* happen. You are likely to be sanctioned, mildly or severely, only if you refuse to adopt the highly cognitive, dominating mode of discourse that everyone identifies as lawyerlike. Nonetheless, the indirect pressure for conformity is intense.

If you, alone in your seat, feel alienated in this atmosphere, it is unlikely that you will do anything about it in the classroom setting itself, however much you gripe about it with friends. It is more than likely that you'll find a way, in class, to respond as the teacher seems to want you to respond— to be a lot like him, as far as one could tell if one knew you only in class, even though your imitation is flawed by the need to suppress anger. And when some teacher, at least once in some class, makes a remark that seems sexist or racist, or seems unwilling to treat black or women students in quite as "challenging" a way as white students, or treats them in a more challenging way, or cuts off discussion when a woman student gets mad at a male student's joke about the tort of "offensive touching," it is unlikely that you'll do anything then either.

It is easy enough to see this situation of enforced cultural uniformity as oppressive, but somewhat more difficult to see it as training, especially if you are aware of it and hate it. But it is training nonetheless. You will pick up mannerisms, ways of speaking, gestures, that would be "neutral" if they were not emblematic of membership in the universe of the bar. You will come to expect that as a lawyer you will live in a world in which essential parts of you are not represented, or are misrepresented, and in which things you don't like will be accepted to the point that it doesn't occur to people that they are even controversial. And you will come to expect that there is nothing you can do about it. One develops ways of coping with these expectations—turning off attention or involvement when the conversation strays in certain directions, participating actively while ignoring the offensive elements of the interchange, even reinterpreting as inoffensive things that would otherwise make you boil. These are skills that incapacitate rather than empower, skills that will help you imprison yourself in practice.

Relations among students get a lot of their color from relations with the faculty. There is the sense of blood brotherhood, with or without sisters, in endless speculation about the Olympians. The speculation is colored with rage, expressed sometimes in student theatricals or the "humor" column of the school paper. ("Put Professor X's talents to the best possible use: Turn him into hamburger." Ha, ha.) There is likely to be a surface norm of noncompetitiveness and cooperation. ("Gee, I thought this would be like *The Paper Chase*, but it isn't at all.") But a basic thing to learn is the limits of that cooperativeness. Very few people can combine rivalry for grades, law review, clerkships, good summer jobs, with helping another member of their study group so effectively that he might actually pose a danger to them. You learn camaraderie and distrust at the same time. So it will be in the law-firm age cohort.

And there is more to it than that. Through the reactions of fellow students—diffuse, disembodied events that just "happen," in class or out of class—women learn how important it is not to appear to be "hysterical females," and that when your moot court partner gets a crush on you, and doesn't know it, and is married, there is a danger he will hate you when he discovers what he has been feeling. Lower-middle-class students learn not to wear an undershirt that shows, and that certain patterns and fabrics in clothes will stigmatize them no matter what their grades. Black students learn without surprise that the bar will have its own peculiar forms of racism, and that their very presence means affirmative action, unless it means "he would have made it even without affirmative action." They worry about forms of bias so diabolical even they can't see them, and wonder whether legal reasoning is intrinsically white. Meanwhile, dozens of small changes through which they become more and more like other middle- or upper-middle-class Americans engender rhetoric about how the black community is not divided along class lines. On one level, all of this is just high school replayed; on another, it's about how to make partner.

The final touch that completes the picture of law school as training for professional hierarchy is the placement process. As each firm, with the tacit or enthusiastically overt participation of the schools, puts on a conspicuous display of its relative status within the bar, the bar as a whole affirms and celebrates its hierarchical values and the rewards they bring. This process is most powerful for students who go through the elaborate procedures of firms in about the top half of the profession. These include, nowadays, first-year summer jobs, dozens of interviews, fly-outs, second-year summer jobs, more interviews, and more fly-outs.

This system allows law firms to get a *social* sense of applicants, a sense of how they will contribute to the nonlegal image of the firm and to the internal system of deference and affiliation. It allows firms to convey to students the extraordinary opulence of the life they offer, adding the allure of free travel, expense-account meals, fancy hotel suites, and parties at country clubs to the simple message of big bucks in a paycheck. And it teaches students at fancy law schools, students who have had continuous experience of academic and careerist success, that they are not as "safe" as they thought they were.

When students at Columbia or Yale paper dorm corridors with rejection letters, or award prizes for the most rejection letters and for the most unpleasant single letter, they show their sense of the meaning of the ritual. There are many ways in which the boss can persuade you to brush his teeth and comb his hair. One of them is to arrange things so that almost all students get good jobs, but most students get their good jobs through twenty interviews yielding only two offers.

By dangling the bait, making clear the rules of the game, and then subjecting almost everyone to intense anxiety about their acceptability, firms structure entry into the profession so as to maximize acceptance of hierarchy. If you feel you've succeeded, you're forever grateful, and you have a vested interest. If you feel you've failed, you blame yourself, when you aren't busy feeling envy. When you get to be the hiring partner, you'll have a visceral understanding of what's at stake, but by then it will be hard even to imagine why someone might want to change it.

Inasmuch as these hierarchies are generational, they are easier to take than those baldly reflective of race, sex, or class. You, too, will one day be a senior partner and, who knows, maybe even a judge; you will have mentees and be the object of the rage and longing of those coming up behind you. Training for subservience is training for domination as well. Nothing could be more natural and, if you've served your time, more fair than that you as a group should do as you have been done to, for better and for worse. But it doesn't *have* to be that way, and remember, you saw it first in law school.

I have been arguing that legal education is one of the causes of legal hierarchy. Legal education supports it by analogy, provides it a general legitimating ideology by justifying the rules that underlie it, and provides it a particular ideology by mystifying legal reasoning. Legal education structures the pool of prospective lawyers so that their hierarchical organization seems inevitable, and trains them in detail to look and think and act just like all the other lawyers in the system. Up to this point I have presented this causal analysis as though legal education were a machine feeding particular inputs into another machine. But machines have no consciousness of one another; inasmuch as they are coordinated, it is by some external intelligence. Law teachers, on the other hand, have a vivid sense of what the profession looks like and of what it expects them to do. Since actors in the two systems consciously adjust to one another and also consciously attempt to influence one another, legal education is as much a product of legal hierarchy as a cause of it. To my mind, this means that law teachers must take personal responsibility for legal hierarchy in general, including hierarchy within legal education. If it is there, it is there because they put it there and reproduce it generation after generation, just as lawyers do.

THE STUDENT RESPONSE TO HIERARCHY

Students respond in different ways to their slowly emerging consciousness of the hierarchical realities of life in the law. Looking around me, I see students who enter wholeheartedly into the system—for whom the training "takes" in a quite straightforward way. Others appear, at least, to manage something more complex. They accept the system's presentation of itself as largely neutral, as apolitical, meritocratic, instrumental, a matter of craft. And they also accept the system's promise that if they do their work, "serve their time," and "put in their hours," they are free to think and do and feel anything they want in their "private lives."

This mode of response is complex because the messages, though sincerely proffered, are not truly meant. People who accept the messages at face value often seem to sense that what has actually transpired is different. And since the law is neither apolitical nor meritocratic nor instrumental nor a matter of craft (at least not exclusively these things), and since training for hierarchy cannot be a matter merely of public as opposed to private life, it is inevitable that they do in fact give and take something different than what is suggested by the overt terms of the bargain. Sometimes people enact a kind of parody: they behave in a particularly tough, cognitive, lawyerlike mode in their professional selves, and construct a private self that seems on the surface to deliberately exaggerate opposing qualities of warmth, sensitivity, easygoingness, or cultural radicalism.

Sometimes one senses an opposite version: the person never fully enters into "legal reasoning," remaining always a slightly disoriented, not-quite-in-good-faith role player in professional life, and feels a parallel inability ever to fully "be" their private self. For example, they may talk "shop" and obsess about the day at work, while hating themselves for being unable to "relax," but then find that at work they are unable to make the tasks assigned them fully their own, and that each new task seems at first an unpleasant threat to their fragile feelings of confidence.

For progressive and left students, there is another possibility, which might be called the denunciatory mode. One can take law school work seriously as time serving and do it coldly in that spirit, hate one's fellow students for their surrenders, and focus one's hopes on "not being a lawyer" or on a fantasy of an unproblematically leftist legal job on graduation. This response is hard from the very beginning. If you reject what teachers and the student culture tell you about what the first-year curriculum means and how to enter into learning it, you are adrift as to how to go about becoming minimally competent. You have to develop a theory on your own of what is valid skills training and what is merely indoctrination, and your ambivalent desire to be successful in spite of all is likely to sabotage your independence. As graduation approaches, it becomes clearer that there are precious few unambiguously virtuous law jobs even to apply for, and your situation begins to look more like everyone else's, though perhaps more extreme. Most (by no means all) students who begin with denunciation end by settling for some version of the bargain of public against private life.

I am a good deal more confident about the patterns that I have just described than about the attitudes toward hierarchy that go along with them. My own position in the system of class, sex, and race (as an upper-middle-class white male) and my rank in the professional hierarchy (as a Harvard professor) give me an interest in the perception that hierarchy is both omnipresent and enormously important, even while I am busy condemning it. And there is a problem of imagination that goes beyond that of interest. It is hard for me to know whether I even understand the attitudes toward hierarchy of women and blacks, for example, or of children of working-class parents, or of solo practitioners eking out a living from residential real-estate closings. Members of those groups sometimes suggest that the particularity of their experience of oppression cannot be grasped by outsiders, but sometimes that the failure to grasp it is personal rather than inevitable. Often it seems to me that all people have at least analogous experiences of the oppressive reality of hierarchy, even those who seem most favored by the system—that the collar feels the same when you get to the end of the rope, whether the rope is ten feet long or fifty. On the other hand, it seems clear that hierarchy creates distances that are never bridged.

It is not uncommon for a person to answer a description of the hierarchy of law firms with a flat denial that the bar is really ranked. Lawyers of lower-middle-class background tend to have far more direct political power in the state governments than "elite" lawyers, even under Republican administrations. Furthermore, every lawyer knows of instances of real friendship, seemingly outside and beyond the distinctions that are supposed to be so important, and can cite examples of lower-middle-class lawyers in upper-middle-class law firms, and vice versa. There are many lawyers who seem to defy hierarchical classification, and law firms and law schools that do likewise, so that one can argue that the hierarchy claim that everyone and everything is ranked breaks down the minute you try to give concrete examples. I have been told often enough that I *may* be right about the pervasiveness of ranking, but that the speaker has never noticed it himself, himself treats all lawyers in the same way, regardless of their class or professional standing, and has never, except in an occasional very bizarre case, found lawyers violating the egalitarian norm.

When the person making these claims is a rich corporate lawyer who was my prep school classmate, I tend to interpret them as a willful denial of the way he is treated and treats others. When the person speaking is someone I perceive as less favored by the system (say, a woman of lower-middle-class origin who went to Brooklyn Law School and now works for a small, struggling downtown law firm), it is harder to know how to react. Maybe I'm just wrong about what it's like out there. Maybe my preoccupation with the horrors of hierarchy is just a way to wring the last ironic drop of pleasure from my own hierarchical superiority. But I don't interpret it that way. The denial of hierarchy is false consciousness. The problem is not whether hierarchy is there, but how to understand it, and what its implications are for political action.

II

SELECTED
FIELDS OF LAW
AND
SUBSTANTIVE
ISSUES

3 KARL E. KLARE

CRITICAL THEORY AND LABOR RELATIONS LAW

ON February 18, 1969, unionized clerks at the Boys Markets supermarket in Cudahy, California observed a supervisor and other nonunion personnel rearranging merchandise in the frozen-food cases. The employees complained that their collective bargaining contract allocated such work to union-represented staff. The union demanded that the counters be stripped of all merchandise and restocked by unionized personnel. Most likely they were unaware that the ensuing events would result in one of the most important labor decisions since the New Deal. [1]

Pejoratively labeled "restrictive practices" by the business-dominated media, work-preservation demands of this kind are often cited to portray the labor movement as "anticonsumer," "antiprogress," and "antipublic interest." The reality for working people is ignored: our public policy takes job scarcity for granted and makes no fundamental commitment to full employment. Because labor has little input into national economic planning, it seeks to protect jobs on an ad hoc, localized basis, through work-preservation rules, alliances with management to obtain favorable tariff and regulatory treatment, and, most recently, through concessions ("givebacks") at the collective bargaining table.

In this particular case, management declined the union's demand that the shelves be restocked. In the ordinary course of events, the union was entitled at this point to file a written grievance to press its interpretation of the contract. The grievance would lead to conferences, and if the parties could not reach agreement, to a ruling by a neutral called an "arbitrator" on whether management had violated the contract. The law is clear, however, that pending resolution of a grievance, the employees must return to work, and, no matter how patently erroneous, management's interpretation of disputed work rules must be obeyed while the grievance is being processed.

For reasons that are obscure, instead of leaving the matter to the grievance process, the supermarket clerks went on strike.

The clerks' grievance strike was in violation of a typical "no-strike clause" contained in the collective bargaining contract, *i.e.*, the union's promise that no work stoppage or "wildcat strike" would occur during the term of the contract. Employees ordinarily do not have legal protection when they strike in breach of a no-strike clause; they can be disciplined or fired. If a union authorizes or provokes a wildcat strike, it is subject to liability for monetary damages. But the delay and costs involved in either replacing employees or suing the union often make these remedies unattractive to employers. What management really wants is to get the employees back on the job. This requires an injunction, a court order compelling the employees to go back to work. Failure to obey such an order is punishable by fines and even prison as contempt of court. In this case, the company went to court for an injunction against the clerks' strike. The question that eventually reached the Supreme Court was whether courts are permitted to enjoin, and thereby to break, grievance strikes.

The "labor injunction" casts a long shadow over American labor history. From the late nineteenth century through the 1930s, employers, assisted by the courts, used the injunction in thousands of cases to combat union organization and strikes. Spontaneity, courage, solidarity, and the acuteness of the sense of grievance are all critical to union success in labor disputes. Since these feelings ebb and flow, timing is obviously a crucial factor. The injunction became employers' favorite legal weapon because it provided a mechanism for nearly instantaneous legal intervention against strikes and a way to obtain long delays in labor disputes. Moreover, the preliminary phases of injunction proceedings could traditionally occur *ex parte* (with only one party—the employer—appearing before the judge) or upon affidavits (without witnesses being subject to cross-examination). There is no right to a jury in injunction hearings. The truth had a way of getting lost in these shabby preliminary proceedings. The union's theoretical right to a subsequent review with full procedural guarantees often was meaningless since an initial, "temporary" injunction could often break a strike. Hostile courts granted employers very broad labor injunctions, as in a famous case involving Eugene V. Debs in which the court order essentially prohibited any person from engaging in any conduct in furtherance of the strike.

The labor injunction became a much-despised symbol of a largely pro-employer judiciary. Generations of antiinjunction agitation finally culminated in the Norris-La Guardia Act of 1932. Section 4(a) of that law expressly prohibits the federal courts from issuing injunctions against peaceful strikes. Many states subsequently passed "little Norris-La Guardia acts" similarly curtailing state court injunctions in labor cases.

But, if the Norris-La Guardia Act forbids injunctions against peaceful strikes, on what possible basis could the Boys Markets company ask for an injunction in the frozen-food-counter case? The company argued that the Norris-La Guardia Act must be "accommodated" to another, subsequent law, section 301(a) of the Taft-Hartley Act of 1947. On its face, section 301(a) deals only with technical jurisdictional issues. It does not say anything about labor injunctions, and its terms certainly do not suggest a repeal of the Norris-La Guardia Act. But by 1970, section 301(a) had been interpreted as expressing a national labor policy of promoting industrial peace by enforcing contractual no-strike clauses and by strengthening grievance-arbitration procedures.

The Supreme Court eventually accepted the company's argument that the policy of industrial peace embodied in section 301(a) takes priority over the explicit antiinjunction provisions of Norris-La Guardia. Despite an act of Congress and generations of popular struggle against the hated labor injunction, the Court held, and the law remains, that employees can be enjoined from utilizing collective action to press their contract grievances, no matter how deeply or wrongly they have been injured by management. The *Boys Markets* doctrine goes so far as to allow the courts to enjoin strikes protesting potentially life-threatening safety hazards.[2]

Cases like *Boys Markets* pose difficulties for all varieties of legal theory. For conventional theory, the task is to find some secure, neutral basis to justify this excess of judicial activism. The embarrassment is that this is a classical instance in which the legislative history and relevant precedents are so ambiguous and conflicting that a respectable formal argument can easily be constructed for either side of the case (indeed, for several conceivable outcomes). The view that the Court's ruling is legally *required* is a good deal less than convincing. Indeed, eight years earlier the Supreme Court had faced the identical question and adopted precisely the opposite approach to that ultimately taken in *Boys Markets*.[3] Had something changed since 1962? As Justice Black acidly commented in his *Boys Markets* dissent: "Nothing at all has changed . . . except the membership of the Court and the personal views of one Justice."[4]

The repertoire of lawyers' formal arguments simply cannot determinately resolve a legal problem of this kind. Judgment is required—judgment not only about the meaning and intent of words, but also about unions and industrial conflict, about where collective bargaining came from and about where it should be going. These are inescapably political judgments. One could acknowledge the ambiguity of the legal materials and still argue, in the current argot, that the *Boys Markets* result "fits" best with the "overall structure" of national labor policy, and that in this sense we can meaningfully say that the result was legally required. But "fit" and "structure" are not

exactly terms of determinative precision. They are terms of judgment, re-
dolent with political meaning. One cannot neatly separate "is" and "ought,"
or "being" and "becoming," in identifying the latent structure of legal doctrine. In this case, the question of "fit" comes down to the relative significance
one assigns the competing antiinjunction and proarbitration principles. One
who gives great weight to Norris-La Guardia tenets can easily make the case
that the 1962 result achieved a better fit with the basic commitments of our
labor law.

Radical critics have not had an easy time explaining legal phenomena
like *Boys Markets* either. It is difficult to argue, in the mode of some commentators, that capitalism requires that grievance strikes be enjoinable, since
the law was otherwise from the 1930s until 1970. Indeed, labor law systems
in the capitalist world exhibit extraordinarily diverse features even as to the
most basic aspects of workplace regulation. Nor was there any discernible
change between 1962 and 1970 in the level or character of class conflict that
might explain the Court's shift. With hindsight we can now identify some
disquieting industrial relations trends that began brewing in that period, such
as increasing efforts by employers to avoid collective bargaining. But it is
hard to imagine that the Court responded to or even registered these then-
obscure developments.

Moreover, there is a particular irony about *Boys Markets*. On its face it
seems clearly to be a repressive, antilabor decision, although we don't really
know for sure what its precise effects have been on the labor-management
balance of power. Yet one can hardly dismiss the case as the product of an
antilabor Court, since unions won numerous momentous victories in that
period. *Boys Markets* itself was the enthusiastic product of one of the most
liberal members of the postwar Court, Justice William J. Brennan. Many
(although not all) of the theoretical underpinnings upon which Brennan built
were developed in a set of Warren era cases brought to and won in the
Supreme Court by unions, not employers.[5] Those precedents were intended
to and did in important ways significantly enhance workers' rights. The
challenge is to develop a theoretical vantage that will enable us to appreciate
a harmful decision like *Boys Markets* as consistent with a legal framework
that is heavily infused with liberal values and that espouses genuine concern
for workers' interests. Neither a more refined doctrinal exegesis, nor a radical
interest/functional analysis, nor an analysis pegged to some metric of class
conflict, will suffice for this purpose.

CRITICAL LEGAL THEORY AND LABOR LAW

The difficulty of explaining the *Boys Markets* case with available theoretical
tools illustrates a broader point about efforts to construct critical perspectives

on law. Critical approaches have always been caught in a tension between the critique of formalism and an aspiration to provide systemic analyses. An instinctive starting point of critical legal theory, particularly when written by lawyers, is the attack on formalism. Antiformalist critique aims to show that the prevailing rules are not preordained by the nature of things, nor are particular case results required by legal logic. To the contrary, the critics argue that legal rules and decisions are contingent and conventional—they are products of human choice. There is always room for discretion, sometimes more, sometimes less, in applying the rules to cases. Following the lead of the Legal Realists, contemporary critics argue that the accepted repertoire of justificatory arguments ("legal reasoning") is sufficiently ambiguous, porous, and contradictory so that particular legal outcomes cannot be understood as required by logic alone. Every instance of rule formulation and rule application involves some component, often subtle and obscure, of moral and political choice and, therefore, of decision-maker responsibility.

This is not to say that radical critics believe (as they frequently are misunderstood or misrepresented as believing) that legal reasoning is indistinguishable from general political argument or that decisional outcomes are simple derivatives of prevailing political interests. Rather, the claim is that legal reasoning is not and cannot be made nearly so autonomous from political and ethical argument as is customarily believed, even by sophisticated thinkers. Critical theory seeks to establish that, consciously or not, legal actors routinely make and express moral and political choices in the course of their work, and that therefore they play a responsible role in constructing the institutional substrata of social and political life. As it happens, this proves remarkably easy to show.

Nor do the critics believe (as they frequently are misunderstood or misrepresented as believing) that either rule-content or decisional outcomes are random and unpatterned. Quite the contrary, critical legal theory has traditionally aspired to show how legal orders systematically reflect, generate, and/or reinforce poverty, class inequality, and patriarchal, homophobic, and racial domination. Regrettably, it is also depressingly easy to show the pervasiveness of class, gender, race, and sex-preference hierarchy in the legal cultures of the advanced democracies, although explaining precisely how law reflects and reinforces invidious domination sometimes proves a more formidable task. But whatever the difficulties, most radical legal theorists adhere to the goal of developing systemic perspectives that situate legal rules and practices within broader, structural accounts of social order and hierarchy. There is an instinctive sense that the systemic approach is what sets radical theory apart from incremental reformism and supplies it with its political bite.

The dilemma, of course, is that the antiformalism collides with and erodes systemic explanation. To attribute observed regularities in legal results to systemic principles or functions, one needs an account of the constraints on routine legal decision making that generate these patterns. That is, systemic theories, whether apologetic or critical, seem to require some version of formalism, some claim or assumption that legal orders have an inbuilt, determinative structure that steers routine decision making. In mainstream theory, the structure is said to be given by the legal culture's overarching philosophical principles. The claim is that properly trained and acculturated legal craftspersons can derive appropriate answers to routine problems by applying a catalogued repertoire of argumentative techniques in order to translate communal norms into legal results. In more critical theories, the role of steering mechanism typically is played either by the basic functional attributes or requirements of the social system, or by "class interest" or some similar form of elite identification. But the radicals' recurring antiformalism aims precisely to demonstrate the pervasiveness of choice, contingency, and personal agency in legal processes. Usually sooner rather than later, the critics' powerful antiformalist arsenal renders all available theories of structural constraint problematic.

Labor law theory illustrates the tension between antiformalism and systemic orientations particularly well. Labor law is often regarded as unusually accessible to radical analysis and criticism. Labor cases frequently evidence quite transparent struggles over power in the workplace. Working people have indelibly imprinted the law of labor relations with their aspirations, values, and struggles, both in victory and anguishing defeat. Accordingly, labor law appears to lend itself naturally to discussion in terms of whether this doctrine or that case expands or diminishes worker power.

But the fact that political issues are so close to the surface in labor law can also be a liability for critical legal theory. The relative ease with which we seem to identify employees' short run, intrasystemic interests in particular legal conflicts may inhibit us from attacking a broader and deeper range of questions: Why did the doctrines and institutions of collective bargaining law develop as they have? What are the historical meanings and social functions of that distinctive institutional and intellectual practice we call labor law? How might we explain labor law's inner tensions and future prospects, particularly in this current period of crisis and transformation in American collective bargaining? How should we evaluate the postwar collective bargaining and labor law systems in terms of their own premises and in light of alternative, expanded conceptions of workplace democracy? What role, if any, can litigation and/or statutory reform play in the ongoing project of advancing workplace democracy? Can we envision radical, postliberal models that will deepen opportunities for self-determination in work while yet preserving the democratic prescripts already impressed upon the law by working peoples' activism? Is there any distinctive role for labor lawyers in conceiving and realizing these new models?

Until recently, those critics who have attempted systemic perspectives usually simply inserted interest analysis into a preformed theoretical structure. The social system, generally designated "capitalism" or "monopoly capitalism," is treated as a historical subject, existing prior to law. It is said to have a "deep" or "intrinsic" structure (e.g., "the relations of production"), and legal results are assumed to derive from this prelegal structure. Some leeway generally is allowed for the impact of social conflict and activism (although the contours of social struggle itself are usually thought to be determined by the conflicts ["contradictions"] of the intrinsic structure). The typical discussion shows, first, that a given set of outcomes was not legally preordained; and then, if employers have won, this is said to reflect the "needs of capital," but if employees were successful, that represents a "heightened level of worker struggle."

Legal theory in this vein is comforting to received wisdom, but not very illuminating. For one thing, by taking for granted that legal phenomena reflect the vagaries of class conflict within an overall structure of system-functional imperatives, the approach avoids all the hard issues and assumes what needs to be proved. The precise questions at stake are whether legal outcomes reflect systemic constraint and social struggle, and if so, why and how this occurs. A methodology premised upon systemic determination of legal interests and outcomes is incapable of even asking these questions. In any event, what the parties' long-run interests are rarely is so transparent as the model supposes.

Moreover, the approach is fundamentally circular. There is no way to describe social structures—deep, intrinsic, or otherwise—without discussing law or lawlike phenomena. There simply is no "prelegal" realm of social life to which legal outcomes can be referred, at least not in the modern age. A particularly embarrassing case of circularity is the ease with which we are told that legal outcomes and processes derive from the underlying relations of production or property ownership, as though production relations or property could meaningfully be defined without reference to legal rules. Finally, the functionalist dimensions of the approach rest on the assumption—shared, ironically, with most mainstream theory—that routine legal practices and results are powerfully determined by constraints on decision makers built into legal orders at some paramount level. But this assumption cannot survive the antiformalist critique.

New approaches are needed to break this theoretical impasse. We surely need to transcend the partial and constricted definitions of employee interests and workplace democracy available within the going system, yet we also need to get beyond prepackaged "class analysis" and unconvincing functionalist or system-logic explanations of the relationships between legal and social orders. Promising debate and new openings have in fact emerged in labor law theory in the past decade. A sense of crisis in the labor movement and signs that the postwar labor relations system is unraveling have added urgency to the discussion. This article presents one new approach, among several appearing in writings by labor lawyers associated with the critical legal studies (CLS) movement.[6]

Conventional legal theory and the older critical approaches share a common difficulty. Both fail to appreciate the pervasiveness of human agency in the construction of legal orders; at the same time, neither adequately explains how human action in legal contexts is socially structured. Mainstream legal theory hardly makes the effort to appreciate the embeddedness of law in social context. Sophisticated postrealists recognize, of course, that law combines reason and fiat. Yet in the conventional image, discoverable logics of social order and of legal justification exist outside of history. The older critical approaches have neither a theory of human agency, nor a convincing account of social determination of legal processes. These approaches explain legal events by reference to some transhistorical logic or metastructure of history, but have great difficulty explaining where the structures come from or how they frame legal processes.

There is a single starting point to resolving these difficulties (a point of departure shared, to be sure, with other, non-CLS approaches that are sociologically or historically oriented). That is to use as the foundation for reconstructing legal theory the most important idea in modern social thought: the concept of the "social construction of reality." A critical approach would aim to understand law as situated in social context. This means an attempt to understand law as a "practice" or form of expression, as a contingent product of human action. Legal processes are meaning-creating activities, in the course of which people try to understand and interpret their experience and to draw connections between their images of how the world works and how people ought to act. Legal actors create symbols, relationships, and institutions. They also create, elaborate, entrench, contest, and resist *understandings*—assumptions, beliefs, and values about human character and capacity, and about social organization and justice.

Social orders are constructed of practices, and, thus, legal practices partially constitute social life. But human action is *situated*, it can only occur in context and through the medium of culturally available forms, symbols, and understandings. Therefore these collectively created structures of recognition, meaning, belief, and relationship pattern and constrain human action and choice, including legal practices. The meaning structures in and through which we have experience orient our perceptions, thoughts, and feelings. They shape imagination and belief about human capacity and fulfillment. Because of this, although the structures and relationships of social life are all contingent products of human action, they often tend to appear as natural and unchangeable.

Given this understanding of legal processes as a form of practice, as situated human action, critical legal theory can deploy the tools utilized in the interpretive disciplines—social history, anthropology, literary criticism, and so on. Interpretive techniques can be used to seek clues regarding the structures of meaning, belief, and power embedded in legal discourse and institutions. All discourses are force fields of power relations. Discourse, including legal discourse, involves peculiar, hierarchical patterns of privileging, silencing, and denial. But critical legal theory aspires to go beyond strictly interpretive methods. It seeks to understand why given legal practices arise in and are sustained by particular social and historical conditions; to understand how various legal practices reinforce prevailing power relations; and to develop theories of transformative practice, of emancipation (and barriers to emancipation) from historically unnecessary restraints upon human freedom and self-realization.[7]

The effort, then, is to go beyond the law's understanding of itself, and also beyond its perceptible, instrumental consequences, to an understanding of the particular vision or visions of the world animating and expressed in a given set of legal practices and institutions, to uncover the assumptions and commitments about politics and social life legal practices embody. The goal is to appreciate how legal discourse and events inform and shape experience and belief, how they sustain and legitimate institutions and power relations. Insofar as legal institutions reinforce hierarchy and inequality in social and political life, and insofar as legal discourse endorses the dominant power arrangements or induces belief in their inevitability, legal culture can be understood as a form of legitimating ideology. While law can be a repository of emancipatory values and aspirations and of questions sharply or subtly critical of the status quo, more typically legal discourse operates to deny us access to our transformative capacities, our power to alter and abolish existing patterns of domination. By exploring, mapping, and criticizing the prevailing forms of legal consciousness, we may hope to release our political imagination and gain access to transformative possibilities immanent in our situation.

BOYS MARKETS AND THE LIBERAL PARADIGM

Ordinarily, legal culture is created and sustained by and in turn largely has effect on people who are regularly engaged in and with the legal arena, e.g., lawyers, judges, politicians, institutional litigants, and certain academics. That is, legal culture for the most part denotes elite culture. For this reason, the approach illustrated here has thus far proved most useful in understanding the coherence and developmental path of legal doctrine itself. But there are important exceptions, historical settings in which other groups in society have influenced the development of legal culture, and cases in which legal ideas and processes have deeply influenced popular culture.[8] There is no question, for example, that American workers have left their imprint on our law of labor relations. Somewhat more controversially, ideas and values about industrial order emanating from the legal arena have sometimes spread beyond professional circles and influenced other participants in our increasingly legalized industrial relations process.

This is particularly true with respect to the postwar, golden age of American collective bargaining law, roughly 1945–1975. In this period, labor law was deeply influenced by a particularly innovative and nuanced set of ideas about the world of work. I will call this the "liberal conception" or "paradigm" of labor law, although this shorthand probably attributes greater clarity and coherence to the ideas than are warranted. While major themes of the liberal approach were developed outside the legal arena, lawyers, judges, and legal academics did play a significant role in elaborating and advancing the paradigm. The liberal worldview never held unchallenged sway; it was attacked from the conservative side throughout the period. Nonetheless, liberal conceptions provided the dominant intellectual influence on the development of postwar labor law. To a considerable extent that influence continues, although many basic assumptions of the liberal model have eroded in the past decade or so.

Liberal labor law thinking surely contributed to and exemplified leading political ideas of the postwar period. Moreover, the liberal paradigm permeated broader, nonelite circles. To a significant, although perhaps unmeasurable extent, values and beliefs associated with this way of thinking about industrial organization were internalized by labor leaders and activists, influencing their perspectives and actions. Many labor leaders accepted assumptions about what is possible and desirable in the workplace that derive from or share themes with the postwar liberal paradigm. This value system therefore forms an important component of the collective unconscious of the American labor movement. To the extent this is so, the latent value system of American collective bargaining law has been a legitimating ideology that has reinforced the dominant institutions for the better part of a generation. "Totalistic" or "reconstructive" criticism of labor law is therefore an indispensable task for those who wish to conceive and work to build alternative forms of workplace democracy. I will consider here three major themes of the liberal paradigm.

CONFINING CONCERTED ACTIVITY

The first is a grudging attitude toward employee participation in workplace governance, and specifically hostility toward the use of employee self-help in dispute resolution. Had the Boys Markets clerks filed a grievance and left their protest at that, the law might well have provided them a remedy. But even liberal judges have limited patience with the use of strike action to vindicate employee rights.

To be sure, strikes and other forms of job action played an enormously significant part in bringing the modern labor law framework into being, and the NLRA resoundingly guarantees employees the right to strike and to engage in other forms of concerted activity. Within the liberal mind-set, it is essential to validate the strike as a fundamental, if residual, right of workers. Justice Brennan has eloquently acknowledged the importance of the reserve right to strike, notably in the case of private sector, "primary economic strikes" (strikes against one's own employer in connection with contract negotiations).[9]

In light of these conflicting pressures, labor law gradually evolved a conception of legitimate collective action that simultaneously *encourages* and *confines* worker self-expression through concerted activity and industrial conflict. Labor law invites and authorizes workers to articulate and advance their interests through self-organization, yet carefully regulates and blunts workers' collective action. The law impedes solidarity and mutual aid and channels collective action into narrow, institutionalized forms. These stylized frameworks of legitimate economic conflict provide rallying points for mobilizing employee energy and commitment, but, particularly as they become bureaucratized and overloaded, they can also exercise a dissipating effect on collective action.

Accepting conflict as a fact of industrial life, postwar liberalism sought to institutionalize and confine it. To meet that goal, labor law theory and doctrine had to (1) fashion a "nonideological" explanation of the causes and purposes of industrial conflict; (2) establish boundaries for the permissible use of economic weapons; and (3) develop alternative dispute-resolution mechanisms that could plausibly claim to be neutral as between capital and labor.

Liberal management theory and social science strips industrial conflict of any class-based or political character and treats it as a by-product of a transnational and transhistorical logic of modernization. Industrial conflict is seen as aimed to advance intrasystemic group or sectoral interests. The precise structure of economic distribution is open to periodic renegotiation, and groups may use self-help weapons in the process. But the fundamental organization of social life is deemed not at stake in or open to revision through industrial conflict. Moreover, it is emphasized that all groups share a common interest in maximizing output (so that the pie from which each gets its slice is as large as possible). Therefore, a basic liberal ground rule is that the strike weapon should not be used to protest midcontract grievances, much less should it be used as a mode of political expression.[10]

Accordingly, the legitimate use of economic force is largely restricted to the periodic ritual of contract negotiation in the private sector, or, in rare cases, to protesting when an employer flagrantly abuses the basic rules of the game. A great deal of labor law doctrine concerns the suppression or weakening of other forms of concerted activity considered to be unacceptably disruptive: forms of worker protest smacking of class-conscious solidarity, such as secondary boycotts; concerted activity through which employees attempt to reorganize the labor process; worker action of a "political" nature transcending the concerns of employees as employees; minority-group dissenting protests; "recognitional" picketing or strikes, designed to cut through the time-consuming legal procedures by which unions obtain representational rights; sit-ins and other trespassory strikes; certain strikes occurring in vital industries; and public employee strikes.[11] Additionally, a central development in modern labor law is the harsh treatment accorded to the midcontract strike, as illustrated by the *Boys Markets* case. The liberal vision of collective bargaining treats the wildcat strike as a basic form of social deviancy, a fundamental industrial crime.

Of course, the liberal model could not simply proscribe wildcat strikes without institutionalizing other means for employees to air their grievances and have them resolved. Just as liberal collective bargaining law prejudices collective employee action, it favors "peaceful" resolution of industrial disputes through formalized, bureaucratic channels, notably grievance arbitration. As Justice Brennan frankly stated in *Boys Markets*:

> As labor organizations grew in strength and developed toward maturity, congressional emphasis shifted from protection of the nascent labor movement to the encouragement of collective bargaining and to *administrative techniques* for the peaceful resolution of industrial disputes.[12]

The most important "administrative" alternative to concerted activity is grievance arbitration. Enforced adherence to no-strike and grievance arbitration agreements became, in Justice Brennan's words, a "dominant motif," indeed, a "kingpin of federal labor policy."[13] *Boys Markets* brought this logic of liberal labor jurisprudence full circle.

Grievance arbitration represents a genuine and in some respects highly effective extension of due process into workplace life. Since employees cannot strike over every grievance, no doubt agreement on an alternative dispute-resolution system is often a good trade-off for employees. The problem is not with arbitration in the abstract but rather with specific features of contemporary doctrine and arbitral processes. For example, the Court has invoked arbitration to divest employees of statutory rights they have *not* waived. There are problems of severe overload and breakdown in our grievance systems. Arbitral due process has significant substantive limitations because the content of arbitral law derives from the contract, that is, from the parties' relative bargaining power, not from open-ended considerations of justice. Above all, there is the tendency of liberal theory to *equate* arbitration with industrial democracy. Without doubting the contribution of a system of informal adjudication and rights enforcement, workplace democracy also requires other institutional forms of a more continuous and participatory nature.

MINIMALIST FREE CONTRACT

The second, somewhat more complicated, theme exemplified by *Boys Markets* is the way contemporary labor law mobilizes the rhetoric of "freedom of contract" and the institution of the labor agreement to reinforce employer power. When it comes to setting wage rates and working conditions, the law most definitely does not favor administrative or regulatory techniques. There are important exceptions, of course, such as minimum wage laws and occupational safety and health requirements, and this list is growing. But insofar as legal policy is concerned, most aspects of wages and working conditions are to be established through freedom of contract, *i.e.*, bargaining processes reflecting the so-called "free play of market forces."

Mainstream labor law theory endorses statutory reform to permit employees to pool their bargaining power in labor markets. As the Court stated in sustaining the NLRA: "union was essential to give laborers opportunity to deal on an equality with their employer."[14] But liberal theory has always been committed to the view that, once labor markets are collectivized, contract should remain the primary source of law and rights in the workplace. Freedom of contract is seen as a basic institutional platform of autonomy and participation in workplace governance.

This position has considerable merit, which is why American workers have fought so determinedly over the years to achieve unionization. When working well, collective contracting offers employees significant and relatively accessible opportunities to participate in determining the content of workplace rules and standards. Collective bargaining offers the advantage of flexible adaptability to local conditions and problems. Centralized administrative bodies can be captured by forces insensitive or hostile to workers' interests. In principle, collective bargaining represents a decentralized, activist alternative to clumsy or antagonistic bureaucratic power.

As will be noted later, the free contract ideal also has serious deficiencies, even when working in optimal fashion. But taking the ideal on its own terms for the moment, it is important to observe that free contract is a very general rubric, consistent with a wide array of actual and conceivable legal regimes. Freedom of contract is simply not a self-defining concept. The lived meaning of a contractual regime can only be determined in social and historical context, and by reference to its specific doctrinal and institutional embodiments. Because of its generality ("indeterminacy"), freedom of contract provided a broad framework during the postwar years within which workers' rights could be advanced on some fronts while they were curtailed and interdicted on others. From a critical point of view, free contract in important aspects came to represent an institutional system that buttresses managerial power. The liberty-enhancing potential of free contract for workers was often blocked, and authoritarian outcomes were fostered instead. To make matters worse, the alluring rhetoric of free contract made it appear as though this control and domination of employees occurred by their own consent.[15]

By way of illustration, one source of indeterminacy within the ideal of free contract is that it simultaneously prizes and protects two conflicting moral values.[16] The first is liberty or freedom of choice, particularly freedom of action in markets. This aspect underlies the attraction of collective bargaining as a framework of employee activism and participation in workplace governance. The second value is security of expectations, the notion that we ought to be able to rely upon others to fulfill their obligations freely undertaken ("a deal is a deal"). Workers, of course, have a great interest in the security of their wages, working conditions, and continued employment that contract, in principle, provides.

The problem is that contract disputes almost invariably put these two values in conflict. Protecting plaintiffs' expectations through enhanced contract enforceability typically detracts from defendants' freedom of choice. Sometimes the predictable plaintiff and defendant groups are more or less the same sorts of people, so that the legal tension evens out in the long run; but often they are not. Resolving contract disputes therefore frequently requires the exercise of judgment about which value to favor in particular contexts, with distinct consequences for different groups in society. This creates room for considerable political play within contract regimes. In the postwar labor context, this political leeway within contract was consistently exploited to favor managerial power and to defeat employees' egalitarian and participatory aspirations.

Boys Markets exemplifies these points. The case involved several relevant contractual promises. The union claimed that management had promised to assign frozen-food work to union personnel, and the employer had also agreed to arbitrate disputes as to the meaning of the contract. The union promised not to strike during the contract term. The employees were obviously concerned for the job security provided by contractual work-assignment rules, but also had an interest in freedom to act in the event they perceived their rights to be violated. The employer relied on the expectation that work would not be interrupted by strikes, but also had an interest in managerial freedom of action in administering the contract and in determining how and by whom work will be carried out. On the surface, one might say that the promises and interests were neatly balanced, and that the free contract ideal necessarily implies that, so long as the employer was willing to arbitrate the grievance, the employees could be required not to strike.

There are at least two "gaps" or points of indeterminacy in the free contract ideal at work here. A first ambiguity involves whose interpretation of the contract should govern pending the arbitrator's definitive ruling. Labor law assumes that management's interpretation prevails, and employees must obey unless and until they win their case (which may be months or even years later, depending upon how backlogged the grievance process is). Nothing in the ideal of free contract or the notion that "a deal is a deal" requires this rule, which profoundly favors managerial freedom to manage at the expense of employee security. Free contract is perfectly consistent with the opposite premise, namely that the employer must restore the status quo and abide by the union's interpretation of the contract, unless and until the arbitrator rules that it is free to do otherwise. That the law nearly consistently takes the former approach reflects a choice in favor of managerial domination.

Second, let us assume that by striking over the frozen-food dispute the employees broke an obligation they had freely entered. It does not follow that the strike was *enjoinable* and the clerks should have been compelled to work. The general notion that we are bound to observe our contractual obligations is quite indeterminate on the point of particular *remedies* for breach. As it happens, the normal remedy for breach of contract is a suit for money damages, not an injunction. The historic position of Anglo-American law, quite apart from Norris-La Guardia strictures, has been to refuse injunctions compelling people to perform service contracts, because compulsion to work intrudes too severely on employees' freedom of action, and ordinarily a suit for damages is thought adequately to protect the employer. By granting the additional and unusual remedy of an injunction, *Boys Markets* favored the employer's security of expectations regarding continuity of work operations over the employees' freedom to take action to protect their working conditions. The decision therefore reflects a distinctly political judgment in favor of workplace hierarchy and against concerted activity.

The "deal is a deal" principle has been conveniently overlooked when strict enforcement of contract terms would limit employer freedom of action. An example is the notorious *Milwaukee Spring*[17] case, which allows employers effectively to walk away from their bargain with a union by transferring the work to a nonunion location. But typically, contract enforcement has been highlighted, at the expense of employee freedom of action, due to a perception that the contract can be useful to management, which "can reasonably expect from a collective labor agreement . . . assurance of uninterrupted operation during the term of the agreement."[18]

The collective bargaining contract is also helpful to management in other ways. Contracts foster long-range economic planning. Contractual grievance procedures provide a device by which higher-level management can monitor and control its own front-line supervisors to ensure compliance with company policy. The arbitral process provides an institutionalized mechanism for generating operating rules for the enterprise and for obtaining a modicum of employee consent and reconciliation to the hierarchical structure of workplace organization. Management can use the threat of damage actions to enlist union officials in efforts to halt wildcat strikes. Thus, the law of the collective contract effectively co-opts unions into the uncomfortable position of performing certain managerial and disciplinary functions. Over the years, the prospect of these and similar advantages to management was deftly invoked by liberal labor theorists to encourage at least a partial employer truce with collective bargaining. *Boys Markets* culminated a long effort to bring the law into conformance with their claims that the liberal model of collective bargaining could be functional for management.

There is another sense in which the free contract ideal was given a rights-narrowing content in the postwar period. Collective bargaining agreements often waive employees' statutory rights; indeed, the collective agreement is a legal device by which employees surrender certain basic democratic rights for a price. Two centerpieces of mature collective bargaining are the union's contractual waiver of the employees' statutory right to strike and the "management's rights" clause, under which the contract carves out a sheltered area of employer prerogative exempted from employee input, protest, and even arbitral review. In effect, employees waive during the term of the contract their statutory right to "coparticipation" in establishing working conditions and rules. These and other waiver rules make the collective bargaining agreement an institutional form by which organized employees consent to their own domination in the workplace.

This is not to suggest that employees should never trade statutory entitlements. Although some workplace rights should be inalienable, surely in other cases employees might be well served by trading statutory entitlements—even the right to engage in certain kinds of concerted activity for limited periods of time—for collectively bargained benefits. But, mainstream theory to the contrary notwithstanding, the mere fact that a waiver is voluntarily bargained does not mean that the resulting arrangement is substantively just or that enforcing the bargain respects or enhances employee autonomy and self-determination. Just because the benefits were preferred to the entitlement under the circumstances does not mean that putting employees to the choice was fair to begin with. There are many circumstances in which preventing certain bargains (child labor, to use an obvious example) might enhance rather than detract from human autonomy. The moral and political significance of contract enforcement cannot be determined a priori, without reference to the social context.

The substantive justice of a bargaining regime and the degree to which it actually respects human autonomy and enhances liberty and self-determination turn on the background distribution of economic and social power and on how the particular rules and institutions constituting the market structure affect the parties' powers, endowments, and vulnerabilities. For example, if the background to bargaining is one of enormous and pervasive inequality (as is typical in the workplace), a legal regime that makes rights under employee protective statutes freely waivable effectively permits employers to deploy their economic power so as to dilute or undermine whatever victories employees have won in the legislature, with the consequence that self-determination is decreased rather than enhanced by free contract. On the other hand, if the legal regime makes it difficult or impossible to waive basic rights (and all free contract regimes restrict or prohibit at least *some* trade-offs), this may enhance employee power and self-determination in the workplace.[19]

Postwar labor law has been exceedingly hospitable to waivers. The dozens of waiver decisions over the years have gradually eroded the statutory rights employees won, at great sacrifice, during and since the New Deal. Cases like *Boys Markets*, vigorously enforcing the waiver of employees' fundamental right to strike, illustrate the process. The waiver rules were promulgated in the name of employee liberty and under the general banner of freedom of contract. But their cumulative effect is to give free contract a specific legal and institutional embodiment that ratifies and reinforces managerial power.

These considerations lead us to some basic deficiences of contracting processes from the workplace democracy standpoint. Like administrative processes, collective bargaining can become overly bureaucratic and insensitive to employee need. Moreover, there is a virtue in the public focus and debate that is encouraged when workplace rights issues are brought explicitly into the political arena. But the chief disadvantage of contracting systems is that the quality of working life and the return to labor are ultimately determined by the broad patterns of distribution of economic power. Although through activism and solidarity employees can influence the bargain in meaningful ways, the overall shape of the bargain is predominantly cast by the background economic context, which in our society is generally one of profound employer/employee inequality and massive corporate power, even throughout most of the dwindling unionized sector. Given this setting, any contract system will inevitably be hostage to the structure of class domination and can never produce a fully adequate or just set of wages and working conditions.

For this reason, workplace reformers have long advocated legislative determination of at least some workplace rights, such as minimum wages, maximum hours, safety protections, and prohibition of race and gender discrimination. In Western Europe, labor and social democratic parties have sponsored much more elaborate programs of noncontract determination of workplace standards. This has led some to assume that progress toward equity in work can *only* be accomplished by a process of gradual statutory encirclement of the field now governed by contract.

This view contains more than one kernel of truth. It properly treats employment relationships as encompassing governance systems and structures of bureaucratic power, as well as bargained arrangements. And it is right to assume that transforming work in enduringly democratic and egalitarian directions will require major changes at the social and political levels. Nonetheless, the left's traditional call for an eclipse of contract is in certain respects seriously misleading. It overlooks the decentralized and participatory virtues of adversary bargaining. It implicitly invokes a fanciful and ultimately undesirable image of an employment system with limited or no scope for individual choices about entry and exit. And hostility to contract, as such, involves the formalist error of treating contract and market too abstractly. Even within a general capitalist framework, market structures and institutions vary widely, and each particular form of market structure or contract regime has distinct, potentially significant consequences for the distribution of power. To use our example once more, whether grievance strikes may be enjoined can make a real difference in the quality of working life, even though enjoinability and nonenjoinability are both variants of a market/contract regime. Critical approaches to legal theory must be sensitive to the distributive consequences of market-structuring rules. The plasticity and variation of such rules can be a source of significant law reform opportunities for workplace democracy advocates.[20]

The notion that markets are structured by legal rules that have significant distributive consequences was a fundamental insight of Legal Realism. Indirectly it influenced the theory of the National Labor Relations Act. A core notion behind the act was to redistribute power in favor of employees by "reconstructing" the background legal regime of labor markets, principally by moving from a system of individual to one of collective bargaining. As I have argued elsewhere, this change was filled with radical potential, even though the framework of labor relations was still conceived predominantly in contractual terms.[21]

The NLRA and related statutes are formulated in quite general terms. Their legal meaning is filled out by thousands upon thousands of interpretive decisions which crucially determine the institutional structure within which labor bargaining takes place. At least in theory, the labor law decisional process could have aimed systematically to reconstruct market ground rules so as to redistribute power and participation opportunities to workers. Such redistributive market reconstruction could have been designed to accord with the principles of contractual autonomy and economic efficiency, and much could have been accomplished consistent with the broad frame of congressional intent.[22] While this was a theoretical possibility, such systematically redistributive market reconstruction was clearly not on the postwar political agenda. The operative spectrum of debate ran between the liberals, who advocated partial market reconstruction, and conservatives, who sought, if not a complete rollback to pre-NLRA days, at least NLRA interpretations involving as little departure as possible from the earlier regime of "unregulated" labor bargaining (that is, labor bargaining regulated by the heavily proemployer common law).

The liberal approach unquestionably advocated reconstruction of labor markets to the extent of fostering collective bargaining and requiring employers to treat with unions. But the prevailing view was that once law set up a collective bargaining process, it should largely recede into the background and refrain from any further attempts to redistribute power or to steer the substantive content of employment contracts. Thus, the liberal approach was a significant but inherently limited attempt to reconstruct labor markets, a position I call "minimalist" or "self-limiting market reconstruction." This diffident and restricted postwar application of the market reconstruction concept is not, as is often believed, a logical corollary of the ideal of autonomous, free collective bargaining. It seems more a reflection of the political context and the decline of social unionism during the Cold War.

Under this gloss on "free contract," liberal collective bargaining law tolerates massive inequality in labor markets, so that the options available to employees, while not negligible, are a shadow of what they could and should be. This has always been a disquieting fact for liberal labor law theory, and its postwar architects have gone to some lengths to deny it. The most common form of denial is the flat assertion that collective bargaining in and of itself rectifies bargaining imbalance and places labor and management on a level playing field.[23] The point of this totally unconvincing though oft-repeated *ipse dixit* is to place an imprimatur of legitimacy on the outcomes of collective bargaining, no matter how parsimonious or inequitable they may be. In this sense, too, the implicit philosophy of collective bargaining law has legitimated and thereby reinforced socially unnecessary hierarchy in the workplace.

BOUNDING EMPLOYEE PARTICIPATION

A third theme, not developed in *Boys Markets* but nevertheless central to postwar labor law, is that its conception of industrial democracy simultaneously *invites* and *limits* employee participation in workplace governance. That there will be employee participation is taken as a given in postwar politics, but the substantive focus of participation is carefully circumscribed. It is deflected away from such concerns as long-range planning for the enterprise, production methods, and the organization of the work process. The "legitimate" involvement of employees tends to be confined to the terms of sale of labor power.

A key legal formulation of these points is the distinction between "mandatory" and "permissive" subjects of collective bargaining. This doctrine determines the circumstances under which an employer is barred from making unilateral decisions and can be compelled to notify the union of proposed changes and bargain with it about them. The permissive subject rule effectively immunizes employers from collective bargaining duties respecting the substance of managerial decisions "fundamental to the basic direction of a corporate enterprise" or those "which lie at the core of entrepreneurial control."[24] The entrepreneurial core, of course, includes most "strategic" decisions, particularly decisions about capital investment in or disinvestment from the enterprise. As a general rule, the more important a management decision is, the less likely that unions can compel employers to bargain about it.[25]

The consequences of deflecting employee participation away from strategic issues have been particularly tragic in recent years with respect to the question of plant closing and relocation. In an incalculably destructive decision, the Supreme Court applied the Reaganomic "cost-benefit" obsession to scope-of-bargaining doctrine. Justice Harry A. Blackmun first provided a remarkably candid description of what he calls the "neutral purposes" of the NLRA—including "defusing and channeling conflict between labor and management"—and then ruled that an employer's decision to close part of its business is outside the mandatory scope of employee participation:

> [I]n establishing what issues must be submitted to the process of bargaining, Congress had no expectation that the elected union representative would become an equal partner in the running of the business enterprise in which the union's members are employed. . . . [I]n view of an employer's need for unencumbered decisionmaking, bargaining over management decisions

that have a substantial impact on the continued availability of employment should be required only if the benefit, for labor-management relations and the collective-bargaining process, outweighs the burden placed on the conduct of the business.[26]

The Court assumes employees have neither the motivation, intelligence, nor ability to participate in or contribute to strategic decision making. Likewise, in legal contemplation, employees make no investment and therefore acquire neither a stake in the direction of their company, nor any legal interest in the fruits of their labor. Nor can the surrounding community, even one dominated by and dependent upon a major enterprise, claim a legal interest to participate in or be protected from crucial capital investment decisions the company makes affecting that community.[27]

Employee participation is also constricted by the basic assumption that enterprises must be organized and directed hierarchically. Employees are bound to obey the employer's commands and operational decisions; this is deemed a natural and eternal feature of the employment relationship. Employees are thought to owe a strong "duty of loyalty" to the employer, although the employer owes no correlative duty to its employees. For example, in many instances employers are privileged in pursuit of their own goals to inflict devastating job-loss upon employees, even sometimes without a business justification, and even sometimes with a motive to retaliate for the exercise of the statutory right to unionize.[28]

Although it is acknowledged to be uniquely suited for communication and social intercourse among employees,[29] the workplace is not treated by law as a place for employees to congregate, express themselves, grow as individuals and collectively, or to experience their creative potential and capacity for self-governance. The legal conception of work is "productivist": the workplace is deemed a place to carry out production under employer command.[30] Though employees may spend the bulk of their waking lives in the plant or office, they acquire no entitlement to regard the workplace as in any sense their own. The workplace—both the physical premises and the existential space—is deemed to "belong" to the employer. The mind-set reflected in these rules and in the grudging approach of American labor law toward employee participation contrasts sharply with the prevailing attitude in Western Europe, where most of the major industrial nations have accorded employee representatives much wider consultative and participatory rights.

THE LIBERAL IMAGINATION AND
POSTWAR COLLECTIVE BARGAINING LAW:
DEFENSIVE DEMOCRACY

Postwar labor law is a complex weave of rights-expanding and rights-restricting doctrines and institutions. It reflects and embodies the aspirations and achievements of popular struggle, and in this respect there are few comparable examples in law. Yet the struggle to humanize and democratize work is incomplete, not only because there were many defeats and compromises along the way, but also because changing times and perceptions constantly alter the potential meanings of and people's hopes for workplace democracy. Thus, postwar labor law provides the foundation for a genuine, but partial and unfinished system of industrial democracy. It is also the foundation of an institutional and ideological complex that legitimates managerial power and reinforces employer control in work.

Labor law's detailed doctrine developed in light of these conflicting directions. Its evolutionary path straddles a tension between its democratizing and hierarchy-reinforcing aspects. It expands but also diminishes and demeans workers' rights. Accommodation of these discordant emphases within a going system required an imaginative effort of applied political theory, one that acknowledged yet co-opted and institutionalized the authentic, emancipatory aspirations of the collective bargaining ideal, yet one that also rejected the repressive approaches constantly urged by conservative and business interests. Postwar labor jurisprudence in the liberal vein, developed in piecemeal fashion by judges, advocates, and academics of the period, elaborated a historically and culturally distinct conception of industrial democracy, what I have called "defensive democracy." Particularly when one recalls the reactionary Cold War climate, the lack of any sort of social democratic political presence, and the decline of CIO-style social unionism, the entrenchment of the liberal collective bargaining paradigm in the 1950s and 1960s was a remarkably successful political initiative.

But the liberal conception of workplace democracy has very substantial in-built ideological and institutional limitations. While employees are guaranteed a voice in establishing working conditions and rules, the power of their voice turns on their strength in the market. Yet as a consequence of the minimalist approach to market reconstruction, employees are permanently subordinated to management in market clout. There are exceptions, of course, cases approaching bilateral monopoly in competition-insulated industries, and cases of strong unions facing weak, fragmented employer groups. But particularly with deregulation and the intensification of world trade competition in recent years, workplace democracy is ordinarily hostage to employers' vastly superior economic resources. To extend Kathy Stone's apt metaphor: workplace democracy in the liberal collective bargaining model is a precarious island of due process surrounded by a constantly threatening sea of class power.[31]

A second, important effect of minimalist market reconstruction has been to promote labor market segmentation—to drive a wedge between the organized and unorganized sectors of the workforce—and to foster the privatization in collective bargaining of welfare functions (e.g., delivering health care) performed by the state elsewhere in the industrial world. By tying welfare to jobs rather than membership in the community, the very success of the postwar labor-management compromise had the effect of uncoupling the concerns of poor people and low-wage workers from the labor movement's political agenda, to the ultimate detriment of both groups. Our collective bargaining policy reflects and also sustains the minimalist American approach to social policy in general. As a result, the United States maintains a dismally low "floor" of welfare entitlements and social benefits. This has had profoundly damaging consequences for the interests of unrepresented and unpaid workers, particularly for women and minority groups. Social welfare minimalism has also damaged the economy by encouraging American firms to indulge in low-wage competitive strategies and, therefore, to waste and injure human capital and to defer the search for the capital-intensive, productivity-enhancing production techniques emphasized by our trade rivals abroad.

Even within its besieged and precarious zone, the liberal model of workplace democracy has in-built limitations. There is an entrenched assumption that control over the strategic level of enterprise decision making is reserved for management. It is likewise assumed that work operations must be organized on an authoritarian basis, so that labor law is indifferent to hierarchy and leaves existing command structures in place.

Finally, the institutional structure of this version of industrial democracy reveals inherent limitations. Through periodic bargaining backed up by the occasional exercise of rights of concerted activity, employee representatives participate from time to time in establishing many of the rules that govern the employment relationship. Employee representatives also participate in negotiating interpretations of contractual rules through the grievance process, when it is working well. However, employees are not invited to participate directly and continuously in firm decision making and governance. Nor are employees routinely entitled to the sorts of business information that would inform and facilitate direct and continuous participation in decision making. To the contrary, in contemplation of law the day-to-day employee role is simply that of command follower. True enough, if management violates the contract, employees can use the grievance process (but not job action) to have the transgression corrected. But in the first instance, and throughout the period pending arbitral review, management manages and employees obey. And because business (as opposed to labor relations) decisions are not ordinarily subject to arbitral review, employees can at most have only an indirect impact on such decisions. Thus, insofar as daily routine is concerned, industrial democracy in the liberal vision is a "defensive" or "reactive" process of rights enforcement within a restricted field, not a form of continuous, open-ended, and participatory democracy. This is surely superior to unconstrained management power, but it is also a good deal less than workplace democracy can and should be.

WORKPLACE GOVERNANCE AND RADICAL VISIONS OF DEMOCRACY

Liberal theorists found in collective bargaining law a superb terrain to develop approaches to general problems of Cold War political theory (e.g., the strategy of institutionalizing conflict, the theory of a common interest in uninterrupted production, technological explanations of modernization). A generation later, critical theorists have an analogous opportunity to derive from the experience of collective bargaining law general approaches to critical legal and political theory.

The richly textured doctrine of labor law that envelops and pervades the daily lives of all union officials and activists induces us to think about workplace problems in ways that inhibit the effort to create industrial freedom. Progressive labor activists must help to forge an entirely new vision of workplace democracy. We must go beyond the liberal legalist conception of industrial justice, in which entitlements ultimately turn on bargaining power rather than human need; in which the prerogatives of capital trump the democratic concerns of employees; and in which employee participation is deflected from the all-important decisions regarding the allocation of society's resources. Our conception of workplace democracy must encompass new notions of the meaning of work. It must center on the idea that work should *have* meaning, that it should be a mode of self-expression and development, that its content and purposes *matter*; on new conceptions of how to reconcile production processes with the needs and rhythms of personal life and of our physical environment; on a new set of values about the uses and allocation of social resources; and on an end to racism, sexism, sex-preference discrimination, and all forms of illegitimate hierarchy in the workplace and in the labor movement.

As part of the effort to construct this new conception of workplace democracy, labor activists must rethink the potential contribution of law. The emphasis here on worker self-activity and my antibureaucratic tone might suggest that my thrust is "antistatist" or, in current parlance, "deregulatory." This is not my intent. In the prevailing political context, deregulation of the workplace (*i.e.*, statutory repeal) means ratification of the preexisting structures of economic inequality and hierarchy, themselves underwritten and maintained by political institutions and background rules of law that by any definition surely constitute a regulatory system. A perspective placing great hope on heightened worker self-reliance and resort to concerted activity does not necessarily entail the conclusion that law and politics (*i.e.*, the collective, institutionalized self-regulation of society) should be disregarded.

The National Labor Relations Act and similar workplace reforms emerged at the intersection of working-class aspirations and elite efforts to rationalize capitalist economic activity. Although they were indelibly marked by workers' struggles, these reforms were in practice largely shaped by those for whom collective bargaining and labor law were modes of reconstituting the liberal capitalist social order. Nonetheless, that the directive institutions of society ("state power") were deployed against workplace inequality and authoritarianism should be seen as a major advance in American political development. The NLRA made a public issue of the structure of power and decision making on the shop floor: this was an exceptional historic achievement.

It is misguided, if not nonsensical, to formulate issues, in labor relations or in any other aspect of the politics of social welfare, in terms of a regulation/deregulation dichotomy. The problem of social policy is not *whether* the organized self-regulatory power of society should be deployed to enhance participation and equality, and to serve our material and spiritual needs. The problem is, rather, what are and should be the *forms* and *content* of such interventions. We must develop an understanding of precisely how and why the exercise of governmental power in the liberal democracies, even in periods of progressive reform, tends to deflect and eviscerate popular participation and often fails to serve or disserves human need. We must develop methodologies for understanding the complex relational, organizational, and communicative patterns embedded in public policy, through which public policy plays its part in constituting capitalist social life as a totality. It is hoped that the analytical and interpretive techniques of critical labor jurisprudence have something to contribute to that task.

Similar considerations apply to needed efforts to fashion a normative political theory consonant with radical images of emancipation. If any conclusion is warranted from the historical trajectory of labor and the law it is that we need a considerably more complex and nuanced theory of the relationship between institutionalized political power and the quest for human freedom than any currently available.

We have inherited two equally unsatisfactory approaches to normative political theory. The statist or technocratic impulse tends to view state power and law as capable of being harnessed instrumentally to the goal of restructuring civil society. The difficulty is that statist approaches break faith with a most fundamental premise: namely, that the highest aspiration of demo-cratic culture should be to generate and nurture in all people the capacity for individual and collective *self*-governance and *self*-realization of their potential.

A contrary, antistatist tradition teaches that freedom consists in the complete subordination of the state to civil society, in "immediate," popular self-management without need for institutional arrangements for organized decision making to ensure popular participation, to resolve disputes, and to secure political and economic guarantees. In this view, freedom is achieved not by the instrumental use of law, but by its withering away. The difficulty with this perspective is its overly sanguine faith in the capacity of direct popular action to restructure and democratize the whole of social life. More-over, there is a failure to appreciate that politics—the evolving of institutions for organizing peoples' collective, self-directive capacities and for nurturing each person's opportunity for and experience of his or her own potential and of the promise of social living—is an essential component of human freedom. If politics is conceived as the processes and the institutions by which com-munities collectively guide their destinies, allocate their resources, resolve their disputes, and guarantee and protect their members' experience of per-sonhood, then politics should flourish, not disappear, in our images of post-liberal democracy.

The conceptions of the relationship between institutionalized power and social life that we inherit from radical and socialist traditions are inadequate both to comprehending our present experience and to projecting images of a free society. Obviously the task of theoretical reconstruction will draw upon the experience of all forms of oppositional political practice and upon learning derived from many fields of social inquiry. For its part, critical labor law reveals that the problem of democratic governance in the workplace is in some respects paradigmatic of the problems of politics and law generally. The effort to conceptualize work as an experience of free, creative, and developmental expression, and the workplace as a locus of democratic self-governance, may suggest general terms in which to conceive lawmaking and institution-building as arenas of human self-development and self-realization. For these reasons, critical labor jurisprudence is inspired by the hope that systematic reflection upon the ebb and flow of alienation and struggle at the intersection of the workplace and the legal process will yield fruitful contributions to the shared theoretical project radicals confront.

NOTES

1. Boys Markets, Inc. v. Retail Clerks Union, Local 770, 398 U.S. 235 (1970).
2. *See* Gateway Coal Co. v. United Mine Workers, 414 U.S. 368 (1974).
3. *See* Sinclair Refining Co. v. Atkinson, 370 U.S. 195 (1962).
4. 398 U.S. at 256.
5. *E.g.*, United Steelworkers of America v. American Mfg. Co., 363 U.S. 564 (1960); United Steelworkers of America v. Warrior & Gulf Navigation Co., 363 U.S. 574 (1960); United Steelworkers of America v. Enterprise Wheel & Car Corp., 363 U.S. 593 (1960) (these cases are known collectively as the "*Steelworkers Trilogy*"); and Textile Workers Union v. Lincoln Mills of Alabama, 353 U.S. 448 (1957).
6. Ken Casebeer and Gary Minda have compiled a bibliography, "Critical Legal Studies and Labor Law," which may be obtained by writing to Professor Ken Casebeer, University of Miami Law School, Coral Gables, Florida 33124-8087. In this article, I am attempting to capture only one strand of CLS work on labor law, not to describe CLS's entire theoretical agenda. The authors cited in the bibliography share many concerns and approaches to labor law, but represent a variety of theoretical perspectives and have disagreed with and vigorously criticized each other's work. Moreover, in addition to theoretical work, CLS labor lawyers also frequently write in a programmatic vein suggesting law reform proposals, institutional alternatives, and strategic approaches. Examples of this type of work are also included in the bibliography.
7. For a discussion of the relationship between and differing aspirations of interpretive and critical social theory, *see* Brian Fay, *Social Theory and Political Practice* (London: George Allen & Unwin, 1975), pp. 70–110.
8. For a classic discussion, see Douglas Hay, "Property, Authority and the Criminal Law," in Douglas Hay, Peter Linebaugh, John G. Rule, E. P. Thompson, and Cal Winslow, *Albion's Fatal Tree: Crime and Society in Eighteenth-Century England* (New York: Pantheon Books, 1975), pp. 17–63.
9. *See, e.g.*, NLRB v. Insurance Agents' International Union, 361 U.S. 477, 488–89 (1960).
10. This summary of the dominant postwar industrial relations theory is drawn from Walter Korpi, "Industrial Relations and Industrial Conflict: The Case of Sweden," in *Labor Relations in Advanced Industrial Societies: Issues and Problems*, ed. Benjamin Martin and Everett M. Kassalow (Washington, D.C.: Carnegie Endowment for International Peace, 1980), pp. 90–93.
11. *See* National Labor Relations Act, as amended, §§ 8(b)(4), (7) and 10(l), 29 U.S.C. §§ 158(b)(4), (7) and 160(l); Labor Management Relations Act, 1947, § 303, 29 U.S.C. § 187 (1976); the "national emergency" provisions of Title II of the Taft-Hartley Act, 29 U.S.C. §§ 176–180 (1976); Elk Lumber Co., 91 N.L.R.B. 333 (1950); International Longshoremen's Ass'n.

v. Allied International, Inc., 456 U.S. 212 (1982); Eastex, Inc. v. NLRB, 437 U.S. 556 (1978); Emporium Capwell Co. v. Western Addition Community Organization, 420 U.S. 50 (1975); Linden Lumber Div., Summer & Co. v. NLRB, 419 U.S. 301 (1974); NLRB v. Fansteel Metallurgical Corp., 306 U.S. 240 (1939).

12. 398 U.S. at 251 (emphasis added).

13. Sinclair Refining Co. v. Atkinson, 370 U.S. 195, 225, 226 (1962) (Brennan, J., dissenting).

14. NLRB v. Jones & Laughlin Steel Corp., 301 U.S. 1, 33 (1937), quoting, with a slight modification, American Steel Foundries v. Tri-City Central Trades Council, 257 U.S. 184, 209 (1921).

15. In earlier work, including the version of this essay appearing in the first edition of this book, I used the phrase "contractualism" to refer to the way free contract supplied the underpinnings of a system of managerial domination. This terminology was misleading (so I now replace it with the phrase "minimalist free contract"), because it suggested that the problem is the abstract concept of contract, rather than its concrete, historical embodiments on which I intended to focus.

16. This argument is developed in Betty Mensch, "Freedom of Contract as Ideology," 33 *Stanford Law Review* 753 (1981).

17. Milwaukee Spring Div. of Illinois Coil Spring Co., 265 N.L.R.B. 206 (1982), *revised*, 268 N.L.R.B 601 (1984), *enforced sub nom.*, United Automobile Workers v. NLRB, 765 F.2d 175 (D.C. Cir. 1985).

18. S. Rep. No. 105, 80th Cong., 1st Sess., at 16 (1947).

19. Law professors commonly object that, a priori, rules prohibiting waivers impair efficiency. Except in trivial cases, this argument is mistaken. In the presence of transaction costs and other forms of market failure, no legal regime will generate a perfectly efficient outcome, nor is it possible to determine the efficiency consequences of legal rules a priori. Whether a particular rule, including a substantive restriction on freedom of contract, will lead to relatively more or less efficient outcomes cannot be determined without detailed, contextualized analysis. That is, the claim that substantive restrictions on freedom of contract are a priori inefficient is false. *See generally*, Duncan Kennedy and Frank Michelman, "Are Property and Contract Efficient?" 8 *Hofstra Law Review* 711 (1980); and Karl Klare, "Workplace Democracy and Market Reconstruction: An Agenda for Legal Reform," 38 *Catholic University Law Review* 1 (1988). It is also a common objection that nondisclaimable terms and prohibitions on waivers must have the consequence of decreasing the welfare of the group intended to be benefited. This argument, too, is mistaken. *See* Duncan Kennedy, "Distributive and Paternalist Motives in Contract and Tort Law, With Special Reference to Compulsory Terms and Unequal Bargaining Power," 41 *Maryland Law Review* 563, 604–14 (1982).

20. Sorting out the complex relationship between contract, bureaucratic power, and legislation as it affects prospects for workplace democracy is obviously

a task beyond the scope of this article. Here I simply wish to underscore the point that radical theory ought not cede the field of contract. For further discussion, see Hugh Collins, "Market Power, Bureaucratic Power, and the Contract of Employment," 15 *The Industrial Law Journal* 1 (1986); and, Klare, "Market Reconstruction," *supra* note 19.

21. *See* Karl Klare, "Judicial Deradicalization of the Wagner Act and the Origins of Modern Legal Consciousness, 1937–1941," 62 *Minnesota Law Review* 265 (1978), and "Traditional Labor Law Scholarship and the Crisis of Collective Bargaining Law: A Reply to Professor Finkin," 44 *Maryland Law Review* 731 (1985).

22. In "Market Reconstruction," *supra* note 19, I advocate a program of "radical market reconstruction" and defend its consistency with the ideal of autonomy and the goal of economic efficiency. While some of my proposals are consistent with the NLRA framework, many others are not and would involve substantial statutory changes.

23. As in the famous dictum of *Jones & Laughlin Steel* quoted above. *See also, e.g.*, NLRB v. City Disposal Systems, Inc., 465 U.S. 822, 835 (1984).

24. Fibreboard Paper Products Corp. v. NLRB, 379 U.S. 203, 223 (1964) (Stewart, J., concurring).

25. *See* Staughton Lynd, "Investment Decisions and the Quid Pro Quo Myth," 29 *Case Western Reserve Law Review* 396, 398–403 (1979).

26. First National Maintenance Corp. v. NLRB, 452 U.S. 666, 681 (1981); *id.* at 674 (footnote omitted); *id.* at 676, 679.

27. For an argument that the law actually does protect, or at any rate, should protect employee and community interests in continuity of investment, *see* Joseph William Singer, "The Reliance Interest in Property," 40 *Stanford Law Review* 611 (1988).

28. *See* Elk Lumber Co., 91 N.L.R.B. 333 (1950); NLRB v. Local 1229, IBEW (Jefferson Standard Broadcasting Co.), 346 U.S. 464 (1953); First National Maintenance Corp. v. NLRB, 452 U.S. 666 (1981); NLRB v. Mackay Radio & Telegraph Co., 304 U.S 333 (1938); Textile Workers Union v. Darlington Mfg. Co., 380 U.S. 263 (1965).

29. *See* NLRB v. Magnavox Co., 415 U.S. 322 (1974).

30. Ford Motor Co., 3 L.A. 779 (1944); Peyton Packing Co., 49 N.L.R.B. 828 (1943), *enforced*, 142 F.2d 1009 (5th Cir.), *cert. den.*, 323 U.S. 730 (1944).

31. *See* Katherine Stone, "The Structure of Post-War Labor Relations," 11 *New York University Review of Law and Social Change* 125, 131 (1982–1983).

4 RAND E. ROSENBLATT

SOCIAL DUTIES AND THE PROBLEM OF RIGHTS IN THE AMERICAN WELFARE STATE

IT was a cool evening in November 1989 as my colleague and I drove through the center of Philadelphia to attend a law school dinner. As we passed one of the city's most elegant hotels we could see, ten feet from the glistening Mercedeses and BMWs parked by the front door, three human forms, wrapped in blankets, stretched out over the steam grates in the sidewalks. In the shadow of a grand church across the street sat two men with plastic cups, looking us in the eyes, motioning with their hands. I thought to myself: if a filmmaker staged scenes like these, we might say they were melodramatic and unbelievable. My colleague spoke: "I don't know what to say to my children when we see things like this. And I'm amazed at how most Americans seem to accept this now as normal."

How do we explain these scenes to our children and to ourselves? One tendency, proclaimed prominently by President Reagan, is to deny any re-

This essay is dedicated to the memory of Edward V. Sparer (1928–1983). Ed Sparer was one of the major architects of modern welfare rights law, and a brilliant and extraordinarily dedicated champion of social justice. He was founder and director of Mobilization for Youth Legal Services, the Columbia Center for Social Welfare Law, and the Health Law Project of the University of Pennsylvania, counsel to the National Welfare Rights Organization, and, at the time of his tragically early death, Professor of Law and Social Welfare at the University of Pennsylvania Law School. Memorial essays and a bibliography of his work are collected in 132 *University of Pennsylvania Law Review* 421 (1984). I also wish to thank the participants in the Work and Welfare Seminar of the University of Pennsylvania's Program for Assessing and Revitalizing the Social Sciences, and Ann Freedman, David Kairys, Sylvia Law, Martha Minow, William Simon, and Robert F. Williams for very helpful comments.

sponsibility on the part of society or its well-off members. It is said that there are jobs available for those who can and will work. For those who cannot work—"the truly needy"—there are "programs" and a "safety net." For those excluded from the major welfare programs, there are shelters and soup kitchens. Anyone left on the streets has therefore chosen to be there. We, the taxpayers, have done all that can be reasonably asked of us. Indeed, if we have any fault, it is that we have been too generous in our past welfare practices, and have thereby unwittingly undermined the will to work and the capacity of self-care.[1]

A different account acknowledges the individual life stories and choices by the homeless, but sees patterns and social choices as well: the flight of capital and manufacturing jobs from the cities; the loss of low-income housing, caused in significant part by tax and other public policies; the fragmented structure of metropolitan government, through which the well-off deny responsibility for the problems of the poor; and the "new class war" launched by the Reagan administration and much of American business on the income, legal rights, social benefits, and bargaining power of vast numbers of low-income Americans. The inability of perhaps three million people to find affordable housing is directly related to several prominent features of this war: the slashing of federal housing subsidies, the failure to increase the minimum wage, and the general budgetary attack on welfare benefits and social services for the poor. According to Robert Hayes, the well-known advocate for the homeless in New York City, the successive waves of the homeless have been those least able to compete in this increasingly social Darwinist society: first the chronically mentally ill, then the young single men with poor job skills, then the single-parent families with young children. Can a federal government that explicitly set out to withdraw seventy billion dollars in benefits from low-income people from 1980 to 1984 seriously claim to be surprised at the increase in homelessness? How can its political leaders deny responsibility for creating, for the first time in American history, mass homelessness and other forms of increased poverty in the midst of general economic prosperity?[2]

This essay is about how contemporary American legal concepts contribute to the debate about social responsibility for poverty and the meaning of social justice. After a brief look at the historical background, I discuss the recent development of two major legal models of government benefits for the poor. The first, termed the welfare entitlement model, was embodied in Supreme Court decisions in the late 1960s and early 1970s, and involved a significant break from the long-standing prior refusal to recognize poor people's legal rights to benefits. Under the entitlement approach, benefits are treated in many contexts as enforceable legal rights, somewhat analogous to property rights and civil liberties. The second model, which I term managerial formalism, is the approach favored by the Reagan/Bush administration and the Rehnquist Court majority, and constitutes a sharp attack on the welfare entitlement model. The core of managerial formalism is that in distributing or denying benefits, and in making a wide range of other decisions involving, for example, land use zoning, mass transit rates, and hospital closings, executive officials and legislators have almost no legal responsibilities to the poor and other vulnerable people, except for those stated very explicitly—hence rarely—in statutes or constitutional provisions. This denial of governmental, and more generally social responsibility with respect to poverty and other human needs, like the similar denial of responsibility for racism and its effects discussed by Alan Freeman in this volume, enhances the economic power of the relatively well-off, preserves the myth that the market operates fairly, neutrally, and apolitically, and reinforces the idea that those who do not succeed economically have no moral or legal claims on the community and only themselves to blame.[3]

Despite their current influence in the Supreme Court and other governmental forums, it is hard to believe that managerial formalism and related conservative perspectives will be adequate, or even perceived to be adequate, for the needs of American society in the 1990s and beyond. The formidable economic challenges posed by Japan and an increasingly integrated Western Europe, and their achievements in technology, living standards, education, and social benefits, are already raising serious questions about American policies that leave so many of our citizens outside the mainstream of economic and social life. Other major challenges facing our society—drugs, crime, environmental hazards, and public health—are also resistant to market-based and privatized solutions. It seems at least possible that a broader concept of social and governmental responsibility will gain strength in the political system, thereby providing a base for the revival and development of a third legal model examined in this essay: that of social duties and group rights, which interact with and supplement the individual entitlement model in interesting ways.

THE LEGACY OF HISTORY: WELFARE, THE LABOR MARKET, AND THE PROBLEM OF RIGHTS AND DUTIES

The major social welfare statute of the New Deal—the Social Security Act of 1935—interacted with existing private property to generate a four-tiered structure of economic and social legitimacy that persists to this day. At the top, predating the New Deal and relatively unrestricted by its tax and regulatory legislation, stands the property of the wealthier members of society, most of which is derived from the "private market"[4]—from inheritance, high salaries, investments, and private pension plans. These forms of wealth are clearly considered private property, and are extensively protected by constitutional, statutory, and judge-made law against many kinds of governmental and nongovernmental encroachment. At a second level stand the vast middle and upper working classes. These households too may have significant private property, notably home equity and some private pension plans. But they also rely heavily on the social insurance programs established by the Social Security Act: old age insurance, disability insurance, unemployment insurance, and (since 1965) Medicare. These programs' benefits are not vested private property in the same sense as property in the first tier, because Congress can change the benefits at any time, subject to powerful political constraints. On the other hand, the social insurance benefits were thought of by the New Deal framers—and continue to be thought of by millions of beneficiaries—as having two "propertylike" characteristics: contribution (through payroll taxes) rather than need as the basis of eligibility, and "definite rules" designed to protect the independence of the beneficiary from the discretion of the bureaucracy by establishing clear, legally enforceable individual entitlements. Such entitlements were not provided to the third tier of citizens, those who fit into the "categories" of need-based welfare assistance created by the Social Security Act, and administered and funded by the states with federal financial assistance and regulatory oversight. These categories—the aged, the blind, the permanently and totally disabled, and single parents with children—constituted the "worthy" or "deserving" poor, who were considered to have socially legitimate reasons for not working, and therefore had some kind of a claim on society for material support. This claim was not, however, explicitly structured as an individual, legally enforceable right. Rather, the complex federal and state administrative and funding mechanisms seemed to contemplate a social duty to be implemented through what might be termed "structured discretion," under which state legislators and bureaucrats would have considerable choice concerning eligibility rules, the amount of benefits, and ad hoc appraisal of individual applicants, subject to more or less clear federal guidelines. The "able-bodied," presumptively "employable" poor, e.g., single adults and two-parent families, were relegated to a fourth tier of state and locally funded "general assistance" in which legislative and bureaucratic discretion was virtually completely unbounded by federal law.[5]

The gradations of rights and social responsibilities generated by the Social Security Act reflected a long and unresolved American debate regarding poverty and social justice. On one side were movements (e.g., labor and populist) and intellectuals expressing communitarian values, rooted in religious traditions and in secular ideals of republicanism and egalitarian democracy, which acknowledged social responsibility for much of poverty and supported extensive private and public effort and expenditure to combat it. One of the most famous expressions of these values was President Franklin Roosevelt's inclusion among the "four freedoms" of "freedom from want." In this broad tradition, relief was sometimes referred to as a "right," although as a practical matter this did not usually mean an individual legal right, but rather a group right or social duty, to be enforced by political pressure and popular protest. On the other side stood many individuals and institutions espousing individualist, laissez-faire values, also rooted in religion and in secular social theories such as social Darwinism, which blamed the poor themselves for their condition and viewed charitable relief as a dangerous addiction that undermined people's willingness to accept whatever the labor market had to offer. In this tradition relief was almost never viewed as a "right," but rather as a "privilege," which the donor (whether governmental or private) could restrict or condition in any way he chose. American social welfare history was, and continues to be, characterized by recurring alternation between these positions: expansion of relief rolls in response to technological change and market dislocations, and then claims by promarket reformers that liberal relief policies *cause* poverty by undermining work incentives, accompanied by new measures to deny benefits and police more strictly the distinction between the deserving (*i.e.*, disabled or otherwise legitimately unemployed) and the undeserving (*i.e.*, employable) poor.[6]

THE MODEL OF WELFARE ENTITLEMENT

Beginning in the 1950s, and gaining momentum in the 1960s, a number of forces led to a new vision of law in the American welfare state. Of foremost importance was the civil rights movement, both because many Black citizens had low incomes, and because the vision of equal rights for all citizens was easily transferable to the poor. Additional (and related) factors included the expanded role of government in social welfare, and, in the 1960s, an organized legal services program, an organized welfare rights movement, the political agenda of the Democratic party, and heightened consciousness among intellectuals and professionals (including some judges) about the need for a more inclusive concept of citizenship.

The concept of legal entitlement to welfare was articulated most influentially by Charles Reich, a professor at the Yale Law School, and Edward Sparer, a founder and director of innovative legal services programs and a law professor at the University of Pennsylvania. In a famous article titled "The New Property," Reich argued that government benefits of all sorts—such as occupational licenses, broadcast licenses, and welfare benefits—were as important to individual liberty as traditional property, and should be accorded the same kinds of procedural and substantive legal protection. Sparer focused specifically on the needs of the poor for human dignity, material resources, and community organization, and showed in detail how recognition of welfare rights could further those goals.[7]

The work of Reich and Sparer generated three concepts of entitlement to government benefits of particular importance to the poor. First, eligibility rules should be understood as defining recipients' rights rather than the limits of welfare officials' discretion; if a person met the income and other eligibility requirements for benefits, he or she should be legally entitled to receive those benefits, without being subject to further discretionary judgments, and with the protection of fair procedures for making relevant decisions. This was already the approach taken in the social insurance programs; the point was to extend this concept of entitlement to the noncontributory, means-tested programs such as Aid to Families with Dependent Children (AFDC).

Second, the right/privilege distinction had to be recognized for what it was—severe coercion—and abandoned. If recipients were to receive benefits as a matter of legal entitlement, and be respected as full citizens, they could not be under constant pressure to waive their rights to privacy, travel, and family autonomy, on pain of losing their means of subsistence. Third, and most ambitiously, Reich argued that because poverty was caused largely by social forces, "when individuals have insufficient resources to live under conditions of health and decency, society has obligations to provide support, and the individual is entitled to that support as of right." A number of legal scholars have subsequently developed extensive arguments to support this and related claims, notably Frank Michelman, Kenneth Karst, and Sylvia Law.[8]

In three landmark cases decided between 1968 and 1970, the Supreme Court accepted the first two meanings of the concept of entitlement in the welfare context. The Court held that states could not impose eligibility requirements that were inconsistent with those contained in the federal Social Security Act, nor could they impose a one-year residency requirement on welfare benefits, or terminate benefits without a hearing that met minimal due process standards. All three cases repudiated the right/privilege distinction and stood for the principle that the substantive and procedural rules of the welfare system had to respect basic constitutional and statutory rights. As important as the Court's formal holdings was its implicit message that the welfare titles of the Social Security Act, drafted largely as a contract between the federal and state governments, created rights that welfare recipients could seek to enforce in federal courts.[9]

However, the third meaning of entitlement—an affirmative right to government assistance to meet basic living needs—was decisively rejected by the Supreme Court as a matter of federal constitutional law. In *Dandridge* v. *Williams*, the Court upheld a state rule limiting AFDC monthly benefits to a maximum of $250 regardless of family size, thereby leaving some large families with less than 60 percent of the state-determined minimum need. The state's justification for this policy was in part as a work incentive; concern was expressed that without a family maximum, the grants to large families would exceed the monthly income earned by full-time work at the minimum wage. But the state conceded that only a very small percentage of welfare recipients were employable, and offered no evidence about how many of the employable adults were in large families burdened by the family maximum. In other words, a very harsh incentive—denial of subsistence benefits—was being imposed on children, including newborns, to affect the behavior of adults most of whom could not respond even if they wished to. Yet with almost no discussion, the Court found the rule to be "rationally based and free from invidious discrimination."[10]

Despite *Dandridge* and other decisions denying claims of welfare rights,[11] the Court's recognition of the possibility of legal entitlement to welfare benefits was enormously important for both practical and symbolic reasons. As a practical matter, the courts' enforcement of federal statutory and constitutional standards protected the grants of millions of needy children, and as a symbolic matter, represented a major step in the effort of the poor to achieve full citizenship. At the same time, the concept of welfare entitlement, and the welfare rights and related movements from which it drew strength, did not succeed in their larger political goal of integrating the poor and minorities into the polity as respected and participating members. On the contrary, welfare recipients, particularly Black welfare recipients, remained the despised "other" in the eyes of much of taxpaying white America, and the identification of the Democrats' "Great Society" with the interests of the Black poor contributed significantly to conservative electoral victories in the 1970s and 1980s. On this political base, the Reagan administration attacked benefits and services of all sorts to low-income people, reducing them sharply so as to provide funds for a vastly expanded military budget, and creating harsh financial pressures for low-wage (and often unavailable) work.[12] The task of the conservative justices in the Burger and Rehnquist eras has been to reconceptualize and revive legal theories justifying official discretion and denial of recipients' rights, to block the expansion of the entitlement model, and to reinterpret it where necessary to make it consistent with conservative values.

THE MODEL OF MANAGERIAL FORMALISM

"Managerial formalism" seems a defensible name for the set of ideas that animates the Rehnquist Court's decisions regarding the poor. Like the Court's decisions in the era of *Lochner* v. *New York* (1905) and *Coppage* v. *Kansas* (1915), these decisions are formalist in maintaining that there is a sharp distinction between government and society, that this and other categories (such as negative versus affirmative rights) are natural, objective, "legal," and nonpolitical, and that judicial and legislative "neutrality" consists in ignoring actual differences in economic and political resources, with the result of reinforcing existing inequalities of economic and political power.

The major difference between classical formalism and its modern descendant lies in their respective treatment of the political process. In the classical period, employers and other property-holders asserted constitutional rights of liberty and property against legislation enacted by political majorities. For these litigants and their judicial allies, the political process was the enemy, and the existing distribution of wealth, including the common law rights associated with it, were defended as "natural" and prepolitical, *i.e.*, as fundamental components of constitutional "liberty" unalterable by mere legislative majorities. In the current era, the litigation roles are often (although by no means always) reversed, with beneficiaries challenging executive and legislative actions. Managerial formalism denies these claims on the asserted grounds of deference to the democratic process, expressed in part through a relentless positivism that recognizes legal rights against the government only in the most explicit legislative and constitutional commands. In addition, modern formalism is "managerial" in that it frequently invokes, and defers to, the "expertise" of legislators and bureaucrats, particularly on issues involving "large social welfare programs" with budgetary implications.[13] Thus while classical formalism saw the distinctions between government and society, public and private as "natural," prepolitical limits on democratic politics, managerial formalism celebrates them as the *products* of democratic politics, and interprets legislative silence as a deep commitment to bureaucratic power.

A recent Supreme Court case dramatically illustrates these themes. In *DeShaney* v. *Winnebago County Department of Social Services*, Joshua DeShaney, a four-year-old boy, was beaten repeatedly by his father, resulting in severe and permanent injuries. The Winnebago Department of Social Services had received many reports that Joshua was being abused by his father, had actually removed him from the home for a time, and had then returned him to his father, after which the social worker assigned to his case continued to chronicle reports of abuse, in the words of Justice Brennan's dissent, "in detail that seems almost eerie in light of her failure to act upon [them]." After his major injury, a federal lawsuit was filed on Joshua's behalf for damages against the state social services department and its employees on the grounds that they had deprived Joshua of his federal liberty right to bodily integrity by failing to intervene to protect him against the known risk of violence from his father.

Conceding that the facts of the case were "undeniably tragic," Chief Justice Rehnquist wrote an opinion for the Court denying all relief. The opinion rests on two major propositions. The first is that the Constitution imposes no "affirmative obligation" on government to do anything about harms that occur between "private actors." The relevance of this statement is at first puzzling; it seems to mean that the state has no constitutional obligation to establish a child protection agency at all, and hence that Joshua has no general federal constitutional right to force the state to provide him with protection. This argument is puzzling because no one was trying to force the state to enter the field; the state *had* established a child protection agency, which had actually involved itself with Joshua's life. On close inspection, however, it becomes evident that the real function of the "no affirmative right" argument is to establish subtly the norms for evaluating the state officials' actual behavior. The Due Process Clause, says Chief Justice Rehnquist, "is phrased as a limitation on the State's power to act, not as a guarantee of certain minimal levels of safety and security," and thus, "[a]s a general matter . . . a State's failure to protect an individual against private violence simply does not constitute a [Due Process] violation. . . ."[14] The slippery terms here are "minimal levels" and "failure," because they cover both the state's doing *nothing at all*, or *nothing with respect to this individual,* and *doing something very incompetently.*

The latent meaning of the no affirmative duty point becomes clear in Chief Justice Rehnquist's second proposition: that the state has not entered into a "special relationship" with Joshua that gives rise to an affirmative duty of protection. One might well ask, why should we not infer a special relationship and duty of care between a government social worker and a helpless four-year-old child she has been assigned to protect? At one level Rehnquist's answer is entirely formal: since the state had not taken physical or legal custody of Joshua, judicial precedents, which dealt with prisoners and hospitalized mental patients, do not require relief. But Rehnquist's more revealing answer is this: that the social worker's inaction did not "cause" Joshua's injuries, because it did not increase his risk of harm beyond what it would have been had the state never established a child protection agency at all. In other words, the state's "right" not to have any child protection agency at all must include the "lesser" right to have one that provides grossly inadequate protection. This is the "right/privilege" distinction in all its glory; because the recipient has no right to force a hypothetical state government to create the benefit at all, she has virtually no rights with respect to how the actual state government defines and administers the benefits it has chosen to provide.

Finally, Rehnquist adroitly links the government/society and affirmative/negative dichotomies to the democratic process, with powerful rhetorical effect. We are told that the Framers, the ultimate source of democratic legitimacy, clearly assigned the question of whether to recognize affirmative rights to the political process, and not to the courts. To question the distinction between negative and affirmative rights is to attack the authority of the "people of Wisconsin," their actual views on the matter being irrelevant to the federal constitutional issue. A case that began as the plea of a severely injured child against a callous or otherwise incompetent child protection agency has been transformed into a defense of the people of Wisconsin against an unrepresentative, potentially self-aggrandizing court. It is a brilliant judicial expression of the imagery so effectively used by President Reagan: we must "get the government off our backs" and return liberty to "the people."

These related themes of managerial formalism—that government has no "causal" responsibility for economic inequality and other "private" harms, no "affirmative duty" to do anything about them or even concern itself with the differential impact of government policies, and virtually no duties with respect to benefits actually provided—permeate the Supreme Court majority's approach to the legal claims of low-income citizens from the mid-1970s to the present. Thus when Congress withdrew federal funding for almost all abortions for low-income women—even those needed to preserve the woman's health—the Court upheld the law on the theory that Congress had not "done" anything to restrict the choices of the women affected.

> . . . [A]lthough government may not place obstacles in the path of a woman's exercise of her freedom of choice, it need not remove those not of its own creation. . . . The [statute] leaves an indigent woman with at least the same range of choice in deciding whether to obtain a medically necessary abortion as she would have had if Congress had chosen to subsidize no health care costs at all.[15]

Similarly, Congress's withdrawal of food stamp benefits from striking workers and their families does not "coerce" workers with respect to their right to strike, but merely "declines to extend . . . assistance" in order to promote government "neutrality" in labor disputes. In another example, a school district's refusal to waive a bus transportation charge for a low-income child living sixteen miles from school is constitutional, because the Constitution does not require bus service to be offered at all, and hence imposes no obligation to offer it for free. In yet another case, low-income disability recipients alleging that government officials illegally and intentionally deprived them of their statutory benefits, causing great hardship for months and even years, are denied any compensatory damages, because of deference to Congress's expertise in managing large social welfare programs.[16]

The Rehnquist Court's approach rests on an extraordinary series of denials. First, there is the denial of the difference between a government decision not to have a service or benefit at all, and a "decision"—or inertia, or callousness, or inattention—that undermines the purpose of the benefit, or that causes preventable harm. To be sure, constitutional doctrines and statutory interpretations requiring certain minimal levels of benefits, services, and competence would have an impact on the programs' budgets, and perhaps on methods of administration. This impact might counsel for only limited and carefully framed duties of this sort, as discussed below with respect to the social duty model. But such an approach would be far more defensible than the strained logic of the right/privilege distinction, which equates a broad policy decision not to provide a benefit at all with the much more focused problem of providing one inadequately or incompetently.

Second, managerial formalism denies the widespread effects of government policies and the pervasive responsibilities that government has actually undertaken. Even in the *Lochner* era, it was false to say that judicial doctrines requiring unregulated labor markets were "neutral" and merely defensive of "natural," prepolitical "liberty," because the "private" rights and resources of employers and workers used in the exercise of that liberty were themselves defined and influenced by humanly fashioned, and hence inevitably political, law. The claim that government refusal to fund food stamps for strikers, or abortions for poor women, is "neutral" seems even less defensible in the 1980s, when significant government subsidies are available to management (in the case of strikes), and for childbirth (in the case of abortions). Indeed, in these cases the claim of government neutrality seems patently false; the evident (and with respect to abortions, explicit) legislative goal of these benefit denials is to pressure recipients to forgo a constitutional right.[17]

Third, the quasi-empirical claim that the government has not "done" anything to people by withdrawing benefits or providing inadequate services, because it has not made their situation worse than it would have been without any government program at all, denies the preemptive or reliance effects of actually providing services. If there were no public school buses in rural North Dakota, presumably extensive networks of carpooling and exchange of services and money would have arisen, in which low-income families would have participated, but not necessarily on a cash basis. With respect to abortions, large-scale federal and state funding of health care for the poor has altered the landscape of health care delivery by raising prices and undermining the pre-Medicaid tradition of public and private charitable care.

The most dramatic example of these reliance effects can be found in the *DeShaney* case. As Justice Brennan demonstrates carefully in his dissent, it is false to say that Joshua was "no worse off" because of the state's inadequate services. State law channeled all reports of child abuse to the local department of social services (DSS), which was given virtually the sole authority to decide what action to take. By relieving other potential sources of care—the neighbors, doctors, and police officers who saw Joshua's injuries—of any sense of obligation to do more than report their concerns to DSS, the state effectively "walled off" Joshua in his father's violent house, and conceivably made his situation worse than if the DSS had not existed at all. As Laurence Tribe puts it:

> From the majority's perspective, the state of Wisconsin operates as a thing, its arms exerting force from a safe distance upon a sometimes unpleasant natural world, in which the abuse of children is an unfortunate, yet external, ante-legal, and pre-political fact. . . . Courts, as passive and detached observers, may reach in to offer a helping hand only when another arm of the state has reached out and shattered this natural, pre-political order by itself directly harming a young child.
>
> Within the majority's stilted pre-modern paradigm, there is no hint that the hand of the observing state may itself have played a major role in shaping the world it observes.[18]

Finally, managerial formalism denies that the federal constitution protects what are termed "affirmative rights." This position relies on the text of the Fourteenth Amendment—that no state shall *deprive* any person of liberty without due process of law—and more fundamentally, on the long tradition of interpreting the 1789 Constitution and the Reconstruction Era amendments as standing for negative rather than affirmative rights. Rehnquist's interpretation has historical support, but it fails to acknowledge and respond to the long communitarian and egalitarian countertradition embodied in numerous legal doctrines, statutes, religious and ethical values, social movements, and most prominently, in what Bruce Ackerman and others have termed a third major constitutional moment: the commitment during the New Deal of all three branches of the federal government, and overwhelming electoral majorities, to an "activist regulatory state." (One might also argue that the civil rights era, including *Brown* v. *Board of Education* and the civil rights legislation of the 1960s, constitutes a fourth constitutional moment, albeit subject to the intense ambiguity explored by Alan Freeman in this volume.) From this view, it is not enough to recite the original intent of the 1789 and 1868 Framers—leaving aside debates about that intent. Rather, contemporary constitutional decision makers must also take into account other commitments of a constitutional and quasi-constitutional nature made since then, notably the vast expansion of the role of government and the further erosion of the government/society distinction. The issue in *DeShaney* is then conceived as analogous to what it was in *Brown* v. *Board of Education*: how do we understand our constitutional principles, textually inscribed in 1789 and 1868, in the light of modern state agencies intervening in, and even monopolizing, matters as fundamental as child protection and education, and in the light of New Deal and civil rights era jurisprudence that added important principles to our earlier constitutional tradition?[19]

The central message of managerial formalism is that consideration of the needs and rights of the poor is a matter of political convenience; callousness and disregard will almost always be found to be "rational" and, under the logic of the right/privilege distinction, "harmless." In addition, managerial formalism has structural implications for all three governmental branches. The position that only precise, mandatory legal texts are enforceable undermines the courts' role as interpreters of broadly framed public values in aid of the disadvantaged, and reduces courts to ratifying not only the explicit choices of the politically powerful, but also "choices" that are at best implicit and ambiguous. Moreover, managerial formalism requires low-income citizens to secure extremely explicit legislative rules and remedies. Although other citizens may be treated similarly by the Court, the poor face unusual and large difficulties in organizing and financing political action. For all of these reasons, the Rehnquist Court's claim that it is simply deferring to political majorities is suspect; its interpretative presumptions help shape the process to which deference is given.

Managerial formalism also implies that we have only two options: either to recognize a full-fledged individual entitlement to a benefit, and thereby greatly reduce political flexibility, or to grant the political branches virtually plenary discretion. This proposition is false; numerous intermediate approaches have been and can be developed that simultaneously recognize social duties to the poor, allow considerable legislative discretion in fulfilling those duties, and shape a process for structuring that discretion.

THE NEED FOR A THIRD MODEL:
THE CRITIQUE OF WELFARE ENTITLEMENTS

For all its virtues, the model of welfare entitlement cannot alone serve as the intermediate model needed to structure but not overly restrict political discretion. First, the concept of entitlement can be and has been turned on its head, with the "clear rules" becoming grounds for denying benefits and creating insecurity, rather than, as Reich and Sparer intended, enhancing it. William Simon recounts "a particularly vivid memory" of a woman with four children whose grant was terminated because she could not produce a letter from one of her children's schools during summer vacation verifying enrollment. When she finally obtained the letter and brought it to her caseworker she was told: "It is too late. There is nothing I can do." Later, after the woman's checks were terminated, the caseworker told Simon that what she had meant was there was nothing that she, as an "ongoing" caseworker, could do. What the worker failed to tell the recepient was that she could have been immediately reinstated by filing an application with the "intake" unit. Simon observes:

> If the literary personification of the pathologies of the old regime [American welfare, 1935–1960] was Dostoyevsky's Grand Inquisitor, with his relentless intimacy and psychological omnipotence, the personification of the pathologies of the new regime is Kafka's Doorkeeper, who stands, passive and inscrutable, before the door to the Law and announces only when it is too late, "this door was intended for you. I am now going to shut it."[20]

Similarly, a recent study that found of the 2,600,000 applicants denied welfare or Medicaid in 1986, almost 60 percent were refused not because their income or assets were too high, but because of "application problems." The study's author suggested "that illiteracy and other language barriers, along with transportation problems and the difficulty of providing necessary documents, were keeping many needy people from help they are qualified for." In another example, Joel Handler eloquently analyzes why a new comprehensive set of nursing home residents' rights is unlikely to provide "the vast majority of residents any protection at all"—because the residents have few resources or capacity to learn about their rights and assert them—and by leading "citizens and policymakers into thinking that they have accomplished something, . . . [may] actually [be] harmful."[21]

To be sure, the advocates of welfare entitlements did not intend to have them administered in a manner hostile or insensitive to recipients' real interests, and there is nothing inherent in the concept that requires this result. But the concept of entitlement according to relatively clear, formal rules does not explicitly address the deeper problems of welfare law and policy—the substantive values and relationships of the programs and of the larger society they reflect—and therefore is vulnerable to this sort of manipulation.[22]

Second, the individualist, possession-based quality of entitlement is both helpful and problematic. On the one hand, welfare recipients, like all other citizens, need for their survival, functioning, and self-respect, to possess individual rights and resources. At the same time, what many low-income persons need and want is not simply "benefits," but also a relationship in which she or he is assisted in meeting her own and society's goals. Moreover, the problems of the poor cannot be solved or even understood solely on an individual basis. The decay of inner-city neighborhoods, the lack of jobs and investment capital, the collapse of inner-city public education, the depressed self-image and low skills of many residents of poor neighborhoods, and the ubiquity of drug addiction and crime are now recognized even by conservative social analysts as social phenomena, larger and more coherent than simply a random clustering of individual life stories. It seems obvious that individual entitlements, such as welfare grants or access to low-cost housing, while necessary to the solution of these problems, are not sufficient, either to assist individuals, or to help build the interracial and interclass coalitions needed for a more egalitarian political consensus.[23]

THE MODEL OF SOCIAL DUTIES AND GROUP RIGHTS

We have been immersed for so long in a model of rights as a matter of individual possession, defended negatively against the rest of the world, that the concepts of social duties and affirmative group rights may appear strange, and hence, as in Rehnquist's *DeShaney* opinion, invisible as part of our constitutional heritage. But in fact the case is not so clear. Social duties to the poor and other disadvantaged groups, enforceable by individuals but not easily reducible to individual rights, have long been part of Western, and specifically American, political, religious, philosophical, and legal traditions. To mention only a few examples, the National Council of Catholic Bishops recently stated that society has a duty to ensure that the basic material needs of its members are met, and that "social institutions be ordered in a way that guarantees all persons the ability to participate actively in the economic, political, and cultural life of the society." Similar formulations can be found in many Western philosophical traditions, notably John Rawls's influential "difference principle." In addition, many modern developments in philosophy and social and legal theory—notably feminism, critical legal studies, critical racial studies, communitarianism, and civic republicanism—question established dichotomies between public and private and advocate self-reflective consciousness on the part of judges and other decision makers concerning the perceptions and needs of groups traditionally defined as subordinate or different. Finally, in recent years state constitutions and statutes have proven to be a richer source of affirmative duties than federal law, in part because of different texts and traditions, and in part because of the influence of conservative political values on the federal judiciary.[24]

Although concepts of social duty embrace a large range of substantive variation, they tend to share certain principles that directly contradict the model of managerial formalism. First, constructs such as "society," "the market," and the "private sphere" are not seen as "natural" and sharply distinct from government, but rather as pervasively structured and influenced by government. Second, in this context, the great ideals of governmental "fairness" and "neutrality," and of acting for the "general welfare," cannot be understood as deferring to a market or a political process in which the strong dominate the weak, but rather as ensuring that all important human interests, including those of the weak, receive fair consideration. Thus the

United States Supreme Court, in reversing the doctrine of liberty of contract in 1937, upheld a state minimum wage law on the grounds that the legislature was entitled to take inequality of bargaining power into account and seek to regulate its consequences. From this perspective, the unequal bargaining power that the *Lochner* court had seen as natural and constitutionally protected was now seen as a social construct subject to legislative change. [25]

The most dramatic example of these two principles—that government pervasively influences society, and has consequently broad social obligations to represent all social interests, including those of the weak—can be found in the New Jersey Supreme Court's *Mount Laurel* decisions on exclusionary zoning. Where Chief Justice Rehnquist cannot see causation and responsibility in the relationship of state social workers to a vulnerable child, the New Jersey Supreme Court sees causation and responsibility in the interplay of state delegation of zoning authority to local governments, local government zoning rules that exclude low- and moderate-income housing from the suburbs, and the desperate conditions of the inner city. Moreover, far from insisting on a mandatory, specific constitutional text as the only basis for affirmative governmental duties, the New Jersey Supreme Court has held that the concept of police powers exercised for the "general welfare" requires the state and its municipalities to take into account the interests of all persons who might need housing in the region, rather than only maximizing the immediate economic interests of a municipality's existing residents.

> . . . [T]hose [zoning] regulations that do not provide the requisite opportunity for a fair share of the region's need for low and moderate income housing conflict with the general welfare and violate the state constitutional requirements of substantive due process and equal protection. . . . The basis for the constitutional obligation is simple: the State controls the use of land, *all* of the land. In exercising that control, it cannot favor rich over poor. It cannot legislatively set aside dilapidated housing in urban ghettos for the poor and decent housing elsewhere for everyone else. The government that controls this land represents everyone. While the State may not have the ability to eliminate poverty, it cannot use that condition as the basis for imposing further disadvantages. . . .[26]

The *Mount Laurel* opinions also reject managerial formalism's bipolar model of constitutionalism and politics, i.e., that there is no middle ground between a clear, mandatory constitutional "right" and wide-open political discretion. Instead, the New Jersey Supreme Court suggests that in implementing this sort of broad social duty, the legislature is a partner with the court in interpreting the constitution, and the relationship between them is less one of hierarchy and more one of dialogue and persuasion.

. . . powerful reasons suggest, and we agree, that the matter is better left to the Legislature. We act . . . because the Constitution of our State requires protection of the interests involved and because the Legislature has not protected them. We recognize the social and economic controversy (and its political consequences) that has resulted in relatively little legislative action. . . . But enforcement of constitutional rights cannot await a supporting political consensus. . . . Our deference to . . . [existing] legislative and executive initiatives can be regarded as a clear signal of our readiness to defer further to more substantial actions.[27]

The *Mount Laurel* decisions do not establish an individual entitlement to affordable housing in the suburbs; rather, they establish a social duty on the part of suburban municipalities to permit a "fair share" of low- and moderate-income housing to be constructed within their borders. This duty is also a group right, enforceable by organizations such as the NAACP, representing potential low-income buyers, and by builders who wish to construct such housing. The effect of the rulings has been a great deal of litigation, the construction of 22,700 units of affordable housing, and the stimulation of the political process to enact a Fair Housing Law, in part to blunt the impact of the court's rulings. Whether the *Mount Laurel* decisions were correct in their analysis of the causes and effects of exclusionary zoning, legitimate interpretations of the state constitution, and successful in helping their intended beneficiaries are hotly debated questions.[28] What seems clear is that without them, there would be less housing diversity in many localities, and much less explicit political consideration of a vital social issue.

A fourth component of the social duty model is that government must respect the logic of its own commitments. At one level this means that executive agencies cannot simply refuse to staff or fund operations dealing with vital human needs, at least not without serious efforts to conserve funds in less destructive ways, and perhaps not without explicit legislative authorization. At another, more controversial level, this means that there may be obligations on the legislature to fund important social benefits and services, such as prisons, hospitals, public education, child protection agencies, welfare benefits, and housing at minimally adequate and equal levels. This is the lesson of the school financing cases, in which ten state supreme courts, including three in 1989, have declared invalid large disparities in locally based education budgets, and required reallocations of millions of dollars.[29]

Recent state court litigation in Massachusetts concerning welfare recipients and the homeless also illustrates this component of the social duty model. A lawsuit was filed against the state welfare department (DPW) under a 1913 state statute providing that welfare benefits "shall be sufficient to enable such parent to bring up such child or children properly in his or her own home

. . . ," and under a second statute requiring DPW to review annually the adequacy of its "standard budget of assistance." Despite these statutes, the state legislature's AFDC appropriations fell increasingly short of rents in Massachusetts' rising real-estate market, contributing significantly to a rise in homelessness. The Massachusetts Supreme Court unanimously held that the 1913 law does not merely state a hortatory goal, but rather creates legal duties on the executive branch to seek to prevent the homelessness of AFDC families by calculating adequate budgetary standards, reasonably using available appropriated funds, and, if appropriations are inadequate to prevent homelessness, notifying the legislature of the deficiency and requesting either additional appropriations or alternative solutions. The state supreme court did not order DPW to pay or the legislature to fund increased benefits, but rather modified the political process by finding a statutory duty on the part of the welfare department to advocate the housing interests of AFDC families in the legislative process. Whether such a duty has any long-term impact remains to be seen; in the short-term, both the court's orders, and the publicity surrounding the litigation, appeared to contribute to some increase in benefits, and to the visibility of the issue. As the New Jersey Supreme Court noted in reaching a similar result, "it is a fact of human experience . . . that not until we see the face of poverty do we react to it."[30]

To be sure, the concept of social duty does not supply simple answers. The definition of the groups to whom such duties are owed, the content of the group rights, and the problems of interpretation and indeterminacy remain formidable.[31] This essay does not attempt to resolve these issues; its goal is rather to show why social duties and group rights are possible and desirable in the context of poverty, and what they might mean.

SOCIAL DUTIES AND THE THREE FACES OF POVERTY

Contemporary American poverty requires three major types of responses.[32] First, poor people need money or in-kind benefits to meet basic human needs, such as food, shelter, clothing, and health care. The concept of entitlement provides important protections with respect to these benefits, but cannot alone assure adequate funding, efficient organization, and political support. Second, for many recipients, supplying funds for basic living needs is not the end of the process, but the beginning; they need extensive additional support to raise their children, free themselves from drugs, take advantage of training opportunities, or, in the case of the disabled elderly, function to their capacities. For them, the social duty model should encompass what William Simon terms "regenerative rights," and Joel Handler calls "empowerment rights." Such rights deliver both commodities—such as housing, job training, nursing home care, or income—and also relationships with guides or advocates committed to helping the recipient overcome external and internal barriers to autonomy and well-being. In this approach, the individual's autonomy is said to be the goal of the relationship, rather than its unrealistic premise or presupposition.[33]

For the most part, rights and duties of this sort cannot be ordered and implemented in detail by courts against recalcitrant agencies. Ideally, such rights and relationships flourish where the guides and advocates themselves have a large degree of autonomy, discretion, and fidelity to their clients, supported by adequate funding and organization supplied by legislative and executive leadership. Courts can, however, give social welfare agencies an incentive to move in this direction by penalizing the harms caused by grossly inadequate alternatives. This is the position taken by Justice Brennan in his dissent in *Schweiker* v. *Chilicky,* in which he advocates imposition of compensatory damages on agencies and officials who deny recipients benefits by grossly disregarding applicable rules, and in his *DeShaney* dissent discussed above. In other contexts, such as the Agent Orange product liability settlement and the Medicare rehabilitation services case, courts have creatively used special masters and other devices to define and implement new kinds of benefits and service relationships.[34]

The third needed response to poverty is the restructuring of major social subsystems—education, housing, metropolitan government, and economic development—to create and expand opportunities and distribute them in a more egalitarian fashion. As suggested by the school financing and *Mount Laurel* litigation, such massive projects primarily rest on a concept of social duty, whose meaning is developed in a complex interplay of the courts, legislatures, bureaucracies, and individuals involved.

Two important caveats concerning the social duty model should be noted. First, the state supreme court cases emphasize the centrality of the legislature, the executive branch, and public opinion as powerful decision makers about the existence and content of social duties. The courts can play an important role, but one more characterized by dialogue and incentives than by hierarchical command. Second, it is important to remember that social duties should be conceived as complements to individual entitlements. The history of the legal and political vulnerability of the poor is so sobering that it would be reckless to abandon or sharply curtail the model of individual entitlements in favor of more discretionary political judgments that might yield some short-term benefits. The challenge is to safeguard and improve the security of individuals while simultaneously expanding the capacity of society to meet their pressing needs.

PROSPECTS FOR THE FUTURE

The existence of a concept of social duty, and of a tradition of thought and action supporting it, does not guarantee that it will prevail against managerial formalism and related conservative perspectives. Indeed, social policy in the United States seems caught between strongly contradictory forces and values. On one side is a suspicion of egalitarian government (although not of governmental power exercised for "traditionalist" ends, such as suppression of flag burning or punishment of abortion) and a corresponding faith in the market (biased toward the rich by bailouts and subsidized speculation, as in the savings and loan industry). Often linked to these views, with great electoral power, are racism, antifeminism, and antigay attitudes. On the other side is widespread concern that the combination of unregulated but perversely subsidized markets cannot adequately manage large sectors of the society— such as the environment or health care—and, as a result, increasing public support for significant and imaginative government action. In addition, there are eloquent and well-organized demands for inclusion and social transformation by previously subordinated groups, and recognition by many of the relatively privileged that the costs of large numbers of underemployed, alienated, unproductive, disabled, and homeless people are very high, in terms of governmental budgets, reduced competitiveness in the international economy, and the spiritual demoralization of American life. From these sources have come new movements for change, and institutional innovation in education, job training, housing, health care, child care, and other social sectors. New technology, the need for more cooperation and human capital in production, and new awareness of systems and methods of decision making may also have considerable impact. Finally, the moderation of conflict with the Soviet Union, and the anticipated "peace dividend" worth billions of dollars, provide a historic opportunity either to reinforce the primacy of the market and the position of the powerful through tax cuts and other measures, or to build new social structures that might further equality and community.[35]

In theory, the emerging efforts among corporations, foundations, universities, state and local governments, public school systems, and state (and some federal) courts to pursue the social duty model and more egalitarian and cooperative goals could coexist with a Congress, an executive, and a Supreme Court still committed to managerial formalism and other expressions of inegalitarian economic and political competition. Such an arrangement seems unlikely to endure, however, for at least two reasons. First, there is a significant "free rider" problem; the institutions engaged in cooperative efforts risk being exploited by other institutions that refuse to contribute, and indeed actively undermine, the cooperative enterprise. Second, as growing numbers of Americans and American institutions attempt to grapple with poverty and other social problems, the idea that these problems are unrelated to government and social choices will become increasingly untenable. What will be done with this realization remains a very open question, but the likely demise of this core principle of managerial formalism offers some hope for the future.

NOTES

1. *See* Steven V. Roberts, "Reagan on Homelessness: Many Choose to Live in the Streets," *The New York Times*, December 23, 1988; Charles Murray, *Losing Ground: American Social Policy, 1950–1980* (New York: Basic Books, 1984); Lawrence Mead, *Beyond Entitlement: The Social Obligations of Citizenship* (New York: Free Press, 1986). For responses to the conservative positions, *see, e.g.*, David T. Ellwood, *Poor Support* (New York: Basic Books, 1988); Fred Block, Richard A. Cloward, Barbara Ehrenreich, and Frances Fox Piven, *The Mean Season: The Attack on the Welfare State* (New York: Pantheon Books, 1987); Michael B. Katz, *The Undeserving Poor: From the War on Poverty to the War on Welfare* (New York: Pantheon Books, 1990).
2. *See* Robert M. Hayes, "Homelessness and the Legal Profession," 35 *Loyola Law Review* 1 (1989); Symposium on the Homeless, 23 *Clearinghouse Review* 104 (1989). *See also* Frances Fox Piven and Richard A. Cloward, *The New Class War: Reagan's Attack on the Welfare State and Its Consequences* (New York: Pantheon Books, 1982); Michael B. Katz, *In the Shadow of the Poorhouse: A Social History of Welfare in America* (New York: Basic Books, 1986); Thomas Edsall, *The New Politics of Inequality* (New York: Basic Books, 1984).
3. *See* Alan Freeman, "Antidiscrimination Law: The View from 1989," in this volume; *see also* Robert Gordon, "New Developments in Legal Theory," and David Kairys, "Introduction."
4. The quotation marks around "private market" refer to the complex character of the adjective "private." On the one hand, economic markets typical of Western capitalist societies do delegate considerable decision-making authority to nongovernmental actors, and reward or penalize individual initiatives. On the other hand, every feature of the "private market," from its formal rules and remedies to the background premises and consciousness of its participants, is directly or indirectly fashioned by the collective experience of the society and often by the government. In addition, actual investment patterns and incentives, including interest rates, monetary supply, tax policy and government spending (*e.g.*, for military production and scientific research) are set or heavily influenced by the government.
5. *See* Social Security Act of 1935, 49 Stat. 620, codified at 42 U.S.C. §§ 301 *et seq.*; Katz, *supra* note 2, at 206–47; Frances Fox Piven and Richard A. Cloward, *Regulating the Poor* (New York: Vintage, 1972), pp. 80–180;

Margaret Weir, Ann Shola Orloff, and Theda Skocpol, eds., *The Politics of Social Policy in the United States* (Princeton, N.J.: Princeton University Press, 1988). *Cf.* William Simon, "The Invention and Reinvention of Welfare Rights," 44 *Maryland Law Review* 1, 14–23 (1985).

6. *See* Katz, *supra* note 2, at 3–84; *The New Class War, supra* note 2, at 44–65; *Regulating the Poor, supra* note 5, at 3–42; *The Mean Season, supra* note 1, at 3–108. *See also* R. H. Tawney, *Religion and the Rise of Capitalism* (Harmondsworth: Pelican Books, 1940; 1st ed. 1926), pp. 228–42 and *passim.*

7. *See* Charles Reich, "The New Property," 73 *Yale Law Journal* 733 (1964); Edward Sparer, "The Role of the Welfare Client's Lawyer," 12 *U.C.L.A. Law Review* 361 (1965); "The Right to Welfare," in *The Rights of Americans,* ed. Norman Dorsen (New York: Pantheon Books, 1971).

8. Charles Reich, "Individual Rights and Social Welfare," 74 *Yale Law Journal,* 1245, 1255 (1965). *See also* Frank Michelman, "On Protecting the Poor Through the Fourteenth Amendment," 83 *Harvard Law Review* 7 (1969); "Welfare Rights in a Constitutional Democracy," *Washington University Law Quarterly* 659 (1979); Kenneth Karst, *Belonging to America: Equal Citizenship and the Constitution* (New Haven: Yale University Press, 1989); Sylvia Law, "Women, Work, Welfare, and the Preservation of Patriarchy," 131 *University of Pennsylvania Law Review* 1249 (1983); Law, "Economic Justice," in *Our Endangered Rights,* ed. Norman Dorsen (New York: Pantheon Books, 1984); Peter Edelman, "The Next Century of Our Constitution: Rethinking Our Duty to the Poor," 39 *Hastings Law Journal* 1 (1987); William Taylor, "*Brown,* Equal Protection, and the Isolation of the Poor," 95 *Yale Law Journal* 1700 (1986).

9. *See* King v. Smith, 392 U.S. 309 (1968); Shapiro v. Thompson, 394 U.S. 618 (1969); Goldberg v. Kelly, 397 U.S. 254 (1970).

10. 397 U.S. 471, 487 (1970).

11. *See* New York State Department of Social Services v. Dublino, 413 U.S. 405 (1973) (interpreting the Social Security Act to permit states to set more restrictive work requirements than those contained in the federal law); Wyman v. James, 400 U.S. 309 (1971) (welfare benefits may be terminated if a recipient refuses to allow a caseworker to enter her home without a warrant or probable cause).

12. *See* Margaret Weir, Ann Shola Orloff, and Theda Skocpol, "The Future of Social Policy in the United States: Political Constraints and Possibilities," in *The Politics of Social Policy in the United States, supra* note 5; *The New Class War, supra* note 2; *The Mean Season, supra* note 1; Katz, *supra* note 1.

13. *See, e.g.,* Schweiker v. Chilicky, 108 S.Ct. 2460 (1988). *Cf.* Mark Tushnet, *Red, White, and Blue: A Critical Analysis of Constitutional Law* (Cambridge, Mass.: Harvard University Press, 1988), pp. 214–46.

14. DeShaney v. Winnebago County Department of Social Services, 109 S.Ct. 998, 1003–1004 (1989).

15. Harris v. McCrae, 448 U.S. 297, 316–317 (1980).
16. Lyng v. International Union, United Auto., Aerospace and Agr. Implement Workers of America, UAW, 108 S.Ct. 1184 (1988); Kadrmas v. Dickinson Public Schools, 108 S.Ct. 2481 (1988); Schweiker v. Chilicky, 108 S.Ct. 2460 (1988).
17. See Cass Sunstein, "Lochner's Legacy," 87 *Columbia Law Review* 873, 882 (1987); Laurence Tribe, "The Curvature of Constitutional Space: What Lawyers Can Learn from Modern Physics," 103 *Harvard Law Review* 1, 24–25 (1989); Kathleen Sullivan, "Unconstitutional Conditions," 102 *Harvard Law Review* 1415, 1500–1501 (1989). See also J.M. Balkin, "The Rhetoric of Responsibility," 76 *Virginia Law Review* 197 (1990).
18. Tribe, *supra* note 17, at 10.
19. See Bruce Ackerman, "Constitutional Politics/Constitutional Law," 99 *Yale Law Journal* 453 (1989); Frank Michelman, "Foreword: Traces of Self-Government," 100 *Harvard Law Review* 1 (1986); Cass Sunstein, "Constitutionalism After the New Deal," 101 *Harvard Law Review* 421 (1987); "Interpreting Statutes in the Regulatory State," 103 *Harvard Law Review* 405, 481 (1989). For a critique of Chief Justice Rehnquist's reading of history in *DeShaney*, see Aviam Soifer, "Moral Ambition, Formalism, and the 'Free World' of *DeShaney*," 57 *George Washington Law Review* 1513 (1989).
20. William Simon, "Legality, Bureaucracy, and Class in the Welfare System," 92 *Yale Law Journal* 1198, 1199 (1983), quoting F. Kafka, *The Trial* 269 (New York: Vintage, 1969).
21. Tolchin, "Many Rejected for Welfare Aid Over Paperwork," *The New York Times*, October 29, 1988 (quoting Sarah Shuptrine); Joel F. Handler, "Community Care for the Frail Elderly: A Theory of Empowerment," 50 *Ohio State Law Journal* 541 (1989).
22. An analysis of Simon's full critique of welfare entitlements, and others' responses to it, is beyond the scope of this essay. Shortly before his death, Sparer responded to an early version of Simon's critique. See Edward V. Sparer, "Fundamental Human Rights, Legal Entitlements, and the Social Struggle: A Friendly Critique of the Critical Legal Studies Movement," 36 *Stanford Law Review* 508, 563–67 (1984). See also Barbara Sard, "The Role of the Courts in Welfare Reform," 22 *Clearinghouse Review* 367, 368, n.6, 380, n.61 (1988).
23. See Kenneth Karst, *supra* note 8; *see also* Lisbeth B. Schorr, *Within Our Reach: Breaking the Cycle of Disadvantage* (New York: Doubleday, 1989) (describing innovative, comprehensive programs that cut across traditional bureaucratic lines); Joel F. Handler, "Dependent People, the State, and the Modern/Postmodern Search for the Dialogic Community," 35 *University of California/Los Angeles Law Review* 999 (1988); Simon, *supra* note 5.
24. See National Conference of Catholic Bishops, *Economic Justice for All* (Washington: United States Catholic Conference, 1986), pp 15, 36–37; John Arthur and William H. Shaw, eds., *Justice and Economic Distribution*

(Englewood Cliffs, N.J.: Prentice-Hall, 1978); Martha Minow, "When Difference Has Its Home: Group Homes for the Mentally Retarded, Equal Protection and Legal Treatment of Difference," 22 *Harvard Civil Rights–Civil Liberties Law Review* 111 (1987); Elizabeth Schneider, "The Dialectic of Rights and Politics: Perspectives from the Women's Movement," 61 *New York University Law Review* 589 (1986); Sylvia Law, "Equality: The Power and Limits of the Law," 95 *Yale Law Journal* 1769 (1986); Handler, "Dialogic Community," *supra* note 23; Charles R. Lawrence, "The Id, the Ego, and Equal Protection: Reckoning with Unconscious Racism," 39 *Stanford Law Review* 317 (1987); Patricia Williams, "Spirit-murdering the Messenger: The Discourse of Fingerpointing as the Law's Response to Racism," 42 *University of Miami Law Review* 127 (1987); Burt Neuborne, "Foreword: State Constitutions and the Evolution of Positive Rights," 20 *Rutgers Law Journal* 877 (1989); Robert F. Williams, "In the Supreme Court's Shadow: Legitimacy of State Rejection of Supreme Court Reasoning and Result," 35 *South Carolina Law Review* 353 (1984).

25. *See* West Coast Hotel Co. v. Parrish, 300 U.S. 379 (1937), reversing Adkins v. Children's Hospital, 261 U.S. 525 (1923). Sunstein, *supra* note 17, at 880–81. *West Coast Hotel* upheld a minimum wage law applicable only to women, but unequal bargaining power rather than gender classification appeared to be the basis of the decision. A contemporary social duty model would reflect developments since 1937 in equal protection doctrine regarding sex-based discrimination, and hence would not uphold a gender classification.

26. Southern Burlington County NAACP v. Township of Mt. Laurel, 92 N.J. 158, 208–9, 456 A.2d 390, 415 (1983) (*Mt. Laurel II*); *see also* 67 N.J. 151, 336 A.2d 713 (1975) (*Mt. Laurel I*).

27. *Id.*, 92 N.J. at 212–13, 456 A.2d at 417. *See also* Hills Development Co. v. Township of Bernards, 103 N.J. 1, 510 A.2d 621 (1986) (upholding New Jersey's Fair Housing Act) (generally referred to as "Mt. Laurel III").

28. *Compare* Harold McDougall, "The Judicial Struggle Against Exclusionary Zoning: The New Jersey Paradigm," 14 *Harvard Civil Rights–Civil Liberties Law Review* 625 (1979), and "*Mount Laurel II* and the Revitalizing City," 15 *Rutgers Law Journal* 667 (1984) with G. Alan Tarr and Russell Harrison, "Legitimacy and Capacity in State Supreme Court Policymaking: The New Jersey Court and Exclusionary Zoning," 15 *Rutgers Law Journal* 513 (1984). *See also* Jeffrey Surenian, Mount Laurel II *and the Fair Housing Act* (Newark: New Jersey Institute for Continuing Legal Education, 1987); Martha Lamar, Alan Mallach, and John Payne, "*Mount Laurel* at Work: Affordable Housing in New Jersey, 1983–1988," 41 *Rutgers Law Review* 1197 (1989); Robert Hanley, "Open Housing Is Mired in Lawsuits Again," *The New York Times*, January 2, 1990.

29. *See, e.g.*, Robinson v. Cahill, 62 N.J. 473, 303 A.2d 273 (1973); Serrano v. Priest, 18 Cal.3d 728, 557 P.2d 929, 135 Cal. Rptr. 345, *cert. denied*, 432 U.S. 907 (1977); Horton v. Meskill, 195 Conn. 24, 486 A.2d 1099

(1985); William E. Thro, "To Render Them Safe: The Analysis of State Constitutional Provisions in Public School Finance Reform Litigation," 75 *Virginia Law Review* 1639 (1989).

30. Massachusetts Coalition for the Homeless v. Secretary of Human Services, 400 Mass. 806, 511 N.E.2d 603 (1987), discussed in Sard, *supra* note 22, at 382–87; Matter of Rulemaking, N.J.A.C. 10:82-1.2, 117 N.J. 311, 566 A.2d 1154, 1160 (1989). *See also* Nancy Morawetz, "Welfare Litigation to Prevent Homelessness," 16 *New York University Review of Law and Social Change* 565 (1987–1988).

31. *See, e.g.*, Owen Fiss, "Groups and the Equal Protection Clause," 5 *Philosophy and Public Affairs* 107 (1976); Mark Tushnet, "Law and Group Rights: Federalism as a Model," in *Law and the Community: The End of Individualism?* ed. Allan Hutchinson and Leslie Green (Toronto: Carswell, 1989), p. 277.

32. *See generally*, Ellwood, *supra* note 1; Marian Wright Edelman, *Families in Peril* (Cambridge, Mass.: Harvard University Press, 1987); William Julius Wilson, *The Truly Disadvantaged* (Chicago: University of Chicago Press, 1987); Lisbeth B. Schorr, *supra* note 23. For conservative disagreement with these policy prescriptions, *see* Murray, *supra* note 1, and Mead, *supra* note 1.

33. *See* Simon, *supra* note 5, at 16; Handler, "Dialogic Community," *supra* note 23, at 1096.

34. *See* In re Agent Orange Product Liability Litigation, 597 F. Supp. 740 (E.D.N.Y. 1984); Fox v. Bowen, 656 F. Supp. 1236 (D. Conn. 1987).

35. *See, e.g.*, Lisbeth B. Schorr, *supra* note 23; Edelman, *supra* note 32; Robert B. Reich, *The Next American Frontier* (New York: Times Books, 1983); William Greider, *The Trouble With Money* (Whittle Direct Books, 1989); David Rosenbaum, "From Guns to Butter: With Cutbacks Likely in Military Spending, Debate Will Center on Where Cash Will Go," *The New York Times*, December 14, 1989.

5 W. HAYWOOD BURNS

LAW AND RACE IN EARLY AMERICA

IN 1855 white men sitting in the Kansas legislature, duly elected by other white men, passed a law that sentenced white men convicted of rape of a white woman to up to five years in prison, while the penalty for a black man convicted of the same offense was castration, the costs of the procedure to be rendered by the desexed.

The penalty of sexual mutilation appears at many points in the annals of American jurisprudence, Kansas in 1855 being but one of the more recent examples. What is special about the sentence of castration is that where it was in force, it was almost universally reserved for blacks (and, in some cases, Indians).

Apart from what this example reveals about the sexual psychopathology of white America, or at least of those in power, it graphically demonstrates the working of law in a racist society. The nexus between law and racism cannot be much more direct than this. Indeed, the histories of the African, Asian, Latin, and Native American people in the United States are replete with examples of the law and the legal process as the means by which the generalized racism in the society was made particular and converted into standards and policies of social control. Going beyond the Kansas example cited, a systematic analysis of racism and law provides keen insight into the operations of both.[1]

In early-seventeenth-century colonial America, blacks and whites often existed and toiled side by side in various degrees of bondage. Though there were gradations of unfreedom, there was, at first, no clearly defined status of "slave." As the century drew to a close, however, the social reality and objective conditions changed sufficiently for the members of the colonial legislatures to recognize officially that the situations of the black person in bondage and the white person in bondage were diverging, with that of the black person becoming more debased. "Free choice" was hardly an issue for either whites or blacks who came in bondage to the New World. Still, there was a considerable difference in being, for example, an Irish indentured servant and a kidnapped African arriving in chains after the unspeakable horrors of the Middle Passage. There are vast differences between a societally enforced discrimination and an entire legal order founded explicitly on racism—a world of difference between "Irish need not apply," as reprehensible as that was, and statutory denial of legal personality, of humanity.

Black people were severed from much of their culture, language, kindred, religion, and all communication with the Old World of their fathers and mothers, from which they had been torn. The ugly sentiments of white racial superiority were beginning to sprout and rear their heads above the native soil. These facts, coupled with a growing understanding of the tremendous economic advantage to be gained from the long-term exploitation of black labor, brought about a social consensus (among whites) that sought to permanently relegate black people to the lowest stratum in a vertical relationship of white over black. This consensus found expressions and implementation in the form of laws passed in colonial legislatures that made slavery for black people both a lifetime condition and a hereditary condition. Thus, through the operation of law, in this case legislated societal racism, the institution of American chattel slavery was created and perpetuated.

With the advent of the detailed and oppressive colonial slave codes of the early eighteenth century, law played a consistent role throughout the period, up to and including the American Revolution. The Revolution, of course, produced a golden opportunity to do business other than as usual. It was, after all, a revolution fought in the name of liberty and egalitarian principles. It was an opportunity that was nonetheless missed or, perhaps better said, rejected. The revolution of Jefferson, Washington, and Madison was never intended to embrace the ebony throngs of captured and enslaved people in their white midsts. It was too much for the eighteenth-century white American mind to view these captured and enslaved people fully as people. It was too much for the Founding Fathers and the economic interests they represented to tamper with that amount of property—even for those who on moral, philosophical, or religious grounds opposed slavery.

Thus, the birth of the new order in the establishment of the Republic brought with it no new day for the African on American soil. In erecting the new state, black people were still consigned to be the hewers of wood, the drawers of water, for there enshrined in the fundamental law of the land, the new Constitution itself was the guaranteed continuation of the slave trade; the guaranteed return of fugitive slaves; and the counting of black persons as three-fifths human beings for purposes of taxation and political representation.

The pre-Revolutionary slave codes were more than ample models for the post-Revolutionary slave codes, which continued their detailed, oppressive harshness into the nineteenth century and into the new and expanding nation. The nineteenth-century slave codes provide an excellent example of law and state operating to impose a given social order. The slave codes legislated and regulated in minute detail every aspect of the life of a slave and of black/white interaction; assured white-over-black dominance; and made black people into virtual nonpersons, refusing to recognize any right of family, free movement, choice, and legal capacity to bring a suit or to testify where the interest of a white person was involved. This legal structure defining a black person's place in society was reinforced by statutes requiring cruel and brutal sanctions for any black man or woman who forgot his or her place and stepped, or even tried to step, out of it.

Even in the so-called Free States there was ample borrowing from the statutory schemes of the slavocracy to enforce a societal (white) view of the black person's rightful station in life. Thus, northern states systematically resorted to legislative devices to impose their collective view on the lives of "free" blacks, restricting them in employment, education, the franchise, legal personality, and public accommodation.

The legal issue of the status of black people in pre–Civil War America came to a head in 1857 in the case of *Dred Scott* v. *Sanford*.[2] It proved to be one of the most important judicial decisions in the history of the black experience with the law. In that case, Dred Scott, a slave who had been taken to a free territory by his master, attempted to sue for his freedom based upon the theory that residence in a free state had made him free.

As Mr. Chief Justice Taney put it, "The question is simply this: Can a negro, whose ancestors were imported into this country, and sold as slaves, become a member of the political community formed and brought into existence by the Constitution of the United States, and as such become entitled to all the rights, and privileges, and immunities, guaranteed by that instrument to the citizen . . . ?"[3]

The Court's answer was, simply, "No." In ruling that Dred Scott, and by extension, any other black person, could not be a citizen under the Constitution, Taney went back to the founding of the Republic, examining what he declared was the public view of the black race at that point and tracing its history through time: ". . . [T]he public history of every European nation displays it in a manner too plain to be mistaken. [T]hey (the black race) had for more than a century before been regarded as beings of an inferior order, and altogether unfit to associate with the white race, either in social or political relations; and so far inferior, that they had no rights which the white man was bound to respect . . ."[4] This ringing Taney dictum dashed the hopes of black people and abolitionists who had looked to the courts to resolve one of the most troubling questions of racial justice of the day. The majority's decision and its view of black people as inferior brought down a rain of criticism on the Court from the North and caused cries of joy to rise from below the Mason-Dixon line. It also set the stage for the oncoming War between the States.

Logically, the Civil War should have made a decided difference in this racial legal dynamic. It did not, for though slavery itself was destroyed by this cataclysmic confrontation, the racism and economic exploitation undergirding slavery remained very much intact. Thus, even after the Emancipation Proclamation, after the war and the Thirteenth Amendment, the South set out to win the peace, despite having lost the war. The states of the South, where well over 90 percent of the nation's black people then lived, countered the emancipation by putting in place a series of laws known as the Black Codes, designed to approximate as closely as possible, in view of the legal abolition of slavery, a white-over-black, master/servant society. This legal order governed movement, marriage, work relations, and most major aspects of the freedperson's life.

In fact, there are many ways in which the Black Codes very much resembled the pre–Civil War slave codes. Laws were instituted against vagabonds to curtail black men from moving away from the land. Sharecropping and the convict-lease laws were designed to keep the former slaves on the land. Unlike other statutes, the vagabond- and convict-leasing statutes were not racial in their terms; however, their purpose and effect were entirely clear. The southern economy was predicated upon a large, exploited black labor force; and except for the brief and bright interregnum of Reconstruction, the law and the state throughout the last years of the nineteenth century and the early years of the twentieth operated to preserve the old order and to wring maximum advantage from white hegemony over an oppressed and economically ravaged black populace.

It was the law as well that played a crucial role in "the strange career of Jim Crow." In an uneven and nonsystematic way, culture and mores had provided for a separation of the races in many aspects of American life. For most of the nation's history, that was not even much of an issue because the presence of slavery took care of any need for social definition. However, during the late 1800s, states began to systematically codify separation of the races, *requiring* segregation literally from the hospital where one was born to the cemetery where one was laid to rest. Segregation no longer was open to local option, custom, and usage but was the state's legal order of the day. These developments occurred at the same point in time that an increasingly conservative Supreme Court was narrowing its interpretation of the Thirteenth, Fourteenth, and Fifteenth Amendments—the Civil War amendments. These trends culminated in the *Plessy* v. *Ferguson*[5] decision of the Supreme Court in 1896, in which "separate but equal" was approved as the law of the land, and the seal of approval of the nation's highest court was placed upon our own American brand of apartheid.

The use of the legal system to create and protect a racially segregated society was coincident with government's manipulation of the law to disenfranchise black citizens. Beginning with the Mississippi constitutional convention of 1890, revising the state's constitution through a series of legal stratagems and artifices—and greatly aided by the extralegal depredations of lynch law—black people were stripped of the ballot and any real semblance of black political power. The poll tax, the literacy test, and the Grandfather Clause were legal devices employed in the service of this racist cause to desired effect.

As a result of state uses of the law in this fashion, black Americans entered the twentieth century segregated, sundered from full and free participation in American life, and politically powerless to do much about it. This situation largely obtained through this century, with minor indications of change and advancement from time to time but with no real major breakthrough in the wall of apartheid and powerlessness until the Supreme Court decision in *Brown* v. *Board of Education.*[6]

Brown and the struggle that followed in its wake—much of which involved use of the law to support and effect positive social change—obviously represent a highly significant advance in black Americans' quest for liberation. It would be an analytical mistake of considerable proportion, however, to view *Brown* as the end of explicitly racist legislation and court decisions, and the advent of civil rights laws as indicative of the end of the relationship among racism and the law and the state. For all our gains, America remains a country deeply infected by racism. Though this racism may not be as explicit or as obvious as it was in earlier times, it is present and no less real. Indeed, the last decade has seen a resurgence of racism in its most virulent as well as sophisticated forms.

NOTES

1. For good general treatment and historical overview, see Derrick Bell, Jr., *Race, Racism, and American Law* (Boston: Little, Brown, 1980); Derrick Bell, Jr., *And We Are Not Saved* (New York: Basic Books, 1987); Albert P. Blaustein, and Robert I. Zangrando, eds., *Civil Rights and the American Negro* (New York: Trident Press, 1968); John Hope Franklin and Alfred A. Moss, Jr., *From Freedom to Slavery* (New York: Alfred A. Knopf, 1988); Paul

Finkelman, *Slavery in the Courtroom* (Washington, D.C.: Library of Congress, 1985); Thomas F. Race Gossett, *The History of an Idea in America* (Dallas: Southern Methodist University Press, 1963); Oscar Handlin, *Race and Nationality in American Life* (Boston: Little, Brown, 1957); A. L. Higginbotham, *In the Matter of Color*, vol. 1 (New York: Oxford University Press, 1980); Winthrop Jordan, *White Over Black* (Chapel Hill: University of North Carolina Press, 1968). Although this short essay focuses mainly on the history of black people and American law, a similar analysis would apply to the historical experiences of other persons of color in the United States.
2. 19 How.(60 U.S.)393 (1857)
3. *Id.* at 403.
4. *Id.* at 407.
5. 163 U. S. 537 (1896).
6. 347 U. S. 483 (1954).

6 ALAN FREEMAN

ANTIDISCRIMINATION LAW: THE VIEW FROM 1989

> One wonders whether the majority still believes that race dis-
> crimination—or, more accurately, race discrimination against
> nonwhites—is a problem in our society, or even remembers
> that it ever was.
>
>
>
> HARRY BLACKMUN
> dissenting in *Wards Cove
> Packing Co.* v. *Atonio*
> (June 5, 1989)
>
>

IN early 1988, shortly after the 125th anniversary of Abraham Lincoln's
Emancipation Proclamation, Anthony Kennedy joined the U.S. Supreme
Court, replacing Lewis Powell, the conservative yet pragmatic appointee of
Richard Nixon. Within a year, this reconstituted Court issued the first of a
number of decisions that would, collectively, amount to the greatest setback
to civil rights progress in a single term of Court since the nineteenth century.
In fact, the impact of the 1989 decisions was so dramatic as to parallel the
post–Civil War Reconstruction Era. Then, it took thirty-three years to go
from the promise of the Emancipation Proclamation in 1863 to the bleak
reality of "separate but equal" endorsed by *Plessy* v. *Ferguson*[1] in 1896. This
time, it has taken thirty-five years to go from the glowing promise of *Brown*
v. *Board of Education*[2] in 1954 to the "Civil Rights Cases" of 1989[3] that
have seemingly enshrined the principle of "unequal but irrelevant."

Indisputably, these decisions were occasioned by the appointment of Justice Kennedy. Yet Ronald Reagan, who appointed Kennedy, also appointed
Justices O'Connor, Scalia, and Rehnquist (as chief justice), all of whom
were selected specifically for, among other things, their opposition to affirmative action. That opposition had been clearly articulated in Reagan's electoral campaign; members of minority groups understood his message and

few supported Reagan. Thus, the demise of the civil rights era signaled by the defeats of 1989 may be just an illustration of the responsiveness of the American political system. The "people" got just what they wanted from their popular president.

To invoke the people by name is to evoke the image of authentic, responsive, participatory democracy. Reality bears no relationship to that image in a country where 10 percent of households own 72 percent of the wealth, where effective political campaigns serve up clever and manipulative stereotypic images that pander to the most irrational fears of voters, where half or fewer eligible voters turn out for national elections, and where there is no national political party that speaks to the aspirations of working people, the poor, the powerless, and the oppressed. Nevertheless, many of those people who voted for Ronald Reagan do believe that racial discrimination is a thing of the past that was abolished by numerous laws enacted in the 1960s, and that racism, if it exists, is not their fault in any event. Many believe as well that blacks and other minorities luxuriate in preferential treatment at the expense of victimized and innocent whites, and that if blacks and others have not benefited from antidiscrimination laws and are still poor and powerless, it's their own fault for not mustering the skill or will to make it. It is tempting to dismiss the proponents of such views as mindless uncaring racists who refuse to acknowledge the objective plight of minorities in America at the close of the 1980s. Yet that temptation must be resisted: the very same views, however despicable, are now enshrined in Supreme Court opinions, and thereby possess a frightening degree of cultural legitimacy.

This essay will suggest that today's views are not the product of recent historical whimsy, but are rather firmly rooted in the contradictory character of antidiscrimination law, the agenda of which was constrained from the outset by abstract principles of formal equality that would surely reassert themselves in time. It is sadly ironic that law, which offered for a time a promise of liberation from America's historic reality of caste-based oppression, and did secure some rights of equality, has also served to legitimize the persistence of rampant, racially identifiable inequality. To understand how that happened, one must look to opinions of the U.S. Supreme Court, a principal source for discovering the meaning of "civil rights."

That Court looms large in our culture. We look to its pronouncements not just for the answers to particular questions of law, but for moral guidance on our most troubling social and political issues. The Court is basically a storytelling institution. Its cases serve as instructive moral parables, presented to most people as stark, melodramatic media distillations. The Court's stories must engage dialectically with other dominant political institutions, with preexisting cultural assumptions, and other sources of cultural authority (e.g., movies). In the long run, the Court offers a vision of America that normalizes the existing patterns of inequality and hierarchy.

This essay will focus on antidiscrimination law as it has evolved in Supreme Court opinions since 1954. After an opening section that depicts the contradictory character of antidiscrimination law, I will trace in some detail the evolution of the legal doctrine in this area to illustrate the complex and dynamic interaction of image and reality. Finally, I will seek to situate the doctrinal history in a larger social and political context as a way of looking to the future.

VICTIM AND PERPETRATOR

Consider the following, all based on actual cases, as stories about the significance of race in American life:[4]

> A multiple-choice test purporting to measure "verbal ability" is used to screen applicants for the D.C. police department. Black applicants fail the test four times more frequently than whites; failure precludes admission to the training academy although the test is not predictive of successful performance on the job.

> At the behest of an *all-white* residential neighborhood in Memphis, Tennessee, bordered on the north by a black neighborhood, city officials close the white neighborhood's only thru north-south street, erecting a barrier at the northern border.

> Mobile, Alabama, with a black population of 30%, refuses to abandon the practice of selecting its three city commissioners on an at-large basis; no black has ever been elected to even one of the positions.

> Richmond, Virginia, one-time capital of the Confederacy, mandates that 30% of its construction contracts go to minority contractors, a decision based on the observation that despite its 50% black population, less than 1% of such contracts had gone to minority contractors in recent years. Aggrieved whites claim the new rule discriminates against them on account of their race.

From the perspective of one who is acquainted with American history and social reality, especially one who is, for example, black, and therefore personally familiar with the experiential reality of racism, these are all easy cases: Given the ugly history of standardized testing in the United States, and the reality that such tests do not even predict job performance, how can it be fair to choose potential police officers with a device that measures little else than their racial and class background? The reality of the street closing is as stark as the whiteness of the neighborhood engineering it, whose success simply confirms the power of whites to use local government to hassle blacks. To say that the Mobile scheme is unassailable is to say that race plays little or no role in voting there, that it is mere coincidence that no black has ever been elected; in other words, to uphold the Mobile procedure requires no less than a denial of reality. As for Richmond, one can only applaud its willingness to compensate for a long and ugly past by redistributing contract access to those who have been denied it for so long.

From the perspective of what has become the dominant voice in antidiscrimination law as articulated by the Supreme Court, the cases are also easy ones: If the test claims to measure verbal ability, then it probably does and that's a good thing; the mere fact of the racially disproportionate failure rate means nothing without evidence that someone employs it *purposely* to exclude blacks. The street closing is just a neutral traffic control decision, unless you can prove that the white people did it to keep *black people* out, instead of just doing it to keep *people* out, most whom *happened to be black*. As for Mobile, it does not matter whether blacks are elected or not, since no race is entitled to representation based on its population percentage; what matters is *why* they chose the at-large system. In this case, since Mobile adopted the system in 1911, the motive could not have been exclusion of blacks from office, since then they did not let blacks vote at all. As for Richmond, its municipal officials must realize that when the Constitution says no to racial discrimination, it does so in color-blind terms, and discrimination against whites is just as illegitimate as the more traditional discrimination against blacks. You can't ask whites as a class to bear responsibility for statistical disparities, unless you can *prove* the whites were purposely excluding blacks from contracts. Absent that evidence, it might be that blacks just didn't want the business, which is their own fault.

The first view, the one rooted in social reality, may be characterized as the "victim" perspective. Central to the victim perspective is an insistence on concrete historical experience rather than timeless abstract norm. For black Americans, that experience has been one of harsh oppression, exclusion, compulsory reduced status, and of being perceived not as a person but as a derogatory cultural stereotype. Years of oppression have left their mark in the form of identifiable consequences of racism: residential segregation, inadequate education, overrepresentation in lowest-status jobs, disproportionately low political power, and a disproportionate share of the least and worst of everything valued most in our materialistic society. From the victim perspective, when antidiscrimination law announces that racial discrimination has become illegal, that law's promise will be tested by the only relevant measure of success—*results*.

The victim perspective focuses on the persistence of conditions traditionally associated with racist practice. The four examples are once again illustrative: racism as traditionally practiced led to discriminatory exclusion from employment, from "white" neighborhoods, from politics, and from government contracts. If those same conditions exist in virtually identical form after antidiscrimination laws have prohibited racial discrimination, the law has not yet done its job. Those conditions are presumptive violations.

The other view, which is the dominant one in American legal culture, may be termed the "perpetrator" perspective. Its concern is with rooting out the behaviors of individual bad actors who have engaged in "prejudicial" discriminatory practices. From the perpetrator perspective, the goal of antidiscrimination law is to apply timeless and abstract norms, unsullied by history or social reality. Its job is to isolate and punish racial discrimination viewed as an instance of individual badness in an otherwise nondiscriminatory social realm. Thus, we cannot find violations of antidiscrimination law in objective social conditions, but only in the actions of identifiable perpetrators who have *purposely* and *intentionally caused* harm to *identifiable victims* who will be offered a *compensatory remedy*.

Central to the perpetrator perspective is the principle of individual (or sometimes institutional) *fault*. All we need do is identify and catch the villains; having done so, we can, with confidence, place responsibility where it belongs. A corollary of this fault principle is that those who, under applicable legal doctrines, are not labeled perpetrators have every reason to believe in their own innocence and noninvolvement in the problem. One who is not a perpetrator can say "It's not my fault; I'm just an innocent societal bystander." Why should the mere bystander be called to account or implicated at all in the business of eradicating the past? This emphasis on fault provides the psychic structure of the "reverse discrimination" issue.

The perpetrator perspective also denies historical reality—in particular, the fact that we would never have fashioned antidiscrimination law had it not been for the specific historical oppression of particular races. Denial leads all too quickly to the startling claim of "ethnic fungibility"—the notion that each of us bears an "ethnicity" with an equivalent legal significance, and with identical claim to protection against "discrimination," despite the grossly disproportionate experience that generated the legal intervention in the first place. Thus, discrimination on the basis of "whiteness" gains the same disreputable status as discrimination against blacks, and efforts to improve conditions for historic victims of discrimination are struck down on grounds of "principle." The key principle is that of "color blindness," which would be the appropriate rule in a future society that had totally eliminated racial discrimination, or, more likely, had never had such a problem at all.

Looking at the four examples from the perpetrator perspective, one sees simply neutral facts. If no bad actors can be identified, then normal principles of individual responsibility apply. Those who are complaining are themselves responsible for their performance on the tests, for their inability to move to other neighborhoods or have a voice in local government, for their political ineffectiveness or failure to obtain contracts: The familiar syndrome is "blaming the victim."[5]

The victim/perpetrator dichotomy may be recast starkly as the difference between equality of results and equality of opportunity, between *de facto* and *de jure* segregation, between substantive and formal equality. Given those choices, American antidiscrimination law has remained firmly within the perpetrator mode, outlawing "intentional" discrimination, guaranteeing equality "before the law," and offering no more than equal opportunity to compete in the game of life. Yet the doctrinal history of antidiscrimination law reveals that the perpetrator form was, for a time, contradicted by results more consistent with the victim perspective. The Supreme Court produced such results not by denying any of the basic tenets of the perpetrator perspective, but by taking advantage of the plasticity of legal characterization. Among the most manipulative legal categories are remedy, causation, and intent. Manipulating all three, the Court for a time seriously toyed with the victim perspective, but never deviated from the perpetrator form. The story begins with the celebrated *Brown* case in 1954.

THE DOCTRINAL SEQUENCE

To understand the puzzling and contradictory character of antidiscrimination law, one may usefully divide the period from 1954 to the present into four "eras" of Supreme Court decision making. The successive eras are neither neat, nor rigid, nor the product of inexorable logic. Yet for each it is possible to describe a particular instance of legal intervention (case or statute) so at odds with received wisdom as to mark a moment of discontinuity. Moreover, within each period, typical decisions serve to characterize the style or cultural assumptions of the era. The four successive eras represent how dominant cultural forces in post–World War II America responded to the pervasive legacy of racism that had revealed itself so starkly to any observer at the beginning of the 1950s. They add up to a story of promise, intervention, retreat, and surrender. Yet the fact of that intervention, despite its contradictory rhetoric, makes it possible to look back and celebrate our success, while ignoring the objective reality of poverty and inequality that remains the pervasive legacy of racism.

THE ERA OF UNCERTAINTY (1954–1965)

Brown v. *Board of Education* clearly marked a break with the past. It made the qualitative leap from merely "equalizing" to declaring that "separate but equal" is "inherently unequal," heralding a period of great promise for improvement in status for black Americans. Nevertheless, despite the hoopla surrounding this most celebrated of all American Supreme Court decisions, the case served as well to usher in a period of great uncertainty. Contributing to such uncertainty were: the elusive rationale of the Court's *Brown* opinion; the Court's all-too-quick refusal to mandate remedies for the violations announced in *Brown*, instead relegating those issues to lower courts; and the consciousness of white liberals, at once utopian and myopic, who saw only the stark "southern" version of America's racial reality.

For the Court, the "question presented" by *Brown* was:

> Does segregation of children in public schools solely on the basis of race, even though the physical facilities and other "tangible" factors may be equal, deprive the children of the minority group of equal educational opportunities?

Its response was affirmative yet enigmatic:

> To separate them from others of similar age and qualifications solely because of their race generates a feeling of inferiority as to their status in the community that may affect their hearts and minds in a way unlikely ever to be undone. . . . "Segregation of white and colored children in public schools has a detrimental effect upon the colored children. The impact is greater when it has the sanction of the law; for the policy of separating the races is usually interpreted as denoting the inferiority of the Negro group. A sense of inferiority affects the motivation of a child to learn. Segregation with the sanction of law, therefore, has a tendency to [retard] the educational and mental development of Negro children and to deprive them of some of the benefits they would receive in a racial[ly] integrated school system." . . . We conclude that in the field of public education the doctrine of "separate but equal" has no place. Separate educational facilities are inherently unequal. . . ."

The quoted passage raises more questions than it answers. Are segregated schools inherently unequal because they make black children feel "inferior" or because kids who are made to feel inferior do not enjoy the benefits of public education? Must schools be integrated in fact to ensure that the black children will no longer feel inferior, and therefore fulfill educational potential? Even if segregation with the "sanction of law" has a "greater" impact on the minority children, does it not have a similar impact when conditions are still segregated despite the removal of such laws?

Unfortunately, these questions are not just rhetorical. They underscore the ultimate and still unresolved uncertainty unleashed by *Brown*. From the standpoint of those who successfully litigated the *Brown* cases, the goal was a pragmatic one—to obtain the best quality education for the nation's previously segregated black children in the least amount of time.[6] In that context, a declaration of per se illegality for segregation seemed much more efficient than case-by-case resource equalization. To integrate previously white schools did not necessarily mean integration for its own sake, but might be understood as just the quickest means of upgrading educational equality. Thus one can regard the *Brown* case as a victory for substantive educational equal opportunity—the idea that all American children should have a chance for educational success, unimpeded by artificial barriers such as racial exclusion. That view of *Brown* finds great support in the opinion itself, with its heavy rhetorical emphasis on the importance of public education, yet within twenty years of *Brown* it was clear that the case did not guarantee equal educational opportunity.[7]

What *Brown* did do, despite its own preoccupation with education, was to outlaw all forms of state-mandated segregation, as the Court made clear in a series of decisions unexplained except by reference to *Brown*.[8] Earnest legal scholars have sought ever since to find the "principle" governing the decisions in *Brown* and its progeny. Among those offered have been "freedom of association," "color blindness," "the antidiscrimination principle," the "group-disadvantaging principle," and the like.[9] These principles, rooted in analytic notions of morality, are offered by their authors as universals against which one can test the particularity of social practices, like "racism." A properly general principle must have a scope of coverage beyond the immediate case that generates its announcement.

An antidote to the endless quest for principle is a close and direct look at social reality. Even the Supreme Court, in a 1967 case dealing with a ban on interracial marriage, conceded that such laws were attempts to institutionalize white supremacy.[10] Thus regarded, segregation, not unlike its counterpart, apartheid, was part of a historically specific and pervasive system of caste-based oppression, serving to subordinate and oppress black Americans.[11] From that perspective, it is fundamentally misguided to keep on asking what principle was implicitly announced by the *Brown* case: what the Court did was to open a window that compelled white Americans to confront at last a particular and revolting social reality.

The Court promoted uncertainty not only with its ambiguous opinion in *Brown*, but also with its nondecision a year later in *Brown II*,[12] when it declined to order remedies for the violations in the five *Brown* cases. Instead, it relegated the remedy issue to the lower courts, who were to proceed "with all deliberate speed." *Brown II* served to usher in the period of "massive resistance" in the South, and postponed the need to confront directly the implicit perpetrator/victim contradiction. On remand, one of the lower courts noted in an all-too-prescient quip that the Constitution "does not require integration. It merely forbids discrimination."[13] The statement is of course an accurate nutshell version of the perpetrator perspective.

The dominant culture of civil rights consciousness, by which I mean that of the northern white liberals whose support for the enterprise was so crucial, further served to inform the period of uncertainty. That culture was, as I have suggested, simultaneously myopic and utopian. The myopic side was the perception of America's "race problem" as constituted by the southern paradigm—state-mandated segregation reinforced by a brutal regime of enforcement, and backed by a white culture infected by "prejudice." While similar instances of prejudice existed elsewhere in the land and might be labeled "racism," the underlying premise was that racist attitudes were an aberration in American life. Typical was Gunnar Myrdal's influential account, which saw a wide gap between American racist behaviors (bad) and the American Creed (good).[14]

The utopian side was a complement to the myopic one—a belief that the race problem would go away if the overt bad behaviors were stopped. The arduous struggles of the black civil rights movement in the South in the 1950s and 1960s, depicted on the nightly news, offered an ongoing morality play to support this consciousness. Bull Connor and Sheriff Clark, with their dogs and fire hoses and cattle prods, were pitted against decent and peaceful Americans merely seeking recognition of their constitutional rights. Ironically, these scenes made the issue of race seem easier than it would appear later on. Then northern liberals could complacently fail to notice the racism that pervaded their own lives and characterized their neighborhoods, their growing suburbs, their schools, their jobs.

Thus the era of uncertainty saw growing national acknowledgment of the egregious sort of racism that fit safely within the perpetrator model, and a gradual increase in the coverage of civil rights law, culminating in the historic enactment of the Civil Rights Act of 1964. Yet all too little attention was paid to either the other-than-southern reality of racism, or the long-delayed question of remedy.

THE ERA OF CONTRADICTION (1965–1974)

During the second era the Court could no longer avoid the perpetrator/victim issue. The perpetrator perspective is indifferent to results: yet, after years of painful struggle, including assassinations and terrorist bombings, it was surely time to deliver on the unfulfilled promise of the 1950s (e.g., *Brown*). The federal government of 1965 formed, however briefly, a unique coalition of commitment to do something about racism. No Chief Executive has ever insisted on substantive racial progress as much as Lyndon Johnson did; the Congress of 1964 and 1965 matched its Reconstruction Era counterpart in the production of civil rights statutes; and even the Supreme Court in 1965 began to wake from its post-*Brown* slumber of remedial avoidance.

In those circumstances, it is hard to imagine that the Supreme Court could have struck down discrimination in voting while leaving black voters as politically powerless as before, "desegregated" schools while leaving them substantially segregated in fact, or invalidated employment discrimination while leaving its victims in the same status as before. Yet the logic of the perpetrator perspective is consistent with "no results" in all three instances: there is no *right* to proportional political representation, there is no *right* to an integrated education, there is no *right* to a job. How could the Court adhere to the perpetrator form while nevertheless ensuring some results? Three legal concepts became crucial: remedy, causation, and intent. The perpetrator perspective insists on a neat correspondence between violation and remedy, proof of objective causation of injury by the perpetrator, and proof of "intent," that is, purposeful discrimination. Yet those three concepts are among the most manipulable in our legal culture. Examples from voting, education, and employment will illustrate how the subtle deployment of those concepts can produce the seemingly contradictory coexistence of perpetrator and victim perspective.

Federal intervention to protect voting rights took a gigantic leap forward with the Voting Rights Act of 1965. That statute was enacted in response to a record of frustration. Blacks were systematically deprived of the right to vote, on the basis of race, and courts were unable to change that reality by merely outlawing specific illegal practices. The statute made its operative provisions depend on voter participation statistics and other nonreviewable administrative findings. While these findings did not constitute evidence of behaviors in themselves violations of any specific civil rights law, they were enough to trigger the act's awesome remedial machinery. The net effect of the act was to create an affirmative right to vote, instead of just a negative right to be free of discrimination in voting.

The value of the right to vote, however, given the reality of racial voting patterns, will depend on whether it translates into political power and influence for the previously disenfranchised minority. That question leads to a remedial focus on "dilution" of minority voting rights, which, in turn, illustrates how the identification of a perpetrator perspective violation can lead to a victim perspective remedy. Suppose, for example, that a municipality has gerrymandered its districts so that the entire black population is in one district while every other district is white, and there is evidence of purposeful discrimination. Suppose further that the court issues an order to the municipality that says "stop doing that," and the response is a redistricting that simply shifts a handful of people but leaves most of the black population in the original district.

If there is no specific evidence of purposeful discrimination this time, how can we decide if the new scheme has "remedied" the violation? A very slight change would seem inadequate, if it left the black community far below its representative potential. But how much is enough? The paradox is that remedy has no coherence in this context unless some notion of racial proportionality is incorporated. Moreover, instead of litigating repetitively to approach the limit of racial proportionality, why not impose such a remedy at the outset? To do so, however, is to incorporate the victim perspective.

A second typical case illustrates how the manipulation of causation to ensure remedial results serves to create victim perspective expectations. The *Brown* case announced the unconstitutionality of legally mandated school segregation; however, by relegating the remedial issues to the lower courts, the Supreme Court did nothing about the actual problem of segregation. While the Court waited, the world changed. Changing neighborhood patterns meant more and more residential segregation. By the time the Court returned to the remedy issue, in 1971 in *Swann* v. *Charlotte-Mecklenburg Board of Education*,[15] to outlaw segregation but do nothing to ensure integration would be embarrassing, and undermining to the Court's credibility. Even Justice Felix Frankfurter had worried publicly during the oral argument in *Brown* that "nothing would be worse" than for the Court "to make an abstract declaration that segregation is bad and then have it evaded by tricks."[16]

But the Court could not go back in time. Thus, it had to order school districts to produce the result—racial balance—that would have followed from immediate and massive enforcement in 1955. By waiting fifteen years, however, the Court knew and simultaneously denied that changes in residential patterns would frustrate all possibility of successful integration through neighborhood school assignment. By insisting on busing to achieve meaningful racial balance, the Court created an expectation that segregation in fact was the evil to be remedied, however tenuous its relation to the historic segregation by law. From the victim perspective, the expectation became an entitlement to integrated schools. The Court rationalized its position by showing, through the use of self-contradictory presumptions, as in *Swann*, how the current conditions were "caused" by the original violation. The Court used similar presumptions in its first northern school desegregation case to extend the remedial obligation from one neighborhood to an entire city: Denver.[17]

The net effect was the creation of a nationwide perception, consistent with the victim perspective, that the problem was not just the practice of legally mandated segregation but the current pattern of racially concentrated schools. That perception gave rise to a right to attend schools in fact integrated, at least for some period of time sufficient to make credible, to black people, the claim that segregation had been outlawed.

The elusive and manipulable notion of intent is best illustrated by the third typical case, *Griggs* v. *Duke Power Co.*,[18] which is the centerpiece of the Era of Contradiction. *Griggs* was the only Supreme Court case that almost incorporated the victim perspective; not surprisingly, it became one of the most repudiated of cases, and may have been substantially overruled in 1989.

Griggs, decided under Title VII of the Civil Rights Act of 1964 rather than the Constitution, involved an ostensibly neutral practice—testing—that was probably being employed for the purpose of racial discrimination. (The employer had explicitly confined black workers to its lowest-status labor department until the effective date of Title VII in July 1965, and immediately thereafter imposed a pair of aptitude test requirements for placement in any department except labor). Yet there was no provable causal link between the racially exclusionary impact of the tests and the employer's blatantly discriminatory prior practice. The Court focused on the test itself as a practice that fell with disproportionate severity on blacks.

Title VII, according to the Court, requires the "removal of artificial, arbitrary, and unnecessary barriers to employment," and proscribes "not only overt discrimination but also practices that are fair in form, but discriminatory in operation." Speaking directly to the question of intent, the Court made it clear that "good intent" or the "absence of discriminatory intent" "does not redeem employment procedures . . . that operate as built-in headwinds for minority groups and are unrelated to measuring job capability." While not going so far as to make such practices automatic violations of the act, Chief Justice Burger's opinion placed the burden of their justification squarely on the employers, and a strict burden it was, requiring proof of *business necessity*: the practice must not only be "related to job performance," but have a "manifest relationship to the employment in question."

Thus *Griggs* set loose some new ideas. Unlike the perpetrator perspective, which inferred nothing from the mere fact of a racially disproportionate result, *Griggs* demanded the justification of ostensibly neutral practices producing such results. The shift from an emphasis on "motivation" to one on "consequences" marks a transformation of the notion of intent in antidiscrimination law. Henceforth, the intentional continuation of a course of conduct producing racially disproportionate results would be actionable, regardless of why the actor chose to continue. To so transform "intent" is to incorporate the victim perspective.

Three aspects of *Griggs* illustrate its implicit potential. With respect to its own factual context, testing, *Griggs* demanded what many knew would be an impossible standard of justification, since written tests are part of a closed world where all they correlate with is each other. Given the centrality of standardized testing in legitimating hierarchy in America, meritocracy itself might come under siege. Furthermore, since *Griggs* was about the very meaning of discrimination, there was no reason to suppose that its doctrine would be cabined. Rather, one expected its application to other employment practices, especially seniority, and to other statutory and constitutional violations, in areas such as school desegregation, voting, housing, land-use regulation, and provision of governmental services. Finally, to the extent *Griggs* presumptively invalidated selection practices with racially exclusionary results, the case subtly coerced the development of explicitly racial affirmative action programs. Employers or schools wanting to retain their "neutral" practices could use affirmative action to compensate for the exclusionary deficiencies of standard selection criteria.

Apart from *Griggs*, the Supreme Court never deviated from the rhetorical form of the perpetrator perspective, even while straining its logic with manipulation of remedy, intent, and causation doctrine. Lower courts, however, went further than the Supreme Court in explicitly extending *Griggs* to other areas. Thus the victim perspective, for a time, crept into federal law.

THE ERA OF RATIONALIZATION (1974–1984)

Without explicitly overruling any of the earlier cases, the Court in the period of rationalization employed a method of containment to defeat any deviant victim perspective expectations. Once again there was an insistence on proof of both intent and causation, coupled with an emphasis on the rhetoric rather than the results of earlier cases. To deal with the subversive *Griggs* decision, the Court arbitrarily declined to extend its logic to other areas, and reduced the defensive burden of proof for employers subject to its rule. Yet it stopped short of overruling the case, leaving it applicable to cases of employment discrimination involving ostensibly neutral hiring and selection criteria.

Thus, with respect to the definition of violation under applicable antidiscrimination law, the perpetrator perspective once again became the norm, subject only to the *Griggs* exception. Simultaneously, however, the Court tolerated and even seemed to encourage vigorous remedial efforts that were in fact at odds with the perpetrator worldview.

The 1974 decision in *Milliken* v. *Bradley*,[19] the Detroit school desegregation case, marks the moment of discontinuity that ushered in the era of rationalization. The case involved the conclusion to be drawn from two rather stark premises: first, that the City of Detroit had for years quite purposely segregated its public school students by race; second, that by the 1990s there would no longer be any white students in the Detroit system. To "desegregate" the Detroit schools, then, would mean no integration at all unless the suburban (and white) school districts in the metropolitan area were made part of the solution. So concluded the district judge; yet the Supreme Court soundly defeated the result-centered expectations created by its own decisions in the Charlotte-Mecklenburg and Denver cases. Taking an atomistic view of state-created jurisdictional units as just so many actors within the perpetrator worldview, the chief justice absolved the suburban districts of responsibility, since they had not been shown to have intentionally caused the segregation in Detroit.

The notion of intent is as elusive as the variety of its forms. From the specific design to harm (associated with criminal law) one can move to "subjective" forseeability ("intentional" torts) to "objective" foreseeability (e.g., negligence in tort) to accountability for the consequences of one's behavior (e.g., "strict" products liability). To insist on the most narrow and purposeful version in antidiscrimination law is to ensure minimalist accountability.

Such was the insistence of the Court in the era of rationalization, when it repeatedly refused to allow an inference of "intentional" discrimination despite dramatic evidence of racially disproportionate consequences. The result was a substantial contraction of the sphere of antidiscrimination law. Three of the "stories" cited in my introduction were cases decided during this period. In 1976, in *Washington* v. *Davis*,[20] the D.C. police case, the justices refused to extend the *Griggs* approach to cases based on constitutional antidiscrimination principles rather than statutory ones. Why? Because "[w]e have never held that the constitutional standard . . . is identical . . . and we decline to do so today."

In addition, in *Davis* the Court summarily overruled all of the lower federal courts that had extended the *Griggs* rule to areas such as housing, zoning, or municipal services.[21] Finally, *Davis* relaxed the *Griggs*-imposed burden of justification, making it easier for employers to validate their otherwise suspect employment practices. A similar insistence on the narrowest definition of intent led to defeat for the black voters subject to Mobile's at-large system, in 1980; and to defeat for the black residents of Memphis burdened by the street closed at their border with the white neighborhood, in 1981.[22]

Despite these defeats, the same Court, during the same period, continued to offer some remedial promise. In 1978, 1979, and 1980, the Court decided its first three affirmative action cases.[23] In each case, affirmative action was challenged by opponents as unlawful "reverse discrimination," and in each case the Court upheld the challenged program. The most publicized of these cases was *Bakke*, involving a university admissions program specifically employing race as a criterion of admission. The Court divided into two warring camps of four justices each, one adamantly opposed, the other as adamantly in favor. Justice Powell, with his oddly pragmatic conservatism, broke the deadlock in a self-contradictory opinion that sought to have it both ways on the perpetrator/victim split.

From the perpetrator view, Powell invoked the most rigid rhetoric of color blindness, with its premise of ethnic fungibility, and rejected the notion that race could be employed in the admissions process for reasons having anything to do with securing racial justice or remedying past discrimination (absent proof of a "violation"). Nevertheless, he decided that an academic concern for the "diversity" of student populations was so compelling as a competing constitutional value, rooted in First Amendment academic freedom, as to trump the equal protection challenge of those charging reverse discrimination. Thus, in the name of a diversity that equates race with being a "farm boy from Idaho," admissions programs could continue to admit largely on the basis of race. Powell's facile assumption of equivalence becomes questionable, however, when one recognizes that the very reason for focusing on race as a relevant characteristic is our specific historical record of discrimination. To allow the admission of students because they are black is to adopt at least in part the victim perspective.

If *Washington* v. *Davis* marks the low point of the rationalization period, its high point was surely the 1979 decision in *United Steelworkers* v. *Weber*, another widely publicized "reverse discrimination" controversy. The case involved a collective bargaining agreement providing for affirmative action efforts to eliminate conspicuous racial imbalances at Kaiser Aluminum plants. The specific controversy arose at a plant in Louisiana where, although the local work force was 39 percent black, only 1.83 percent of skilled craftworkers were black. The plan at issue provided for training of production workers to become skilled craftworkers, with 50 percent of the trainees to be black, regardless of seniority, until the percentage of black craftworkers matched that in the local population. Weber, a white production worker with more seniority than some of the black trainees, charged the union and company with unlawful racial discrimination under Title VII of the 1964 Civil Rights Act.

In a 5 to 2 decision, the Court upheld the plan as a laudable effort to break down old patterns of segregation and hierarchy by creating job openings for blacks in areas of traditional exclusion. Implicit in this decision were two key assumptions consistent with the victim rather than the perpetrator perspective, both of which were ignored in Justice Brennan's plurality opinion.

The first assumption was that statistical disparity (the 1.83 percent compared with the 39 percent) was itself enough to make out a *prima facie* case of violation under *Griggs*, which remained applicable to hiring and promotion practices. The second was that a court finding such a violation (assuming the employer could not defend the disparity) would order an affirmative action remedy not unlike the one negotiated by union and management in *Weber*. To treat the statistical disparity as a presumptive violation is to say that, given our history and social reality, conditions that *look* like those traditionally associated with racist practice are to be regarded as such. This approach relieves aggrieved members of the victim group (blacks, in this case) from the impossible perpetrator perspective burden of bringing forth specific individuals who can show they would have been trained as skilled craftworkers *but for* specific selection practices purposely utilized by the employer. By so defining the violation, its remedy follows: the employer must take affirmative steps to change the racial balance of its craftworker work force. There is no pretense of satisfying the perpetrator perspective demand that specific and identifiable victims be compensated; the remedy is a group remedy designed to confer on black workers a fair share of jobs. *Weber* thus illustrates how the *Griggs* rule and its remedial implication kept the victim perspective alive, albeit contained, at the close of the era of rationalization.

THE ERA OF DENIAL (1984–????)

To complete the dismantling process that had begun in the period of rationalization, the Court needed to reconsider, and reject, the implicit assumptions of *Weber*. Once statistical disparities cease to be presumptive violations, and remedies mandating numerical results are no longer required (or even permitted), the reality of inequality experienced by black Americans becomes just another neutral feature of our socioeconomic landscape.

The remedial question arose first in *Firefighters* v. *Stotts*,[24] in 1984, where the Court, speaking through John F. Kennedy appointee Byron "Whizzer" White, rejected the application of an affirmative action hiring plan (mandated by a consent decree) to a layoff situation. The district court had decided that a budget-induced layoff plan should be applied so as to preserve the percentage gains made by the affirmative action hiring required by the consent decree. Thus, according to the Supreme Court:

> The issue at the heart of this case is whether the District Court exceeded its powers in entering an injunction requiring white employees to be laid off, when the otherwise applicable seniority system would have called for the layoff of black employees with less seniority.

Just as the Court had refused in 1977 to extend the logic of the *Griggs* rule to seniority cases, the Court in *Stotts* concluded that despite the affirmative action consent decree, it was "inappropriate to deny an innocent employee the benefits of his seniority in order to provide a remedy . . . in a suit such as this."

This conclusion followed from a cold, clinical, perpetrator perspective analysis of the situation. Even though the black workers had been hired pursuant to an affirmative action plan adopted as part of a consent decree in a lawsuit charging racial discrimination in hiring, "there was no finding that any of the blacks protected from layoff had been a victim of discrimination . . ." If they were not "victims," why had their hiring been mandated by the affirmative action plan?

The doctrine of *Stotts* was simply inconsistent with numerically grounded race-conscious affirmative action as upheld in *Weber*. Nevertheless, in the years following *Stotts*, the Court entered into a period of incoherent doctrinal instability, deciding five more affirmative action cases in 1986 and 1987. In four of them, involving hiring and promotion, the Court upheld the plans,[25] often citing *Weber* with approval, yet without any consistent majority voice. In one, the 1986 *Wygant*[26] decision, the justices followed *Stotts* in another layoff situation, largely because Justice Powell, placing pragmatism ahead of coherence, chose to insist on the perpetrator perspective only in seniority cases, while Justice O'Connor, who had joined the Court in 1984, moved only slowly and haltingly toward opposition to affirmative action.

Yet during this period of instability a new and strident voice had joined the Court. Justice Scalia, appointed in 1986 when Rehnquist was elevated to Chief Justice, was unambiguously rooted in the perpetrator perspective. In 1979 he had written:

There [are] many white ethnic groups that came to this country in great numbers relatively late in its history—Italians, Jews, Irish, Poles—who not only took no part in, and derived no profit from, the major historic suppression of the currently acknowledged minority groups, but were, in fact, themselves the object of discrimination by the dominant Anglo-Saxon majority. [To] be sure, in relatively recent years some or all of these groups have been the beneficiaries of discrimination against blacks, or have themselves practiced discrimination. But to compare their racial debt—I must use this term since the concept of "restorative justice" implies it; there is no creditor without a debtor—with that of those who plied the slave trade, and who maintained a formal caste system for many years thereafter, is to confuse a mountain with a molehill.[27]

Dissenting in one of the 1987 affirmative action cases, Scalia made it clear that his programmatic agenda is nothing less than the full restoration of the perpetrator perspective as the only approach to antidiscrimination law.

With a predatory flair for sniffing out the vulnerable points in prior opinions, Scalia's stinging dissent in *Johnson* v. *Transportation Agency*[28] demands that *Weber* be overruled. For him, the affirmative action plan upheld in that case was nothing less than "intentional discrimination on the basis of race." According to Scalia, racially disproportionate statistical disparities are at most evidence of "societal discrimination." Societal discrimination is not only irremediable under antidiscrimination law, which requires identifiable perpetrators and victims, but is also irremediable through voluntary affirmative action plans. The latter amount to no more than insistence on racial proportionality—an unconstitutional goal. Scalia also denounced *Griggs* for coercing employers fearful of lawsuits directed at their numerical disproportion into adopting affirmative action programs that are themselves illegal "reverse discrimination," and he denounced *Bakke* for its pretense that race is just one of many "diversities."

However harsh the sound of that dissent, its voice had been present all along, though occasionally and inconsistently muted. In 1989, that voice acquired the votes needed for implementation of its remaining agenda.

Of the six major civil rights defeats issued by the Supreme Court in 1989, three are directed to the lingering victim perspective assumptions that perpetuated the viability of at least some affirmative action programs. The three, *Wards Cove Packing Co.* v. *Atonio*,[29] *Martin* v. *Wilks*,[30] and *City of Richmond* v. *J. A. Croson Co.*,[31] amount collectively to a repudiation of the implicit principles, if not the actual results, of both *Griggs* and *Weber*. These decisions compel us to deny that starkly racial differences in status have anything to do with "discrimination"; to believe that affirmative action programs amount to "reverse discrimination" against white people and as such are just as pernicious as the historical and persistent discrimination that generated civil rights law in the first place; and to deny that results matter as a measure of whether antidiscrimination law has been successful.

As described earlier, a key feature of the era of rationalization was the surgical containment of *Griggs* v. *Duke Power Co.* through the Court's renewed insistence on proof of (purposeful) intent. Examples were the refusal to find even presumptive violations in the D.C. police case (*Washington* v. *Davis* [1976]), the Mobile voting case (*Mobile* v. *Bolden* [1980]), and the Memphis street-closing case (*Memphis* v. *Greene* [1981]). Last term's decision in *Wards Cove*, the Alaska cannery case, was in one sense just a logical extension of those three cases, with the scalpel applied not just to contain but to remove *Griggs* from the body of our civil rights jurisprudence. So described, the decision surely deserves to be called a major civil rights setback:

yet, it is even more dismal than that. There is a Dickensian quality to the opinion, with its excessive solicitude for employer-defendants, and its preoccupation with legal technicality (intent, causation, burden of proof) which serves to distance the victims from their own case. Its tone of reassurance—the law is still there for plaintiffs with the well-pled case—is in context about as reassuring as a promise from Uriah Heep. Justice White may have authored the opinion, but its outlook is that of Justice Scalia.

The case involved the seasonal operation of a cannery in Alaska. Even the majority conceded the existence of a two-tiered hierarchial workforce, with jobs categorized as "cannery" (unskilled and low-status) or "noncannery" (mostly skilled and higher-status). The district court found "significant disparities between the at-issue jobs (*i.e.*, noncannery jobs) and the total workforce at the canneries." These disparities were explained specifically by the fact that "nearly all employed in the 'cannery worker' department are nonwhite." The nonwhites whose lawsuit had begun fifteen years earlier included persons of Samoan, Chinese, Filipino, Japanese, and Alaska Native descent, all but one of whom were American citizens. The racial disproportion was underscored by the fact that the employer used separate hiring channels to fill the two categories, and segregated the workers by category in housing and eating facilities.

Despite overwhelming evidence of a tradition of racial separation, which Justice Stevens characterized as bearing "an unsettling resemblance to aspects of a plantation economy," Justice White concluded that the plaintiffs had not proved even enough to require an explanation from the employer. In so doing, he deployed virtually every ideological component of the perpetrator perspective. He rebuked Justices Stevens and Blackmun for their "hyperbole," since no one had ever shown that the employer practiced "intentional" discrimination. As to the readily observable *Griggs*-type consequences, White announced that the plaintiffs could not rely on aggregates, but had to show instead how any particular hiring practice specifically *caused* discriminatory results, being sure to show how many "qualified" nonwhites were available for the jobs at issue (as opposed to requiring the employer to justify its practices as ones that selected those who are "qualified").

He reminded us that we do not wish to hold employers accountable for racially disparate situations that are not their "fault"; that if we compelled them to defend racial imbalance in lawsuits, they might take affirmative steps to create racial balance, which would of course be illegal and discriminatory; and, that we would not want employers to be "potentially liable for 'the myriad of innocent causes that may lead to statistical imbalances in the composition of their work forces.'" He later characterized these undesirable and untoward consequences as a "host of evils" to be avoided. Accordingly, he substantially reduced the burden of explanation on employers once a successful case has been made out (if it ever can be under the new standards), and, in a stunning coup de grace, he reversed the *Griggs* rule that placed the burden of proof on such employers.

Wards Cove thus obliterates the implicit assumption in *Weber* that serious statistical disparities are presumptive violations of Title VII. In fact, there is very little left of the *Griggs* notion that discriminatory results should compel persuasive justification. Instead, except to the extent that *Griggs* still applies (which may be no further than North Carolina employers who adopted test and diploma requirements in 1965), the notion of "violation" has been placed firmly within the perpetrator perspective. Instead of confronting social and historical reality, antidiscrimination law has been reduced to the status of just another intentional tort, albeit one with unusually strict intent and causation requirements.

The other two 1989 cases dealt with "reverse discrimination" challenges to affirmative action programs. One case focused on procedure, the other on substance. Their combined effect is the elevation of reverse discrimination claims to a status identical to claims on behalf of discrimination's historic and traditional victims; in short, the law has been turned on its head.

In the procedural case, *Martin* v. *Wilks*, the Court allowed a group of white fire fighters claiming reverse discrimination to challenge a consent decree that had been entered into by the city of Birmingham, Alabama, in 1981, settling litigation begun in 1974 and providing for affirmative action hiring and promotion for black fire fighters. Seven of the nine federal appeals courts ruling on that issue had precluded such attacks as "impermissible collateral attack." The Supreme Court, by a vote of 5–4, took the opposite view. This "procedural" decision serves to invite legal attack by aggrieved whites on long-standing affirmative action programs originating in litigation, conferring on the whites a continuing right to complain about reverse discrimination in court.[32] Its substantive implication is that this is so serious a social problem that we must offer those aggrieved a chance to vindicate their "rights."

That last observation surely gains credence from the Court's substantive decision in *City of Richmond* v. *J. A. Croson Co.*, involving the 30 percent set-aside for minority contractors in Richmond, Virginia, and described in my introduction. The Court struck down the program as illegal reverse discrimination under the equal protection clause of the Constitution, reasoning that the mere fact that less than 1 percent of contracts had gone to minority contractors in a city with a 50 percent black population was insufficient evidence of racial discrimination to serve as justification for the program. The opinion has a "good cop/bad cop" quality, with Justices O'Connor, White, and Rehnquist playing the former role, and, not surprisingly, Justice Scalia the latter, and with Justice Kennedy somewhere in between.

These internal differences may well be more rhetorical than real. The key point is that remedial racial classifications are henceforth to be treated as "suspect," and subjected to the same "strict scrutiny" applied in racial discrimination cases. They must justify themselves, if at all, by demonstrating the existence of a "compelling" governmental interest, which was found lacking in Richmond. Scalia would go even further and apply a per se rule of invalidity to affirmative action programs, allowing only the compensation of specific victims who have proved discrimination against themselves.

Richmond thus institutionalizes the worldview of "ethnic fungibility" so central to the perpetrator outlook. Only in the messy particularity of historical and current social reality can one rediscover what it means and has meant to be black in America. Yet there is a feature of the *Richmond* opinion that is even worse than its resort to abstract, timeless, and ahistorical principle. In a singular instance of callous racial insensitivity, Justice O'Connor deviates from "principle" and becomes willing to infer discrimination from structure. She reminds us that blacks comprise 50 percent of the population of Richmond, and hold five of nine seats on the city council, leading to a "concern that a political majority will more easily act to the disadvantage of a minority." With a white majority in similar circumstances (e.g., *Mobile*), we are not even permitted to infer a racial problem. While one could dismiss O'Connor's point as facile legal argument, it may well be a warning to urban blacks who are gaining political power (as I write, a black candidate has just been elected mayor of New York City) that if they try to serve their own constituencies by remedying historic inequalities largely perpetrated by white political majorities serving their constituencies, they will be hauled into court as racists.

THE POLITICS OF RACE AND RIGHTS

To label the recent Supreme Court decisions as instances of denial is to imply the existence of a reality to which the Court is seeking to cut off our access through its rhetorical ploys. In fact, even *Time* magazine recently characterized the past decade as one of "willful denial of the realities of white-black relations."[33] Those realities are two: substantive inequality and the intractable persistence of racism. As to the former, a recent and massive study sponsored by the National Research Council noted that "Since the early 1970s, the economic status of blacks relative to whites has, on average, stagnated or deteriorated."[34] As to the latter, there is the continuing witness of blacks who have won their middle-class credentials yet find themselves still subjected to the humiliating practices that signal racism's lasting power, as they are denied entrance to stores or apartment houses by security guards, or left waiting for taxicabs in the rain while white passengers are picked up.

Those twin realities amount to a grim reversal of the utopian expectation predicted by Gunnar Myrdal, whose massive study, *An American Dilemma*, both captured and informed the white liberal consciousness whose support was so crucial for any racial progress. Central to Myrdal's conception of America's "race problem" was the "principle of cumulation," or the "vicious circle," which implied that the persistence of racial stereotypes in the minds of whites served to perpetuate the poverty and powerlessness of blacks, while the actuality of poverty and powerlessness served to reinforce the stereotypes. Myrdal predicted that the "vicious circle" could be turned on its head and redirected toward racial progress: If whites would allow their own better natures to operate, they would cease to perceive blacks through a stereotypical lens, which would, in turn, open up new political and economic possibilities for blacks, which would, in turn, expose the falsity of the racial stereotypes, etc.

This reformist and turnabout version of the vicious circle proved flawed in two basic ways. The view that changes in white consciousness would follow from changes in black status depends upon a model of white racism as a consciously held "mistaken" view, one that is educationally correctable, and at odds with one's better self: in short, racism is a personal moral dilemma in the white mind. Recent experience suggests that racism persists at a level much deeper than the superficial one depicted by Myrdal's model—that it is an unconscious, culturally transmitted, and seemingly intractable feature of American life.[35]

The flip side of Myrdal's expectation is equally flawed. That changes in consciousness (as, e.g., civil rights laws) will lead to significant changes in status depends upon a tenuous proposition—the availability of equality of opportunity. As suggested earlier, the important white advocates of what has been termed "liberal interracialism"[36] were at once myopic and utopian. In a sense, they hoped to get results "for free." Their modest, reformist goal was that the socioeconomic stratification of black Americans would come to resemble that of whites. Once the obstacle of irrational racial "prejudice" was removed, blacks would advance through the rational, impersonal workings of meritocracy, facilitated by a system of public education that gave everyone an equal start. This was a vision that denied, and suppressed, the possibility that there was, in America, a *class* structure, with cultural as well as economic dimension. That structure significantly reduced upward mobility, and served to perpetuate the dominant position of those already controlling wealth and power.

Central to liberal attitude and hope, then, was what may be the single most important myth that rationalizes American social, cultural, and economic reality—formal individualistic equality of opportunity.[37] It was the abiding faith of folks as disparate as John Locke, Abraham Lincoln, Hubert Humphrey, and Richard Nixon. It serves not only to rationalize but to celebrate inequality, while compelling those who fail to "make it" to internalize a despairing lack of self-worth. It facilitates our callous indifference to the reality of adult inequality by loading the burden of advancement onto our children, mediated by a system of education that systematically denies the extent to which the odds of success are overwhelmingly stacked against those who start at the bottom—white or black.

No practice symbolizes the seemingly objective and neutral character of meritocracy so much as the standardized test. In this context one might better understand the Supreme Court's decision in *Griggs* not as necessarily insisting on equality of *results*, but as demanding a more credible system of equality of *opportunity*. Notably, Chief Justice Burger expressed a deep skepticism about mechanistic credentialism ("History is filled with examples of men and women who rendered highly effective performance without the conventional badges of accomplishment in terms of certificates, diplomas, or degrees"). No doubt he was influenced by his own background in having attended, unlike most of his judicial colleagues, a "night" law school (William Mitchell College of Law in St. Paul, Minnesota). The Court may have been rejecting mechanistic credentialism, but hoping for methods of testing that would really correlate with occupational performance.

Whatever optimism may have been the basis for *Griggs*, however, was quickly doused by the reality of post-*Griggs* litigation involving tests. In case after case, the tests demonstrably failed to satisfy the job-relatedness standard.[38] In fact, litigation revealed that the only thing such tests measure is test-taking ability, so that one test will often correlate well with another test, yet fail in any statistical way to predict actual job performance. Moreover, the tests used for tracking in public schools, or for college and university admissions, like the SAT, correlate best with one's socioeconomic background, thereby disproportionately excluding blacks and other minorities, and rewarding those who already own the predominant share of the nation's "cultural capital."[39] Thus the educational system, claiming to offer equality of opportunity, with its objective and neutral criteria of evaluation, serves instead to provide the ruling class with a "theodicy of its own privilege."[40] In that context, it is hardly surprising that the Court in *Washington* v. *Davis* acted quickly (within five years) to confine *Griggs* to Title VII cases—lest it be applied, as it surely would have, to SATs, and even bar exams—and, simultaneously, to make clear that the job-relatedness standard might be satisfied even if one test did no more than correlate, even weakly, with just another test. Any other result would have been seriously destabilizing to the whole structure of American meritocracy.

Having diminished the *Griggs* threat to meritocratic pretension, the Court still faced the dilemma of whether substantive civil rights gains for blacks could be achieved without challenge to the belief systems that rationalize our inequality generally. That dilemma serves to explain the dissonant character of the period of rationalization, and the instability implicit in the affirmative action issue. Affirmative action offers an inside-out version of one of the traditional Marxist lines on American racism. Marxists have argued that racism serves to "divide the working class" by keeping lower-class blacks and whites at odds with one another, which plays into the hands of an accordingly less-threatened ruling class. According to this theory, the interest of the ruling class lies in promoting and maintaining racism, while the working classes might prevail if only they could see their commonality of oppression.[41]

Ironically, however, it has surely been in the enlightened self-interest of the American ruling class, at least since the 1950s, to do something real and visible about the "race problem." In the early Cold War period, most Soviet anti-American propaganda focused on racism; American leaders were desperate to counter that propaganda.[42] Today, American multinational corporations are competing, and not too successfully, in markets where multiracial staff, as well as management, would bolster their image and profits. For corporate leaders, the civil rights agenda has been a high priority.

Unlike the utopian liberals described earlier, most pragmatic capitalists know that equality of opportunity is largely a sham, a grandiose rhetoric that rationalizes their own hierarchical advantage. Therefore, they recognize that to produce substantive results—*i.e.*, visible jobs for blacks—without dismantling class-based obstacles for the lower class generally requires a conscious, race-based redistribution of opportunity. The paradigm of such was the affirmative action plan in *Weber*, adopted by the employer (along with the union) and upheld by the Court. It makes perfect sense, if *Weber* is viewed this way, that Justice Potter Stewart, who regularly voted to support, with some pragmatic care, the interests of capitalists, gave the majority its fifth vote. Under *Weber*, an employer may specifically correct a racial imbalance in its skilled work force, using moderate but not excessive means, without otherwise subjecting its selection criteria to scrutiny or challenge.

But such redistributive schemes are ultimately destabilizing. The race-conscious effort to increase the presence of blacks is also a concession that equality of opportunity does not work on its own. Moreover, to offer to blacks opportunities that would have otherwise gone to whites is to take away what individuals experience as vested rights or expectations even if they are more accurately regarded as unfair advantages in their social and historical context. The closer such programs come to redistribution of vested rights the more threatening they become to a mainstay of American hierarchy.

From this perspective, the seemingly contradictory behavior of Justice Powell makes sense. Powell supported affirmative action in hiring and promotion, as well as university admissions (though barely), in a manner seemingly consistent with the victim perspective; yet he adopted the perpetrator perspective with a vengeance in joining the Court's majority in *Stotts*, the seniority layoff case that introduced the era of denial. From the perspective of the pragmatic capitalist, a worker's seniority is an asset (or investment) equivalent to one's own stocks, bonds, or plants. As it had in 1977 refused to extend the *Griggs* rule to Title VII seniority cases, the Court declined to extend its tolerance of affirmative action to defeating seniority protection against layoffs, even where that refusal meant the defeat of gains realized through previously upheld affirmative action. The hiring/layoff distinction became a symbolic line separating affirmative action as the seemingly non-threatening extension of opportunity from affirmative action as total destabilization of hierarchy.

That compromise line was inherently fragile. The Court tried to maintain it in 1986 and 1987, by striking down affirmative action in another layoff case, yet upholding it in four more hiring and/or promotion cases, with a series of fragmented opinions and increasingly bitter dissents. The line was bound to unravel, for if equality of opportunity were reality, not just mythology, then affirmative action at the hiring and promotion stage was no less "unfair" than affirmative action at layoff. Or, if equality of opportunity *was* just mythology, then *all* existing hierarchy was illegitimate.

The political genius of Reagan was to rally the American people around their most cherished illusions, including the illusion of equal opportunity. He convincingly portrayed affirmative action as out of line with traditional American notions of fair play and protection of rights. Reagan's victory meant short-term gain for capitalists liberated from regulation. Nevertheless, on some issues, including affirmative action, it may have split the ruling class. With a striking purity of spirit, the Reagan team found Supreme Court justices who would take American mythology seriously, and would not bend the rules to accommodate even the pragmatic interests of sophisticated corporate executives and politicians who understood the long-term advantages of racial diversity.

The clearest example is Scalia, who infuses his opposition to affirmative action, rooted in the perpetrator worldview, with a populist appeal to lower-class white "victims." For him the pragmatic capitalists are no better than the liberals:

> Yet [it] is precisely *these* groups [white ethnics not part of the "dominant Anglo-Saxon majority"] that do most of the restoring. It is they who, to a disproportionate degree, are the competitors with the urban blacks and

Hispanics for jobs, housing, education—all those things that enable one to scramble to the top of the social heap where one can speak eloquently (and quite safely) of restorative justice.

The 1989 cases can best be understood, then, as reaffirming the myths that normalize inequality as the outcome of impersonal, neutral forces. *Wards Cove*, by reprocessing what looks like rampant racial inequality into a happenstance statistical distribution occasioned by applicant "preferences" or the size of "qualified" pools, reassures us that equality of opportunity is working, except in the rare case where specific inappropriate behaviors can be identified. By rendering even serious racial imbalance irrelevant, *Wards Cove* undermines the legitimacy of efforts to redress such imbalance through affirmative action.

Richmond, though decided earlier, may be regarded as a logical conse- quence of *Wards Cove*, for the fact that less than 1 percent of the city's construction contracts went to minority contractors over a five-year period in a city with a 50 percent black population is just as irrelevant as the racially imbalanced structure of the cannery and noncannery jobs in the later case. By trivializing the statistics, the Court almost automatically delegitimizes the 30 percent set-aside program. From the standpoint of federal law, the two cases are of a piece, since affirmative action remedies will no longer be compelled by statistical disparities that are not even arguable violations. *Wilks*, moreover, virtually ensures that even judicially mandated affirmative action, whose status has also become doubtful, will be challenged as "reverse discrimination." Given these decisions, along with the fact that Ronald Reagan appointed more than half of the current federal judiciary, it is in- creasingly difficult to regard federal courts as hospitable forums for the vin- dication of civil rights.

One response may be a rebirth of federalism, with principal efforts directed at creating new solutions at the state and local level. Recent state court decisions suggest the existence of such a trend.[43] Yet even those efforts may be undercut by the recent Supreme Court cases, especially *Richmond*. Given the rhetoric of the Reagan years, the *Richmond* decision may be characterized as an exercise in hypocrisy. No claim was advanced so loudly with respect to judicial appointments as the one calling for an end to the "judicial ac- tivism" that had legitimized abortions and outlawed school prayer in the name of federal rights. In *Richmond*, now that there is a solid conservative majority, one can see a complete reversal of liberal and conservative positions on judicial activism as opposed to state autonomy.

The set-aside program in *Richmond* was not mandated by any federal law or court; it was voluntarily adopted by the democratically elected legislature of the city of Richmond to redress a long-standing local problem of inequality through a modest redistribution of access. In as blatant an instance of judicial activism as one can find, the Supreme Court deployed federal rights theory to override local process. Although using language of equality ("reverse discrimination"), the right protected was more in the nature of an economic right—freedom of contract. Thus the federal courts are once again playing their historic role of protecting vested interests against the excesses of democracy.[44]

I have sought in this essay to offer the corrosive clarity of realism. The goal of that effort is not, however, to promote despair, but to advocate an energetic redirection of activity. If the federal courts are to become, as they were in the past, little more than reactionary apologists for the existing order, we should treat them with the contempt they deserve. One can only hope that other political institutions will be reinvigorated.

NOTES

1. 163 U.S. 537 (1896). I will with some frequency use black-white as the model of race in America, because I find it impossible to think about the topic without drawing heavily from the black experience, although, of course, Native Americans, Hispanics, Asian-Americans and other "nonwhites" also have suffered severe racial discrimination.
2. 347 U.S. 483 (1954).
3. Six 1989 cases stand out in this regard. The three major ones, all of which will be discussed in this essay, were City of Richmond v. J. A. Croson Co., 109 S. Ct. 706 (1989); Wards Cove Packing Co. v. Atonio (June 5, 1989); and Martin v. Wilks (June 12, 1989). The Court limited civil rights law in three cases of statutory interpretation: Lorance v. AT&T Technologies, Inc., Patterson v. McClean Credit Union, and Jett v. Dallas Independent School Dist. (all decided in June 1989), where it insisted on strict filing-time requirements for civil rights plaintiffs, limited the coverage of an 1866 civil rights law, and limited the availability of damage remedies.
4. The four cases are: Washington v. Davis, 426 U.S. 229 (1976); Memphis v. Greene, 451 U.S. 100 (1981); City of Mobile v. Bolden, 446 U.S. 55 (1980); City of Richmond v. J. A. Croson Co., 109 S. Ct. 706 (1989).
5. *See generally*, William Ryan, *Blaming the Victim* (New York: Pantheon Books, 1972).
6. *See, e.g.*, Robert Carter, "A Reassessment of *Brown v. Board*," in *Shades of Brown*, ed. Derrick Bell (New York: Teachers College Press, Columbia University, 1980).
7. *See* San Antonio Ind. School Dist. v. Rodriguez, 411 U.S. 1 (1973) (wealth

discrimination does not violate equal protection to the point of invalidating school financing through local property taxation, despite substantial disparities between districts in per-pupil expenditure), along with Milliken v. Bradley, 418 U.S. 717 (1974), discussed later in this essay.

8. *See, e.g.*, Gayle v. Browder, 352 U.S. 903, *aff'g per curiam* 142 F. Supp. 707 (M.D. Ala. 1956) (buses); Holmes v. City of Atlanta, 350 U.S. 879, vacating *per curiam* 223 f.2d 93 (5th Cir. 1955) (municipal golf courses); Mayor of Baltimore v. Dawson, 350 U.S. 877, aff'g *per curiam* 220 F.2d 386 (4th Cir. 1955) (public beaches and bathhouses).

9. *E.g.*, Herbert Wechsler, "Toward Neutral Principles of Constitutional Law," 73 *Harvard Law Rev.* 1 (1959); Richard Posner, "The DeFunis Case and the Constitutionality of Preferential Treatment of Racial Minorities," 1974 Sup. Ct. Rev. 1, 21–26; Paul Brest, "In Defense of the Antidiscrimination Principle," 90 *Harvard Law Review* 1 (1976); Owen Fiss, "Groups and the Equal Protection Clause," 5 *Philosophy and Public Affairs* 107 (1976).

10. Loving v. Virginia, 388 U.S. 1, 11 (1967).

11. *See, e.g.*, Charles Black, "The Lawfulness of the Segregation Decisions," 69 *Yale Law Journal* 421 (1960). For a comparative history of racism in the United States and South Africa, *see* George Fredrickson, *White Supremacy: A Study in American and South African History* (New York and Oxford: Oxford University Press, 1981). *See also* Cornel West, "Marxist Theory and the Specificity of Afro-American Oppression," in *Marxism and the Interpretation of Culture*, ed. C. Nelson and L. Grossberg (Urbana and Chicago: University of Illinois Press, 1988).

12. Brown v. Board of Education, 349 U.S. 294 (1955).

13. Briggs v. Elliott, 132c F. Supp. 776, 777 (E.D.S.C. 1955).

14. Gunnar Myrdal, *An American Dilemma* (New York: Harper and Row, 1944). For a thorough, comprehensive, and sophisticated study of Myrdal's work that reveals its origins, context, production, ideology, reception, and impact, *see generally*, D. Southern, *Gunnar Myrdal and Black-White Relations: The Use and Abuse of An American Dilemma, 1944–1969* (Baton Rouge and London: Louisiana State University Press, 1987). Chap. 6, for example, traces its importance for civil rights litigation, culminating with its citation in Brown v. Board of Education's famous footnote 11.

15. 402 U.S. 1 (1971).

16. Quoted in Richard Kluger, *Simple Justice* (New York: Alfred A. Knopf, 1976), p. 572.

17. *See* Keyes v. School District No. 1, 413 U.S. 189 (1973).

18. 401 U.S. 424 (1971).

19. 418 U.S. 717 (1974).

20. 426 U.S. 229 (1976).

21. The Court expressed its "disagreement" with such cases in n. 12 of the *Davis* opinion. Examples of such cases are Norwalk CORE v. Norwalk Redevelopment Agency, 395 F.2d 920 (2d Cir. 1968) (urban renewal and

housing); Kennedy Park Homes Ass'n, Inc. v. City of Lackawana, 436 F.2d 108 (2d Cir. 1970), *cert. denied*, 401 U.S. 1010 (1970) (zoning); Hawkins v. Town of Shaw, 437 F.2d 1286 (5th Cir. 1971), *aff'd on rehearing en banc*, 461 F.2d 1171 (1972) (municipal services).

22. City of Mobile v. Bolden, 446 U.S. 55 (1980); Memphis v. Greene, 451 U.S. 100 (1981).

23. Regents of the Univ. of California v. Bakke. 438 U.S. 265 (1978); Weber v. Kaiser Aluminum and Chemical Corp., 433 U.S. 193 (1979); Fullilove v. Klutznick, 448 U.S. 448 (1980) (federal law mandating 10 percent set-aside for minority-owned business enterprises).

24. 467 U.S. 561 (1984).

25. Sheet Metal Workers v. EEOC, 478 U.S. 421 (1986); Firefighters v. Cleveland, 478 U.S. 501 (1986); United States v. Paradise, 480 U.S. 149 (1987); Johnson v. Transportation Agency, 480 U.S. 616 (1987).

26. Wygant v. Jackson Board of Education, 476 U.S. 267 (1986).

27. Scalia, "The Disease as Cure," 1979 *Washington University Law Quarterly* 147, 152.

28. 480 U.S. at 657–77.

29. U.S. Sup. Ct., June 5, 1989.

30. U.S. Sup. Ct., June 12, 1989.

31. 109 S. Ct. 706 (1989).

32. In striking contrast to the Court's continuing insistence on strict timing rules for traditional civil rights plaintiffs. *See, e.g.*, Lorance v. AT&T Technologies, Inc. (U.S. Sup. Ct., June 12, 1989).

33. *Time*, August 7, 1989, pp. 12–15.

34. Gerald Jaynes and Robin Williams, Jr., eds., *A Common Destiny: Blacks and American Society* (Washington: National Research Council, 1989). *See also* Derrick Bell, *And We Are Not Saved* (New York: Basic Books, 1987); Kimberle Crenshaw, "Race, Reform and Retrenchment: Transformation and Legitimation in Antidiscrimination Law," 101 *Harvard Law Review* 1331 (1988).

35. *See, e.g.*, Charles Lawrence, "The Id, the Ego, and Equal Protection: Reckoning with Unconscious Racism," 39 *Stanford Law Review* 317 (1987); Richard Delgado, "Words that Wound: A Tort Action for Racial Insults, Epithets and Name-Calling," 17 *Harvard Civil Rights-Civil Liberties Law Review* 133 (1982). For a powerful experiential account, *see* "Anthony Walton, Willie Horton and Me," *The New York Times Magazine*, August 20, 1989 (§ 6), p. 52. *See also* Mari Matsuda, "Public Response to Racist Speech: Considering the Victim's Story," 87 *Michigan Law Review* 2320 (1989).

36. *See generally*, J. Kirby, *Black Americans in the Roosevelt Era* (Knoxville: University of Tennessee Press, 1980).

37. For a more extensive discussion of this issue, *see* Alan Freeman, "Racism, Rights and the Quest for Equality of Opportunity," 23 *Harvard Civil Rights-Civil Liberties Law Review* 295 (1988).

38. *E.g.*, Chance v. Board of Examiners, 458 F.2d 1167 (2d Cir. 1972); Bridge-

port Guardians v. Bridgeport Civil Service Comm'n, 482 F.2d 1333 (2d Cir. 1973).

39. See, e.g., McGeorge Bundy, "The Issue Before the Court: Who Gets Ahead in America?" *The Atlantic Monthly*, November 1977, p. 48; James Fallows, "The Tests and the 'Brightest': How Fair Are the College Boards?" 245 *Atlantic* 37 (1980). On the reality of equality of opportunity, see Richard DeLone, *Small Futures* (New York and London: Harcourt Brace Jovanovich, 1979).

40. See Pierre Bourdieu, *Outline of a Theory of Practice* (Cambridge: Cambridge University Press, 1977), p. 188.

41. For a general discussion, see Richard C. Edwards, Michael Reich, Thomas E. Weisskopf, *The Capitalist System* (Englewood Cliffs, N.J.: Prentice-Hall, 1972), pp. 287–321. See also David M. Gordon, *Problems in Political Economy: An Urban Perspective* (Lexington, Mass.: D. C. Heath, 1977), pp. 143–205.

42. See Mary Dudziak, "Desegregation as a Cold War Imperative," 41 *Stanford Law Review* 61 (1988). See also Vincent Harding, *The Other American Revolution* (Los Angeles: Center for Afro-American Studies, University of California, 1980), pp. 143–44. Derrick Bell, *Race, Racism and American Law*, 2d ed. (Boston: Little, Brown, 1980), pp. 40–44.

43. E.g., in October 1989, the Texas Supreme Court became the tenth state court to strike down its state's school financing as unconstitutional under state law, despite the U.S. Supreme Court's refusal to do so under federal law in its 1973 *Rodriguez* decision, which involved the same Texas system.

44. *Richmond* is in the grand tradition of Fletcher v. Peck, 10 U.S. (6 Cranch) 87 (1810), where an activist Supreme Court deployed federal rights theory to prevent a state legislature from redistributing corruptly acquired property rights.

   Nor is there anything new about the rhetoric of "reverse discrimination." For a decision, and an opinion, not unlike the currently expressed views of Justice Scalia, see Frankfurter, J., in Hughes v. Superior Court, 339 U.S. 460 (1950).

7
NADINE TAUB AND
ELIZABETH M. SCHNEIDER

WOMEN'S SUBORDINATION AND THE ROLE OF LAW

THE Anglo-American legal tradition purports to value equality, by which it means, at a minimum, equal application of the law to all persons. Nevertheless, throughout this country's history, women have been denied the most basic rights of citizenship, allowed only limited participation in the marketplace, and otherwise denied access to power, dignity, and respect. Women have instead been largely occupied with providing the personal and household services necessary to sustain family life.

The work women perform in the domestic sphere is barely acknowledged, let alone valued. Institutional arrangements that preclude women's economic and sexual autonomy ensure that this work will be done primarily by women. Often, though not always, these institutions are expressed in legal form.

This chapter explores two aspects of the law's role in maintaining women in an inferior status. It first considers the way the law has furthered male dominance by explicitly excluding women from the public sphere and by refusing to regulate the domestic sphere to which they are thus confined. It then examines the way the law has legitimized sex discrimination through the articulation of an ideology that justifies differential treatment on the basis of perceived differences between men and women.

THE LEGAL ORDER AND THE PUBLIC/PRIVATE SPLIT

Excluded in the past from the public sphere of marketplace and government, women have been consigned to a private realm to carry on their primary

The authors gratefully acknowledge the assistance of Ann Freedman, Associate Professor of Law, Rutgers Law School, Camden, New Jersey, and David Kairys in the development of this article.

responsibilities, *i.e.*, bearing and rearing children, and providing men with a refuge from the pressures of the capitalist world. This separation of society into the male public sphere and the female private sphere was most pronounced during the nineteenth century, when production moved out of the home.[1] But even today, women's opportunities in the public sphere are limited by their obligations in the private domestic sphere.

Men dominate both the public sphere and the private sphere. Male control in the public sphere has often been consolidated explicitly by legal means. The law, however, is in large part absent from the private sphere, and that absence[2] itself has contributed to male dominance and female subservience. In discussing the role of law in relation to this public/private split, this section first reviews the legal means by which women have been excluded from the public sphere, and then considers the law's absence from the private sphere and how that absence furthers male dominance.[3]

LEGAL EXCLUSION FROM THE PUBLIC SPHERE

The most obvious exclusion of women from public life was the denial of the franchise. Although in colonial times unmarried, propertied women were technically entitled to vote on local issues, all state constitutions that were adopted after the War of Independence, with the temporary exception of New Jersey's, barred women from voting. This initial exclusion gained even greater significance in the 1820s and 1830s, when the franchise was extended to virtually every white male regardless of property holdings. Even after the Civil War, when black men gained the right to vote, women of all races continued to be denied the ballot. The Nineteenth Amendment, giving women the vote, finally became law in 1920 after what has been described as "a century of struggle."[4]

The amendment's passage, however, did not mean that women were automatically accorded the rights and duties that generally accompanied elector status. For example, the exclusion of women from jury duty was upheld as late as 1961, when the Supreme Court explicitly rejected the equal-protection claim of a woman accused of murdering her husband. The Court found Florida's exclusion of women who did not voluntarily register for jury service "reasonable," since:

> Despite the enlightened emancipation of women from the restrictions and protections of bygone years, and their entry into many parts of community life formerly considered to be reserved to men, woman is still regarded as the center of home and family life.[5]

Even today, women are excluded from what is viewed as a crucial test of citizenship—armed combat duty.[6] As a result, women who wish to participate on an equal basis in the military cannot do so. Moreover, because combat exclusion is used to justify an all-male draft registration system,[7] women are also exempted from the fundamental responsibility of deciding whether to join or resist their country's military efforts.

Women have likewise been excluded from full participation in the economy. Under English common law, not only were they barred from certain professions (such as law), but, once married, they were reduced to legal nonentities unable to sell, sue, or contract without the approval of their husbands or other male relatives.[8] Although these disabilities were initially rigidified by codification of laws, which began in the 1820s, they were gradually lifted in the middle and latter part of the nineteenth century. Starting in the 1840s, various states passed laws that gave women the right to hold certain property in their own name. Subsequent legislation, enacted over the following half-century, afforded them the right to conduct business and retain their own earnings. The enactments were, however, repeatedly subjected to restrictive judicial interpretations that continued to confirm male dominance in business matters.

Even as women moved into the paid labor force,[9] they were limited in their work opportunities and earning power by the ideological glorification of their domestic role reflected in the law. Women have been consistently excluded from certain occupational choices and denied equal earning power by statute and other governmental action.[10] Such explicit exclusions persist today despite the promise of equal treatment contained in the Fourteenth Amendment and affirmative antidiscrimination legislation enacted in the 1960s and 1970s.[11] For example, in 1977 the Supreme Court found it legal to deny women jobs as guards in maximum-security prisons on the ground that the very presence of women would prompt sexual assaults.[12] In so holding, the Court simply ignored the fact that all guards are subject to assault by virtue of being guards and that a prison relies on the threat of future sanctions to maintain order. Women have also been and continue to be excluded from educational opportunities requisite to participation on an equal basis with men in the economy. As late as 1977, the Supreme Court upheld without opinion an appellate court decision finding that Philadelphia's two sex-segregated elite high schools were separate but essentially equal and that Philadelphia did not deny females equal protection by maintaining the dual schools.[13] Post–New Deal social-welfare legislation has likewise imposed barriers to women's participation in the public sphere. Reflecting and reinforcing the assumption that men are breadwinners and women are homemakers, Social Security legislation has denied female workers fringe benefits available to male workers.[14] Based on the same assumption, welfare and job programs have given men priorities in job placement and job training, with the result that women seeking work have been forced to stand by and watch the most desirable positions go to men.[15]

Legislation denying women the right to determine whether and when they will bear children has also served to exclude women from the public sphere. Beginning in the 1870s, legislative restrictions began to reinforce and supplement existing religious and cultural constraints on birth control. The Comstock Law forbidding obscene material (expressly including contraceptive devices) in the United States mail was invalidated in 1938,[16] while the Supreme Court did not invalidate state restrictions on the marital use of contraceptives until 1965[17] and their distribution to single persons until 1972.[18] Similarly, in the middle and late nineteenth century, most states enacted criminal statutes against abortion, although the procedure, at least in the pre-"quickening" stage, had not been a crime at the common law.[19] While a number of these statutes were liberalized in the 1960s, criminal sanctions remained in force until they were invalidated by the 1973 Supreme Court decisions.[20] Since then, provisions have been upheld that exclude abortion from Medicaid coverage and require the parents of many minors to be notified.[21] And in 1989, the Supreme Court once again signaled to the states that they would uphold restrictions on abortion.[22]

Many nongovernmental practices also help to exclude women from the public sphere. Commercial concerns have refused women credit and work; trade unions and professional associations have excluded women from skilled employment; public accommodations and business clubs have denied women entrance. Only very recently and very incompletely have governments acted to remedy this discrimination.[23] As the introduction to this book points out, in distinguishing only between governmental and nongovernmental agencies, and ignoring distinctions based on power, the law has tolerated and tacitly approved discriminatory conduct by a variety of powerful institutions.

THE ABSENCE OF LAW IN THE PRIVATE SPHERE

While sex-based exclusionary laws have joined with other institutional and ideological constraints to directly limit women's participation in the public sphere, the legal order has operated more subtly in relation to the private sphere to which women have been relegated. On the one hand, the legal constraints against women retaining their earnings and conveying property—whose remnants endured well into the twentieth century—meant that married women could have legal relations with the outside world only through their husbands. In this sense, the law may be viewed as directing male domination in the private sphere. On the other hand, the law has been conspicuously absent from the private sphere itself. Despite the fundamental similarity of conflicts in the private sphere to legally cognizable disputes in the public sphere, the law generally refuses to interfere in ongoing family relationships. For example, the essence of the marital relation as a legal matter is the exchange of the man's obligation to support the women for her household and sexual services. Yet contract law, which purports to enforce promissory obligations between individuals, is not available during the marriage to enforce either the underlying support obligation or other agreements by the parties to a marriage to matters not involving property. A woman whose husband squanders or gives away assets during the marriage cannot even get an accounting. And while premarital property agreements will be enforced on divorce, courts' enormous discretion in awarding support and distributing property makes it highly unlikely that these decisions will reflect the parties' conduct during the marriage in regard to either the underlying support obligation or other agreements. It is as if in regulating the beginning and the end of a business partnership the law disregarded the events that transpired during the partnership and refused to enforce any agreements between the partners as to how they would behave.[24]

Similarly, tort law, which is generally concerned with injuries inflicted on individuals, has traditionally been held inapplicable to injuries inflicted by one family member on another. Under the doctrines of interspousal and parent-child immunity, courts have consistently denied recoveries for injuries that would be compensable but for the fact that they occurred in the private realm.[25] In the same way, criminal law declined to punish intentional injuries to family members. Common law and statutory definitions of rape in many states continue to carve out a special exception for a husband's forced intercourse with his wife. Wife beating was initially omitted from the definition of criminal assault on the ground that a husband had the right to chastise his wife. Even today, after courts have explicitly rejected the definitional exception and its rationale, judges, prosecutors, and police officers decline to enforce assault laws in the family context.[26]

While in recent years, there has been some modification of these doctrines, the idea that law is inappropriate in the private sphere persists. A modern example of this phenomenon is the idea that family disputes are best suited for mediation rather than more formal legal proceedings.[27]

The state's failure to regulate the domestic sphere is now often justified on the ground that the law should not interfere with emotional relationships involved in the family realm because it is too heavy-handed. Indeed, the recognition of a familial privacy right in the early twentieth century has given this rationale a constitutional dimension. The importance of this concern, however, is undercut by the fact that the same result was previously justified by legal fictions, such as the woman's civil death on marriage. More importantly, the argument misconstrues the point at which the law is invoked. Legal relief is sought when family harmony has already been disrupted. Family members, like business associates, can be expected to forgo legal claims until they are convinced that harmonious relations are no longer possible. Equally important, the argument reflects and reinforces powerful myths about the nature of family relations. It is not true that women perform personal and household services purely for love. The family is the locus of fundamental economic exchanges, as well as important emotional ties.

Isolating women in a sphere divorced from the legal order contributes directly to their inferior status by denying them the legal relief that they seek to improve their situations and by sanctioning conduct of the men who control their lives. For example, when the police do not respond to a battered woman's call for assistance or when a civil court refuses to evict her husband, the woman is relegated to self-help, while the man who beats her receives the law's tacit encouragement. When the law does not allow for wage attachments or other standard collection devices to be used to enforce orders for child support, it leaves women in desperate financial straits.

But beyond its direct, instrumental impact, the insulation of women's world from the legal order also conveys an important ideological message to the rest of society. Although this need not be the case in all societies, in our society the law's absence devalues women and their functions: women simply are not sufficiently important to merit legal regulation. This message is clearly communicated when particular relief is withheld. By declining to punish a man for inflicting injuries on his wife, for example, the law implies she is his property and he is free to control her as he sees fit. Women's work is discredited when the law refuses to enforce the man's obligation to support his wife, since it implies she makes no contribution worthy of support. Similarly, when courts decline to enforce contracts that seek to limit or specify the extent of the wife's services, the law implies that household work is not real work in the way that the type of work subject to contract in the public sphere is real work. These are important messages, for denying woman's humanity and the value of her traditional work are key ideological components in maintaining woman's subordinate status. The message of women's inferiority is compounded by the totality of the law's absence from the private realm. In our society, law is for business and other important things. The fact that the law in general has so little bearing on women's day-to-day concerns reflects and underscores their insignificance. Thus, the legal order's overall contribution to the devaluation of women is greater than the sum of the negative messages conveyed by individual legal doctrines.

Finally, isolating women in a world where the law refuses to intrude further obscures the discrepancy between women's actual situation and our nominal commitment to equality. Like other collective ideals, the equality norm is expressed predominantly in legal form. Because the law as a whole is removed from women's world, the equality norm is perceived as having very limited application to women. In this way, people are encouraged to favor equality in the public sphere of government and business (e.g., "equal pay for equal work") while denigrating the need for any real change in social roles ("I'm not a woman's libber"). The law can thus purport to guarantee equality while simultaneously denying it.

In short, the law plays a powerful role, though certainly not an exclusive role, in shaping and maintaining women's subordination. The law has operated directly and explicitly to prevent women from attaining self-support and influence in the public sphere, thereby reinforcing their dependence on men. At the same time, its continued absence from the private sphere to which women are relegated not only leaves individual women without formal remedies but also devalues and discredits them as a group.

Acknowledging that the public/private split currently promotes male dominance is very different from suggesting that no division between the public and private is ever acceptable. While the concern that a rigid system of legal rights and wrongs will stifle feelings is a real one, a key aspect of women's present subordinate status is the failure to recognize work now performed in the domestic sphere as a real economic contribution rather than a spontaneous and gratuitous product of emotion. Our limited understanding of patriarchal relations makes it difficult to foresee the precise institutional arrangements, and thus the legal formulations, that will mark the end of male dominance; but it is apparent that the value of "women's work" will have to be acknowledged in a fundamental sense. Much of this work will most likely move out of the home. Consequently, a large portion of the activity that now takes place in the private sphere should come to be governed by law to the same extent as activities already located in the public sphere.

Delineating the extent of human relationships and activities that should ultimately escape collective judgments and prescribing the degree to which the "personal" and the "human" should be reserved to a special private realm is even more difficult. In other areas of the law, it has been argued that there is a continued role for organized institutional political power in the quest for human freedom and that law may enhance, rather than stifle, self-realization.[28] The recognition that immunizing the family realm has thus far reinforced women's identity as man's property and obscured her subordination should spur our efforts to explore this possibility.

LEGAL CONTROLS ON REPRODUCTION AND THE PUBLIC/PRIVATE SPLIT

The relationship between legal controls on reproduction and the public/private split is not a simple one. Until 1965, a number of laws dating from the latter part of the nineteenth century that restricted access, use, and even information about contraception and abortion remained in place at both the state and federal level. In that year, a fragmented Supreme Court struck down as violative of the Constitution Connecticut's ban on use of birth control in the case of *Griswold* v. *Connecticut*.[29] Though no one rationale emerged clearly from the multiple opinions in *Griswold*, subsequent decisions made plain that restrictions on the procreative choice, like other family decisions, ran afoul of a constitutional right of privacy. Important among these was the 1973 *Roe* v. *Wade*;[30] decision, which invalidated a Texas criminal abortion law and spelled out relatively stringent standards for other abortion laws. Over the next decade and a half, with the crucial exception of prohibitions on Medicaid funding, the Court struck down a variety of restrictions on abortion.

In terms of the public/private split, this process of invalidation is complex. On the one hand, the Court responded to the women's movement and other political pressures to allow women to exercise greater autonomy. On the other hand, in so doing it ignored other legal grounds for the decision, which had been offered by women's groups, in favor of a rationale that reaffirmed the public/private split. And over the next sixteen years antiabortion forces mobilized and exerted enormous pressure on the Court to overrule *Roe* v. *Wade*. The impact of these efforts is seen in the 1977 and 1980 decisions upholding restrictions on Medicaid funding for abortions[31] and the changes in Court personnel that have caused the strong pro-choice majority to dwindle.

In July 1989, the Supreme Court decided *Webster* v. *Reproductive Services*,[32] upholding various restrictions on access to abortion imposed by the state of Missouri. While the Court stopped short of reversing *Roe* v. *Wade* outright, the case has been generally understood as a significant retrenchment on constitutional guarantees for abortion rights. The plurality opinion by Chief Justice Rehnquist, with separate concurrences by Justices O'Connor and Scalia, upheld provisions prohibiting the use of public employees, facilities, and public funds to perform or assist any abortion not necessary to save the woman's life and requiring physicians to perform specified tests to determine fetal viability at twenty or more weeks. Two other provisions— the preamble to the law dating the beginning of human life from the moment of conception and a prohibition on the use of public funds, facilities, and employees for encouraging or counseling abortion—were left standing as a majority agreed they were not properly before the Court. Thus, at a minimum, the Court has made clear that at least some governmental interference with women's ability to decide whether and when they will bear children is permissible.

The effect of *Webster* on the public/private split is also complex. It is clear that the law plays an important role in maintaining the public/private split when it denies women reproductive autonomy. As a practical matter, the inability to determine whether or when they will have children combined with the sex-based assignment of childrearing responsibilities has prevented women from participating fully in the public sphere. Women's ability to engage in political life has been constrained, and their work and educational opportunities have been limited.

Moreover, the legal rationale currently relied on for cutting back on the constitutional protection afforded procreative choice itself reflects the notion that women do not belong in the legally protected public sphere. The cutback turns on the argument that only those rights specifically mentioned in the Constitution, the Bill of Rights, and subsequent amendments should be recognized and enforced by the judiciary. In this view, recognition of the abortion right in *Roe* v. *Wade* was an improper, judge-made departure from the Constitution. A particularly extreme version of this argument, the argument from original intent, gained currency during the Reagan period. Under this approach, constitutional protection should be given only those rights of importance to the decision makers at the time the Constitution was drafted or amended. Concerns of importance to those historically excluded from the decision-making process, such as reproductive autonomy, would continue to be denied protection. The state and federal officials using this argument today to defend restrictions on abortion look to the historical record and insist that neither the Founding Fathers nor the framers of the Fourteenth Amendment regarded the right to abortion as fundamental. In so doing, of course, they ignore the inevitable consequence of their approach: to permit those already in the public sphere to limit the ability of others to join them.

Reproductive laws have functioned to maintain the public/private split in the past as well. As 281 historians told the Supreme Court considering *Webster*,[33] abortion was particularly prevalent and visible in the nineteenth century and was not illegal for much of this nation's history. From 1820 to 1860, abortion regulation in the states rejected broader English restrictions and sought to protect women from particularly dangerous forms of abortion. The nineteenth-century movement to regulate abortions, which culminated in the enforcement of restrictive legislation of the 1860s and 1870s, was one chapter in a campaign by "regulars"—the men who ultimately became practitioners and proponents of scientific medicine and who formed the American Medical Association (AMA)—to drive out the frequently female "irregulars."

One important reason the AMA succeeded in its antiabortion efforts was its ability to persuade male political leaders that "abortion constituted a threat to social order and to male authority."[34] The AMA played upon popular fears generated by the nineteenth-century movement for women's suffrage and equality that women were departing from their purely maternal role.

As described by the AMA's Committee on Criminal Abortion, in 1871 [the woman who seeks abortion] becomes unmindful of the course marked out for her by Providence, she overlooks the duties imposed on her by the marriage contract. She yields to the pleasure—but shrinks from the pains and responsibilities of maternity; and, destitute of all delicacy and refinements, resigns herself, body and soul, into the hands of unscrupulous and wicked men. Let not the husband of such a wife flatter himself that he possesses her affection. Nor can she in turn ever merit even the respect of a virtuous husband. She sinks into old age like a withered tree, stripped of its foliage; with the stain of blood upon her soul, she dies without the hand of affection to smooth her pillow.[35]

Denying abortion was thus a way of keeping women in their place.

How, then, do legal controls on reproduction square with the general notion that the absence of law from the private sphere has furthered women's subordination? Developments in the law governing reproduction must obviously be viewed two ways. There is no question that *Webster* and its like authorize legal intrusions into the private sphere and that such intrusions undercut the claim that the private sphere has been characterized by an absence of law. But at the same time, such intrusions must be understood as both a cause and effect of the public/private split. Thus in the reproductive area, unlike other areas, an absence of any state regulation seems to enhance the autonomy of many women. However, collective support will ultimately be necessary to ensure that all women have the resources necessary to effectuate their reproductive choices and enable them to participate fully in all aspects of life. It is difficult to see how such support will be forthcoming so long as reproduction is regarded solely as a matter for the private sphere.

THE LEGAL IDEOLOGY OF SEXUAL INEQUALITY

As we have seen, the law has enforced male dominance through its direct impact on the lives of individual women and men, and its symbolic devaluation of women and their functions. The law has also perpetuated inequality through the articulation of an ideology that camouflages the fundamental injustice of existing sexual relations. Because the law purports to be the embodiment of justice, morality, and fairness, it is particularly effective in performing this ideological function.

Historically, women's subservient status has been associated with a view of differences between the sexes and differential legal treatment. A succession of Supreme Court decisions[36] has legitimized that subservient status by upholding laws which, on their face, mandate that the sexes be treated differently. This section examines the principal doctrinal bases used by the Court by focusing on three illustrative Supreme Court decisions.[37] In an 1873 decision, differences between men and women were expressed in terms of gross overgeneralizations reflecting moral or religious views of women's nature and proper role. The ideology masked women's inferior treatment by glorifying women's separate role. In 1908, the differences focused to a much greater extent on the "facts" of women's physical limitations necessitated by their reproductive functions and their consequent dependence on men. These deficiencies called for special treatment for women to be on an equal footing with men. Present-day ideology is even more subtle. The Supreme Court espouses a concern for sexual equality and purports to reject stereotypical overgeneralizations about the sexes; yet it refuses to recognize classifications based on reproductive capacity as sex-based, and it regards legal and social disabilities that have been imposed on women as realistic differences sufficient to justify differential treatment. By continuing to make differential treatment appear fair, the current Court provides a rationale for present inequalities.

WOMEN'S "SEPARATE SPHERE": BRADWELL V. ILLINOIS

In *Bradwell* v. *Illinois*,[38] the Supreme Court upheld the Illinois Supreme Court's decision to refuse Myra Bradwell admission to the Illinois bar because she was a woman.[39] She studied law under her husband's tutelage; raised four children; ran a private school; was involved in civic work; and founded a weekly newspaper, the *Chicago Legal News*, which became an important legal publication. A feminist active in women's suffrage organizations, Myra Bradwell played an important role in obtaining Illinois legislation that removed women's legal disabilities. She took her case to the Supreme Court, arguing that admission to practice law was guaranteed by the privileges and immunities clause of the recently adopted Fourteenth Amendment.

The *Bradwell* litigation took place within the context of a particular conception of sex roles. Although women were in no way the equals of men during the colonial and Revolutionary periods, the nature of their subordination, particularly in the middle classes, changed dramatically between the end of the eighteenth century and the middle of the nineteenth century.[40] The early stages of industrial capitalism involved increasing specialization and the movement of production out of the home, which resulted in heightened sex segregation. Men went out of the house to work; and women's work, influence, and consciousness remained focused at home. Although women continued to be dependent on and subservient to men, women were no longer placed at the bottom of a hierarchy dominated by men. Rather, they came to occupy women's "separate sphere," a qualitatively different world centered on home and family. Women's role was by definition incompatible with full participation in society.

"Separate-sphere" ideology clearly delineated the activities open to women. Women's role within the home was glorified, and women's limited participation in paid labor outside the home[41] was most often in work that could be considered an extension of their work within the home. For example, native-born mill girls in the 1820s and 1830s, and immigrant women in the 1840s and 1850s, worked in largely sex-segregated factories manufacturing textiles, clothing, and shoes. Likewise, after a period of time, teaching became a woman's occupation. Unpaid charitable and welfare activities, however, were encouraged as consistent with women's domestic responsibilities.

Although ultimately quite constraining, the development of women's separate sphere had some important benefits. While the emphasis on women's moral purity and the cult of domesticity tended to mask women's inferior position, it also allowed women a certain degree of autonomy. It gave them the opportunity to organize extensively into religious and secular welfare associations, afforded access to education, and provided them with a basis for uniting with other women. Evaluations of the cult of domesticity and women's separate sphere by feminist historians have consequently ranged from the view that women were victims of this ideology to the recognition that women found a source of strength and identity in their separate world.[42]

The development of separate-sphere ideology appears in large measure to have been a consequence of changes in the conditions of production. Behavior was then further channeled by a vast cultural transformation promoted through books and magazines. The law does not seem to have played an overt role in the initial articulation of the separate-sphere ideology; but to the extent that the ideological transformation that occurred in the early part of the nineteenth century was a reaction to a strict hierarchy imposed by the previous legal order, the legal system may well have played an important part at the outset.

In any event, the law appears to have contributed significantly to the perpetuation of this ideology. Immediately following the Civil War, feminists attempted to have women expressly included in the protections of the Fourteenth and Fifteenth amendments. The failure of the Fourteenth and Fifteenth amendments to address the needs of women, and indeed for the first time to write the word "men" into the Constitution, resulted in a long-lasting division in the women's movement, which reflected differences regarding both ends and means, and which lasted at least until the 1890s. Feminists aligned with the Republican party stressed black suffrage and saw women suffrage as coming through a constitutional amendment at some future time. The more militant and effective National Woman Suffrage Association favored legal and political efforts to obtain a judicial or congressional declaration that the Wartime Amendments also secured rights for women.[43] Although Myra Bradwell's legal challenge was not known to be part of an organized strategy, her attempt to use the Fourteenth Amendment to challenge state prohibitions on occupational choices legally reflected this tack. By invoking the cult of domesticity as a legal rationale for rejecting this demand, the courts enshrined and reinforced separate-sphere ideology while deferring women's rights.

In rejecting Myra Bradwell's challenge to Illinois's prohibition on occupational choice, the Supreme Court had two options: to construe the new constitutional guarantees narrowly so as to defeat all comers, or to find special reasons for treating women differently. The majority adopted the first approach. It held that the decision was controlled by the Court's decision (the day before) in the *Slaughter-House Cases*,[44] which held that, even after the adoption of the Fourteenth Amendment, states retained the unmediated right to regulate occupations.

However, Justice Joseph Bradley, who dissented in *Slaughter-House*, opted for the second approach. His concurring opinion is the embodiment of the separate-sphere ideology:

> [T]he civil law as well as nature itself, has always recognized a wide difference in the respective spheres and destinies of man and woman. Man is, or should be woman's protector and defender. The natural and proper timidity and delicacy which belongs to the female sex evidently unfits it for many of the occupations of civil life. . . . The constitution of the family organization, which is founded in the divine ordinance, as well as in the nature of things, indicates the domestic sphere as that which properly belongs to the domain and functions of womanhood. The harmony, not to say identity, of interests and views which belong, or should belong, to the family institution is repugnant to the idea of a woman adopting a distinct and independent career from that of her husband. . . .
>
> It is true that many women are unmarried and not affected by any of the duties, complications, and incapacities arising out of the married state, but these are exceptions to the general rule. The paramount destiny and mission of woman are to fulfill the noble and benign offices of wife and mother. This is the law of the Creator. And the rules of civil society must be adapted to the general constitution of things, and cannot be based upon exceptional cases.[45]

Glorification of women's destiny serves to soften any sense of unfairness in excluding women from the legal profession. Since this "paramount destiny and mission" of women is mandated by "nature," "divine ordinance," and "the law of the Creator," the civil law need not recognize the claims of women who deviate from their proper role. By conceiving of the law as the means of enforcing reality as it "is or should be," Bradley can concede that some women do live apart from men—or even that some women who live with men are capable of functioning in the public domain—without exposing the law as unreasonable.

WOMEN'S PHYSICAL DIFFERENCES: *MULLER* v. *OREGON*

In the nineteenth century, the persisting separate-sphere ideology legitimized and reinforced women's marginal and secondary status in the work force. Working women were suspicious, inferior, and immoral. Those women who joined the work force were predominantly single or widowed, and confined to "women's jobs," serving as a reserve supply of cheap labor. The primary identification of women with the home also provided an ideological basis for keeping women out of unions.

With industrialization and urbanization in the late nineteenth century came deplorable work conditions for all workers, which prompted unions and social reformers to press for legislation regulating conditions of work, hours, and wages. By the turn of the century, both sex-neutral and sex-based protective laws had been passed and sustained against legal challenge. Women-only protective laws were enacted with the express support of such reform groups as the National Women's Trade Union League, the General Federation of Women's Clubs, and the National Consumers' League, which merged the energies of wealthy and working women. Although sex-based legislation might have conflicted with suffragists' initial argument that women were entitled to the role because they were fundamentally equal to men, it was entirely consistent with the more expedient position they had adopted in the 1890s, to the effect that women should be given the vote because their special perspective would benefit society.

Protective-labor legislation was countered legally by conservatives who, led by the American Bar Association, revived the natural-law notion of freedom of contract and located it in the due process clause of the Fourteenth Amendment. The effort culminated in *Lochner* v. *New York*,[46] a decision that, in striking down maximum-hour legislation for bakers by relying on the "common understanding" that baking and most other occupations did not endanger health, cast doubt on the validity of all protective legislation.

Advocates of state "protective" legislation for women could take two routes after *Lochner*: one, to displace the "common understanding" in *Lochner* with scientific evidence that all industrial jobs, when performed more than ten hours a day, were dangerous to a worker's health; or two, by arguing that women's need for special protection justified an exception to *Lochner*.[47] In *Muller* v. *Oregon*,[48] the Supreme Court was faced with a challenge to an Oregon statute that prohibited women from working more than ten hours a day in a laundry. The National Consumers' League, which played the major role in the middle- and upper-class reform movement, filed an *amicus* brief, written by Louis Brandeis, Josephine Goldmark, and Florence Kelly,[49] which attempted to combine both approaches. The brief portrayed as common knowledge pseudoscientific data regarding physical differences between men and women, emphasizing the "bad effects" of long hours on women workers' health, "female functions," childbearing capacity, and job safety, and on the health and welfare of future generations. Adopting the view urged by the *amici,* the Court upheld the challenged legislation:

> that woman's physical structure and the performance of maternal functions place her at a disadvantage in the struggle for subsistence is obvious. This is especially true when the burdens of motherhood are upon her. Even when they are not, by abundant testimony of the medical fraternity continuance for a long time on her feet at work, repeating this from day to day, tends to injurious effects upon the body, and as healthy mothers are essential to vigorous offspring, the physical well-being of woman becomes an object of public interest and care in order to preserve the strength and vigor of the race. . . .
>
> Still again history discloses the fact that woman has always been dependent upon man. . . . As minors, though not to the same extent, she has been looked upon in the courts as needing special care that her rights may be preserved. . . . Though limitations upon personal and contractual rights may be removed by legislation, there is that in her disposition and habits of life which will generate against a full assertion of these rights. She will still be where some legislation to protect her seems necessary to secure a real equality of right. . . . Differentiated by these matters from the other sex, she is properly placed in a class by herself, and legislation designed for her protection may be sustained, even when the legislation is not necessary for men and could not be sustained.[50]

Muller expresses a view of women as different from and more limited than men because of their "physical structure" and "natural functions." Although this view of women is every bit as fixed as that expressed in *Bradwell,* it purports to be grounded in physical fact. Legal reforms, such as the removal of "limitations upon personal and contractual rights," would be ineffective in changing women's rights because of women's "disposition and habits of life." These differences in physical structure and childbearing capacity are thus sufficient for women to be "properly placed in a class by themselves." Women's primary function as mother is now seen as physically incompatible with the demands of equal participation in the work force. Special work conditions for women are therefore justified.

Both social reformers and legal realists regarded the statute's survival and the Supreme Court's recognition of economic and social facts as important victories. However, as organized labor lost interest in protective legislation for men, the primary legal legacy of *Muller* was a view of women that justified excluding women from job opportunities and earning levels available to men.[51] The Court's focus on the apparently immutable facts of women's physique obscured the exploitation of workers generally and the social discrimination that assigned full-time responsibility for the household to women. As an ideological matter, the notion that women's different physiology requires special protection continues to legitimize a division of labor in which men are primary wage earners entitled to draw on the personal services of their wives, and women remain marginal workers available to replace more expensive male workers.[52]

UNEQUAL EQUAL PROTECTION: MICHAEL M. v. SONOMA COUNTY

Although Supreme Court opinions of the 1960s began to acknowledge some changes in woman's position,[53] it took the rebirth of an active women's movement in the 1960s and the development of a legal arm to obtain a definitive legal determination that sex-based discrimination violated the equal-protection clause of the Fourteenth Amendment. In 1971, the Supreme Court, in *Reed* v. *Reed*,[54] for the first time invalidated a statute on the ground that it denied women equal protection. The Court unanimously struck down an Idaho statute preferring males to females in the performance of estate administration, refusing to find generalizations about women's business experience adequate to sustain the preference. Although the actual dispute involved a relatively trivial duty, a statute that already had been repealed, and facts that presented no major threat to the established social order, the opinion appeared to voice a view of women that seemed radically different from previous judicial expressions.

Equal protection rests on the legal principle that people who are similarly situated in fact must be similarly treated by the law.[55] In *Reed* the Court for the first time held that women and men are similarly situated. The Court recognized the social reality, through "judicial notice," that "in this country, presumably due to the greater longevity of women, a large proportion of estates . . . are administered by women.[56] By recognizing a departure from traditional social roles as so obvious as to be able to rely on judicial notice, the Court appeared to presage the erosion of the "differences" ideology.

Over the last ten years, in upholding equal-protection challenges to sex-based legislation, the Supreme Court has repeatedly rejected overgeneralizations based on sex.[57] For example, in *Frontiero* v. *Richardson*,[58] the Court upheld an equal-protection challenge to the military's policy of denying dependency benefits to male dependents of female servicewomen. The plurality opinion criticized *Bradwell* as reflective of an attitude of "romantic paternalism" that "in practical effect, put women not on a pedestal but in a cage."[59] Similarly, in *Stanton v. Stanton*,[60] the Court upheld an equal-protection challenge to a state statute specifying a greater age of majority for males than females with respect to parental obligation for support. In so doing, the Court appeared to understand the effect of stereotypes in perpetuating discrimination and the detrimental impact that differential treatment has on women's situation.[61]

However, the Supreme Court's developing application of equal protection has not lived up to its initial promise. The Court has adopted a lower standard of review for sex-based classifications[62] than for race-based classifications, reflecting its view that race discrimination is a more serious social problem than sex discrimination. The Court has rejected only those stereotypes that it perceives as grossly inaccurate. Indeed, the Court has developed a new and more subtle view of "realistically based differences," which encompasses underlying physical distinctions between the sexes, distinctions created by law, and socially imposed differences in situation, and frequently confuses the three. In these cases, the Court simply reasons that equal protection is not violated because men and women are not "similarly situated."

The paradigmatic physical distinction between the sexes, women's reproductive capacity, has been consistently viewed by courts as a proper basis for differential treatment. The present Court does so by refusing to recognize that classifications based on pregnancy involve sex discrimination and by ignoring the similarities between pregnancy and other temporary disabilities. In *Geduldig v. Aiello*,[63] the Supreme Court rejected an equal-protection challenge to California's disability insurance system, which paid benefits to persons in private employment who were unable to work but excluded from coverage disabilities resulting from pregnancy. The Court noted that

> [w]hile it is true that only women become pregnant, it does not follow that every legislative classification concerning pregnancy is a sex-based classification like those considered in *Reed, supra* and *Frontiero, supra*. Normal pregnancy is an objectively identifiable physical condition with unique characteristics. Absent a showing that distinctions involving pregnancy are mere pretexts designed to effect an invidious discrimination against the members of one sex or the other, lawmakers are constitutionally free to include or exclude pregnancy from the coverage of legislation such as this on any reasonable basis, just as with respect to any other physical condition.[64]

This position was effectively reaffirmed in *General Electric v. Gilbert*,[65] in which the exclusion of pregnancy from General Electric's disability program was upheld in the face of a challenge under Title VII of the Civil Rights Act.

Similarly, the present Court finds differential treatment justified by women's special circumstances, even when those circumstances reflect legislatively[66] or socially imposed burdens.[67] In *Parham* v. *Hughes*,[68] a plurality of the Court upheld a Georgia statute that allowed an unwed mother to sue for the wrongful death of her child, but disallowed such suits by an unwed father unless he had procured a court order legitimating the child. The Court found that treating men and women differently in this fashion did not constitute impermissible sex discrimination because the two sets of parents were not similarly situated in two respects. First, under Georgia law, unwed fathers, but not unwed mothers, could legitimate their children by a unilateral act. This difference is, of course, imposed by law, not by biological necessity. Second, the Court pointed to the difficulty in ascertaining the father's identity. Here the difference in situation results primarily from socially imposed differences in childrearing patterns, since, as a physiological matter, unless the woman is observed giving birth, there is little reason to put more faith in a woman's claim to be a particular child's parent than in a man's claim to be that child's parent. The Court's reliance on these societally imposed differences reflects its present willingness to uphold distinctions that are generally accurate though unfair to individuals and likely to perpetuate existing sex roles.

The most recent expression of the Court's current ideology of equality is a 1981 Supreme Court case, *Michael M.* v. *Sonoma County*,[69] upholding California's statutory rape law, challenged by a seventeen-year-old male, which punished males having sex with a female under eighteen. The thrust of his attack on the statute was that it denied him equal protection since he, not his partner, was criminally liable.

Statutory rape laws have rested historically on the legal fiction that young women are incapable of consent. They exalt female chastity and reflect and reinforce archaic assumptions about the male initiative in sexual relations and the weakness and naïveté of young women.[70] Nevertheless, the Court in *Michael M.* found no violation of equal-protection guarantees and upheld the differential treatment as reasonably related to the goal of eliminating teenage pregnancy.

Although the Court in *Michael M.* cited its prior decisions rejecting sex-based classifications without proof of a "substantial relationship" to "important governmental objectives," it did not, in fact, apply them. No legislative history was produced in California or elsewhere to show that the purpose of the sex-based classification was to eliminate teenage pregnancy. Moreover, the experience of other jurisdictions showed that the criminalization of male, but not female, conduct bore little relation to the goal of eliminating teenage pregnancy. Instead, the Court simply stated that because females become pregnant and because they bear the consequences of pregnancy, "equalization" via differential punishment is reasonable.

> We need not be medical doctors to discern that young men and young women are not similarly situated with respect to the problems and risks of sexual intercourse. Only women may become pregnant and they suffer disproportionately the profound physical, emotional and psychological consequences of sexual activity.[71]

Thus, the Court asserts, the sex-based classification, which "serves roughly to 'equalize' the deterrents on the sexes,"[72] realistically reflects the fact that the sexes are not similarly situated.

Justice Potter Stewart's concurring opinion in *Michael M.* develops the crux of this new ideology of realistically based classifications:

> The Constitution is violated when government, state or federal, invidiously classifies similarly situated people on the basis of the immutable characteristic with which they were born. . . . [W]hile detrimental gender classifications by government often violate the Constitution, they do not always do so, for the reason that there are differences between males and females that the Constitution necessarily recognizes. In this case we deal with the most basic of these differences: females can become pregnant as the result of sexual intercourse; males cannot. . . .
>
> "[A] State is not free to make overbroad generalizations based on sex which are entirely unrelated to any differences between men and women or which demean the ability or social status of the protected class." Gender-based classifications may not be based upon administrative convenience or upon archaic assumptions about the proper role of the sexes. . . . But we have recognized that in certain narrow circumstances men and women are *not* similarly situated and in these circumstances a gender classification based on clear differences between the sexes is not invidious, and a legislative classification realistically based upon these differences is not unconstitutional. . . .
>
> Applying these principles to the classification enacted by the California legislature, it is readily apparent that [the statute] does not violate the Equal Protection Clause. Young women and men are not similarly situated with respect to the problems and risks associated with intercourse and pregnancy, and the statute is realistically related to the legitimate state purpose of reducing those problems and risks.[73]

Yet, the classification at issue in *Michael M.* had very little to do with biological differences between the sexes. As is seen from the total absence of supportive legislative history, the statute was not designed to address the problem of teenage pregnancy. Moreover, as Justice John Paul Stevens points out, if criminal sanctions are believed to deter the conduct leading to pregnancy, a young woman's greater risk of harm from pregnancy is, if anything, a reason to subject her to sanctions. The statute instead embodies and reinforces the assumption that men are always responsible for initiating sexual intercourse and females must always be protected against their aggression. Nevertheless, the Court's focus on the physical fact of reproductive capacity serves to obscure the social bases of its decision. Indeed, it is striking that the Court entirely fails to treat pregnancy as sex discrimination when discrimination really is in issue, while using it as a rationale in order to justify differential treatment when it is not in issue.

Like *Bradwell* and *Muller, Michael M.* affirms that there are differences between the sexes, both the physical difference of childbearing capacity and women's social role, which should result in differential legal treatment. However, because this affirmation comes at the same time as the Court claims to reject "overbroad generalizations unrelated to differences between men and women or which demean [women's] ability or social status," the Court's approval of differential treatment is especially pernicious. The fact of and harms caused by teenage pregnancy are used by the Court to avoid close analysis of the stereotypes involved and careful scrutiny of the pregnancy rationale. The role that the challenged statute plays in reinforcing those harms is never examined. The Court accepts as immutable fact that men and women are not similarly situated, particularly when pregnancy is involved. The Court then appears to favor equal rights for women, but for one small problem—pregnancy.

As an ideological matter, the separation of pregnancy and childbearing capacity, social discrimination, and even legally imposed discrimination from "invidious" discrimination, in which differential treatment is unrelated to "real" differences between men and women, perform an important function of legitimizing discrimination through the language of equality.[74] Although its doctrinal veneer is different, the Court's current approach has the same effect as *Bradwell* and *Muller.* If both pregnancy and socially imposed differences in role always keep men and women from being similarly situated— thereby excluding sex-based differences from the purview of equal protection—then the real substance of sex discrimination can still be ignored. Childbearing capacity is the single greatest basis of differential treatment for women—it is a major source of discrimination in both work and family life, and the critical distinction on which the ideology of both separate spheres and physical differences rests. Yet, by appearing to reject gross generalizations about proper roles of the sexes exemplified by both *Bradwell* and *Muller*, current ideology attempts to maintain credibility by "holding out the promise of liberation."[75] By emphasizing its reliance on a reality that appears more closely tied to physical differences and the hard facts of social disadvantage, e.g., the consequences of teenage pregnancy for young girls, the Court appears sensible and compromising. Indeed, the message of the Court's approach is merely to reject "ultra feminist" androgyny while favoring equality generally. However, by excluding the core of sex discrimination, the Court is effectively removing women entirely from the reach of equal protection.

This new ideological approach must be viewed, as were *Bradwell* and *Muller*, in its historical context. Although the women's movement provided the triggering change in consciousness, and an understanding of the nature and forms of sex stereotyping on which the sex-discrimination challenges of this period have been based,[76] many of the sex-discrimination cases decided by the Supreme Court have not arisen from feminist struggles and have been presented to the Court by men, not women. As a result, these cases, including *Michael M.*, did not always develop the harm perceived by women for the Court, either as a factual or legal matter. Moreover, in the absence of a sustained mass movement, the Supreme Court has been able to use feminist formulations to justify the status quo. During much of the 1980s, with the advent of a visible right-wing, antifeminist, and antiabortion movement, the women's movement appeared to be losing public support. Indeed, the strategy of these conservative groups to separate immediate claims for parity, such as equal pay, from more fundamental demands relating to the necessary conditions for real equality, such as the Equal Rights Amendment and reproductive control, seemed successful in reinforcing a tendency of some within the women's movement to separate reproduction from other sex discrimination issues.[77] The Court's new approach tends to strengthen this separation of issues within the women's movement and reward the most conservative tendencies. The political activism and public support for reproductive choice sparked by the *Webster* decision seem to reflect a clearer understanding of the critical relationship between reproductive control and equality, and it will be interesting to see how the Court responds.

Although the legal ideology of equality shows some progression from *Bradwell* to *Michael M.*, there is less than might be expected. Certainly the Court's view of women, and the ways in which it sees the sexes, has moved from an overt view of women's separate roles to a more subtle view of limited differences, but this new view is more dangerous precisely because it appears so reasonable. The Court's perception of differences that suffice to justify discrimination has altered somewhat, but it remains equally fixed. The Court continues to validate inequality by legitimizing differential treatment.

NOTES

1. As David Kairys explains in the Introduction to this book, American legal doctrine distinguishes sharply between the public and the private sectors. Focusing on the question of governmental versus private control, the distinction plays an important role in disguising the very limited nature of the rights afforded people in general. A distinction between public and private spheres also characterizes the law relating to women, but in this context "public" has a much broader and "private" a much narrower meaning. "Public" refers to governmental and market matters, while "private" refers to the domestic or family realm.

2. There is some evidence that during colonial times, when the household was the unit of production, the law intervened more directly in the home. Thus, it may be more appropriate to speak of the law's withdrawal rather than its absence from the domestic sphere.

3. This section draws heavily on Kathryn Powers's article "Sex Segregation and the Ambivalent Directions of Sex Discrimination Law," 1979 *Wisconsin Law Review* 55 (1979).

4. Eleanor Flexner, *A Century of Struggle*, rev. ed. (Cambridge, Mass.: Harvard University Press, 1975).

5. Hoyt v. Florida, 368 U.S. 57, 61 (1961). In Taylor v. Louisiana, 419 U.S. 522 (1975), a case involving a male rape defendant, the Supreme Court tacitly overruled *Hoyt* but avoided the question of equal protection for women, relying instead on the defendant's Sixth Amendment right to a fair trial.

6. 10 U.S.C. §6015; 10 U.S.C. §8549 (Navy and Air Force). The Army and Marine Corps preclude the role of women in combat as a matter of established policy; Rostker v. Goldberg, 101 S. Ct. 2646, 2657 (1981) (upholding the all-male draft registration scheme).

7. *Id.*

8. There is a dispute as to whether women's actual status during the colonial period corresponded to the position accorded them by law. Initial research suggested that women were able, as a practical matter, to function as managers, traders, artisans, and even attorneys. Thus, despite their exclusion from formal political processes, they were granted a basic and integral, though subservient, role in the community. The same research suggested that women's position declined with the growth of commercial capitalism and specialization. Subsequent research, however, argues that women's crucial economic role failed to translate into power and influence, and that sex roles were far more rigidly defined than had been thought. *Cf.* Mary Ryan, *Womanhood in America*, 2d ed. (New York: New Viewpoints, 1979) and Albie Sachs and Joan Hoff Wilson, *Sexism and the Law* (New York: The Free Press, 1978) *with* Mary Beth Norton, *Liberty's Daughters: The Revolutionary Experience of American Women* (Boston: Little, Brown, 1980).

9. By 1978, 56 percent of all women over sixteen worked at least part of the year, while in 1950 the figure was below 30 percent. Excluding farm workers, before 1900 less than 20 percent of all women were in the paid labor force. Alice Kessler-Harris, *Women Have Always Worked: A Historical Overview* (Old Westbury, N.Y.: The Feminist Press, 1981), pp. 70, 147.

10. *See, e.g.*, the discussion of Myra Bradwell's exclusion from the Illinois bar, and of protective legislation, *infra*.

11. The Equal Pay Act of 1963 and Title VII of the Civil Rights Act of 1964 provided civil remedies for employment discrimination, while private discrimination in the housing and credit markets was prohibited in 1974.

12. *See* Dothard v. Rawlinson, 433 U.S. 321, 336 (1977). *See also* Phillips v. Martin Marietta Corp., 400 U.S. 542 (1971), suggesting that a company could legally deny jobs to women with preschool children if it could show that such children interfered more with female workers as a group than with male workers as a group.

13. *See* Vorchheimer v. School District of Philadelphia, 430 U.S. 703 (1977) (affirmed by an equally divided court). By contrast, the doctrine of separate but equal was rejected in the racial context in 1954. *See* Brown v. Board of Education, 347 U.S. 483 (1954).

14. *See, e.g.*, Weinberger v. Wiesenfeld, 420 U.S. 636 (1975); Califano v. Goldfarb, 430 U.S. 199 (1977); Califano v. Westcott, 443 U.S. 76 (1979).

15. *See* Barbara A. Babcock et al., *Sex Discrimination and the Law: Causes and Remedies* (Boston: Little, Brown, 1975), pp. 782–800.

16. United States v. Nicholas, 97 F.2d 510 (2d Cir. 1938); *see generally*, Linda Gordon, *Woman's Body, Woman's Right* (New York: Penguin Books, 1977).

17. Griswold v. Connecticut, 381 U.S. 479 (1965).

18. Eisenstadt v. Baird, 405 U.S. 438 (1972).

19. Roe v. Wade, 410 U.S. 113 (1973).

20. *Id.*; Doe v. Bolton, 410 U.S. 179 (1973).

21. Maher v. Roe, 432 U.S. 464 (1977); H. L. v. Matheson, 450 U.S. 398 (1981).

22. Webster v. Reproductive Services, 109 S. Ct. 3040 (1989).

23. *See* note 11 *supra*. On the federal level, for example, discrimination on the basis of race but not sex is forbidden by the Civil Rights Act of 1964.

24. *See* Powers, *supra* note 3, at 76, for a similar analogy.

25. Recent limitations on interspousal immunity may be due in part to the recognition of the role played by insurance, a factor that removes the situation from the private sphere and places it in the public realm.

26. The law's absence from the realm of personal relationships is even more conspicuous when the relationships lack official sanction. Lesbians, for example, are not barred from relief by intrafamily immunity doctrines only because the law does not allow them to solemnize or otherwise gain public recognition of their relationship.

27. Lisa Lerman, "Mediation of Wife-Abuse Cases: The Adverse Impact of

Mediation on Women," 7 *Harvard Women's Law Journal* 57, 58 (1984) (citing Frank Sander).

28. *See* in particular chapter 3.
29. 381 U.S. 479 (1965).
30. 410 U.S. 113 (1973).
31. Maher v. Roe, 432 U.S. 464 (1977); Harris v. McCrae, 448 U.S. 297 (1980).
32. 109 S.Ct. 3040 (1989).
33. Brief of 281 American Historians as Amici Curiae Supporting Appellees in Webster v. Reproductive Services.
34. Carol Smith-Rosenberg, *Disorderly Conduct* (New York: Alfred A. Knopf, 1985), p. 235.
35. Brief of 281 Historians, *supra* note 33.
36. The Supreme Court is by no means the exclusive source of legal ideology. Indeed, it is arguable that in the area of women's rights, Supreme Court opinions are not the best or most accurate source of prevailing views of women, since few Supreme Court cases prior to 1970 involved assertions of equal rights by women.
37. Much of the material regarding the first two cases has been drawn from Babcock et al., *supra* note 15.
38. Bradwell v. Illinois, 83 U.S. (16 Wall.) 130 (1873).
39. Arabella Mansfield, in Iowa, had become the first woman regularly admitted to practice law in the United States in 1869.
40. *See* Ryan, *supra* note 8; Nancy F. Cott, *The Bonds of Womanhood* (New Haven: Yale University Press, 1977); Kessler-Harris, *supra* note 9.
41. Only about 10 percent of all women worked in the paid labor force in the mid-1840s. The percentage did not rise above 20 percent before 1900. Kessler-Harris, *supra* note 9, at 61, 70.
42. *See* Cott, *supra* note 40, pp. 197–99.
43. *See generally*, Ellen C. DuBois, *Elizabeth Cady Stanton and Susan B. Anthony: Correspondence, Writings and Speeches* (New York: Schocken, 1981).
44. 83 U.S. (16 Wall.) 130 (1873).
45. *Id.* at 141–42.
46. Lochner v. New York, 198 U.S. 45 (1905).
47. Babcock et al., *supra* note 15, at 28.
48. Muller v. Oregon, 208 U.S. 412 (1908).
49. This brief has mistakenly come to be known as the first Brandeis brief, since Louis Brandeis actually filed it, although Josephine Goldmark, Florence Kelly, and other volunteers assembled the data. Babcock et al., *supra* note 15, at 29.
50. Muller v. Oregon, 208 U.S. at 421–22.
51. Sex-based protective legislation was considered valid until a series of court decisions between 1968 and 1973 invalidated such statutes. A few statutes, however, remain on the books today.

52. *See* Heidi Hartmann, "Capitalism, Patriarchy and Job Segregation by Sex," 1 *SIGNS* 137 (1976).
53. *See, e.g.,* Hoyt v. Florida, 368 U.S. 57 (1961).
54. Reed v. Reed, 404 U.S. 71 (1971).
55. *See generally,* Joseph Tussman and Jacobus TenBroek, "The Equal Protection of the Laws," 37 *California Law Review* 341 (1949).
56. Reed v. Reed, 404 U.S. at 75.
57. Most of these cases have involved assumptions built into government benefit statutes that the male was the breadwinner and the female the dependent at home. *See* Frontiero v. Richardson, 411 U.S. 677 (1973); Weinberger v. Wiesenfeld, 420 U.S. 636 (1975); Califano v. Goldfarb, 430 U.S. 199 (1977); and Califano v. Westcott, 443 U.S. 76 (1979).
58. Frontiero v. Richardson, 411 U.S. 677 (1973).
59. *Id.* at 684.
60. Stanton v. Stanton, 421 U.S. 7 (1975).
61. *Id.* at 14–15.
62. In Craig v. Boren, 429 U.S. 190, 197 (1976), the Court articulated the standard that "to withstand constitutional challenge, . . . classifications by gender must serve important governmental objectives and must be substantially related to achievement of those objectives."
63. Geduldig v. Aiello, 417 U.S. 484 (1974).
64. *Id.* at 496, n. 20.
65. General Electric v. Gilbert, 429 U.S. 125 (1976). The Supreme Court's view of pregnancy expressed in *Gilbert* was promptly rejected by Congress. The Pregnancy Discrimination Act, 26 U.S.C. §3304(a) (12) (1976), was passed by Congress to overturn the *Gilbert* decision. This suggests that the Supreme Court's ideology concerning pregnancy as a permissible basis for differential treatment in employment was not widely accepted. It underscores the tenuousness of relying on Supreme Court opinions as a source of prevailing views on women. *See supra* note 36.
66. *E.g.,* in both Schlesinger v. Ballard, 419 U.S. 498 (1975), and Rostker v. Goldberg, 453 U.S. 57 (1981), the Supreme Court rejected equal-protection challenges to sex discrimination in the military on the grounds that since sex-based differential treatment already existed in the military, men and women were not "similarly situated" to begin with. In *Rostker,* the Court particularly emphasized that since the perpetuation of this differential treatment was fully considered by Congress and not "unthinking," it was permissible. *Supra* at 2655.
67. Ironically, despite his actual vote, Justice Potter Stewart's dissent in Caban v. Mohammed, 441 U.S. 380, 398 (1979), at least gives lip service to the need to differentiate between inherent physical differences and societally imposed differences in roles.
68. Parham v. Hughes, 441 U.S. 347 (1979).
69. Michael M. v. Sonoma County, 450 U.S. 464 (1981).
70. Note, "The Constitutionality of Statutory Rape Laws," 27 *UCLA Law*

Review 757, 761 (1980); Michael M. v. Sonoma County, 159 Cal. 3d 340, 601 P.2d 572 (1979); (Mosk, J., dissenting). Leigh Bienen, "Rape III: National Developments in Rape Reform Legislation," 6 *Women's Rights Law Reporter* 170, 189 (1981). However, as Bienen points out, the women's movement has sometimes been ambivalent as to whether these laws helped or hurt women. Bienen, *supra* at 180.

71. Michael M. v. Sonoma County, 450 U.S. at 471.

72. *Id.* at 473.

73. *Id.* at 477–79.

74. *See* in particular, chapter 6; Alan Freeman, "Legitimizing Racial Discrimination Through Antidiscrimination Law: A Critical Review of Supreme Court Doctrine," 62 *Minnesota Law Review* 1050 (1978).

75. *Id.* at 1052.

76. Indeed, feminist legal strategies are still evolving. For a thorough presentation of the principle that each person is entitled to equal treatment based on equal performance without regard to sex, *see* Barbara Brown et al., "The Equal Rights Amendment: A Constitutional Basis for Equal Rights for Women," 80 *Yale Law Journal* 871 (1971). Concern that the equal-rights approach allows a few exceptional women to satisfy the criteria for success and thus escape subordination while their individual success serves to justify the reality that most women remain in an inferior position has been expressed in Powers, *supra* note 3; Catherine MacKinnon, *Sexual Harassment of Working Women: A Case of Sex Discrimination* (New Haven: Yale University Press, 1979); and Ann E. Freedman, "Housework, Childcare and the Limits of Equality Theory" (Paper presented at the Critical Legal Studies Conference, Minneapolis, Minnesota, May 1981). For a discussion of alternate formulations, see these sources and Nadine Taub, Book Review, 80 *Columbia Law Review* 1686 (1980).

77. *See* Mary Dunlap, "Harris v. McRae," 6 *Women's Rights Law Reporter* 165 (1981).

RHONDA COPELON

A CRIME NOT FIT TO BE NAMED: SEX, LIES, AND THE CONSTITUTION

A STORY

ALTHOUGH he entered the overwhelming world of law school wanting, like everyone else, not to be scrutinized, Rob was—almost immediately. It began with appearance: he wore glasses with rather bold black frames, and earrings; he didn't dress jock. There was his manner: he was a bit too aloof from the carousing of some of the younger men. After a while, there were his words: in class discussion about discrimination, Rob risked noting the failure to mention lesbians and gays. Then the questions began: "Why do you wear earrings? Does that signal you're available for sex? Are you gay? Do you like gay bars? Why won't you answer our questions?" Their own motives and unease unacknowledged, some claimed that the questions were an attempt to make Rob feel comfortable. One student, purporting to reassure, told him, "I don't like gays, but I don't let it affect the way I treat them."

The discomfort was unbearable. Rob exchanged his bold black frames for ordinary wire rims. But he was isolated. A faculty member to whom Rob turned told him, "Unpopularity is the price we pay for our politics." To Rob, the price he was paying for his life was hate. He tried to take it on. He put up a sign—"Heterosexism Can Be Cured." It was torn down. To some, this confirmed he had only gotten what he deserved; he had insulted heterosexuality. Nobody was responsible, except Rob. In lawyerly fashion,

I wish to thank Nan Feyler, Dorothy McCarick, David Nadvorney, Sharon Thompson, and David Kairys for their comments, Laurie Beck for her insightful research, and writer Maureen McCafferty for transforming my prosaic version of the "story" into pointed prose.

some began to defend: the First Amendment protects even offensive speech. But they missed the point. The harassment—the hate—was largely unseen and uncriticized. Few defended his right to respect, or to peace.

The semester ended, and, shaken, Rob traveled home. One night someone never to be known or confronted trashed Rob's desk. Half the student body met to protest, while others blamed Rob for disrupting their studies. Doubt was expressed that this was a homophobic act. A few people suggested that maybe Rob did it.

Rob's story is a stigma contest which pits the power of the stigmatizer against the resistance of the stigmatized.[1] It typifies the dynamic of deviance creation, and particularly, of homophobic harassment. Gay men, lesbians, and bisexuals may choose to be "out," or they may wish not to self-identify and yet will not or cannot bury their self sufficiently to escape notice. Attention is drawn to culturally determined indicators of "otherness"—dress, joviality, manner, and the mention of gay and lesbian concerns. By violating the "norm," the gay person threatens the conventions of gender identity, the boundaries of gendered sexuality, and heterosexuality itself. One becomes an object of curiosity and of derision, the cause, rather than the victim, of division and distraction. Harassment helps to consolidate the righteousness of the threatened majority; their prejudice is exalted, but never examined. The homophobia that underlies feelings, reactions, words, and even assault is trivialized and denied. The harassers draw power from the discomfort and, ultimately, the silent complicity of others, the very fear of the word. The only alternatives are retreat or resistance; the only safety rests in support.

Lawsuits, too, are stigma contests, and the judicial opinions they generate are stories. Civil rights suits challenge exclusion and stigmatization, both practically and symbolically. Lesbian and gay rights advocates challenge homophobia and heterosexism[2] and the multitude of harms these processes wreak. Judges bring to the resolution of these claims a deep and often unrecognized homophobia that leads to a similar, albeit more subtle, process by which norms are reinforced and variety is stigmatized.

This essay is about the way the judiciary resolves the stigma contest over sexual orientation, and, in so doing, reveals the societal tension between bigotry, tolerance, and affirmation. The focus here is on several leading privacy decisions both because they provide an essential text on homophobia and because they demonstrate some of the pitfalls of seeking liberation through the liberal concept of negative rights.[3]

> . . . the question is more akin to whether those suffering from measles
> have a constitutional right, in violation of quarantine regulations, to as-
> sociate together and with others who do not presently have measles . . .
> —Chief Justice William Rehnquist[4]

To compare homosexuality and contagious disease, as the Chief Justice did in a 1978 opinion, is quintessential homophobia. If a "disease," homosexuality is, according to the dictionary, an "impairment of the normal state of the living animal," a "disorder or derangement," an "alteration that impairs the quality of a product." To be labeled diseased is to be inferior and to evoke revulsion, avoidance, anger, and pity. But the notion that homosexuality might be "contagious"—"communicable by contact," "spreading," "catching," and, tellingly, "exciting similar emotions or conduct in others"[5]—challenges the norm of dichotomized gender identity and the superiority of heterosexuality itself, and calls for the sternest measures. First to contain sin, then to contain sickness, Western society has, at different times, branded and hanged sodomites, burned witches, jailed "deviants," and tortured gays and lesbians with shock treatment and behavior modification.[6] The imposition of such punishments does not aim to rout out all the "wrongdoers," however; draconian measures create stigma, stereotypes, marginalization, invisibility, and denial.

Whether caught in the sting of church, state, or medical enforcement, or in the oppressive but also subversive refuge of secrecy and dissemblance, gay women and men have braved enormous odds simply to love, to share pleasure, to survive, and to resist. In the last twenty years this resistance has burst into the open. Nurtured by the underground societies of the 1950s, the experience of the civil rights movement, and the courage of thousands of "comings-out," the lesbian and gay movement of our time embraces open, collective, and multifaceted resistance to antigay measures and practices as well as to the invisibility and degradation they entrain.[7]

In the courts, the movement launched a multifaceted attack, a centerpiece of which was the challenge to the criminal sodomy laws, for the criminalization of gay sexuality is a cornerstone of the legal and societal oppression of gay people. With the caution that judicial confrontations are but a small part of broader conflict over homophobia in everyday life, the focus here is primarily on the 1986 decision of the Supreme Court in *Bowers* v. *Hardwick*,[8] the case in which the Court answered, for the nonce, the fundamental question whether gay people have a protected right or a contagious disease. A majority of five ruled that the constitutional right of privacy provided no protection, and, in doing so, upheld the criminalization of sodomy, the symbolic quarantine of gays and lesbians. Some lesbians and gay men are likely to be jailed as a result of the *Hardwick* decision. But even more terrible is the fact that it gives constitutional approval to the criminalization of gay love and sex; brands lesbian, gay, and bisexual people as evil or sick; threatens their right to hold on to their children and jobs, and to obtain housing and benefits; legitimizes violence and degradation; and denies the very right to be.

The majority position in *Hardwick* operates as "law," but it was the product of a deeply divided Court. Four justices joined in a landmark dissent recognizing that the right to choose one's intimate relationships is central to authenticity and self-realization. Justice Blackmun, who only eight years earlier had wondered with Chief Justice Rehnquist whether homosexuality was a contagious disease, wrote that dissent. *Hardwick* reflects not only the power of the majoritarian norm of heterosexuality but also the strength of the lesbian/gay movement both in the fear that threads the majority decisions approving criminalization and in the sharp split on the Court for which the movement can claim substantial credit.

Michael Hardwick seemed to present the perfect "test" case. He was in his bedroom having oral sex with a man when he was interrupted by a police officer who had come to his house purportedly to serve him a summons for a traffic violation and was unwittingly let in by Hardwick's roommate. Ordered to dress under the scrutiny of the officer and then held for ten hours in the local jail, Hardwick and his partner were charged under the Georgia statute which makes sodomy—"any sexual act involving the sex organs of one person and the mouth or anus of another"—a felony punishable by a term of one to twenty years. Though he was never formally charged, Hardwick brought a civil rights action challenging the law, and the lower court agreed with his claim that it violated the constitutional right of privacy. The only question before the Supreme Court in the *Hardwick* case was whether gay sex should be protected within the right of privacy.

There were many ways for the Court to have recognized a right of privacy in this case. It could have emphasized the geographical location of Hardwick's arrest as a paradigmatic example of privacy, compatible at least to the use of obscenity in the home which drew constitutional protection in *Stanley v. Georgia*.[9] It could have used the facts of this case to deplore the horrors of invading the bedroom, as it did in *Griswold v. Connecticut*,[10] which invalidated prohibitions on contraceptive use as an invasion of marital intimacy. It could have recognized that sheltered sexual activity and the intimacy of association involved is akin to the values underlying the recognition of privacy in the contraception and abortion cases.[11] To do this, however, the Court would have had to acknowledge something it consistently avoided in those cases—that the protection of procreative choice is inextricable from recognition of the right to sexual pleasure independent of reproduction or marriage.

The majority refused all these routes. And while it claimed to do so as an exercise of judicial restraint, its reasoning is an example of homophobic excess. The majority decision, written by Justice White, explicitly disclaims at the outset to have any position on the wisdom of criminal sodomy laws or the propriety of legislative repeal. White argues that he is only declining to recognize rights for which there is no explicit textual support and, thereby, preserving the proper relationship between the Court and the legislatures. But White does not usually subscribe to the originalist school of interpretation which sacralizes the Founding Fathers and the text of the Constitution as the fount of wisdom.[12] Although some form of originalism, which would resurrect the patriarchal value system that dominated the eighteenth and nineteenth centuries, is nearly dominant on the Court with the addition of Justices Scalia and Kennedy, *Hardwick* is not simply a product of its growing ascendance. Because White supports the contraception decisions and abhors the abortion decisions, and because Justice Powell, the swing vote in *Hardwick*, supported them both, the task of the majority was to draw lines. The invocation of judicial restraint is but a thin veil for the condemnation of gay and lesbian sexuality; it is homophobia, not jurisprudence, that drives the majority's analysis.

The majority's negative characterization of the right at stake is the first indication of homophobia. Rather than fairly describing Hardwick's claim to a right of privacy encompassing sexual choices or intimate association, White characterizes Hardwick's claim as a "right to engage in homosexual sodomy" or as a "claimed constitutional right of homosexuals to engage in acts of sodomy."[13] The term "sodomy" is, of course, a shocker, an explicit reference to the unredeemable evil of Sodom and Gomorrah.[14] The term "homosexual"—a phrase developed by doctors and sexologists to describe an unfortunate condition—rather than "gay" or "lesbian," positive terms originating in the community, signals discomfort, social distance, and judgment.[15] Finally, by using the terms "acts of sodomy," legal terminology common to criminal indictments and suggestive of harm or nonconsent, the majority denies the possibility that gay sex might be fluid and loving.

This implicit equation of gay sexuality with evil and danger underpins White's rejection of Hardwick's argument that the protection previously recognized by the Court for marriage, procreation, and family relationships logically extends to sexual intimacy. To deny this claim would seem to require some explanation. Instead, White baldly asserts that there is no "resemblance" or "connection between family, marriage, or procreation on the one hand and homosexual activity on the other.[16] The gay person is served up as a creature apart, and gay intimacy is treated as unrelated to heterosexual intimacy whether it be a one-night stand or a lasting relationship.

The danger of gay sexuality is also underscored by the Court's rejection of the claim that gay sex, like obscenity, should at least be protected in the home. Although obscenity is sexually explicit material which is unprotected by the First Amendment, and, therefore, subject to criminal sanction, *Stanley* v. *Georgia* protected it because it was found in the home. Nonetheless, the *Hardwick* majority reinterpreted *Stanley* as a First Amendment decision, distinguishing sexual speech from sexual conduct (and ignoring that sexual conduct often accompanies the use of sexually explicit materials in the home). It emphasized that the home does not confer immunity for criminal conduct, comparing gay sex first to drugs, firearms, and stolen goods and then to adultery, incest, and bigamy.[17] In so doing, the Court evoked images of dissolution, fear, seizure, and instability.

The confusion between consensual sodomy and nonconsensual, exploitative sexuality such as incest echoes the stereotypical fear of gay men as predators and child molesters, even though the incidence of child molestation and sexual harassment is disproportionately committed by heterosexual males. The analogy to adultery reflects fears that gay sexuality challenges the traditional monogamous heterosexual family. By contrast, Justice Blackmun excoriates the majority's choice of analogies and its failure to explain why it did not use nonthreatening analogies such as private, consensual heterosexual activity or even sodomy within marriage for comparison.[18] While for feminists the notion of privacy in the home has been fraught with danger, as is the ambiguity of consent in the domestic or sexual sphere,[19] the kind of privacy claimed in *Hardwick*—the right of sexual self-determination—is precisely that which has been legally denied to women and gay people.

Thus in rejecting Michael Hardwick's claim that his constitutional right of privacy was infringed, the majority advances, mostly by implication, its view of gay sexuality as unrelated to recognized forms of sexual activity or intimate relationship, and as exploitative, predatory, threatening to personal and social stability. In so doing, it echoes the stereotypes at the heart of homophobia—the portrayal of gay people as dangerous as well as subhuman "others."

Although professing fidelity to legislative intent, Justice White had to do some fancy footwork to confine the case to one involving only "homosexual sodomy." The Georgia statute under which Michael Hardwick was arrested is gender-neutral; it prohibits all sodomy—heterosexual as well as same-sex. Hardwick was challenging the constitutionality of the entire statute—the criminalization of oral and anal sex for both heterosexuals (including the married) and gays and lesbians. By limiting the case to "homosexual sodomy," the Court read into the Georgia statute a special and separable condemnation of gay sex never intended by the legislature.

Moreover, like the Georgia statute at issue in *Hardwick*, most proscriptions on sodomy were not gender-based. In the thirteen colonies, only three singled out sodomy between men, and two had no prohibitions at all. In 1868, when the Fourteenth Amendment was ratified, there were still only three states that had singled out same-sex sodomy. Most statutes only applied to anal intercourse, whether homosexual or heterosexual; and thirty-two states excluded oral sex from their prohibitions until the last decade of the nineteenth century. The object of these condemnations was not same-sex sex, but non-procreative sex, to which medical authorities of the nineteenth century ascribed inheritable physical defects. Indeed, some treatises considered sodomy in marriage to be equally punishable for these reasons.[20] Thus, the particular animus of the Court toward same-sex sodomy distorted the historical facts and purposes of the criminalization of sodomy.

The majority opinion constructs another historical fallacy—that the condemnation of homosexual sodomy is unbroken and unambiguous. White argues that the proscription of same-sex sex has "ancient roots," thereby ignoring the tradition of ancient tolerance. The Greek attitude was very complex and varied with historical time, place of residence, social class, age, and with whether the man was effeminate or played the passive, receptor role.[21] Roman men could marry each other until A.D. 32. Moreover, sexual acts between men were tolerated during the early Middle Ages as well as among the elite in eighteenth-century France.

Most importantly, the notion of a "homosexual" as a kind of person is an artifact of the nineteenth century. Before that sodomy was something a person did, not something a person was. Indeed, the homosexual/heterosexual distinction was developed, in part, as a consequence of industrialization. The possibility of economic independence from the family permitted men and a smaller number of women to live outside the matrix of the traditional family.[22] Doctors and analysts advocated the homosexual/heterosexual dichotomy in part to protect those with same-sex preferences from being treated as sinners or criminals by characterizing their desire as hereditarily or psychosexually determined and, therefore, beyond their control.[23]

Thus armed with its own certainty of the inexorable evil of gay sex, the Court concluded that the claim that gay intimacy is protected is "at best, facetious."[24] This is the language not of reasoned analysis or reluctant restraint but of anger and trivialization. By distorting the historical record and defining the right in terms of engaging in criminal conduct, the Court manufactured a false and unbroken chain of condemnation.

In its narrow approach both to defining the right and to examining history, the Court laid the groundwork for a radical departure in the methodology of evolving rights that are not explicit in the text of the Constitution. Whereas the task of the Court was to decide whether the criminalization of sodomy is consistent with the Constitution, the majority treated the fact of past criminalization as determinative. Rather than examine the nature of liberty, the Court searched for proscription. Rather than examine "ancient proscriptions" in light of modern values or the relation between the state and the individual to see whether their premises merited continued respect, the Court constitutionalized the prejudices of (or rather, attributed to) the past. It had no answer to Justice Blackmun's contention that by such lights, the Court should have no authority to invalidate miscegenation laws—prohibiting interracial marriage—as a denial of fundamental liberty.[25] The anger that drives the majority in *Hardwick* has thus sharpened a methodology that may render a history of sanction impermeable to constitutional challenge at least where the claims are held in similar contempt by a majority of the Court.[26]

The concurring opinions in *Hardwick* reveal the homophobia of the Court in different ways. Justice Burger purports to add force to the majority opinion by reliance on the Judeo-Christian tradition, surely a suspect basis in an antiestablishmentarian state. He also relies on Blackstone's Commentary, which describes sodomy as "the infamous crime against nature" of "deeper malignity" than rape, and "a crime not fit to be named."[33] The reference is both chilling in its deprecation of women (since, under the common law, only an unmarried woman could be raped), and paranoid in its equation of sodomy with supreme evil. It is hard not to hear it as the voice of a man fearing the sexual interest of another man as the ultimate assault on masculinity, identity, and power.

By contrast, Justice Powell—the swing vote in *Hardwick*—advocates the stigmatizing function of the sodomy laws in a more controlled but no less insidious fashion. Noting that the twenty-year penalty imposed by the Georgia statute might be cruel and unusual, he nonetheless deems it unnecessary to decide the question. And further noting that Georgia's interest is undercut by the failure to have enforced the law for several decades, he nevertheless upholds the law because it involves "conduct that has been condemned for hundreds of years." In other words, it is wholly acceptable to use the criminal law purely for the symbolic purpose of delegitimation.[27]

Justice Blackmun's dissenting opinion for four justices stands in sharp contrast. The right involved is the "most comprehensive of rights and the right most valued by civilized men, namely the right to be let alone."[28] While he acknowledges the geographical claim to the privacy of the bedroom, his focus is on decisional privacy, autonomy from state-dictated conformity in matters of intimate association. The relation between the essence of marriage, family, and procreational liberty is acknowledged. Moreover, the concept of privacy embraced by the Blackmun dissent transcends secrecy or the negative concept of privacy that is the constraint of tolerance; it reflects a positive concept of privacy, an affirmation of the significance of sexual self-definition:

> Only the most willful blindness could obscure the fact that sexual intimacy is a sensitive, key relationship of human existence, central to family life, community welfare and the development of human personality. . . . The fact that individuals define themselves in a significant way through their intimate sexual relationships with others suggests, in a nation as diverse as ours, that there may be many "right" ways of conducting those relationships, and that much of the richness of a relationship will come from the freedom the individual has to choose the form and nature of these intensely personal bonds.[29]

It is not surprising that the *Hardwick* majority opinion—which ranks among the most brutal constitutional decisions—is countered by one of the most sweeping and egalitarian dissents in favor of human dignity.

If the Court had recognized the right of privacy, it could not have sustained the sodomy law without finding it justified by a compelling state interest. In recent decades, this has required more than ancient or religious moralism. But when the Court fails to find a protected right, as it did in *Hardwick*, it defers to the legislature so long as the law is "rational" or reasonably related to a legitimate governmental purpose. While this level of scrutiny is extremely minimal, the rationality test suggests, at the least, that some effort at explanation is due. The State of Georgia offered one, arguing:

> [H]omosexual sodomy is anathema of [*sic*] the basic units of our society—marriage and the family. To decriminalize or artificially withdraw the public's expression of its disdain for this conduct does not uplift sodomy, but rather demotes these sacred institutions to merely alternative lifestyles.[30]

To Hardwick's argument that "majority sentiments about the morality of homosexuality should be declared inadequate," the Court says merely: "We do not agree, and are unpersuaded that the sodomy laws of some 25 States should be invalidated on this basis."[31] With this remarkable sleight of hand, the Court justifies the criminalization of gay people's most intimate relationships.

The Court's refusal to explain is unprincipled in the extreme. It is a canon of its legitimacy that judicial power is justified by a willingness to provide reasons. But homophobia commonly operates to make gay and lesbian sexuality unmentionable. It is successfully nurtured by whispered disapproval. As recently as 1972, a state court upheld against a claim of unconstitutional vagueness a criminal statute which used the terms "unnatural or perverted sexual practice," "because it is unnecessary to describe in detail practices which are matters of common knowledge."[32] To treat something as unmentionable because it is a matter of common knowledge is oxymoronic. A socially endorsed secret, however, sows heightened shame. It feeds denial and demands invisibility. It controls the expression of gays and lesbians, labeling as "flaunting it" conduct that is viewed as romantic and heartwarming when enjoyed by heterosexuals.

Moreover, to explain why it is "rational" to criminalize gay sex involves relinquishing the authority simply to label difference as deviance. It undercuts the hegemonic quality of the norm; the unquestioned superiority of heterosexuality and its indisputed power to pronounce all alternatives as not only inferior, but immoral. It eliminates the need to explicate why sex between people of the same sex is unnatural or disgusting; why it is not simply a variant on nonprocreative sex; why it is threatening to personal or social stability. It is hard to answer these questions without sounding uptight, vulnerable, paranoid, fundamentalist, obsessed, excited, or just plain silly. To be required to explain runs the risk of diffusing both the authority of the speaker and the horror that attends the unspeakable.

When courts have sought to explain the rationality of criminalizing or excluding gay people, the premises that underlie homophobia are writ large. Unlike *Hardwick*, the lower federal court cases upholding the mandatory discharge of gay people from the military do try to explain the "rationality" of exclusion. The original regulations required discharge for any involvement in "homosexual acts"; notably, they were amended to include touching for the purpose of sexual gratification and to exclude a single act unaccompanied by the desire to repeat it.[34] These regulations and decisions provide a window into the fears that abound in high places. Perhaps the judges are more forthright in this context because they can rely on the myth that military life, even in peacetime, is different from nonmilitary life in ways that make privacy less obtainable, the protection of masculinity and the gender hierarchy more pressing, and nonconformity a national security risk. Perhaps they are more forthright because they cannot endow military authorities, as opposed to the legislatures, with power to dictate morality; or, perhaps, because as lower federal court judges, they do not enjoy the supreme power to settle the issue.

Whatever the reason, the answers are illuminating, not of the "unique needs of the military,"[35] but of a more pervasive need to preserve the hegemony of heterosexuality. Two opinions, *Dronenburg* v. *Zech*,[36] by failed

Supreme Court nominee Robert Bork, and *Beller* v. *Mittendorf*,[37] by the victor in that process, now Justice Anthony Kennedy, are illustrative.

In *Dronenburg*, Judge Bork asserts that the facts of the case exemplify the problem. But the only facts he gives us are that a twenty-seven-year-old petty officer had sex with a nineteen-year-old seaman recruit and then broke off the relationship. From this he concludes:

> Episodes of this sort are certain to be deleterious to morale and discipline, to call into question the even-handedness of superiors' dealings with lower ranks, to make personal dealings uncomfortable where the relationship is sexually ambiguous, to generate dislike and disapproval among many who find homosexuality morally offensive, and, it must be said, given the powers of military superiors over their inferiors, to enhance the possibility of homosexual seduction.[38]

In *Beller*, Kennedy accepted the Navy's assertion that retaining known homosexuals would create tensions with other members who "despise/detest homosexuality"; authority problems because a homosexual officer might not command respect or trust; undue influence as a result of the emotional relationship; and a possible adverse impact on recruiting.[39] What we have in these justifications is not only the endorsement of bald prejudice, but fear—fear of sexual ambiguity, seduction, and chaos. None of the allegedly "certain" consequences were proven in the cases. The exemplary records of the discharged plaintiffs were ignored.

The concerns expressed about "homosexuality" are not dissimilar to the traditional fears expressed about having women on ships or in combat, in leadership as opposed to in brothels. Echoing Justice Burger's invocation of Blackstone in *Hardwick*, the judges show inordinate sensitivity to sexual harassment, which, in the heterosexual context, has, until most recently, been viewed as harmless sport. Indeed, the denunciation of consensual gay and lesbian sexuality serves the same purpose as acceptance of the heterosexual harassment of women: both preserve gender dimorphism and the power difference attached to stereotypical masculinity (the sexual aggressor) and femininity (the sexual receiver). Ultimately, both preserve the boundaries and the hegemony of heterosexuality.

The argument that suppression of gay and lesbian sexuality is essential to preserve heterosexuality is sometimes explicit. In *People* v. *Onofre*[40] the New York Court of Appeals rejected the district attorney's argument that the criminalization of same-sex sodomy protects the institution of marriage. The court upheld the right of privacy, rejecting this argument because there was no empirical evidence that the gay sexuality would substitute for marriage.

In these contests over the sanctity of heterosexual marriage, some gay and lesbian rights advocates stress the immutability of sexual orientation to minimize the threat. The argument, however, is a self-defeating one.[41] While a lessening of the legal burdens on gays and lesbians would not likely usher in the age of polymorphous sexuality, it must be acknowledged that social control is not without effect. Monogamous heterosexual marriage is a hotbed of sexual lies and hypocrisy, and heterosexuality is itself highly programmed from infancy.[42] Justice Blackmun's response in *Hardwick* that "there may be many 'right' ways of conducting . . . [intimate sexual relationships], and that much of the richness of a relationship will come from the freedom an individual has to choose the form and nature of these intensely personal bonds[,]" takes a different tack. It elevates integrity over form, diversity over norms.

THE LIMITS OF PRIVACY

It is astonishing that, in 1986, the Court would not see fit to protect voluntary sexual activity in the bedroom. From the perspective of the liberal theory of rights, Michael Hardwick was not asking for much—only that the state not punish cloistered private choices. Under this view, private choices are tolerable because they are of great import to the individual, but of little consequence to society. By protecting these private choices, the law is saved from the embarassment of widespread disrespect and unenforceability. The trade-off is small because recognition of a negative right of privacy does not require that society renounce its prejudices. The liberal view of privacy is perfectly consistent with the view that homosexuality is "deviant" and "disgusting," but "OK so long as it doesn't show."

Rob's story, however, illustrates the illusiveness of this notion of privacy. Just as he could not conceal the possibility of his different sexuality without denuding his identity, so sexual self-definition must cross the bounds of privacy. While privacy implies secrecy and shame, the choice of sexual partners of the same sex is no more intrinsically private than the identity of one's spouse. Nor is this choice easily confined to the private realm of the bed or the closet. It involves not only sexual, but also social and familial identity—who one is in public as well as in private and what the legal norms are. To accept mere tolerance of hidden sexual difference is not only degrading; it is ultimately self-defeating.

Beyond the inefficacy of secrecy, the liberal notion of privacy reinforces the hierarchy embodied in heterosexism. To protect sexual "difference" reminds us that heterosexuality is the norm, the preferred and privileged status, while a same-sex or bisexual orientation is aberrant, inferior, tolerated at best. The protection of sexual "difference" does not protect the expression of variety in everyday life. It carves out an exception to the norm; it preserves deviance by the very act of permitting it limited scope.

To critique the liberal notion of privacy does not mean that the loss of such protection in *Hardwick* is not of enormous significance. In the realm of sexuality—fraught as it is with taboo—the notion of a sphere of noninterference with consensual activity is a necessary, albeit insufficient, condition for self-determination. The terrible penalties imposed on gays and lesbians in the past are warning enough of the dangers of sexual repression. Beyond that, there is no doubt that even the recognition of a narrow right of privacy in *Hardwick* would have had broad social impact. No longer could the criminal law be invoked as source of stigma or as a basis for denying people their children or their wherewithal to live. While discrimination and certainly prejudice would not magically be eradicated, the protection of privacy would inevitably spill over into greater safety in everyday life, greater legitimacy in public.

Herein lies the paradox that privacy authorizes too little and challenges too much. Although the notion of privacy parades as a value-free basis for decision, *Hardwick* demonstrates that the agnostic stance of liberal privacy as to the value of the protected activity does not survive where prejudice and fear are deep. It is doubtful that any of the students harassing Rob or standing by in silence would have argued that he had no right to choose his sexual partners. But their actions indicate, as do all opinions of the majority Justices in *Hardwick*, that privacy is not tolerable when it suggests a proud alternative to social norms.

Without underestimating the raw threat of sexuality, it is important to underscore the relationship between the stigmatization of gays and the preservation of the differentiation between men and women. As both stories demonstrate, same-sex intimacy is threatening to gender identity, gendered sexual boundaries, the expectation of heterosexuality, and the power relations it embodies. A heterosexist culture goes to elaborate lengths to construct distinct gender identities as well as the propensity toward heterosexuality. It may be that the very fragility of the channeled sexual self heightens the danger presented by crossing the line; that precisely because sexual identity and heterosexuality are not preordained but encultured and even chosen, those who deviate from the heterosexual norm must be stigmatized and excluded.

To acknowledge the flaws in the liberal concept of privacy not only refuses the legal closet and reveals the sources of prejudice; it also suggests alternative strategies more consonant with the original goals of the movements for sexual and women's liberation. It requires insistence on the right of expression rather than of privacy. And it requires a demand—suggested by Justice Blackmun's dissent—that people's sexual and intimate choices be equally honored and supported by the society. It means talking straight about sex as well as dismantling the complex social apparatus that channels sexuality into preferred forms. As Adrienne Rich has written:

> Heterosexuality as an institution has also drowned in silence the erotic feelings between women. I myself lived half a lifetime in the lie of that denial. That silence makes us all to some degree, into liars . . . The possibilities that exist between two people . . . are . . . the most interesting things in life. The liar is someone who keeps losing sight of these possibilities.[43]

Challenging the dynamic of homophobia and the systemization of heterosexual privilege thus contains the possibility of not only undoing stereotypes and oppression but also fostering more authentic and ultimately more secure sexual choices—whether gay, straight, or bisexual—for everyone. Privacy provides but a small and dangerously limited step in the much larger project of liberation, and its ultimate success will depend more on the progress of the larger project than on the effort to closet its potential.

TRANSCENDING HARDWICK

Though the 5–4 decision in *Hardwick* appears to have resolved the stigma contest, it is far from the last word. In one sense, *Hardwick* can be seen as a desperate attempt to maintain the status quo in the face of new claims of human rights, and, as such, it is one in a line of infamous decisions rejecting claims to full citizenship on the part of different groups. In *Dred Scott* v. *Sandford*[44] a former slave sought recognition as a free citizen. Relying on the constitutional framers' view and hoping to defuse the burgeoning abolition movement, the Court rejected his claim and pronounced the constitutional inferiority of African-American people, fixing "a stigma, of the deepest degradation, . . . upon the whole race.[45] Twenty years later, in *Bradwell* v. *Illinois*[46] the Court heard the first claim of women to the rights of citizenship, a claim that came on the heels of the defeat of the first wave of the feminist movement. While the majority ruled on grounds fairly applicable to both men and women, a concurring opinion which appears to have influenced the law for almost a hundred years, declared that by virtue of divine ordinance and natural law, women could have no rights inconsistent with their "paramount destiny" as wives and mothers.[47] And less than twenty-five years later, after the radicalism of post–Civil War Reconstruction had been systematically dismantled, the Court, in *Plessy* v. *Ferguson*,[48] interred the promise of the Civil War by declaring that racial segregation, premised again on the inferiority of African-Americans, would survive under the ruse of "separate but equal." It took almost a hundred years to begin to undo the premises of each of these latter decisions.

Hardwick, like *Dred Scott*, was decided not after a movement had peaked, but at a point when it was on the rise. Obviously, the status of gay people will not be determined by a civil war, but rather through a process of gradual emancipation. Despite the set-back dealt and intended by the Court majority, *Hardwick* has not dampened the ardor of nor decimated participation in the lesbian and gay rights movement. Paradoxically, it may have radicalized segments of the gay movement who were economically comfortable and less cognizant of their vulnerability. While *Hardwick* surely drove many people into deeper secrecy, it has also been a catalyst for others to come out. The "safety" of the closet and the false security of material comfort have been shattered by AIDS and by the homophobic action and inaction that it produced. It is a testimony to the strength of this movement that in this new panic over contagion, draconian proposals for mandatory testing and quarantine have made slow progress. And it is a testimony to the need of lesbians and gays to both live and die with honor that recognition of familial rights traditionally the preserve of heterosexuals—to procreate, keep custody of one's children, enjoy partnership benefits, exercise guardianship, and perhaps even marry—proceeds in state courts and legislative bodies. Just as *Hardwick* was in part the product of organizing a movement which refused to be maligned, so its consequence and longevity, will be determined by the courage of lesbians and gay men and their demand that everyone acknowledge and transcend homophobia and heterosexism, sexual lies, gendered straightjackets, and ultimately, perhaps, sexual classification itself.

NOTES

1. Edwin Shur, *The Politics of Deviance: Stigma Contests and the Uses of Power* (Englewood Cliffs, N.J.: Prentice-Hall, 1980).
2. These and some other terms should be defined. As used here, heterosexism is the systematic implementation, through law, custom, and other vehicles, of the view that heterosexuality is "natural" and that lesbian and gay sexuality are morally and socially inferior. The division of sex, family, and social life and work into two distinct and impermeable genders is an essential component of heterosexism. Heterosexism is distinct from, though fed by, homophobia, the fear and loathing of lesbians and gay men. It is also important

to distinguish between tolerance and affirmation. Tolerance implies that something negative must be put up with, whilst affirmation embraces difference as a neutral fact and, in a hostile climate, as a positive one.

3. I will not canvass all the theories or the dilemmas with using the Constitution to secure lesbian/gay rights, but note simply that they are numerous. The recognition of lesbian/gay rights has been pressed on a number of constitutional grounds. Statutes have been challenged on vagueness grounds. Lesbian/gay rights advocates have urged that classifications based on sexual orientation ought to be treated as "suspect" or at least with heightened scrutiny under the equal protection clause because of the dangerous prejudice produced by homophobia. The First Amendment has been invoked to protect both advocacy of lesbian/gay rights and the assertion of a lesbian or gay identity. And, given the sexism inherent in homophobia, discrimination on the basis of sexual orientation has been characterized as irreducibly gender discrimination. From the blatant to the subtle—from the vagueness claims to the gender claims—these arguments are being regularly rejected or are hanging by a gossamer thread in the federal courts today.

4. Ratchford v. Gay Lib, 434 U.S. 1080 (1978) (Rehnquist and Blackmun, JJ., dissenting from the Supreme Court's refusal to review a lower federal court order requiring university recognition of a gay rights group).

5. Webster's Third New International Dictionary (Springfield, Mass.: G. & C. Merriam Co., 1981).

6. J. N. Katz, Gay American History (New York: Avon Books, 1976); Peter Conrad and Joseph Schneider, Deviance and Medicalization: From Badness to Sickness (St. Louis, Mo.: C.V. Mosby, 1980), pp. 173–213.

7. John D'Emilio, Sexual Politics, Sexual Communities: The Making of a Homosexual Minority in the United States (Chicago: University of Chicago Press, 1984), pp. 173–213.

8. Bowers v. Hardwick, 487 U.S. 186 (1986).

9. 394 U.S. 557 (1969).

10. 381 U.S. 479 (1965).

11. Ibid.; Eisenstadt v. Baird, 405 U.S. 438 (1972); Carey v. Population Services, 431 U.S. 678 (1977); Roe v. Wade, 410 U.S. 113 (1973).

12. See, e.g., Paul Brest, "The Misconceived Quest for the Original Understanding," 60 Boston University Law Review 204 (1980). See Rhonda Copelon, "Unpacking Patriarchy," in A Less Than Perfect Union: Alternative Perspectives on the U.S. Constitution, ed. Jules Lobel (New York: Monthly Review Press, 1988).

13. 478 U.S. at 191.

14. Genesis, 19:1–11. See, e.g., Conrad and Schneider, supra note 6, at 173–74.

15. It is enormously refreshing to read judicial decisions which use the terminology "gay" instead of homosexual and "straight" as well as heterosexual for contrast. The ones that I have seen emanate from federal courts in the Bay Area, which is a testament to the impact of a strong and proud lesbian

and gay community not only on the language but also the outcomes in the courts. *See e.g.*, Watkins v. U.S. Army, 837 P. 2d. 1428 (9th Cir. 1988); High Tech Gays v. Defense Indus. Sec. Clearance Office, 668 F. Supp. 1361 (N.D. Cal. 1987). The term "homosexual" is used in this article only when referring specifically to that characterization of gays and lesbians.

16. 478 U.S., at 190–91.
17. *Hardwick*, 478 U.S. at 195.
18. *Id*. at 209, n. 4.
19. Taub and Schneider, "Women's Subordination and the Rule of Law," in this volume.
20. *See* Vern Bullough and Bonnie Bullough, *Sin, Sickness and Sanity: A History of Sexual Attitudes* (New York: New American Library, 1977), pp. 55–73, 201–9; Anne Goldstein, "History, Homosexuality, and Political Values: Searching for the Hidden Determinants of Bowers v. Hardwick," 97 *Yale Law Journal* 1073, 1083–85 (1988) (hereinafter "Hidden Determinants").
21. "Hidden Determinants" at 1087, n. 77.
22. J. D'Emilio, "Capitalism and Gay Identity," in *Powers of Desire: The Politics of Sexuality*, ed. A. Snitow, C. Stansell, and S. Thompson (New York: Monthly Review Press, 1983) (hereinafter "Powers of Desire"); and Lilian Faderman, *Surpassing the Love of Men* (New York: William Morrow, 1981), pp. 178–230.
23. "Hidden Determinants," *id*. at 1087–88 for sources; Conrad and Schneider, *supra* note 6, pp. 181–87; J. Katz, "The Invention of Heterosexuality," 121 *Socialist Review* 7 (February 1990).
24. *Hardwick*, 478 U.S. at 194.
25. Loving v. Virginia, 388 U.S. 1 (1967).
26. *See, e.g.*, Michael H. v. Gerald D., 109 S. Ct. 233 (1989).
27. *Hardwick*, 478 U.S. at 198.
28. *Id*. at 199, citing Olmstead v. United States, 277 U.S. 438, 478 (1928) (Brandeis, J., dissenting).
29. *Hardwick*, 478 U.S. at 205.
30. Brief of Petitioner Michael J. Bowers, Attorney General of Georgia, at 37–38.
31. *Id*. at 196.
32. Hughes v. State of Maryland, 14 Md. App. 497, 287 A. 2d 299 (1972), *cert. denied*, 409 U.S. 1025 (1972).
33. *Hardwick*, 478 U.S. at 194, 4 W. Blackstone, *Commentaries** 215.
34. SECNAV Instruction 1900.9C excerpted in Beller v. Mittendorf, 632 F. 2d 788, 802, n.9 (9th Cir. 1980). In suppressed reports leaked to the press, a research arm of the Department of Defense has criticized the military's discrimination against lesbians and gays as unjustified. *See* DOD Personnel Security Research and Education Center, "Nonconforming Sexual Orientation and Military Suitability" (December 1988) and "Preservice Adjustment of Homosexual and Heterosexual Military Accessions: Implications

for Security Clearance Suitability" (January 1989); "Rethinking DOD Policy on Gays," *Washington Post*, November 6, 1989.

35. 741 F. 2d 1388, 1398 (D.C. Cir. 1984).

36. *Id.* at 1398.

37. 632 F.2d. 788 (D.C. Cir. 1980).

38. 741 F. 2d at 1398.

39. 632 F. 2d at 811.

40. 51 N.Y.2d 476, 415 N.E. 2d 936, 941 (1980).

41. The notion that sexual orientation is immutable is extremely reassuring to many people, both gay and straight. Whereas some gays and lesbians experience their sexuality as determined from childhood and immutable, others experience it as a choice. Beyond this experiential difference, it is important not to win rights through appeals to pity rather than respect, to comfort rather than authenticity. *See* J. Halley, "The Politics of the Closet: Towards Equal Protection for Gay, Lesbian and Bisexual Identity," 36 *UCLA Law Review* 915 (1989).

42. Adrienne Rich, "Compulsory Heterosexuality and Lesbian Existence," in *Powers of Desire, supra* note 22, p. 177.

43. Adrienne Rich, *On Lies, Secrets and Silence: Selected Prose, 1966–1978* (New York: W.W. Norton & Co., 1979), pp. 190–93.

44. 60 U.S. (19 How.) 393 (1857).

45. *Id.* at 409.

46. 83 U.S. (16 Wall.) 130 (1873).

47. *Id* at 139–42 (Bradley, J., concurring).

48. 163 U.S. 537 (1896).

9 KIMBERLE CRENSHAW

A BLACK FEMINIST CRITIQUE OF ANTIDISCRIMINATION LAW AND POLITICS

THE title of one of the very few Black women's studies books, *All the Women Are White, All the Blacks Are Men, But Some of Us Are Brave*,[1] sets forth a problematic consequence of the tendency to treat race and gender as mutually exclusive categories of experience and analysis. This tendency is perpetuated by a single-axis framework dominant in antidiscrimination law and reflected in feminist theory and antiracist politics that distorts the multidimensionality of Black women's experiences and undermines efforts to broaden feminist and antiracist analyses.

THE ANTIDISCRIMINATION FRAMEWORK

One way to approach the problem at the intersection of race and sex is to examine how courts frame and interpret the stories of Black women plaintiffs. Indeed, the way courts interpret claims made by Black women is itself part of Black women's experience; consequently, a cursory review of cases involving Black female plaintiffs is quite revealing. To illustrate the difficulties inherent in judicial treatment of intersectionality, I will consider three employment discrimination cases: *DeGraffenreid* v. *General Motors, Moore* v. *Hughes Helicopter and Payne* v. *Travenol.*[2]

This chapter originated as an address given at the Conference on New Developments in Feminist Legal Theory, sponsored by the Chicago Legal Forum in October 1988. An earlier version that is more heavily footnoted appears in 1989 *Chicago Legal Forum* 139 (1989). I would like to thank Neil Gotanda, Kendall Thomas, Stephanie Phillips, Darcy Calkins, and the West Coast Fem Crits for their comments and support. I am especially indebted to David Kairys and Richard Yarborough, whose invaluable assistance made this contribution possible.

In *DeGraffenreid*, five Black women brought suit against General Motors, alleging that the employer's seniority system perpetuated the effects of past discrimination against Black women. Although General Motors did not hire Black women prior to 1964, the court noted that "General Motors has hired . . . female employees for a number of years prior to the enactment of the Civil Rights Act of 1964." Because General Motors did hire women—albeit *white women*—during the period that no Black women were hired, there was, in the court's view, no sex discrimination that the seniority system could conceivably have perpetuated. Moreover, reasoning that Black women could choose to bring either a sex or a race discrimination claim, but not both, the court stated:

> The legislative history surrounding Title VII does not indicate that the goal of the statute was to create a new classification of "black women" who would have greater standing than, for example, a black male. The prospect of the creation of new classes of protected minorities, governed only by the mathematical principles of permutation and combination, clearly raises the prospect of opening the hackneyed Pandora's box.

The court's conclusion that Congress did not intend to allow Black women to make a compound claim arises from its inability to imagine that discrimination against Black women can exist independently from the experiences of white women or of Black men. Because the court was blind to this possibility, it did not question whether Congress could have meant to leave this form of discrimination unredressed. Assuming therefore that there was no distinct discrimination suffered by Black women, the court concluded that to allow plaintiffs to make a compound claim would unduly advantage Black women over Black men or white women.

This negative conclusion regarding Black women's ability to bring compound claims has not been replicated in another kind of compound discrimination case—"reverse discrimination" claims brought by white males. Interestingly, no case has been discovered in which a court denied a white male's reverse discrimination claims on similar grounds—that is, that sex and race claims cannot be combined because Congress did not intend to protect compound classes. Yet, white males challenging affirmative action programs that benefit minorities and women are actually in no better position to make a race and gender claim than the Black women in *DeGraffenreid*: If white men are required to make their claims separately, they cannot prove race discrimination because white women are not discriminated against, and they cannot prove sex discrimination because Black males are not discriminated against. One would think, therefore, that the logic of *Degraffenreid* would complicate reverse discrimination cases. That Black women's claims raise the question of compound discrimination while white males' reverse discrimination claims do not suggests that the notion of "compound class" is somehow relative or contingent on some presumed norm rather than definitive and absolute. If that norm is understood to be white male, one can understand how Black women, being "two steps removed" from being white men, are deemed to be a compound class while white men are not. Indeed, if assumptions about objectivity of law are replaced with the subjective perspective of white males, one can understand better not only why Black women are viewed as compound classes and white men are not, but also why the boundaries of sex and race discrimination doctrine are defined respectively by the experiences of white women and Black men. Consider first that when a white male imagines being a female, he probably imagines being a white female. Similarly, a white male who must project himself as Black will no doubt imagine himself to be a Black male, thereby holding constant all other characteristics except race.

Antidiscrimination law is similarly constructed from the perspective of white males. Gender discrimination, imagined from the perspective of white men, is what happens to white women; race discrimination is what happens to Black men. The dominance of the single-axis framework, most starkly represented by *DeGraffenreid*, not only marginalizes Black women but simultaneously privileges the subjectivity of white men. Under this view, Black women are protected only to the extent that their experiences coincide with those of either of the two groups. Where their experiences are distinct, Black women will encounter difficulty articulating their claims as long as approaches prevail which completely obscure problems of intersectionality.[3]

Moore v. *Hughes Helicopters, Inc.* presents a different way in which courts fail to understand or recognize Black women's claims. *Moore* is typical of cases in which courts refused to certify Black females as class representatives in race *and* sex discrimination actions.[4] In *Moore*, the plaintiff alleged that the employer, Hughes Helicopter, practiced race and sex discrimination in promotions to upper-level craft positions and to supervisory jobs. Moore introduced statistical evidence establishing a significant disparity between men and women, and somewhat less of a disparity between Black and white men in supervisory jobs.

Affirming the district court's refusal to certify Moore as the class representative in the sex discrimination complaint on behalf of all women at Hughes, the Ninth Circuit noted approvingly:

> . . . Moore had never claimed before the EEOC that she was discriminated against as a female, *but only* as a Black female. . . . [T]his raised serious doubts as to Moore's ability to adequately represent white female employees.

The curious logic in *Moore* reveals not only the narrow scope of antidiscrimination doctrine and its failure to embrace intersectionality, but also the centrality of white female experiences in the conceptualization of gender discrimination. The court rejected Moore's bid to represent all females apparently because her attempt to specify her race was seen as being at odds with the standard allegation that the employer simply discriminated "against females." However, the court failed to see that the absence of a racial referent does not necessarily mean that the claim being made is a more inclusive one. A white woman claiming discrimination against females may be in no better position to represent all women than a Black woman who claims discrimination as a Black female and wants to represent all females. The court's preferred articulation of "against females" is not necessarily more inclusive—it just appears to be so because the racial contours of the claim are not specified.

The court's preference for "against females" rather than "against Black females" reveals the implicit grounding of white female experiences in the doctrinal conceptualization of sex discrimination. For white women, claiming sex discrimination is simply a statement that but for gender, they would not have been disadvantaged. For them there is no need to specify discrimination as *white* females because their race does not contribute to the disadvantage for which they seek redress. The view of discrimination that is derived from this grounding takes race privilege as a given.

Discrimination against a white female is thus the standard sex discrimination claim; claims that diverge from this standard appear to present some sort of hybrid claim. More significantly, because Black females' claims are seen as hybrid, they sometimes cannot represent those who may have "pure" claims of sex discrimination. The effect of this approach is that even though a challenged policy or practice may clearly discriminate against all females, the fact that it has particularly harsh consequences for Black females places Black plaintiffs at odds with white females.

The *Moore* court also denied the plaintiffs' bid to represent Black males, leaving Moore with the task of supporting her race and sex discrimination claims with statistical evidence of discrimination against Black females alone. Because she was unable to represent white women or Black men, she could not use overall statistics on sex disparity at Hughes, nor could she use statistics on race. Proving her claim using statistics on Black women alone was no small task, due to the fact that she was bringing the suit under a disparate impact theory of discrimination.

The court's rulings on Moore's sex and race claim left her with such a small statistical sample that even if she had proved that there were qualified Black women, she could not have shown discrimination under a disparate impact theory. *Moore* illustrates yet another way that antidiscrimination doctrine essentially erases Black women's distinct experiences and, as a result, deems their discrimination complaints groundless.

Finally, Black female plaintiffs have sometimes encountered difficulty in their efforts to win certification as class representatives in some race discrimination actions. This problem typically arises in cases where statistics suggest significant disparities between Black and white workers and further disparities between Black men and Black women. Courts in some cases[5] have denied certification based on logic that mirrors the rationale in *Moore*: The sex disparities between Black men and Black women created such conflicting interests that Black women could not possibly represent Black men adequately. In one such case, *Payne* v. *Travenol*, two Black female plaintiffs alleging race discrimination brought a class action suit on behalf of all Black employees at a pharmaceutical plant. The court refused, however, to allow the plaintiffs to represent Black males and granted the defendant's request to narrow the class to Black women only. Ultimately, the district court found that there had been extensive racial discrimination at the plant and awarded back pay and constructive seniority to the class of Black female employees. But, despite its finding of general race discrimination, the court refused to extend the remedy to Black men for fear that their conflicting interests would not be adequately addressed; the Fifth Circuit affirmed.[6]

Even though *Travenol* was a partial victory for Black women, the case specifically illustrates how antidiscrimination doctrine generally creates a dilemma for Black women. It forces them to choose between specifically articulating the intersectional aspects of their subordination, thereby risking their ability to represent Black men, or ignoring intersectionality in order to state a claim that would not lead to the exclusion of Black men. When one considers the political consequences of this dilemma, there is little wonder that many people within the Black community view the specific articulation of Black women's interests as dangerously divisive.

In sum, several courts have proved unable to deal with intersectionality, although for contrasting reasons. In *DeGraffenreid*, the court refused to recognize the possibility of compound discrimination against Black women and analyzed their claim using the employment of white women as the historical base. As a consequence, the employment experiences of white women obscured the distinct discrimination that Black women experienced.

Conversely, in *Moore*, the court held that a Black woman could not use statistics reflecting the overall sex disparity in supervisory and upper-level labor jobs because she had not claimed discrimination as a woman, but "only" as a Black woman. The court would not entertain the notion that discrimination experienced by Black women is indeed sex discrimination—provable through disparate impact statistics on women.

Finally, courts such as the one in *Travenol* have held that Black women cannot represent an entire class of Blacks due to presumed class conflicts in cases where sex additionally disadvantaged Black women. As a result, in the few cases where Black women are allowed to use overall statistics indicating racially disparate treatment, Black men may not be able to share in the remedy.

Perhaps it appears to some that I have offered inconsistent criticisms of how Black women are treated in antidiscrimination law: I seem to be saying that in one case, Black women's claims were rejected and their experiences obscured because the court refused to acknowledge that the employment experience of Black women can be distinct from that of white women, while in other cases, the interests of Black women were harmed because Black women's claims were viewed as so distinct from the claims of either white women or Black men that the court denied to Black females representation of the larger class. It seems that I have to say that Black women are the same and harmed by being treated differently, or that they are different and harmed by being treated the same. But I cannot say both.

This apparent contradiction is but another manifestation of the conceptual limitations of the single-issue analyses that intersectionality challenges. The point is that Black women can experience discrimination in any number of ways and that the contradiction arises from our assumptions that their claims of exclusion must be unidirectional. Consider an analogy to traffic in an intersection, coming and going in all four directions. Discrimination, like traffic through an intersection, may flow in one direction, and it may flow in another. If an accident happens in an intersection, it can be caused by cars traveling from any number of directions and, sometimes, from all of them. Similarly, if a Black woman is harmed because she is in the inter-section, her injury could result from sex discrimination or race discrimination or both.

Providing legal relief only when Black women prove that their claims are based on race or on sex is analogous to calling an ambulance for the victim only after the driver responsible for the injuries is identified. But it is not always easy to identify the driver: sometimes the skid marks and the injuries simply indicate that they occurred simultaneously, frustrating efforts to de-termine which driver caused the harm. In these cases the tendency seems to be that no driver is held responsible, no treatment is administered, and the involved parties simply get back in their cars and zoom away.

I am suggesting that Black women can experience discrimination in ways that are both similar to and different from those experienced by white women and Black men. Black women sometimes experience discrimination in ways similar to white women's experiences; sometimes they share very similar experiences with Black men. Yet often they experience double discrimina-tion—the combined effects of practices which discriminate on the basis of race, and on the basis of sex. And sometimes, they experience discrimination as Black women—not the sum of race and sex discrimination, but as Black women.

DeGraffenreid, Moore, and *Travenol* are doctrinal manifestations of a common political and theoretical approach to discrimination which operates to marginalize Black women. Unable to grasp the importance of Black women's intersectional experiences, not only courts, but feminist and civil rights thinkers as well have treated Black women in ways that deny both the unique compoundedness of their situation and the centrality of their experiences to the larger classes of women and Blacks. Consequently, their needs and perspectives have been relegated to the margin of the feminist and Black liberationist agendas. While it could be argued that this marginalization represents an absence of political will to include Black women, I believe that it reflects an uncritical and disturbing acceptance of dominant ways of thinking about discrimination.

Underlying dominant conceptions of discrimination, which have been challenged by a developing approach called critical race theory,[7] is a view that the wrong which antidiscrimination law addresses is the use of race or gender factors to interfere with decisions that would otherwise be fair or neutral. This process-based definition is not grounded in a bottom-up commitment to improve the substantive conditions for those who are victimized by the interplay of numerous factors. Instead, the dominant message of antidiscrimination law is that it will regulate only the limited extent to which race or sex interferes with the process of determining outcomes. This narrow objective is facilitated by the top-down strategy of using a singular "but for" analysis to ascertain the effects of race or sex. Because the scope of antidiscrimination law is so limited, sex and race discrimination have come to be defined in terms of the experiences of those who are privileged *but for* their racial or sexual characteristics. Put differently, the paradigm of sex discrimination tends to be based on the experiences of white women; the model of race discrimination tends to be based on the experiences of the most privileged Blacks. Notions of what constitutes race and sex discrimination are, as a result, narrowly tailored to embrace only a small set of circumstances which do not explicitly include the experiences of Black women.

To the extent that this general description is accurate, the following analogy can be useful in describing how Black women are marginalized in the interface between antidiscrimination law and race and gender hierarchies: imagine a basement which contains all people who are disadvantaged on the basis of race, sex, class, sexual preference, age and/or physical ability. These people are stacked—feet standing on shoulders—with those on the bottom being disadvantaged by the full array of factors, up to the very top, where the heads of all those disadvantaged by a singular factor brush up against the ceiling. Their ceiling is actually the floor above which only those who are *not* disadvantaged in any way reside. In efforts to correct some aspects of domination, those above the ceiling admit from the basement only those who can say that "but for" the ceiling, they too would be in the upper room. A hatch is developed through which those placed immediately below can crawl. Yet this hatch is generally available only to those who—due to the singularity of their burden and their otherwise privileged position relative to those below—are in the position to crawl through. Those who are multiply burdened are generally left below unless they can somehow pull themselves into the groups that are permitted to squeeze through the hatch.

As this analogy translates for Black women, the problem is that they can receive protection only to the extent that their experiences are recognizably similar to those whose experiences tend to be reflected in antidiscrimination doctrine. If Black women cannot conclusively say that "but for" their race or "but for" their gender they would be treated differently, they are not invited to climb through the hatch but told to wait in the unprotected margin until they can be absorbed into the broader, protected categories of race and sex.

Despite the narrow scope of this dominant conception of discrimination and its tendency to marginalize those whose experiences cannot be described within its tightly drawn parameters, this approach has been regarded as the appropriate framework for addressing a range of problems. In much of feminist theory and, to some extent, in antiracist politics, this framework is reflected in the belief that sexism or racism can be meaningfully discussed without paying attention to the lives of those other than the race-, gender-, or class-privileged. As a result, both feminist theory and antiracist politics have been organized, in part, around the equation of sexism with what happens to white women and the equation of racism with what happens to the Black middle class or to Black men.

Looking at historical and contemporary issues in both the feminist and the civil rights communities, one can find ample evidence of how both communities' acceptance of the dominant framework of discrimination has hindered the development of an adequate theory and praxis to address problems of intersectionality. Not only does this adoption of a single-issue framework for discrimination marginalize Black women within the very movements that claim them as part of their constituency but it also makes the illusive goal of ending racism and patriarchy even more difficult to attain.

FEMINISM AND BLACK WOMEN:
"AIN'T WE WOMEN?"

Oddly, despite the relative inability of feminist politics and theory to address Black women substantively, feminist critics and scholars borrow considerably from Black women's history. For example, "Ain't I a Woman" has come to represent a standard refrain in feminist discourse.[8] Yet the lesson of this powerful oratory is not fully appreciated because the context of the delivery is seldom examined.

In 1851, Sojourner Truth declared "Ain't I a Woman?" and challenged the sexist imagery used by male critics to justify the disenfranchisement of women.[9] The scene was a Women's Rights Conference in Akron, Ohio; white male hecklers, invoking stereotypical images of "womanhood," argued that women were too frail and delicate to take on the responsibilities of political activity. When Sojourner Truth rose to speak, many white women urged that she be silenced, fearing that she would divert attention from women's suffrage to emancipation. Truth, once permitted to speak, recounted the horrors of slavery, and its particular impact on Black women:

> Look at my arm! I have ploughed and planted and gathered into barns, and no man could head me—and ain't I a woman? I could work as much and eat as much as a man—when I could get it—and bear the lash as well! And ain't I a woman? I have born thirteen children, and seen most of 'em sold into slavery, and when I cried out with my mother's grief, none but Jesus heard me—and ain't I a woman?[10]

By using her own life to reveal the contradiction between the ideological myths of womanhood and the reality of Black women's experience, Truth's oratory provided a powerful rebuttal to the claim that women were categorically weaker than men. Yet Truth's personal challenge to the coherence of the cult of true womanhood was useful only to the extent that white women were willing to reject the most racist attempts to rationalize the contradiction; such rationalizations were premised on the belief that because Black women were something less than real women, their experiences had no bearing on true womanhood. Thus, this nineteenth-century Black feminist not only challenged patriarchy, but she also challenged white feminists wishing to embrace Black women's history to relinquish their vested interest in whiteness.

To inherit the legacy of Truth's challenge to patriarchy, contemporary white feminists must also accept Truth's challenge to their forebears. Even today, white women's difficulty in sacrificing racial privilege renders them susceptible to Truth's critical question. When feminist theory and politics that claim to reflect *women's* experience and *women's* aspirations do not include or speak to Black women, Black women must ask: "Ain't *We* Women?" If this is so, how can the claims that "women are," "women believe," and "women need" be made when such claims are inapplicable or unresponsive to the needs, interests and experiences of Black women?

The value of feminist theory to Black women is diminished because it evolves from a white racial context that is seldom acknowledged. Not only are women of color in fact overlooked, but their exclusion is reinforced when *white* women speak for and as *women*. The authoritative universal voice—usually white male subjectivity masquerading as nonracial, nongendered objectivity[11]—is merely transferred to those who, but for gender, share many of the same cultural, economic, and social characteristics. When feminist theory attempts to describe women's experiences through analyzing patriarchy, sexuality, or separate-spheres ideology, it often overlooks the role of race. White feminists thus ignore how their own race functions to mitigate some aspects of sexism and, moreover, how it often privileges them over and contributes to the domination of other women.[12] Consequently, feminist theory remains *white*, and its potential to broaden and deepen its analysis by addressing nonprivileged women remains unrealized.

An example of how some feminist theories are narrowly constructed around white women's experiences is found in the separate spheres literature. The critique of how separate spheres ideology shapes and limits women's roles in the home and in public life is a central theme in feminist legal thought.[13] Feminists have attempted to expose and dismantle separate spheres ideology by identifying and criticizing the stereotypes that traditionally have justified the disparate societal roles assigned to men and women. Yet this attempt to debunk ideological justifications for *women's* subordination offers little insight into the domination of Black women. Because the experiential base upon which many feminist insights are grounded is white, theoretical statements drawn from them are overgeneralized at best, and often wrong.[14] Statements such as "men and women are taught to see men as independent, capable, powerful; men and women are taught to see women as dependent, limited in abilities, and passive," are common in this literature. But this "observation" overlooks the anomalies created by crosscurrents of racism and sexism. Black men and women live in a society that creates sex-based norms and expectations which racism operates simultaneously to deny; Black men are not viewed as powerful, nor are Black women seen as passive. An effort to develop an ideological explanation of gender domination in the Black community should proceed from an understanding of how crosscutting forces establish gender norms and how the conditions of Black subordination wholly frustrate access to these norms. Given this understanding, perhaps we can begin to see why Black women have been dogged by the stereotype of the pathological matriarch or why there have been those in the Black liberation movement who aspire to create institutions and to build traditions that embrace and celebrate patriarchy.[15] For example, Black families have sometimes been cast as pathological largely because of Black women's divergence from the white middle-class female norm. The most infamous rendition of this view is found in the Moynihan report (discussed below), which blamed many of the Black community's ills on a supposed pathological family structure.

Because ideological and descriptive definitions of patriarchy are usually premised upon white female experiences, feminists and others informed by feminist literature may make the mistake of assuming that since the role of Black women in the family and in other Black institutions does not always resemble the familiar manifestations of patriarchy in the white community, Black women are somehow exempt from patriarchal norms. For example, Black women have traditionally worked outside the home in numbers far exceeding the labor participation rate of white women.[16] An analysis of patriarchy that highlights the history of white women's exclusion from the workplace might permit the inference that Black women have not been burdened by this particular gender-based discrimination. Yet the very fact that Black women *must* work outside the home has conflicted with normative expectations that women remain in the home, often creating emotional strife within their personal lives. Thus, Black women are burdened not only because they often have to take on responsibilities that are not traditionally feminine but, moreover, because their assumption of these roles has sometimes been interpreted within the Black community as either Black women's failure to live up to patriarchal norms or as another manifestation of racism's scourge upon the Black community.[17] This is one of the many aspects of intersectionality that cannot be understood through an analysis of patriarchy rooted in white experience.

Another example of how theory emanating from a white context obscures the multidimensionality of Black women's lives is found in feminist discourse on rape. A central political issue on the feminist agenda has been the pervasive problem of rape. Part of the intellectual and political effort to mobilize around this issue has involved the development of a historical critique of the role that law has played in establishing the bounds of normative sexuality and in regulating female sexual behavior.[18] Early carnal-knowledge statutes and rape laws are understood within this discourse to illustrate that the objective of such statutes traditionally has not been to protect women from coercive intimacy but to protect and maintain a propertylike interest in female chastity. Although feminists quite rightly criticize these objectives, to characterize rape law as reflecting male control over female sexuality is for Black women an oversimplified and ultimately inadequate account.

Rape statutes generally do not reflect *male* control over *female* sexuality, but *white* male regulation of *white* female sexuality. Historically, there has been absolutely no institutional effort to "protect" Black female chastity.[19] Courts in some states had gone so far as to instruct juries that unlike white women, Black women were not presumed to be chaste. For example: "What has been said by some of our courts about an unchaste female being a comparatively rare exception is no doubt true where the population is composed largely of the Caucasian race, but we would blind ourselves to actual conditions if we adopted this rule where another race that is largely immoral constitutes an appreciable part of the population."[20] Also, while it was true that the attempt to regulate the sexuality of white women placed unchaste women outside the law's protection, racism restored a fallen white woman's chastity where the alleged assailant was a Black man.[21] No such restoration was available to Black women.

The singular focus on rape as a manifestation of male power over female sexuality tends to eclipse the use of rape as a weapon of racial terror.[22] When Black women were raped by white males, they were being raped as Black women specifically: their femaleness made them sexually vulnerable to racist domination, while their blackness effectively denied them any protection.[23] This white male power was reinforced by a judicial system in which the successful conviction of a white man for raping a Black woman was virtually unthinkable.

In sum, both the failure of feminism to address the interplay of race and gender in constructing Black and white female sexuality and the failure to appreciate fully the close connection between historical constructions of white female sexuality and racial terrorism contribute to feminism's inability to politicize sexual violence in ways that speak to and include Black women. Sexist expectations of chastity and racist assumptions of sexual promiscuity thus combined to create a distinct set of issues confronting Black women.[24] These issues have seldom been explored in feminist literature; nor have they been prominent in antiracist politics. The lynching of Black men, the institutional practice legitimized by the oppositional representations of Black male and white female sexuality, has historically occupied the Black agenda on sexuality and violence. Consequently, those who attempt to address sexual violence against Black women are caught between members of the Black community who, perhaps understandably, view with apprehension attempts to litigate questions of sexual violence and a feminist community that reinforces this suspicion by focusing on white female sexuality. Black concerns on this issue are premised on the historical fact that the protection of white female sexuality was often the pretext for terrorizing the Black community.[25] The difficulty is further compounded by the failure of some white feminists to acknowledge adequately the relationship between the constructed images of white female sexuality and racial terrorism.

Susan Brownmiller's discussion of the Emmett Till case illustrates the problem created by a solipsistic approach to rape that places white women's sexuality at the center of the analysis.[26] Despite Brownmiller's quite laudable efforts to discuss elsewhere the rape of Black women and the racism involved in much of the hysteria over the Black male threat, her analysis of the Till case places the sexuality of white women, rather than racial terrorism, at center stage. Brownmiller states: "Rarely has one single case exposed so clearly as Till's the underlying group-male antagonisms over access to women, for what began in Bryant's store should not be misconstrued as an innocent flirtation. . . . In concrete terms, the accessibility of all white women was on review." Later, Brownmiller argues:

> And what of the wolf whistle, Till's "gesture of adolescent bravado"? We are rightly aghast that a whistle could be cause for murder but we must also accept that Emmett Till and J. W. Millam shared something in common. They both understood that the whistle was no small tweet of hubba-hubba or melodious approval for a well-turned ankle. Given the deteriorated situation . . . it was a deliberate insult just short of physical assault, a last reminder to Carolyn Bryant that this black boy, Till, had a mind to possess her.

While Brownmiller seems to categorize the case as one that evidences a conflict over possession, it is regarded in African American history as a tragic dramatization of the South's pathological hatred and fear of African Americans. Till's body, mutilated beyond recognition, was viewed by thousands so that, in the words of Till's mother, "the world could see what they did to my boy." The Till tragedy is also regarded as one of the historical events that bore directly on the emergence of the civil rights movement. Juan Williams characterized its effect well: "[W]ithout question it moved black America in a way the Supreme Court ruling on school desegregation could not match. . . . [T]he murder of Emmett Till had a powerful impact on a generation of blacks. It was this generation, those who were adolescents when Till was killed, that would soon demand justice and freedom in a way unknown in America before."[27] Brownmiller's remarkable insensitivity to the horror of the Till case illustrates how centering the perspective of white women in feminist discourse can operate to minimize racial oppression and to alienate Black women.

This contributes to the fear among some Black women that antirape agendas may undermine antiracist objectives. The politization of rape in both feminist and antiracist discourse also illustrates how Black women are caught between ideological and political currents that coalese and often collide in the intersection of race and gender. The multidimensional experiences and interests created by these cross currents are marginalized within feminist and antiracist politics framed around unidimensional analyses.

INTEGRATING AN ANALYSIS OF SEXISM INTO BLACK LIBERATION POLITICS

Anna Julia Cooper, a nineteenth-century Black feminist, coined a phrase that has been useful in evaluating the need to incorporate an explicit analysis of patriarchy in any effort to address racial domination.[28] Cooper often criticized Black leaders and spokespersons for claiming to speak for the race, but failing to speak for Black women. Referring to one of Martin Delaney's public claims that where he was allowed to enter, the race entered with him, Cooper countered: "Only the Black Woman can say, when and where I enter . . . then and there the whole Negro race enters with me."[29]

Cooper's words bring to mind a personal experience involving two Black men with whom I had formed a study group during our first year of law school. One of our group members, a graduate from Harvard College, often told us stories about a prestigious and exclusive men's club that boasted memberships of several past United States presidents and other influential white males. He was one of its very few Black members. To celebrate completing our first-year exams, our friend invited us to join him at the club for drinks. Anxious to see this fabled place, we approached the large door and grasped the brass door ring to announce our arrival. But our grand entrance was cut short when our friend sheepishly slipped from behind the door and whispered that he had forgotten a very important detail. My companion and I bristled, our training as Black people having taught us to expect yet another barrier to our inclusion; even an informal one-Black-person quota at the establishment was not unimaginable. The tension broke, however, when we learned that *we* would not be excluded because of our race, but that *I* would have to go around to the back door because I was a female. I entertained the idea of making a scene to dramatize the fact that my humiliation as a female was no less painful and my exclusion no more excusable than had we all been sent to the back door because we were Black. But, sensing no general assent to this proposition, and also being of the mind that due to our race a scene would in some way jeopardize all of us, I failed to stand my ground. After all, the club was about to entertain its first Black guests— even though one would have to enter through the back door.

Perhaps this story is not the best example of the Black community's failure to address problems related to Black women's intersectionality seriously. It would be more apt if Black women, and only Black women, had to go around to the back door of the club and if the restriction came from within and not from outside the Black community. Still, this story does reflect a markedly decreased political and emotional vigilance toward barriers to Black women's enjoyment of privileges that have been won on the basis of race but continue to be denied on the basis of sex.[30]

The story also illustrates the ambivalence among Black women about the degree of political and social capital that should be expended toward challenging gender barriers, particularly when the challenges might conflict with the antiracism agenda. While there are a number of reasons—including antifeminist ones—why gender has not figured directly in analyses of the subordination of Black Americans, a central reason is that race is still seen by many as the primary oppositional force in Black lives.[31] If one accepts that the social experience of race creates both a primary group identity as well as a shared sense of being collectively assaulted, some of the reasons that Black feminist theory and politics have not figured prominently in the Black political agenda may be better understood.[32]

The experience of racial otherness that Black women share with Black men prevent Black feminist consciousness from patterning the development of white feminism. For white women, the creation of a consciousness that was distinct from and in opposition to that of white men figured prominently in the development of white feminist politics. Yet Black women, like Black men, live in a community that has been defined and subordinated by color.[33] Even though patriarchy clearly operates within the Black community, these shared experiences of white domination render the creation of a political consciousness that is oppositional to Black men untenable.

Yet while it is true that the distinct experience of racial otherness militates against the development of an oppositional feminist consciousness, the assertion of racial community sometimes supports defensive priorities that marginalize efforts to address and dismantle patriarchy within the Black community. This marginalization is apparent where artistic portrayals of sexism within the Black community meet with stiff resistance, or where discussions about economic and family policy uncritically embrace patriarchal values that compromise the interests of Black women. Examples of both of these tendencies can been seen in recent debates over dominant images of the Black family. The *Color Purple* controversy centered on allegations that Black men were categorically denigrated in Alice Walker's novel chronicling a Black woman's struggle against domestic abuse.[34] While it is clear that Black women are not immune from domestic violence, many critics viewed the story as dangerous to the interests of the Black community because it gave credence to violent stereotypes of Black males.[35] In short, the story of a Black woman's quest to overcome physical and emotional abuse was viewed by many as oppositional to the larger interest in combatting racism. Such issues—to the extent that they were valid concerns—should remain private, critics claimed.

The tendency to hold patriarchal values constant in the defense of Black interests is also illustrated in the ongoing debate over the alleged pathology of the Black family. This can be seen in the reaction to sociological and political characterizations of the Black family as the source of many of the Black community's social ills.

Daniel Moynihan's 1965 diagnosis of the ills of Black America depicted a deteriorating Black family, foretold the destruction of the Black male house-holder, and lamented the creation of the Black matriarchy.[36] His conclusions prompted a massive critique from liberal sociologists and from civil rights leaders.[37] Surprisingly, while many critics characterized the report as racist for its blind use of *white* cultural norms as the standard for evaluating *Black* families, relatively few responses argued that the report was sexist for its endorsement of a *patriarchal* vision of the family in which men hold tra-ditional dominant roles.[38]

This relative insensitivity to questions of patriarchy can be seen in the more recent controversy over the televised special *The Vanishing Black Fam-ily.*[39] In this Bill Moyers special, the Moynihan image of the dysfunctional Black family was rehearsed along with familiar images of promiscuous, in-dependent women and sexually irresponsible, immature Black men.[40] One apparent theme of the special was that welfare was in part responsible for the "vanishing" Black family because the government, through monthly payments, replaced the role of the male in the family. This has permitted Black men to father children carelessly and has simultaneously allowed Black women to choose state dependency over the more appropriate choice of settling with a husband.

Like the criticism lodged against the Moynihan report decades earlier, critics attacked the racist packaging of the program. Yet few challenged the patriarchal assumptions upon which the conclusions of pathology were based, such as the a priori association of female-headed families with dysfunction-ality and the implicit assumption that the answer to welfare dependence is to reinstitute the male as the family head. White feminists were equally culpable. There was little, if any, published response to the Moyers report from white feminist critics. Perhaps they were under the mistaken assumption that since the report focused on the Black community, the problems high-lighted were racial, not gender based. Whatever the reason, the result was that the ensuing debates over the future direction of welfare and family policy proceeded without significant feminist input. The absence of a strong feminist critique of the Moynihan/Moyers model not only impeded the interests of Black women but also compromised the interests of growing numbers of white women heads of household who find it difficult to make ends meet.

William Julius Wilson's *The Truly Disadvantaged* modified much of the moralistic tone of this debate by reframing the issue in terms of a lack of marriageable Black men.[41] According to Wilson, the decline in Black marriages is not attributable to poor motivation, bad work habits, or irresponsibility, but instead is caused by structural economics which have forced Black unskilled labor out of the work force. Wilson's approach represents a significant move away from that of Moynihan/Moyers in that he rejects their attempt to center the analysis on the morals of the Black community. Yet he too considers the proliferation of female-headed households as dysfunctional per se and fails to explain fully why such households are so much in peril. Because he incorporates no analysis of the way the structure of the economy and the work force subordinates the interests of women, especially childbearing Black women, Wilson's suggested reform begins with finding ways to put Black men back in the family. In Wilson's view, we must change the economic structure with an eye toward providing more jobs for Black men.

My criticism is not that providing Black men with jobs is undesirable; indeed, this is necessary not only for Black men themselves but for an entire community that is depressed and subject to a host of sociological and economic ills that accompany massive rates of unemployment. But as long as we assume that the massive social reorganization Wilson calls for is possible, why not think about it in ways that maximize the choices of Black women? For instance, Wilson only mentions in passing the need for day care and job training for single mothers. No mention at all is made of other practices and policies that are racist and sexist, and that contribute to the poor conditions under which nearly half of all Black women must live.[42] A more complete theoretical and political agenda for the Black underclass must take into account the specific and particular concerns of Black women; their families occupy the bottom rung of the economic ladder, and it is only through placing them at the center of the analysis that their needs and the needs of their families will be directly addressed.

EMBRACING THE INTERSECTION

If any real efforts are to be made to free Black people of the constraints and conditions that characterize racial subordination, then theories and strategies purporting to reflect the Black community's needs must include an analysis of sexism and patriarchy. Similarly, feminism must include an analysis of race if it hopes to express the aspirations of nonwhite women. Neither Black liberationist politics nor feminist theory can ignore the intersectional experiences of those whom the movements claim as their respective consituents. In order to include Black women, both movements must distance themselves from earlier approaches in which experiences are relevant only when they are related to certain clearly identifiable causes (for example, the oppression of Blacks is significant when based on race, of women when based on gender). The praxis of both should be centered on the life chances and life situations of people who should be cared about without regard to the source of their difficulties.

I have stated earlier that the failure to embrace the complexities of compoundedness is not simply a matter of political will, but is also due to the influence of a way of thinking about discrimination which structures politics so that struggles are categorized as singular issues. Moreover, this structure imports a descriptive and normative view of society that reinforces the status quo.

It is somewhat ironic that those concerned with alleviating the ills of racism and sexism should adopt such a top-down approach to discrimination. If their efforts instead began with addressing the needs and problems of those who are most disadvantaged and with restructuring and remaking the world where necessary, then others who are singularly disadvantaged would also benefit. In addition, it seems that placing those who currently are marginalized in the center is the most effective way to resist efforts to compartmentalize experiences and undermine potential collective action.

It is not necessary to believe that a political consensus to focus on the lives of the most disadvantaged will happen tomorrow in order to recenter discrimination discourse at the intersection. It is enough, for now, that such an effort would encourage us to look beneath the prevailing conceptions of discrimination and to challenge the complacency that accompanies belief in the effectiveness of this framework. By so doing, we may develop language which is critical of the dominant view and which provides some basis for unifying activity. The goal of this activity should be to facilitate the inclusion of marginalized groups for whom it can be said: "When they enter, we all enter."

NOTES

1. Gloria T. Hull, et al., eds., *All the Women Are White, All the Blacks Are Men, But Some of Us Are Brave* (Old Westbury, N.Y.: Feminist Press, 1982). For other works setting forth a feminist analysis of law from a nonwhite perspective, *see* Judy Scales-Trent, "Black Women and the Constitution: Finding Our Place, Asserting Our Rights (Voices of Experience: New Responses to Gender Discourse)," 24 *Harvard Civil Rights–Civil Liberties Law Review* 9 (1989); Regina Austin, "Sapphire-Bound," 1989 *Wisconsin Law Review* 539 (1989); Angela Harris, "Race and Essentialism in

Feminist Legal Theory," 42 *Stanford Law Review* 581 (1990); Paulette Caldwell, "A Hair Piece" (unpublished manuscript on file with author); Taunya Banks, "Dangerous Women: African-American Women Lawyers— The Ethics of Exclusion and Marginalization" (unpublished manuscript on file with author).

2. 673 F.2d 798 (5th Cir. 1983). These are all statutory cases pursuant to Title VII of the Civil Rights Act of 1964, 42 U.S.C. §2000e, *et seq.* as amended (1982).

3. Not all courts that have grappled with this problem have adopted the *DeGraffenreid* approach. Indeed, other courts have concluded that Black women are protected by Title VII. *See, e.g.*, Jeffries v. Harris Community Action Ass'n., 615 F.2d 1025 (5th Cir. 1980). However, the very fact that the Black women's claims are seen as aberrant suggests that sex-discrimination doctrine is centered in the experience of white women. Even those courts that have held that Black women are protected seem to accept that Black women's claims raise issues that the "standard" sex-discrimination claims do not. See Elaine W. Shoben, "Compound Discrimination: The Interaction of Race and Sex in Employment Discrimination," 55 *NYU Law Review* 793, 803–4 (1980), criticizing the *Jeffries* court's use of a sex-plus analysis to create a subclass of Black women.

4. *See also* Moore v. National Association of Securities Dealers, 27 EPD (CCH) §32.238 (D.D.C. 1981); but *see* Edmondson v. Simon, 86 FRD 375 (N.D. Ill. 1980), where the court was unwilling to hold as a matter of law that no Black female could represent without conflict the interests of both Blacks and females.

5. *See* Strong v. Arkansas Blue Cross and Blue Shield, Inc. 87 FRD 496 (E.D. Ark. 1980); Hammons v. Folger Coffee Co., 87 FRD 600 (W.D. Mo. 1980); Edmondson v. Simon, 86 FRD 375 (N.D. ill. 1980); Vuyanich v. Republic National Bank of Dallas, 82 FRD 420 (N.D. Tex. 1979); Colston v. Maryland Cup Corp., 26 Fed. Rules Serv. 940 (D. Md. 1978).

6. 416 F. Supp. 248 (N.D. Miss. 1976), aff'd., 673 F.2d 798 (5th Cir. 1982).

7. This interpretation of antidiscrimination law is part of a larger critique loosely termed critical race theory. While no determinative definition of this work is yet possible, one can generally say that the literature focuses on the relationship between law and racial subordination in American society. It shares with liberal race critiques a view that law has provided an arena for challenging white supremacy. Critical race theory goes beyond the liberal critiques, however, in that it exposes the facets of law and legal discourse that create racial categories and legitimate racial subordination.

   Other broad themes common to critical race theory include the view that racism is endemic to, rather than a deviation from, American norms. This developing literature reflects a common skepticism toward dominant claims of meritocracy, neutrality, objectivity, and color blindness. Critical race theory embraces a contextualized historical analysis of racial hierarchy as part of its challenge to the presumptive legitimacy of societal institutions.

The work manifests an appreciation of the role of the lived experience of people of color in constructing knowledge about race, law, and social change.

Critical race theory draws upon several traditions, including poststructuralism, postmodernism, Marxism, feminism, literary criticism, liberalism, and neopragmatism and discourses of self-determination such as Black nationalism and radical pluralism. The work is thus aggressively interdisciplinary in an effort to understand more fully how race is constructed, rationalized, and experienced in American society. Critical race theory goes beyond liberal understandings of race and racism by exploring those of its manifestations that support patriarchy, heterosexism, and class stratification. The normative stance of critical race theory is that massive social transformation is a necessary precondition of racial justice.

Work by scholars of color in this developing tradition includes: John Calmore, "Toward Archie Shepp and the Return of Fire Music: A Discourse on Critical Race Theory, Housing Law, and the African-American Predicament" (unpublished manuscript on file with author, 1990); Kimberle Crenshaw, "Race, Reform, and Retrenchment in Antidiscrimination Law," 101 *Harvard Law Review* 1331 (1988); Richard Delgado, "Storytelling for Oppositionalists and Others: A Plea for Narrative," 87 *Michigan Law Review* 2411 (1989); Neil Gotanda, "A Critique of 'Our Constitution Is Color Blind': Racial Categories and White Supremacy" (unpublished manuscript on file with author, 1990); Charles Lawrence, "The Id, the Ego, and Equal Protection: Reckoning with Unconscious Racism," 39 *Stanford Law Review* 317 (1987); Mari Matsuda, "Public Response to Racist Speech: Considering the Victim's Story," 87 *Michigan Law Review* 2320 (1989); Kendall Thomas, " 'Rouge et Noir' Reread: A Popular Memory of Herndon v. Georgia" (forthcoming in *Duke Law Journal*); Gerald Torres, "Local Knowledge, Local Color: Critical Legal Studies and the Law of Race Relations," 25 *San Diego Law Review* 1043 (1988); Patricia Williams, "Spirit-Murdering the Messenger: The Discourse of Fingerpointing as the Law's Response to Racism," 42 *Miami Law Review* 127 (1987); Robert Williams, "Taking Rights Aggressively: The Perils and Promise of Critical Legal Theory for Peoples of Color," 87 *Law & Inequality: A Journal of Theory and Practice* 103 (1987). Other work that shares some of these basic tenets includes: Alan Freeman, "Legitimizing Racial Discrimination Through Antidiscrimination Law: A Critical Review of Supreme Court Doctrine," 62 *Minnesota Law Review* 1049 (1978); Duncan Kennedy, "Comment: A Cultural Pluralist Case for Affirmative Action in Legal Academia" (forthcoming in *Duke Law Review*); Gary Peller, "Race Consciousness" (forthcoming in *Duke Law Journal*).

8. *See* Phyliss Palmer, "The Racial Feminization of Poverty: Women of Color as Portents of the Future for All Women," 11 *Women's Studies Quarterly* 3–4 (Fall 1983), posing the question why "white women in the women's movement had not created more effective and continuous alliances with

Black women when "simultaneously . . . black women have become heroines for the women's movement, a position symbolized by the consistent use of Sojourner Truth and her famous words, 'Ain't I a woman?' "

9. See Paula Giddings, *When and Where I Enter: The Impact of Black Women on Race and Sex in America* (New York: William Morrow & Co., 1984), p. 54.

10. Eleanor Flexner, *Century of Struggle: The Women's Rights Movement in the United States* (Cambridge, Mass.: Belknap Press, Harvard University Press, 1975), p. 91. See also Bell Hooks, *Ain't I a Woman?* (Boston: South End Press, 1981).

11. " 'Objectivity' is itself an example of the reification of white male thought." Hull et al., eds., *But Some of Us Are Brave*, p. xxv.

12. For example, many white females were able to gain entry into previously all-white male enclaves, not through bringing about a fundamental reordering of male versus female work, but in large part by shifting their "female" responsibilities to poor and minority women.

13. Feminists often discuss how gender-based stereotypes and norms reinforce the subordination of women by justifying their exclusion from public life and glorifying their roles within the private sphere. Law has historically played a role in maintaining this subordination by enforcing the exclusion of women from public life and by limiting its reach into the private sphere. *See, e.g.*, Deborah L. Rhode, "Association and Assimilation," 81 *Northwestern University Law Review* 106 (1986); Frances Olsen, "From False Paternalism to False Equality: Judicial Assaults on Feminist Community, Illinois 1869–95," 84 *Michigan Law Review* 1518 (1986); Martha Minow, "Foreword: Justice Engendered," 101 *Harvard Law Review* 10 (1987); Nadine Taub and Elizabeth Schneider, "Perspectives on Women's Subordination and the Role of Law," in this volume (and pp. 117–39 of the first edition).

14. This criticism is a discrete illustration of a more general claim that feminism has been premised on white middle-class women's experience. *E.g.*, early feminist texts such as Betty Friedan's *The Feminine Mystique* (New York: W.W. Norton & Co., 1963) placed white middle-class problems at the center of feminism and thus contributed to its rejection within the Black community. *See* Hooks, *Ain't I a Woman?*, pp. 185–96.

15. *See* Hooks, *Ain't I a Woman?*, pp. 94–99, discussing the elevation of sexist imagery in the Black liberation movement during the 1960s.

16. See generally Jacqueline Jones, *Labor of Love, Labor of Sorrow: Black Women, Work, and the Family from Slavery to the Present* (New York: Basic Books, 1985); Angela Davis, *Women, Race, and Class* (New York: Random House, 1981).

17. As Elizabeth Higginbotham noted, "women, who often fail to conform to 'appropriate' sex roles, have been pictured as, and made to feel, inadequate—even though as women they possess traits recognized as positive when held by men in the wider society. Such women are stigmatized because their

lack of adherence to expected gender roles is seen as a threat to the value system"; Elizabeth Higginbotham, "Two Representative Issues in Contemporary Sociological Work on Black Women," in Hull et al., eds., *But Some of Us Are Brave*, p. 95.

18. *See* generally Susan Brownmiller, *Against Our Will* (New York: Simon & Schuster, 1975); Susan Estrich, *Real Rape* (Cambridge, Mass.: Harvard University Press, 1987).

19. See Note, "Rape, Racism, and the Law," 6 *Harvard Women's Law Journal* 103, 177–23 (1983), discussing the historical and contemporary evidence suggesting that Black women are generally not thought to be chaste. See also Hooks, *Ain't I a Woman?*, p. 54, stating that stereotypical images of Black womanhood during slavery were based on the myth that "all black women were immoral and sexually loose"; Beverly Smith, "Black Women's Health: Notes for a Course," in Hull et al., eds., *But Some of Us Are Brave*, p. 110, noting that "white men for centuries have justified their sexual abuse of Black women by claiming that we are licentious, always 'ready' for any sexual encounter."

20. Dallas v. State, 76 Fla. 358, 79 So. 690 (1918), quoted in Note, 6 *Harvard Women's Law Journal* at 121 (*supra*, n. 19). Espousing precisely this view, one commentator stated in 1902: "I sometimes hear of a virtuous Negro woman but the idea is so absolutely inconceivable to me . . . I cannot imagine such a creature as a virtuous Negro woman." (ibid., p. 82). Such images persist in popular culture. See Paul Grein, "Taking Stock of the Latest Pop Record Surprises," *Los Angeles Times*, July 7, 1988, recalling the line "Black girls just wanna get fucked all night." Opposition to such negative stereotypes has sometimes taken the form of sexual conservatism. "A desperate reaction to this slanderous myth is the attempt . . . to conform to the strictest versions of patriarchal morality"; Smith, "Black Women's Health," in Hull et al., eds., *But Some of Us Are Brave*, p. 111. Part of this reaction is reflected in the attitudes and policies of Black schools, which have been notoriously strict in regulating the behavior of female students. See Gail Elizabeth Wyatt, "The Sexual Experience of Afro-American Women," in *Women's Sexual Experience: Exploration of the Dark Continent*, ed. Martha Kirkpatrick (New York: Plenum Publishing Corp., 1982), p. 24.

21. Because of the way the legal system viewed chastity, Black women could not be victims of forcible rape. One commentator has noted that "[a]ccording to governing stereotypes, chastity could not be possessed by Black women. Thus, Black women's rape charges were automatically discounted, and the issue of chastity was contested only in cases where the rape complainant was a white woman"; Note, 6 *Harvard Women's Law Journal* 126. Black women's claims of rape were not taken seriously regardless of the offender's race. A judge in 1912 said: "This court will never take the word of a nigger against the word of a white man [concerning rape]" (*ibid.*, p. 120). On the other hand, lynching was considered an effective remedy for a Black man's

rape of a white woman. Since rape of a white woman by a Black man was "a crime more horrible than death," the only way to assuage society's rage and to make the woman whole again was to brutally murder the Black man (*ibid.*, p. 125).

22. See "The Rape of Black Women as a Weapon of Terror," in Gerda Lerner, *Black Women in White America* (New York: Pantheon Books, 1972), pp. 172–93. *See also* Brownmiller, *Against Our Will*. Even where Brownmiller acknowledges the use of rape as racial terrorism, she resists making a "special case" for Black women by offering evidence that white women were raped by the Klan as well (*ibid.*, p. 139). Whether or not one considers the racist rape of Black women a "special case," such experiences are probably different.

23. Lerner, *Black Women in White America*, p. 173.

24. Paula Giddings notes that the combined effect of sexual and racial stereotypes: "Black women were seen as having all of the inferior qualities of white women without any of their virtues"; Giddings, *When and Where I Enter*, p. 82.

25. A cogent and insightful analysis of Black women's ambivalence with respect to the antirape movement, drawing on contemporary incidents like the Charles Stuart hoax in Boston and the Central Park jogger case, is offered by Valerie Smith, "Split Affinities: The Case of Interracial Rape," in *Conflicts in Feminism*, ed. Maryanne Hirsch and Evelyn Fox Keller (Routledge, Chapman, and Hall, 1990).

26. Brownmiller, *Against Our Will*, p. 272.

27. See Juan Williams, "Standing for Justice," in *Eyes on the Prize* (New York: Viking Press, 1987).

28. See Anna Julia Cooper, *A Voice from the South* (Ohio: Aldine Printing House, 1892; reprint ed., Westport, Conn.: Negro Universities Press, 1969).

29. *Ibid.*, p. 31.

30. To this one could easily add class.

31. An anecdote illustrates this point. A group of female law professors gathered to discuss "Isms in the Classroom." One exercise led by Pat Cain involved each participant listing the three primary factors that described herself. Almost without exception, white women in the room listed their gender either primarily or secondarily; none listed their race. All of the women of color listed their race first, and then their gender. This would suggest that identity descriptions seem to begin with the primary source of opposition with whatever the dominant norm is. See Pat Cain, "Feminist Jurisprudence: Grounding the Theories" (unpublished manuscript on file with the author), pp. 19–20.

32. For a comparative discussion of Third World feminism paralleling this observation, see Kumari Jayawardena, *Feminism and Nationalism in the Third World* (London: Zed Press, 1986).

33. For a discussion of how racial ideology creates a polarizing dynamic which subordinates Blacks and privileges whites, see Kimberle Crenshaw, "Race,

Reform, and Retrenchment: Transformation and Legitimation in Antidis-crimination," 101 *Harvard Law Review* 1331, 1371–76 (1988).

34. Jack Matthews, "Three 'Color Purple' Actresses Talk About Its Impact," *Los Angeles Times*, January 31, 1986; Jack Matthews, "Some Blacks Critical of Spielberg's 'Purple'," *Los Angeles Times*, December 20, 1985. But *see* Gene Siskel, "Does 'Purple' Hate Men?" *Chicago Tribune*, January 5, 1986; Clarence Page, "Toward a New Black Cinema," *Chicago Tribune*, January 12, 1986.

35. A consistent problem with any negative portrayal of African Americans is that they are seldom balanced by positive images. On the other hand, most critics overlooked the positive transformation of the primary male character in *The Color Purple*.

36. Daniel P. Moynihan, *The Negro Family: The Case for National Action* (Office of Policy Planning and Research, United States Department of Labor, 1965).

37. See Lee Rainwater and William L. Yancey, *The Moynihan Report and the Politics of Controversy* (Cambridge, Mass.: MIT Press, 1967), pp. 427–29, 395–97.

38. See Jacquelyne Johnson Jackson, "Black Women in a Racist Society," in *Racism and Mental Health* (Pittsburgh: University of Pittsburgh Press, 1973), pp. 185–86.

39. *The Vanishing Black Family*, PBS Television broadcast, January 1986.

40. Columnist Mary McGrory, applauding the show, reported that Moyers found that sex was as common in the Black ghetto as a cup of coffee; McGrory, "Moynihan was Right 21 Years Ago," *Washington Post*, January 26, 1968. George Will argued that oversexed Black men were more of a menace than Bull Connor, the Birmingham police chief who in 1968 achieved international notoriety by turning fire hoses on protesting school-children; Will, "Voting Rights Won't Fix It," *Washington Post*, January 23, 1986.

41. William Julius Wilson, *The Truly Disadvantaged: The Inner City, the Underclass, and Public Policy* (Chicago: University of Chicago Press, 1987).

42. Nor does Wilson include an analysis of the impact of gender on changes in family patterns. Consequently, little attention is paid to the conflict that may result when gender-based expectations are frustrated by economic and demographic factors. This focus on demographic and structural explanations represents an effort to regain the high ground from the Moyers/Moynihan approach, which is more psychosocial. Perhaps because psychosocial explanations have come dangerously close to victim blaming, their prevalence is thought to threaten efforts to win policy directives that might effectively address deteriorating conditions within the working class and poor Black communities. See Kimberle Crenshaw, "A Comment on Gender, Difference, and Victim Ideology in the Study of the Black Family," in *The Decline of Marriage Among African Americans: Causes, Consequences, and Policy Implications* (forthcoming 1990).

10 MARK TUSHNET

THE POLITICS OF CONSTITUTIONAL LAW

MOST of us think about constitutional law in two ways. Often we think of constitutional law as the expression of the deepest and most enduring values of the people of the United States, embodying our commitments to justice, fairness, and the like. Yet, perhaps as often we think of constitutional law as a form of politics, describing justices as "conservative" or "liberal" in the same way that we describe senators as conservative or liberal. These two ways of thinking about constitutional law sit uneasily together, but to understand constitutional law, and particularly for political activists interested in social change, it's important to keep them clearly distinct. This chapter begins by sketching the structure of the Constitution and follows with a brief constitutional history of the United States, to show how the two ways of thinking about the Constitution have arisen and how they maintain themselves by capturing different aspects of the Constitution's structure and history. The final section deals in somewhat more detail with the idea of constitutional rights, using as its central example the Supreme Court's decision that our constitutional principle of free speech was violated by a statute making it illegal to burn a flag as part of a political protest.[1]

The flag-burning case illustrates the tension between the two ways of thinking about the Constitution particularly well, because it is a typical "liberal" result, with an opinion, written by the liberal Justice William Brennan and a dissent written by the conservative Justice William Rehnquist, and yet the majority also included the conservatives Justice Antonin Scalia and Anthony Kennedy. A second focus will be the recent historical experience of the Warren Court in the 1960s, which suggests that, at least on occasion, the courts, and constitutional law, can be instruments of progressive political change used against reluctant politicians.

The combination of historical and structural arguments developed here may explain how the two perspectives operate. In the end, however, criticism and defense of the constitutional system must rest on political judgments about its ability to sustain progressive values in the future. I will suggest that progressives ought to be skeptical about becoming too deeply committed to a defense of the existing constitutional system, though some commitment is appropriate in light of the historical evolution of constitutional systems. Progressives should, of course, continue to be sensitive to the possibility that the constitutional system provides certain strategic advantages in particular political struggles, but should be skeptical about a *general* defense of that system.

THE STRUCTURE OF THE CONSTITUTION

When the drafters of the Constitution met in Philadelphia in 1789, most of them agreed that the system of government under which they were living was seriously inadequate.[2] Most government occurred through the state governments, and these, most of the framers believed, were incompetent at best and dangerous at worst. They were primarily concerned that state governments were too easily dominated by popular majorities, who then enacted legislation that promoted their own interest at the expense of the interests of the more stable and nationally oriented members of the community. For example, after the Revolution, many small farmers and craftsmen went into debt so that they could expand their production to meet the demands let loose by the onset of peace. Economic conditions, particularly in connection with trade with Europe, were unstable, though, and these debtors frequently found themselves hard-pressed to pay back what they owed on schedule. As a result, they pressured their state governments to adopt various forms of debt relief, such as postponements of repayment or even complete suspension of debts. And, on one important occasion when debtors were unable to obtain relief from their state government, they took up arms in what is known as Shays' Rebellion. Farmers in western Massachusetts, led by Daniel Shays, marched on local courthouses and attempted to prevent creditors from using established legal processes to collect their debts. When Massachusetts was able to suppress Shays' Rebellion only with some difficulty, the framers took the lesson to be that a stronger national government was needed.

State governments were causing trouble in other ways. Again because they were controlled by local, ordinarily popular, interests, state governments adopted policies dealing with trade and manufacturing that attempted to advance local interests without concern for the impact on other states. Local regulations frequently interfered with the development of a secure system of international trade. Economic development seemed to require, in addition, the growth of a nationwide market, for which some sort of national monetary system seemed necessary. But, again, state governments issued their own forms of money, sometimes refusing to recognize the money issued by other states.

As the framers saw it, perhaps people would eventually understand that the policies they had their state governments adopt were foolish, and that, by making economic development difficult, the people were not advancing their own long-term interests. But, the framers feared, it might take too long to learn that lesson. In the meantime, various European powers were watching the United States, eagerly awaiting the opportunity to dismantle the new nation and recolonize it.

The solution to these difficulties appeared to be a stronger national government. Such a government could override local interests and promote the broader national interest; it could have at its command sufficient military force to suppress internal rebellions and to thwart potential foreign conquerors; it could thereby open the way for secure economic development.

It was not all that difficult to identify what had to go into a new and more powerful national government, though working out the details in a way that satisfied all the interests within the nationalist coalition proved to be harder. First, the new Constitution should contain provisions that barred states from adopting the kinds of policies that had caused all the difficulties. To prevent the recurrence of the adoption of debtor relief statutes, the Constitution says that states may not adopt laws that impair the obligation of contracts. It also keeps them from issuing their own money. In an important provision that was the subject of later controversy, the Constitution also authorizes Congress to regulate commerce among the several states, or with foreign nations. For many years after the Constitution was adopted, lawyers and judges believed that this provision, on its own, made it unconstitutional for states to enact any laws regulating interstate commerce; it certainly authorized Congress to override localistic laws; and the courts soon took it to mean that they could invalidate local legislation that interfered with interstate and international commerce even if Congress had not acted.

The commerce clause, though, signals an important problem that the framers had to face. To accomplish their goals, they had to create a national government that was strong enough to override local policies of the sort that had caused the problems they were reacting to. Those policies, however, were adopted by popular majorities in the states. The framers then faced two problems. First, how were they to persuade those same popular majorities that a new national government should be created that would be able to frustrate the desires those majorities had been expressing in the states? Second, and more important in the long run, how were the framers to guarantee that the same popular majorities would not unite to control the new, and newly powerful, national government? Then indeed they would have jumped from the frying pan into the fire; state governments could create bad policy within their boundaries, while other states might still adopt good policies, but if the national government adopted bad policies everyone would suffer.

The framers were able to secure the adoption of the Constitution for a number of reasons. The adoption of the new Constitution was a much closer thing than most people now realize. The majorities in key states such as New York and Virginia were paper-thin. The proponents of the new Constitution were simply better politicians than its opponents. They were able to manipulate the timing of key votes, for example, and, perhaps more important, were better at manipulating the symbols of nationhood than the opponents of the Constitution. Finally, the nation did face serious difficulties, and the new Constitution was the only thing around that purported to be a solution to those difficulties. The framers knew, that is, how hard it is to beat something—their proposal—with nothing—the status quo that, it was widely agreed, was unsatisfactory.

The framers attempted to control popular majorities by combining several strategies that had the overall effect of making it extremely difficult for popular majorities to adopt effective policies to control the productive activities of the private sector. These strategies, still prominent in the contemporary constitutional system, were *federalism*—the allocation of substantial law-making power to state governments—and the *separation of powers*—the division of authority within a national government consisting of a president, a House of Representatives, a Senate, and an independent judiciary. The judiciary, in turn, was to have the power of *judicial review*, enabling it to overturn legislation that, in the view of the judges, violated the Constitution. The national government could act aggressively, through Congress and the courts, against local legislation that impaired the goals of national economic development, but federalism and the separation of powers would make it difficult for the national government itself to regulate the economy.

The framers were almost forced to build federalism into their system. Local attachments to state governments were too strong to overcome, so any successful restructuring of the national government would have to have important federalistic elements. Nonetheless, once the more powerful national government was created, federalism had a new role. State governments could not adopt regulations of commerce that interfered with economic development. They could, however, adopt what came to be known as "police power" regulations. These were laws designed to promote the health, safety, and general welfare of the state's population. A good example in modern times is provided by legislation aimed at reducing the adverse social impact of plant closings. The existence of many states in itself places a limit on the kinds of police power regulations states can adopt, at least once economic development reaches the point where there is a large national market for capital. The limit arises because, if the owners of capital are unhappy with the police power regulations one state adopts, they can relocate to another state with more favorable regulations. The mere threat of relocation constrains states from adopting police power regulations that substantially interfere with the decisions the owners of capital wish to make. In the past, this threat limited the ability of states to adopt effective programs of social insurance and even wages-and-hours limitations, and more recently it inhibited the adoption of effective local plant-closing legislation. The general effect of federalism in a developed economy, then, is to make it difficult for local majorities to adopt substantial social welfare programs.

What about the powerful national government? Even if federalism makes it difficult for individual states to adopt social welfare programs through the exercise of their police powers, the national government can adopt even more substantial programs applicable throughout the country. The fact that the social welfare system of the United States is significantly narrower in scope than similar systems in other advanced economies, and the much more limited scope of legislation dealing with plant closings in the United States compared to legislation in Western Europe, suggests that there is something about the structure of the national government that makes it hard to get such programs enacted. Constitutional structures are not the only source of the difference, of course, but the existence of a system of separation of powers on the national level is one part of the explanation. Another is the well-established practice, not itself required by the Constitution, of choosing members of Congress by plurality votes in single districts.

The different elements in the national government are selected in different ways, giving them different constituencies. For example, members of the House of Representatives are elected for the relatively short period of two years, and they represent the smallest units or districts in the national system. For this reason, the framers thought, the House of Representatives would be the branch most often dominated by popular majorities of the sort that had caused difficulties in the states. Somehow, the House had to be kept under control. The Senate and the presidency were the means of control. In the original Constitution, senators were elected indirectly, chosen by state legislatures. The thought was that, in order to obtain the support of a state legislature, a senator would have to be a relatively elite member of the state's governing class, and such people, the framers hoped, would be able to take a broader view than the members of the House of Representatives. Even after the Seventeenth Amendment replaced indirect election of senators with their direct election by the people in the states, the fact that senators serve for six rather than two years provides some check on popular control of Congress. In addition, of course, the cost of running a statewide campaign is so great, even compared to the extremely high cost of running for the House of Representatives, that few populist candidates can afford to run for the Senate.

The president, too, is elected indirectly. The framers' hope that the Electoral College would actually play a serious role in selecting the president was defeated almost from the outset. Once again, however, the fact that the president is selected by the largest constituency, the nation as a whole, for a longer period than the House of Representatives imposes some limits on the development of a national popular program.

Plurality elections in single districts lead directly to the creation of a two-party system, whose effect is to make it more difficult for dissident voices to receive serious political consideration. In a plurality system, a vote cast for a third party is almost always "wasted," in the sense that the third-party candidate rarely has a real chance of winning the election. In other democratic systems, the existence of many parties has been a source of important social initiatives (not all of them progressive, of course). In the United States, third parties have been indirectly influential, as when socialists in the early years of the twentieth century forced the major parties to develop programs responsive to the needs of workers in the new highly industrialized economy. This sort of indirect influence, however, while important, operates more slowly than direct participation in the formation of governments.

Another limit on the power of the national government arises from the separate constituencies of the president and Congress. Because they have different bases of political support, the president and members of Congress are under no real political pressure to develop a coordinated national party program. If a member of Congress "delivers" to his or her constituency, by securing defense contracts or other subsidies for locally important industries, the member can almost completely ignore the president's desires on other issues. Popular forces cannot just work within a national party structure, as they can in parliamentary systems; they must assemble majorities both nationwide and in many local districts as well, a task that has been beyond the limited financial resources available to most popular movements in the history of the United States.

To see the effect of this scheme of separation of powers, consider the problem of plant closings. Each plant closing has an impact on a particular community, and eventually there may be enough plant closings for people throughout the country to believe that some sort of legislative response is required. What do they have to do to get such a program adopted by the national government? They must persuade majorities in the House and Senate, and they must make sure that the president is sympathetic to their concerns. Because the entire House of Representatives is elected every two years, in theory at least a nationwide popular majority can elect a sympathetic House in one election. Only one-third of the Senate is elected in each national election; to gain control over the Senate, then, the popular majority must hold together for at least four years. Similarly, because the president's term is four years, the same majority must be in place for that period. Given the advantages incumbents have in elections, creating a majority in all the branches of the government for a new program is likely to be, and indeed has proven to be, quite difficult.

Experience has shown that new coalitions, such as Franklin Delano Roosevelt's New Deal coalition, can be assembled only over a period of eight to ten years at the quickest. In this way the separation of powers serves the goal of obstructing the ability of popular majorities to gain control of the powerful national government.

And even after popular majorities do gain control, there is another hurdle: judicial review of the legislation they manage to enact. Judicial review is, among other things, the power to declare statutes unconstitutional and thereby to place a legal obstacle in the path of implementing the program embodied in the statutes. The judges of the federal courts, including the Supreme Court, are formally independent of the control of political majorities, at least in the sense that the judges cannot be removed from office if popular majorities disagree with their actions (as majorities can remove elected officials, by voting for their opponents in the next election). The judiciary is, however, indirectly dependent upon popular majorities, because federal judges are nominated by the president and must be confirmed by the Senate before they can take office. As judges retire, resign, or die, they are replaced by new judges who are in tune with the political forces then in control. The effect of life tenure for judges, then, is analogous to the longer terms for senators: It means that a political majority must hold together for a long enough time to gain control, not only of the Congress and the presidency, but also the courts, if it is to implement its program without obstruction. Historically, it takes about a decade for a political majority to get control of the courts; if a new coalition cannot hold together for that long, it will be unable to take over the government as a whole.

The structure of the Constitution, including federalism, the separation of powers, and judicial review, makes it difficult, though not impossible, for new political majorities to replace old coalitions. Judicial review in particular is, in the overall scheme of the Constitution, not really a mechanism for vindicating some predetermined set of individual rights—and in particular not the rights advanced by progressive forces at any particular time—but is rather either a way to block the programs of new majorities that are not strong enough to sustain themselves for more than a decade or a means of smoothing out the period of transition from one political majority to another. The constitutional history of the United States confirms this interpretation of the constitutional structure.

A BRIEF CONSTITUTIONAL HISTORY OF THE UNITED STATES

We have already seen how the Constitution was designed to unify the nation behind a program of economic development. For about a generation after the framing, roughly until 1835, the political coalition that had supported the original Constitution continued to dominate the national political process. Congress was content to let economic development occur in a relatively unguided way, and the states, under the influence of the philosophy of the Constitution, rarely attempted to interfere with interstate or international trade. The Supreme Court endorsed the nationalist economic program by upholding the constitutionality of the government's primary instrument of economic control, the Bank of the United States, in an opinion that also cast doubt on the constitutionality of state efforts to interfere with commerce.[3]

By the 1830s the original nationalist coalition was coming under strain. Throughout the nation, popular majorities supported the programs of Jacksonian Democracy, which sought, in a modest way, to displace the entrenched economic elites and to replace them with a more dynamic entrepreneurial element. Here, too, the Supreme Court came to the aid of the newly dominant political coalition, by allowing states to eliminate monopolies they had granted in earlier years, in favor of unrestricted competition.[4] (As might be expected, given the dynamics of the constitutional structure described earlier, the Court was divided over this and other issues implicated in the Jacksonian program, because not all of the justices who were part of the prior generation's politically dominant coalition had been replaced by the time the Jacksonians became dominant elsewhere in the government.)

In addition, and more important in the long run, the issue of slavery began to fracture the nation. The framers of the Constitution knew that the problem of slavery was likely to be divisive; it had, among other things, caused enormous difficulties in the design of the details of representation at the constitutional convention. The framers believed that they had developed a system of government in which the interests of states—especially the southern states—would be permanently protected. The growth of abolitionist sentiment in the North made southerners extremely nervous and, although in fact they continued to control the national government—including the Supreme Court—up to the election of Abraham Lincoln in 1860, they became more and more dissatisfied with the constitutional system. Somewhat ironically, one important branch of the abolitionist movement, led by William Lloyd Garrison, also found the Constitution unsatisfactory, calling it a "covenant with death" because, as the Garrisonians understood, the structure of the Constitution did indeed provide substantial protection for the continued existence of slavery.

The Civil War must be understood, in constitutional terms, as a demonstration of the failure of the Constitution. The carefully designed balance of powers, through federalism and separation of powers, turned out to be unable to manage the conflict over slavery. The Supreme Court used its power of judicial review in a futile effort to take the issue of slavery out of national politics by holding, in the notorious *Dred Scott* case, that Congress had no power to regulate slavery.

Once the North defeated the Southern rebels, they returned to the original Constitution, modifying it in order to eliminate, as best they could, the legacy of slavery in the Southern and national political systems. The Thirteenth Amendment abolished slavery, the Fourteenth Amendment provided a charter of national liberty to be protected against encroachment by the states, and the Fifteenth Amendment guaranteed blacks the right to vote. These amendments demonstrate that the constitutional system can incorporate sustained popular pressures, yet, coming as they did only after a bloody war, they also show how difficult it is for progressives majorities to have their way. For about a decade, the so-called Reconstruction of the South promised to restructure power in the South and, therefore, in the nation. The national commitment to the elimination of the legacy of slavery waned and, after 1876, neither Congress nor the courts were terribly interested in using the three Civil War amendments to continue to protect the interests of blacks.

The Fourteenth Amendment soon became the vehicle for protecting a new set of individual rights—not the rights of blacks to be free of terrorism or white domination, but the rights of corporate investors to be free of interference from political majorities who wished to control their investments. The Fourteenth Amendment provides that states shall not "deprive any person of life, liberty, or property, without due process of law." In a series of decisions culminating in *Lochner* v. *New York*,[5] the Supreme Court held that the due process clause limited not only the procedures states could use but also their substantive power to regulate corporations, finding that certain kinds of regulations unconstitutionally interfered with capital's "liberty" to enter into contracts freely. Although the Court upheld regulations of wages and hours in situations where it believed there to be a real possibility of an imbalance of bargaining power—in cases involving miners and women workers—in *Lochner* it invalidated a wages-and-hours law that applied to what it took to be ordinary male workers because, as the Court saw it, such a law was simply an effort to reallocate power from capital to labor.

The Court's abandonment of the cause of blacks after 1876 was consistent with the political tenor of the nation, as the structure of the Constitution suggests it would be. And, for a time, the exuberant economic growth of the nation in the last quarter of the nineteenth century made the Court's support of capital consistent with what politically dominant elites desired, even in the face of substantial opposition from working people.[6] By the turn of the century, though, the Progressive movement had begun to support a more modern form of governmental regulation of capital to promote the long-term interests of capital against the shortsightedness of individual capitalists. Progressives, in gradually taking control of state legislatures and influencing Congress and several presidents, came to see the Supreme Court as a serious obstacle to their political programs.

Until the New Deal, the Supreme Court's course was one of erratic opposition to Progressive reforms, a course that mirrored the inability of Progressives to sustain a political coalition that controlled the other branches of the national government. With the onset of the Depression, though, and the creation of Roosevelt's New Deal coalition, the Court's opposition to reform caused a constitutional crisis. The Court invalidated central elements of the New Deal program—elements, to be sure, that almost certainly did little to alleviate the economic causes or effects of the Depression—and Roosevelt attacked both the Court's decisions and the Court itself. Roosevelt proposed to "pack" the Supreme Court by appointing several new justices who he assumed would support his programs. The Court-packing plan failed, at least in the sense that it was not enacted, but the Court itself came around to support New Deal programs, first by a strategic change in vote by Justice Owen Roberts and then, again as the constitutional structure would suggest, by timely retirements from the Court.

After the New Deal, the distinctive form the welfare state had in the United States was in place, and the Court retreated from its opposition to governmental regulation of capital. It withdrew from the supervision of what it came to call "economic and social legislation." Almost at the same time, though, the Court began to develop a new constituency. The capitalists who had been the Court's supporters had lost the battle, and it made little political or structural sense for the Court to continue to fight on behalf of their interests. Because a new coalition was in place, one that included blacks and political liberals, the Court developed a constitutional theory that made the protection of the members of the newly dominant coalition the Court's primary task. As Justice Harlan Fiske Stone put it in what has become the most famous footnote in the Court's history, the Court would be especially alert to legislation that adversely affected the interests of "discrete and insular minorities."[7]

The New Deal coalition continued to dominate national politics through the 1950s and early 1960s, and the Court continued to play its appointed role. Most dramatically, of course, the Court invalidated the system of racial segregation in the South. Yet, despite the opposition that the desegregation decisions generated in the South, eliminating segregation was, first of all, consistent with Stone's theory of constitutional protection of New Deal interests, and, second, eliminated a regional source of embarrassment to a nation engaged in a worldwide ideological struggle over "democracy" with the Soviet Union. When the very same Court confronted basic challenges to the constitutional order that, it believed, were posed by American Communists, it firmly upheld most of the efforts to suppress domestic communism. Strikingly, in a series of parallel cases involving on the one hand efforts by Congress and state legislatures throughout the nation to suppress the Communist party and on the other hand otherwise barely distinguishable efforts by southern legislatures to suppress the black movement, the Court issued a series of decisions whose bottom line was, as Professor Harry Kalven put it, that the Communists always lost and the NAACP never did.[8]

The picture changed a bit during the 1960s. The Court became less suspicious of domestic dissent, largely because, to the extent that dissent was linked to international communism it was a failure and, to the extent that dissent was linked to black protest, it seemed consistent with the full development of the New Deal program. More important, the Court continued to promote the program of the New Deal coalition, particularly in its Great Society version of a more robust welfare state, when that coalition was in the process of disintegration.

The election of Richard Nixon and his appointment of Warren Burger as chief justice, and subsequent appointments of three other conservative justices, effectively terminated the alliance that the Court had struck with the increasingly devitalized New Deal coalition. Yet, until the late 1980s, no new political coalition replaced the New Deal coalition, as the continued domination of Congress by the Democratic party showed. Not surprisingly, then, with no clear direction forthcoming from the elected branches of government, the Supreme Court limped along, on the whole taking a moderately conservative line but occasionally making some progressive decisions, as in the abortion cases of 1973.

By the end of the 1980s the Supreme Court appeared to have taken a definitive turn in the conservative direction. In one sense this too was to be expected, for the Democratic party came to reflect, as the Republicans already did, the domination of the political system as a whole by increasingly conservative elites. And yet, the political situation may be sufficiently fluid to make it possible for progressive forces to recapture the Supreme Court for their programs if they succeed in capturing the elected branches of the government, and even in the absence of a large-scale political transformation, to find the Court an occasional ally in political struggles.

The history of the Supreme Court, and of constitutional law, shows that the structure the framers put in place actually worked in the way they hoped it would. The Supreme Court has acted as a brake on overly quick political change, and so has been largely a conservative force in the society. But it has also come around to support and even advance progressive programs when the other branches of the government supported such programs consistently enough. The rhythm of politics in the Supreme Court and constitutional law is somewhat more sedate than that of politics elsewhere in the government, but in the end constitutional law is, and always has been, a reflex of politics.

CONSTITUTIONAL RIGHTS IN PROGRESSIVE POLITICS

The structure and history of the Constitution, as recounted above, suggest that progressives ought to be skeptical about their ability to utilize constitutional law as a means of advancing their programs. Skepticism, though, may seem inappropriate in light of the relatively recent—though apparently now abandoned—role of the Supreme Court in supporting first the black civil rights movement and then, somewhat less forcefully but crucially on the central issue of the right to procreative choice, the women's movement. And, for several reasons, progressives are right in refusing to write off the appeal to constitutional rights as one of their modes of political action. Yet, there are also reasons to be quite self-conscious about the risks of that appeal.

As the brief history of constitutional law suggested, the Supreme Court's support for the civil rights and women's movements reflected the array of political forces in the political system generally. In the long view, the Warren Court was an unusual and brief instance in which the Court happened to come under control of progressive interests to a somewhat greater extent than those forces sustained elsewhere in the political system. One lesson of the brevity of the Warren Court—conservatives have now dominated the Supreme Court for a longer period than Earl Warren was chief justice—is that progressive advance through the use of the courts cannot be sustained in the absence of progressive advance through other forms of politics. Another lesson of the Warren Court experience, though, is that there are times when the political system as a whole is sufficiently open to progressive change that appeals to constitutional rights can be effective not only in politics but in the courts as well. Of course, those times of relative openness may themselves be brief, in which case the opportunity for progressive use of the courts may be quite limited, or they may be fairly sustained, in which case more might be accomplished in the courts.

In addition, appeals to constitutional rights can sometimes work quite effectively in the rhetoric of political discourse. As a general matter, popular respect for the ideas of rights means that an argument phrased as an appeal to constitutional right has at least a little greater initial force than an argument phrased solely in terms of what is a good thing for the society to do. People get indignant, or at least understand others' being indignant, when they feel that their rights have been infringed, in a way that they don't when they are told merely that there are better ways to do things. And, from the relatively narrow point of view of progressive lawyers, there's not much else they can contribute to progressive political activity than arguments premised on the possibility that the legal system will recognize rights: That's just about the only argument that lawyers, as distinct from other political activists, can make.

Appeals to rights can be effective beyond rhetoric. As the example of desegregation litigation indicates, sometimes they can be used to produce concrete victories for progressive forces. The victories can be won in court directly, or small victories in court can be used as a focus for organizing a progressive constituency for further action seeking more extensive changes, both in additional court cases and through legislative action brought on by pressure from the mobilized community. Indeed, sometimes *defeats* in court can effectively mobilize a group, by demonstrating to them that they can't rely on any government institution, as those institutions are currently composed, to advance their interests so they better organize to change the government. Consistent with the general propositions I have presented about the role of the courts in the government, the desegregation example shows that the beneficial effects of court victories by invoking rights depend on a particular array of political forces—there a South whose political elites were out of step with the national political elites to which the Supreme Court was responding. (The related point about the occasional usefulness of court defeats should be clear.)

Appeals to the Constitution, then, are an appropriate part of the repertoire of progressive politics. Their limitations, though, deserve attention, too. First, conservatives can appeal to rights just as well as progressives can. The Supreme Court over the course of its history has been quite sensitive to claims by capital that progressive legislation infringes the right to private property, for example, and the Supreme Court has recently found in the Constitution a right, held by white men, to be protected against racial discrimination in the form of affirmative action.[9] Preserving the possibility of progressive invocations of constitutional rights has, probably, in the long run contributed to the effectiveness of progressive movements, but the practical ability of conservatives to get the courts to help them, over the course of constitutional history, makes the question substantially closer than a nostalgic reverence for the Warren Court sometimes leads progressives to think.

Second, not all appeals to the Constitution are equally effective. Progressives have tried to argue that there is a constitutional right to a minimum standard of living, or to minimal provision of shelter. Not only have these arguments had extremely limited success in the courts; even more, the rhetoric of rights doesn't seem to have been particularly effective in the general political domain either. Where "rights" to food and shelter are involved, appeals to individual and collective responsibility seem to have worked somewhat better than appeals to rights per se, though as the conditions in the cities of the United States attest nothing has worked very well for the victims of United States capitalism in decline. Of course there are many reasons for the ineffectiveness of appeals to such rights; for example, the array of political forces is not hospitable to the basic claims, no matter how they are phrased, and were the political forces to change, the rhetoric of rights might then become more effective.

Yet, without attributing too much to the defects of an appeal to rights as a general matter, we may note that, in an important way, appeals to rights are inherently limited. Such appeals operate within the legal system, or at least within a rhetorical structure shaped in large measure by what the legal system has already done. The precedents, which do of course recognize some rights and provide the basis for arguing that additional rights should be recognized, also help to define the limits of permissible extensions of existing rights. Some things, such as a right to shelter, simply "go too far" in light of what the legal system has already done. What exactly "too far" means is determined in specific contexts, but in general it will be strongly affected by the sound common sense of the community of professional lawyers. Because of the social origins and affiliations of most of its members, and because of who pays its bills, the legal community is on the whole a rather conservative group, in the sense that it always thinks that the limits of "responsible" reform are much closer to existing arrangements than many progressives do. Thus, because the effectiveness of appeals to rights will be substantially affected by the views of a relatively conservative community of professional lawyers, such appeals will almost inevitably be effective only within fairly narrow limits.

The role of rights and court victories in political organizing is also more complex than it might seem at first. For, although victories in courts can mobilize constituencies to further action, they can sometimes demobilize constituencies, in essence making the victory too easy or premature in terms of the overall development of political support for progressive programs. Here the abortion controversy may provide a simplified example. In 1973, when the Supreme Court found that a woman's right to choose to have or not have an abortion was protected against substantial state regulation by the Constitution, the women's movement was not fully formed. The Court, and the segments of the political elite to which it was reponsive, may have seen the women's movement as a potential source of support, worth encouraging by giving it a victory on a crucially important issue. Yet, among the consequences of the Court's decision was, perhaps ironically, a relative weakening of the women's movement. The abortion decision generated a counterrights movement, invoking the language of rights to call itself the "right to life" movement. And, because pro-choice forces could rely on the courts to invalidate legislation that the antichoice forces pushed through legislatures, they had relatively less need to sustain the kind of organizing pressure that leads legislatures to act—in short, they had relatively less need to continue to mobilize their constituency for political action. By 1989, when the Court appeared ready to reconsider the premises of the 1973 abortion decisions, the pro-choice movement had to gear up and use forms of political action that it had not entirely abandoned but had played down in recent years. In the short run, this placed it at a disadvantage in the legislative arena, though the ultimate outcome remains uncertain.

A final problematic dimension of appeals to ideas of rights arises precisely from the fact that appealing to rights comes quite naturally to lawyers, including progressive lawyers. Of course there is no particular reason why a progressive political movement should involve lawyers at all, but to the extent that it does, the lawyers' contribution may be to shift the language of the movement in the direction of appeals to rights. That may not always be to the good, as the conservative appropriation of the language of rights to attack affirmative action shows. That is, to the extent that a movement's rhetoric relies on appeals to rights, it becomes vulnerable to redefinitions of the rights that are at stake. And, once again, the structural fact that the courts, as part of the political system, most often reflect existing arrays of power, means that redefinitions to the disadvantage of progressive movements are rather likely to occur. Appealing to rights may be all that lawyers can contribute to progressive movements, but sometimes the movements should reject the contribution.

The Supreme Court's decision finding it unconstitutional for the government to punish flag desecration, which occurred as part of a political protest, illustrates in a particular setting some of the difficulties I have described above in general terms. Gregory Johnson, who describes himself as a revolutionary Communist, burned a flag during a demonstration against the policies of the Reagan administration. The Supreme Court held that the First Amendment's protection of free speech meant that Johnson could not be punished for his actions.

Even on the surface, the Court's decision is somewhat ironic. As the

Court's analysis demonstrated, governments make flag burning illegal only because so many people are offended by the message of contempt for the existing government that flag burning conveys to them.[10] Yet, if Johnson can assert a free speech defense to his prosecution, it becomes harder for him to convey that message. "After all," viewers may think, "because he can't go to jail for burning the flag, nothing much is really at stake here—including his protest against the government and its policies." Although the flag-burning case may present an extreme example, the dynamic I have described has almost certainly affected the development of protest activity in the United States. Once the courts defended the rights of protestors to hold marches on city streets and the like, "ordinary" marches became less effective as methods of attracting uncommitted people to the protest movement; protest marches became routine, almost not worth noticing, and therefore not that effective. As a result, marches have to be massive before people pay attention to them, and a march that attracts a fair number of people can be a failure because it doesn't attract as many people as its predecessor. Or, protestors have to develop novel ways of attracting attention, through street theater such as "sleep-ins" in parks to bring the problem of homelessness to the attention of policymakers and the public. As a result, either protest becomes routinized and thereby domesticated—something that the political system puts up with precisely because it is ineffective—or it becomes so out of the ordinary that it is not protected by the right of free speech and so is made ineffective by being suppressed.

Justice Brennan's opinion for the Court in the flag-burning case moved the use of free speech to discredit protest to an even deeper level. He suggested, as the argument so far has also done, that the Court's vindication of Johnson's free speech claim in itself demonstrated the invalidity of his criticism of the United States. The message is something like this: "After all, if the Constitution protects Johnson from prosecution for doing something so offensive to almost everyone in the country as burning the flag, that shows what a great country this is—and therefore shows that Johnson is wrong."[11] Justice Brennan went further. He suggested that people should use, not the vindication of Johnson's claim in the Supreme Court, but the very moment when he burned the flag as an occasion for celebrating the nation's strength. Observers should have saluted the flag as Johnson burned it, Justice Brennan said, and then given it a respectful burial. Obviously, were people to respond to Johnson's action in that way, it would completely lose its effectiveness as an act of criticism of the government and its policies.

Justice Brennan is a liberal, and, as a member of the Supreme Court, he is a part of the nation's political elite. His opinion in the flag-burning case shows that he has a quite subtle understanding of the role that the vindication of rights has in maintaining the existing political system against those who would disrupt or replace it. Others, like Chief Justice Rehnquist, would simply suppress the flag burning. We might fairly ask, "Which course is more likely to serve the long-term interests of political elites?" I have suggested that the vindication of rights, as illustrated in the flag-burning decision, does so. That, of course, would once again be consistent with the overall role of the Constitution and the Supreme Court in stabilizing the political system.

CONCLUSION

The skepticism about the Constitution suggested by the structure and history of the Constitution should be overcome in some situations, as when the political situation is fluid enough that progressives can reasonably expect their interests to be advanced by appeals to constitutional rights. That might not happen very often, and progressives should always be aware of the risks, such as the possibility of a conservative assertion of counterrights, that attend the reinforcement of the rhetoric of rights. Even more, they should be aware that when they "succeed" in the courts, they may lead the courts to generate formulations about rights that, in the long run, may stand in the way of progressive political advance.

Of course one also takes one's political victories where one finds them. I suspect that in the next decade progressives are going to find few victories in constitutional law, in which case the skepticism I have described, while appropriate, will hardly be worth worrying about.

NOTES

1. Texas v. Johnson, 109 S.Ct. 2533 (1989).
2. The most subtle elaboration of the views of the framers of the Constitution is *The Federalist Papers*, particularly the classic numbers 10 and 51. The general perspective developed in this section is strongly influenced by Charles Beard, *An Economic Interpretation of the Constitution* (New York: Macmillan, 1913), a classic work which remains valuable even though its particular thesis about the origins of the Constitution has been discredited. The most important modern work for students of the origins of the Constitution is Gordon Wood, *The Creation of the American Republic* (Chapel Hill: University of North Carolina Press, 1969).
3. McCulloch v. Maryland, 17 U.S. (4 Wheat.) 316 (1819).
4. *See* Proprietors of Charles River Bridge v. Proprietors of Warren Bridge Co., 36 U.S. (11 Pet.) 420 (1837); James Willard Hurst, *Law and the Conditions of Freedom in Nineteenth Century America* (Madison: University of Wis-

consin Press, 1956); Stanley Kutler, *Privilege and Creative Destruction* (Philadelphia: J. B. Lippincott Co., 1971).

5. 198 U.S. 45 (1905).
6. *E.g.*, the Court creatively—a critic might even say lawlessly—construed the Constitution to allow the government to penalize the labor leader Eugene Debs for leading a strike against the Pullman railroads. In re Debs, 158 U.S. 564 (1894).
7. United States v. Carolene Products, Inc., 304 U.S. 144, 152 n. 4 (1938).
8. Harry Kalven, *A Worthy Tradition* (New York: Harper and Row, 1988), p. 259.
9. Not to mention the invocation of the rights of the fetus in the antichoice literature.
10. It's probably worth noting, too, that in an important sense Johnson shares with the people he offended exactly the same sense, that the flag is an extremely important symbol of the government and policies of the United States.
11. This suggests that (putting the personal impact on him aside—which an outsider to his political decision can't do) Johnson may have made a political error in asserting, up to the Supreme Court, a free speech defense of what he did. An alternative view of the fact that Johnson did assert such a defense is that it shows the deformations progressive movements face when they rely on lawyers whose only professional tool is the invocation of rights.

11 DAVID KAIRYS

FREEDOM OF SPEECH

HISTORIANS and legal scholars acknowledge that there have been incidents and periods in our history in which freedom of speech has been
denied, but these events are usually described as aberrations and blamed on
some overzealous individual or group that was out of step with American
traditions. It is commonly assumed in the courts and law reviews that there
were no significant court decisions on freedom of speech before the First
World War, and that shortly thereafter speech was legally protected by the
Supreme Court and has remained so ever since. Popular literature extends
these views posited in the legal literature to embrace the idea that freedom
of speech is a cornerstone of the Constitution and the basis of our country
that has been faithfully enforced by the courts throughout our history.

However, despite persistent but nonspecific references to "our traditions"
in legal and popular literature, no right of free speech as we know it existed,
either in law or practice, until a basic transformation of the law governing
speech in the period from about 1919 to 1940. Before that time, one spoke
publicly only at the discretion of local, and sometimes federal, authorities,
who often prohibited what they, the local business establishment, or other
powerful segments of the community did not want to hear.

From the adoption of the First Amendment (1791) to the beginning of
the basic legal transformation (1919), a variety of social and religious activists
demanded recognition of freedom of speech. The most significant of these—
the abolitionists, the anarchists, the Industrial Workers of the World (IWW,
or Wobblies), the Socialist party, and the early labor and women's movements—were sometimes successful in speaking, gathering, and distributing
literature publicly. Federal and state courts, however, repeatedly refused to
protect any form of speech.

The transformation of the law of free speech between 1919 and 1940
resulted primarily from the activities of the labor movement, the first mass-

I appreciate the helpful comments on early drafts of this chapter provided by Thomas
Emerson, Marge Frantz, Victor Rabinowitz, David Rudovsky, and James Weinstein.

based movement posing a credible challenge to the existing order that de-manded freedom of speech. The labor movement viewed free speech as a necessary component of the right to organize unions; and the seminal Su-preme Court decisions constitutionally protecting free speech came in the late 1930s as part of a general social, political, and legal shift in favor of labor that included, in the legislative arena, the adoption of the National Labor Relations Act (NLRA). The primary periods of stringent enforcement and enlargement of speech rights by the courts, the 1930s and the 1960s, correspond to the periods in which popular movements demanded such rights.

This history and the social role of the law regarding freedom of speech are presented, first, in a brief history of the law and practice from 1791 to 1940; second, in an analysis of legal decision making in two Supreme Court cases that best illustrate the basic change in speech law; and, third, in a discussion of the contemporary social and ideological role of freedom of speech.

A BRIEF HISTORY OF FREE SPEECH IN THE UNITED STATES, 1791 TO 1940

> Liberty . . . does not reside in laws, nor is it preserved by courts. Yet the ordinary citizen is so neglectful of the protection of his [or her] own liberties that the legal profession almost alone concerns itself with their interpre-tation. This is unfortunate—for lawyers are not commonly lovers of liberty.
>
> —*Leon Whipple (1927)*[1]

For all that has been written about freedom of speech, there is little that acknowledges the pre–World War I history or recognizes the profound change in the law in this century, and even less that attempts to analyze the change. But many primary and secondary sources document the specific incidents, practices, and court rulings that comprise this history.[2] The incidents and periods discussed here, while they concern a variety of speech, press, and religious activites, do not constitute a comprehensive treatment of speech. A particular aspect—speaking, gathering, and distributing literature in public places—has been emphasized because it is the subject of the Supreme Court cases that best illustrate the transformation in the law and because this aspect played a major role in the events leading to the transformation.

THE TRANSFORMATION IN LEGAL DOCTRINE

In 1894, the Reverend William F. Davis, an evangelist and longtime active opponent of slavery and racism, attempted to preach the Gospel on Boston

Common, a public park. For his first attempt, Davis was incarcerated for a few weeks in the Charles Street Jail; the second time, he was fined and appealed the sentence.

The hostility of the Boston authorities toward Davis probably stemmed from his espousal of the Social Gospel, a popular religious trend of the time that emphasized social responsibility and often condemned the corruption of city officials. In any event, Davis believed there was a "constitutional right of citizens to the use of public grounds and places without let or hindrance by the City authorities."[3]

The Supreme Court of Massachusetts disagreed.[4] In an opinion by Oliver Wendell Holmes—later a justice of the Supreme Court of the United States known for his decisions protecting freedom of speech—the court upheld Davis's conviction based on a city ordinance that prohibited "any public address" on public grounds without a permit from the mayor. Holmes, like almost all state and lower federal court judges,[5] viewed such an ordinance as simply a city regulation of the use of its park, which was within the city's rights as owner of the property. Davis had no basis, in the Constitution or elsewhere, to claim any limits on this property right:

> That such an ordinance is constitutional . . . does not appear to us open to doubt. . . . For the Legislature absolutely or conditionally to forbid public speaking in a highway or public park is no more an infringement of the rights of a member of the public than for the owner of a private house to forbid it in his house.

The Supreme Court of the United States unanimously affirmed, quoting Holmes's analogy to a private house.[6] In the only reference to the Constitution, the Court said it "does not have the effect of creating a particular and personal right in the citizen to use public property in defiance of the Constitution and laws of the State." Nor did the Court find any constitutional or other limit on the mayor's authority to deny permission selectively or for any reason: "The right to absolutely exclude all right to use, necessarily includes the authority to determine under what circumstances such use may be availed of, as the greater power contains the lesser."

Forty years later,* the labor movement, like Reverend Davis, believed that the government should hold and maintain public streets, sidewalks, and parks for the use of the people. Labor organizers had regularly been denied freedom of speech, except in cities with progressive or socialist mayors. After Congress passed the NLRA in 1935, the Congress of Industrial Organizations

---

* There were intervening related decisions; these cases and the process of change are discussed in later portions of this chapter.

(CIO) sought to explain its provisions and the benefits of unions and collective bargaining to working people throughout the country. Nowhere was their reception more hostile than in Jersey City, New Jersey, the turf of political boss Frank Hague.

The CIO planned to distribute literature on the streets and host outdoor meetings, but permits for these activities were denied by Hague. Hague was an early supporter of the less militant American Federation of Labor and of the New Deal, which provided him with resources for distribution to local communities and political allies. But by the mid-1930s he had firmly allied himself with the manufacturing and commercial establishments. He made it clear that labor organizers were not welcome in Jersey City, and many were cast out of town, usually by being put on a ferry to New York. Local businesses were promised that they would have no labor troubles while he was mayor; his response to the CIO was: "I am the law."[7]

The CIO brought suit against Hague, resulting in a Supreme Court ruling in favor of the CIO.[8] The Court said:

> Wherever the title of streets and parks may rest, they have immemorially been held in trust for the use of the public and, time out of mind, have been used for purposes of assembly, communicating thoughts between citizens, and discussing public questions. Such use of the streets and public places has, from ancient times, been a part of the privileges, immunities, rights, and liberties of citizens.

This was a direct repudiation of both the doctrinal basis and the result in *Davis*, and it first established the basic concept of free speech now taken for granted. However, the Court did not explicitly overrule *Davis*,[9] discuss the lack of free speech prior to its decision, or even acknowledge that it had made a fundamental change in legal doctrine. Rather, the opinion was an inspiring exposition of a right to freedom of speech based on natural law. Like all natural-law-based principles, it is essentially timeless and without a social context.

In the quoted passage, the streets and parks have "immemorially" been held for the people and used for speech "time out of mind," and the right of free speech stems "from ancient times." The Court apparently was some-what defensive and wished to emphasize this point, since it is repeated three times in the crucial passage of the opinion. But there is no indication as to what time or place the Court was referring; it certainly had never been so in the United States before this very case, as the Court had itself ruled in *Davis*. One can almost feel sorry for Boss Hague: like most of his contem-poraries, even those who never reached the level of boss, and city admin-istrators throughout American history, Hague prohibited speech he or the local establishment did not want to hear, surely unaware that he was tampering with rules "from ancient times."

The Court made an essentially political and social judgment to change the law, but it was presented as based solely on required, preexisting, and legal principles, and directed at a scapegoat rather than at a systematic social practice.

BEFORE THE TRANSFORMATION

Davis is the only Supreme Court decision addressing these basic free-speech issues before the transformation began, but state and lower federal court decisions, as well as the practice throughout the country, confirm that there was no tradition of or legally protected right to free speech as we know it prior to the transformation. The supposed existence of such a tradition and such rights is a longstanding myth.

The Constitution and the Early Popular Understanding of Freedom of Speech. The Constitution, as ratified in 1787, does not mention freedom of speech, although historians and legal scholars generally agree that the Bill of Rights, in the form of amendments adopted four years later, was promised and necessary to secure ratification.

There is considerable controversy, however, about how the framers of the Constitution and the population generally viewed freedom of speech before and during the constitutional drafting and ratification process.[10] The traditional view that freedom of speech was widely supported—which has been translated into the current popular notion that free speech was the founding principle of our country—is usually documented, if at all, by reference to eloquent but largely rhetorical writings in this century by Harvard law professor Zechariah Chafee, Jr. This view has been challenged based on convincing historical research, principally by historian Leonard Levy.

The controversy has suffered from a lack of concreteness: freedom of speech as we know it consists of several specific concepts and rules guaranteeing, most basically, the ability, without restraint, punishment, or content-based limitation, to criticize government and public officials and private institutions and individuals; to express one's views in public places; and to associate with others for political purposes. While the Constitution and the First Amendment were popularly understood to embody basic notions of political freedom, including at least a repudiation of judicial or other actions that prohibit in advance publication by the press (called prior restraints), the other aspects of free speech as we know it developed throughout our two-hundred-year history.

For example, English and American law at the time of the Constitution essentially rendered criticism of the government or its officials a criminal act. This offense, called seditious libel, was based on the conception of a monarch and government as divine and above reproach. The truth of a criticism was considered a basis for aggravation rather than mitigation of the crime because a correct criticism was more likely to create discord and contempt for the government. While seditious libel is completely incompatible with our current conception of free speech, it was a crime in every state at the time the Constitution was adopted. Furthermore, Levy's review of the writings and speeches of the framers of the Constitution and the leaders of the Revolution shows that none of them—including even Thomas Jefferson and Thomas Paine—opposed criminalization of seditious libel. Some of the framers advocated reforms of the law of seditious libel, including adoption of truth as a defense and the determination of libel by the jury, but still favored the criminalization of criticism of the government and its officials.[11]

Levy suggests, rather convincingly, that the First Amendment, alone among the provisions of the Bill of Rights in being explicitly directed at and limiting only Congress, was not viewed by its framers as changing existing law and merely constituted a reservation to the states of the power to regulate speech and press. The seeds of popular belief in free speech as we know it came later, perhaps in response to the Sedition Act of 1798 (discussed below).

In any event, the experience of revolution and the emergence of the new nation generated a wave of intolerance immediately before and after the adoption of the Constitution. To some extent this is understandable and typical of revolutions that have occurred elsewhere: after a violent struggle and in the wake of victory, there is a yearning for consensus, or at least conformity that appears to reflect consensus. But the very nature of the new nation seems to have accentuated rather than restrained this process. Belief and pride in the attainment of freedom were turned against itself; nonconformity and dissent were greeted with extreme, legally sanctioned, and sometimes violent intolerance.

Although the issue of the relationship of the colonies to England was hotly and publicly debated before and during the war, any sign of even an early questioning of independence tended to be viewed as disloyalty. Many people had sentimental, familial, and economic allegiances to England, which was often also their birthplace. Because they believed or hoped differences could be settled without war, they were treated as traitors, regardless of whether they had actually acted or sided with England during the Revolution. They were subjected to special taxes, loyalty oaths, banishment, and violence; and laws in most states prohibited them from serving on juries, voting, holding office, buying land, or practicing certain designated professions. The pacifism of the Quakers was also regarded as treasonous. Their religious services were banned, and they were frequently imprisoned, banished, and subjected to mob violence.[12] This pattern of repression based on a false equation of disloyalty with ancestry, religion, or expression of opposition to established policy would be repeated throughout this history.

The Federalists—Our First Party. While the ink on the First Amendment was barely dry, the Federalist party attempted to silence its opponents with prosecutions for the common-law offense of seditious libel. In a turnabout, the Republicans later used the same device to prosecute Federalists, including a minister who criticized Jefferson in a Thanksgiving Day sermon.[13]

The Federalists, undaunted by the First Amendment to their Constitution, became dissatisfied with the ineffectiveness of these seditious libel prosecutions due to doubts raised about whether federal courts have common-law jurisdiction. In 1798, they pushed through Congress, by a narrow margin, the Sedition Act, which made it a crime to

> . . . write, print, utter or publish . . . any false, scandalous and malicious writings against the government of the United States, or either House of Congress . . . or the President with the intent to defame . . . or to bring them into contempt or disrepute . . . [14]

Although the act also contained two protective devices—truth was made a defense, and the jury was to decide whether the words were seditious—Federalist judges quickly negated their effect. They refused to distinguish between statements of fact and opinion, and they ruled that the defendant must prove the truth of every minute detail to establish the truth defense. Overall, they treated the First Amendment as if it only codified preexisting law and prohibited only prior censorship, which had been prohibited in England since 1695 and in the colonies since 1725.[15]

The most prominent person prosecuted under the Sedition Act was Matthew Lyon, a member of Congress critical of the Federalists. Lyon was imprisoned and his house sold to pay his fine (nevertheless he was reelected in the next election). The longest prison term, two years, was served by a laborer for erecting a sign on a post that read, in part, No Stamp Act, No Sedition . . . downfall to the Tyrants of America, peace and retirement to the President. The act was "never invoked against alien enemies, or possible traitors, but solely against editors and public men whom the Federalists under President Adams desired to silence or deport in order to suppress political opposition."[16]

The act and consequent prosecutions were extremely unpopular, and convictions were difficult to obtain without manipulation of the composition of juries (which, as a result, were comprised almost entirely of Federalists) and active bias by Federalist judges. "Popular indignation at the Act and the prosecutions wrecked the Federalist Party."[17]

Jefferson pardoned all those convicted, and the government repaid their fines. The Supreme Court never reviewed any of the common-law or statutory sedition cases, but several legal doctrines that restricted expression were adopted by the lower courts and would be repeatedly resurrected later. The two foremost were the "bad-tendency" doctrine, which allowed prosecution for words that could, in however remote or indirect a fashion, contribute to disorder or unlawful conduct sometime in the future; and the "constructive-intent" doctrine, which ascribed to the speaker or writer the intent to cause such remote and indirect consequences. Perhaps most important, in this infancy of the Constitution, the law proved to be a willing partner in repression.

The Mob as an Expression of Public Opinion, 1830–1860. During the early 1800s, the relatively new and abstract ideas of liberty and democracy that had fueled the Revolution seemed less important than pressing social problems primarily related to urban centralization and immigration. Democracy came to be viewed as sanctioning, or even requiring, the use of any means necessary to thoroughly and quickly implement the will of the majority. Again, the perceived righteousness of American democracy became its undoing, as the majority claimed "their final right to settle with the minority."[18] Any person who differed from the majority—by ancestry, religion, appearance, or disagreement with majority positions—was suspect and blamed for social problems, which usually took the heaviest toll on them. The goal was to eliminate differences, which were perceived as the cause of social disorders; the means was mob violence. "The early governing autocrats had tried to limit liberty by stifling interpretation of the Constitution or by appeals to English precedents. The people simply appealed to force."[19] And the government, including the courts, offered no protection.

Discrimination against minorities was not unusual. In New York, Masons were prohibited from serving on juries until 1927; in many states Jews were excluded from juries, professions, and public office until the mid–1800s; and blacks were still slaves. But the broad range of "Native American" movements during this period unleashed a ferocious reign of terror against each wave of new immigrants and, not coincidentally, cheap labor. In this nation of immigrants, "native" was defined, it would appear, not as the original population (American Indians) but on a continuum, so that groups could claim nativity vis-à-vis all other groups of more recently immigrated ancestry.

Among the Native American persecutions,[20] none was more ferocious than the persecution of Irish Catholics, which included the random killings and raids of the Know-Nothing party. The Irish, as so many other minorities, absorbed the Native American ideology rather than develop a tolerance born of experience. Later, when they ascended to power in parts of California, they persecuted the Chinese.

Mormons, seen as dangerous first for their savvy land purchases and later for their practice of polygamy, were banished, randomly beaten, and killed in several states. In Missouri the governor ordered them "exterminated," and men, women, and children were massacred in a series of pogroms. They moved to Illinois, where their leader, Joseph Smith, was murdered by a mob while in jail. They then moved to Utah, where they became the natives and proceeded to persecute others, including blacks.

Social reformers of this period, including people favoring abolition of slavery, free education, birth control, and temperance, were treated similarly.[21] Statutes in every southern state forbade any speech or writing that questioned slavery. These were uniformly enforced by the courts; such speech or writing was held possibly to lead to slave insurrections and was therefore prohibitable based on the bad-tendency doctrine.

Alongside this legal suppression, citizens' committees and vigilante activities were widespread and unchecked by legal authorities. There were many lynchings and beatings of abolitionists, and the citizens' committees kept track of even the mildest expression of antislavery views. A slaveholder in Grayson County, Virginia, who defended a minister's sermon against slavery, was tarred and feathered by the local committee. When he sought warrants for the arrest of some committee members he recognized, the committee threatened his lawyers and the judge, and disrupted a hearing. Subcommittees were subsequently formed throughout the county to report any "suspicious opinions," and the courts were instructed not to act in cases of crimes against abolitionists. It became common in the South after 1840 to repudiate the notion of natural rights and the Declaration of Independence, which were both seen as based on Jefferson's "radicalism."[22]

There were no similar statutes and few lynchings in the North, but mobs accomplished the same goals. Most notable were riots in Philadelphia and Illinois, where Elijah Lovejoy, the editor of an antislavery newspaper, was murdered by a mob.[23]

In 1837, after a series of lengthy and embarrassing petitions against slavery were presented to Congress, it banned presentation of all such petitions in order that "the agitation of this subject should be finally arrested, for the purpose of restoring tranquillity to the public mind."[24] Basic notions of freedom and democracy—and the First Amendment right "to petition the Government for redress of grievances"—were, it seems, secondary in importance to the tranquility of a public mind that apparently was undisturbed by widespread mob violence and slavery.

The Early Labor Movement. The labor movement was accustomed to hostility from the legal system; in the early 1800s, the courts generally regarded unions and strikes as criminal conspiracies. By the 1870s, the labor movement began to focus on freedom of speech, which it viewed as a necessary component of the right to organize. Peaceful labor demonstrations were regularly and often violently broken up by the police. For example, during the depression of 1873–1874, a large group of unemployed workers demonstrating in New York were attacked by police. The city had granted a permit but revoked it minutes before the demonstration. Demonstrators, unaware of the revocation, were beaten with clubs by platoons of police, who rushed into the crowd. Two meetings in a private hall called to protest the police action at the demonstration were also broken up by the police. By a contemporary account, "the aggrieved working men and their sympathizers felt as though they had no rights which the municipality was bound to respect."[25]

The Anarchists. Beginning in 1897, Emma Goldman and other anarchists toured the country speaking on a range of topics, from politics to literature and the arts. They were regularly prohibited from speaking, on streets or in public or private halls, or limited to certain topics. The process became so routinized that Goldman, who called it a struggle for "liberty without strings," incorporated it into her condemnations of governmental power and coercion. Usually, radicals, liberals, and some conservatives would rally to support her right to speak.

For example, in 1909 Goldman was to deliver a lecture entitled "Henrik Ibsen as the Pioneer of Modern Drama" at Lexington Hall in New York City. The police, present in the private hall leased by Goldman, said she could speak so long as she addressed the topic. However, the first time she mentioned "Ibsen," a police sergeant mounted the speaker's platform and said she was deviating from the topic. Her protestations that she must mention Ibsen's name to discuss Ibsen and drama were to no avail. The large crowd, at first amused by the absurdity of the police order, was roughly cleared from the hall with the use of clubs.[26]

The "Free-Speech Fights" of the IWW. From 1909 to 1915, the IWW conducted a nationwide campaign to challenge denials of the right to speak on public streets, sidewalks, and parks.[27] Seeking to reach mainly migratory workers in the only places possible, the Wobblies saw themselves in a "struggle for the use of the streets for free speech and the right to organize." This struggle became the focal point for employer resistance to the Wobblies' organizing efforts.

The strategies for the free-speech fights derived from earlier successful efforts by members of the IWW, Socialist party, and Socialist Labor party. In 1908, they had together won the repeal of a ban on street speaking in Los Angeles by repeatedly violating the ban until the jails were filled. This was systematized in 1909 by drawing on hundreds, and sometimes thousands, of workers from around the country with announcements in the Wobbly newspaper, *Industrial Worker*.

Each person would mount a soapbox and begin a speech with the usual Wobbly greeting, "Fellow workers and friends." These four words ordinarily sufficed to result in arrest, after which the next person would mount the soapbox. The jails would soon be filled, as would schools and other buildings used for the overflow. The struggle was seen as political, not legal, and early on elected committees decided not to "waste" their limited resources on lawyers' fees.

The first major fight, in Missoula, Montana, was led by Elizabeth Gurley Flynn. In 1909, the Wobblies were speaking on the streets and distributing literature to protest employment agencies that charged unemployed workers a fee for nonexistent jobs. When the agencies and local businesses persuaded the city council to pass an ordinance banning street speaking, the *Industrial Worker* issued a national call, and a "steady stream of Wobblies flocked into Missoula, 'by freight cars—on top, inside and below.' " As the jails filled, the Wobblies received support from a variety of sources, including Senator Robert LaFollette, university professors, and townspeople worried about the costs of incarcerating so many persons. The authorities eventually relented: all of the criminal charges were dropped, and, as Flynn later wrote, "We returned to our peaceful pursuit of agitating and organizing the I.W.W."[28]

Beginning the next year, twelve hundred people were arrested in a Spokane, Washington, free-speech fight that lasted several months. In response to Wobbly street speaking, also directed primarily against corrupt employment agencies (which had, for example, sent five thousand fee-paying workers to a company that employed only one hundred), the city council prohibited "public meetings on any of the streets, sidewalks, or alleys." A local court upheld the ban while carving out an exception for the Salvation Army. The free-speech prisoners were beaten in jail, and some were placed in chains and forced to work on a rock pile. Three died in an unheated school that was used after the prisons had been filled. When the police shut down the *Industrial Worker* office and arrested Flynn (then noticeably pregnant) though she had not violated the ordinance, the fight became "front-page news in every newspaper in the country,"[29] and hundreds more headed for Spokane. The ordinance was repealed, the *Industrial Worker* was allowed to publish, nineteen employment agencies lost their licenses, and two particularly brutal prison guards were fired. After another successful fight the following year in

Fresno, California, the Wobblies were often able to win the de facto right to speak and organize with only a threat of a national call in the *Industrial Worker*.

Employers on the West Coast then organized the Merchants and Manufacturers Association to oppose free speech for the Wobblies, and they openly advocated a tactic that was first widely used in the Fresno fight: vigilantes, working with the police, would routinely beat the street speakers and throw them out of town. This became the regular practice, with the vigilante mobs often headed by leading business and banking figures. The most brutal actions occurred in San Diego in 1912, where anti-Wobbly vigilantes included leading members of the chamber of commerce and real-estate board, as well as a variety of merchants and bankers. These vigilantes regularly attacked the Wobblies as they entered town on freight trains, and made them kiss the flag and walk through gauntlets of men swinging clubs. One Wobbly was shot to death; others were tarred and feathered or had "IWW" branded on their bodies. However, throughout this and other, frequent attacks, the Wobblies persisted nonviolently and were almost always successful, including major victories in Cleveland, Denver, Detroit, Philadelphia, Omaha, Kansas City, Des Moines, San Francisco, Vancouver, Hawaii, and Alaska.

The *Industrial Worker* summed up the Wobbly experience with the legal system: "A demonstration of working men in the interests of the constitutional right of freedom of speech is judged a 'riot' by the courts; but violence and terrorism on the part of the capitalists and their tools is 'law and order.' "[30] While the Wobblies did not achieve widespread or legal protection of the freedom to speak, they did achieve major successes and brought the issue to the public consciousness. They also made it quite clear that continued refusal to allow and protect free speech would lead to major confrontations into which significant segments of society would be drawn to support the labor movement as well as free speech.

The Women's Movement. Advocates of women's rights were particularly harassed by local and federal officials. In the early 1900s, Margaret Sanger and Emma Goldman were frequently arrested and sometimes fined or imprisoned for distributing leaflets with information on birth control. Newspapers that offended the postmaster—which included almost anything on the subject of sex or women—were denied the use of the mails. The publisher of a socialist newspaper in Oklahoma received a six-month sentence, under a federal obscenity statute, for publishing an ad for a pamphlet that criticized the popular view of women as sex objects and explained "why the Socialists believe women are human beings."[31] This conviction was affirmed on appeal,[32] and in a later case federal censorship of the mails was approved by the Supreme Court.[33]

In 1917 participants in the women's suffrage movement came to the White House seeking President Wilson's endorsement of a constitutional amendment granting women the right to vote. When their efforts failed, they set up a picket of six women with banners at the White House gates. The women were convicted of "obstructing traffic," which they had not done, and imprisoned for three days after refusing to pay fines. During the weeks that followed, others were similarly convicted and sentenced for obstructing traffic or disorderly conduct, and some were sent to a distant prison. Months later, more women were arrested in a public park across from the White House, many of whom were mistreated in jail and staged hunger strikes in protest.[34]

The repressive measures of this period were investigated by the U.S. Commission on Industrial Relations, a body with business and labor representatives established by Congress in 1912 to investigate the conflict between labor and capital and related causes of social unrest. The commission concluded that

> [O]ne of the greatest sources of social unrest and bitterness has been the attitude of the police toward public speaking. On numerous occasions in every part of the country, the police of cities and towns have either arbitrarily or under the cloak of a traffic ordinance, interfered with, or prohibited public speaking, both in the open and in halls, by persons connected with organizations of which the police or those from whom they receive their orders, did not approve. In many instances such interference has been carried out with a degree of brutality which would be incredible if it were not vouched for by reliable witnesses.
>
> . . . [The] long list of statutes, city ordinances, and military orders abridging freedom of speech and press . . . have not only not been interfered with by the courts but whenever tested have almost uniformly been upheld by State and Federal courts.[35]

The courts justified these decisions with both an expanded notion of the "police power," which gave the states enormous powers of repression in the name of preservation of safety and order, and the bad-tendency doctrine, whereby almost any expression of a different view was depicted as undermining law and order. Leon Whipple, a leading historian of civil liberty in the United States, described this mode of thought well:

> It proceeds from preserving the peace to preserving the status quo. This force for safety soon translates safety into "law and order" and this into

"the established order." It changes health into comfort, and comfort into peace of mind, which means no agitation, no freaks, no tampering with things as they are.[36]

THE TRANSFORMATION: 1919—1940

The Espionage Act of 1917 made it a federal crime to "willfully make or convey false reports or false statements with intent to interfere with the operation or success of the [armed forces of the United States] or to promote the success of its enemies," to "willfully cause or attempt to cause insubordination, disloyalty, mutiny, or refusal of duty," or to "willfully obstruct . . . recruiting or enlistment."[37] The next year, more offenses were added, including "uttering, printing, writing, or publishing any disloyal, profane, scurrilous, or abusive language, or language intended to cause contempt, scorn, contumely or disrepute as regards the form of government of the U.S., the Constitution, the flag, the uniform of the Army or Navy, or any language intended to incite resistance to the U.S. or promote the cause of its enemies."[38]

These acts, designed for use against opponents of American participation in World War I, constituted yet another example in this repressive history. However, for the first time, they prompted some justices of the Supreme Court to raise First Amendment problems with the criminalization of dissent; this was the beginning of the transformation of speech law, which proceeded case-by-case over the course of the next twenty years.

The judicial response to the Espionage Acts began with business as usual. A Second Circuit decision, *Masses Publishing Co.* v. *Patten*,[39] approved of the postmaster's refusal to deliver a newspaper to its subscribers because it expressed negative opinions about the purposes and conduct of the war. This and over two thousand criminal prosecutions were justified with the bad-tendency and constructive-intent doctrines. Professor Chafee examined these prosecutions in detail and concluded that

> [T]he courts treated opinions as statements of fact and then condemned them as false because they differed from the President's speech or the resolution of Congress declaring war. . . . [I]t became criminal to advocate heavier taxation instead of bond issues, to state that conscription was unconstitutional . . . , to urge that a referendum should have preceded our declaration of war, to say that war was contrary to the teachings of Christianity. Men have been punished for criticizing the Red Cross and the Y.M.C.A. . . .[40]

None of the Espionage Act convictions was reversed by the Supreme Court on First Amendment grounds, but the first signs of change came in the opinions of Justices Louis Brandeis and Oliver Wendell Holmes. In 1919 Justice Holmes articulated his "clear-and-present-danger" test in *Schenck* v. *United States*.[41] This was seemingly at least a partial repudiation of the bad-tendency doctrine, and it was set out in a unanimous opinion.

However, the *Schenck* test, which is still with us today, hardly provides a precisely defined or clearly applied standard. While the *Schenck* opinion was widely hailed by liberal commentators,[42] its exaggerated importance was evident in the decision itself. All that Schenck, a Socialist party leader, had done was distribute a leaflet to draftees criticizing the war, challenging the draft as unconstitutional, and urging them to challenge their conscription on legal grounds and by legal means. There would seem to be no danger, since the courts could adjudicate such challenges, and whatever consequences there might be were neither clear nor present. Yet, Holmes's opinion affirmed the conviction, and it would be regularly cited in later cases to justify convictions for mere dissent.[43]

Holmes's votes with the majorities in two subsequent affirmances of convictions further undercut the meaning and importance of the *Schenck* test: one involved the author of critical articles on the constitutionality of the draft and the purposes of the war, and the other sent Eugene Debs to prison on a ten-year sentence for a speech at a socialist rally in which he mildly condemned the war as a contest between competing capitalist classes.[44] The *Debs* case raised a public outcry because of the stature of Debs and the fact that his supposed crime was an attempt to cause insubordination in the military and to obstruct recruiting, although he did not speak to soldiers or urge resistance to the draft. While in prison, Debs received more than 920,000 votes for president as the Socialist party candidate in the election of 1920, more than he had received in any of four prior elections.

Holmes and Brandeis began their famous series of dissents in *Abrams* v. *United States*.[45] In that case, the conviction of mainly Russian-born and Jewish defendants for aiding the Germans was based on a leaflet that condemned U.S. military intervention in the Soviet Union in 1918. The majority of the Court held that the actions advocated, such as a general strike, would affect the war effort against Germany even though that intent, as required by the Espionage Act, was clearly not present. In this and subsequent cases,[46] Brandeis and Holmes masterfully set out in dissents and concurrences the fundamental social, historical, and political bases for free speech that have survived to this day. Quoting Justice Brandeis:

> Those who won our independence believed that the final end of the State was to make men free to develop their faculties; and that in its government the deliberative forces should prevail over the arbitrary. They valued liberty both as an end and as a means. They believed liberty to be the secret of

happiness and courage to be the secret of liberty. They believed that freedom to think as you will and to speak as you think are means indispensable to the discovery and spread of political truth; that without free speech and assembly discussion would be futile; that with them, discussion affords ordinarily adequate protection against the dissemination of noxious doctrine; that the greatest menace to freedom is an inert people; that public discussion is a political duty; and that this should be a fundamental principle of the American government. They recognized the risks to which all human institutions are subject. But they knew that order cannot be secured merely through fear of punishment for its infraction; that it is hazardous to discourage thought, hope and imagination; that fear breeds repression; that repression breeds hate; that hate menaces stable government; that the path of safety lies in the opportunity to discuss freely supposed grievances and proposed remedies; and that the fitting remedy for evil counsels is good ones. Believing in the power of reason as applied through public discussion, they eschewed silence coerced by law—the argument of force in its worst form. Recognizing the occasional tyrannies of governing majorities, they amended the Constitution so that free speech and assembly should be guaranteed.[47]

After World War I and the Russian Revolution, various forms of American radicalism blossomed, and there was a period of hysterical reaction, usually referred to as the "Red Scare." On the state level, there were new sedition, criminal anarchy, and syndicalism laws; thirty-two states forbade the flying of a red flag; and the New York legislature expelled five socialists. Socialist Victor Berger was twice denied a seat in the House of Representatives; the federal government deported many aliens for their beliefs; and in 1920 the attorney general (assisted by a young federal agent named J. Edgar Hoover) conducted the infamous Palmer raids. Private institutions and individuals, often acting with the government, engaged in similar repression. Harvard alumni and Justice Department officials sought to have Professor Chafee fired for his criticism of the *Abrams* decision in a law review article; charges that he was "unfit as a law school professor" were rejected, but only after a hearing at the Harvard Club.[48]

Holmes and Brandeis continued their articulation of a broad-based right of expression, although, as in *Schenck*, the votes they sometimes cast affirming convictions conflicted with their eloquence.[49] In 1925 a majority finally said the First Amendment was applicable to the states.[50] However, the breakthrough in results came in 1931 in *Stromberg* v. *California*,[51] where the Court reversed a state conviction for displaying a red flag at a Young Communist League summer camp. That same year the Court first prohibited prior restraints by the states on the press.[52]

Subsequently, freedom of expression was enlarged throughout the decade. The leading decisions spanned only five years (1936–1940), during which time the Court (in addition to *Hague*): invalidated a state tax on the press, reversed a conviction for a peaceful assembly, reversed a conviction for an attempt to promote "resistance to lawful authority" by distribution of a pamphlet advocating a separate black nation in the South, invalidated the conviction of a Jehovah's Witness for violating an ordinance requiring a permit for distributing literature, invalidated an ordinance banning all leafleting, protected a Jehovah's Witness's right to solicit door-to-door without a permit, and protected the right to picket.[53] Probably the most libertarian decision in the Court's history, in its reasoning if not also in its result, came in 1943, when it invalidated a state compulsory flag-salute law.[54]

In these cases, the bad-tendency and constructive-intent doctrines and the notion of seditious libel were repudiated, and a multifaceted right of expression was established. As the decade wore on, the natural-law-based rationale of *Hague* was emphasized, and the rich history of the struggle for free speech was transformed into a natural right from ancient times, guaranteed by the Constitution and enforced, with some unfortunate exceptions, by the courts.

THE FREE-SPEECH MOVEMENT

It is so common to view free speech as a legal rather than political issue that we tend to overlook the fact that there was—and is today—a free-speech movement that played an important role in the struggle for free speech.

While the political and religious groups and activists who were denied freedom of expression usually viewed it as secondary in importance to their substantive demands, they and many others organized efforts to more effectively raise the free-speech issue. There were a number of ad hoc groups, such as the Free Speech Committee, which held a meeting of two thousand people in 1909 following a series of incidents highlighted by the refusal to allow Emma Goldman to speak on Ibsen's writings in New York. About the same time, the IWW started its free-speech fights, which combined labor organizing with the free-speech demand, and Theodore Schroeder formed the Free Speech League, which primarily produced theoretical writings. In the early 1930s, the International Labor Defense focused on various civil liberties issues predominantly in the South (and brought national and international attention to the Scottsboro case).

Though surely significant, none of these efforts was broadly based, able to command consistent national attention, or systematic in its strategies or approach to the free-speech issue. What the free-speech movement lacked was a mass base, a national organization, and effective organizing; it found all three in the labor movement, the National Civil Liberties Bureau (which became the American Civil Liberties Union in 1920), and Roger Baldwin.[55]

Baldwin, whose upper-middle-class family could claim an ancestor on the *Mayflower*, was a pacifist with a strong commitment to personal freedom and social justice. His philosophic and political thinking was deeply affected by Emma Goldman and other anarchists, although he did not oppose all forms of government. He also differed from the anarchists in his approach; as he told me, "I was essentially a pragmatist. I did things that I thought would work. Emma was essentially an idealist, and she did things that she thought were right."

In 1917 Baldwin and Crystal Eastman, a leader of the American Union Against Militarism (AUAM), convinced the board of AUAM to form an adjunct, called the Civil Liberties Bureau, that would be primarily concerned with the prosecutions and treatment of conscientious objectors during World War I. The bureau was generally greeted with hostility, including a denunciation in the *New York Times* for "antagonizing the settled policies of our government,"[56] which caused controversy within AUAM and resulted in its separation from AUAM a few months later. As an independent entity, the National Civil Liberties Bureau (NCLB) was headed by Baldwin and included on its board several nationally known reformers, socialists, and lawyers, including Clarence Darrow and Norman Thomas.

The NCLB immediately took on the toughest civil liberties issues of the day: protection of conscientious objectors and the Espionage Act prosecutions. The federal government responded by raiding the NCLB office and seizing all its files. Also in this initial period, Baldwin served a year in jail for draft resistance, after which he remarked, "I am a graduate of Harvard, but a year in jail has helped me recover from it."[57]

When he returned to the NCLB, Baldwin insisted on a new approach that emphasized labor-related civil liberties issues and an alliance with the labor movement. The NCLB issued a pamphlet on the IWW, which, though containing a disclaimer, clearly indicated where the organization stood on the conflict between labor and capital:

> [There have been] deliberate misrepresentations by employing interests opposed to organized labor, who have . . . paint[ed] the I.W.W. as a terrorist organization of "anarchists." They thus frighten the public into an alliance with them instead of with labor. . . . [V]iolence has been much more commonly used against the I.W.W. than by it; . . . the violence used by employers is open, organized, deliberate and without any excusable provocation; . . . the I.W.W. have almost never retaliated even in the face of outrages ranging from murder to mass deportations. . . . [The disloyalty and treason charges against the I.W.W. are based on] simply the ordinary activities of labor-unions struggling to get better wages and conditions. . . .[58]

This pamphlet was banned from the mails and almost led to an Espionage Act prosecution, but, in one of the few successful legal challenges of the period, the NCLB won a court order overturning the ban.[59]

Baldwin led the NCLB through a reorganization in 1920 that emphasized the alliance with labor. The NCLB had long tried to unite liberal and left groups around the free-speech issue, but many identified the NCLB with pacifism or even disloyalty, and its strong image provoked criticisms from the left and right. The reorganized NCLB, to be named the American Civil Liberties Union, would, according to the reorganization memorandum written by Baldwin,[60] institute a "dramatic campaign of service to labor" with a National Executive Committee composed of a core of labor leaders and labor sympathizers. One major tactic would be IWW-type free-speech fights where employers or local governments denied labor organizers free speech. "A few well-known liberals, for instance, going into the strike districts of western Pennsylvania and exercising their right to speak in defiance of sheriff-made law ought to dramatize the situation effectively." And so it did; there were successful labor-related free-speech fights sponsored and supported by the ACLU in the 1920s and 1930s in Connecticut, New Jersey, Pennsylvania, and West Virginia.[61]

The new National Executive Committee, all of whose members were prolabor, consisted of a core of labor leaders and many well-known socialists, communists, and liberals.[62] They had succeeded in uniting a coalition of labor and the left, which sought and found support from all levels of society.

Baldwin told me he viewed the free-speech issue as primarily political and only secondarily legal, and as inseparable from the rights of workers to organize and bargain collectively. The reorganization scheme was aimed at increasing the power and political effectiveness of the ACLU.

> [O]rganization was the basis of our service in the ACLU. [We] as an organization were powerless and therefore we had to attach ourselves to the defense of movements that had power. . . .
>
> If we had been a legal aid society helping people get their constitutional rights, as such agencies do their personal rights, we would have behaved quite differently. We would have stuck to constitutional lawyers [and] arguments in courts. We would not have surrounded [the NCLB and the ACLU] with popular persons. But we did the opposite thing. We attached ourselves to the movements we defended. We identified ourselves with their demands . . . [and] we depended on them . . . for money and support.

Thus constituted and directed,[63] the ACLU proceeded to challenge and organize around, for example, antievolution statutes in the *Scopes* case, the Espionage Act prosecution of Communist Benjamin Gitlow, the Sacco-

Vanzetti prosecutions—and, in 1937, the antilabor and antifree-speech actions of Boss Hague.

LEGAL DECISION MAKING: EXPLAINING THE TRANSFORMATION

The fundamental conflict between the *Davis* and *Hague* decisions raises the basic questions about legal decision making: How do judges make decisions? How and why does the law change?

An appropriate starting point is the explanations given by the justices themselves: that their decisions were determined by legal reasoning and analysis. Indeed, if the law is separate from political and social forces, as it purports to be, there should be a coherent *legal* explanation. The primary source of law in these cases was, of course, the Constitution, but the operative constitutional provisions, the First and Fourteenth amendments, were identical in both cases. *Hague* held that the First Amendment, prohibiting any "law abridging freedom of speech" and operating against the states through the Fourteenth Amendment, establishes an individual right to speak on public streets, sidewalks, and parks; *Davis*, with the same provisions in effect, held the opposite.

It might be argued that there was a legal barrier to enforcement of the First Amendment against the states prior to the Supreme Court's incorporation of the First Amendment into the Fourteenth Amendment in 1925.[64] But this only begs the question; the same provisions were in effect since the Civil War, and thereafter an incorporation decision could have been made whenever the Court chose to make it. In fact, the Court had clear opportunities and discussed the issue even before the *Davis* case.[65] The incorporation of the First Amendment was not a legally required or determined phenomena; rather, it was, chronologically and actually, a manipulation of legal doctrine that was part of the transformation, more an effect than a cause.

Another possible legal explanation might be found in the prior decisions that interpreted the general language of the First Amendment. However, in both periods there were precedents and reasoning supporting each side. Moreover, since precedents and reasoning can be distinguished, modified, or discarded, they do not require any particular rule or result. This is particularly clear in *Hague*, since *Davis* was a direct precedent that the Court chose to avoid. There is no legal explanation for that choice; the law merely provides a variety of stylized rationalizations for justifying choices made on other grounds. This would still be true had the Court decided to follow *Davis*, because that would also be a choice nowhere required in the law, and the question would still be why the Court made that choice.

Other possible explanations focus on the character, intelligence, and historical sophistication of Justice Holmes; perhaps Holmes was simply smarter or more in touch with the framers of the Constitution than other judges. There is, however, no basis for assuming that Holmes had any less character or intelligence when he wrote the *Davis* Massachusetts opinion than when he dissented as a Supreme Court justice in *Abrams*. Nor could any connection with the framers offer a sensible explanation, since the framers wrote and passed the Sedition Act and conceived and articulated the bad-tendency doctrine.

There is no legally required rule or result, and despite endless attempts by judges and legal scholars to find transcendent legal principles, there simply are none. But one can make sense of these decisions by examining the social and political contexts in which they were made, and by viewing legal decision making and law as political processes.

Davis asked the Court to overturn a longstanding local practice sanctioned by many lower federal and state court decisions; and the Supreme Court, without even a dissent, simply repeated the result and doctrine developed by the lower courts. But society underwent fundamental changes between *Davis* and *Hague*. Industrialization, the First World War, the Depression, the New Deal, and the left and labor movements led to basic shifts in consciousness and social and power relations. These shifts affected judges as well as society generally, and some of the judges, though from the same strata of society as the judges of the *Davis* era, came to see the justice of at least some progressive demands. Justice Holmes's reassessment of speech rights would seem to exemplify this kind of change. In the early 1920s, he revised his thinking about freedom of speech, and the author of the *Davis* opinion in the Massachusetts Supreme Court became the U.S. Supreme Court's foremost spokesman for free speech. This was not the result of more legal research or any legal principle but of his and society's altered consciousness.

Such a social change is transmitted to and affects individuals in various ways—through mass media, public and private associations, professional groups, and peer pressures. Such influences on Holmes probably included a particularly critical meeting with Professor Chafee, who was very upset about the *Debs* decision.[66] The judges, like Holmes, who came to place considerable value on freedom of speech (and it was surely not all of them) did so because they, as people living and working in society, were affected by historical and social changes and the events and people surrounding them. Due to the peculiar nature of our legal system and the socialization, education, and experience of our judges, these judges would generally express this new consciousness in legal terms, and many of them would honestly deny its newness and honestly believe it stemmed from legal analysis.

Furthermore, Davis was an isolated individual, while the left and labor movements were broad-based, national, and politically powerful. A significant measure of sympathy, understanding, and legitimacy flows from power; demands and speakers that were once regarded as extremist become legitimate as they crystallize into a movement that gains numbers and power. Whipple, in his examination of freedom of speech as practiced from colonial days to the First World War, concluded that "whoever has power, economic or political, enjoys liberty."[67]

The power of such a movement also places judges in a bind. Though most were likely to be hostile or ambivalent toward the labor and left movements and their demands, the demand for free speech had clear historical roots and was seen as appropriate by many people. To deny this demand, a judge would have to risk fomenting a major confrontation in a period already fraught with the possibility of revolution. Moreover, it would be clear that if labor could not speak and organize legally, it would do so illegally and perhaps adopt a strategy similar to the IWW free-speech fights, which won considerable support for the IWW as well as for the Constitution. Although some judges might welcome the confrontation, others—even those born and raised on Wall Street—would find it preferable to bring these activities within and under the control of the established order, as Congress had done with the NLRA.

The power of this movement and the precedents favoring local control over speech would also raise institutional concerns. To uphold the right of free speech would require contradicting longstanding precedents and widespread practice. On the other hand, to deny a demand so widely supported would raise a public outcry, undermine the Court's authority, and perhaps stimulate support for Roosevelt's court-packing scheme announced in 1937. These institutional concerns amount to a choice between rejecting (or avoiding) a precedent and widespread practice and ruling against the mainstream of political thought. That the latter would be a major and perhaps predominant concern is clear if one looks closely at the context: there was a widespread controversy about the courts in this period, and the Court's recent trend was in the direction of the mainstream of society in several related decisions;[68] the law's blatant pro-business slant was seen in some upper-class circles as undermining its power and authority; Congress had enacted the NLRA in 1935, and in 1936 Congress established a committee to investigate "violations of the right of free speech and assembly and undue interference with the right of labor to organize and bargain collectively" (reflecting, among other things, the fact that these two rights were widely viewed as inseparable);[69] and an *amicus* brief filed by the American Bar Association favored the CIO's position.

The various factors discussed here would not necessarily operate intentionally or even consciously, nor would the justices necessarily see themselves as engaged in anything other than a legal analysis. Rather, they would be quite accustomed to expressing social and political concerns and values as legal arguments and to implementing changes of society's rules expressed in legal terms and not necessarily even self-understood as changes. Their socialization, education, and experience, their perception of their role, and their understanding of the needs of the society they serve could lead to this change in the law as easily as a conscious political decision to bring within the system and to regulate labor protest and other dissent.

THE REALITY AND IDEOLOGY OF FREE SPEECH

The basic principle that individuals and groups have the ability to express different and unpopular views without prior restraint or punishment is a necessary element of any democratic society. To the extent that we have enforced this principle in the roughly fifty years since the transformation—which we have, to an unprecedented degree, since the early 1960s—we can and should be proud. I do not question the principle or its importance and validity under any system of social relations.

However, free speech means much more than this in American politics and culture. Free speech is discussed as if it defined an economic or political system, or even a religion, rather than a series of rules prohibiting governmental limits on individual expression. It is what makes us good, and better (than other countries and people). Freedom of speech is at the core of our national identity.

Yet, the American celebration of free speech is unsettling, contradictory, and quite complex. The invocation of free speech gains wide acceptance when formulated generally and abstracted from current controversies, or when aimed at specific repressive practices in other countries. But specific applications in the United States are regularly greeted with contempt, evident in the recurring controversies over flag burning and demonstrations by Nazis. There is considerably less than a consensus about or a widespread understanding of the basic aspects of American speech law that truly distinguish it from more restrictive laws and practices prevalent almost everywhere else in the world. The rejection of seditious libel and other limits on unfettered dissent and criticism, the content barrier, expression in a variety of places and a variety of ways, the primacy of expression over competing concerns—all are controversial on the home field of free speech and may not command a majority of the population or, more certainly these days, the Supreme Court.

Simultaneously, the shortcomings of American speech law are generally ignored, even by some of its ardent advocates. The ideal is often assumed to be—or confused with—the reality. In fact, not only has the history of free speech been regularly misrepresented; the ability of our people to communicate meaningfully based even on the most libertarian version of free speech accepted by our courts has been greatly exaggerated. Moreover, the courts failed to provide an effective barrier in the most repressive period since the transformation (the 1950s); and in the last fifteen years, the central insights and distinguishing rules of American speech law have been substantially undercut by the Supreme Court without noticeable public debate or interest.

SINCE THE TRANSFORMATION

Throughout the posttransformation period, the basic approach set out in *Hague* and other cases of that era has been more or less followed depending mostly on the historical context. Thus, in the 1950s, Senator Joe McCarthy, the House Un-American Activities Committee, and many others resurrected the pretransformation tradition, and the judiciary essentially collapsed.[70] Unpopular ideas and associations again became illegal; dissenters were jailed and lost jobs. The courts abdicated in the face of a reactionary media blitz,[71] leading Justice Hugo Black to say:

> It has been only a few years since there was a practically unanimous feeling throughout the country and in our courts that this could not be done in our free land. . . . [The ultimate question is] whether we as a people will try fearfully and futilely to preserve democracy by adopting totalitarian methods, or whether in accordance with our traditions and our Constitution we will have the confidence and courage to be free.[72]

On the other hand, during the 1960s, the civil rights movement demanded and obtained stringent enforcement and enlargement of speech rights. This is best exemplified by the Supreme Court decisions expanding the right to picket, protecting the press, and protecting even a demonstration with signs inside a public library.[73]

However, even in the most libertarian periods, freedom of speech has been exclusively defined by the historically and culturally specific set of speech rights developed in the transformation period (mainly the 1930s), whose scope and importance in contemporary society are regularly exaggerated. First, the speaker, demonstrator, and writer must cope with the clear-and-present-danger standard and First Amendment balancing tests (in which the interest in speech is "balanced" against competing concerns). The clear-and-present-danger standard can easily be used, as it was in the opinions that first articulated it, to justify repression and punishment of dissent—to allow the bad-tendency doctrine in by the back door.[74] Since the scope of the dangers referred to has never been meaningfully defined (or even limited to unlawful activities), the clear-and-present-danger formulation amounts to the notion that speech loses its protection when it becomes persuasive or effective concerning something a judge views as dangerous.[75] First Amendment balancing tests, while purporting to require particular, legally determined results, provide, in the words of Professor Thomas Emerson, only "various considerations [that can] be enumerated but not weighted. There [is] no standard of reference upon which to base a reasoned, functional determination."[76] This often reduces to a question of whether the speech at issue, given all the circumstances, will likely or potentially cause disruption, which means "harmless" and "futile" speech is protected while speech that is effective, persuasive, or apt to provoke a response is not.[77] These rules tend to allow expression only if it is abstract and ineffective.[78]

The effectiveness and usefulness of our speech rights are also diminished by the reality that effective communication in modern society is expensive. People of ordinary means must rely on the Constitution for a means of communication and organization. People with power and money do not need to picket, demonstrate, or distribute leaflets on the street. The mass media continuously express their perspectives, both explicitly and implicitly, by "more respectable"—and more effective—means.

But most basically, freedom of speech as we know it simply does not provide people of ordinary means entrée to society's dialogue on the issues of the day. Rather, they—we—are allowed to demonstrate, picket, hand out literature, gather in the streets, sing, chant, yell, and scream—all of which effectively amounts to a *display of displeasure or discontent*, without the means to explain why we are displeased much less to actually participate in any social dialogue. This display often will not even gain a spot on the local news unless some violation of the law, injury, destruction of property, or stunt accompanies it. If it does appear, it will usually be unexplained, without description of its context, and frequently misrepresented. Our ability to communicate is haphazard, burdensome, lacking an effective means to explain or persuade; and our messages are filtered, edited, and censured by media organizations mostly interested in pleasing the public and making profits rather than communication, education, or social dialogue. It should not be surprising that so many Americans—across the political spectrum—perceive themselves and their views as excluded from public discourse.

Essentially, the law and society have frozen the scope and nature of our speech rights at levels appropriate to the 1930s, when specific audiences, like factory workers, were geographically centered, and speaking, gathering, and distributing literature in public places were the primary means of communication. The speech rights conceived in that period do not provide access to our current means of communication. Technological, social, and cultural changes have rendered the fruits of the free-speech struggle somewhat obsolete. Television, radio, newspapers (increasingly concentrated and limited in number and diversity), and direct mail now constitute the battleground, and the marketplace of ideas. In the absence of mass-based demands, we have allowed no meaningful inroads into these media for people or groups without substantial money or power.

The scope and reality of our speech rights as a means of communication and persuasion are thus limited by these legal, economic, and practical barriers. I would not relinquish these rights—with considerable patience and persistence, they can and have been meaningful, and often they are all we have. But the ordinary person or group of ordinary persons has no means, based in the Constitution or elsewhere, to engage meaningfully in that dialogue on the issues of the day that the First Amendment is so often heralded as promoting and guaranteeing.

THE RECENT RETRENCHMENT

In recent years, free-speech law has shifted drastically further from its transformation-period emphasis on enhancing the ability of ordinary people to express themselves meaningfully. While some previous rulings protecting speech have been (narrowly) reaffirmed,[79] the media and public have been inexplicably silent as the Rehnquist-Burger Court has experimented with what may be a dismantling of the basic system of free speech. There has been a conservative speech retrenchment in recent years with three major elements: the Court has increasingly narrowed and restricted the free-speech rights available to people of ordinary means, enlarged the free-speech rights of wealthy people and corporations, and erected a free-speech barrier to public access to the media and to important electoral, economic, and social reforms.

At the forefront of the Court's speech rulings over the last fifteen years has been a systematic restriction of the range of places and contexts in which speech is protected. The Court has overruled earlier decisions protecting leafleting in shopping centers; upheld a blanket prohibition of posting signs on any city-owned buildings, poles, or other property; approved limits on expression at state fairgrounds, residential neighborhoods, open portions of military facilities maintained like civilian communities, and areas near foreign embassies; limited access for competing viewpoints to a government-sponsored fundraising drive and an administrative communications network; cast serious doubt about expression at airports and other terminals; imposed content limits on speech by public employees; and approved censorship of school newspapers.[80]

These decisions have been largely based on a new principle created by the Court that generally allows expression only in places and contexts the Court decides are "public forums." The majority opinions and results in these cases are reminiscent of the *Davis* case, repudiated in the transformation era—particularly the emphasis the Court has placed on the government's authority to wholly or selectively restrict access for the purpose of expression to governmental property and facilities that are otherwise open to the public or to government approved speech.[81]

In recent cases the Court has also cast serious doubt on the content barrier—the cornerstone of our speech law that prohibits the government from limiting speech based on its content. The Court has held that a restriction on speech based on content can be constitutional if the *purpose* is directed at other, legitimate "secondary effects," like traffic congestion or litter. This new doctrine was initially applied to speech that is only marginally protected, but one of the recent cases signals a willingness among at least three of the conservative justices to apply it to all speech.[82]

The opinions distinguishing forums from nonforums and allowable from prohibited content restrictions are tedious and draw vague lines that lack any substantial basis or connection to free-speech principles; it is clear only that previously protected speech is no longer protected. The underlying free-speech concerns are hardly discussed, except in frequent dissents by Justices Brennan and Marshall, who recently characterized one of the new developments in speech law as "ominous."[83]

These speech cases are consistent in their basic approach to individual rights and the Constitution with the Court's limiting decisions in a variety of other areas. The fundamental focus of the conservative justices is not whether constitutional rights have been violated or an injustice has been done but whether that bad result was the *specific motivation or purpose* of the unconstitutional conduct. Thus, exculpatory evidence destroyed by a prosecutor in violation of a defendant's clear constitutional rights will not be remedied unless the prosecutor's purpose was to wrongfully convict the defendant; a city's acquiescing to the wishes of a white neighborhood to close a main street to an adjoining black neighborhood will not be remedied unless the purpose is to keep out the traffic of black people as opposed to keeping out traffic that happens to be black; and there is no remedy for constitutional violations by police officers if they "reasonably" believed their conduct was lawful.[84] Now free speech can be denied if the purpose is not to deny free speech. Such malicious purposes can seldom be proved, of course; benign motives are available to explain malignant acts, and in many of these cases, the Court does not even look at or require an explanation if malice cannot be proved or a benign purpose can be imagined.

Simultaneously and without apparent concern for motives, the Court has expanded the free-speech rights of wealthy people and corporations. The Court has extended free speech protections to corporations, as if they were people, even as to issues unrelated to their businesses; invalidated as a violation of free speech a Florida statute providing a limited right to reply in a newspaper to candidates who have been criticized; and invalidated as violations of free-speech limits on the amount of money an individual can spend to support a candidate.[85]

In the public access cases, television networks and local stations and large newspapers—owned by fewer and fewer large corporations with little experience or concern with journalism or public discourse—claim absolute protection not only from government censorship (protection that is appropriate) but also from any claims to access by the people. Although they monopolize the idea marketplace, the courts have protected them against claims to access as if they were individuals handing out leaflets on a street corner. Limited rights to access, such as a right to reply, are common in Western Europe, and they would probably improve quality and audience interest as well as enhance democracy.

The conservative shift over the last decade has included a decrease in popular access to media and increased "privatization" of the means of communication. This trend is exemplified by the downfall of the "fairness doctrine" and the privatization and exclusiveness of cable television (which involves a tremendous waste of resources as an additional set of wires is crisscrossing the American landscape to transmit a medium whose technological hallmark is the lack of any necessity for wires) and newer technologies, such as fiber optics. This has all occurred even as the content of our major media has degenerated; the corporate standardbearers of free speech acknowledge and sometimes glorify their avoidance of ideas or controversy. A much broader range of people and ideas must gain access to our media.[86]

We are moving toward a regime in which the Constitution yields substantially enlarged rights and power for corporations and wealthy individuals, but the ordinary citizen has no enforceable constitutional rights unless he or she can prove the government has acted maliciously and the government cannot suggest an alternative, plausibly benevolent purpose. The essence will be enhanced governmental power to suppress and impose its will on the people. The rationale and rallying cry for this new regime will be, as it was for the Reagan decade, freedom—a magnificent word and idea being steadily reduced to its opposite.

THE IDEOLOGY OF FREE SPEECH

As we stray further from the ideal of free speech we celebrate, it becomes easier to see the ideological aspects of free speech in the United States. The struggle for free speech up to the transformation, waged largely by progressives and finally realized by the labor, civil rights, and other progressive movements, has been falsely redefined as a set of preexisting natural rights whose essence and history are legal rather than political. A false pride in the legal system has displaced a source for genuine pride in the people, who fought business interests and the government—including the courts—to achieve recognition of free speech.

This recast version of freedom of speech serves in our society to validate and legitimize existing social and power relations and to mask a lack of real participation and democracy. In all capitalist countries, a sharp distinction is drawn between a person's "private" and "public" life. In the public sphere, which includes selection of government officials and political expression, basic concepts of freedom, democracy, and equality are applicable. However, in the private sphere, which encompasses almost all economic activity, we allow no democracy or equality and only the freedom to buy and sell.[87] Fundamental social issues, such as the use of our resources, investment, the environment, the work of our people, and the distribution of our goods and services, are all left to "private"—mainly corporate—decision makers.

The ideology of free speech is basic to widespread acceptance of this public/private split. Whatever the state of our economy and people, this ideology tells us that we are free and our society is democratic because we can vote and we have free speech. Like all effective ideology, this reflects as well as distorts reality. Thus, while freedom of speech is essential to any free and democratic society, so is the ability to participate meaningfully in the formulation of social policies and priorities and the provision of basic needs for shelter, health care, nutrition, education, and meaningful work.

But voting in elections increasingly dominated by fleeting, contentless media images and free speech that allows no meaningful entrée into the social dialogue are presently the only ways to participate in societal decisions that affect our lives. We have drawn the line defining the "private" sphere with a uniquely broad brush. Wider participation, on issues like workplace governance, plant closings, and environmental protection, already exists in a variety of forms in many countries. After two hundred years—and with democracy fueling revolts around the world—American democracy must mean more than voting every four years in elections devoid of content or context and the right to picket when you're really upset.

The ideological development and use of free speech in the United States have rendered this hard-won principle of liberation also an instrument of delusion: its reality is far less impressive than its rhetoric; its attainment and continued vitality depend more on popular movements than judges or courts; and its seeming embodiment of individual power and democracy masks powerlessness and society's refusal to allow real participation in the decisions that affect our lives. Our celebration of free speech should be tempered by the realization that its continued vitality even here is not at all assured, and channeled into efforts to protect transformation-era speech rights and to expand public access to the media and participation and democracy regarding the decisions that affect our lives.

NOTES

1. Leon Whipple, *Our Ancient Liberties* (New York: Da Capo Press, 1972), vol. 8.
2. *See generally*, Leon Whipple, *The Story of Civil Liberty in the United States* (Westport, Conn.: Greenwood Press, 1927); Zechariah Chafee, Jr., *Free Speech in the United States* (Cambridge, Mass.: Harvard University Press, 1941); Norman Dorsen, Paul Bender, and Burt Neuborne, *Emerson, Haber and Dorsen's Political and Civil Rights in the United States* (Boston: Little, Brown, 1976), 1:20–51; Thomas Emerson, *The System of Freedom of Expression* (New York: Random House, 1970); John Roche, *The Quest for the Dream* (New York: Macmillan, 1963); Jerold Auerbach, *Labor and Liberty* (New York: Bobbs-Merrill, 1966); Jerold Auerbach, "The Depression Decade," in *The Pulse of Freedom*, ed. Alan Reitman (New York: W. W. Norton, 1975); Paul Murphy, *World War I and the Origin of Civil Liberties in the United States* (New York: W. W. Norton, 1979); David Rabban, "The First Amendment in Its Forgotten Years," 90 *Yale Law Journal* 514 (1981).
3. *Boston Globe*, May 11, 1897.
4. Commonwealth v. Davis, 162 Mass. 510, 511 (1895).
5. The leading cases are collected and discussed in Rabban, *supra* note 2.
6. Davis v. Massachusetts, 167 U.S. 43 (1897).
7. Dayton McKean, *The Boss* (Boston: Houghton Mifflin, 1940); Irving Bernstein, *The Turbulent Years* (Boston: Houghton Mifflin, 1970); Richard Connors, *A Cycle of Power* (Metuchen, N.J.: Scarecrow Press, 1971).
8. Hague v. CIO, 307 U.S. 496 (1939). Of the seven justices participating, five concurred in the substantive aspects of Justice Owen Roberts's plurality opinion, which is considered the opinion of the Court for present purposes.
9. The Court said it did not have to "determine whether . . . the *Davis* case was rightly decided" because Davis did not apply for a permit and the purpose of the *Davis* ordinance was not "directed solely at the exercise of the right of speech and assembly" but also included regulation of the park for the "public convenience." However, while these facts are correct, the *Davis* court clearly based its decision on the property rights of the city, a basis the *Hague* court rejected. Moreover, both ordinances set up permit systems that the Court had already invalidated only months earlier, Lovell v. Griffin, 303 U.S. 444 (1938), and the *Hague* ordinance was ruled void on its face

because individuals have a constitutional right to speak and assemble on public streets, sidewalks, and parks. The decisions are inconsistent. *See also* Jamison v. Texas, 318 U.S. 413 (1943).

10. *See generally* Whipple, *supra* note 1; Whipple, *supra* note 2; Zechariah Chafee, Jr., *How Human Rights Got into the Constitution* (Boston: Boston University Press, 1952); Chafee, *supra* note 2; Leonard Levy, *Emergence of a Free Press* (New York, Oxford University Press, 1985); Leonard Levy, *Legacy of Suppression: Freedom of Speech and Press in Early American History* (Cambridge, Mass.: Harvard University Press, 1960); Leonard Levy, "The Legacy Reexamined," 37 *Stanford Law Review* 767 (1985); David Rabban, "The Ahistorical Historian: Leonard Levy on Freedom of Expression in Early America," 37 *Stanford Law Review* 795 (1985).

11. *Emergence of a Free Press*, *supra* note 10.

12. Claude Van Tyne, *Loyalists in the American Revolution* (New York: Macmillan, 1902); John Fiske, *The Critical Period of American History* (Boston: Houghton Mifflin, 1896); Whipple, *supra* note 2, at 10–11.

13. Whipple, *supra* note 2, at 19–22; James Stephens, *Digest of the Criminal Law*, 6th ed. (New York: Macmillan, 1904), pp. 96–99.

14. Act of June 25, 1798, 1 Stat. 570; Act of July 14, 1798, 1 Stat. 596.

15. Frank Anderson, "The Enforcement of the Alien and Sedition Laws," *Annual Report of the American Historical Association* (1912), pp. 113–26; Whipple, *supra* note 2, at 25–27; Chafee, *supra* note 2, at 18.

16. Whipple, *supra* note 2, at 21, 26–27.

17. Chafee, *supra* note 2, at 27.

18. Whipple, *supra* note 2, at 49.

19. *Id.*, at 51.

20. *Id.* at 57–63, 71–73.

21. *Id.* at 73–75, 90; Russell Nye, *Fettered Freedom* (Lansing: Michigan State University Press, 1963), pp. 154–57, 174–76.

22. Nye, *supra* note 21, at 187, 227–29.

23. Whipple, *supra* note 13, at 93–100; Nye, *supra* note 21, at 145–50.

24. XII Register of Debates 28 (1837); Nye, *supra* note 21, at 41–85.

25. Quoted in Whipple, *supra* note 2, at 222.

26. Richard Drinnon, *Rebel in Paradise* (Chicago: University of Chicago Press, 1962), pp. 121–42; "Policemen Stop Emma Goldman; Clear the Hall," *New York World*, May 21, 1909, p. 1 (retrieved and available from The Emma Goldman Papers, University of California at Berkeley, which has extensive materials on Goldman's free-speech struggles).

27. This description is drawn from Philip Foner, *History of the Labor Movement in the United States* (New York: International Publishers, 1965), 4: 172–213; Philip Foner, ed., *Fellow Workers and Friends, I.W.W. Free-Speech Fights as Told by Participants* (Westport, Conn: Greenwood Press, 1981); Whipple, *supra* note 2, at 223–24; Paul Brissenden, *The I.W.W.* (New York: Russell & Russell, 1957), pp. 262–66; Joyce Kornbluh, *Rebel Voices* (Ann Arbor: University of Michigan Press, 1964), pp. 94–126; Edwin Witte,

The Government in Labor Disputes (New York: McGraw-Hill, 1932), p. 202.

28. Foner, *supra* note 27, at 176–77.
29. *Id.* at 183.
30. *Industrial Worker*, February 1, 1912.
31. Whipple, *supra* note 2, at 277–80.
32. Coomer v. United States, 213 Fed. 1 (8th Cir. 1914).
33. *Ex parte* Jackson, 96 U.S. 727 (1877).
34. Whipple, *supra* note 2, at 312–17.
35. *Final Report of the U.S. Commission on Industrial Relations*, at 98, 49 (1915). The commission recommended "that Congress forthwith initiate an amendment to the Constitution securing these rights against encroachment by Federal, State, or local governments or by private persons and corporations." *Id.* at 50.
36. Whipple, *supra* note 2, at 267.
37. Act of June 15, 1917, c. 30, I, § 3, 50 U.S.C. 33 (Repealed 1948).
38. Act of May 16, 1918, c. 75, § 1, 40 Stat. 553, 1359–60.
39. 245 F. 102 (2d Cir. 1917). The court reversed a ground-breaking libertarian ruling by District Judge Learned Hand.
40. Chafee, *supra* note 2, at 51.
41. 249 U.S. 47 (1919).
42. E.g., Zechariah Chafee, Jr., "Freedom of Speech in War Time," 32 *Harvard Law Review* 932 (1919).
43. *See, e.g.*, Abrams v. United States, 250 U.S. 616, 619 (1919); Schaefer v. United States, 251 U.S. 466, 477 (1919).
44. Frohwerk v. United States, 249 U.S. 204 (1919); Debs v. United States, 249 U.S. 211 (1919).
45. 250 U.S. 616 (1919).
46. *See* Schaefer v. United States, 251 U.S. 466 (1919); Peirce v. United States, 252 U.S. 239 (1920); Gilbert v. Minnesota, 254 U.S. 325 (1920); United States *ex rel.* Milwaukee Social Democratic Publishing Co. v. Burleson, 255 U.S. 407 (1921); Gitlow v. New York, 268 U.S. 652 (1925).
47. Whitney v. California, 274 U.S. 357, 375–76 (1927) (Footnote omitted).
48. Chafee, *supra* note 2, Dorsen, Bender, and Neuborne, *supra* note 2, at 39–46; Robert Murray, *Red Scare: A Study of National Hysteria, 1919–1920* (Minneapolis: University of Minnesota Press, 1955); William Preston, *Aliens and Dissenters: Federal Suppression of Radicals, 1903–1933* (Cambridge, Mass.: Harvard University Press, 1963); Donald Johnson, *The Challenge to American Freedoms, World War I and the Rise of the American Civil Liberties Union* (Lexington: University Press of Kentucky, 1963), pp. 119–48; Peter Irons, "Fighting Fair: Zechariah Chafee, Jr., The Department of Justice, and the 'Trial at the Harvard Club,' " 94 *Harvard Law Review* 1205 (1981).
49. *See* Whitney v. California, *supra* note 47.

50. Gitlow v. New York, 268 U.S. 652 (1925). Technically, this was dictum, since it was not necessary to the decision.
51. 283 U.S. 359 (1931).
52. Near v. Minnesota, 283 U.S. 697 (1931).
53. Grosjean v. American Press Co., 297 U.S. 233 (1936); DeJonge v. Oregon, 299 U.S. 353 (1937); Herndon v. Lowry, 301 U.S. 242 (1937); Lovell v. Griffin, 303 U.S. 444 (1938); Schneider v. Irvington, 308 U.S. 147 (1939); Cantwell v. Connecticut, 310 U.S. 296 (1940); Thornhill v. Alabama, 310 U.S. 88 (1940).
54. West Virginia State Board of Education v. Barnette, 319 U.S. 624 (1943). The justices were probably affected by the widespread news in this period (withheld from the public earlier) of the Holocaust in Germany, to which they seemed to refer: "Those who begin coercive elimination of dissent soon find themselves exterminating dissenters. Compulsory unification of opinion achieves only the unanimity of the graveyard." *Id.* at 641.
55. *See generally* Johnson, *supra* note 48; Drinnon, *supra* note 26; Auerbach, *Labor and Liberty* and "The Depression Decade," both *supra* note 2; Peggy Lamson, *Roger Baldwin: Founder of the American Civil Liberties Union* (Boston: Houghton Mifflin Co., 1976). In this account, I have also relied on a personal interview with Baldwin. At ninety-seven and only several months before his death, he still exhibited the clarity and vigor he brought to bear on the free-speech issue. The interview was conducted on May 5, 1981, at Baldwin's home in New Jersey. I appreciate the assistance of my friend Candace Falk, who had me invited to an interview of Baldwin originally planned to cover only her book, *Love, Anarchy, and Emma Goldman* (New York: Holt, Rinehart and Winston, 1984).
56. *The New York Times*, July 4, 1917, p. 8, col. 4.
57. Johnson, *supra* note 48, at 48.
58. NCLB, *The Truth About the I.W.W.* (April 1918).
59. Johnson, *supra* note 48, at 74–78.
60. NCLB memorandum, "Proposed Reorganization of the Work for Civil Liberty," December 31, 1919, quoted *id.* at 146.
61. *See* Auerbach, *Labor and Liberty, supra* note 2. *See also* Paul Murphy, "Communities in Conflict," in Reitman, *supra* note 2.
62. The labor leaders included James Maurer (president of the Pennsylvania Federation of Labor), Henry Linville (president of the Teachers Union of New York), Duncan McDonald (president of the Illinois Federation of Labor), A. J. Muste (National Organizer for the Amalgamated Textile Workers Union), Julia O'Connor (National Organizer for the Telephone Operators Union), and Rose Schneiderman (Women's Trade Union League). Not all of organized labor was part of this effort; generally, the more progressive unions participated. Many unions also used their own lawyers instead of or in addition to the ACLU lawyers. Other committee members included Jane Addams, Albert DeSilver (codirector with Roger Baldwin),

Elizabeth Gurley Flynn, Felix Frankfurter (then a professor of law at Harvard), Helen Keller, Walter Nelles (attorney), and Norman Thomas.

63. Since the transformation, the ACLU has had a very different posture: it emphatically does not identify with, or care about, its clients' substantive demands or politics. But that position was adopted and tenable only after the political process that led to the transformation.

64. See Rabban, supra note 2.

65. See Spies v. Illinois, 123 U.S. 131 (1887); United States v. Cruikshank, 92 U.S. 542 (1875). Another good opportunity was lost in Patterson v. Colorado, 205 U.S. 454 (1907).

66. Fred Ragan, "Justice Oliver Wendell Holmes, Jr., Zechariah Chafee, Jr., and the Clear and Present Danger Test for Free Speech: The First Year, 1919," 58 Journal of American History 24, 43 (1971); Irons, supra note 48, at 1211–12. Holmes apparently was also affected by Judge Learned Hand, with whom he corresponded, and an article in The New Republic. See Robert Cover, "The Left, The Right and The First Amendment: 1918–1928," 40 Maryland Law Review 349 (1981).

67. Whipple, supra note 1, at vi.

68. E.g., N.L.R.B. v. Jones & Laughlin Steel Corp., 301 U.S. 1 (1937). The ABA amicus, and the list of its prestigious signatories, is summarized at 307 U.S. at 678.

69. Pursuant to the resolution, S. Res. No. 266, 74th Cong., 2d Sess. (1976), the Senate Committee on Education and Labor created its Subcommittee on Violations of Free Speech and the Rights of Labor. The subcommittee, as its title and the resolution suggest, viewed freedom of speech and the right of workers to organize and bargain collectively as inseparable. See. S. Rep. No. 1150, 77th Cong., 2d Sess. (1942); S. Rep. No. 398, 78th Cong., 2d Sess. (1944). See generally Auerbach, Labor and Liberty, supra note 2.

70. See, e.g., Barenblatt v. United States, 360 U.S. 109 (1959); Uphaus v. Wyman, 360 U.S. 72 (1959); Dennis v. United States, 341 U.S. 494 (1951); American Communications Association v. Douds, 339 U.S. 382 (1950); Lawson v. United States and Trumbo v. United States, 176 F.2d 49 (D.C. Cir. 1949), cert. denied, 339 U.S. 934 (1950) (the Hollywood 10 case). The courts also capitulated to a wave of hysterical reaction only a few years after the transformation. See Korematsu v. United States, 323 U.S. 214 (1944), approving the imprisonment of all Japanese-Americans on the West Coast.

71. The ACLU and Baldwin also succumbed. Baldwin played a leading role in the ACLU's expulsion of Elizabeth Gurley Flynn from the ACLU board because of her membership in the Communist party. Jerold Auerbach, "The Depression Decade," supra note 2; Corliss Lamont, The Trial of Elizabeth Gurley Flynn by the American Civil Liberties Union (New York: Horizon Press, 1968); Lucille Milner, Education of an American Liberal (New York: Horizon Press, 1954). The ACLU rescinded and repudiated this action in 1976.

72. Barenblatt v. United States, 360 U.S. at 147 (dissenting).
73. *See* Cox v. Louisiana, 379 U.S. 536 (1965); *The New York Times* v. Sullivan, 376 U.S. 254 (1964); Brown v. Louisiana, 383 U.S. 131 (1966).
74. *See* Dennis v. United States, 341 U.S. 494 (1951); Emerson, *supra* note 2, at 112–21.
75. *See* Alexander Meiklejohn, *Political Freedom* (New York: Harper & Brothers, 1960), pp. 29–50; Dorsen, Bender, Neuborne, *supra* note 2, at 57–58.
76. Emerson, *supra* note 2, at 117. *See also* Dorsen, Bender, and Neuborne, *supra* note 2, at 58.
77. *See, e.g.*, Heffron v. Intern. Soc. of Krishna Consciousness, 452 U.S. 640 (1981); Roseman v. Indiana University of Pennsylvania, 520 F. 2d 1364 (3d Cir. 1975), *cert. denied*, 424 U.S. 921 (1976). *See also* Richard Harris, *Freedom Spent* (Boston: Little, Brown, 1976).
78. *See, e.g.*, N.L.R.B. v. Retail Store Employees Union, Local 1001, 447 U.S. 607 (1980) (limits on number of peaceful, nonobstructive pickets); N.L.R.B. v. United Mineworkers of Amer., 429 F.2d 141 (3d Cir. 1970) (prohibiting peaceful "secondary boycott").
79. *See, e.g.*, Texas v. Johnson, 109 S.Ct. 2533 (1989) (symbolic flag burning protected).
80. *See* Hudgens v. NLRB, 424 U.S. 507 (1976); Members of City Council and Taxpayers v. Vincent, 466 U.S. 789 (1984); Heffron v. Intern. Soc. for Krishna Consciousness, 452 U.S. 640 (1981); Frisby v. Schultz, 108 S.Ct. 2495 (1988); Greer v. Spock, 424 U.S. 828 (1976); Boos v. Barry, 108 S.Ct. 1157 (1988); Cornellius v. NAACP Legal Def. and Educ. Fund, 473 U.S. 788 (1985); Perry Educ. Assn. v. Perry Local Education Assn., 460 U.S. 37 (1983); Airport Comrs. of L.A. v. Jews for Jesus, 107 S.Ct. 2568 (1987); Connick v. Myers, 461 U.S. 138 (1983); Hazelwood Sch. Dist. v. Kuhlmeier, 108 S.Ct. 562 (1988). There have been exceptions, mostly involving expressive activities highly valued by conservatives. *See* Widmar v. Vincent, 454 U.S. 263 (1981) (religious meetings in schools).
81. For a good summary of the historical development of the public forum doctrine, *see* Robert Post, "Between Governance and Management: The History and Theory of the Public Forum," 34 *UCLA Law Review* 1713, 1718–58 (1987).
82. City of Renton v. Playtime Theatres, Inc., 475 U.S. 41 (1986); Boos v. Barry, 108 S.Ct. 1157 (1988) (plurality opinion extending "secondary effects" analysis to political speech). A number of the "forum" cases also involve content issues. Compare an earlier leading case on the content barrier, Police Dept. of Chicago v. Mosley, 408 U.S. 92 (1972).
83. Boos v. Barry, 108 S.Ct. at 1173.
84. Arizona v. Youngblood, 109 S.Ct. 33 (1988); Memphis v. Greene, 451 U.S. 100 (1981); Anderson v. Creighton, 483 U.S. 635 (1987).
85. First Nat. Bk. of Boston v. Bellotti, 435 U.S. 765 (1978); Miami Herald v. Tornillo, 418 U.S. 241 (1974); Buckley v. Valeo, 424 U.S. 1 (1976). This phenomenon is not limited, of course, to the courts. For example, President

Reagan justified his veto of the Children's Television Act of 1988, which limited some advertising techniques directed at children, with appeals to freedom of speech.

86. The access issue is not new. *See* Jerome Barron, "Access to the Press—A New First Amendment Right," 80 *Harvard Law Review* 1641 (1967).

87. In feminist analysis, the public-private split is drawn differently; the public sphere includes all work outside the home.

12 JULES LOBEL

FOREIGN AFFAIRS AND THE CONSTITUTION: THE TRANSFORMATION OF THE ORIGINAL UNDERSTANDING

ON July 9, 1985, Attorney General Edwin Meese unveiled a theory of constitutional jurisprudence centered on the doctrine of original intent.[1] Drawn from the writings of conservative judges and constitutional scholars, the Reagan administration's perspective would require judges to interpret the Constitution strictly based upon the document's text and the intent of its framers. Several months later, the Justice Department's fidelity to its newly found constitutional theory was tested in a federal court sitting in Boston. Several American businessmen had challenged the president's embargo of Nicaragua and termination of the Treaty of Friendship, Commerce and Navigation between the two countries, arguing that the intent of the Framers of the Constitution and early leaders of the Republic was to deny the president sole power to terminate a treaty between the United States and another country. The president could only do so, they argued, with the assent of Congress or the two-thirds of the Senate required to enter into the treaty in the first place. The Justice Department attorney responded with the argument that the original history was essentially irrelevant since twentieth-century U.S. presidents have continuously terminated treaty obligations.[2]

Indeed they have, and the recent history of U.S. foreign policy can only be described as directly incompatible with the Constitution and the intent of its framers. In a wide variety of foreign policy contexts—the use of military force overseas, making and breaking treaty commitments, compliance with international law—modern presidents have dramatically expanded their powers beyond those allotted by the original constitutional scheme. They have argued that the expansion of executive power is necessitated by the changing international context of the world in which we live. For example, while the proponents of the War Powers Resolution in 1973 emphasized the intent of the Framers of the Constitution, opponents of the bill cited the necessity for rapid executive action in a nuclear age and the repeated exercise of executive war powers during the nineteenth and twentieth centuries. Similarly the Johnson administration argued that the president had the unilateral constitutional power to send troops to Vietnam because the interdependence of the twentieth-century world required an expansion of the eighteenth-century's understanding of the executive's power to defend the country from attack.[3] While occasionally supporters of the imperial presidency attempt to fashion an argument based on the Framers' intent,[4] their main defense of executive power relies on "the gloss which life"[5] has written on the Constitution.

The growing gap between the original separation of powers framework of the Constitution and the contemporary conduct of United States foreign policy calls for an explanation. The dissonance between constitutional design and current practice is fundamentally a result of the tension between the quest for empire and the democratic ideal. While that tension has been present throughout our country's history, it was greatly exacerbated by the United States rise as a world power in the late nineteenth century and emergence as the dominant power after World War II. The aggressive assertion of U.S. power throughout the globe, and the perceived fears, crisis, and responsibilities wrought by that power, places severe and perhaps overwhelming strains on our constitutional structure. For that structure, designed to limit and constrain power, is now seen as a hindrance to the United States' new role in the world.

The debate over original intent, therefore, is not, nor can it be, simply a "neutral," jurisprudential dialogue. For the so-called objective legal principle of original intent merely masks a basic political dispute over competing values. In the areas of privacy or racial discrimination, that tension is between individual liberty and equality and the original sexism and racism that pervaded the Constitution; in the area of foreign affairs the conflict is posed between the original republican values of the Constitution and our quest for empire. We must therefore eschew a talismanic invocation of original intent in favor of an analysis which asks what were the original values, why they were important to the framers, and are they still relevant today.

THE ORIGINAL INTENT

The newly independent America was a weak military power having strong commercial interests and opportunities. At the time Washington assumed the presidency, the United States Army consisted of fewer than 840 men. As commander in chief, Washington was without any U.S. naval forces to command. Only at the end of Washington's tenure in office were several large frigates, constituting the beginning of a navy, nearing completion.[6] Faced with stronger European powers threatening to drag the country into warfare, and a decentralized political system made up of fractious and bickering state governments, a cautious foreign policy based on respect for international norms was a necessity. Early United States foreign policy was therefore designed to avoid, as much as possible, political entanglements in European affairs. As Attorney General Randolph observed in 1795,

> An infant country, deep in debt; necessitated to borrow in Europe; without manufacture; without a land or naval force; without a competency of arms or ammunition; with a commerce, closely connected beyond the Atlantic, with a certainty of enhancing the price of foreign productions, and diminishing that of our own; with a constitution more than four years old; in a state of probation, and not exempt from foes[—]such a country can have no greater curse in store for her than war. That peace was our policy has been admitted by Congress, and by France herself.[7]

Foreign policy was a major concern underlying the convocation of the Constitutional Convention in Philadelphia. Various state governments were violating international law and treaty agreements, provoking retaliatory actions by European powers. Randolph opened the main business of the convention by listing the defects of the Articles of Confederation, the first of which included "that they could not cause infractions of treaties or of the law of nations to be punished."[8] Madison echoed this theme, asking whether the proposed constitutional plan will "prevent those violations of the law of nations and treaties which if not prevented must involve us in the calamities of war."[9]

The constitutional arrangements arrived at in Philadelphia reflect the strategic goal of extending commerce with Europe while avoiding political entanglements and war with European powers. The foreign affairs provisions contain several important themes: maintaining a strong central government capable of conducting foreign policy and asserting U.S. sovereignty, dividing power within that central government so that the president could not unilaterally involve the new republic in disastrous overseas engagements, and ensuring that the United States foreign policy be based on law, including international law.

The constitutional Framers understood the connection between procedure and substance; their procedural choices were designed to achieve certain substantive goals. To ensure that U.S. force be used only to counter serious threats to national security, Congress, not the president, was given the power to commit the United States to armed conflict. To James Madison, the executive branch was more likely to involve us in warfare since "war is, in fact, the true nurse of executive aggrandizement."[10] Thomas Jefferson desired an "effectual check to the Dog of War," James Madison noted that Congress would be "clogging rather than facilitating war," and James Wilson, a key figure at the convention argued that the Constitution was designed not to "hurry us into war."[11] The president's power to use armed force was narrowly circumscribed to that of defending against an attack on U.S. armed forces or territory. The constitutional commitment of the power to declare war to Congress was not premised solely on the perceived value of democratic decision making and open debate that the legislature could provide, it also represented a substantive judgment on the part of the framers that entry into war should be difficult. That substantive judgment was conditioned on both general principle and the historical circumstances the leaders of the Republic found themselves in.

Moreover, the Constitution gives Congress broader war powers than simply the power to declare war. It also, for example, provides Congress the authority to issue letters of marque and reprisal. This now-forgotten power was viewed by our early leaders as the authority to authorize a broad spectrum of armed hostilities short of declared war. For example, Thomas Jefferson included within the congressional power to issue letters of marque and reprisal the power to order general reprisals against a foreign nation using the public armed forces.[12] Similarly, James McHenry, John Adams's secretary of war, and Alexander Hamilton agreed that any executive exercise of American naval force beyond defending the nation's seacoast, American vessels, or commerce within American waters "come[s] within the sphere of reprisals and . . . require[s] the explicit sanction of the branch of government which is alone constitutionally authorised to grant letters of marque and reprisal."[13] More generally, many statesmen of the period used marque and reprisal to refer to a state of "imperfect war," by which they meant any state of armed hostilities that did not rise to the level of declared war.[14] Thus, it can be argued that uses of force short of war, such as covert paramilitary warfare, come within the sphere of the Framers' concern.

The Framers were also wary of providing the executive with unilateral power over the other key area of U.S. foreign policy in the eighteenth century—the making and terminating of treaties with foreign countries. As Alexander Hamilton noted, the "history of human conduct does not make it wise to commit interests of so delicate and momentous a kind [entering into treaties] to the sole disposal . . . of a president."[15] Thus, the Constitution expressly limits the executive's role in forming a treaty by requiring the advice and consent of two-thirds of the Senate.

Significantly, Article VI of the Constitution confers on treaties the status of supreme law of the land. While primarily intended to make treaties binding on the states, the status of treaties as domestic law also suggests that they could not be repealed or violated by executive action alone. For it is the executive's constitutional obligation to "take care that the laws be faithfully executed," he is not empowered to repeal or ignore the law. While the text of the Constitution is silent on the issue of who could abrogate a treaty, the early leaders of the Republic and drafters of the Constitution believed that the president could not do so alone. As vice president, Jefferson argued that "Treaties being declared equally with the law of the United States, to be the supreme law of the land, it is understood that an act of the legislature alone can declare them infringed and rescinded." Sitting on circuit, Justice James Iredell, who had led the fight for adoption of the Constitution in North Carolina, stated that only Congress could declare a treaty void, and that absent such a declaration the treaty was still in effect.[16]

Indeed, when the United States decided to abrogate its treaties of alliance and friendship with France during the quasi-war with that country in the late 1790s, all agreed that annulling the treaties could not be undertaken by the executive alone. The unanimous view in Congress was expressed by Congressman Sewall who noted that "In most countries it is in the power of the Chief Magistrate to suspend a treaty whenever he thinks proper; here Congress only has that power."[17] The executive branch also concurred in the view that the president could not annul the French treaties. In an executive memorandum responding to questions from President Adams, Secretary of War James McHenry advised that suspending the treaties with France would "require the deliberation of Congress."[18] Writing to Madison, Vice President Jefferson noted that he was glad "to hear it admitted on *all hands* that the legislature is the only power which can control a treaty."[19] Rather than rely on executive action, the administration's supporters introduced a bill into Congress to annul the treaties, reflecting their understanding of the Constitution's distribution of power.

The Framers also viewed international law as providing a legal restraint on executive and even congressional acts.[20] While international law, then referred to by the term law of nations, was not explicitly made part of the supreme law of the land, the Framers clearly considered it to have such status. Justice Marshall's opinion in the *Neriede* stated the common understanding that the law of nations "is a part of the law of the land."[21]

In their famous debate on the authority for President Washington's Proclamation of Neutrality of 1793, Madison and Hamilton both recognized that international law's status as domestic law gave rise to an executive duty to enforce international law. Five years later Madison again argued that the executive was without power to act in derogation of international law. The Adams administration had prohibited the arming of ships in U.S. ports as a violation of neutrality, but as tensions mounted between France and the

United States, the executive revoked its prohibition, thereby granting "an indirect license to arm." Congress had not yet acted. Madison complained that the executive had no power to grant such an indirect license:

> The first instructions were no otherwise legal than as they were in pursuance of the Law of nations, and, consequently in execution of the law of the land. The revocation of the instructions is a virtual change of the law, and consequently a usurpation by the Executive of a legislative power.[22]

During the ensuing debate over relations with France, various congressmen noted, without contradiction, that the president could use the nation's armed forces only in a "manner authorized by the law of nations."[23]

Justice Story agreed that the law of nations bound the executive even in the exercise of war powers. In a dissent to *Brown* v. *United States* discussing the executive's powers to wage the War of 1812 with Great Britain, Story noted that the president "has a discretion vested in him, as to the manner and extent; but he cannot lawfully transcend the rules of warfare established among civilized nations. He cannot lawfully exercise powers or authorize proceedings which the civilized world repudiates and disclaims."[24] Chief Justice Marshall's majority opinion did not dispute this point. It held that the scope of the president's constitutional war powers should be construed consistently with the law of nations to require congressional authorization prior to executive seizure of alien property.

The judiciary also played an important role in restraining executive adventurism. In *Little* v. *Barreme*, a unanimous Supreme Court upheld the imposition of individual liability on a naval commander for his seizure of a merchant ship suspected of trading with the French during the quasi-war with France in the late 1790s.[25] The Court imposed liability on the commander despite the fact that he had acted pursuant to a presidential order, because his acts violated a congressional statute.

The series of legal restraints imposed on the executive flowed from the founding generation's understanding of the world in which they lived and America's role in that world. The leaders of a weak and newly independent nation recognized the need to rely heavily on international law to guide foreign policy. Benjamin Franklin's advice in 1775 that the "circumstances of a rising state make it necessary frequently to consult the law of nations," was followed throughout the latter part of the eighteenth century.[26] Similarly, the predominance of foreign policy issues in the constitutional debates of the 1790s reflected the critical importance of foreign policy to the new Republic and the perceived value of the Constitution in providing a framework for conducting a judicious, cautious, and prudent policy toward other countries. In the debates over Washington's policy in 1793–1794 of remaining neutral in the Franco-British War, the Jay Treaty with Britain in 1795–1796, or the conduct of the undeclared war with France in the latter 1790s, constitutional understandings were always a critical issue in the congressional and executive disputes over U.S. policy. A modern observer would be surprised to discover the substantial percentage of the annals of Congress in the 1790s devoted to foreign policy debates about relatively technical issues of constitutional or international law. That President Washington requested each member of his cabinet to present an opinion of the duties required by international law to maintain neutrality, and upon failing to reach a consensus presented the questions to the Supreme Court for an advisory opinion (which the Supreme Court refused to render thus establishing the doctrine that the Court will not render such advice), attests to the importance of these issues. It is hard to imagine modern presidents or Congresses behaving similarly.

Even in the early years of the Republic, the Constitution's foreign policy strictures were subject to differing interpretations and at times stretched by presidents. The Madison administration's fomenting of rebellion in Florida in the early 1800s in order to obtain the territory from Spain is but one example of executive conduct of a dubious constitutional nature. Indeed, the early leaders both were cautious internationally yet dreamed of empire. Jefferson claimed that "I am persuaded no constitution was ever before so well calculated as ours for extensive empire and self-government."[27] The conflict between a desire for empire and American military and political weakness with respect to Europe produced executive action that often bordered on or even exceeded the constitutionally permissible. This was particularly true with respect to weaker powers on our borders: Indian tribes, at times Spain, and later Mexico.

Yet despite these inconsistencies, the first few decades of American foreign policy were characterized by joint executive-Congress participation in most foreign policy decisions and generally cautious executive use of U.S. military force. Abraham Sofaer, who exhaustively studied those early years, concludes that while presidents took the lead in foreign affairs activities and sometimes engaged in activities that "exceeded the bounds of behavior by which they publicly purported to be governed," "at no time did the executive claim 'inherent' power to initiate military actions . . . Furthermore, no President or other official of the executive branch ever claimed that Congress lacked power to control or dictate executive conduct."[28]

EMERGENCE OF THE IMPERIAL PRESIDENT

In the late nineteenth and early twentieth centuries, however, the United States turned toward globalism and international power. With the extrusion of American power abroad, the limitations on presidential power, so carefully guarded by the early leaders of the Republic, began to erode. The United States' assertive exercise of military power abroad, the increasing use of executive agreements to bypass the treaty procedure, and the unilateral executive use of force beyond merely protecting American citizens contributed to the evisceration of the limitations on executive power. Observers as diverse as author James Bryce, editor E. L. Bodkin, and military strategist Captain Alfred Thayer Mahan worried that the Constitution was inconsistent with these new imperial aspirations. [29]

A critical theoretical transformation began to unfold during these early years of globalism. Inherent presidential power to meet crises was for the first time seen as emanating from within the Constitution. President Theodore Roosevelt articulated a broad theory of executive emergency power. Roosevelt, unlike Jefferson, grounded this emergency power on a notion of inherent constitutional authority, stating that the president had the "legal right to do whatever the needs of the people demand, unless the Constitution or the laws explicitly forbid him to do it."[30]

The Supreme Court provided encouragement to the theory of inherent executive constitutional power to meet exigencies. In 1890, in the course of ruling that the president had the power to provide the justices with personal bodyguards, the Court noted that the president possessed broad, implied, constitutional powers beyond the execution of treaties and congressional acts. [31]

The scholarly community also recognized that America's new role required constitutional changes in the traditional constitutional model. For an astute academic such as Woodrow Wilson, the assertion of power abroad "changed the balance of [constitutional] parts," projecting the president "at the front of government." According to Wilson, the traditional theory of the Constitution was premised on Newtonian science, a paradigm that viewed the universe as composed of opposite forces balancing each other to create symmetry and order. [32] The metaphor of Newtonian physics underscored a dualist conception of politics and constitutional law that imposed a strict boundary on executive power. [33] Wilson, recognizing the constitutional transformation wrought by rising American power, substituted Darwin for Newton, elastic adaptation and modification to environment for formalistic dualities, as the mainspring of American constitutionalism. Wilson thus provided an intellectual framework for the practical shading of legal boundaries limiting executive power.

The process that started at the end of the nineteenth century culminated after World War II. The United States' new role as the world's dominant superpower fed an obsession with crisis. American dominance altered our notion of national security. Every challenge to United States hegemony anywhere in the world began to be perceived as a threat to national security. Those perceived threats to United States power generated a profound sense of crisis, leading William Fulbright and others to argue that traditional democratic separation of powers principles had to yield to the need for strong executive power to meet the new situation and maintain United States power.[34] The distinguished historian Arthur Schlesinger analogized the United States perspective to the state of mind of the Roman Empire:

> There was no corner of the known world where some interest was not alleged to be in danger or under actual attack. If the interests were not Roman, they were those of Rome's allies; and if Rome had no allies, then allies would be invented . . . Rome was always being attacked by evil-minded neighbors, always fighting for a breathing space.[35]

National Security Council (NSC) Paper 68, issued in April 1950 as "the first comprehensive statement of a national strategy after World War II," foresaw "an indefinite period of tension and danger."[36] In response, the NSC called for a massive military buildup, and, as President Truman later wrote, "a great change in our normal peacetime way of doing things."[37]

Modern presidents have developed broad, elastic theories of executive power to justify their expansion of power. Three key constitutional sources have emerged: the "executive power" clause, the commander in chief clause, and the executive's implied power over foreign affairs.

Presidents such as Theodore Roosevelt, Harry Truman, and Richard Nixon have asserted that since Article I limits congressional power to those powers "herein granted," while Article II's grant of "executive power" has no such limitation, the president has inherent power to do either anything necessary to preserve the United States, or, even more broadly, anything not explicitly forbidden by the Constitution. Even though this "executive power" clause argument has been condemned by commentators and some courts, the executive has continued to rely on it to assert broad power over the conduct of American foreign policy. The ill-defined breadth of these presidential arguments was accurately foreseen by Daniel Webster in his 1835 address to the Senate: "Executive power is not a thing so well known, and so accurately defined, as that the written constitution of a limited government can be supposed to have conferred it in the lump. What is executive power? What are its boundaries?"[38]

The executive has also justified broad emergency power through resort to the commander in chief clause of Article II. The traditional limit of the commander in chief's power to that necessary to repel sudden attack or resist invasion until Congress has declared war no longer controls after the Cold War. The Justice Department argued that the president had the unilateral power to send troops to Vietnam because the interdependence of the twentieth century world meant that all warfare anywhere in the world might "impinge directly upon the nation's security."[39] Therefore, modern presidents have articulated a constitutional power to send forces into combat whenever they detect threats to national security. Under this model, the commander in chief's powers, in Dean Rusk's approving words, "are as large as the situation requires."[40] If any threat to United States security around the world activates the executive's war powers, then the distinction between the executive emergency power to repel an attack and congressional power to authorize the introduction of U.S. forces into hostilities loses significance.

Finally, the executive branch has often relied on the president's generic and ill-defined power as "the sole organ of foreign affairs," articulated by dicta in *United States* v. *Curtiss-Wright Export Corp.* in 1936,[41] to justify broad assertion of power over foreign policy. Recent administrations have asserted forcefully that the Constitution limits congressional authority to restrain the exercise of the president's power as the "sole organ" of foreign affairs power.[42]

Congress and the judiciary have in most cases assented to this assertion of executive power. Congress has delegated broad power to the president to authorize activities such as covert actions or embargoes of trade with foreign countries and has refused to enforce statutes such as the War Powers Resolution which provide limits on executive action. The judiciary has often refused to intervene in cases challenging U.S. foreign policy, as was the case during the Vietnam War. Instead, judges have sought refuge in the "judicially created" political question doctrine to avoid review. A recent case brought by owners of a Norwegian vessel seeking damages for the destruction of their ship by mines placed in Nicaraguan harbors by the CIA is instructive. The Norwegian ship was a neutral vessel, whose captain had no warning that mines had been placed around Nicaraguan ports. The case is analogous in certain key aspects to the already discussed 1804 Supreme Court opinion in *Little* v. *Barreme*. In both cases, executive officials had acted in disregard of congressional legislation and caused damage to a commercial vessel. While the Supreme Court in 1804 held the captain liable for damages, the Second Circuit Court of Appeals affirmed a decision that the Nicaraguan case presented a political question which courts should not decide.[43] The Supreme Court refused to hear the Norwegian shipowner's appeal.

The result of executive assertiveness, congressional compliance, and judicial abstention has been a reworking of the original constitutional understandings. Post–World War II executives have repeatedly used U.S. forces without congressional authorization, allegedly for "defensive" purposes pursuant to their commander in chief power. Moreover the 1950s witnessed the rise of covert operations involving the use of paramilitary troops to overthrow or support foreign governments as an important instrument of U.S. foreign policy. Between 1953 and 1973 the CIA used paramilitary troops in at least eight major efforts against foreign governments.[44] Because of the post-Vietnam political and legal objections to using American troops to achieve foreign policy goals, the Reagan administration increasingly turned to paramilitary operations to execute foreign policy, as is evident in our relations with Nicaragua, Afghanistan, Cambodia, and other countries. These covert operations are not initiated pursuant to congressional authorization, thus violating the constitutional mandate that all U.S. uses of force be authorized by Congress.[45]

Similarly, separation of powers in the making and breaking of treaties has been undermined. There has been a spectacular rise in the number of executive agreements with other nations, agreements that do not require ratification by two-thirds of the Senate. While the first 150 years of our nation's history produced a rough equivalence between the number of executive agreements and official treaties entered into by our government, since 1939, close to 95 percent of all international agreements entered into by the United States have been executive agreements, not treaties.[46] Congressional efforts to curtail such agreements, such as the Bricker Amendment in the 1950s, have been easily brushed aside.

The president's purported power to unilaterally terminate treaties is also primarily premised on twentieth-century practice. In *Goldwater* v. *Carter*, a case involving President Carter's termination of the treaty with Taiwan, the administration claimed that there had been thirteen prior instances in which a president terminated a treaty without congressional participation. Eleven of those cases occurred since the end of World War I.[47]

Finally, the role of international law as a restraint on governmental conduct also has been undermined in the modern era. In the 1880s and 1890s, the courts held that Congress could violate treaties and customary international law.[48] While the Supreme Court did strike down an executive act in violation of international law in 1900, the reporter's note to the present Restatement of Foreign Relations holds that "there is authority for the view that the President has the power, when acting within his constitutional authority, to disregard a rule of international law or an agreement of the United States," and the Eleventh Circuit Court of Appeals has recently affirmed that position.[49] The United States, as a dominant world power, now perceives international law to be more of a hindrance than a central focus of U.S. foreign policy.

DEMOCRACY AND THE QUEST FOR EMPIRE

The twin disasters of Vietnam and Watergate created pressure to restore limitations on executive powers. Even strong supporters of the growth of executive power during the 1940s and 1950s, such as Arthur Schlesinger and William J. Fulbright, began to question whether the pendulum had swung too far.[50] Congress sought to reassert its power in a series of post-Vietnam statutes, such as the War Powers Resolution of 1973, which provided automatic withdrawal of U.S. forces after sixty days absent explicit congressional approval, the Hughes-Ryan Amendment asserting oversight over covert action, and the International Economic Emergencies Powers Act (IEEPA).[51]

So far, less than two decades after Congress initiated these efforts, these statutes lie in shambles, wrecked by presidential defiance, congressional acquiescence, and judicial undermining. Virtually all observers recognize the War Powers Resolution to be a failure. No president has ever filed a report starting the sixty-day clock running, despite repeated executive introduction of armed forces into hostile situations in Indochina, Iran, Lebanon, Central America, Grenada, Libya, and most recently the Persian Gulf. Congress has challenged this noncompliance only once, without a decisive result.[52] The judiciary has refused to adjudicate claims challenging executive action as violative of the resolution, most recently holding that a challenge by over a hundred congressmen to the armed presence in the Persian Gulf was nonjusticiable.[53] Senator Robert Byrd recently introduced legislation to amend the resolution by repealing its most important operative measures, including the sixty-day clock. That "amendment" appears motivated by a growing conviction that the resolution is unworkable. As John Hart Ely put it, "[r]epeal *is* one way to increase compliance."[54]

Supporters of the reformist initiatives of the 1970s can be grouped into two camps, labeled by Kenneth Sharpe as the "aberrationists" and the "legalists."[55] The aberrationists blame the failure to comply with the Constitution or law on individual mistakes. The majority report of the Iran-Contra Committee, for example, argues, "[T]he Iran-Contra Affair resulted from the failure of individuals to observe the law, not from deficiencies in existing law or in our system of governance."[56]

Yet while any one scandal can always be blamed on individual mistakes, the inability of the reform statutes to check executive abuse in a wide variety of foreign policy contexts simply cannot be the product of individual dishonesty, corruption, ambition, or stupidity. As Professor Harold Koh perceptively comments, the Iran-Contra affair represented not simply an aberration, "but deeper systemic flaws in the current legal structure of our foreign policymaking process."[57]

The legalist responses to the reformist failure primarily urge a process oriented approach. Professor Koh advocates a new national security "charter," which would "seek to alter recurrent patterns of executive behavior by re-structuring the *institutional* attributes" that contribute to executive excesses. [58] His design would encourage Congress and the judiciary to become involved in foreign policy issues. The legalist proposals, while recognizing a systemic pattern, still fail to address the basic problem leading to both the events of the Iran-Contra affair and the failure of reform efforts.

The reason for the failure of the post-Vietnam reforms lies in the very forces and substantive policies that underlie the transformation of our original constitutional understandings in the late nineteenth century. The reformist failure is not only a legal or institutional failure, but primarily caused by an aggressive United States assertion of power in the international arena. To restore republican thought in the area of foreign affairs requires not merely procedural change but substantive reevaluation.

Old lessons have to be constantly relearned. The debate over the Iran-Contra scandal narrowly focused on such issues as what the president knew, whether the law was violated, and whether new legislation is needed. Commentators have generally ignored the causal connection between the persistent failure of the executive to heed constitutional or legal limitations in its efforts to overthrow the Nicaraguan government and an aggressive view of American power in the world. Yet two decades ago, the Vietnam War vividly brought this lesson into focus.

As the war in Vietnam dragged on, thoughtful commentators began to question whether our constitutional assumptions could withstand the quest for empire. The doubts that had earlier appeared in the 1890s as to whether the Constitution could function "for a conquering nation" reappeared forcefully in the 1960s. Henry Steele Commager wrote that the "abuse of power by Presidents is a reflection, and perhaps a consequence, of abuse of power by the American . . . nation." In the long run, "abuse of executive power cannot be separated from abuse of national power. If we subvert world order and destroy world peace, we must inevitably subvert and destroy our own political institutions first." The answer to abuse of executive power, was and still is, neither the removal of evil people, nor the reform of insufficient laws, but rather the dissipation of the "forces, motives and fears which underlie the exercise and the rationale of excessive presidential power." [59]

The Vietnam War also led William Fulbright to reevaluate dramatically his earlier views on empowering the presidency. The failure in Vietnam provided an occasion to rethink the messianic anticommunism that drove the United States to unilaterally intervene anywhere in the world in the name of national security. For Fulbright the conflict was clear. If "America is to become an empire, there is very little chance that it can avoid becoming a virtual dictatorship as well."[60]

While better presidents, advisers, and laws are both necessary and significant in curbing executive power, the failure of legal reforms reflects the nation's failure to dramatically alter its substantive worldview. The procedural constraints the Constitution places on executive action reflect a substantive vision of America's place and role in the world. That vision no longer comports with our role as the dominant world power.

Our relative power to shape world affairs has declined since the 1950s; a spate of recent scholarship suggests that the decline will continue. The continued quest for dominance will therefore surely bring with it continued crisis. The more forcefully America strives to maintain hegemony, the stronger the perception of crisis will be. The policy of hegemonic maintenance is simply inconsistent with reinvigorating the carefully balanced limitations on power encapsulated in our constitutional assumptions.

Revitalizing the liberal legal paradigm requires a substantive redefinition of United States national security that does not necessitate the present imperial responsibility which inevitably leads to continued crisis. As the Senate Foreign Relations Committee recognized in proposing war powers legislation in 1973, the bill would not restore checks and balances without substantive changes in American foreign policy: "If the country is to be continually at war, or in crisis, or on the verge of war, or in small-scale, partial or surrogate war, the force of events must lead inevitably toward executive domination despite any legislative roadblocks that may be placed in the executive's way."[61]

Such a transformation would involve several related components. First, the pervasive anticommunism that has been so central to the foreign policy of each of the past eight administrations must be discarded. Second, the United States must relinquish the prevailing assumption that our national security requires the prevention or overthrow of leftist revolutionary governments throughout the world.[62] Third, in response to Gorbachev's initiatives, we must move to end the Cold War and substitute cooperation for containment in our relations with the Soviets.[63] Finally, a different foreign policy requires recognizing and adapting to the economic and political interdependence of nation-states, requiring increased United States reliance on multilateral political, economic, and judicial institutions to resolve international problems.

While substantive changes in U.S. foreign policy could somewhat restore the original perspective of our constitutional provisions relating to international affairs, a long-term transformative vision must insist on two very different, but complementary changes from our present situation. The first would be the further development of the international system of governance, supplementing nation-states and simultaneously weakening the "us-versus-them" perspective that characterizes the present nation-state system. The second change would involve reviving communalist politics, in which the citizenry, often acting through local communities, plays a more active role in determining our relations with peoples of other nations. Both changes undermine the liberal system's basis in distinct national rules: one by internationalizing government, the other by localizing it and making the citizenry into active participants in the decision-making process.

These changes would supplement and ultimately transform traditional separation of power restraints. The constitutional restraints on the executive are the product of a fear of unilateral decision making by any one person. In an effective multinational system, unilateral United States executive power would be restrained by international, political, and legal processes. Moreover, active citizen and local participation in foreign policy-making would reduce the power of the centralized government, rendering unrestrained executive adventurism less likely. The legal restraints currently provided horizontally within the national government by separation of powers would be supplemented by vertical restraints imposed by international society and popular community pressures.

The resulting normative vision would probably rely more on community interaction and less on fixed rules to govern our lives. Eschewing a reliance on fixed rules to order our lives requires decision making that focuses on the particular consequences of the concrete alternative possibilities in discrete situations.[64] Professor Michelman argues that much of our constitutional dialogue occurs outside the formal channels of electoral and legislative politics: for example, in town meetings, voluntary organizations, and local government agencies. "Those are all arenas of potentially transformative dialogue."[65] To citizen activists of the last few decades, law is not merely the positivistic command of the sovereign, but a product of the community's experiences and values that they articulate.[66] That different vision of law as deriving from community interaction is more multidimensional and particularized than the traditional model of liberal constitutional thought.

The possibility of these transformations lies within the shadows of the present.[67] While the bright hopes of a world government that accompanied the establishment of the United Nations have faded, Gorbachev's new perspectives, the increasing interdependence of the world's economies, and awareness of the vulnerability of the global environment have renewed interest in multilateral institutions and cooperative approaches. In addition, the revival of scholarly interest in citizenry participation in government has proceeded apace with an actual revival of citizen participation in foreign affairs issues.[68] Localities have begun passing resolutions on foreign policy issues, adopting sister cities in other parts of the world, and actively refusing to cooperate with federal emergency plans. Citizens across the country have engaged in acts of civil disobedience to display their disapproval of policies in Central America.[69] Antinuclear activists have also taken to the streets and jails to protest the United States continuation of the nuclear arms race. While these efforts are on the margin of current mainstream thought on foreign affairs, it is possible that the current citizen's movement will move from the margin to the center in the twenty-first century.

The changes that the twentieth century have wrought in our original constitutional foreign affairs framework illustrates the connection between substantive policy and procedural mechanisms. It is this connection that fundamentally underlies the bankruptcy of the new jurisprudence of originalism. Under the guise of neutral jurisprudence, this theory attempts to obscure substantive choices as to the nature of our society. Questions of whether the government should interfere in women's decision making as to reproduction, or whether our government should torture people abroad or commit aggression against other nations are issues which go to the heart of how we constitutionally define ourselves and limit our government. Those choices cannot be made by merely looking at the original intent of the framers without understanding the nature of the historical and social circumstances of the age in which they lived. The attempt to mask broad substantive choices by reference to a jurisprudence of original intent can no more succeed now than it did in 1857 when Judge Taney used it to deny blacks U.S. citizenship in the *Dred Scott* case.[70]

The twentieth-century changes in that framework call for a renewed debate over the current relevance and importance of those values, not for a blind obedience to original intent. To the extent that our nation really wants to relearn how to live peacefully with other countries instead of lording over them, the procedural mechanisms set up in the Constitution ought to be restored and revitalized.

NOTES

1. Address of Attorney General Edwin Meese III, before the American Bar Association, July 9, 1985.
2. Beacon Products v. Reagan, 633 F. Supp. 1191, 1198–99 (D. Mass. 1986). I was cocounsel for the plaintiffs in this case on behalf of the Center for Constitutional Rights.
3. S. Rep. No. 220, 93rd Cong. 1st Sess. 7 (1973). Office of the Legal Adviser, Dept. of State, "The Legality of United States Participation in the Defense of Vietnam," 75 *Yale Law Review* 1985 (1965).

4. *See* Symposium, 43 *University of Miami Law Review* 5 (1988).

5. The phrase comes from Justice Frankfurter's concurring opinion in Youngstown Sheet & Tube v. Sawyer, 343 U.S. 579, 610 (1952) (Frankfurter, J., concurring).

6. A. Sofaer, *War, Foreign Affairs and Constitutional Power* (Cambridge: Ballinger, 1976), p. 116.

7. Letter From Randolph to James Monroe (June 1, 1795) cited in Lobel, "The Rise and Decline of the Neutrality Act: Sovereignty and Congressional War Powers in United States Foreign Policy," 24 *Harvard International Law Journal* 1, 21 (1983); *see also* F. Wharton, A *Digest of International Law of the United States*, 2d ed. (Washington, D.C.: Government Printing Office, 1887), 3: 514.

8. *The Records of the Federal Convention of 1787*, ed. M. Farrand (New Haven: Yale University Press, 1911), 1: 19.

9. *Id.*, p. 316.

10. Helvidius No. 4, in *Writings of James Madison*, ed. G. Hunt (New York: G.P. Putnam's Sons, 1906), 6: 174.

11. *The Papers of Thomas Jefferson*, ed. J. Boyd (Princeton: Princeton University Press, 1951), 15: 397; *Records, supra* note 8, pp. 319, 528.

12. Opinion of Sec'y of State (May 16, 1793) (Thomas Jefferson), reprinted in J. Moore, A *Digest of International Law* (Washington, D.C.: Government Printing Office, 1906), 7: 123.

13. Letter from James McHenry to John Adams (May 18, 1798), reprinted in A. Sofaer, *supra* note 6, p. 155. Letter from Alexander Hamilton to James McHenry (May 17, 1798), reprinted in *The Papers of Alexander Hamilton*, ed. H. Syrett (New York: Columbia University Press, 1979), 21: 461–62. *See also* The Defence, No. 37, vol. 20 *supra*, at 17.

14. *See* J. Kent, *Commentaries on American Law*, ed. O. W. Holmes (Boston: Little, Brown & Co., 1873; 1st ed., 1826), p. 71.

15. A. Hamilton, *The Federalist*, No. 75, ed. J. Cooke (Middletown, Conn.: Wesleyan University Press, 1961), pp. 505–6. *See also* J. Story, *Commentaries on the Constitution of the United States*, 5th ed. (Boston: Little, Brown & Co., 1905), 2: § 1512.

16. Jefferson's Manual of Senate Procedure, reprinted in Senate Manual, S. Doc., 94th Cong., 1st Sess. 668 (1975); Ware v. Hylton, 3 U.S. (3 Dall.) 199, 261 (1796) (opinion of Iredell, circuit justice), *rev'd on other grounds*, *id.* at 285.

17. 5 Annals of Cong. 2120 (1798). *See also* 5 Annals at 1901–2 (remarks of Congressman Sitgreaves) and at 2123 (remarks of Congressman Dana).

18. Adams Papers, Reel 387, March 14, 1798.

19. Letter of Jefferson to James Madison, May 31, 1798, *Writings of Thomas Jefferson*, ed. A. Lupscomb (Washington, D.C.: Thomas Jefferson Memorial Assoc., 1903), vol. 10 (emphasis added).

20. Lobel, "The Limits of Constitutional Power: Conflicts Between Foreign Policy and International Law," 71 *Virginia Law Review* 1971 (1985).

21. 13 U.S. (9 Cranch) 388, 423 (1815).
22. Letter from James Madison to Thomas Jefferson, April 2, 1798, reprinted in *Writings of James Madison*, ed. G. Hunt (New York: G. P. Putnam's Sons, 1900), 2: 313.
23. 5 Annals of Cong. 1807 (1798) (Congressman Robert Williams); *id.* at 1806 (Congressman Abraham Venable).
24. 12 U.S. (8 Cranch) 110, 129, 153 (1814) (Story, J., dissenting).
25. 6 U.S. (2 Cranch) 170 (1804).
26. Letter of B. Franklin to Dumas, December 19, 1775, reprinted in *The Revolutionary Diplomatic Correspondence of the United States* (Washington, D.C.: Government Printing Office, 1889), 2: 64. *See also* G. Lint, "The American Revolution and the Law of Nations, 1776–1789," 1 *Diplomatic History* 20, 33 (1977) (American weakness made policy based on law of nations the only realistic choice.) *See generally*, D. Lang, *Foreign Policy in the Early Republic: The Law of Nations and the Balance of Power* (Baton Rouge: Louisiana State University Press, 1985), pp. 11, 67, 90.
27. Cited in W. Lafeber, "The Constitution and U.S. Foreign Policy: An Interpretation," in *A Less Than Perfect Union: Alternative Perspectives on the U.S. Constitution*, ed. J. Lobel (New York: Monthly Review Press, 1988), pp. 221, 226.
28. A. Sofaer, *supra* note 6, at 378–79.
29. *See generally*, Lafeber, *supra* note 27, pp. 229–34; A. Schlesinger, *The Imperial Presidency* (Boston: Houghton Mifflin, 1973), pp. 85–91.
30. T. Roosevelt, *Theodore Roosevelt, An Autobiography* (New York: C. Scribner, 1913), p. 464.
31. *In re* Neagle, 135 U.S. 64 (1890).
32. W. Wilson, *Constitutional Government in the United States* (New York: Columbia University Press, 1908), pp. 55, 59; Lafeber, *supra* note 27, pp 231–34.
33. P. Goldstene, *The Collapse of Liberal Empire: Science and Revolution in the Twentieth Century* (New Haven: Yale University Press, 1977), pp. 11–12.
34. J. W. Fulbright, "American Foreign Policy in the 20th Century Under an 18th-Century Constitution," 47 *Cornell Law Quarterly* 1, 7 (1961); *see* S. Hoffman, *Gulliver's Troubles?, Or the Setting of American Foreign Policy* (New York: McGraw-Hill, 1968). W. Lippmann, *The Public Philosophy* (Boston: Little, Brown & Co., 1955), pp. 23–24, 29, 48; *see also* T. Bailey, *The Man in the Street* (Gloucester, Mass.: P. Smith, 1964), p. 13. *see generally*, S. Rep. No. 797, 90th Cong., 1st Sess. 6 (1967) (perception of crisis is most important cause of executive assertion of virtually unlimited war power and congressional acquiescence).
35. A. Schlesinger, *supra* note 29, p. 184 (quoting J. A. Schumpter, *Imperialism and Social Classes* (New York: A. M. Kelly, 1951), p. 51.
36. S. Ambrose, *Rise to Globalism* (Baltimore: Penguin Books, 1971), p. 190;

see also Lafeber, *supra* note 27, p. 222 (NSC-68 became the blueprint of U.S. policy after 1950).

37. S. Ambrose, *supra* note 36, pp. 189–91.

38. Myers v. United States, 272 U.S. 52, 229–30 (1926) (Reynolds, J., dissenting) (emphasis in original) (quoting from D. Webster, *The Works of Daniel Webster* (Boston: C.C. Little and J. Brown, 1851), 4: 186).

39. Office of the Legal Adviser, Dept. of State, "The Legality of United States Participation in the Defense of Viet Nam," 75 *Yale Law Journal* 1085 (1965).

40. A. Schlesinger, *supra* note 29, p. 169.

41. 299 U.S. 304, 320 (1936).

42. *See, e.g., U.S. Intelligence Agencies and Activities: Risks and Control of Foreign Intelligence: Hearings Before the House Select Committee on Intelligence,* 94th Cong., 1st Sess. 1729–34 (1975) (statement of Mitchell Rogovin, special counsel to director of CIA under President Ford); *Hearings Before the Senate Select Comm. on Intelligence,* 96th Cong. 2d Sess. 15–19 (1980) (statement of Stansfield Turner, director of the CIA under President Carter) (requirement of prior notification of all covert actions would amount to excessive intrusion into executive's constitutional powers); *The Intelligence Community,* ed. T. Fain, K. Plant, and R. Milloy (New York: R. R. Bowker Co., 1977), p. 714; *Intelligence Oversight Act of 1988 Hearings Before the House Comm. on Foreign Affairs,* 100th Cong., 2d Sess. 114–15 (1988) (testimony of Mary Lawton, counsel for intelligence policy, Justice Department).

43. Chaser Shipping Corp. v. United States, 649 F. Supp. 736 (S.D.N.Y. 1986), *aff'd,* 819 F.2d 1129, *cert. Denied,* 108 S. Ct. 695.

44. Church Committee Report, S. Rep. No. 755, 94th Cong., 2d Sess. 145 (1977).

45. *See* J. Lobel, "Covert War and Congressional Authority: Hidden War and Forgotten Power," 134 *University of Pennsylvania Law Review* 1035 (1986).

46. *Treaties and Other International Agreements: The Role of the U.S. Senate,* S. Prt. 98–205, 98th Cong. 2d Sess., (Washington, D.C.: Senate Foreign Relations Committee, 1984), pp. 37–40.

47. 617 F.2d 697, 723 (D.C. Cir. 1979) (McKinnon, dissenting). The administration's claims have been disputed. Even assuming the accuracy of such claims, the past practice demonstrates the twentieth-century nature of executive treaty termination.

48. Whitney v. Robertson, 124 U.S. 190 (1888); *Chinese Exclusion Case,* 130 U.S. 581 (1889). *See also* U.S. *ex. rel.* Pfefer v. Bell, 248 F.2d 992, 995 (E.D.N.Y. 1918). Compare with framers attitudes, Lobel, 71 *Virginia Law Review, supra* note 20, at 1076–1100.

49. Rest. 3rd, Restatement of the Foreign Relations Law of the United States, 115 Reporter's Note 3; The Paquete Habana, 175 U.S. 677, 700 (1900); Garcia-Mir v. Meese, 788 F.2d 1446 (11th Cir. 1986), *cert. denied,* 107 S.Ct. 289 (1986). But see Fernandez v. Wilkinson, 505 F. Supp. 787, 798

(D. Kan. 1980), *aff'd on other grounds*, 654 F.2d 1382 (10th Cir. 1981) for the opposing position.

50. A. Schlesinger, *supra* note 29.

51. Pub. L. No. 93–148, 87 Stat. 555 (1973) (codified at 50 U.S.C. §§ 1541– 1548 (1982)). Pub. L. No. 95–223, 91 Stat. 1625 (1977) (codified at 50 U.S.C. Supp. V §§ 1701 *et seq.* (1982)).

52. Ely, "Suppose Congress Wanted a War Powers Resolution That Worked," 88 *Columbia Law Review* 1379, 1381, and n. 8 (1988). The one occasion was the Lebanon crisis, when Congress negotiated a "compromise" with the Reagan administration permitting troops to remain in Lebanon for eighteen months.

53. Lowry v. Reagan, 676 F. Supp. 333 (D.D.C. 1987); Crockett v. Reagan, 720 F.2d 1355 (D.C. Cir. 1983); Sanchez-Espinoza v. Reagan, 568 F. Supp. 596 (D.D.C. 1983), *aff'd*, 770 F.2d 202 (D.C. Cir. 1985).

54. Ely, *supra* note 52, at 1384.

55. K. Sharpe, "The Real Cause of Irangate," 68 *Foreign Policy* 19, 34 (1987).

56. *Iran-Contra Report*, S. Rep. No. 216, H. Rep. No. 433, 100th Cong., 1st Sess. 667, 669 (1987), at 423. The minority report agreed "that the underlying cause of the Iran-Contra Affair had to do with people rather than with laws." *Id.* at 583 (minority report).

57. H. Koh, "Why the President (Almost) Always Wins in Foreign Affairs: Lessons of the Iran-Contra Affair," 97 *Yale Law Journal* 1255, 1257 (1988).

58. *Id.* at 1323.

59. H. Commager, *The Defeat of America* (New York: Simon and Schuster, 1968), p. 57. Presidential adviser and well-known historian Arthur Schlesinger arrived at a similar conclusion in *The Imperial Presidency*, writing that the imperial "vision of the American role in the world, unbalanced and overwhelmed the Constitution." A. Schlesinger, *supra* note 29, pp. 168– 69.

60. 115 Cong. Rec. 16618 (June 19, 1969).

61. S. Rep. No. 220, 93rd Cong., 1st Sess. 20 (1973).

62. Sharpe, *supra* note 55, at 41; *see also* W. Williams, *The Tragedy of American Diplomacy* (Cleveland: World Publishing Co., 1959), p. 212 (essence of different foreign policy would be open door for revolutions).

63. Many commentators from across the political spectrum have recently called for ending the Cold War. R. Barnet, "Fear of Soviet Changes Sells America Short," *Los Angeles Times*, December 19, 1988, § II at 5, col. 4; S. Cohen, "Will We End The Cold War? The Next President's Historic Opportunity," 247 *The Nation* 293 (1988); S. Cohen, "Centrists Lack the Guts to Respond to Gorbachev," *New York Times*, September 19, 1988; M. Parks, "To Clear Cold War Leftovers," *Los Angeles Times*, October 2, 1988; A. Rosenthal, "Gorbachev in Motion," *The New York Times*, December 11, 1988; W. W. Rostow, "Five Great Goals for the Next Generation," *Wall Street Journal*, September 6, 1988; R. Ullman, "Ending the Cold War," 72 *Foreign Policy* 130 (1988).

64. L. Mazor, "The Crisis of Liberal Legalism," 81 *Yale Law Journal* 1032, 1052–53 (1972).

65. F. Michelman, "Law's Republic," 97 *Yale Law Journal* 1493, 1531 (1988).

66. *See* R. Cover, "The Supreme Court, 1982 Term—Foreword: Nomos and Narrative," 97 *Harvard Law Review* 1 (1983) (law stems from community).

67. R. Falk, "The Grotian Quest," in *International Law, A Contemporary Perspective* ed. R. Falk, F. Kratochwil, S. Mendlovitz (Boulder: Westview Press, 1985), p. 36.

68. B. Barber, *Strong Democracy, Participatory Democracy for a New Age*, (Berkeley: University of California Press, 1984); *see, e.g.,* F. Michelman, *supra* note 65; P. Brest, "Constitutional Citizenship," 34 *Cleveland State Law Review* 175 (1986); P. Brest, "Further Beyond the Republican Revival: Toward Radical Republicanism," 97 *Yale Law Journal* 1623 (1988).

69. M. Shuman, "Dateline Main Street: Local Foreign Policies," 65 *Foreign Policy* 154 (Winter 1987). *See* R. Falk, Introduction, in F. Boyle, *Defending Civil Resistance Under International Law* (Dobbs Ferry, N.Y.: Transnational Publishers, 1987).

70. In *Dred Scott*, the Supreme Court argued that "No one, we presume, supposes that any change in public opinion or feeling, in relation to this unfortunate (Black) race, in the civilized nations of Europe or in this country, should induce the court to give to the words of the Constitution a more liberal construction in their favor than they were intended to hear when the instrument was framed and adopted." Dred Scott v. Sandford, 60 U.S. (19 How.) 393 (1857).

13 ELLIOTT CURRIE

CRIME, JUSTICE, AND THE SOCIAL ENVIRONMENT

NO one should doubt that violent crime constitutes an American epidemic. Crime—and the violent drug trade with which it's often connected—have brought tragedy and devastation to America's cities, especially to poorer and minority communities. The continuing massacre on the streets, brought home daily by gruesome portraits in the newspapers and on the TV screen, has produced a climate of fear and outrage—and stimulated an increasingly punitive response. Legislators have pressed for stiffer prison terms, harsh mandatory sentences for drug offenders, the death penalty for drug dealers and violent children. Public officials have rushed to spend ever-growing proportions of their limited budgets on prisons and jails: this year, the states' spending on corrections rose faster than any other category of expenditure— twice as fast, for example, as money for schools.[1] President Bush's much-touted antidrug strategy, announced at the close of the eighties, was topheavy with spending for corrections, proposing several times as much federal funding for prison cells as for drug treatment programs. In this climate, many Democratic officeholders have scrambled to appear even "tougher" on crime and drugs than the Republican administration.

All of this may give the illusion of momentum against the crime and violence that plague America in the last years of the twentieth century. It does not, however, offer a realistic remedy. For what's generally ignored in the legislative stampede for more punishment is that we have been system-atically following similar policies for many years; and those policies have failed, massively and tragically. In this article I'll describe the dimensions of that failure, and sketch the outlines of an approach to violent crime that can be both effective and progressive.

I

The basic thrust of American crime policy in recent years dates roughly from the beginning of the 1970s, with the emergence of what we can fairly call the "conservative revolution" in criminology. That revolution was only one facet of a much broader transformation in American social thought and policy on domestic issues. To place it in context, we need to look briefly at what had come before. During the 1950s and 1960s, a more broadly liberal understanding of crime and criminal justice was dominant in the United States, at least on the intellectual level—though it had less consistent impact on the way the criminal justice system worked in practice.

What most characterized the mainstream of liberal thinking in that era— what I'll here call "liberal realism"—was the fundamental understanding that crime was a *social* problem. As the President's Commission on Law Enforcement and the Administration of Justice—established by Lyndon Johnson in 1966—put it, "Crime is a social problem that is deeply interwoven with almost every aspect of American life." In particular, violent crime on the American level—which the commission recognized was far worse than in other industrial societies—was a symptom of basic social inequalities that had been allowed to fester for too long. This was not just a simple matter of widespread unemployment and poverty, but of a deeper and more disturbing disintegration of basic social institutions, especially for the urban poor: "The social institutions generally relied on to guide and control people in their individual and mutual existence," the commission wrote, "simply are not operating effectively in the inner city." In particular, "every effort" needed to be made to strengthen the family, now "often shattered by the grinding processes of urban slums." The commission accordingly declared that the most important single objective the nation should pursue if it wished to "significantly" reduce crime was to "seek to prevent crime before it happens by assuring all Americans a stake in the benefits and responsibilities of American life."[2]

The commission didn't neglect the problems and needs of the police, courts, and prisons. But it did not simply call for more of them. Instead it focused on what it regarded as the key failing of the justice system in general, and the prisons in particular; they were not doing much to prepare offenders for purposive, constructive lives on the outside. Indeed, if anything, the prisons often rendered them less fit to return to society when they came out than when they went in. The most pressing need was for a "substantial upgrading" of the correctional system, and its reorientation "toward integration of offenders into community life."[3]

The conservative "revolution" stood these themes on their head. It defined crime as largely a criminal justice problem, and it rejected both social explanations of the causes of crime and social solutions to it. By the mid-seventies, that "revolution" had come to dominate American thinking and policy on crime to an astonishing degree. It had dethroned social explanations of the causes of crime, cast the idea of the rehabilitation of offenders into the category of the antique and faintly disreputable, relegated the belief that social programs might help prevent crime to the margins of public discourse, and simultaneously elevated the idea that crime could be best reduced by deterrence and incapacitation to a central place in social policy.

The thrust of the conservative argument was hardly new. It reached back to the social Darwinism of the nineteenth century, and beyond. Crime, in this view, was caused by the absence of sufficient punishment. Often this was couched in the framework of the belief in a fundamentally "wicked" human nature, as the conservative Harvard scholar James Q. Wilson put it in a hugely influential book, *Thinking About Crime*, in the mid-seventies.[4]

In the United States in recent years, conservatives argued, a pervasive permissiveness had worn down most of the institutional controls on the darker human appetites—permissiveness spawned by the misguided ideals of liberalism and the hedonistic and indulgent culture of the sixties. To understand the spread of crime in America, therefore, we needed to look to the indulgent, "child-centered" family and school and, above all, to the leniency of the criminal justice system. Crime could only be held in check if that system punished offenders with sufficient certainty, swiftness, and severity. But in the United States we had largely abandoned those aims in favor of an overemphasis on the rights of criminals.

The other side of this argument was the contention that the adverse social factors invoked by liberal criminologists to explain America's stunningly high crime rate were either irrelevant or, in some cases, worked in the opposite direction from what liberals believed. Conservative criminologists denied that there were strong connections between crime and such key staples of the liberal explanation as economic deprivation, social inequality, and inadequate labor markets: at the extreme, some went so far as to deny that there were social causes of crime at all. Others argued that the liberal explanations were themselves partly to blame for rising crime: the emphasis on social causes of crime had eroded the sense of individual responsibility.

These arguments drew ammunition from the undeniable fact that, though our incarceration rate remained far higher than other countries', it had fallen during the sixties—just as crime rates were rising. Even more importantly, the conservative argument was boosted by what its advocates often described as a basic "paradox" of crime in the sixties—by what the British criminologist Jock Young calls the "etiological crisis."[5] What Young means is that the liberal view of the causes of crime, and of appropriate remedies for it, was undermined by the apparent paradox that crime rates rose just when a number of things which, by this view, ought to have reduced crime were improving substantially—at least on paper and in the aggregate. Incomes were rising, unemployment (on the national level) was falling, and we were beginning to devote significant governmental resources to social programs for the disadvantaged. If the liberal view was correct, conservatives gleefully argued, crime should have fallen; that it didn't do so opened the door to a view that blamed the rise in crime primarily on the leniency of the criminal justice system (and to a lesser extent the family and the schools) while simultaneously arguing that liberal programs were at best irrelevant, at worst part of the deepening culture of permissiveness and indulgence that bred crime.

But the conservative revolution likewise began to sputter in its tracks in the mid-1980s, when it became apparent to all but the most ideologically stalwart that the model wasn't working. Despite the huge increases in incarceration we witnessed in the seventies and eighties, criminal violence remained devastatingly high, and in many places rising; whole communities were shredded and turned nightmarish by drugs and gang violence. This was, after all, one of the largest experiments in social engineering we've ever seen in the United States (though it was rarely acknowledged as such); and so its failure has been an event of considerable moment. Let's step back for a moment and consider the magnitude of the changes the "revolution" has brought—and the magnitude of the crisis it has left us.

On the criminal justice side, the effect of the conservative revolution is most starkly evident in the rapidly rising rate of incarceration in the United States. We tripled the prison population nationally from the early seventies to the present, and the rate of increase was even greater in some states. Between 1980 and 1987 *alone*, the prison population increased by 210 percent in Alaska, 179 percent in California, 146 percent in New Jersey, 142 percent in Arizona.[6] By the end of 1988, as the number of Americans behind bars in state and federal prisons, local jails, and public juvenile facilities on any given day approached the one-million mark, that population amounted to a "city" of the incarcerated nearly the size of Detroit. Outside the prison walls, the number of those under the control of parole or probation authorities—almost triple the number behind bars, and increasingly under stringent conditions like home detention and electronic monitoring—rose by 95 percent between 1980 and 1987 alone.[7] And since these are aggregate numbers, they don't convey the degree to which the correctional system has come to loom over the daily life of what we euphemistically describe as "high-risk" communities. Almost one in four black men between the ages of twenty and twenty-nine were in custody, on probation, or on parole on any given day in the late 1980s.[8] Nor should it be thought that these increases simply correspond to equal increases in the crime rate, with which the criminal justice system is struggling to keep up. On the contrary, the level of imprisonment *per crime* has risen sharply—for violent crimes and burglary, by 72 percent between 1980 and 1986 nationwide, *192 percent* in New York, 127 percent in California.[9]

The other side of the conservative revolution was the systematic withdrawal of social supports and public services from the most distressed communities and most disadvantaged families in America, justified by the vague assertion that doing so would free the forces of the private market economy to provide for them what government intervention had not. I can only note here some of the most significant of those changes. Between the end of the seventies and the mid-eighties alone, the average welfare benefit under the Aid to Families with Dependent Children program (AFDC) fell by a fifth, while the proportion of poor children receiving those benefits fell from 72 to 60 percent: the proportion of low-income families brought above the federal poverty line by some combination of AFDC, Social Security, and unemployment insurance fell from about one in five to one in nine—casting about half a million families into poverty. Meanwhile, there were simultaneous and severe cuts in public medical and social services. From 1978 to 1984, federal spending on maternal and child health·care and community health centers dropped by a stunning 32 percent. Between 1981 and 1988, federal funding under the Title XX Social Services Block Grant—which supports, among other things, child abuse prevention and child protective services—fell by a third.[10]

But it has by now become starkly clear that this course of action has not revitalized America's cities, or transformed and motivated the urban underclass, or taken back the streets. On the contrary, no one needs to be reminded of the tragic, sometimes nearly incomprehensible social disintegration and violence that still confront us in the streets and homes of so many of our cities. The FBI's Uniform Crime Reports show overall violent crime up by almost 45 percent from 1978 to 1988. After a lull in the early eighties, violence has risen relentlessly, almost mimicking the similar rises in incarceration. Overall violent crime rose 4 percent from 1984 to 1985, 12 percent from 1985 to 1986, 5 percent from 1987 to 1988. Aggravated assaults rose 6 percent from 1984 to 1985, a startling 15 percent from 1985 to 1986, another 9 percent over the next two years. A number of cities—New York and Washington prominent among them—attained all-time high numbers of homicides in 1988—despite the 192 percent increase in prison admissions per violent offense in New York and a 106 percent increase in the District of Columbia.[11] The rises in crime in the mid-to-late 1980s, moreover, also took place in spite of the continued shrinking of the proportion of the American population in the younger, more crime-prone age groups, a result of the "baby bust" of the sixties and early seventies. That decline, as many criminologists predicted, should have lowered the crime rate—and probably did, other things being equal. But other forces kept it up stubbornly.

The conservative revolution, then, didn't fail for lack of implementation. It failed because its premises were wrong. The conservative explanation of America's crime rate depended on the assertion that the criminal justice system in the United State was extraordinarily lenient—at least by impli- cation, more so than that of other countries. But in fact the United States imprisoned a far higher proportion of its citizens than any advanced industrial society outside the Soviet bloc, even in the sixties. By the beginning of the eighties we were incarcerating up to ten times the proportion in the Neth- erlands and several times that of other European nations; and we were suffering homicide rates not less than three and up to ten times higher.[12]

Our high and rapidly increasing levels of incarceration also cast doubt on the more specific conservative argument that an excessive concern with the rights of criminals was "hobbling" the courts. Those doubts were confirmed by careful studies of what actually went on in the criminal courts (most recently, a survey by the American Bar Association) which repeatedly showed that the proportion of criminal cases "lost" because of procedural restrictions was minuscule.[13])

The other central conservative assertion—that crime had little or nothing to do with the social and economic deficits and distortions of American society—also depended on evidence that, to put matters politely, was less than robust. Conservative writers often tried to evade these links between crime and social structure in part by denying that there was anything unusual about America's crime rate. James Q. Wilson, for example, rejected the idea that high rates of crime were linked to particular kinds of social organization on the ground that "virtually every nation in the world, capitalist, socialist, or communist, has experienced in recent years rapidly increasing crime rates."[14] But the assertion was misleading on two counts: a number of coun- tries, including Japan and several European nations, had *not* experienced sharp rises in violent crime: and even those that had were left with rates of serious criminal violence so far below our own that the differences vastly outweighed the similarities. Faced with the weakness of that argument, some conservatives have more recently begun to argue that differences between countries (and between groups within them) in crime may be partly due to biological characteristics—that they reflect what Wilson and the psychologist Richard Herrnstein describe as "underlying distributions of constitutional factors."[15] But neither Wilson and Herrnstein nor anyone else has been able to turn up "constitutional" factors that can explain why violent crime is so much higher in the United States than in Europe, in Detroit than in Toronto, or in the 1980s than in the 1950s.

Meanwhile, study after study continued to affirm the connections between America's crime rate and its high levels of economic insecurity and inequality. Those connections, to be sure, were often more complex than liberal criminologists had generally believed in the fifties and sixties. Evidence that a simple connection existed between crime and the national level of unemployment, for example, was not strong. But there *was* strong evidence that the experience of being trapped in a life without the prospect of stable or dignified work was closely linked to crime. Likewise, the most careful research rarely turned up *simple* links between levels of poverty and levels of crime; what it more clearly showed was a strong connection between extremes of social and economic *inequality* and high levels of criminal violence.[16]

These findings help explain the apparent "paradox" of rising crime amidst the prosperity of the sixties which was so important to the conservative argument. For the broad statistics portraying rising incomes and employment for the nation as a whole masked the deepening marginalization of some groups in American society—especially the minority poor in the inner cities—who were increasingly denied the fruits of the "affluent" society which, with great frustration, they saw growing all around them. And those findings also help us understand why the net effect of the conservative revolution has been to increase violent crime, not reduce it. For even the huge increases in incarceration could not contain the violent results of years of policies that systematically aggravated so many of the social factors known to be implicated in crime: policies that increased inequality, eliminated vast numbers of stable, well-paying jobs, and magnified the economic and social stresses on American families.

II

The failure of the conservative strategy against crime offers an opening for the development of an approach adequate to the genuine crisis that confronts us—one that both builds on and goes beyond the lost mainstream of what I've called "liberal criminology." The heart of that revitalized approach must be a reaffirmation of the central idea that crime is indeed a *social* problem—one that, on its devastating American level, is rooted in deep strains and contradictions in our social structure. It is not by accident that the United States has by far the highest rates of serious crime in the developed world while simultaneously standing out among industrial societies on a host of other troubling measures—child poverty, infant mortality, inadequate public services, extremes of economic inequality. Mounting a serious attack on the violence that plagues us means confronting those multiple social deficits head-on.

That kind of "social-environmental" strategy must include measures to address the problems of individuals and families "at risk," but must also move beyond them to the tougher level of social control over the larger forces now increasingly undermining American communities and placing families "at risk" in the first place. As that suggests, there can be no "quick fix" for the American crime problem. The level of social devastation in the communities that have been most affected by the destruction of solid labor markets, the withdrawal of preventive social services, and the flood of hard drugs is now beyond anything we've seen before in this country; and it will require responses of a breadth and depth we've not yet seriously contemplated.

Let me sketch out some of the most crucial—and most promising—of those responses. Some of those I'll list involve changes in the criminal justice system; others move beyond it. Some of them involve interventions on the close-in level of families and individuals; others address more complex and longer-range issues of community stability, of political economy, and even of culture. Some are long-term; others could have an immediate impact on crime and the fear it creates. The list is meant to be illustrative, not exhaustive; I want simply to draw, in broad brushstrokes, what I think ought to be some key priorities for a progressive agenda on crime.

1. We need to devote more resources to *public safety* in the cities. There is a crying need for more community protection in the face of the twin crises of violence and drugs in recent years—both to reduce the intolerable risks to residents of inner-city neighborhoods and to create enough breathing room to enable longer-term strategies against crime and community deterioration to be put in place. We need to insist that communities have a fundamental right to the best protection against violence and fear we can offer; and that the erosion of resources for public safety that has often resulted from the fiscal starvation of the cities is unacceptable. That means more, and more visible, law enforcement. But it isn't enough simply to call for more money for local law enforcement without thinking through more clearly what we want law enforcement to accomplish—and how it will be made more accountable to community concerns.

The most important priority for enhanced public safety in the cities isn't to produce more arrests; we already arrest far more people—especially for minor drug offenses—than the courts can handle. The most important priority should be to protect neighborhood residents from violence and intimidation by dealers and from predation by drug users; secondarily, to disrupt local drug markets and drive them underground, or out of the community. No one imagines that this is anything other than a short-term strategy, which under current conditions is most likely to divert and displace, rather than to eliminate, the problem. But short-term displacement can have an important function in an emergency situation. Dealing can be driven away from residential areas and schools and off the public streets, where it is both harder to find and less likely to pose risks to the community.

To do this we'll need to spend more. But we can increase the reach of that spending by civilizing more police tasks and by developing effective civilian patrols that work closely with local police. We have some encouraging evidence that community patrols can significantly improve the sense of security in a neighborhood, given sufficient resources.[17] We should explore them more consistently.

2. We need a commitment, real rather than rhetorical, toward accessible, nonpunitive *drug abuse treatment* for those who need it—both within and outside of the criminal justice system. Like our approach to the family, the way we think about hard drugs has been deeply shaped by broader ideological agendas rather than a level-headed reading of the evidence. Some variants of what I've called liberal criminology often failed to take the drug problem seriously, finding more to worry about in the public reaction to drug abuse than in the effects of hard drugs themselves on communities and individuals—particularly the disadvantaged who were (and are) the chief victims of the spread of hard drugs. The Reagan administration put most of its cards on strategies—especially interdiction and harsh mandatory sentencing—that had already proven spectacularly unsuccessful, while simultaneously slashing resources for drug treatment. The Bush administration's drug plan promised a slight tilt of federal resources away from interdiction, deterrence, and incapacitation toward treatment and prevention. But it also adamantly refused to raise new revenues to pay for more treatment—and promised to aggravate the drug-crime problem by taking scarce resources from other preventive social programs to cover the costs of the drug "war."

But the problem goes deeper than financing. An effective strategy against hard drugs cannot simply throw new money at the existing treatment system; it must also reform that system and redefine its aims. We need to ensure that treatment is of high quality, intensive, accompanied by serious outreach to addicts, by after-care that supports them once out of treatment, and by advocacy in the community for their broader needs with respect to housing, health care, and employment. We've learned that it's not that hard to get people off drugs; what's hard is to *keep* them off, and that tougher goal must be a main thrust of a progressive drug policy. Addicts typically come to treatment with many other social and personal disadvantages; if these underlying problems aren't addressed, we perpetuate the recycling of addicts from treatment to the social conditions that bred their addiction in the first place, and back again—as the conventional treatment system too often does today.

3. I've suggested that we should push for expanded drug treatment within the criminal justice system as well as in the community. The marginal cost

of providing treatment to offenders in institutions, in particular, is very low—
and the potential returns in reduced crime and increased chances of success
on release are very high. But there is a more general principle here. We
should reaffirm and strengthen the Crime Commission's insistence that our
chief need is to *upgrade* the correctional system and reorient it toward helping
offenders, where possible, to become productive and contributive—not simply to expand its capacity to contain the consequences of social neglect. The
commonsense idea that we should do something constructive with people
after they've broken the law fell out of fashion, almost into oblivion, in the
1970s. But there is growing evidence for a more encouraging view. [18]

One of the most glaring failings of the conservative approach to the justice
system has been its gutting of the services—both inside and outside the system
itself—that could help offenders toward more productive lives. The lack of
resources has especially crippled the potential of probation and parole. A
National Institute of Justice survey in 1988 found that the great majority of
probation and parole agencies were unable to offer the community resources
offenders needed. Eight out of ten mentioned the lack of sufficient drug
programs and housing referrals; seven out of ten included job training, mental
health services, and alcohol programs. "Serious questions must be raised,"
the study concludes, "about the system's present capacity to absorb additional
offenders. Large and difficult caseloads coupled with a lack of staff and a
shortage of community resources reflect a criminal justice subsystem strained
to its limits." [19]

We should aim higher. On the most immediate level, we can begin to
deliver more consistently the *basic services* many young offenders often need.
Within the juvenile justice system in particular, we should finally insist that
more constructive use be made of the time that young offenders are under
supervision. We ought to think of that time as a resource, which we may
profitably use to see to it that they leave a little smarter, a little healthier, a
little more sober than they came in. This is particularly important given
what some research suggests about the links between low skills and poor
verbal abilities and serious delinquency. [20] We know how to raise those skills,
and we should insist that no young person is left languishing idle and illiterate
in any juvenile institution in the country.

4. We need a much greater commitment to *family-support programs*, and,
especially, real rather than rhetorical support for comprehensive programs
against child abuse and domestic violence. The debate over the family's role
in crime and delinquency has been shaped, even more than other crimi-
nological issues, by the shifting ideological currents of recent years. The
liberal criminology of the fifties and sixties tended to shy away from acknowledging the family's importance as a crucible of character formation.
The conservative criminology of the seventies and eighties revived interest

in the family's role in developing character and competence, but also detached the family and its functioning from the social and economic forces that powerfully affected it. A revitalized progressive criminology must recognize that the family is both a crucial shaping force and one that is in turn shaped by forces far larger than itself. That recognition is especially important in the face of the massively increased strains on American families in the past fifteen years under the impact of adverse economic shifts and conservative social policy. Accordingly, we will need both a genuinely pro-family economic policy at the national level—about which more in a moment—and far greater attention to interventions at the level of individual families.

Since the seventies, there has been encouraging evidence that family-support programs can improve childrearing skills; we also have promising results from innovative programs for child-abusing families. But once again, if the emerging evidence on what we *could* do is encouraging, the level of implementation is not. In the case of child abuse, it is pitifully weak: we are quite simply allowing a massive and at least partly preventable tragedy to play itself out in soul-shattering ways, on children whose other social and economic disadvantages render them both vulnerable and largely invisible. This is not only a major crime in itself, but one which tends disturbingly often to recapitulate itself as many abused children become abusive parents in their turn.[21] To be sure, there is nothing inevitable about that progression, as the developmental psychologists Joan Kaufman and Edward Zigler have reminded us. But their own best estimate suggests that perhaps a third of severely abused children are likely to become severely abusive parents—a rate six times that of the population as a whole.[22]

Meanwhile, children at high risk of abuse have also been among the worst—if least vocal—victims of the conservative Darwinist approach to social policy. The Reagan years saw massive cutbacks in federal funding for child-abuse prevention and child protective services, forcing much of the responsibility for the problem onto states and localities just when their resources were shrinking and the risks to children—from rising family poverty, homelessness, parental drug abuse—were sharply increasing. Any serious anticrime strategy must work to reverse that legacy—and to repair, where possible, the damage it has caused.

5. We should also expand *health and mental health services* for vulnerable children—and their parents—including high-quality prenatal and postnatal care. We should do this anyway, but there's good reason to believe that it can be a meaningful part of a comprehensive, "ecological" strategy against crime and delinquency. The evidence is complex, but suggestive that childhood injuries to the central nervous system and severe, untreated psychiatric problems (often related to child abuse) may be implicated in some of the most troubling and destructive forms of delinquency.[23] In their study of

fourteen juveniles condemned to death for especially brutal crimes, for example, Dorothy Lewis and her colleagues conclude that these children are typically "multiply handicapped": they "tend to have suffered serious CNS injuries, to have suffered since early childhood from a multiplicity of psychotic symptoms, and to have been physically and sexually abused." At the same time, "the clinical and legal services necessary to try to uncover these vulnerabilities are *routinely unavailable* to this population of juveniles"— much less, of course, the services necessary to even begin to *treat* them.[24]

6. [We should expand high-quality, intensive *early childhood education*] along the model of Head Start and the Perry Preschool project. There is by now a consensus that these programs are one of the most effective (and cost-effective) means we have of preventing delinquency; they also produce other positive results, including improved jobs and earnings and reduced welfare dependency.[25] There is indeed some evidence that these programs have a positive effect on the psychological and social functioning of *parents* as well as children.[26] But the proportion of eligible children served by these programs is now about 18 percent.

It's important not to claim *too* much for these programs. Their advocates sometimes place excessive expectations on approaches to the problems of inner-city children which do not confront the larger social and economic context in which those problems originate. And they share a traditional American tendency to overemphasize educational solutions to social problems.[27] A preschool on every ghetto corner won't overcome the structural disintegration of the surrounding communities—a disintegration whose sources lie well beyond the disadvantaged child and family, beyond the local community, and beyond the reach of the school, and which may intensify in the coming decades. But on their own terms, these programs have demonstrated their effectiveness; we should expand them.

III

The accumulating evidence suggests that all of these measures can be important in reducing crime, if they are done with the necessary seriousness and intensity. But a serious anticrime strategy must also be bold enough to confront the deeper and often more complex social deficits that underlie the widespread disintegration of family and personality in the United States— and that will, if left unaddressed, surely cripple and compromise even our best efforts to work with vulnerable individuals and families. Here, therefore, are three long-term goals for the twenty-first century. All of them are worthy of support for many reasons—but not least because they have the potential to alter the context of individual and family development in ways that promise to diminish crime.

First, we must move to *reduce inequality and social impoverishment.*

We know that the gap between affluent and poor has been increasing in the United States—in part because of widening differences in earnings among people who work, in part because of the reductions in income support I've touched on above.[28] And the bare figures on the growing income gap understate the growth in inequality because they do not include the bifurcation of social services that has simultaneously taken place—the withdrawal of the public sector from the poor and the near-poor, especially the young. We will need to reverse this trend—not least because the evidence continues to grow, from both cross-national and domestic studies, that extremes of inequality—especially when coupled with excessive mobility and the fragmentation of community and family life—are fertile ground for the growth of violent crime.[29] Reducing inequality is a tall order: but it's not an impossible one. Many other nations have done it. And though we can't simply transfer their approaches to our own very different social and historical context, we can learn much from their experience that is vital to our own efforts to create a society that is both more just and more secure.

So far, our hesitant legislative efforts to mitigate the extremes of inequality in the United States have met with stiff resistance. Witness the recent legislative battle to restore the value of the minimum wage, which has fallen close to 30 percent in real terms since the early 1980s. The fight for a decent minimum floor on earnings should continue, but we also need to do much more; ultimately, to move toward what in Scandinavia is called a "solidaristic" wage policy—one that raises the floor enough to ensure every working adult the means to a dignified livelihood—and to narrow the demoralizing and criminogenic abyss between affluent and poor.[30]

That strategy should include—as it has, for example, in Sweden—an explicit effort to raise the earnings of women closer to those of men, in order to reduce the intolerable deprivations faced by families headed by single women in the United States, and to provide the indispensable material foundation for other efforts to enhance family life—and to reduce the toll of domestic violence. As it stands, low-income women are especially likely to be trapped in a cycle of repeated assaults in the home, because they have few realistic options on the outside to help them move out from under abusive relationships. Improving those options by increasing women's capacity for self-support is an essential complement to other strategies, in the community and the justice system, against domestic crime.

Second, and closely related to the reduction of inequality and deprivation, we should move toward an *active labor market policy* aimed at upgrading the work available to disadvantaged Americans. Again, there is strong evidence that poor jobs—unstable, dead-end, with low wages—are linked to many kinds of crime. And the effects tend to accumulate when several generations remain trapped with few opportunities beyond those jobs, in good part because of long-term, corrosive effects on the mediating institutions of family and neighborhood.[31] That being the case, it's difficult to feel sanguine about the much-touted high rate of job creation in the United States in recent years, for it's painfully clear that an increasing proportion of those jobs have been low-wage and often part-time.[32] This kind of economic "growth" can do little or nothing to address the roots of social pathology among those now disadvantaged by low earnings and shattered links to more sustaining and stable livelihoods.

As we move toward the next century, we'll have to acknowledge—as some European countries have long done—that a sufficient supply of good, stable jobs does not flow automatically from the operation of the private market, but requires active intervention by government. In the United States, the most critical need is for publicly supported, community-oriented job creation, particularly in the provision of essential public services to disadvantaged communities. Among other things, a serious commitment to public job creation would help us accomplish some of the key anticrime strategies I've just advocated—expanded early education, improved childhood mental-health services and family support programs, expanded and enhanced drug treatment. *Without* a public policy to create community-sustaining jobs, those crucial services will inevitably be skimpy and starved of enough resources to do their jobs. *With* that policy, we could begin to build a viable economic infrastructure in "high-risk" communities that could serve as the base for overall economic development—while simultaneously delivering the basic reparative and socializing services without which neither social peace nor economic development in those communities will be possible.

That kind of community-service-driven economic development could also, importantly, provide challenging and rewarding roles in the community for young people now ensnared by the lures of the inner-city drug culture. The negative job shifts of the past fifteen years have substantially diminished the number of truly rewarding jobs they can hope for, while creating vast numbers of low-paying jobs in the private retail and service economy that typically lead nowhere—and that cannot offer a compelling alternative to the multiple attractions of dealing and delinquency. A broad, serious commitment to hire the young to help transform their stricken communities *could* offer an alternative. For the appeal of the drug trade in the inner city is not just money; it's also challenge and respect. If we fail to provide those, we can be assured that the urban young will find them where they can.

Let me emphasize that this is a more difficult and long-term task than most criminologists have been willing to acknowledge. Liberal criminologists have sometimes implied that simply reflating the national economy to bring down the overall unemployment rate, or launching another summer job program for ghetto kids, could overcome the accumulated effects on family and personality of several generations of long-term economic deprivation and social impoverishment—and the relentless influence of a broader culture of predatory consumption. That's an unrealistic hope. I believe there is still time to turn that complex of adversities around. But no one should underestimate how hard it will be.

Third, we should work toward a genuinely *supportive national family policy*.

There is much rhetoric about "strengthening the family" in the United States. Beneath it is the reality of an ongoing disaster for American families, especially those in the bottom third of the income distribution, increasingly put at the mercy of a destabilizing and destructive economic and social environment. And the adverse forces in that environment—growing economic deprivation, excessive mobility, the retreat of accessible housing, the corrosive effects of alcohol and drugs—are by no means confined to the inner cities. They now reach upward well into parts of the old "middle" strata of American society. Left alone, those forces are likely to intensify in the future. I've argued that we should put more resources into supportive programs for "high-risk" children and families; but if we make no simultaneous effort to control the forces that undermine families in the first place, we'll be stuck continually at the level of picking up the pieces.

The employment and income policies I've just suggested are themselves key elements of a humane and progressive family policy for the next decades. But we also need national policies devoted specifically to reducing the stresses caused by the present conflicts between family and work. It's well known that we are one of the only remaining countries in the advanced industrial world that doesn't officially recognize the human, social, and even economic value of freeing up time for working parents to spend with families and children.[33] Our traditional practice has been to squeeze every ounce of paid working time out of parents in the service of private economic gain and to resist fiercely the rather innocuous idea that private business bears some responsibility for the impact of the conditions of work on their employees' families. Our first effort at national legislation in this direction, which would have mandated companies to provide up to ten weeks of *unpaid* leave, over two years, to parents at the birth of a child or in the event of a child's illness (some European countries mandate a paid leave of up to several months) has at this writing died once again in Congress, a casualty of the view that it represented unwarranted government interference in the economy.

But the reality is that our lack of a humane national policy to mitigate the conflicts between family and work—a lack which distinguishes us, again, from virtually every other advanced society—amounts to a massive subsidy to private business, in that it requires the rest of us to pay for the social costs of the resulting strains on families—the costs of physical and mental illness, domestic violence and delinquency. We will need to press not only for a family leave policy that finally drags us, kicking and screaming, into the last third of the twentieth century, but also, more broadly, for the idea that Americans who work have a fundamental right to sufficient family time— in order, among other things, to make possible the attentive and unharried care of the young.

IV

Some may object that these strategies go well beyond the customary bound- aries of criminology. But a strategy against crime that can hope to make headway against the deepening crisis of America's cities must transcend the disciplinary and bureaucratic fragmentation that now cripples both our think- ing and our policy toward crime. Our conventional approach is to isolate crime and criminal justice from their social setting—to think of "crime policy" as something quite separate from a family policy, an employment policy, an antipoverty policy. Nothing could be more fruitless. In human societies, as in the natural environment, things are *connected* to each other. What we do (or don't do) in the realm of economic policy in particular has a profound impact on the social institutions through which individuals are brought up healthy or damaged, compassionate or unfeeling, contributive or predatory. Making a serious attack on criminal violence, in the home and on the street, means restoring the integrity of that social environment by harnessing our material and technological resources to ends more supportive of community, family, and human development. And it means challenging some long-standing cultural attitudes that are deeply implicated in the dev- astating levels of violent crime in American society. We often think of culture as rigid and unchangeable—a permanent fact of life. But in the last generation alone we've seen major changes in American culture; in the way we think about the social role of women, or the status of people of color; in the way we think about our relationship to the natural environment or about health and nutrition. For the next generation, we should aim for changes of com- parable magnitude in some aspects of American culture that may now seem set in stone: the degree of social deprivation and inequality we tolerate; the degree of violence we consider normal and acceptable in the course of childrearing—or of marriage; the level of access to social and health services we deem to be the minimum responsibility of civilized society; the relative balance of private gain versus cooperative endeavor as esteemed personal motives, of private economic "choice" versus the stability and socializing competence of communities and families.

Just as we have now—belatedly—begun to understand that we cannot systematically ravage or neglect the natural environment, or our bodies, without terribly destructive and self-defeating consequences, so we should come to understand that the *social* environment requires a level of sustenance and stewardship far beyond what can be provided as a residual product of economic growth. The big job for progressives in the coming years will be to place the integrity of the social environment firmly at the top of the political and intellectual agenda, and keep it there.

There is some encouraging evidence that the stark consequences of a decade of neglect have produced at least the stirrings of a reaction against the hard conservative Darwinism of the 1980s. By the end of the decade, majorities of the American public, according to opinion polls, supported greater investment in educational, employment, and health care strategies to help the disadvantaged into more productive roles in American life. And they were more willing to pay for those strategies than to pour more resources into an already bloated military. Opinion research also suggests that what the public most wants is for crime to be prevented before it happens; and that they tend to believe that crime is most often caused by remediable social problems.[34]

Nor have the implications of continuing urban disintegration been lost on those whose job is to govern the cities, or to do business in them. *Business Week* magazine, in a 1988 cover story on what it called the crisis of "human capital" in America, warned that "The U.S. may now be entering an era when neglect of the bottom half of society begins to threaten the welfare of the entire nation".[35] The magazine went on to propose substantially increased public spending—for preschool education, prenatal care, intensive job training for the disadvantaged young, and more. In the same year, *U. S. News and World Report*—again, a magazine not previously noted for its bleeding-heart sympathies—chided the Reagan government for offering "too many promises, too little help" to the children of the inner cities.[36] The Committee for Economic Development, an influential policy-making voice for America's corporate elite, similarly urged billions of dollars in new funding for Head Start, child health care, and other active public policies for high-risk children.[37] Even George Bush, in his 1988 campaign for the presidency, called on the nation to "invest in children," while the Republican party platform called for "large" increases in funding for Head Start.

Skepticism about the depth of some of these claims is in order, of course; especially those made in the midst of a presidential campaign. Nevertheless, I believe the shift from the hard, unalloyed "free-market" social Darwinism of the Reagan years is a real one.

But it is also a fragile one. There are other, less encouraging, possible responses to the continuing violence in America's streets. One troubling possibility is that we could go backward. We could adopt the view that the failure of our recent strategies toward street crime—and toward the problems of the "high-risk" urban poor generally—indicates that the problems are much more intractable than we had supposed. We might locate the source of this intractability in the biological or cultural insufficiencies of those who still fail to make it into the increasingly elusive mainstream of American society. And we might use that explanation to justify a kind of urban triage: an even greater withdrawal of resources from the most stricken communities and a tacit policy of allowing them to spiral still further downward, while simultaneously unleashing the repressive power of an expanded criminal justice system to contain the resulting violence and disorder. I don't think that will happen; I think its potential social costs are too enormous and too widely understood. But I don't think it's inappropriately alarmist to bring it up as a possibility. It is, after all, not so far removed from the strategy we've in fact been following for some years. It should be clear that none of these possible outcomes are inevitable: the prospects for the safety of our cities and for the integrity of our criminal justice system in the coming decades will depend crucially on our ability to build a broad, lasting, and effective movement for social change.

NOTES

1. "States Spending Fastest on Jails", *The New York Times*, August 9, 1989.
2. President's Commission on Law Enforcement and the Administration of Justice, *The Challenge of Crime in a Free Society* (Washington, D.C., Government Printing Office, 1967), p. vi.
3. Ibid., p. 183.
4. James Q. Wilson, *Thinking About Crime* (New York: Random House, 1975).
5. Jock Young, "Recent Developments in Criminology," in *Developments in Sociology*, ed. M. Haralambos (London: Causeway Press, 1988).
6. U.S. Bureau of Justice Statistics, *Prisoners in 1987* (Washington, D.C., Government Printing Office, 1988), p. 3.
7. Calculated from *Statistical Abstract of the United States, 1987* (Washington, D.C.: U.S. Government Printing Office, 1988), p. 173, and U.S. Bureau of Justice Statistics, *Correctional Populations in the United States, 1987* (Washington, D.C.: U.S. Department of Justice, 1989), cover chart.
8. Marc Mauer, *Young Black Men and the Criminal Justice System* (Washington, D.C.: The Sentencing Project, 1990), p. 1.
9. Bureau of Justice Statistics, op. cit., p. 6.
10. U.S. Congress, House Select Committee on Children, Youth, and Fam-

ilies, *Children and Families: Key Trends in the 1980s* (Washington, D.C., Government Printing Office, 1988), p. 44; Center on Budget and Policy Priorities, *Impact of Government Benefit Programs Declines, Adds to Number of Poor Families* (Washington, D.C., 1988); U.S. Congress, Office of Technology Assessment, *Healthy Children: Investing in the Future* (Washington, D.C., Government Printing Office, 1987), p. 43; Center on Budget and Policy Priorities, *Still Far From the Dream* (Washington, D.C., 1988), p. 37.

11. Federal Bureau of Investigation, *Uniform Crime Report 1988*, Preliminary Annual Release, April 1989.

12. U.S. Bureau of Justice Statistics, *International Crime Rates* (Washington, D.C.: Government Printing Office, 1988), p. 5.

13. American Bar Association, *Criminal Justice in Crisis* (Washington, D.C., 1988).

14. Wilson, op. cit., p. xiii.

15. James Q. Wilson and Richard J. Herrnstein, *Crime and Human Nature* (New York: Simon and Schuster, 1985), p. 88.

16. For a review of this research, *see* Elliott Currie, *Confronting Crime: An American Challenge* (New York: Pantheon Books, 1985), chaps. 4 and 5.

17. One community patrol in New York City is described in Milton S. Eisenhower Foundation, *Twenty Years Later: Progress on the Unfinished Agenda* (Washington, D.C., 1990).

18. For a review of research on the rehabilitation of offenders, *see* Paul Gendreau and Robert Ross, "Revivification of Rehabilitation: Evidence from the 1980s," *Justice Quarterly*, vol. 4, no. 3, September 1987.

19. U.S. National Institute of Justice, *Difficult Clients, Large Caseloads Plaque Probation, Parole Agencies* (Washington, D.C., 1988), p. 8.

20. *See, e.g.*, Gordon Berlin and Andrew Sum, *Toward a More Perfect Union: Basic Skills, Poor Families, and Our Economic Future* (New York: Ford Foundation, 1988).

21. Richard J. Gelles and Murray A. Straus, *Intimate Violence* (New York: Simon and Schuster, 1988).

22. Joan Kaufman and Edward Zigler, "Do Abused Children Become Abusive Parents?" *American Journal of Orthopsychiatry*, vol. 57, no. 2, April 1987.

23. *See*, Dorothy O. Lewis et al, "Biopsychosocial Characteristics of Children Who Later Murder: A Prospective Study," *American Journal of Psychiatry*, vol. 142, no. 10, October 1985.

24. Dorothy O. Lewis et al, "Neuropsychiatric, Psychoeducational, and Family Characteristics of 14 Juveniles Condemned to Death in the United States," *American Journal of Psychiatry*, vol. 145, no. 5, May 1988.

25. J. R. Beruetta-Clement et al., "The Effects of Early Educational Intervention on Crime and Delinquency in Adolescence and Early Adulthood," in *Prevention of Delinquent Behavior*, ed. John D. Burchard and Sara N. Burchard (Beverly Hills: Sage, 1987).

26. Faith Parker, Chaya S. Piotrowski, and Lenore Peay "Head Start as a Social

Support for Mothers: The Psychological Benefits of Involvement," *American Journal of Orthopsychiatry*, vol. 57, no. 2, April 1987.

27. Cf. Martin Woodhead, "When Psychology Informs Public Policy: The Case of Early Childhood Intervention," *American Psychologist*, vol. 43, no. 6, June 1988.

28. For a general discussion of these trends, see Elliott Currie, Robert Dunn, and David Fogarty, "The Fading Dream: Economic Crisis and the New Inequality," in *Crisis in American Institutions*, ed. Jerome Skolnick and Elliott Currie (Glenview: Scott, Foresman/ Little, Brown, 1988); Bennett Harrison, Chris Tilly, and Barry Bluestone, "Rising Inequality," in *The Changing American Economy*, ed. David Obey and Paul Sarbanes (New York: Basil Blackwell, 1986).

29. *See generally*, Currie, *Confronting Crime*, chap. 5; most recently, William R. Avison and Pamela Loring, "Population Diversity and Cross-national Homicide Patterns; the Effects of Inequality and Heterogeneity," *Criminology*, vol. 24, no. 4, 1986.

30. On the Swedish experience, *see* Gosta Rehn, "Swedish Active Labor Market Policy: Retrospect and Prospect," *Industrial Relations*, vol. 24, Winter 1985.

31. *See generally*, Michele Sviridoff and Jerome McElroy, *Employment and Crime: A Summary Report* (New York: Vera Institute of Justice, 1985); Currie, *Confronting Crime*, chap. 4.

32. Barry Bluestone and Bennett Harrison, "The Grim Truth About the Job Miracle," *The New York Times*, February 1, 1988; Sar Levitan and Elizabeth Conway, "Shortchanged by Part-time Work," *The New York Times*, February 27, 1988.

33. Pauline Hopper and Edward Zigler, "The Medical and Social Science Basis for a National Infant Care Leave Policy," *American Journal of Orthopsychiatry*, vol. 58, no. 3, July 1988.

34. *See, e.g.*, John Doble and Keith Melville, "The Public's Social Welfare Mandate," *Public Opinion*, January/February 1989; Richard Morin, "A Sea Change on Federal Spending," *Washington Post*, National Weekly Edition, August 28–September 3, 1989. On the public view of crime prevention, *see* John Doble, *Crime and Punishment: The Public's View* (New York: Public Agenda Foundation, 1987).

35. *Business Week*, September 19, 1988, p. 103.

36. *U.S. News & World Report*, November 7, 1988.

37. Committee for Economic Development, *Children in Need: Investment Strategies for the Educationally Disadvantaged* (New York, 1987).

14 DAVID RUDOVSKY

THE CRIMINAL JUSTICE SYSTEM AND THE ROLE OF THE POLICE

THERE is a widely held perception that the criminal justice system is too lenient and that it impedes law enforcement. This claim is surely curious in a society that sends a higher proportion of its people to prison for longer periods of time than any country other than South Africa and the Soviet Union. (In 1990 over one million persons, or three times the number of just fifteen years ago, were in our prisons and jails; the rates in Britain and West Germany were each less than one-third of the American rate.)[1] Nevertheless, in a turnabout that deflects attention from our social and economic inequities, aspects of the criminal justice system that, in principle, secure fairness and equality often are *blamed* for creating or exacerbating the problem of crime and violence.

It is not unusual for government officials, law enforcement officers, and others to exploit the public's legitimate fear of crime for partisan political purposes. Ethnic and minority groups are often blamed for crime, regressive and harshly punitive legislation is passed in the name of crime control, the courts are attacked for being too soft, and the police are encouraged to use extralegal methods to control crime and criminals. Rarely do these measures actually reduce levels of crime or increase public safety; instead, they enable their proponents to demonstrate their "toughness" and "concern" on this issue.

Over the past decade, we have spent billions of dollars on the law enforcement side of the war on drugs. The result: more arrests, hundreds of thousands more in prison, diversion of money from social programs, and yet even more drugs and drug-related crimes than at any time in our history. Even more pernicious is the fact that the war on drugs is becoming "a war on black people." Despite abundant evidence that cocaine use is as frequent in white communities as it is in black areas, it is minority communities that have been targeted by the police and the media as the problem. Black America is being criminalized at an astounding rate (one in four black men in their twenties are in prison or under parole supervision as compared to 6 percent of white men in the same age group), in no small part because of the racially disproportionate impact of drug policies. As Atlanta Police Chief Eldrin Bell commented: "If we started to put white America in jail at the same rate that we're putting black America in jail, I wonder whether our collective feelings would be the same, or would we be putting pressure on the President and our elected officials not to lock up America, but to save America."[2] Undaunted, President Bush urges a continuation of this pathetically ineffective and shortsighted policy.

While the debate over the issues of crime, law enforcement and individual rights is not new, it has become more intense ever since the Warren Court established a set of basic procedural protections that limited police powers and created a modest level of fairness and equality in the criminal justice system. In reaction, political and legal forces have sought to denigrate the principles of due process, the right to counsel, privacy, and the privilege against self-incrimination. This attack is part of a larger program that seeks to subordinate democratic rights to claims of order, efficiency, and executive power. Its target is the judiciary's role in defining fundamental liberties, and it has successfully mobilized sentiment against the fragile structure of fairness that the Constitution provides in the criminal justice system.

As Elliott Currie's chapter demonstrates,[4] the much heralded conservative program, with its emphasis on punishment and incapacitation, may have satisfied our need for retribution, but as the social and economic conditions of significant parts of our society have become increasingly ruinous, even the most extreme punishment can provide only marginal protection. For every thief we send to prison, scores of others are being nurtured in the dangerous and often hopeless conditions of a permanent underclass. Our society simply lacks the elementary social and economic fairness to make possible a solution to the problem of crime without a radical restructuring of our social system. As Kenneth B. Clark aptly put it, if we continue to mug our schools, communities, and neighborhoods, we should not be surprised if those who turn to crime increase "in number, defiance, and venom."[5]

The essential task is to develop a program that promotes fairness and equality, treats the accused, the convicted, and the victim with dignity, *and* controls and deters crime and violence. While sharply conflicting attitudes toward crime and violence are understandable, an inability to analyze and confront extremely difficult issues, including some that challenge deeply held beliefs, has left progressives without a credible voice in this discussion.

What should the response be when inexplicable violence and serious crime disrupt and damage so many lives? That corporate and political criminals are not punished for their acts is not an excuse for condoning violent crime; that the police brutalize as well as protect is not an insurmountable barrier to demanding adequate police protection; that discrimination, lack of opportunities, abusive relationships, and inequality may lead to the creation of an underclass from which stems a disproportionate amount of crime may not be sufficient reason for not incapacitating or otherwise deterring those convicted of serious crimes. The central problem is to differentiate between legitimate and illegitimate uses of police and state power.

THE RIGHTS OF THE ACCUSED AND THE NEEDS OF LAW ENFORCEMENT

The notion that law enforcement and police obedience to law are mutually exclusive goals has led to excesses that violate constitutional norms, with very little gain in law enforcement. Moreover, because our political democratic rights are inextricably linked to the rights of the accused, to allow community prejudice and fear to override the Constitution will inevitably weaken the fabric of rights and protections that are essential to freedom and democracy in all societies.

It is not surprising that the debate over the impact of constitutional rights on the incidence of crime is of relatively recent vintage. Before the Court articulated basic constitutional protections for the accused, there was no right to appointed counsel, limited remedies for illegal police arrest, search, or interrogation practices, no protection against unfair identification procedures, and the prosecutor did not even have an obligation to divulge exculpatory evidence. Under these circumstances crime could hardly be blamed on the Constitution.

The Warren Court made substantial changes in criminal procedure, but it did not always side with the accused and it often deferred to law enforcement interests. For example, the Court limited the defense of entrapment by adopting a rule that focuses on the intent of the defendant to commit a crime, thus permitting broad overreaching by agents—even the creation of a crime—if the defendant had some "predisposition" toward criminal activity. Similarly, the Court declined to restrict police use of agents and stoolpigeons to manipulate personal, political, and business relationships, and to intrude into homes and offices.[6]

In addition, the Court framed several of its significant rulings in a manner that allowed the police, prosecutors, and lower courts to ignore or undermine constitutional protections. A notable example was the Court's failure to require disclosure and identification of police informers who allegedly provided information in support of search warrants.[7] Many warrants are based only on the assertion of a police officer that an "informant" observed criminal activity. By crediting this assertion without determining whether the informant even exists, the Court, in the words of one observer, winked its eye at the police "perjury routine."[8]

Indeed, the decisions of the Warren Court that provoked the most pointed criticism, *Miranda* v. *Arizona*[9] and *Mapp* v. *Ohio*,[10] formulated rules that were easily avoided, even before the Court expressly limited them. Almost immediately, the mandate of these cases was circumvented at trial by a fact-finding process that slants decision making in favor of particular classes of litigants. For example, the implementation of these protections hinges on such questions as: Were the *Miranda* warnings given? Did the suspect waive his right to counsel? Did the defendant act in a manner that gave the police officer "probable cause" for his arrest?

It is quite easy for an officer to assert that *Miranda* warnings were given or that the defendant was acting in an illegal or suspicious manner. Judges regularly choose to accept even blatantly unbelievable police testimony. After the *Mapp* decision, which required courts to exclude from trial illegally seized evidence, defendants who had previously submitted to police searches apparently altered their behavior patterns such that, upon seeing an officer, they felt compelled to toss away incriminating evidence. Judicial acceptance of such testimony allows the police to circumvent *Mapp* with a technicality: one who throws away evidence has "abandoned" it and cannot claim that he was unlawfully searched; however, he can be convicted of having possessed it.

The enormous controversy surrounding the exclusionary rule is certainly not explicable on the theory that it unduly interferes with law enforcement. To the contrary, it has only the most minimal impact on conviction rates. The General Accounting Office has concluded that only 2 percent of all federal cases are lost because of exclusion of evidence.[11] Of course, if the exclusionary rule is seen as a symbolic law-and-order issue, one can readily understand why some urge its demise, although the message such a repeal would send to largely uncontrolled police officers is troublesome to contemplate. In fact, the acceptance by police and other government officials of widespread illegal police practices demonstrates that it is the underlying constitutional principles and not the exclusionary rule that is the primary target of the police establishment. Whether or not evidence is excluded at trial is not the significant issue; rather, it is the power of the police to act in an unbridled and uncontrolled fashion. Nevertheless, because the basic principle is politically more difficult to attack, enforcement mechanisms become the target.

The attack on the exclusionary rule is an example of the way the public's perception of the criminal process has been consciously manipulated. The distortion of the actual impact of this rule on conviction rates and (if, in fact, any relationship exists) on public safety diverts the focus from the illegal police conduct and leads the public to believe that constitutional principles are simply too dangerous to enforce.

RETRENCHMENT AND REACTION

The Burger-Rehnquist Court has not rejected every claim made on behalf of the accused, but it has made serious inroads on the Warren Court precedents, rationalizing the denial of constitutional protections on the basis of asserted needs of public safety and law enforcement.

PREVENTIVE DETENTION

In 1987, the Court for the first time approved pretrial preventive detention of "dangerous" defendants.[12] The debate on this issue has focused almost exclusively on those who are released and arrested for new crimes (as opposed to those who spend months in jail, only to be found not guilty at trial), and the danger to the public has been greatly exaggerated. In a study in Washington, D.C., it was determined that only 2 percent of those charged with violent crimes were arrested for a violent or property crime while on bail.[13] Indeed, given the difficulty of predicting dangerousness with any accuracy, to be confident of preventing one person from committing a violent crime while on bail we would have to incarcerate up to ten who would not.

Justice Marshall pointed to the real dangers of preventive detention:

> Such statutes, consistent with the usages of tyranny and the excesses of what bitter experience teaches us to call the police state, have long been thought incompatible with the fundamental human rights protected by our Constitution. Today a majority of this Court holds otherwise. Its decision disregards basic principles of justice established centuries ago and enshrined beyond the reach of governmental interference in the Bill of Rights. . . .
>
> Throughout the world today there are men, women and children interned indefinitely, awaiting trials which may never come or which may be a mockery of the word, because their governments believe them to be "dangerous."

Moreover, those who believe that only "dangerous" criminals will be confined should understand the significant precedent that incarceration without conviction can have for people who vigorously oppose governmental policies, particularly in time of war. The Court's opinion contains this ominous reference:

We have repeatedly held that the government's regulatory interest in community safety can, in appropriate circumstances, outweigh an individual's liberty interest. For example, in times of war or insurrection . . . the government may detain individuals whom the government deems to be dangerous.

ARREST, SEARCH, AND SURVEILLANCE

The history of Fourth Amendment interpretation is hardly one of acute sensitivity to personal rights. In 1961, in *Mapp* v. *Ohio*, the Court ruled that where the police violate the Fourth Amendment by improperly seizing evidence, that evidence must be excluded from any criminal prosecutions. For the better part of 175 years prior to *Mapp*, most states provided no remedy for unlawful police arrests or searches.

The Court's Fourth Amendment decisions of the 1960s, although hardly of one piece and hardly without important limitations grounded in deference to law enforcement needs, established several basic propositions. The centerpiece was *Katz* v. *United States*,[14] where the Court broadened the scope of the Fourth Amendment by ruling that electronic surveillance constituted a search even where no physical trespass had occurred. Placing an electronic amplifier on a telephone booth "violated the privacy upon which [the user of the booth] . . . justifiably relied." Personal privacy, not narrow property notions, was now the touchstone of the Fourth Amendment.

In a vivid demonstration of the ways in which legal doctrine can be manipulated, the Court soon transformed the *Katz* principle from one that broadened and deepened our notions of privacy into rules that have decimated Fourth Amendment protections. The Court's emphasis on personal privacy provided the basis for its conclusion in *Katz* that "what one seeks to preserve as private may be constitutionally protected." *Katz* expanded the scope of the Fourth Amendment by making explicit the notion that it was intended to protect our privacy from unreasonable government intrusion.

Quite rapidly the doctrine underwent a subtle but significant change: the Court required the individual to show both a subjective expectation of privacy and a claim that society is prepared to say is reasonable. It is doubtful that anyone can claim even a subjective expectation of privacy in most aspects of everyday life given the disclosures over the past twenty years of governmental spying, disruption of political dissidents, intrusive surveillance techniques, and the increasing use of technology to trace our steps and activities. And how are we to determine whether the public is prepared to say that one's expectation of privacy is legitimate? Who is to define when you have a "legitimate" expectation of privacy? Can the government defeat privacy interests by simply stating that it will search all persons in particular areas (e.g., airports or "high-crime areas")? How do we decide whether our private conversations with friends or associates are protected from governmental overhearing, bugging, or the use of informers?

We are told by the Court that we have no legitimate expectation of privacy in personal bank accounts, that we should not be surprised if the telephone company makes our records available to the police, that as passengers in cars or guests in homes we may not have a sufficient interest to object to unlawful police intrusions, and that a fenced-in backyard is not protected against aerial searches.[15] Further, the Court has ruled that society is not prepared to recognize the right of a prisoner to even limited privacy with respect to items kept in his cell—a Bible, photos of his family, personal letters, or books. There is no plausible empirical or other basis for these conclusions.[16]

One of the most troublesome anomalies in Fourth Amendment jurisprudence—and its most serious weakness with respect to the rights of the political opposition—is the distinction the Court has drawn between intrusions into our homes, offices, and political and personal relationships by a police officer, which are fully subject to the Fourth Amendment, and the use of agents and informers, which remains virtually unregulated. By affording law enforcement free reign to use informers and agents, the Court has told us not to expect privacy in our relationships, including our political associations. The distortion of Fourth Amendment doctrine that results is succinctly described by Anthony G. Amsterdam: "I can conceive of no rational system of concerns and values that restrict the government's power to rifle my drawers or tap my telephone but not its power to infiltrate my home or my life with a legion of spies."[17]

The Court has justified this practice by saying that you "assume the risk" that the people you deal with may be agents of the police. But is that the kind of society we want to build? There is a crucial difference, grounded in notions of liberty, between the normal risk we all take that a friend today may be a turncoat tomorrow, and the risk of faithlessness that is incurred when the police bribe, threaten, or otherwise convince our associates to become informers and enter our lives and premises as police agents? Nor is there any difference between the injury to privacy caused by bugging or wiretapping and that achieved by police spies who record everything we say. The price of privacy has been raised to an intolerable level: the total shutdown of communication. Justice Harlan has pointed out that the issue is not simply whether *criminals* place unjustified reliance on so-called friends:

> By casting its "risk analysis" solely in terms of the expectations and risks that a "wrongdoer" or "one contemplating illegal activities" ought to bear, the plurality opinion, I think, misses the mark entirely. . . . The interest [to be protected] is the expectation of the ordinary citizen, who has never engaged in illegal conduct in his life, that he may carry on his private

discourse freely, openly, and spontaneously without measuring his every word against the connotations it might carry when instantaneously heard by others unknown to him.[18]

The debate over the proper interpretation of the Fourth Amendment holds serious implications for important issues that are just now appearing. What limits, if any, should be placed on drug and AIDS testing? As technology advances, how do we balance the increased capabilities of law enforcement to invade and monitor our lives with the privacy rights of individuals? Can the government continue to infiltrate and monitor political organizations through the use of agents and informers? Are the interests protected by notions of autonomy and privacy the kind of fundamental democratic rights that are critical to any fair society? It is important to note that each incursion on civil liberties discussed above was justified by the government or courts as a necessary crime-control measure, yet the incremental impact of this trend will be a substantial lessening of political liberties for all.

IDENTIFICATIONS

The Court has subverted other important constitutional principles, including the requirement that pretrial identification procedures be conducted fairly, with a lawyer present at a lineup, and without unnecessarily suggestive conditions. This principle that is designed to make the identification process more reliable and thus enhance the truth-finding aspect of the criminal justice system.

Since so many cases turn on the issue of identification and since mistaken identification is probably the single greatest cause of conviction of the innocent, it might have been thought that a Court that stressed reliability of the trial process in weakening the exclusionary rule would embrace procedures designed to make the trial verdict more accurate. But the Court has ruled that only postindictment lineups require a lawyer (most lineups are preindictment), and has further held that even unnecessarily suggestive identifications can be used at trial.[19] These decisions not only strike a serious blow at fairness but they demonstrate that "reliability of the fact-finding process," which has been used as a justification for denying certain rights, will itself be subordinated to state claims of efficiency and police control.

REMEDIAL MECHANISMS

Not satisfied with its erosion of the substantive protections of the Fourth Amendment, the Court has also restricted the remedial mechanisms that are necessary for effective vindication of Fourth Amendment rights. The exclusionary rule has been substantially restricted.[20] Further, the Court has created doctrines that reduce the efficacy of civil remedies for constitutional violations. One such doctrine is qualified immunity which allows a court to deny civil damages to persons arrested or searched without probable cause if the officer in "good faith" believed cause to exist even if it did not.[21] Compensation for the victim of a constitutional violation is thereby given a subordinate position in our hierarchy of values.

The Court has also made it extremely difficult to obtain injunctive relief from proven unconstitutional police actions. For example, in *Los Angeles v. Lyons*,[22] a plaintiff had been rendered unconscious as a result of a police "choke hold," after the police stopped his car for a motor vehicle violation. The plaintiff had offered no threats or resistance. He sued for an injunction against the use of this police practice in similar situations and supported his claim with evidence of fifteen deaths (mostly of blacks) that had occurred as a result. The Court refused to issue an injunction since Lyons could not prove that he would *again* be subjected to such a hold in the future. If he was, the Court assured him he could sue for damages (or, if he was so unfortunate to die, his family could sue). Showing little concern for the deadly consequences of this unconstitutional police practice, the Court blithely reasoned:

> Of course, it may be that among the countless encounters between the police and the citizens of a great city such as Los Angeles, there will be certain instances in which strangleholds will be illegally applied and injury and death unconstitutionally inflicted on the victim. . . . it is no more than conjecture to suggest that in every . . . encounter between the police and a citizen, the police will act unconstitutionally and inflict injury without provocation or legal excuse. And it is surely no more than speculation to assert either that Lyons himself will again be involved in one of those unfortunate instances, or that he will be arrested in the future and provoke the use of a choke hold by resisting arrest, attempting to escape, or threatening deadly force or serious bodily injury.[23]

LIBERTY, FREEDOM, AND BASIC FAIRNESS

The work of the Warren Court was not a function of radical political or legal theory. Rather, that Court's insistence on fair procedure, equal rights for the indigent, elimination of racial bias, and limits on overbearing police procedures were based on conventional notions of due process, equality, and fairness. The Court never questioned the legitimacy of police authority or of most penal sanctions.

On the other hand, the political and legal theories that animate prevailing criminal justice policies virtually ignore the social changes needed to ameliorate causes of crime. Further, these policies subordinate our basic freedoms to enhance largely unrestrained police practices.

In this respect, the legal system reflects a view of state power that has been espoused by some in the most privileged segment of our society. Asserting property interests over individual rights, they assume their own individual rights are not at risk. Testimony by the president of the Philadelphia Chamber of Commerce before the United States Commission on Civil Rights provides a good example:

> [M]ost businessmen feel that the protection which business receives in this city is so outstanding that they are willing to put up with instances which *had they occurred to somebody in their own family or in their employment they would consider unbearable.* It's not difficult to differentiate between something that happens to either you or somebody with whom you're very close where police brutality is involved, and where you have righteous indignation and you want instant action, and something that happens to somebody else, where you shrug your shoulders and say, "Well, I'm afraid that's something we just have to accept in return for adequate police protection." The average businessman does feel that he is willing to put up with "a little brutality" in return for what he considers adequate protection.[24]

There is also an integral relationship between the rights of the accused and other democratic rights, such as freedom of speech. Recall in the court's preventive detention decision the assertion that "in times of war or insurrection . . . the government may detain [dangerous] individuals." One would have thought that the Japanese relocation experience of World War II had been the last of such intolerable policies. The liberties provided to criminal suspects are part of a broader scheme of political rights, and their significance extends beyond the issue of the proper balance of powers and rights between the state and criminal defendants. Conservative forces in this country certainly recognize this distinct relationship. Consider the statements by former Attorney General Edwin Meese, in a 1986 report calling for the overturning of the *Miranda* decision. Notwithstanding abundant evidence that *Miranda* does not hamper law enforcement and is if anything too deferential to the police, the attorney general states that *Miranda* should be discarded:

> An abrogation of Miranda would be of broader import because of its symbolic status as the epitome of Warren Court activism in the criminal law area. We accordingly regard a challenge to Miranda as essential, not only in overcoming the detrimental impact caused directly by this decision, but also as a critical step in moving to repudiate a discredited criminal

jurisprudence. Overturning Miranda would, accordingly, be among the most important achievements of this administration—in restoring the power of self-government to the people of the United States in the suppression of crime.[25]

The conservative crime control model—with its emphasis on governmental and police power, restriction of individual rights, and its disparagement of the social and economic cause of crime—has failed to stem the rising tides of crime and drugs. In a society that marginalizes the lives of millions of poor and minority people, this is not a surprising result. At the same time, the legal system, in adopting and implementing doctrine that is governed by these political and social theories, has put in jeopardy fundamental rights and liberties. Ultimately, the costs of the current approach will not only be increased economic inequality and unchecked violence, but a weakening of the constitutional guarantees of liberty and equality.

NOTES

1. National Institute of Justice, *American Prisons and Jails* (Washington, D.C.: U.S. Government Printing Office, 1980); Benjamin H. Renshaw, Department of Justice Press Release, July 2, 1981; American Institute of Criminal Justice, *Just the Facts* (Philadelphia, 1890); Elliot Currie, "Crime and Ideology," *Working Papers*, May 1982.
2. See Ron Harris, "Blacks Feel Brunt of Drug War," *Los Angeles Times*, April 22, 1990.
3. *See, e.g.*, Mapp v. Ohio, 367 U.S. 643 (1961); Gideon v. Wainwright, 372 U.S. 335 (1963); Brady v. Maryland, 373 U.S. 83 (1963); Miranda v. Arizona, 384 U.S. 436 (1966).
4. "Crime, Justice, and the Social Environment," chapter 13.
5. *The New York Times*, January 14, 1985, Op-Ed page.
6. See Sherman v. United States, 385 U.S. 293 (1966); Hoffa v. United States, 385 U.S. 293 (1966).
7. McCray v. Illinois, 386 U.S. 300 (1967).
8. Irving Younger, "The Perjury Routine," *The Nation*, May 8, 1967.
9. 367 U.S. 643 (1961).
10. 384 U.S. 436 (1966).
11. U.S. General Accounting Office, *Impact of Exclusionary Rule on Federal Criminal Prosecutions* (Washington, D.C.: U.S. Government Printing Office, 1979).
12. United States v. Salerno, 481 U.S. 739 (1987).

13. "Pretrial Release: An Evaluation of Defendant Outcomes and Program Impact" (1981), cited in David Bazelon, "The Crime Controversy: Avoiding Realities," 35 *Vanderbilt Law Review* 487, 494 (1982).
14. 389 U.S. 347 (1967).
15. United States v. Miller, 425 U.S. 435 (1976); Smith v. Maryland, 422 U.S. 735 (1976); California v. Ciraolo, 106 S.Ct. 1809 (1986).
16. Hudson v. Palmer, 468 U.S. 517 (1984).
17. Anthony G. Amsterdam, "Perspectives on the Fourth Amendment," 58 *University of Minnesota Law Review* 349, 365 (1974).
18. United States v. White, 401 U.S. 745, 789 (1971) (dissenting opinion).
19. Kirby v. Illinois, 406 U.S. 682 (1972); Manson v. Brathwaite, 432 U.S. 98 (1977).
20. *See, e.g.,* Leon v. United States, 418 U.S. 897 (1984); Rakas v. Illinois, 439 U.S. 138 (1978); Stone v. Powell, 428 U.S. 475 (1976).
21. Anderson v. Creighton, 483 U.S. 635 (1987). See D. Rudovsky, "The Qualified Immunity Doctrine in the Supreme Court: Judicial Activism and the Restriction of Constitutional Rights," 138 *University of Pennsylvania Law Review* 23 (1989).
22. 461 U.S. 95 (1983).
23. *Id.* at 110.
24. U.S. Commission on Civil Rights, *Who Is Guarding the Guardians?* (Washington, D.C.: U.S. Government Printing Office, 1981).
25. *Report to the Attorney General on the Law of Pre-Trial Interrogation,* Office of Legal Policy, February 12, 1986, p. 115.

15 RICHARD L. ABEL

TORTS

TORTS are injuries for which the law awards money damages. The law does not compensate all experiences that victims and society perceive as injurious: exceptions include social rebuffs or the pain of witnessing the death of a close friend. Torts overlaps with many other bodies of law and is best grasped in relation to them. Some events are both torts and crimes, such as a drunk driver striking a pedestrian; the state will prosecute the offender, from whom the victim may seek damages. But some torts are not crimes because the actor lacked the wrongful state of mind, such as a car driver who is merely negligent. And some crimes are not torts because no one was injured, such as speeding on an empty highway. Victims who seek compensation for property damage may have to argue about the extent of their rights—that ownership of land includes the right to be free from the noise of an adjacent airport, for example; but tort claims are not the usual means of settling property disputes. Most tort claims arise in situations where the parties have not agreed in advance what will happen in case of conflict—again, a two-car accident is the best illustration. But sometimes tort claims arise out of a contract, such as the sale of a defective product or the failure of an insurer to pay an insured. And agreements may limit as well as expand

I am grateful for the comments of Emily Abel, Jay Feinman, Sandra Segal Ikata, David Kairys, Mark Kelman, William Simon, and Mark Tushnet. All still would disagree with some of what I have written and some with all of it. Adequate documentation of my arguments would more than double the length of this chapter; a fully documented version is forthcoming as "A Critique of Torts," 37 *UCLA Law Review* 785 (1990). Interested readers will find much of the evidence cited in my earlier articles: "A Critique of American Tort Law," 8 *British Journal of Law and Society* 199 (1981); "A Socialist Approach to Risk," 41 *Maryland Law Review* 695 (1982); "Risk as an Arena of Struggle," 83 *Michigan Law Review* 772 (1985); "Blaming Victims," 1985 *American Bar Foundation Research Journal* 401; "£'s of Cure, Ounces of Prevention," 73 *California Law Review* 1003 (1985); "Should Tort Law Protect Property Against Accidental Loss?" 23 *San Diego Law Review* 79 (1986); "The Real Tort Crisis—Too *Few* Claims," 48 *Ohio State Law Journal* 443 (1987).

the right to sue in tort—as when a parking lot successfully disclaims liability for damage to cars. Although tort law is created by judges, they often are influenced by rights found in statutes and even the Constitution. I stress the overlaps between torts, criminal law, property, contracts, constitutional law, and regulation because the law school curriculum typically conveys the misleading impression that these are watertight compartments.

A VERY BRIEF HISTORY

Before the modern era, tort law was preoccupied with intentional wrongs (it still is in regions relatively unaffected by industrialization, urbanization, capitalism, and the state). Because people did not control large amounts of energy, accidents rarely caused serious injury. In societies where the means and relations of production did not generate great differences in wealth, status was differentiated by reputational criteria. Intentional wrongs and the response to such affronts significantly shaped reputation. Even misfortunes we now call accidents—such as a snake bite, lightning bolt, or fatal disease—often were attributed to a human agent, through beliefs in witchcraft and sorcery, or to the wrath of ancestors or gods. In the absence of a state, redress often depended on the victim's capacity to mobilize supporters (based on kinship, residence, or age grouping), who were more likely to be outraged by intentional wrongs.

The social, economic, political, and cultural changes of the last few centuries have transformed tort law. Technological development made it possible for inadvertence to inflict previously unimaginable misery. Individuals can do so when driving cars or starting fires (in office towers or hotels, for instance). Collectivities (both public and private) can cause much greater damage, whether through momentary events (the Exxon oil spill, the Bhopal disaster) or ongoing activities (the manufacture and sale of asbestos, thalidomide, and cigarettes; the dumping of nuclear waste). The concentration of both private capital and political power, together with autocratic structures of control, have greatly augmented the potential effects of carelessness (social organization compounding technological change).

Mass migration and urbanization have produced a nation of strangers. They cannot enhance their standing by inflicting or revenging intentional injuries; indeed, they stand to lose status (except within deviant subcultures). Most anonymous wrongs are motivated by material gain. Its victims, similarly, are more interested in compensation than personal revenge; but tort actions offer little redress because few criminals can pay damages. Concern about status relationships is concentrated within the family, which is increasingly nuclear. Violence and emotional abuse are endemic within that domain, but the state is reluctant to intervene for fear of undermining intimacy, in the absence of consensus about normative standards, and because those wielding power within the family (men and parents) strongly resist interference. Status competition obviously is endemic to politics and the market, but in both it is mandated, not penalized.

The same social structural changes that reduce the salience of intentional torts simultaneously increase the importance of negligent injuries. Strangers have less incentive to exercise care toward each other and greater difficulty in resolving conflict when injury occurs. Both features are aggravated by the deepening divides of class and race. The rise of capitalism, technological development, and the division of labor all have increased the social distance between those who make what Calabresi calls the "decision for accidents" and their potential victims: workers and consumers of goods, services, and environmental amenities (such as air and water). Tortious behavior has come to resemble modern warfare in this respect.

As the focus of tort law has shifted from intentional wrongs among intimates to unintentional injuries among strangers, the moral tone also has changed. Although scholars disagree about the standard of care demanded by preindustrial tort law, few would deny that nineteenth-century judges adopted a highly moralistic rhetoric, allowing recovery only if defendants were morally culpable and victims wholly innocent. In the last hundred years these moral judgments have been subordinated to an equally explicit concern with compensation. Damages have been awarded to victims who previously would have been barred from recovery: charitable hospital patients, social guests or trespassers on the land of another, passengers in another's car, and those who were contributorily negligent or assumed the risk. Similarly, those who caused injuries have been held liable without fault simply because they were employers or manufacturers or engaged in abnormally dangerous activities.

Changes in the experience of injury have profoundly shaped the contours of tort damages: lost earnings, medical expenses, property loss, and intangible damages. Capitalism has created a proletariat that must sell its labor for wages in order to live. Capitalists, by contrast, must minimize labor costs by discarding workers whose productivity is diminished. Because unemployment is tantamount to destitution, lost earnings (past and future) are an essential element of compensatory damages. Because capitalism erodes the obligations of mutual support outside the nuclear family and increasingly compels both spouses to work, those disabled by accident must purchase care from strangers. Increases in the technical competence of medical professionals have been accompanied by deskilling of the laity. At the same time, medical costs have been inflated by the monopoly the state confers on professionals. Capitalism and mass production have disseminated consumer goods widely among the general public. Not only is there more to be destroyed but most goods are thoroughly fungible (indistinguishable from others of the same kind): they are bought rather than made and readily replaced—indeed, the newer the better (the totaled car replaced by the latest model, for instance). Finally, as we will see more fully below, the commodity form has been extended from goods, labor, and care to all forms of human experience—everything can (and increasingly must) be bought. Consequently, tort damages are granted for physical pain, disfigurement or loss of bodily function, fear, and damage to emotional relationships. The growing importance of damages for intangible injury reflects the fact that postindustrial society promises everyone a perfect life, unimpaired by accidents, and elevates leisure and consumption above work and production.

Social fragmentation has made it very difficult for victims to mobilize group support for their claims, increasing their dependence on the state and on the commodified assistance they must buy from lawyers. Both eagerly accept the responsibility. The state always has sought a central role in norm enforcement and conflict resolution, progressively asserting its monopoly over the use of force. The vociferous campaign for "law and order" waged by politicians and the media justifies the continuing expansion of state coercion. Powerful bureaucracies—courts, prosecutors, police, and prison officials— develop vested interests in processing crime. The victim becomes an embarrassing anachronism—necessary to set the process in motion but an inconvenience thereafter. Criminal prosecutions virtually supplant civil actions for intentional tort. In recent decades, the state has extended its protective role to the workplace, the environment, and the market. Private practitioners specialized in representing tort victims develop their own vested interests. The economic manifestation is the contingent fee—plaintiffs' lawyers take a proportion of the victim's recovery (typically 25 to 50 percent). The political manifestation is uncritical support for fault-based private law remedies by the Association of Trial Lawyers of America and its state counterparts.

The Marxist critique of capitalism as a system of production that exploits and alienates workers offers suggestive analogies with contemporary tort law. In precapitalist society injury, like work, is experienced as "use value"—it is not mediated by the market. Intimates feel obligated to care for victims; social groups diminished by the injury support the victim's demand for redress. The capitalist state asserts a monopoly of force, undermining private collective action. The legal system, which constructs the market for labor, capital, land, and commodities, also constructs the market for injuries. Just as capitalism separates workers from the means of production, so legal professionalism separates tort victims from the means of redress and medical professionalism separates victims and intimates from responsibility for care. In each instance a fraction of the dominant class mobilizes state power to protect its property—capital or professional credentials. Just as the owner of capital combines it with the worker's labor to produce a commodity (a good or service) with exchange value in the market, so the lawyer combines the state-created monopoly of legal representation and advice with the victim's injury to produce a commodity—a tort—that has exchange value in both the state-created market (the court) and the dependent markets it engenders (negotiated settlements). (Physicians also package the victim's injury with their own socially constructed expertise and the labor of subordinates for sale to third-party payers.) Just as the capitalist insists on "managerial prerogatives" in the workplace, so the private practitioner and prosecutor demand total control over legal production; the victim (like the worker) has little say over how injuries are made into torts and crimes. Most victims, like most workers, receive the bare minimum needed for survival. Just as the capitalist expropriates the surplus value created by the worker, so the lawyer expropriates a fourth to a half of the victim's recovery, sometimes sharing it with other professionals, such as physicians.

CRITIQUE

There is broad agreement that the purposes of tort law are to pass moral judgment on the wrong committed, respond to the victim's needs, and encourage future safety. It does a poor job of all three.

MORAL JUDGMENT

Moral judgment historically was the core of tort law. Few would deny that endangering or injuring another merits condemnation or that the victim's suffering deserves public recognition. Furthermore, those held liable clearly experience tort damages as punishment. Yet tort liability is incoherent as a moral system.

It consistently violates the basic principle of proportionality between the wrongfulness of the defendant's conduct and the magnitude of the penalty imposed. Because punishment is a function of harm caused it is either too severe or too lenient. It is too severe when momentary inadvertence results in catastrophic injury—drivers who take their eyes off the road to tune the radio, causing automobile accidents that inflict a lifetime of agony on others (usually on several others). It is too lenient when egregiously unsafe conduct happens to cause little or no injury—by chance or through the intervention of others. Courts deal with these inequities haphazardly: judges invoke doctrines of proximate cause and duty to curtail liability; juries stretch notions of causation to extend liability. But many injustices are not corrected, and all the moral intuitions lack a principled basis. Similar problems arise when the law allows defenses based on victim misconduct; again courts make ad hoc accommodations, adjusting the standard of care to the victim's capacity (measured by age and physical or mental disability), making crude comparisons between the fault of the parties, or acknowledging environmental constraints on volition (such as an employer's domination of employees, or the few choices enjoyed by poor people).

Notions of fault constructed when individuals were the significant actors and technology was simple are inadequate to assign responsibility today. Many torts, particularly the most serious, are caused by corporate entities, both public and private. The doctrine of respondeat superior (holding employers strictly liable for negligent employees) ensures victim compensation, but it also obviates the need to determine which employee was responsible. Liability insurance pays most damages, but it also insulates the wrongdoer from moral judgment. Many injuries are caused by the independent acts of several unrelated defendants, among whom there is no principled basis for apportioning responsibility. Indeed, the very notion of individual responsibility is inconsistent with probabilistic theories of causation. Consequently, the imposition of liability on DES manufacturers, all of whom *might* have injured the victims but most of whom clearly did not, seems to violate basic principles of fairness.

Tort theory and practice affront the moral intuitions of laypeople. Survey research reveals that both victims and the general public believe that compensation ought to be divorced from fault. On one hand, those injured deserve and need compensation regardless of their own behavior. On the other, compensation should be paid by those who can most easily afford it (because they are wealthy or can spread the burden) or who benefit from the activity (such as employers, manufacturers, or sellers). The attribution of fault becomes a mere rationalization for this more compelling ethical goal. Tortfeasors are even more hostile to the role of moral judgment. Most cases are settled rather than adjudicated, and those settlements often explicitly deny any acknowledgment of fault. This contrasts sharply with many non-Western societies, in which the response to injury focuses on the causal actor's admission of guilt, apology, and plea for forgiveness.

The ethical incoherence of torts is accentuated by the proliferation of different standards of care for particular situations unconnected by any explanation for why each is appropriate. In preindustrial societies, liability sometimes was predicated on fault and sometimes was imposed without fault, while in other instances fault went unpunished. Although nineteenth-century judges invoked fault to narrow liability, even they did not embrace fault unconditionally, as shown by the persistence of strict liability for ultrahazardous activities. The last hundred years have seen continued tension between fault and nonfault principles. Nonfault recovery has expanded through workers' compensation, products liability, ultrahazardous activity, and no-fault automobile insurance. Some defenses have been restricted (such as assumption of risk or agreements not to sue) and others modified (comparative fault largely displaced contributory negligence). And a few jurisdictions have created comprehensive compensation programs. Yet fault principles have reappeared within every nonfault scheme: employee intoxication or employer breach of safety regulations in workers' compensation; notions of the appropriateness of ultrahazardous activities; the concept of a defect and comparative fault in products liability; criminal activity in comprehensive compensation programs.

The inconsistencies detailed above all reflect difficulties in the dominant ethical framework of utilitarianism (measuring acts by their consequences). When tort law instead reflects an essentialist or nonconsequentialist ethic, the results are even less satisfactory. The obligation to help another in danger is one of the most intractable problems in tort law. Our inability to find an acceptable position highlights the basic contradiction between egoism and altruism: we can neither embrace one of the extremes nor find any principled position between them. We have just as much difficulty combining utilitarian and nonutilitarian ethics. We require informed consent before medical procedures out of respect for the patient's autonomy (a nonutilitarian value); but we impose liability only when the information withheld would have persuaded a *reasonable* person to reject the procedure; and the quantum of damages measures the physical injury caused by the procedure rather than the violation of autonomy (both rules emphasize consequences). We impose a general duty of reasonable care, but we also respect parental rights to raise children according to personal beliefs (even when these may endanger the child) and religious scruples against medical treatment (although these may conflict with the duty to mitigate damages).

Partly in response to these difficulties, but also because liberalism is uncomfortable with moral arguments that express patent and seemingly irreconcilable value dissensus, tort law has turned to the language of economics, replacing moral fault with the efficient allocation of resources, a concept that appears scientific and apolitical. I discuss below the empirical obstacles to a cost-benefit analysis of injury. But I also find it ethically unacceptable to make safety a commodity, which potential victims consume according to idiosyncratic preferences. Such "choices" inevitably reflect the enormous differences in both individual wealth and socialization.

In fact, tort law rejects many of the pivotal recommendations of economic analysis. It penalizes victims who choose too little safety (by reducing or denying recovery) but fails to punish those who choose too much, although their behavior is just as inefficient. Economics would argue for symmetrical treatment of plaintiffs and defendants, but tort law is much more solicitous of victims. Economics would be indifferent to context, but tort law is contextually specific, recognizing that a consumer's "choice" of an unsafe product differs from a worker's "choice" of an unsafe job. Indeed, the Coase theorem—a foundation of law and economics—sees tort liability as superfluous whenever plaintiff and defendant could have negotiated safety: in the workplace or the purchase of such products and services as air travel, pharmaceutical products, home appliances, and medical care. Although economics would disregard the characteristics of the parties, tort law imposes different obligations on corporate entities and individuals, entrepreneurs and consumers. Although economics would simply aggregate all the "costs of accidents" in calculating desired levels of safety, tort law treats personal injury differently from property damage and lost profits. Although economics views all choices as equally "free," tort law recognizes resource constraints in the purchase of "essential" goods and services. In sum, economics offers neither an accurate description of existing tort law nor a morally superior alternative.

COMPENSATION

If moral judgment is the origin of tort law, compensation is the contemporary preoccupation. Victims need money—often desperately—to replace lost earnings and pay medical expenses; only after this is assured are they concerned to allay their sense of outrage and ensure that the tortfeasor has been properly punished. Jurors (and many judges) are equally preoccupied with helping needy victims. Yet tort law is an unsatisfactory mechanism of compensation, both in its material consequences and as ideology.

Tort law cannot adequately compensate needy victims because liability is a function of fault rather than need. A victim injured by someone not at fault will remain uncompensated. A victim at fault can never receive more than partial compensation. And even when the victim is found to be innocent and the defendant at fault, the consequences of liability depend on the material circumstances of plaintiff and defendant. If the defendant lacks resources, a tort judgment is an empty remedy. If the defendant is no wealthier than the plaintiff, there is no *social* gain in shifting the financial burden from one to the other. Indeed, the goal is not to compensate the victim but to spread the financial burden among as many people as possible. But tort liability does so only when the victim is an uninsured individual and the tortfeasor is either insured or a large corporate entity whose damages will be shared by many customers, shareholders, employees, or taxpayers.

Given the legal and financial obstacles to recovery, it is not surprising that relatively few victims succeed. The best empirical investigation examined English accident victims disabled for at least two weeks and found that only 12 percent recovered *any* tort damages. Although there are many reasons why the American claims rate might differ, several studies confirm that recovery is infrequent here as well. Lawyers are essential to successful claims, but they are prohibited from initiating contact with accident victims. Because the vast majority of claims are settled out of court, even the small fraction of victims who seek compensation recover only part of their damages. Economic incentives encourage tortfeasors to overcompensate small claims (because of their nuisance value) and undercompensate large ones (because victims need immediate payment while the legal system allows defendants to delay for years). Since other sources of compensation also are inadequate (loss insurance, sick pay, welfare, disability benefits, and pensions), many victims and their families are severely impoverished.

Tort damages not only are inadequate as compensation, they also are unequal, thereby symbolizing, reproducing, and intensifying existing in equalities. Because liberalism rejects status inequalities, tort law gradually has eliminated *de jure* distinctions between patients injured in charitable and profit-making hospitals, fee-paying passengers and gratuitous guests injured in automobile accidents, and business and social guests injured by landowner negligence. Yet the legal proclamation of formal equality obscures the persistence of real inequality. This has many sources.

First, some people are more likely than others to be victimized by tortfeasors who cannot or will not pay compensation. Crime victims, for instance, are disproportionately poor, racial minorities, women, and adolescent or elderly. Sovereign immunity often protects government from tortious liability; its victims are likely to be charitable patients, criminal accused, prison inmates, welfare recipients, and veterans.

Second, the process of making a claim is institutionalized to varying degrees in different settings. Automobile accidents are governed by reasonably clear behavioral rules (traffic laws); because they occur in public, witnesses usually are available; they create physical evidence (such as skid marks and dents); the police often are summoned and make written reports; and at least one party is likely to be insured. Compensation almost always is available for work accidents; fellow workers encourage victims to claim and also act as witnesses; trade unions provide assistance and legal representation; and class relations create a sense of entitlement. When other accidents occur—in the home or during leisure activities—the claims process is much less thoroughly institutionalized: there may be no witnesses; victims tend to blame themselves; and there is no obvious defendant. The English study found that 29 percent of road accident victims and 19 percent of work accident victims recovered some damages but only 2 percent of other victims (who represented 86 percent of those accidentally disabled for two weeks or more). Women, the young and old, and the unemployed are more likely to fall in the last category.

Third, the measure of damages is unequal. Tort damages are far more generous than workers' compensation payments, crime victim compensation schemes, or veterans' benefits for those disabled in the military. Victims in the last three categories are more likely to be manual workers, poor, or racial minorities. Tort damages deliberately reproduce the existing distribution of wealth and income. Those who question its legitimacy may be troubled that the state is using its coercive power to re-create inequality. Furthermore, the cost of preserving privilege is borne by everyone buying liability insurance, purchasing products and services, and paying taxes. Thus, *all* insured car owners pay the cost of compensating the privileged few who drive Rolls-Royces or earn half a million dollars a year. They also pay for the superior medical care consumed by victims from higher socioeconomic strata. Because nonpecuniary damages often are calculated as a multiple of pecuniary damages (generally two to five times as much), the privileged also recover more for their pain and suffering. Finally, it seems likely that jurors are more solicitous of those who have lost privilege than those who never enjoyed it.

Because these biases cumulate, tort law intensifies social inequality. Among English accident victims disabled for two weeks or more, men recovered tort damages almost twice as often as women, victims between the ages of twenty-five and fifty-four three times as often as those younger or older, the employed more often than the unemployed, and housewives less than a third as often as their proportion of the injured population would predict. The mean sick pay award to women was less than half that of men.

The decision to compensate is inescapably political and unprincipled. Three illustrations must suffice. First, when adjacent property owners seek to put their land to inconsistent uses—a cattle feed lot and a residential development, for instance—one must give way. But no legal principle can choose between them. Second, the consequences of tortious behavior ramify indefinitely in time and space and across social relations. The decision about where to terminate liability is hopelessly arbitrary: spouses can recover loss of consortium but children, parents, and siblings cannot; one who witnesses the injury of an intimate can recover for emotional distress but not one who arrives on the scene minutes later or is a friend rather than a relative; a homeowner whose house is burned by a fire next door can recover but not the neighbor one house farther away. Third, courts have been unable to explain when lost profits will be compensated.

Even if all these problems could be overcome (and they cannot), tort liability would be an extraordinarily inefficient mechanism for compensating victims. A very large proportion of the money paid by defendants is consumed by private loss and liability insurers, courts, and of course lawyers. Victims receive only a small fraction.

From the perspective of compensation, tort damages are no more satisfactory on the level of ideology. Their fundamental justification is thoroughly inadequate: money cannot restore victims to their status quo ante. Damages paid after prolonged delay are not the same as the wages lost or property destroyed years earlier (even if prejudgment interest is added). All goods are not fungible. Reimbursement for the cost of medical treatment is hardly identical with never having to undergo it. But perhaps the most telling objection is that money cannot be equated with nonpecuniary loss. We can better appreciate the historical contingency and cultural specificity of contemporary American tort damages by contrasting them with other responses: African customary law, for instance, which "compensated" death by the payment of livestock proportioned to the bridewealth necessary to affiliate a child to "replace" the deceased; or a workers' compensation scheme in which a lost toe is worth sixteen weeks' wages.

If all legal remedies transmit cultural messages, what do American tort damages say? First, they reaffirm the existing distribution of resources. By compensating owners for property loss, tort damages uphold the belief in private property and its concomitant—that a victim's worth is proportional to the value of property owned. By preserving the income streams of those who suffer physical injury, tort damages endorse the legitimacy of the existing income distribution and the intergenerational reproduction of inequality (when children claim for the wrongful death of a parent). By excluding some victims and injuries and discouraging others from claiming, tort law suggests that they are less highly valued. By relegating injured employees to workers' compensation, the law treats them like pure labor value, implicitly denying that they suffer the pain for which we compensate tort victims or enjoy the pleasures whose loss often is a significant element of tort damages. Tort law proclaims the class structure of capitalist society: you are what you own, what you earn, and what you do.

Second, by monetizing intangible injuries tort law extends a fundamental concept of capitalism—the commodity form—from the sphere of production (work) to that of reproduction (producing workers). Damages for pain and suffering extrapolate Bentham's hedonic calculus to its logically absurd conclusion, insisting that every pain suffered can be offset by an equivalent pleasure, which can be bought for money. Jurors, therefore, must simulate a market in sadomasochism by asking what they would charge to undergo the victim's misfortune. Tort law thus extracts an involuntary present sacrifice (injury) in exchange for future gain (damages), reflecting bourgeois notions of delayed gratification and an instrumental view of the self—the very characteristics Weber stressed in identifying capitalism with the Protestant ethic.

Damages commodify unique experience by substituting the universal equivalent, money—as when a plaintiff's attorney asks the jury to assign a monetary value to each second of the victim's pain and then aggregate it over a lifetime of suffering. This dehumanization is particularly striking in two diametrically opposed situations. When injuries shorten a victim's life expectancy, money damages are rationalized as enhancing present pleasure in lieu of years forgone—a secular version of the Faustian compact. A child born illegitimate or seriously disabled, who sues for wrongful life, is claiming money damages for the net detriment of painful experience over the alternative of nothingness. Large awards for severe pain and suffering have several additional consequences: they salve the guilt of the unimpaired at having been spared such torment (the survivor syndrome) and rationalize their selfish desire to avoid and ignore the disabled (our new "invisible man"). Rather than evoking compassion for victims, large awards awaken envy for what is seen as a windfall and convey the erroneous impression (deliberately fostered by the insurance industry) that the tort system is working well—if anything, too well.

If damages for pain and suffering commodify experience, their recent extension to injuries to relationships commodifies love. Damages are now paid for loss of the society and companionship of a parent in wrongful death actions; loss of the consortium of an injured spouse, lover, parent, or child; the experience of witnessing or learning about an injury to a loved one; mistreatment of the corpse of a loved one; misinformation about the death of a loved one; misinformation causing the breakup of a marriage; even the sorrow following damage to loved objects.

Such payments proclaim several messages. All relationships have a monetary equivalent and hence can be bought and sold. The value of the relationship depends on the extent to which the "other" approaches societal ideals of physical beauty, mental acuity, athletic ability, and emotional normality. Tort damages assume, and help construct, a single scale along which everyone can be ranked—extrapolating adolescent obsession with popularity, universalizing 1950s rating-dating. The implicit assumption is that an impaired partner will be discarded, like any other consumer product in our throwaway society, and a replacement purchased with the money damages received—the tort analogy to no-fault divorce. All relationships become a form of prostitution—the semblance of love exchanged for money—a generalization of feminist critiques of marriage. Just as society awards pain and suffering damages so that the injured victim can purchase the companionship that will no longer be extended out of love, so it gives damages to those who loved the victim, returning their lost "investment" so that they can reinvest in unimpaired "human capital."

SAFETY

If moral judgment was historically the stimulus for tort claims and compensation is the contemporary preoccupation, safety actually should be our greatest concern. Many folk sayings capture this: safety first; better safe than sorry; an ounce of prevention is worth a pound of cure. Calabresi forcefully argued this twenty years ago, convincing most scholars that reducing the cost of injuries must take priority. Were we not concerned to foster safety, indeed, private law remedies would be hard to justify: criminal law expresses moral judgment more forcefully, and no-fault schemes compensate victims more efficiently.

Although tort law is not the only means of fostering safety, every alternative encounters serious problems. The ideal mechanism would be self-interest: victims controlling the risks to which they are exposed. But the extreme division of labor associated with technological development, mass production of consumer goods, and the separation of workers from ownership and control of the means of production under capitalism make this impossible. Nor can we rely on altruism to inspire concern for safety in those with the power to inflict harm. Social distance, cultural difference, and class divisions undermine solicitude for others. And profit seeking in a competitive market compels entrepreneurs to cut corners on safety.

Recognizing these limitations, we have created an elaborate regulatory apparatus that charges the state with protecting safety at work, in consumer goods and services, transportation, the environment, and recreational activities. Yet the deficiencies of regulation are manifold and notorious. Victims are not the only concern of regulators, who are swayed by political pressure, bureaucratic convenience, good relations with the regulated, and of course outright corruption. Regulation is slow and legalistic. Regulators generally have less information and expertise than the regulated and lack sufficient resources to inspect, investigate, and prosecute. Both regulators and courts are reluctant to impose severe penalties.

Legal theorists representing very different political persuasions have responded to this predicament by arguing that tort liability should be the central mechanism for promoting safety. Although they disagree whether liability ought to be strict or based on fault, they concur that the most efficient way to achieve an optimum level of safety is to internalize accident costs by making tortfeasors liable for their consequences. At least since Learned Hand offered his famous formula more than forty years ago, judges, lawyers, and legal scholars have argued that fear of liability will compel potential tortfeasors to engage in a cost-benefit analysis, taking just those safety precautions that cost less than the accidents they prevent. Yet the scientific facade of this economic formulation conceals a number of fundamental theoretical flaws and empirical problems.

First, although theoretically it is possible (if often difficult) to calculate the costs of safety precautions, it is not possible to calculate the benefits of accident avoidance. Economists cannot tell us the value of bodily integrity or emotional well-being because these are not defined by the market. The costs of accidents can only be determined collectively—after the fact by a judge or jury, before it by a legislature or regulatory agency. All of these are political decisions, not the findings of positive economics. Even those elements of damage that have market values—lost earnings and medical expenses—are extremely difficult to predict in the future. Actuarial methods can only tell us how a large population will behave, not the outcome of an individual case. Thus a central element in the cost-benefit analysis is irretrievably indeterminate.

Second, tort liability necessarily translates unequal recoveries (discussed above under "compensation") into unequal exposure to risk. An entrepreneur in a competitive market *must* spend less to protect those who are either less likely to claim or whose damages will be lower, *i.e.*, the poor, unemployed, racial minorities, noncitizens, inadequately educated, young and old, and women. Thus, cheap consumer products and services are not only less effective and attractive but also more dangerous; low-paid workers suffer more frequent and more serious injuries and illnesses at work; and the underprivileged are exposed to greater environmental pollution. Whether or not the Bhopal disaster was an "accident," it was no accident that its victims were among the poorest in the Third World. Nor is it chance that toxic waste dumps are overconcentrated in black ghettos in the United States.

Third, the threat of tort liability can elicit the optimum level of safety only if the potential tortfeasor knows that the trier of fact (judge or jury) will perform the cost-benefit analysis correctly. But that calculation is theoretically impossible. The trier of fact must determine whether the defendant failed to take specified safety precautions that would cost-effectively have avoided the injury that actually occurred. Yet cost-benefit analysis requires potential tortfeasors engaged in ongoing activities to evaluate *all* possible safety precautions for their contribution to reducing the costs of the entire population of accidents that *may* occur (both their number and intensity). Only a legal regime of true strict liability would place the decisional burden where it properly belongs—on the potential tortfeasor to evaluate the safety of an activity in advance rather than on the trier of fact to assign responsibility for an injury after the fact.

Fourth, every tort system, whether based on fault or strict liability, must determine whether this defendant caused this plaintiff's injury. But both the natural and the social sciences describe causation in terms of probabilities. Therefore, we can only talk meaningfully about the connection between populations of causes and effects. By singling out just some of the totality of causal agents, tort judgments inevitably hold them liable for injuries for which they were only partly responsible and fail to impose liability on others who share that responsibility. How, for example, should a court decide which injuries were caused by exposure to asbestos?

Fifth, safety sometimes must defer to the other two goals—moral judgment and compensation. Courts often invoke the highly malleable concepts of duty and proximate cause to curtail liability because the consequences seem disproportionate to the defendant's moral culpability. Less often they interpret negligence and causation broadly to impose liability because they find the defendant's behavior particularly reprehensible. Courts often look for the "deep pocket" defendant (large public or private entities or those likely to be insured) and then construe negligence and causation in order to rationalize the imposition of liability. Sometimes, by contrast, they refuse to find negligence or causation because the defendant seems less capable of bearing the burden than the plaintiff.

This focus on compensation distorts the promotion of safety in another way. When a large public or private entity is held liable (partly because it is a "deep pocket"), its organizational structure profoundly shapes the way in which the liability message is communicated to those who actually caused the injury. Only the willfully naive could maintain that the result will be "optimum safety"—or even that this concept has any meaning. And in the very large number of cases where insurance pays the bill, there are many reasons why liability is *not* accurately reflected in premium levels. Indeed, if insurance perfectly transmitted liability costs to insureds much of its raison d'être would disappear.

Sixth, the efficacy of tort liability in encouraging safety rests on several dubious assumptions about economic rationality and market conditions. Some actors are not maximizers in any simplistic sense. Charitable and governmental entities do not seek profits; indeed, an adverse judgment may augment the budget of a government department and actually increase the power of its bureaucrats. Most individuals so rarely cause accidents that they have little incentive to seek information about their frequency and severity or how to avoid them. Liability is no threat to those who are judgment proof. Even profit-seeking enterprises may be able to transfer liability costs to consumers rather than enhance safety if demand is relatively inelastic (the good or service is a necessity), the market is highly concentrated (there are few producers or sellers), or accident costs are an insignificant proportion of price. Reliance on economic incentives creates another dilemma: it argues for denying or reducing damages in order to motivate careless victims to be safer; but this necessarily undermines the safety incentives of tortfeasors. Furthermore, such reasoning makes the counterintuitive assumption that victims and tortfeasors are similarly motivated.

Seventh, and perhaps most important, tort liability produces optimum safety only if *all* victims recover *all* their damages from those who negligently caused their injuries. Yet we saw above that only a fraction of victims recover anything—just 12 percent of those disabled for at least two weeks in England (and doubtless even fewer of those who suffered less serious injuries). A rational entrepreneur *must* discount safety expenditures by the likelihood of being forced to pay damages—in England such an entrepreneur would spend less than 12 percent of the optimum amount on safety. If the market is perfectly competitive (as deterrence theory presupposes), it will drive out of business anyone who indulges in a higher level of safety. Most entrepreneurs are very unlikely ever to be sued: half of all products liability litigation between 1973 and 1986 was directed at just eighty companies, and only 9 percent of manufacturers were sued in that last year.

Furthermore, the threat of damages encourages entrepreneurs to minimize *liability*, not accident costs. It creates perverse incentives: to conceal information about danger, take actions that maximize success in litigation (practicing defensive medicine by ordering unnecessary, costly, and perhaps even harmful tests), resist legitimate claims (especially those that may establish unfavorable precedents), use economic power to wage a war of attrition against claimants, delay, and conclude settlements that limit publicity. How else can we explain why Ford produced a Pinto whose gasoline tank it knew was explosive, Johns-Manville subjected workers to asbestos for decades after it knew they were suffering lung damage and cancer, and McDonnell-Douglas produced and American Airlines flew a DC–10 they knew contained a faulty pylon and other design defects? Studies of the deterrent effect of criminal sanctions repeatedly demonstrate that certainty is more important than severity. Because full damages are rarely collected, tort liability encourages suboptimal safety.

Tort law fails as deterrence even when evaluated by its own criteria. Economic theory argues that governmental regulation ought to be unnecessary: contract can allocate risk more efficiently when the cost of transactions between the parties is low; and the threat of tort liability should achieve optimum safety in the remaining cases. Yet even the most ardent advocate of laissez-faire economics would hesitate to eliminate all speed limits, end medical malpractice liability, and abolish the Food and Drug Administration and the Federal Aviation Administration. Furthermore, if deterrence theory worked perfectly there would be *no* tort litigation: fear of liability would ensure optimum safety, and meritless lawsuits would not be brought. Yet conservatives loudly proclaim (and denounce) what they insist is a tort litigation explosion.

Reliance on a private law mechanism like tort to promote safety has other unfortunate consequences. The focus on liability to the individual victim subverts a collective response by all those endangered. Damages are paid only to individuals; group reparations and class actions rarely are available to those injured by the same polluter, manufacturer, common carrier, or employer. Because liability arises only when an injury has occurred, tort law fails to address the underlying problem of risk. Under capitalism, private law, like private medicine, is obsessed with individual cure at the expense of collective prevention because capitalism creates a market for the former while opposing state involvement in the latter. Money damages undermine the collective interest in safety both by perpetuating the lie that they restore the victim to the status quo ante (so that greater safety is unnecessary) and by arousing jealousy toward the newly wealthy victim, thereby diluting the sympathy and solidarity of others who are potential victims.

At the same time that law individualizes victims (actual and potential), it collectivizes tortfeasors—through the corporate form, the doctrine of respondeat superior, expansive interpretations of proximate cause (that seek a "deep pocket"), and the spread of liability insurance. This aggregation reflects the fact that tort damages have grown too large to be paid by individual defendants. The legal system further accentuates the power imbalance between individual victims and collective tortfeasors. Although the collective liability insurer can aggressively badger the individual victim for a release, the plaintiff's lawyer cannot approach victims to offer representation. Group legal service plans established in the 1930s to represent automobile accident victims were outlawed for several decades. Corporations often refuse to bargain collectively with unions over safety practices on the ground that these are "management prerogatives." Thus the individual victim (consumer, worker, traveler, breather of air, and drinker of water) confronts a collective tortfeasor (enterprise, insurer, government) in the struggle over risk, whether the conflict occurs in the legislature, regulatory agency, or court, or at the negotiating table.

PROPOSALS

Criticism can lead in two directions: concrete limited reforms capable of implementation within the existing political framework and more adequate solutions that would require a fundamental restructuring of society. I will offer both responses, organized like the critique (even though some issues overlap and all responses to risk must reconcile tensions between the goals).

MORAL JUDGMENT

Tort law fails almost entirely to pass moral judgment on the infliction of risk and injury. Negligent behavior is a public as well as a private wrong, since it endangers many people besides the chance victim. It therefore merits the official disapproval that only the state can express, in order to reaffirm the norms of safety. Prosecutors and administrative agencies must pursue safety offenders more vigorously. Because both respond to political pressure, actual and potential victims must organize to demand effective enforcement. Trade unions and consumer and environmental groups already do this; given the substantial free rider problem (people can enjoy benefits without contributing), they deserve state financing and legislative support.

Victims require a different kind of moral response. First, this must recognize their injury and sense of grievance; damages not only fail to do this, they suggest that the victim has enjoyed a windfall. Second, tortfeasors must acknowledge wrongdoing and apologize. In complex organizations it will be necessary to trace responsibility throughout the chain of command, from the employee who physically caused the injury up to top management. Settlements resolve the vast majority of claims; instead of denying culpability they must explicitly accept it. Third, moral judgment must occur *every* time someone is injured or endangered; even if general deterrence changed tortfeasor behavior (a doubtful proposition) it would not respond to the needs of victims. This means that all victims must be strongly encouraged to claim—by lawyers, the legal system, cultural norms, and support groups.

Finally, we must stop blaming victims. We do so now through legal doctrines like contributory negligence, comparative fault, assumption of risk, dangerous jobs, and agreements not to sue as well as through economic arguments that workers receive a "risk premium" or consumers "choose" to purchase dangerous products and services. Liberalism fosters these misconceptions by locating all constraint within the state, while portraying "private" behavior as free. But victims "choose" risk and injury within an environment of limited and grossly unequal economic resources; they are influenced by divergent cultural norms about their entitlement to safety; and many suffer an acute sense of political powerlessness. The concept of choice could become morally compelling only after we equalized individual circumstances— a profound challenge to those who take liberalism seriously. Furthermore, even if we agreed that individuals should be free to choose risk, this would not logically entail that they have forfeited our sympathy when they are injured. Suffering seems more than adequate punishment for carelessness (if any is deserved). And it still may be morally appropriate to criticize tortfeasors and expect them to apologize.

COMPENSATION

Accidents will happen even in utopia. The popular preoccupation with compensation accurately reflects the severe personal and social dislocations they can cause. But taking compensation seriously will require a total restructuring of the legal mechanisms. Only governmental programs can meet the criteria advanced below.

First, compensation should respond to *what* happened rather than *how* it happened, to need rather than cause or fault. It should be universally available: to those suffering congenital disability and illness as well as injury, whether or not they can identify a culpable agent, and even if they themselves are to blame. That, after all, is how we respond to the misfortunes of those we love. We must view compensation as a social good, to be encouraged if not required, because compensation, like education or preventive medicine, also benefits others by helping the victim resume productive activities and social relationships (it has what economists call positive externalities). Victims should not have to struggle through an obstacle course to extract compensation from a reluctant bureaucracy or adversary. Lawyers, support groups, and government should reach out to those in need in order to overcome the differences in culture and civic competence that make some more ready to claim than others.

Second, state compensation should affirm the equal humanity of victims, both materially and symbolically. Comprehensive medical care (broadly defined to include physical and psychological therapy) should be freely available according to need. The state should restore all victims to the same level of income and property—whatever minimum society believes it can afford. Enlightened self-interest should make that fairly generous, since accidents happen to everyone. Those who enjoy the privileges of greater wealth and income should bear the burden of losing them or protecting them through loss insurance; this also would reduce the inefficiencies of requiring potential victims to carry loss insurance and potential tortfeasors to carry liability insurance.

Third, there should be *no* compensation for intangible harm. Despite propaganda campaigns by trial lawyers' associations seeking to convince the public that pain and suffering damages are the inalienable birthright of every freedom-loving American, virtually inscribed in the Constitution, surveys of victims repeatedly demonstrate that most do not want it, though they do want defendants to acknowledge the wrong inflicted. Just as the present system of compensating pecuniary loss treats equals unequally (all people are created equal), so compensation for intangibles treats unequals equally (every human experience is unique). Nonpecuniary damages also dehumanize the response to misfortune, substituting money for compassion, arousing jealousy instead of sympathy, and treating experience and love as commodities.

The three reforms just proposed not only are mutually compatible but also reinforce each other. The trade-off between the quantum of damages awarded each victim and the number of victims benefited is not only logical but also documented by historical experience. Workers' compensation, automobile no-fault insurance, the Swedish no-fault medical malpractice scheme, and New Zealand's comprehensive compensation program all offer reduced benefits but serve more victims. Eliminating the adjudication of causation and fault and the calculation of past and future income and property loss, medical expenses, and intangible damages will enormously reduce transaction costs. It will obviate the need for lawyers (an original goal of workers' compensation). And it will drastically reduce delay, which presently inflicts great hardship on victims, forcing them to accept inadequate settlements.

I do not want to slight the difficulty of implementing these reforms or exaggerate what they will achieve. They will elicit vigorous opposition from both the plaintiffs' bar and private liability insurers (traditional adversaries who might forge an unholy alliance to defeat them). But though both are adept at manipulating symbols and wield formidable material resources, their hypocritical posturing has seriously eroded their public credibility. Nor do they deserve sympathy. American lawyers always have been very creative in finding new sources of business, and insurers who lose liability policies probably can make more money writing loss insurance for those wishing to protect their high income streams and substantial property holdings. Besides, reformers may be able to enlist the support of capital, which would gladly unload on the state the burden of health insurance, liability insurance, workers' compensation, and sick pay.

Even were these reforms implemented, they would represent only a social democratic solution to the problem of risk—ameliorating rather than eliminating the rigors of capitalism. They would reallocate the *cost* of accidents but not the accidents themselves. True, the legal system no longer would encourage tortfeasors to inflict greater risk on underprivileged victims whose liability costs are lower (because they recover fewer or smaller awards). But those endowed with greater material, social, or educational resources still would be able to translate their privileges into lower risk when choosing consumer goods and services, a workplace, and environmental amenities, just as they would be able to buy better medical care and insure their superior wealth and income against loss.

SAFETY

Without denigrating the reforms proposed above, I fully subscribe to the view that safety must be our first priority. We want to prevent accidents, not respond to them with moral condemnation and social support; and the more we prevent the less important those responses become. I offer two contradictory proposals: one could be pursued incrementally within the existing social framework, while the other would require a radical transformation.

The first takes seriously the role of tort liability in deterring unsafe behavior. Many of the deficiencies I criticized can be ameliorated or eliminated. First, liability should be strict rather than based on fault. A strict liability regime encourages the tortfeasor to reduce *accident costs* rather than liability. It places responsibility for the decision for accidents on the entrepreneur (who is familiar with the risks and safety precautions) rather than the jurors (who are chosen for their ignorance of these matters). It encourages research on safety. It internalizes the cost of *all* accidents (not just those caused by the defendant's fault) in the price of the good or service, allowing the market mechanism of consumer choice to reduce the quantity of accident-causing behavior to the optimum level. And it reduces transaction costs by eliminating the hotly contested issue of fault (although it intensifies disputes about cause and increases the total number of claims).

Second, victim behavior should not bar or diminish recovery. Self-interest (the axiomatic foundation of economics) sufficiently discourages potential victims from exposing themselves to risk; there is no evidence that the denial of compensation makes them safer.

Third, damages should reflect *all* costs of the accident, however these ramify through chance circumstance, emotional bonds, or economic interdependence. Doctrines of duty and proximate cause should not terminate liability; indeed, I would eliminate them altogether.

Fourth, claims should be actively encouraged—certainly by bar associations, possibly by individual lawyers. As claimants pursue their selfish interests they simultaneously perform a public service. Furthermore, claiming is learned behavior and should be reinforced. And encouragement will have the greatest effect on those who have been least likely to claim, helping to equalize claims rates.

Many objections will be raised to this proposal. Some will maintain we cannot afford it: courts will be overburdened, prices inflated, and companies driven out of business. But these are captious criticisms. Courts exist to hear valid claims—we do not close schools because there are too many students, libraries because there are too many readers, or roads because there are too many drivers. When police, prosecutors, and prisons are overextended by rising crime rates we increase their budgets; we should be at least as generous when private individuals mobilize the law. If consumers purchase fewer goods or services when their prices reflect accident costs as well as labor and materials, we have simply moved closer to the efficient allocation of resources. If we want to subsidize goods or services, there are fairer, more effective ways to do so than by leaving the random victim uncompensated. In any case, liability costs contribute little to the price of most goods and services. Others will decry anything that fuels American "litigiousness" and increases social conflict. But Americans actually exhibit relatively low and fairly constant rates of civil litigation. And social conflict could be reduced much more effectively if tortfeasors stopped causing so many injuries and promptly acceded to claims when they were made. We don't reduce the crime rate by telling victims to stop complaining so much; why should we respond to the tort rate that way?

Perhaps the most telling objection to this proposal is its inconsistency with my earlier endorsement of no-fault compensation. But politics is not logic, and I see no practical obstacles to pursuing both reforms simultaneously: encouraging a 100 percent claims rate under a strict liability regime while gradually mobilizing support for universal public medical care and income maintenance. Indeed, movement toward strict liability (which merely extrapolates laissez-faire economics) may create enthusiasm for no-fault compensation. If forced to choose, I would sacrifice the former to achieve the latter: the unquestionable good of universal compensation outweighs the uncertain deterrent of tort liability, especially given its very high administrative costs.

But even a strict liability regime with a 100 percent claims rate (an empirical impossibility) remains seriously flawed. It reproduces inequality, since tortfeasors still find it cheaper to endanger the poor. It violates autonomy, since the state still determines the cost of accidents and the tortfeasor decides whether to inflict them. And it undermines community, since victims must claim as individuals. Fidelity to these three ideals in the confrontation with risk will require a commitment to democratic socialism—the extension of democracy from the polity to all of social life.

Human autonomy is the foundation of Kantian ethics. Contemporary tort law reflects this inspiration in its insistence that those exposed to danger ought to be as autonomous as possible in the confrontation with risk. The doctrine of informed consent seeks to protect the autonomy of patients. Potential negligence victims cannot "assume" that risk unless they act with adequate knowledge and volition; the difficulty of realizing these conditions in the workplace persuaded legislatures to abrogate the doctrine. "Agreements" not to sue are unenforceable when the good or service is a necessity. Warnings put consumers on notice of risk only when they effectively communicate the danger.

The goal of autonomy in the encounter with risk can be realized in the workplace only through worker ownership and control of the means of production. Only in producer cooperatives will those exposed to risk also profit from that exposure and have the power to perform the cost-benefit analysis advocated by law and economics.

Rawlsian theories of justice call for equality of benefits and burdens—risk among them. This principle also is reflected in daily life. Many countries, including our own, require universal military service (at least for young men during wartime) in the belief that the threat of death or disability ought to be borne by all (however imperfectly that ideal is realized). None explicitly allows the wealthy to buy an exemption or substitute, as occurred during the nineteenth century; and many Americans remain deeply ashamed that the privileged were able to avoid military service in the Vietnam War. State guarantees of a minimal level of medical care express a rudimentary notion of equal entitlement to physical well-being. Americans are properly horrified when they read that Third World countries tolerate markets in bodily organs or that a physician proposed to create one here.

Risk in the workplace can be equalized only by substantially reducing the division of labor by rotating tasks—headwork and handwork, safe and dangerous. At the very least, everyone should periodically perform the most dangerous jobs—only that will awaken self-interest in reducing risk and foster empathetic understanding of the dangers that fellow workers encounter daily.

Liberalism conceptualizes the encounter with risk as a matter of individual choice: where to work, how to travel, what to consume, how to spend one's leisure, where to live. But individuals choose within a framework constructed by others. The most important decisions about risk—environmental pollution, the organization of work, the range of consumer goods and services—are made by collectivities (private enterprise and government). Consequently, those exposed to risk also must respond collectively. Together they can mobilize far more information than any individual could master; collective decision making also will compel individuals to reexamine their idiosyncratic risk preferences and aversions.

The organizational form best suited to promote autonomy, equality, and community in the encounter with workplace risk is the producer cooperative, whose members share ownership and management, rotate tasks, and decide collectively. Consumer cooperatives might perform a similar role, although the lesser salience of consumption (compared to production) and the multiplicity of goods and services will make it difficult to sustain the interest and develop the expertise of members. It is so hard to organize the diffuse public exposed to environmental risk that only state regulation can respond adequately. In each domain, equality of risk presupposes a high degree of social, political, economic, and cultural equality.

CONCLUSION

Contemporary tort law, not surprisingly, reflects the dominant traits of late-twentieth-century America: capitalist relations of production, individualism, extreme division of labor, and commodification. The unfortunate consequences for the incidence and distribution of risk and injury could be ameliorated within the existing social framework. Conservative rhetoric about law and order justifies harsher, more certain punishment for those who endanger or injure others. Numerous countries have shown that social democratic programs of health care and income maintenance are fully compatible with advanced capitalism and political liberalism. Laissez-faire ideology justifies strict liability as a means of promoting efficient resource allocation.

But if we take seriously the values of autonomy, equality, and community in the encounter with risk we must give equally serious consideration to democratic socialism: worker ownership and management, consumer co-operatives, equalization of benefits (resources) and burdens (risks), and a state sufficiently powerful to regulate environmental pollution.

16 REGINA AUSTIN AND SHARON DIETRICH

EMPLOYER ABUSE OF LOW-STATUS WORKERS: THE POSSIBILITY OF UNCOMMON RELIEF FROM THE COMMON LAW

THE workplaces of the 1990s will not all be boardrooms and courtrooms; nor will every employee be concerned with perks, power breakfasts, and tax shelters. Despite the media's fixation with wealthy white-collar managers and "thirtysomething" professionals, many workers still struggle to make it through the workday at jobs that provide them with neither status nor a decent wage. They will continue to do so in the 1990s. Little attention is paid to the terms and conditions under which they are employed. This chapter explores how a flexible common-law remedy might play a role in the struggle of these workers for dignity and fair treatment in the workplace.[1]

Consider those who staff "no-frills" assembly lines. The typical assembly line worker is presumed to be engaged in the manufacture of large durable items like automobiles or heavy industrial equipment. He (as opposed to she) is generally thought to be a white man who endures monotonous work in exchange for high wages and a middle-class life-style. He is also zealously protected from mistreatment and arbitrary discharge by his union. But assembly line work in less lucrative trades is quite common. On the no-frills assembly lines, workers may pack a different piece of candy in a box of assorted bonbons or stick an empty liquor bottle on a fast-moving conveyer belt. An apparel sweatshop where compensation is tied to production quotas is similar to a no-frills assembly line; here the workforce may consist of women, many of them Latino and Asian immigrants, directed by a white male management. On assembly lines of the no-frills kind, workers suffer through the endless tedium of their jobs without the financial rewards typically received by their white male blue-collar counterparts. Though the workplace may be covered by a collective bargaining agreement, ardent union advocacy is a mirage because the union considers itself lucky even to keep the workplace organized and worries about what the next negotiations will bring.

Not all white-collar employees are high-status executives earning large salaries. Consider the untold number of personnel who push the paper and answer the phones in the customer service, accounts receivable, or claims departments of large bureaucratic organizations like public utilities, banks, and insurance companies. Production quotas exist in this setting as well. Employees are told how many forms must be photocopied or how many complaints must be processed in an hour. Strict work rules govern everything from bathroom breaks to the removal of office supplies having a value of less than a dollar. Nonconformity is unacceptable. The bureaucratic structure that might be expected to protect the workers' interests often proves to be suffocating and inexplicable, with one department acting in complete contradiction with another and trapping the employee in the middle.

Finally, there are the large commercial laundries, retail establishments, fast-food restaurants, hotels, and casinos, where unskilled service workers experience what might be termed a "plantation" style of supervision. Harassment, sexual, racial, and otherwise, is an accepted fact of life. There are no unions or bureaucratic safeguards. Unhappy workers quit and move on. Management expects them to go and is undisturbed by their passing because they are easily replaced.

Despite affirmative action and antidiscrimination legislation, black and brown women and men and white women continue to occupy a disproportionate number of the positions in workplaces situated such as these, at the bottom of the employment ladder. Because there are few legal entitlements sheltering workers not covered by collective bargaining agreements and employment contracts, the law as reported in cases or propounded in treatises is not a very good witness to the struggles of those whose abuse slips through the cracks in the civil rights statutes.

It is commonly assumed that workplace supervision and the common law that supports it work in pretty much the same way—from the top down. The law performs both a structuring function and an ideological function in according employers wide latitude in controlling their employees. It does this through common law rules neutral on their face and pernicious in effect. The conventional wisdom, which the law reflects, holds that workplaces would not run smoothly and efficiently if employers did not have the right to fire at will (subject to a few public policy exceptions) or to inflict forms of discipline that carried an emotional "sting." The workers for their part are assumed to passively accept the natural necessity of the employers' rule, and by staying on the job agree to be so governed. The consent of the workers legitimates both the authority of the law and that of the employers.

Yet, the stories that low-status workers actually tell about their bosses, their working conditions, and their responses to both suggest that the orthodox view is at best a fantasy and at worst an outright deception. According to the workers, unfair discharges, abusive conditions, and exploitative behavior abound in the offices and on the assembly lines where they labor. For example, employees in some offices are routinely "papered" when they displease their superiors, so that there will be something in their personnel files, however minor the infraction or however long ago it happened, that will support a decision to discharge them. Workers find such behavior on the part of employers objectionable.

As a general matter, low-status minority and/or female workers are more likely to be maligned for their supposed stupidity, indolence, and rebelliousness than praised for their resilience in the face of poor pay or respected for their restraint in combating oppressive working conditions. In spite of this, many workers accept neither the negative characterization of themselves nor the presumption that they deserve supervision that is harsh and arbitrary. Furthermore, because supervisors and bosses produce all kinds of grief and worry for the workers, the workers cause a bit of trouble in return; to expect them to do otherwise is to condone their oppression.

Nonetheless, the workers' criticisms of their working conditions and their resulting oppositional behavior often create the basis for their acceptance of the prevailing hierarchy in the workplace. Their "consent" is achieved not merely through a recognition of the rightful authority of those in control, but by a complicated process that includes both more resistance on the part of the workers and more overt coercion on the part of the bosses than are usually acknowledged.

Rich accounts of the injustice and unfairness low-status female and/or minority workers experience on the job and their responses to such treatment can be found in social science literature, popular texts, and the files of legal services lawyers. The customs, practices, discourses, and values by which these women and men assess, tolerate, and resist workplace abuse have two sources. One is local to the confines of the workplace, the product of the social interaction at the particular job site or at job sites of the same kind. Evidence of this work culture is reflected in the consensus workers share about the production goals they can reasonably be expected to meet or the scrutiny an employer may appropriately use to detect improper employee conduct. The second source is broader. Those whose lives are circumscribed by racism, ethnocentricity, and sexism develop mechanisms by which they defend their persons and maintain their pride in a range of hostile situations, including the employment context. The strategies that women employ in coping with harassment on the street or that blacks use in dealing with department store security surveillance may be called into play in the workplace. The solidarity that group culture promotes off the job carries over into work life. For example, acting both as workers and as women, the secretaries at a particular job site may informally adopted strategies for collectively responding to child-care emergencies that arise during work hours.

Both work culture and minority group culture facilitate the development of critical perspectives of workplace operations and supervision that are at odds with those employers and the law espouse. The workers formulate standards of merit and achievement that prize skills that the employer will never acknowledge with praise or pay. Job descriptions and supervisory disparagement do not inhibit the development of self-esteem in workers performing what are considered the most menial tasks. The workers' appreciation of their own dedication and skill gives them a sense of dignity. Thus, a black line supervisor who was fired because he lacked verbal skills, paid too little attention to his paperwork, and coddled his supervisees was highly respected by those who worked at the plant because he had a functional understanding of plant operations and was willing to pitch in and do a share of the dirty work.

The workers' criticism can produce behavior that seems antagonistic to the interests of employers. Employees who maintain a telephone grapevine by which to alert one another of the whereabouts of the boss and jewelry factory operatives who playfully throw their employer's wares at one another are acting on their negative appraisals of their supervision and/or of their employers' product.

Unfortunately, the attempts at opposition sometimes miscarry by making working conditions more palatable for the workers while facilitating the employers' objectives. The masculine norms that working-class males invoke to elevate the status of hard manual labor over white-collar paper pushing make it easier for employers to send them into environments polluted with carcinogens or to supply them with heavy equipment they must operate in an unsafe manner. An employer may accommodate employees who resort to pilferage to compensate for low wages rather than pay them more. The employees in such a case have not gained a measure of power over the employer, though they may think that they have; in fact, they are more vulnerable because they have given their employer a justification for firing them at any time.

The critical core of work and group culture supports a redefinition of the worth of work and conduct of a seemingly oppositional nature; yet it also thereby produces in the workers a sense that they are laboring by choice. Though the values workers hold contradict those of employers, the behavior these values prompt most often fail to transform power relations or greatly affect the distribution of the proceeds of the enterprise as between workers and owners. Genuine change in the workplace very likely requires more specific, confrontational conflict in the workplace and more widespread political opposition, at the local level and beyond.

The limitations of cultural resistance, of course, are not the sole explanation for the fact that the opposition which low-status workers mount remains confined to a narrow band of options of very low visibility and limited efficacy. The material context in which such workers exist reduces their disruptive capacities.

The nature of the enterprises by which they are employed, the significance of the work they perform, the skills they bring to the job, the way in which their supervision is structured, and their overall social and economic standing function to reduce the amount of trouble those who occupy the bottom rungs of the labor force are able to generate.[2] The jobs they fill, sometimes referred to as secondary market jobs, are nonunionized positions in manufacturing, consumer services, trade, clerical work, and migrant agricultural labor. Such jobs require few skills, pay little, and provide no job security, rewards for seniority, or prospects for advancement. Workplace supervision is typically of a type known as "simple control," which places the worker at the mercy of the supervisor who unilaterally controls job assignments, wage rates, discipline, and termination decisions. Simple control gives an employer a great deal of flexibility in adjusting the size and salaries of its work force as demand changes. The workers have little choice but to adjust to the vagaries of simple control because they are dependent on their wages, are hindered in securing other employment by multiple forms of discrimination, and can easily be replaced by the vast number of unskilled and low-skilled minority and/or female workers seeking employment.

Yet the coercion that is a structural aspect of so-called secondary market jobs subject to regimes of simple control is not entirely incompatible with choice, nor does it totally stifle conflict, even on the part of the most expendable and the most exploitable employees. "Bad jobs" produce oppositional behavior which is very often functional insofar as the employer is concerned because it facilitates the workers' accommodation to poor working conditions. A certain amount of opposition is healthy for the enterprise and will be tolerated. Though "bad," the jobs may nonetheless be the best jobs the workers can find; they accordingly have an incentive to struggle to make them better. There is always the possibility that through resistance the workers will "turn the joke and slip the yoke" as it were, *i.e.*, outwit the boss and reap small gains in terms of improved working conditions.

Larger, more permanent gains depend upon there being material openings that can be exploited to increase the economic costs of worker discord and to expand the workers' bargaining power. There are some hopeful signs on the material horizon. Service sector jobs are proliferating and demographic changes suggest that employers will be looking to minority women and men and white women to fill them.[3] News reports indicate that employers are responding with increased interest in the cultural diversity of their work forces.[4] Those at the bottom of the status hierarchy should be among the beneficiaries of this newfound interest in "difference" and greater attention should be paid to their critiques about offensive supervision. But worker abuse has existed in times of low as well as in times of high unemployment, and it is unlikely that abuse will be reduced, let alone alleviated, without large-scale worker protest.

The effort to mobilize workers and to increase the impact of their local resistance will require a thoroughgoing critical ideology that supports their demands for more generous terms and conditions of employment. The workers would benefit from a manifesto that captures their sense of insult and embraces their criticism and anger in language the workers would use. The ideology should start with the workers' collective sense of when an employer or supervisor has "gone too far," "crossed the line," and "asked more of a worker than the salary she or he is paid can excuse." It should be spouted by institutions and actors at the highest level of visibility, not merely to counter the impact of the dominant ideology on low-status workers, but also to reaffirm the correctness of their local experiences of exploitation and of the need to respond with defiance.

It is in this regard that the common law might prove useful. The law, like society generally, has viewed abuse of low-status workers as normal and uneventful, negating their dignity and, on a basic level, their humanity. However, given its flexibility, the law could easily accord low-status workers the same concern for their emotional and physical well-being long provided to people higher on the social ladder. In doing this, the law might provide the occasion for capturing the tales workers have to tell about offensive working conditions and passing them down the line in a more formal, comprehensive form that retains the essence of the workers' rhetoric and consciousness. Concurrently emphasizing the material openings that suggest that the time is ripe for change would perform a service that the workers may be unable to perform for themselves. Additionally, stating the workers' demands in the form of a legal entitlement might be useful in the effort to organize the cynical and the disheartened. A lawsuit by a single discharged worker challenging abusive supervision can encourage those employees still in the job to think about their circumstances and to maneuver to improve their lot through less formal mechanisms.

Not too much can be made of the law, however. Courts are not likely to recognize rights and entitlements without the impetus provided by worker mobilization and action. Yet the quest for legal remedies often deflects the energies of grass-roots agitators and facilitates compromises among elites. Lawsuits may be of limited usefulness to workers who wish to remain on the job. Moreover, legal terminology that bears little resemblance to the language ordinary people would use in discussing a problem is of little assistance in informal mobilization. Those who are not directly privy to the process of law's creation and implementation have reason to be skeptical about its impact in reducing their subordination and economic exploitation.[5] Lawyers and worker-clients must work out an accommodation in pursuing a joint project for workplace reform that contains components of informal and formal engagement with employers. The struggle, of course, is ultimately the workers'.

The tort of intentional infliction of emotional distress or outrage is one of many that might be used to check disciplinary abuse by supervisors. Under existing law, a worker can recover only if she or he proves that the supervisor's behavior was "outrageous" and that she has suffered severe harm as a consequence. Consideration of the workers' needs, civility, and reasonable, articulated justifications for discipline are not mandated by the tort despite the psychological harm their absence may cause workers. Only the most extraordinary departures from the norm, those bordering on the absurd and the abominable, currently support a cause of action for intentional infliction of emotional distress. Threatening to fire waitresses in alphabetical order until the person responsible for a theft is discovered satisfied the requirement;[6] firing the waitresses without explanation probably would not have been actionable.

There are various ways in which the outrageousness standard could be applied to reflect the norms of work and minority group cultures to produce a more worker-centric assessment of mistreatment and harassment on the job. For example, if we were to listen to minority workers of both sexes and women workers of all colors, they might not describe the sort of shockingly crass discrimination that is covered by Title VII of the Civil Rights Act of 1964. Kinder and gentler forms of supervision that expressly avoid overt expressions of racist and sexist antagonism merely reflect subtler and more pernicious modes of bigotry. Actions that workers attribute to white supremacist thinking and the follies of patriarchy fall easily into the broad category of nonspecific capricious malevolence. In fact, employers defend themselves by admitting that they are arbitrary and mean-spirited, which is legal, whereas racial and sexual discrimination are not. The lower the status of the workers the more justifiable unexplained or harsh supervision seems. Instead of straining to categorize supervisory conduct in terms of racism and sexism, it would make sense simply to condemn it as being the illegitimate exercise of the prerogatives of superior class status and to proclaim that *no one* should be treated that way. The workers' experiences support an expansive definition of worker harassment that would cover not only those workers of color and/ or women whose abuse falls outside of the scope of existing antidiscrimination law, but also those potential white and male allies who presently have no protection whatsoever.

Worker culture incorporated into tort law would provide a basis for debunking notions that the nature of supervision may properly vary with the race, sex, age, and color of collar of the workers. Cussing out blue-collar males and tormenting them with "horseplay"; calling secretaries "girl" or "honey" and factory operatives, "animals"; and closely scrutinizing young blacks because they might be thieves can be every bit as insulting and degrading as racial epithets and sexual touching. And such conduct should be every bit as actionable. All workers are due respect and neither false nor true assumptions about their proclivities and mores in interacting with each other should justify conduct falling below the minimum accorded employees who are white or male or otherwise privileged. It follows that "ridicule, humiliation, exaggerated disparagement, orders compelling subservient behavior for its own sake, and insensitivity to the personal and social needs of workers"[7] should receive across-the-board censure by the courts.

The tort of outrage should allow for the redress of the full range of abusive conduct, racial, sexual, and otherwise, that afflicts the workers at a single job site. As the law now stands, slight variations in an overall pattern of abuse can produce different outcomes for different employees when they pursue litigation. The harassment of some, of course, assures the oppression of the many. The common plight and resulting solidarity of a work group should translate into recoveries for emotional harm that are premised on a totality of the circumstances of employer mistreatment.

In addition to providing an alternative measure of outrageousness, reliance on the cultural modes and mores of workers would change other aspects of the way in which the outrage tort is presently applied. For example, the requirement that one bringing a claim of outrage show "severe" emotional harm discriminates against those who can least afford to fall apart and those who, through extraordinary effort, maintain their sanity and stability. Therapy is not cheap. It also discriminates against workers who have the support of a strong work group. The mere fact that a worker has had to marshal her or his psychological and social resources should be sufficient proof of emotional harm. Anger, resentment, and disdain should be added to the array of emotional responses that evidence distress.

It is not uncommon for employers to justify abusive discipline by reference to the conduct of the employees. A cultural analysis might show that acts the trier of fact considers deviant are justifiable forms of resistance to oppressive supervision or approved informally agreed-upon terms and conditions of employment. Thus, it should be recognized that "abusing" bathroom and of employment. Thus, it should be recognized that "abusing" bathroom and coffee break privileges may represent a legitimate response to an employer's inflexible control of the pace of work. Similarly, black women who stand up to the supervisor and "mouth off" are neither hostile nor evil. Talking back and responding in kind can be legitimate responses to oppressive supervision.

Low-status workers have not unthinkingly acceded to their employers' demands for unfettered regulation of their behavior on the job. Despite the structural constraints of their work environments and their tenuous socio-economic positions, they criticize and resist the efforts of supervisors and bosses to manage their behavior and manipulate their senses of self-worth. The common law of the workplace could be reshaped to capture their critical perspectives and to provide workers with some support as they attempt to escalate their local attack on unacceptable working conditions. Worker-centered causes of action would cut across racial, ethnic, and gender lines to condemn employer harassment that is now justified on the basis of class privilege and become a rallying point for a wide range of workers. If disseminated on a broad scale, the legal ideology has the potential for being a useful tool for organizing bottom-up justice in the workplaces of low-status workers of all colors and both genders.

NOTES

1. Extensive references and documentation supporting this chapter are set out in Regina Austin, "Employer Abuse, Worker Resistance, and the Tort of Intentional Infliction of Emotional Distress," 41 *Stanford Law Review* 1 (1988).
2. *See generally*, R. Edwards, *Contested Terrain* (New York: Basic Books, 1979); D. Gordon, R. Edwards, and M. Reich, *Segmented Work, Divided Workers* (Cambridge: Cambridge University Press, 1982).
3. Current predictions of future workforce trends envision a slower increase in the numbers joining the labor pool than at any time since the 1930s. As a result, a shortage of workers is anticipated. White males are expected to constitute as little as 15 percent of the net additions to the workforce. Thus, employers will be forced to recruit and retain women and/or minorities to satisfy their personnel demands. To do so, employers will be required to take affirmative steps to attract these workers. *See generally*, the Hudson Institute, *Opportunity 2000: Creative Affirmative Action Strategies for a Changing Workforce* (prepared for the Employment Standards Administration, U.S. Department of Labor, September 1988); R. Kutscher, "Overview and Im-

plication of the Projections to 2000," *Monthly Labor Review*, September 1897, pp. 3, 6, 89; G. Silvestri and J. Lukasiewicz, "A Look at Employment Trends to the Year 2000," *Monthly Labor Review*, September 1987, pp. 46, 59.

4. *See* Solomon, "Firms Address Workers' Cultural Variety," *Wall Street Journal*, February 10, 1989.

5. *See* G. Lopez, "The Work We Know So Little About," 42 *Stanford Law Review* 1, 8–9 (1989).

6. Agis v. Howard Johnson Co., 371 Mass. 140, 355 N.E.2d 315 (1976).

7. *Id*.

17 MORTON J. HORWITZ

THE DOCTRINE OF OBJECTIVE CAUSATION

WHEN the first-year law student is taught to distinguish sharply between "actual" or "but for" causation and "proximate" or "legal" cause, the student is learning a system that did not crystallize until the 1920s. Before the successful attack of Legal Realism on the objectivity of causation, judges and lawyers thought in terms only of "actual" causes, of "chains of causation," which could be "broken" by "intervening" or "supervening" events. This historical essay is about how this paradigm of objective causation came into being and was challenged during the late nineteenth century.

THE EARLY CONCEPTUALIZATION AND CHALLENGE

At the conceptual center of all late-nineteenth-century efforts to construct a system of private law free from the dangers of redistribution was the idea of objective causation. In tort law especially, where the dangers of social engineering had long been feared, the idea of objective causation played a central role in preventing the infusion of "politics" into law.

If tort law was to be private law, legal thinkers reasoned, its central legitimating function had to be corrective justice, the restoration of the status quo that existed before any infringement of a person's right. The plaintiff in a tort action should recover only because of an unlawful interference with his right, not because of any more general public goals of the state.

The idea of vindication of individual rights was intimately connected with the notion of objective causation. Only if it was possible to say objectively that A caused B's injury would courts be able to take money from A and give damages to B without being charged with redistribution. Without objective causation a court might be free to choose among a variety of possible defendants in order to vindicate the plaintiff's claim. If the question of which of several acts "caused" the plaintiff's injury was open to judicial discretion, how could private law stay clear of the dangers of the political uses of law for purposes of redistribution?

There were two basic metaphors used by legal thinkers to express the idea of objective causation. The first was the notion of there being a distinction between "proximate" cause and "remote" cause. The idea had worked its way into the common law from Lord Bacon's *Maxims of the Law*, the first of which was: "In law, look to proximate, not remote, causes." The second, related notion, taken over from the natural sciences, was that there were objective "chains of causation" from which judges could scientifically determine which acts, in a complicated series of events, really "caused" the plaintiff's injury. A number of related legal doctrines also sought to classify situations in which separate acts constituted "intervening" or "supervening" causes sufficient to break the "chain" and hold another defendant liable. But, above all, it was necessary to find a single "scientific" cause and thus a single responsible defendant, for any acknowledgment of multiple causation would open the floodgates of judicial discretion.

The earliest attacks on this system of causation can be traced back to the 1870s and to efforts of young American philosophers to counter a growing movement in America toward philosophical idealism.

Along with his fellow members of the informal Metaphysical Club, Oliver Wendell Holmes, Jr., "had come very early to share their deep distrust and antagonism to the a priori categories of Kant and the conceptual dialectic of Hegel. A philosophy of law, an analysis of legal history, which was built on Kantian or Hegelian foundations must be repudiated and cast aside."[1] Together with future Harvard philosophers William James and Chauncey Wright, Holmes shared membership in the Metaphysical Club with a young instructor at Harvard Law School named Nicholas St. John Green.

In the midst of his Metaphysical Club speculations in 1870, Green published an article in the recently established *American Law Review* on "Proximate and Remote Cause," which, so far as I know, was by far the earliest direct challenge to orthodox legal notions of objective causation, and was not to be repeated for another fifty years. Green disputed the fundamental Baconian maxim that the law could objectively distinguish between "proximate" and "remote" causes in order to assign legal liability in a nondiscretionary manner. "The phrase 'chain of causation,' . . . embodies a dangerous metaphor," wrote Green.

> It raises in the mind an idea of one determinate cause, followed by another determinate cause, created by the second, and so on, one succeeding another till the effect is reached. The causes are pictured as following one upon the other in time, as the links of a chain follow one upon the other

in space. There is nothing in nature which corresponds to this. Such an idea is a pure fabrication of the mind.

There is no single objective "proximate" cause, Green argued. "To every event there are certain antecedents. . . . It is not any one of this set of antecedents taken by itself which is the cause. No one by itself would produce the effect. The true cause is the whole set of antecedents taken together."

In a passage typical of those that have led historians to see the roots of pragmatism and skepticism in these early speculations of the Metaphysical Club, Green declared: "When the law has to do with abstract theological belief, it will be time to speculate as to what abstract mystery then may be in causation; but as long as its concern is confined to practical matters it is useless to inquire for mysteries which exist in no other sense than the sense in which every thing is a mystery."[2] "When a court says this damage is remote, it does not flow naturally, it is not proximate," he wrote four years later, "all they mean, and all they can mean, is, that under all the circumstances they think the plaintiff should not recover. They did not arrive at that conclusion themselves by reasoning with those phrases, and by making use of them in their discussion they do not render that decision clear to others."[3]

It is important to note nevertheless that Green did not dispute the possibilities of objective causation in the physical sciences, where "there is a search for what may with some propriety, perhaps, be called proximate cause." In the sciences, he conceded, it was possible to use causation as "not an absolute but a relative term," signifying "the nearest known cause considered in relation to the effect, and, in contrast to some more distant cause."

Green surveyed the uses of causation in various fields of law to demonstrate how courts manipulated the terms "proximate" and "remote" to accomplish other purposes. In contract cases, courts employed these terms to determine what damages might "reasonably be supposed to have been contemplated by the parties." In negligence cases, "misconduct is called the proximate cause of those results which a prudent foresight might have avoided." But above all, there is "no settled rule" in tort because the determination of causation "often varies in proportion to the misconduct, recklessness or wantonness of the defendant."[4] In law, moral conceptions constantly intruded upon scientific ones.

Green thus not only anticipated Holmes's famous "prediction theory" of law. He also previewed[5] what a half-century later would be the most powerful argument of the legal realists against the continued insistence of legal orthodoxy on the objective character of causation in law: that because judges and jurists inevitably imported moral ideas into their determinations of legal causation, they were making discretionary "policy" determinations under the guise of doing science.

There are many reasons why the later legal realists' critique of causation doctrine largely succeeded while Green's challenge seems to have been ignored.[6] In the realm of ideas, however, one important difference between the two periods stands out. While Green was prepared to concede that the notion of objective causation "may with some propriety" be used in the physical sciences, his legal realist successors were to witness an internal challenge to causation in the natural sciences themselves. Without its pretensions to scientific foundations, legal conceptions of objective causation became increasingly vulnerable.

THE POLITICS OF CAUSATION: ENTREPRENEURIAL LIABILITY AND ECONOMIC GROWTH

The underlying political issues in the controversy over legal causation were directly confronted in 1874, four years after Green wrote, by the orthodox treatise writer Francis Wharton. The recent appearance of John Stuart Mill's *Autobiography*, Wharton wrote, had "revived . . . the controversy on causation" originally stirred up by the publication of Mill's *Logic* (1843).[7] "The doctrine advocated by . . . Mill that the cause of an event is the sum of all its antecedents," Wharton argued, was "irreconcilable with the principles of Roman and of Anglo-American law." Besides, he maintained, the inevitable result of a doctrine of multiple causation was "communism."

Wharton's major argument was that the theory of causation was different in law than it was in the natural sciences. "[P]hysicists who treat all antecedents as causes, and who can only judge of material forces, can afford no aid to jurisprudence when it undertakes to distinguish those conditions of which are material, and therefore merely consecutive, from those which are moral and causal." Given the fact that the scientific definition of causation "has not, with rare exceptions, been considered, by Anglo-American courts, to call even for discussion, this shows that so far as concerns practical life, the materialists' view of causation has no ground on which to stand."

Thus far, it should be noticed, Wharton's main strategy was simply to dissociate legal causation from scientific causation. There was not yet an attempt to argue that the claims of legal "science" can or should be grounded on those of the natural sciences. For Wharton, the distinctively legal emphasis on "moral" causation was connected with the search for a "free agency" among the multiple antecedent causes. By the "levelling of all antecedents to the same parity," by failing both to "distinguish . . . between physical and moral forces" and to "require . . . that physical forces be directed in conformity with moral law," Mill was "denying man's moral primacy over and responsibility for nature. . . ."

The result was "the practical communism which this theory of the causal character of all antecedents promotes."

> Here is a capitalist among these antecedents; he shall be forced to pay. The capitalist, therefore, becomes liable for all the disasters of which he is in any sense the condition, and the fact that he is thus held liable, multiplies these disasters. Men become prudent and diligent by the consciousness that they will be made to suffer if they are not prudent and diligent. If they know that they will not be made to suffer for their neglects; if they know that though the true cause of a disaster, they will be passed over in order to reach the capitalist who is a remoter condition, then they will cease to be prudent. . . . No factory would be built. . . . Making the capitalist liable for everything, therefore, would end in making the capitalist, as well as the non-capitalist, liable for nothing; for there would be soon no capitalist to be found to be sued.[8]

One will be startled at the seemingly sudden leap that Wharton makes from the technical question of legal causation to his warnings of destruction of capitalism only if he or she fails to understand the systemic character of legal thought in the later nineteenth century.

Mill himself had attacked the existing doctrine of objective causation because it was associated with German idealist metaphysics, which he later noted was, "in these times, the great intellectual support of false doctrines and bad institutions. . . . There never was such an instrument devised for consecrating all deep-seated prejudices. And the chief strength of this false philosophy in morals, politics, and religion, lies in the appeal which it is accustomed to make to the evidence of mathematics and of the cognate branches of physical science."[9]

Wharton's defense of objective causation and his insistence on a single responsible legal cause were repeated by all late-nineteenth-century treatise writers. For Wharton's generation the ideas of "moral" causation and of "free agency" were still regarded as intelligible and objective a priori categories. That Nicholas St. John Green alone could argue that the confusion of scientific and moral notions was precisely what made legal doctrines about causation unintelligible is evidence of his premature skepticism. In the 1870s few were yet prepared to agree that the infusion of moralism into law made it political. Indeed, it was the "amoral" that Wharton identified with communism. By the end of the nineteenth century, however, orthodox legal thinkers would begin to downplay the "moral" element in causation while emphasizing the scientific basis of objective causation in law. But as they thereby implicitly conceded their own growing skepticism about the objectivity of moral categories, they laid themselves open for the final assault on causation by the legal realist heirs of Nicholas Green, who would now not only show the illicit moralism of legal causation but also the collapse of causation in the natural sciences as well.[10]

There were few occasions before the twentieth century when the political problems underlying the question of objective causation burst forth with the clarity of a Green or a Wharton. By and large, orthodox judges and jurists continued to invoke the metaphors of "chains of causation" and "natural and probable consequences" as if these were concepts capable of objective determination.

But the skepticism of Green found another channel: the prediction theory of law articulated by Oliver Wendell Holmes. There are two separate elements in Holmes's theory. The first, expressed by his famous aphorism from "The Path of the Law" (1897), is that "the prophecies of what courts will do in fact, and nothing more pretentious, are what I mean by the law." Indeed, as early as in his Harvard University lectures of 1871–1872, Holmes first expressed a similar idea virtually contemporaneously with Green's, which does suggest a reciprocal influence between Green and Holmes. Above all, Holmes's emphasis on the probabilistic nature of prediction was an effort to deny the claims of the legal system to logical or "mathematical" certainty.[11]

But there was another similar but far more practically significant shift to a prediction theory in Holmes's thought: his emphasis on foresight in the law of torts. Not only is Green's influence quite clear but, as we shall see, the function of foresight in both Green and Holmes was to avoid the problems inherent in any claims to objectivity in legal cause.

A shift to "foresight" as a substitute for "natural sequence" had begun to appear in the case law of the 1860s. By the early 1870s, there were already "two views," Wharton noted, concerning liability for negligence.

> The first view is that a person is liable for all the consequences which flow in ordinary natural sequences from his negligence; the second, that he is liable for all the consequences that could be foreseen as likely to occur.[12]

Wharton opposed the foreseeability view and insisted on "ordinary natural sequence" as the basis for determining causation and hence liability. "If the consequence flows from any particular negligence according to ordinary natural sequence, without the intervention of any independent human agency, then such consequence, whether foreseen as probable or unforeseen, is imputable to the negligence."[13]

More than any other writer, Wharton was responsible for clearly formulating the orthodox view of objective causation that would continue to dominate late-nineteenth-century legal thought. Only a half-century later would legal critics derisively refer to this formula as "negligence in the air."[14]

By that time, the idea of negligence as "relational" concept had completely triumphed, and the notion of objective causation had begun to disintegrate. While he himself was something of a transitional figure with respect to the moralistic foundations of negligence, Wharton basically continued to draw on the earlier notion that it was simply just to hold an immoral actor liable for the proximate consequences of his act.

For the late nineteenth century, one judicial decision stood out as a radical rejection of the idea of objective causation; and every treatise writer, including Wharton, was forced to take a stand on its merits. In *Ryan v. New York Central Railroad* (1866),[15] the New York Court of Appeals had held that a railroad that negligently caused a fire was liable only to the owner of an adjacent house and not to subsequent owners whose houses were destroyed in the path of the spreading fire.

The court had employed traditional language in rejecting the claim of the second house owner. Only the destruction of the first house was the "proximate" result of the railroad's negligence; all of the remaining injuries were "remote," the court declared. Yet, even the use of traditional language offered little comfort to believers in the nondiscretionary and self-executing character of the orthodox categories. The result, limiting liability to the first house, seemed contrary to any common sense understanding of the difference between proximate and remote consequences. And even more importantly, the court spent far more time explaining why any other result "would . . . create a liability which would be the destruction of all civilized society."[16]

The New York court, Judge Thomas Cooley contemptuously noted, was "apparently . . . more influenced in their decision by the fact that the opposite doctrine 'would subject to a liability against which no prudence would guard, and to meet which no private fortune would be adequate,' than by a strict regard to the logic of cause and effect."[17]

The decision in *Ryan* is one of many in the period after 1840 limiting the liability of the agents of economic growth, especially the railroad. Yet, the typical judicial strategies for extending entrepreneurial immunity had rarely dealt so cynically with the idea of causation. While virtually all judges and jurists of the nineteenth century had also promoted doctrines limiting entrepreneurial liability, the *Ryan* decision nevertheless remained an outcast through the entire period.[18]

The explanation gives us some insight into the relative autonomy of legal ideas. The conception of objective causation was too central to the legitimation of the entire system of private law for it to be abandoned even in the interest of erecting another barrier to entrepreneurial liability. Many judges, to be sure, manipulated the proximate-remote distinction in other cases to limit entrepreneurial liability, but few did so as brazenly as *Ryan*, threatening to bring the entire intellectual system into disrepute.

Wharton seems to have come closer than any treatise writer to defending the *Ryan* decision. While never explicitly endorsing it, he did cite it as illustrative of the slightly different orthodox principle that the intervention of an "independent responsible human agency" relieves a negligent defendant from liability. "If a house is properly built, if it is properly watched, if a proper fire apparatus is in operation, it can be prevented, when a fire approaches from a neighboring detached house, from catching the fire."[19] From this Wharton seems to have concluded that the owner of the second house was, in effect, contributorily negligent and thus produced a break in the chain of causation. But unlike the court in *Ryan*, even Wharton recognized a Michigan court's assertion that without an intervening cause, "the principle of justice, or sound logic . . . is very obscure, which can exempt the party through whose negligence the first building was burned from equal liability for the burning of the second."[20]

Wharton thus sought to absorb the *Ryan* case into his own orthodox paradigm of objective causation. Indeed, he devoted considerable energies to demonstrating the terrible consequences of failing to relieve entrepreneurs of liability when an "intervening cause" broke the negligent "chain of causation."

"Whether a railroad company is to be liable for all fires of which its locomotives are the occasion," he wrote, "is a question so important to the industrial interests of the land. . . ." Unless abutting landowners are "held to be personally responsible for the consequences of placing combustible materials by the side of a railroad," the "noncapitalists" will be "skipped over" and "the rich corporation" will be "attacked."

> Capital, by this process is either destroyed, or is compelled to shrink from entering into those large operations by which the trade of a nation is built up. We are accustomed to look with apathy at the ruin of great corporations, and to say, "well, enough, they have no souls, they can bear it without pain, for they have nothing in them by which pain can be felt." But no corporation can be ruined without bringing ruin to some of the noblest and most meritorious classes of the land. Those who first give the start to such corporations are men of bold and enterprising qualities, kindled, no doubt, in part by self-interest, but in part also by the delight which men of such type feel in generous schemes for the development of public resources, and the extension to new fields of the wealth and industry of the community. Those who come in, in the second place, to lend their means to such enterprises after these enterprises appear to be reliable objects of investment, are the "bloated bond-holders," consisting of professional

men of small incomes, and widows and orphans whose support is dependent on the income they draw from modest means left to them by their friends. Nor is it these alone who are impoverished by the destruction of the corporations of which I here speak. The corporation may itself be soulless, and those investing in it may deserve little sympathy, but those whom it employs are the bone and sinew of the land. There is no railroad, no manufacturing company that does not spend three-fourths of its income in the employment of labor. When the corporation's income ceases, then the laborer is dismissed. We hear sometimes of the landlord's caprice. But there are no evictions which approach in vastness and bitterness to those which are caused by the stoppage of railway improvements or of manufacturing corporations; in few cases is there such misery to the laboring classes worked, as when one of these great institutions is closed. I think I may, therefore, safely say that the question before us relates eminently to the industrial interests.[21]

It was the doctrine of independent, intervening causes on which Wharton staked his entire hopes for limiting entrepreneurial liability within the orthodox paradigm of objective causation. And it was here that the emerging doctrine of foreseeability seemed to him to pose the greatest danger. "The consequence" of any foreseeability test, Wharton wrote, "would be that the capitalist would be obliged to bear the burden, not merely of his own want of caution, but of the want of caution of all who should be concerned on whatever he should produce." If courts could argue that even intervening causes of an injury were foreseeable, the result "would be traced back until a capitalist is reached. . . . If this law be good, no man of means could safely build a steam engine, or even a house."[22]

But whether or not the choice between "natural sequence" and "foreseeability" tests had, in fact, any real effect on aggregate levels of liability, it is clear that any formulation of causation in terms of foresight presented major dangers.

We have already seen that Wharton regarded the "natural sequence" idea as a major intellectual barrier against multiple causation, which he identified as leading to "communism." But Wharton also saw an entirely different threat emanating from any reliance on a foreseeability test: the potential of redistribution through a theory of strict liability.

There existed

certain necessary though dangerous trades, of which we can say statistically that in them will be sacrificed prematurely the lives not merely of those who voluntarily engage in them, but of third persons not so assenting. Yet in such cases (e.g., gas factories and railroads), we do not hold that liability for such injuries attaches to those who start the enterprise foreseeing these consequences.[23]

In a statistical world, Wharton saw, any foreseeability test would lead to the conclusion that all risks were predictable in the aggregate. Indeed, though he was not alarmed at the prospect, Green saw similar results from a shift to a prediction theory and noted that "[w]ith events of this kind underwriters deal."[24]

In a world of randomness, where there is no necessary connection between particular causes and effects, all we can hope to do is to statistically correlate acts and consequences in the aggregate. Wharton's individualistic notions of "moral causation" and "free agency" had begun to yield to a world of probabilities and statistical correlations.

When, in 1897, Holmes declared that in law "the man of the future is the man of statistics, and the master of economics,"[25] he already clearly understood the implications that flowed from the radical change in the conception of responsibility that a prediction theory entailed.

Earlier, in *The Common Law* (1881), Holmes had opposed turning the state into "a mutual insurance company against accidents" that would "distribute the burden of its citizens' mishaps among all its members." Not only was "state interference . . . an evil, where it cannot be shown to be a good"; more importantly, "the undertaking to redistribute losses simply on the ground that they resulted from the defendant's act" would "affront the sense of justice," since it was based on "the coarse and impolitic principle that a man acts always at his peril."[26]

Now, however, he recognized both the pressure of organized labor for workmen's compensation laws and "the inclination of a very large part of the community . . . to make certain classes of persons insure the safety of those with whom they deal." For Holmes, the issue of strict liability versus negligence had become, by the turn of the century, simply "a concealed, half conscious battle on the question of legislative policy," which could not "be settled deductively." Most injuries

with which our courts are kept busy today are mainly incidents of certain well-known businesses. They are injuries to person or property by railroads, factories, and the like. The liability for them is estimated, and sooner or later goes into the price paid by the public. The public really pays the damages, and the question of liability, if pressed far enough, is really the question how far it is desirable that the public should insure the safety of those whose work it uses.[27]

Without objective causation, the problem of assigning liability had become simply a question of the fairness of the distribution of risks, "a concealed half-conscious battle on the question of legislative policy." Liability for injury had become just another cost of doing business, which could be "estimated," insured against, and ultimately included in "the price paid by the public." The individualistic world of Wharton's "moral causation" and "free agency" had begun to be transformed into a world of liability insurance in which the "legislative" question of who should pay would ultimately undermine the self-contained, individualistic categories of private law.

NOTES

1. Mark DeWolfe Howe, *Justice Oliver Wendell Holmes: The Proving Years* (Cambridge, Mass.: Belknap Press, 1957), p. 151.
2. Nicholas St. John Green, "Proximate and Remote Cause," 4 *American Law Review* 201 (1870). Reprinted in *Essays and Notes on the Law of Tort and Crimes* (Menasha, Wis.: G. Banta, 1933).
3. Book Review in 8 *American Law Review* 508; *Essays*, p. 82.
4. Green, *supra* note 2, at 213–15.
5. Jerome Frank edited an edition of Green's writings, *Essays and Notes on the Law of Tort and Crimes*, *supra* note 2.
6. Though we may pay tribute to Green's prescience and originality, his direct influence on legal doctrine seems to have been nonexistent. If we are to find Green's influence, we must trace it through a more indirect process by which a number of his perceptions were taken up by others and gradually accumulated into a critical whole. Brilliant and original as Green was, if he is to be allowed any measure of immortality, it must be either specifically, through his effect on Holmes, or more generally, because of his contributions to the development of pragmatism.
7. John Stuart Mill's challenge to orthodox ideas of causation was first presented in his *System of Logic* (1843), bk. 6, chap. 11, and his *Examination of Sir William Hamilton's Philosophy* (1865). Mill's ideas on causation came to Wharton's attention through Rowland G. Hazard's *Letters on Causation and Freedom in Willing* (London: Longmans, 1869), which contests Mill's ideas. *See* Francis Wharton, *A Treatise on the Law of Negligence*, 2d ed. (Philadelphia: Kay, 1878), p. 137, n. 1. The issue was apparently revived for Wharton by the posthumous publication of Mill's *Autobiography* (1873). The significance of Mill's epistemology for American philosophy is discussed in Bruce Kuklick's *The Rise of American Philosophy: Cambridge, Mass., 1860–1930* (New Haven, Conn.: Yale University Press, 1977), pp. 16–21. Just as Wharton's *Treatise on the Law of Negligence* (Philadelphia: Kay

& Brother, 1874) was about to be published, he wrote a separate pamphlet, *A Suggestion as to Causation* (Cambridge, Mass.: Riverside Press, 1874), which he intended as an appendix to his *Treatise*. In addition to his *Treatise*, his ideas on causation are elaborated in "Remote and Proximate Fires," 1 *Southern Law Review* (n.s.) 729 (1875).

8. Wharton, *A Suggestion as to Causation, supra* note 7, p. 11.
9. John Stuart Mill, *Autobiography* (Indianapolis: Liberal Arts Press, 1957), p. 145.
10. We may consider Judge Benjamin Cardozo's famous 1928 decision in the *Palsgraf* case as the culmination of Legal Realist attacks on the objectivity of causation. I hope, on another occasion, to spell this out. You should refer to G. Edward White's excellent discussion of *Palsgraf* in *Tort Law in America: An Intellectual History* (New York: Oxford University Press, 1980), pp. 92–102.

It is important to see that the collapse of causation in the natural sciences was occurring at virtually the same time as *Palsgraf* was decided.

When Friedrich Waissman lectured at Oxford University on the subject "The Decline and Fall of Causality," he pinpointed 1927 as the year that "saw the obsequies" of causality in contemporary science. The death-blow, for Waissman, came with Heisenberg's enunciation of the uncertainty principle in 1927.

See William A. Wallace, *Causality and Scientific Explanation* (Ann Arbor: University of Michigan Press, 1972), 2: 163.

Moving beyond the natural sciences, Thomas L. Haskell, in *The Emergence of Professional Social Science* (Urbana, Ill.: University of Illinois Press, 1977), points to a general decline of causal analysis in American social thought beginning around the turn of the century. The attack on formalism, he argues, was, at bottom, an attack on causation by a new generation of thinkers who "from their concrete social experience in an urbanizing, industrializing society" understood the world as radically more interdependent. "Where all is *inter*dependent," Haskell writes, "there can be no *in*dependent variables. To insist on the interconnectedness of social phenomena in time and in social space is to insist on the improbability of autonomous action" (p. 13). Haskell continues (p. 40):

Things near at hand that had once seemed autonomous and therefore suitable for causal attribution were now seen as reflexes of more remote causes. Those factors in one's immediate environment that had always been regarded as self-exacting, spontaneous entities—causes: things in which explanations can be rooted—now began to be seen as merely the final links in long chains of causality that stretched off into murky distance. One's familiar institutions were drained of causal potency and made to appear merely secondary and proximate in their influence on one's life.

In law, the contemporary distinction between "actual" and "legal" cause emerged under these influences.

11. Max Frisch, "Justice Holmes, The Prediction Theory of Law, and Pragmatism," 39 *Journal of Philosophy* 85 (1942); Howe, *supra* note 1, pp. 74–76; Kuklick, *supra* note 7, pp. 48–50.

12. Wharton, *Treatise on the Law of Negligence, supra* note 7, p. 112.

13. *Id.* at 63.

14. Cardozo quoting Pollock, *Torts* in Palsgraf v. Long Island Rail Road, 248 N.Y. 339 (1928): "Proof of negligence in the air, so to speak, will not do."

15. 35 N.Y. 210 (1866).

16. 35 N.Y., at 217.

17. Thomas M. Cooley, *A Treatise on the Law of Torts* (Chicago: Callaghan & Co., 1906), 1: 116–17.

18. The decision was rejected in England and most American states. Cooley, *supra* note 17, pp. 117–18. Only in New York and Pennsylvania, Pennsylvania Rail Road v Kerr, 62 Penn. St. 353 (1869), adopted the *Ryan* rule. Even in New York, the case was "limited and explained away" by subsequent cases: Thomas G. Shearman and Amasa A. Redfield, *A Treatise on the Law of Negligence*, 4th ed. (New York: Baker, Voorhis, 1888), p. 32, n. 4; Cooley, *supra* note 17, at 117, n. 13, and "the weight of this case as a precedent was somewhat diminished" by subsequent Pennsylvania decisions as well. *Id.* at 117–18, n. 14.

19. Wharton, *supra* note 7, p. 125.

20. *Id.* at 135, quoting Judge Christiancy in Hoyt v. Jeffers, 30 Mich. 181 (1874).

21. "Liability of Railroad Companies for Remote Fires," 1 *Southern Law Review* (n.s.) 729 (1875).

22. Wharton, *supra* note 7, pp. 114–15.

23. *Id.* at 63.

24. Green, *supra* note 2, at 215.

25. Oliver Wendell Holmes, "The Path of the Law," in *Collected Legal Papers* (New York: Harcourt, Brace & Howe, 1920), p. 187.

26. Oliver Wendell Holmes, *The Common Law* (Boston: Little, Brown, 1963), pp. 77–78, 124.

27. Holmes, *supra* note 25, pp. 182–83.

18 JAY M. FEINMAN AND PETER GABEL

CONTRACT LAW AS IDEOLOGY

IN 1915 the United States Supreme Court struck down a Kansas statute that prevented employers from requiring their employees to quit or refrain from joining unions because the statute interfered with the "freedom of contract" protected by the Fourteenth Amendment to the Constitution.[1] In *Coppage* v. *Kansas* the Court said:

> The principle is fundamental and vital. Included in the right of personal liberty and the right of private property—partaking of the nature of each— is the right to make contracts. . . . The right is as essential to the laborer as to the capitalist, to the poor as to the rich . . .[2]

The right of freedom of contract expressed in this opinion conveys a sense of personal autonomy, projecting a free market in which laborer and capitalist, rich and poor can freely transact to get what they want, unfettered by the needs of others or the dictates of government. At the same time, the image also conveys a sense of social solidarity, suggesting that the market is an arena of mutual respect in which people can hammer out their collective destiny through firm handshakes enforceable in a court of law.

The view of contract in *Coppage* v. *Kansas* is now generally regarded as incomplete. Under modern contract law, "society may restrict the individual's freedom to contract. . . . At the very least, the state may strive to ensure that [people making contracts] do in fact bargain in acceptable ways and are not so powerful as to substitute coercion for bargain."[3] The principle of personal autonomy underlying freedom of contract has been supplemented by modern principles of cooperation and fairness to ameliorate the harshest aspects of market exchanges. The modern image of contract conveys a new

This is a revision by Jay Feinman of the essay that Peter Gabel and Jay Feinman wrote for the first edition of this book.

sense of autonomy and solidarity, in which people are both free to act and protected from the most harmful consequences of their actions and the actions of others.

Social images like these are not restricted to contract law. When Ronald Reagan promised to "lift government off of the backs of the people," he presented a utopian image much like the traditional image of freedom of contract. The image signified that it had only been "government" that had been preventing us from realizing our personal desires, and that now we could once again stand as free and equal individuals, ready to take whatever action serves our respective self-interests. Now George Bush calls for a "kinder, gentler America," in which the altruism of volunteers will provide "a thousand points of light" that will restore a sense of community purpose and serve the needs of the underprivileged. Like the modern image of contract, this vision presents a way of achieving both autonomy and community.

Traditional freedom of contract and modern contract law, like the politics of Reagan and Bush, express elements of people's authentic yearning for personal autonomy and social solidarity. However, the images also mask the extent to which the social order makes it difficult to achieve true autonomy and solidarity. The truth is that we live within social and economic hierarchies that often leave us feeling powerless, alienated from one another, and locked into the routines of everyday activities so that it is difficult to achieve increased personal power and freedom and genuine social connection and equality. And the truth also is that this impoverishment of our human possibilities can be overcome not by the implementation of an abstract legal principle or a political slogan but only by our own sustained efforts to transform these hierarchies, to take control over the whole of our lives, and to shape them toward the satisfaction of our real human needs. This sort of concrete, practical movement would embody the realization of the utopian content of images like these. However, the law denies the oppressive nature of the existing hierarchies, suggests instead that inequality, powerlessness, and alienation are consequences of what people have chosen through their own actions, and therefore retards the achievement of the utopian ideals.

The law is one of many vehicles for the development and transmission of ideological imagery. In order to understand the historical and present nature of the legal system, and of contract law as a part of this system, one must grasp the relationship between the utopian images transmitted through legal ideas and the socioeconomic context with which the images have been associated. This essay provides a brief introduction to a method for understanding this ideological power of law by tracing the history of contract law over the last two hundred years.

CONTRACT LAW IN THE EIGHTEENTH CENTURY

Eighteenth-century contract law would be barely recognizable to the modern lawyer. The core of eighteenth-century contract law was not the enforcement of private agreements but the implementation of customary practices and traditional norms. Indeed, in his *Commentaries on the Law of England,* written in the 1760s, Sir William Blackstone did not consider contracts to be a separate body of law at all.

In part, contracts was that portion of the law of property concerning the transfer of title to specific things from one person to another—the process by which "my horse" became "your horse." Because of this present-oriented title theory, legal enforcement of an executory agreement (an agreement under which the parties promised to render their performances at some time in the future) was not generally available. Contract law also concerned customary obligations between people related to status, occupation, or social responsibilities. For example, a patient was "contractually" obligated by custom to pay for a physician's services whether or not he actually had promised to pay prior to the rendering of the services. In all types of contracts cases, the substantive fairness of the agreement or relation was subject to scrutiny by a lay jury applying community standards of justice. If a physician sued for his fee or a seller of goods for her price, the jury could decide that even an amount agreed to by the parties was excessive and inequitable, and so award a smaller sum instead.[4]

Thus, eighteenth-century contract law did not encourage commercial exchange. The traditional image of the world presented by contract law regarded the enforcement of market transactions as often illegitimate, so a seller could never be guaranteed the price he or she had bargained for, and liability might be imposed in the absence of agreement when required by popular notions of fairness. Such a system could exist because the development of a system of production founded upon universal competition in national and world markets had not yet fully emerged, and the political worldview that justified the relatively static property relations of traditional, precapitalist society had not yet been entirely overturned.

Between the latter part of the eighteenth century and the middle of the nineteenth century, the economic and political relations that had been associated with eighteenth-century contract law were burst asunder. In this period the system of economic and social relations known as free-market capitalism achieved a full development begun several centuries earlier, and the political climate was explosively transformed in the service of those social and economic developments with the aid of violent revolutions in America and Western Europe. These changes dramatically transformed the life situations of people in Western society and brought about an equally dramatic transformation in contract law.

CONTRACT LAW IN THE NINETEENTH CENTURY

In the nineteenth century, the key changes in society were its split into capital-owning and nonowning classes, and the dissolution of traditional patterns of social relations. As to the first, the social and economic positions of those who owned capital in the form of land, money, and machinery, and those who, having been thrown off the land or out of their traditional crafts, owned only their minds and bodies, increasingly diverged. Business owners were driven irrespective of their personal will or greed to compete with one another for markets for their products and to extract, with the assistance of a developing mechanical technology, the greatest possible production from their workers at the lowest possible cost. Workers were forced to sell their labor power to owners for a wage in order to survive and thereby to subject much of their daily lives to the owners' control; at the same time, competition among them often drove wages down to bare survival levels.

The second great change in society was the dissolution of many of the traditional bonds among people that had characterized the social relations of earlier periods. The social meaning of work, property, and community were increasingly fragmented as socioeconomic processes that were characterized by competition and individual self-interest reorganized the social universe. Traditional social environments had hardly been idyllic and certainly embodied forms of alienation and class domination that ought not to be idealized. But the rise of capitalism—with its universal market in which people and things were everywhere made subject to the exigencies of money exchange—and the transformation of traditional society—a profound disruption of people's everyday experience in their homes, work, and social life—generated a dramatic and dislocating social upheaval. Within a short stretch of historical time, people experienced and were forced to adapt to the appearance of the factory and the slum, the rise of the industrial city, and a violent rupture of group life and feeling that crushed traditional forms of moral and community identity. While part of this transformation was an attempt to overturn the repressive aspects of a traditional, hierarchical society, it also created that blend of aggression, paranoia, and profound emotional isolation and anguish that is known romantically as the rugged individual.

How could people have been persuaded or forced to accept such massive disruptions in their lives? One vehicle of persuasion was the law of contracts, which generated a new ideological imagery that sought to give legitimacy to the new order. Contract law was one of many such forms of imagery in law, politics, religion, and other representations of social experience that concealed and denied the oppressive and alienating aspects of the new social and economic relations. Contract law denied the nature of the system by creating an imagery that made the oppression and alienation appear to be the consequences of what the people themselves desired.

Denial and legitimation were accomplished by representing reality in ideal terms, as if things were the way they were because the people wished them to be so.[5] This representation was not the product of conspiratorial manipulation by power-mad lawyers and judges. Instead, the legal elites tended to identify with the structure of the social and economic order because of what they perceived to be their privileged position within it, and they expressed the legitimacy of that structure when arguing and deciding cases in their professional roles. During this period important members of the bench and bar associated themselves emotionally and intellectually with the new socioeconomic order and expressed in their professional activities the essential nature of the new system. In arguing and deciding cases, they fit the situation presented within that system to resolve the conflict represented by the dispute at issue. Those resolutions tended to legitimate the basic social relations, no matter how unjust, oppressive, and alienating they actually were. In the process of resolving many cases, legal concepts were built up that embodied the new social relations. The result was a system of contract law that appeared to shape economic affairs according to normative principles but that was, in fact, only a recast form of the underlying socioeconomic relations.

"Freedom of contract," later expressed in *Coppage* v. *Kansas*, was the legitimating image of classical contract law in the nineteenth century. It projected an ideal of free competition as the consequence of wholly voluntary interactions among many private persons, all of whom were in their nature free and equal to one another. From one point of view this was simple truth, for the practical meaning of the market system was that people conceived of as interchangeable productive units ("equality") had unfettered mobility ("freedom") in the market. From an ideological point of view, this ideal expressed the sense of personal freedom involved in the destruction of the traditional social order with its status relations and hierarchies, but it also constituted denial and apology.[6] It did not take account of the practical limitations on market freedom and equality arising from class position or unequal distribution of wealth. It also ignored other meanings of freedom and equality having to do with the realization of human spirit and potential through work and community. The legitimation of the free market was achieved by seizing upon a narrow economic notion of freedom and equality, and fusing it in the public mind with the genuine meaning.

The legal consequences of this legitimating mystification were the separation of contract law from the law of property and the law of nonconsensual relations, the representation of all social relations as deriving from the free and voluntary association of individuals without coercion by the state, and the allocation of responsibility for the coercion worked by operation of the market to personal merit or luck. In an economy founded upon the accumulation of capital through exchange transactions occurring in a competitive market, the proper role of the state was conceived to be that of the relatively passive enforcer of the "free will" of the parties themselves, of their "freedom of contract." As a result, the nineteenth-century law of contracts consisted of a series of forms ostensibly designed solely to realize the will of free and equal parties, as that will was objectively manifested in agreements.[7]

Some leading contracts cases taught to first-year law students illustrate the power and effects of this mystification. The rules for contract formation and performance were extensions of the principle of objectively manifested free will. A son and his wife worked for his father on the father's farm for some twenty-five years without pay, in the expectation that the father would will the farm to him on his death. When the father died without a will, the farm was divided among all his heirs. Could the son, like the eighteenth-century physician, recover in contract, if not for the farm, at least for the value of his services? No, because there was no clear expression of an agreement between father and son, without which the court would be invading the freedom of the parties if it imposed liability.[8] On the other hand, where the parties had made a definite agreement, it bound them absolutely. Thus, a builder contracted to build a schoolhouse; the partly finished building was blown down by a windstorm; and after being rebuilt, it collapsed again due to soil conditions that could not be remedied. Was the builder liable for failure to build a third time? Indeed he was, for "where a party, by his own *contract*, creates a duty or charge upon himself, he is bound to make it good if he may, notwithstanding any accident by inevitable necessity."[9]

The most important and in some ways the most peculiar rules of classical contract law concerned the doctrine of "consideration," which grew out of the principles of freedom and equality. Since the market was the measure of all things, only those promises were enforceable that represented market transactions—those for which the person making the promise received something, a "consideration," in return. Thus, a promise to make a gift was not enforceable because it was gratuitous.[10] Further, if a person offered to sell his house to another and agreed to give the other person until Friday to decide whether to buy or not, he could change his mind and revoke the promise because it was, like a gift, a gratuity.[11] Conversely, when a bargain had been struck, it was firm, and the courts would not inquire into the "adequacy of consideration," *i.e.*, the fairness of the bargain. If a person promised to pay a large sum of money in return for a worthless piece of paper, the nineteenth-century court, unlike the eighteenth-century jury, would "protect" the exercise of free will between supposedly equal parties and bind him without weighing the substantive fairness of the transaction.[12]

The results in these cases may seem unfair or irrational today, but to the judges of the time they were neither. The courts could not easily have intervened to protect a party or to remedy unfairness without violating the ideological image that the source of social obligation rests only upon the bargain that the parties themselves have evinced, not upon the community's version of justice. This imagery, drawn as it was from the experience of competitive exchange and the privatization of the social order, served to deny the oppressive character of the market and the lack of real personal liberty experienced by people in their private and work lives. Most important, it served to deny that there was a system at all that was coercively shaping and constricting the social world, because the imagery made it appear that this world was simply the perpetual realization of an infinite number of free choices made by an infinite number of voluntary actors.

CONTRACT LAW IN THE TWENTIETH CENTURY

Today judges applying contemporary contract law would probably reach different results in these cases. The son might receive a recovery for the value of the services conferred on the father. Liberalized doctrines of excuse for nonperformance might relieve the builder. In many circumstances, a "firm offer," such as the offer to sell the house upon acceptance before Friday, is binding without consideration; in other cases, the court might not enforce the offer but would at least compensate the buyer for expenses incurred in reliance on the offer. And, purportedly, courts today will in extreme cases correct any gross unfairness in a bargain.

Contemporary contract law views these cases differently not because twentieth-century judges are wiser or smarter than their nineteenth-century counterparts, or because a new and more equitable style of legal reasoning has somehow sprung into being through a progressive maturation of the judicial mind. The old rules disintegrated for the same reason they were conceived: there has been a transformation of social and economic life that has brought about a parallel transformation in the ideological imagery required to explain it.

The transformation from the nineteenth-century to the twentieth-century forms of American capitalism was the consequence of a variety of factors that can only be summarized here: competition among businesses produced ever larger concentrations of capital within fewer and fewer companies; workers organized in response to their collective dependence on these emerging monopolies and challenged in a revolutionary way the myths of freedom and equality; exploitation of the Third World, advancing technology, and efficient organization of production facilitated the partial assimilation of the

American labor movement, allowing for the payment of higher wages while deflecting more radical labor demands; this increase in the level of wages, the use of part of the economic surplus for unemployment insurance, Social Security, and other types of welfare benefits, and the greater psychological control of consumer purchases through the mass media helped to alleviate the system's persistent tendency toward underconsumption. The basic requirement for understanding contemporary contract law is to look at the socioeconomic system thus produced and to observe its transposition, through the medium of law, into an imaginary construct that accommodates the progressive elements of the attack on classical law while ultimately securing the system's appearance of legitimacy.

The essential characteristic of contemporary capitalism is a shift toward greater integration and coordination in the economy and away from the unbridled competition of the free market. Coordination is accomplished first by very large corporations that are vertically and horizontally integrated (meaning there are relatively few "horizontal" corporations at the top of the major industries that own the capital that controls "vertically" production and distribution in each industry); and second, by a massive involvement of the state in regulating and stabilizing the system. In place of the unrestricted mobility of productive units that characterized the operation of the market in the nineteenth century, we now have integration, coordination, and cooperation to maintain systemic stability through more pervasive and efficient administration.

The rise of the coordinated economy has created a major problem for the law—how to transform the ideology of "freedom and equality" and its adjunct, "freedom of contract," into a new image that might retain the legitimating power of the older images while modifying them to conform more closely to the actual organization of daily life in the modern era. The method of addressing this problem has been to transform contract law into a relatively uniform code for business transactions that is predominantly defined not by the individualist principle of unregulated free competition but by the more collective principle of competition regulated by trade custom.[13] Since most "trades" (whatever nostalgia for a bygone era that term may evoke) are actually integrated production networks subject to supervision by dominant firms, the modern law of contracts is able to retain the legitimating features of private agreement while effectuating the regulatory and stabilizing component that is a central principle of the contemporary economy.

The principle of regulated competition leads to different results in the kinds of cases mentioned earlier. The twentieth-century counterpart to the case of the son who could not recover from his father's estate because of the absence of an express promise is the 1965 Wisconsin case of *Hoffman* v. *Red Owl Stores*.[14] The Hoffmans were small-town bakers who were induced to sell their bakery and move to a new town in reliance on the promises of an agent of the Red Owl supermarket chain that they would be granted a franchise, which never came. Under classical contract law, the Hoffmans would be without a remedy because the formal franchise contract had never been executed; in the twentieth century, however, the Wisconsin court discarded that restricted notion of agreement and held that they could recover because their reliance on the agent's representation had been commercially reasonable. The strict nineteenth-century requirement of bargain was rejected in favor of a broader standard of social obligation more expressive of the realities of the late-capitalist economy.

Hoffman v. *Red Owl* is a leading case for the principle that atomistic, concrete agreement is no longer the sole principle of contract law; people's tendency to act in reliance on less formal representations must be protected as well. It also illustrates the doctrine that private economic actors have a duty to act in "good faith." Both principles embody the ethic of cooperation and coordination reflective of the modern economy.

These principles apply in other cases also. The promise to keep open until Friday an offer to sell a house would now frequently be enforced because that is recognized as an appropriate and necessary way to do business today.[15] In rare cases, courts can even be moved to inquire into the fairness of a bargain—into the adequacy of consideration—under the recently developed doctrine of unconscionability. While this doctrine has more theoretical significance than practical effect, sometimes consumers and other parties with little economic power can be protected from the more outrageous excesses of economic predators.[16] In sum, people are conceived to be partners in a moral community where equity and the balancing of interests according to standards of fair dealing have supplanted the primitive era, when every moral tie was dissolved in "the icy waters of egotistical calculation."[17] And the state as passive enforcer of private transactions has become the state as active enforcer of the newly conceived notion of the general welfare.

CONCLUSION

The chart on page 383 may help to summarize this three-stage transformation of the economic and legal world. It shows how at each stage in our history the ideological imagery of contract law served to legitimate an oppressive socioeconomic reality by denying its oppressive character and representing it in imaginary terms.[18]

This is a very different explanation of the role of contract law from liberal or leftist instrumental analyses, which suggest that particular rules of law or particular results "helped" capitalists by providing a framework for legal enforcement of market activity. Instrumental analyses of contract law confuse the role of direct force with the role of law in the development of socio-historical processes. Social processes like "free-market capitalism" do not get "enforced" by "laws." Rather, these processes are accepted through social conditioning, through the collective internalization of practical norms that have their foundation in concrete socioeconomic reality. Since these norms are in part alienating and oppressive, the process of collective conditioning requires the constant threat of force and the occasional use of it. For example, if you fail to perform your part of a bargain, it *may* be the case that a sheriff with a gun will attach your bank account to pay the aggrieved party his or her damages. The occasional deployment of direct force serves to maintain the status quo as well as to get people to accept its legitimacy.

"The law" does not enforce anything, however, because the law is nothing but ideas and the images they signify. The law justifies the practical norms and thus contributes to the collective conditioning process. In addition, the law contributes to constituting and reconstituting the norms and the social reality that they represent, as occurred with the transformations among the historical epochs discussed above.

One important way that this justification process occurs is through judicial opinions. Judicial opinions "work" as ideology by a rhetorical process in which oppressive practical norms are encoded as "general rules" with ide-ological content; these "rules" then serve as the basis for a logic ("legal reasoning") that supposedly determines the outcome of the lawsuit. A key social function of the opinion, however, is not to be found in the outcome and the use of state power which may follow from it, but in the rhetorical structure of the opinion itself, in the legitimation and reconstitution of the practical norm that occurs through the application of it in the form of a "legal rule." That enforcement of bargains was much more likely to occur under nineteenth-century contract law than under eighteenth-century law is, of course, true; but this does not mean that the function of nineteenth-century contract law was to "enforce bargains." The reverse expresses the truth more accurately—that the enforcement of bargains functioned to permit the elaboration of contract law as legitimating ideology.

The central point to understand from this is that contract law today con-stitutes in large part an elaborate attempt to conceal what is going on in the world. Contemporary capitalism bears no more relation to the imagery of contemporary contract law than did nineteenth-century capitalism to the imagery of classical contract law. Contemporary capitalism is a coercive system of relationships that more or less corresponds to the brief description given here. The proof of this statement inheres in the situations we all face in our daily lives in the functional roles to which we are consigned: lawyer, secretary, student, tenant, welfare recipient, consumer of the products and services of Exxon, Citibank, and Sears. Despite the doctrines of reliance and

	Socioeconomic Reality	Ideological Imagery
Eighteenth Century	The social order is organized through traditional statuses and hierarchies, creating relations of class domination determined primarily by distribution of landed wealth, fixed occupation, and inherited social position.	The social order is organized through hierarchies based upon "natural" class position, which exist prior to human intervention; and the legal system implements customary moral and religious principles, which support the natural hierarchies.
Nineteenth Century	The social order is organized through free competition, made coercive through the operation of an unregulated market, creating relations of class dominance determined primarily by the ownership of capital.	The social order is organized through the formation of voluntary contracts among free and equal citizens, with whose choice the state will not interfere, creating a classless society where everyone has equal opportunity for personal gain and happiness.
Twentieth Century	The social order is organized through the predominant control by large enterprises of all aspects of production, with the help of regulatory planning and "stabilization" by the state, creating relations of class domination determined primarily by the ownership of capital.	The social order is organized through the voluntary cooperation of different groups in the economy (big business, labor, franchisees, the unemployed, etc.) whose good-faith cooperation the state seeks to coordinate purposively toward the general administration of a fair society where class inequalities are compensated for through regulation and redistribution.

good faith, large business corporations daily disappoint our expectations as to how they should behave. Despite the doctrine of unconscionability, unfairness is rampant in the marketplace. In this reality our narrow functional roles produce isolation, passivity, unconnectedness, and impotence. Contract law, like the other images constituted by capitalism, is a denial of these painful feelings and an apology for the system that produces them.

Most of the time the socioeconomic system operates without any need for law as such because people at every level have been imbued with its inevitability and necessity. When the system breaks down and conflicts arise, a legal case comes into being. This is the "moment" of legal ideology, the moment at which lawyers and judges in *their* narrow, functional roles seek to justify the normal functioning of the system by resolving the conflict through an idealized way of thinking about it.

But this also can be the moment for struggle against the narrow limits imposed in law on genuine values such as freedom, equality, moral community, and good faith.

We can see glimpses of that sort of struggle in the transformation from classical to modern contract law. Classical legal thought represented the world in its image of freedom of contract. Because of the socioeconomic transformation and because of their own perception of the falseness and injustice of that image, lawyers developed the modern image of contract, which includes more elements of interdependence, trust, and cooperation than did classical law. However, instead of holding out these ideals as a goal, in its legitimating function contract law presents them as standards of the marketplace that have been achieved.

The critical approach to law exposes the limits imposed on law by the ideological nature of the system and questions whether the legal system helps or hinders the actual realization of authentic values in a meaningful sense in everyday life. For example, consider the doctrine of reliance as the basis of enforcement of a promise exemplified in *Hoffman* v. *Red Owl*. The current doctrine is artificially constrained by focusing on a discrete promise and a discrete act of reliance, as when the Hoffmans sold their bakery specifically because they had been promised a Red Owl franchise. We might instead recognize that people rely in intangible ways on more diffuse promises and representations; indeed, some of the most important ways people rely on each other is expressed in the continuity of behavior within institutions that are important to their lives. Workers rely on their employers to treat them fairly in everyday events and to consider their interests when making decisions of major importance. Accordingly, contract law might prohibit an employer from firing a worker without good cause even in the absence of a specific contractual provision requiring the employer to do so,[19] and it might even prohibit a company from closing a plant in one area without taking adequate account of the importance of its continued operations to the workers and to the local community.[20]

Recently courts and legislatures have begun to recognize the power of these arguments, but in each of these instances, the power of legal ideology has constrained the recognition. In the plant closing situation, for example, workers at a U.S. Steel plant in Youngstown, Ohio, and their lawyers buttressed their political action and community organizing with legal claims that U.S. Steel was prohibited by contract law and property law from simply closing the plants that were the lifeblood of the community. Although the federal trial and appeals courts recognized the enormity of the situation and the power of the workers' arguments, they failed to provide a remedy because "the mechanism [to do so] . . . is not now in existence in the code of laws of our nation."[21] In fact, it was not the law that restrained the judges, but their own beliefs in the ideology of law. By recognizing the possibilities for social responsibility and solidarity which are immanent in the doctrine of reliance, they could have both provided the workers a remedy and transformed the ideology of contract law.

New developments in contract law such as these would have positive instrumental effects. But consistent with this essay's emphasis on the ideological role of contract law, their greater importance would be in exposing the legitimating function of traditional doctrines and providing a forum for peoples' struggle to achieve freedom, connection, and authenticity. The law's treatment of a worker's rights in his or her job is intimately connected with the economic and social power structures that define what it means to be a worker and an employer. Critically rethinking contract law permits us to expose the limits of the system and to explore the possibility of a different order of things.

NOTES

1. Coppage v. Kansas, 236 U.S. 1 (1915).
2. 236 U.S. at 14.
3. E. Allan Farnsworth, Contracts 23 (Boston: Little, Brown, 1982).
4. Morton Horwitz, *The Transformation of American Law, 1780–1860* (Cambridge, Mass.: Harvard University Press, 1977), chap. 6.
5. *See* Peter Gabel, "Reification in Legal Reasoning," 3 *Research in Law and Sociology* 25 (1980).
6. *See* Duncan Kennedy, "The Structure of Blackstone's *Commentaries*," 28 *Buffalo Law Review* 205 (1979).
7. *See* Friedrich Kessler and Grant Gilmore, *Contracts: Cases and Materials*, 2d ed. (Boston: Little, Brown, 1970), pp. 2–6.
8. Hertzog v. Hertzog, 29 Pennsylvania State Reports 465 (1857).
9. School Trustees of Trenton v. Bennett, 27 New Jersey Law Reports 513 (1859).
10. Kirksey v. Kirksey, 8 Alabama Reports 131 (1845).
11. Dickinson v. Dodds, 2 English Law Reports, Chancery Division (Court of Appeal 1876). For the way in which American contract theorists manipu-

lated this and other English precedents to support their ideas, *see* Grant Gilmore, *The Death of Contract* (Columbus: Ohio State University Press, 1974).

12. Haigh v. Brooks, 113 English Reports 119 (Queen's Bench 1839, Exchequer 1840).

13. *See* Eugene Mooney, "Old Kontract Principles and Karl's New Kode: An Essay on the Jurisprudence of Our New Commercial Law," 11 *Villanova Law Review* 213 (1966).

14. 26 Wisconsin Reports 2d 683, 133 Northwestern Reports 2d 267 (1965).

15. New York General Obligations Law, §5-1109 (McKinney 1978); Uniform Commercial Code, §2-205; Restatement (Second) of Contracts, §87(2) (1981).

16. *See* Arthur Leff, "Unconscionability and the Code: The Emperor's New Clause," 115 *University of Pennsylvania Law Review* 485 (1967).

17. Karl Marx and Friedrich Engels, *The Communist Manifesto* (New York: Washington Square Press, 1964), p. 62.

18. The chart, like the rest of this essay, focuses on economic elements of the socioeconomic reality, so it does not include references to the importance of race, gender, and social class in organizing the social order to create relations of domination.

19. In the last few years courts have granted some employees limited rights against unjust termination, but they have done so without questioning the basic structure of employment. *See* Kenneth Casebeer, "Teaching an Old Dog New Tricks: *Coppage v. Kansas* and At-Will Employment Revisited," 6 *Cardozo Law Review* 765 (1985).

20. For a discussion and critical analysis of the law on plant closings, *see* Joseph William Singer, "The Reliance Interest in Property," 40 *Stanford Law Review* 611 (1988).

21. Local 1330, United Steel Workers v. United States Steel Corp., 631 F.2d 1264, 1266 (6th cir. 1980). For an account of the workers' struggle, *see* Staughton Lynd, *The Fight Against Shutdowns: Youngstown's Steel Mill Closings* (San Pedro, Calif.: Single Jack Books, 1982).

19 WILLIAM H. SIMON

CONTRACT VERSUS POLITICS IN CORPORATION DOCTRINE

THE traditional corporation law doctrine expounded in the law schools and the law reviews tends to disappoint both those looking for vocationally relevant technical instruction and those looking for theoretical insight into the vital business institutions of capitalism. The type of deconstructive or "trashing" analysis associated with critical legal studies that finds tension and contradiction underlying a veneer of doctrinal coherence and confidence seems to have been preempted here. Mainstream lawyers have dismissed the field in terms as radical as those of the most implacable trasher. "We have nothing left," wrote Bayless Manning, "but our great empty corporation statutes— towering skyscrapers of rusted girders, internally welded together and containing nothing but wind."[1]

While the widely held belief that corporation doctrine needs overhauling is surely correct, traditional doctrine does have more significant content than Manning's remark implies. Perhaps the most important content is an implicit map of the universe of business law that situates various disparate elements of doctrine in a way that influences the way people learn and manipulate them. A striking feature of this map is its tendency to relegate considerations of power and public value to the periphery. The explicit content of the corporations course seems resolutely apolitical, but the implicit map expresses a vision that seems an unmistakably conservative one.

Most of the recent efforts inspired by economics to revise business doctrine have not challenged its basic premises or its political vision. They have, however, made these premises more explicit and given them more theoretical substance. This is a real achievement, but an ambitious reform effort ought to consider, not only fleshing out the conventional subject matter, but also redefining it to include a broader range of political perspectives.

In this essay I try to identify the central themes of corporation doctrine. I then try to bring to the surface some tacit political commitments of this doctrine by describing another set of concerns, once considered central to the study of business organization in America, that contemporary corporation doctrine excludes. Finally, I speculate that recent developments in business practice and economic theory might be conducive to the revival of the older, explicitly political tradition of discourse about the coporation.

WHAT CORPORATION DOCTRINE IS ABOUT—
PRIVATE ORDERING

The introductory law school business course is typically called Corporations, and even when it has a broader title, such as Business Associations, it is focused largely on corporation law. Moreover, within this field, it is prin-cipally concerned with a special kind of corporation—the large publicly held enterprise. Relatively little attention is devoted to small, closely held cor-porations. The premise that corporations is the core business law field and that, within the field, large, publicly held businesses are central is also reflected in the allocation of scholarly effort and attention.

Throughout most of the period since World War II, corporations has been treated as, in effect, a specialized branch of contract law. This branch is concerned with the mutual adjustment or private ordering of relations among investors, lenders, and managers.

Among corporation lawyers, contract rhetoric is favored by people who tend to support judicial and legislative deference to ostensibly voluntary business arrangements, and it is sometimes resisted by those who tend to support state intervention to protect investors. But the positions of both groups can be readily embraced within contemporary mainstream contract doctrine, with its princples of fraud, duress, and unconscionability and its associated panoply of implied-in-law, nonwaivable rights and duties.[2] Both the inter-ventionists and the noninterventionists are contractual in the sense used here. They are both primarily focused on investors, lenders, and managers, and they both treat informed bargaining among these parties as the ideal way to define relations among them (however much they differ about the extent to which practical obstacles to such bargaining warrant regulation).

From the contract perspective, the distinctive feature of corporate orga-nization is that it involves large numbers of people engaged in a relatively long-term collaboration. Since basic contract rhetoric tends to presuppose small numbers of individuals, arm's length bargaining, and short-term re-lations, adjustments seem needed in the corporate field. Corporation doctrine is focused primarily on two sorts of adjustments. One has to do with the extent to which the corporation should be personified, that is, the extent to which various actors associated with the corporation should be treated as a unity. The other has to do with constraining the ability of corporate actors to abuse their discretion to take advantage of each other.

Personification. A problem of formality arises from the difficulty of adapting the basically individualistic rhetoric of American private law to deal with large-scale collective activity. A highly influential though largely mistaken response to this problem might be called the naive view of corporate formality. The naive view suggests that once a business fulfills certain prescribed procedural steps it should be treated as a legal "person" indistinguishable from a natural individual. Moreover, the naive view holds that the decision to treat a business as a corporate person in this manner resolves a host of specific legal issues.

Much of the modern history of corporation law has been preoccupied with a war against the naive view.[3] The war has nearly been won, but fighting continues on a few fronts, and some portion of the law school corporation course is devoted to reenacting prior victories.

From the late nineteenth century through the Depression, the debate over corporate formality was intensely politically charged. The naive view was associated with a conservative politics hostile to business regulation. Conservatives relied on the naive view of corporate personality in support of arguments that incorporated businesses should have the same rights of privacy as natural individuals, despite the relatively impersonal, materialistic nature of the businesses, and that they should have the same rights of property as natural individuals, despite the relatively greater power businesses achieved through centralized control of the property of large numbers of people.

Many who fought the naive view believed that its defeat would necessarily entail the adoption of a view of business organization more favorable to regulation. But others cautioned that rejecting the naive view did not preclude you from arguing against regulation. It just forced you to come up with a substantive reason against regulation. Moreover, the rhetorical sleight of hand involved in the naive view could be used to support regulation, and rejecting the naive view opened up as many misleading arguments against regulation as it closed. You could concede the portrayal of the corporation as a person and portray it as a rapacious, irresponsible one in need of punishment or discipline; you could deny that the corporation was a person and argue that it was just a collection of individuals, some of them widows and orphans, trying to achieve some financial security.

The critics prevailed over the naive view, but only incompletely. The battle against the naive view still has to be fought. Consider, for example, the Supreme Court's 1978 decision in *First National Bank of Boston* v. *Bellotti,* which struck down a state statute prohibiting corporations in certain lines of business from making political expenditures in connection with referenda on tax issues. Justice Powell's opinion for the majority seems to flirt with the naive view when it relies on earlier decisions upholding First Amendment claims by natural individuals without considering the differences between individuals and corporations that might be relevant to the First Amendment.[4] On the other hand, Justice Rehnquist's dissent, which vigorously rejects the naive view and insists on viewing the corporation as an "artificial being," seems to make the related mistake of attributing substantive significance to the *refusal* to characterize the corporation as a person.[5] In arguing for the statute as an exercise of the state's distinctively broad regulatory powers over corporations, he slights the question of whether the statute might infringe the free speech and associational rights of the shareholders.

Bellotti is something of an anachronism because it deals with an explicitly political issue, and the case is rarely found in courses or treatises on corporation law. The critique of the naive view usually occurs in connection with issues concerning the internal relations of participants in corporate activities. Consider, for example, the following:

■ Is a contract purportedly negotiated on behalf of a corporation by one of its organizers prior to the completion of the incorporation process binding on the subsequently incorporated business? An answer inspired by the naive view is the contract is not binding since, if the corporation did not exist at the time it was made, it could not bind itself or authorize anyone else to do so for it.

■ Can creditors of a corporation reach assets formally held by separate corporations when the corporations are affiliated by ownership, management, and operations in what appears to be functionally a single business? The naive view suggests that they cannot be reached since the assets belong to someone other than the debtor.

■ Is a contract purportedly made on behalf of a corporation binding when it would involve the corporation in an area of activity outside those specified in the statement of purposes in its charter? A naïf would be content to answer no on the ground that the corporation lacked the capacity to enter such a contract.

■ May a corporate officer buy stock on the basis of undisclosed inside information? Under the naive view, one can say yes, because the officer's corporate duties are to the corporation, not to the stockholders.

■ May a corporation sue an officer under antifraud provisions of the federal securities statutes for failure to disclose material facts in a transaction in which the officer sold something to the corporation. Under the naive view, one might say it cannot sue because, since the officer was an agent of the corporation, his knowledge is imputed to the corporation, and the corporation thus could not have been deceived.

In such cases, the answer associated with the naive view is wrong, at least insofar as it is offered as a substantive argument, rather than a summary of an independently grounded conclusion. Courses in corporate doctrine use such issues to teach that, while it is often convenient to treat the corporation as a unitary entity or fictional person, one must resist the temptation to read substantive significance into this practice.

Thurman Arnold, a famous critic of the naive view, argued that the destruction of that view should lead to an understanding of the corporation as a political entity, "an integral part of our government," as he put it.[6] Arnold was not making the mistake here of attributing substantive significance to a formal matter. He simply assumed that once people stopped conflating corporations with natural individuals it would be apparent to them that the distinctively interesting issues about corporations had to do with the social effects of concentrated economic power.

But he was wrong. The naive view has been replaced by a view of the corporation, not as an aggregation of power or a center of governance, but as a "nexus of contracts." What is pernicious about the naive view to contemporary corporations scholars is not its tendency to obscure economic power, but its tendency to obscure conflicts of interest among shareholders, managers, and creditors. Contemporary doctrine would address these conflicts in contract terms. And this turns out to mean that one looks for convergent expectations of the parties, or when none are found, to solutions that promote efficiency.

Discretion. Although the corporate form is available to businesses of nearly every functional description, contemporary corporation doctrine focuses on large corporations with hierarchically organized management and a large number of dispersed investors who are not active in corporate affairs. Since shares in these corporations are regularly traded in public capital markets, the shareholders are a constantly changing class.

If the paradigm contract is a bargained for specification of the parties' rights and duties, then the relations of participants in large corporations seem deviant in two respects. First, the great mass of shareholders have no practical opportunities to bargain directly with each other or with the officers of the corporation. Second, it is not feasible to specify the duties of corporate officers; they need discretion to respond to myriad and largely unforeseeable contingencies. There are similar, though perhaps less intense, concerns about the relation of creditors with officers and managers and about the relation of shareholders among themselves. Contemporary corporation doctrine takes as its central problem the task of constraining the abuse of the discretion that results when direct bargaining and contractual specification are not feasible. Abuse here means the failure to maximize the value of the firm to managers, shareholders, and creditors or the expropriation by some of these participants of returns due to others.

The main focus of doctrine is on the problem of preventing officer exploitation of shareholders. The doctrine takes two general perspectives: one focuses on internal institutional mechanisms of officer accountability; the other focuses on the constraints and opportunities that result from the fact that the large corporation's shares are traded in organized national markets.

The two principal internal mechanisms devices to protect shareholders from managerial discretion are fiduciary duties and voting rights. The basic idea of fiduciary duties is that officers owe unspecified, open-ended obligations to maximize the value of corporate ownership and to distribute this value in proportion to the size of shareholdings. Such duties are enforceable by shareholders through derivative suits in which a single shareholder can challenge a breach on behalf of the "corporation," that is, the body of shareholders. Voting rights enable the shareholders to elect and remove the board of directors, which in theory has general managerial power over the corporation and appoints its senior officers.

But these devices have problems. While fiduciary duties by their nature do not have to be specified in advance, effective compliance and enforcement requires some degree of consensus about the conduct they prohibit, and outside the more blatant forms of officer self-dealing, this has proved difficult to achieve. Moreover, because officers of large corporations control large amounts of wealth, most of it belonging to other people, the potential loss from bad decisions is enormous relative to the returns officers expect from their own salaries and shareholdings when things go well. It is thus difficult to prescribe liability for breach of duty that is sufficiently severe to deter improper conduct while preserving incentives for taking on the job. (This is particularly true of the job of the "independent" director—a part-time outsider as opposed to the inside director who is also a manager—but it is also a problem with inside directors.)

Voting rights suffer from basic recurrent dilemmas of collective action among self-interested individuals. To make effective use of voting rights the shareholder needs to invest in research about the corporation and in communication and coordination efforts with other shareholders. However, the gains from voting that effectively polices managerial responsibility accrue to all shareholders, and shareholders benefit from the efforts of their peers whether they contribute to them or not. Thus, shareholders tend to be "rationally apathetic." They usually do not engage in active monitoring either because the returns to the holdings of any one shareholder from monitoring would not warrant the costs to that shareholder (even though shareholders would benefit in the aggregate from monitoring by more than its costs) or because shareholders who would gain enough individually to justify efforts hope to "free-ride" on the efforts of their peers.

Moreover, to the extent shareholders do become active, there is a risk they will exploit other shareholders by seeking gains disproportionate to their holdings. If a majority of the shares can bind the corporation, then an individual or group that holds a majority can make decisions that disproportionately benefit themselves at the expense of the minority. (For example, they can have the corporation sell things to or buy things from other entities they own at prices favorable to the other entities.) If the rules try to constrain such exploitation by giving the minority a veto, the danger arises that the minority will threaten to block profitable moves (the loss of which would cost it less than the majority) unless they receive a disproportionate share of the gains.

In recent years, a large literature has emerged that is relatively indifferent to or dismissive of internal institutional mechanisms of accountability and relatively sanguine about the pressures that arise from public securities markets. A shareholder can express dissatisfaction with management more easily by selling her shares than by organizing an electoral campaign. To be sure the price she receives may be discounted because of the managerial practices she disapproves of, but the fact that the securities markets continuously price the corporation's shares based in part on evaluation of managerial decisions makes the market an engine of accountability. Improper manager decisions will lower the price of shares. The fear of such a reaction will often act as a deterrent to improper decisions. If this deterrent is ineffective, the market provides a second one—the takeover. If a corporation's shares decline because of bad management, an outsider can profit by buying sufficient shares to enable her to replace existing management with a better one.

However, there are a variety of problems with this view.[7] For the market to operate as an engine of accountability, prices have to be based on rational estimates of future earnings rather than simply on fad or mob psychology, though some believe that the latter play decisive roles in price determination. Even conceding that prices are good estimates of future earnings, there are evident limitations on their ability to discipline managers. For one thing, managerial compensation in large corporations typically depends only to a small extent on stock price; thus, the incentives from price per se are weak.

The takeover threat may be more formidable, but the takeover strikes many as a crude accountaility mechanism, creating as many abuses as it checks. Takeovers (including the preliminary stage of identifying targets) are slow enough and expensive enough that at best they allow managers a considerable range of ineptitude before they become a serious threat.

There is, moreover, the difficulty in designing an effective takeover process. If takeovers are made too easy, acquirers may be able to stampede target shareholders into selling at unreasonably low prices or exploit minorities once they assume control; if they are made too difficult, management will be able to immunize itself from challenge. And it may be that some takeovers themselves constitute managerial ineptitude or malfeasance by acquiring corporation executives who want to expand their empires even at the cost of corporate profitability. If they act quickly enough, they can do so without turning themselves into takeover targets.

Contemporary corporation doctrine thus consists largely of a standard repertory of institutional responses to the problem of discretion—vaguely specified contractual duties—in the relations of managers, shareholders, and creditors. There is a large range of variations and combinations of the standard responses, and no one is especially stable or commands consensus. Within the dominant perspective, debates occur between those with greater confidence in internal accountability mechanisms and those with greater confidence in capital market mechanisms, between those more concerned about managerial ineptitude and malfeasance and those more concerned about shareholder passivity and malfeasance, and between those who most fear target management self-entrenchment and those who most fear acquirer management empire building.

Critical legal studies critiques often suggest that mainstream doctrine tends to induce complacency about or confidence in institutions by lending a false sense of coherence and completeness to the doctrines that describe them.[8] I think this point applies less strongly to corporations than other subjects. Corporation doctrine is distinctively contentious and relatively openly chaotic. A student emerging from the corporations course would be unlikely to have a lot of confidence in the ability of any particular combination of the standard responses to deal adequately with the problem of discretion among managers, shareholders, and creditors. But such a student might well take for granted that the central problem of corporation doctrine is in fact or ought to be controlling discretion in these relationships. At least, hardly anything in the course would encourage him to think that there might be other equally important problems for corporate doctrine.

WHAT CORPORATION DOCTRINE IS NOT ABOUT—POLITICS

We can get some insight into the premises of contemporary business law doctrine by comparing the current conception of the subject matter of corporations to an earlier one. Throughout much of the nineteenth century, the subject of the nature and social function of the corporation occupied a central place in popular discourse about public affairs. It was treated as an intensely political subject. While the legal treatment of the corporation was never as openly or intensely political as the popular one, it did reflect some of the popular concerns. During this period, a large portion of the more important corporate doctrine was treated as public, often constitutional, law. As today, the subject was identified with large, managerially controlled businesses with dispersed ownerships, but in contrast to today, the most salient issues concerned the political implications of such enterprises.[9]

One perspective that fueled much of the debate might be identified—at some risk of oversimplification—as economic republicanism. This perspective took a variety of forms and influenced positions at many points of the political spectrum. Some of its distinctive themes can be found in the polemics and programs of Jeffersonian republicanism, Jacksonian democracy, the radical republicanism of the Reconstruction Era, the Populism of the Farmer's Alliance, and the labor radicalism of the Knights of Labor.[10]

The conception of business organization in economic republicanism was political rather than contractual. First, republicanism focused on the effects of business organization on, not just investors, lenders, and managers, but on a variety of other constituencies and the larger surrounding society. Second, while bargaining among affected constituencies played a role, that role was subordinated to criteria of economic democracy. These criteria were expressed most distinctively in inalienability rules and government support for particular kinds of enterprises.

Like socialists, the republicans focused attention on the economic basis of a democratic political order, and they saw democracy as incompatible with a drastically unequal distribution of productive resources. Like classical liberals, the republicans also emphasized the danger of a large and powerful state to democracy, and they saw an important role for private property as a bulwark against state power. They appealed to a vision of an economy designed to encourage small-scale, internally egalitarian enterprise and to protect small capital against both the state and large capital.

Their notion of the typical economic actor was inspired by ideals of citizenship as well as of productive efficiency: a single individual or group of equals working at their own direction with their own productive resources. Widely distributed property was considered essential to secure the average citizen from subordination to an economic elite in both the public sphere and the workplace, which was itself viewed as a forum of political self-expression and solidarity.

In this vision, the state acted to support the political ideal of an independent citizenry in part through the definition of property entitlements. For example, scale could be constrained through agrarian (acreage limitations and residency requirements in public land and water grants) and antimonopoly laws.

The state also established banking and credit institutions responsive to the needs of small enterprise and provided technical and marketing assistance that remedied some disadvantages of small-scale production.

Economic republicanism implied a strong preference for investment in human capital, i.e., education, as opposed to physical capital. This meant, for one thing, a system of universal public education. It also meant institutions to facilitate the sharing and development of specialized knowledge within firms and occupations. These goals were animated by overlapping ideals of the skilled worker and the knowledgeable citizen. The skilled worker views work both as a form of self-expression and as creative participation in an occupational culture. The knowledgeable citizen takes a similar view toward participation in the political processes of the community and the larger society.

The role of the market in this vision was complex. On the one hand, a primary economic process was contractual exchange among private parties. Such a process was seen as conducive to productive efficiency. Equally important, it was also seen as necessary to sufficiently decentralize the social system to ensure meaningful participation by producer-citizens in both the workplace and the community. But the market, depending on how it was defined and regulated, could also be a threat to efficiency and decentralization. For example, if contractual exchange produced far-flung, hierarchically controlled, large-scale enterprises, they undermined the goal of decentralization and threatened the autonomy of workers and local political communities. And when exchange processes left local firms and political communities defenseless against the pressures of volatile national and world markets, they further threatened autonomy.

Unrestricted exchange could also create radical uncertainty and instability incompatible with productive efficiency as well as political autonomy. In the classical tradition associated with James Harrington, nineteenth-century American economic republicans viewed investment in nonmovable or locally rooted assets as the material foundation of a prosperous, participatory polity. As with the classicists, land was the paradigmatic immovable asset, but certain kinds of education in knowledge specific to craft or occupational communities or long-term trading or collaborative relations with local partners might also qualify. Such investments gave the individual the kind of stake in the community that would motivate materially productive and political activity and the kind of independence that would protect him from subordination. (One reason why republicans considered black slavery a threat to the independence of whites was that the comparative mobility of slave as opposed to landed property discouraged slaveholders from making material or personal investments in local communities and encouraged them to oppose politically the types of public investments necessary to a vital public culture.)

Such locally rooted investments are interdependent to a greater extent than investments in readily redeployable assets. An individual would be reluctant to undertake such an investment to the extent that others seem unable or unlikely to undertake complementary investments or to the extent that others seem able and likely to withdraw their complementary investments. Unrestricted exchange threatens the solvency of the community by eroding the rootedness of investments and increasing the danger of a situation in which individuals who would want to stay if the others would stay stampeded into withdrawing their investments because they are unable to collectively commit to stay. One reason for the hostility to speculators and intermediaries in economic republicanism is that they introduce a community-threatening liquidity to investments. (This problem is most familiar today in connection with investment in residential neighborhoods—for example, the destabilizing effects of "blockbusting" real estate brokers who induce homeowners to sell quickly at low prices for fear that, if their neighbors sell before they do, prices will go still lower.)

A related concern about unrestricted exchange is that it might permit the citizen to alienate the kind of autonomy necessary to her effective functioning as a producer-citizen. This type of concern survives in contemporary prohibitions against selling one's self into slavery or slightly milder forms of subordination (e.g., debt peonage or specifically enforceable personal service obligations), but nineteenth-century republicanism had broader notions of the proper scope of inalienability. For example, the notorious "crop lien" that required the farmer to surrender the control of the growing and marketing of his crop to financial intermediaries was considered a politically objectionable infringement of autonomy.

The republican attitude toward monopoly differed from the currently dominant one in two respects. First, republicanism was suspicious of large-scale enterprise even in competitive markets where the power to restrict output and raise price above cost was small. Second, republicanism was sympathetic to certain constraints on price and wage competition that encouraged or protected small enterprise and employment relations. This sympathy was partly motivated by noneconomic concerns, but partly by notions of efficiency. Contemporary mainstream economists tend to see an exceptional role for monopoly rights, such as those conferred by patent and copyright, as an inducement to important forms of investment. The republicans had an analogous intuition, but the types of investment they focused on were different. They were especially concerned with investments in skills, in long-term cooperative business relations, and in product quality reputations. Constraints on wage and price competition were seen as an inducement to make such investments, as a way of channeling competition toward innovation in products and production (rather than toward sweating labor and shaving product quality), as well as an approach to smoothing the process of economic adjustment.

The republican ideal of economic association was most fully expressed in the late-nineteenth-century rhetoric of "cooperation." Cooperation implied a kind of flexible, solidaristic (but not radically altruistic) collaboration among equals. Cooperation could take the form of a "cooperative," a worker owned and managed a firm, but the firm was a less important category in republican rhetoric than it is in the business rhetoric of today. In agriculture, where the cooperative ideal was most influential, cooperation was most visible in purchasing and marketing associations formed by independent owner-operator farmers. In the program of industrial cooperation of the Knights of Labor, producer cooperatives were linked to each other through unions and to their suppliers, customers, and communities through a variety of ties of varying degrees of formality.

In republican rhetoric, corporation was an antonym for cooperation. The corporation appeared as a threat to the republican program. It fostered concentration and centralization of economic power. It tended to subordinate workers to the status of wage earners and order followers. It threatened to subject local affairs to the control of managers and owners not connected to the community and to the vicissitudes of volatile, far-flung markets. And by creating highly dispersed and liquid ownership interests, it tended to preclude the republican role of ownership as a solvent of local relationships.

The concerns of republican discourse about business organization contrast strikingly with those of contemporary legal doctrine. In both visions, the corporation is central, less because of its technical legal features, than because of its connotation of large-scale, hierarchical, managerially controlled enterprise. But the issues associated with the corporation differ radically in the two visions. Political concerns are nearly invisible in contemporary corporations doctrine. So are some of the social roles that economic organization plays in the republican view, such as the reinforcement of community ties. And many of the actors who play prominent roles in the republican view—workers, suppliers, customers, local communities—have disappeared.

Now, the fact that doctrinal concerns have changed since the nineteenth century is not in itself surprising, but the extent to which the older concerns have receded in business law calls for some explanation. Although many have long regarded some features of the republican vision as anachronistic or discredited, some features, such as the emphasis on the political significance of large corporate enterprise and the concern about the possibilities of personally satisfying work in such organizations, remain prominent in the discussion of the corporation in popular discourse and in academic fields such as political science and sociology.

Nor does the fact that the concerns of the republican vision are peripheral to the preoccupations of practicing business lawyers explain their treatment in contemporary doctrine. Legal doctrine, as expounded in the law reviews and taught at the law schools, has always been somewhat aloof from practical lawyering concerns. It has rarely been reluctant to deal with matters of political or policy significance when such matters are considered important.

Moreover, the contemporary contours of corporations doctrine do not seem any more attuned to practical lawyering needs than a republican counterpart would likely be. It is widely believed that the law school corporations course is out of touch with practice. The doctrinal content of the course is really quite skimpy, and neither its curricular centrality nor the amount of time devoted to it could be justified in practical terms. And a variety of matters of fundamental practical importance—noncorporate business forms, agency, close corporations matters, nonprofit enterprise, and finance and employment matters subject to distinctive contract practices—are skimmed or ignored. In two recent books offering introductory surveys of the knowledge lawyers need for business practice, corporate doctrine gets 20 percent or less of the coverage.[11] Yet, corporate doctrine continues to receive the great majority of attention, sometimes all of it, in the great majority of introductory law school business courses.

The marginalization of partnership in contemporary doctrine is especially striking. The presumptive form of the partnership—for example the one provided by the Uniform Partnership Act in the absence of contrary agreement—is a fairly egalitarian worker cooperative (with the qualification, also characteristic of many other types of worker cooperatives, that some workers are not owner/partners). This form corresponds substantially to the economic republican enterprise vision. However, it is also quite well established in a variety of important, quite nonutopian business contexts in contemporary America. Perhaps the most important of these is the large law firm of the sort where most graduates of elite law schools go on to practice. You would think that these students would have an intense practical interest in the dynamics of such organizations, but they have been largely invisible in the law school business curriculum.[12] (This may be changing, though most of the change seems to be prompted by a 1986 revision to the Internal Revenue Code that created incentives for enterprises organized on the conventional corporate model to try to squeeze themselves into the partnership form to achieve tax advantages. The interesting issues from the republican point of view—for example, the need to balance incentives for productivity with the goal of maintaining an egalitarian, solidaristic organization—receive little attention.)

Surely part of the explanation for the definition of corporation doctrine and its central place in business law generally lies, not in practical vocational concerns, but rather in ideological ones. This doctrine and this arrangement express tacitly a vision of the social order that holds sway over legal and business elites. By taking as paradigmatic the large, hierarchically organized enterprise owned by outside investors, mainstream doctrine implies that other forms of enterprise are relatively uninteresting, marginal, or nonviable. And the relegation of political concerns and concerns for constituencies other than the three privileged ones to the periphery at worst implies that these concerns are relatively unimportant and at best suggests a limited vision of how they might be dealt with. The implication is that these outside concerns are to be dealt with either through contractual specification or through conventional forms of regulation. The republican notion that such concerns might be dealt with through the structuring of enterprises—either by general constraints on enterprise form and scale or by government support for favored structures—is implicitly denied.

The recently intensified tendency to situate corporations doctrine in the context of capital markets (and to integrate it with securities law) as opposed to situating in the context of, for example, labor markets (and integrating it with employment law) or local communities (and integrating it with local government law) encourages the marginalization of distributive issues. Some corporation scholars have generated moral interest in the various ways by which managers exploit investors, but when we consider that most of the victims of this exploitation are rich—most individually held stocks are held in the top few percentile of the income distribution—and/or foolish—much exploitation could be costlessly avoided by investing through diversified funds run by professional intermediaries—it is hard to see such problems as fundamental issues of social justice. (The distributive issues with respect to investments held by intermediaries, and especially pension funds, are more interesting and important, but these are excluded from mainstream core doctrine.)

Conventionally defined doctrine seems incapacitated to confront the critical distributive issues that arise from one of the more important recent developments in connection with the large corporation—the flight of capital to the Sunbelt and abroad and the attendant erosion of the manufacturing sector of the Northeast and Midwest. The focus of corporation doctrine on investors, capital markets, and neoclassical economics makes it easy to emphasize the advantages of capital mobility. Traditional capital suppliers have benefited from many of the changes involved here. And the capital markets, with commodified products, large numbers of buyers and sellers, and widely disseminated information, lend themselves distinctively to modeling in terms of neoclassical theories that assert the efficiency of unrestrained alienation.

On the other hand, the disadvantages associated with recent mass capital movement have been visited largely on workers and local communities, who do not appear in corporation doctrine. Moreover, the limitations of neoclassical economic models that become quite apparent when the relations of corporations with workers and communities are considered are more easily ignored when these actors are banished.

Of course, legal doctrine does not entirely ignore the relations of large-scale business enterprise with workers and communities or the effects of corporate power on democratic values. There are, after all, plenty of legal rules that apply to these relations. Doctrine as expounded in the law schools and the law reviews purports to deal with these rules outside the corporation field. But in fact these rules are often peripheral and are sometimes invisible in academic doctrine.[13]

Economic concentration is the focus of antitrust law, and while the quintessentially republican concerns that influenced the passage of the major statutes typically get some acknowledgment, the subject is currently dominated by an explicitly apolitical concern with consumer welfare. Concern about the influence of corporate power on the electoral and administrative processes surfaces in the law concerning campaign finance, lobbying, and official conflict of interest. Though they sometimes get attention in constitutional and administrative law, they are treated as specialized subjects.

The only major doctrinal field devoted to workers is labor law. But this field has long been preoccupied with unionized workers who have never been a majority of the work force and are now a rapidly dwindling minority. Nonunionized workers have always been nearly invisible in the law schools and the law reviews. And municipal law has remained a specialized backwater, marginalized both by the preoccupations of the general run of elite legal academics with national government and with the judiciary and by the preoccupations of several of the few practitioners of the subject with narrowly technical matters.[14]

The core business field in which redistribution is a central focus is tax. The relegation of distributive issues to tax seems to express tacitly a preference for the tax/transfer system as a means of redistribution. (The transfer part of this mechanism, of course, gets almost no attention, but that is another story.) Republicanism traditionally opposed reliance on taxes and transfers in favor of a strategy of achieving distributive goals through the rules that determine the distribution of primary incomes, including both labor law and the rules that determine the availability of credit and assistance to small businesses. From the republican point of view, the tax/transfer approach has the dual disadvantage of increasing the dependence of ordinary citizens on the state and of leaving unconstrained the political power of the wealthy that results from their control over the investment process.

The case for broadening the perspective of corporations doctrine does not depend on belief in the superiority of the republican vision or the cooperative program. Those who have recently reconsidered elements of the program differ widely over their merits.[15] But the preeminence of the corporate mode in contemporary doctrine does not rest on any widespread agreement about its superiority, but simply on the a priori exclusion or marginalization of alternatives and the undefended refusal to consider many of the issues that republicans considered essential to the appraisal of economic organization. Thus, the main argument for broadening the focus is to encourage greater reflectiveness about the premises of economic organization.

PROSPECTS FOR CHANGE

Recent developments in economic practice and theory suggest that the time may be auspicious for a redefinition of the field of corporate doctrine to include some of the concerns and issues emphasized in economic republicanism.

Two sets of practical developments have changed the landscape of large enterprise in ways that put increasing pressure on the boundaries of traditional corporation doctrine.

One is the growth of financial intermediaries, and especially pension funds. An increasingly large portion, now approaching about half in terms of value, of ownership claims on publicly held businesses are held by banks, insurance companies, mutual funds, and pension funds. These organizations have both expertise and ability to aggregate claims that make active exercise of shareholder rights more plausible than in the case of dispersed, small-stakes shareholders. Many of these intermediaries hold their shares in trust for middle- and working-class individuals. This is notably true of pension funds whose managers hold shares to finance the current income of retirees and the retirement income of current workers. About half of private sector workers are currently covered by some pension plan, and a substantial and growing share of the nation's capital is owned by these funds.

The notion of large blocks of claims on corporate capital held by middle- and working-class people, most of them employees of large corporations, has inspired the vision of a major transformation of the economy into "pension fund socialism." These suggestions are exaggerated. Without drastic changes in the rules of the game, pension funds will not claim anything approaching a majority of corporate wealth in the foreseeable future. To the extent that socialism implies that workers have control over as well as beneficial interests in capital, the current arrangements are rarely socialistic. Plans typically are not structured to permit beneficiaries to exercise shareholder rights directly. Moreover, most plans do not focus their investments in the companies in which their beneficiaries' work; rather they diversify their holdings so that they do not hold more than a small fraction of the shares of any given company. (In strictly financial terms, such diversification helps beneficiaries by lowering the risk of their investments.)

Nevertheless, the growth of pension capital seems to challenge the traditional boundaries of corporate doctrine. At the least it has brought to prominence a new set of shareholders—the intermediaries—whose structure and conduct have to be taken into account. Moreover, even in the conventional diversified funds, situations sometimes arise where a pension fund in which a firm's workers have substantial beneficial interests has a significant voting block on an issue, such as a takeover by an acquirer expected to initiate layoffs, in which the workers are interested. Such situations raise issues that erode the traditional distinction between shareholders and workers and the relegation of workers to separate peripheral fields.

Moreover, the growth of pension finance at least raises the possibility—and has provided a few examples—of more dramatic shifts to worker ownership. Unlike the conventional diversified fund, the employee stock ownership plan focuses its investments in the stock of the beneficiaries' employer. Such plans have been encouraged in recent years by a tax subsidy. The subsidy is structured so that employers can often capture its financial benefits without giving significant control to employees, and while a significant portion of the work force now participates in such plans, few involve serious worker control. Nevertheless, there have been some notable examples, including a few large firms, of substantial worker ownership and control, and while the tax subsidy is not conditioned on serious shifts in control, it at least legitimates them.[16]

The second set of developments that challenges traditional doctrinal contours concerns both business practice and economic theory. The developments in business practice I have in mind are often discussed in connection with the pressures of intensified foreign competition, the attenuation of demand for standardized mass-produced consumer goods, and the relative decline of the manufacturing in relation to the service sector of the economy.[17] These trends have increased the premium on the ability to make rapid adjustments to volatile market signals and to diversify products. The prototypical large enterprise throughout the period in which corporate doctrine took its modern form was a manufacturing business engaged in very long runs of standardized goods with machinery dedicated to specific operations operated by narrowly skilled workers. But this pattern seems to be changing.

At the enterprise level, managers are insisting that increased product market competition and volatility precludes them from guaranteeing wage and benefit levels of the order to which the more successful unionized manufacturing workers were once accustomed. They also claim that traditional job classifications and work rules designed to protect workers from abusive managerial discretion prevent the kind of prompt, flexible adjustment to market signals that the new environment demands. And at the same time, some of these managers are seeking better trained and motivated workers with more general skills and the capacity for judgment and discretion.

For their part, workers are pressing demands for kinds of job security that impinge on managers' traditional discretion over levels of employment, investment, redeployment of capital, and subcontracting.

One set of responses to these tensions involves the extension to workers of some of the traditional incidents of ownership. These include both financial incidents, such as profit sharing, bonuses, and other forms of contingent compensation. They also include various opportunities for participation in decision making either at the shop-floor level in forms such as quality-of-worklife programs, or at the senior governance level, in forms such as representation on the board of directors. In addition, contractual provisions over matters such as subcontracting and plant closing now occasionally restrict discretion over matters previously considered the prerogatives of managers and owners. These developments make it increasingly difficult to separate owner/creditor/manager relations from employee relations. They also make it harder to understand employee relations in terms of contractual specification.[18]

These developments have involved analogous changes with other constituencies such as suppliers, customers, and governments. Firms are developing increasingly complex and flexible relations with suppliers involving joint investments and complex, flexible coordination (and firms are decentralizing internally by giving autonomy to divisions in ways that sometimes erode the distinction between division and supplier or customer). Governments, especially at the state and local level, have experimented with sponsoring industrial districts or regional economic networks in ways that make them active participants in the enterprises involved.[19]

At the same time economic doctrines that have begun to filter into the law schools have taken a parallel direction, in part, of course, in response to the developments in practice. In 1970, Albert Hirschman succeeded in making intelligible to neoclassical economists the centuries-old republican commonplace that encumbrances on mobility and alienation (barriers to "exit" in his jargon) can promote productive activity by increasing the relative incentives for internal participatory efforts ("voice") to improve the organization or community.[20]

Since then other economists have taken account of the role that long-term relations cemented by relatively immobile investments play in resolving important practical problems ignored in neoclassical economics. Such problems include the viability of executory bargains in a world where litigation is costly and uncertain, and the ability of people with differing levels of knowledge and information to bargain with each other.[21] The solutions to such problems often lie in mutual investments that make the parties dependent on and vulnerable to each other.

Consider, for example, the question of training workers in skills that are specific to the operations of an employer. If the employer finances the training, it risks losing its benefits because the worker may leave. If the worker finances the training, she risks losing its benefits because the employer may discharge her. Moreover, the most effective trainers may be experienced employees, and they may be unwilling to cooperate because they fear that newly trained workers will compete against and replace them. A fully specified long-term employment contract would be unenforceable against the worker and might excessively constrain the employer's ability to change or reduce employment levels in accordance with economic conditions. One response to this situation is a semiformal bargain that includes compensation arrangements that reward seniority, giving the employee an incentive to remain after the training period, and a seniority rule for layoffs, giving workers some protection against discharge before they reach the point of relatively generous compensation and neutralizing the threat of competition from junior workers.

In these circumstances, the firm has made an illiquid investment in the worker by training her; the worker has made an illiquid investment in the firm by giving up other learning and job opportunities and by accepting deferred compensation. The new institutional economists see such semiformal arrangements of mutual interdependence as material bases for the kind of flexible cooperation that obviates full contractual specification and reliance on official enforcement procedures. Once workers are seen in this manner as investors in the firm, their exclusion from the central focus of business organization seems arbitrary.

To the extent these developments in theory and practice continue, they will challange the boundaries that have defined corporations doctrine. While they push toward a different definition of the core concerns of the doctrine, this need not necessarily be a republican one. Indeed the best-known model of an economy built partly on flexible long-term relations—Japan—seems decidedly unrepublican in its acceptance of hierarchy and paternalism.

Nevertheless, the developments in both theory and practice have an affinity for republicanism in at least some respects. First, the business reform ideal of the broadly skilled worker with discretion in the workplace is shared by economic republicanism, which associates it both with economic productivity and effective citizenship.

Second, the contemporary economists' concern with grounding long-term productive cooperative relationships in interdependent investments and their related idea of long-term employment as an investment that may require the kind of security conventionally associated with capital investments somewhat overlap the republican ideal of securing independent membership in a political community through property rights.

Third, both innovative business practice and republicanism tend to subvert the priority given in both legal doctrine and neoclassical economics to the firm as a focus of analysis by shifting attention to relations involving actors such as suppliers, customers, and local governments who are not formal members of the firm.

Fourth, both the new economic practices and republicanism challenge some conventional notions about decentralization in analogous ways. The conventional notions tend to portray decentralization in terms either of the restriction of government regulation and the enhancement of the autonomy of property generally or in terms of the devolution of government power to state and local government. They tend to take for granted that business organizations be internally centralized, and they tend to be relatively indifferent to the kind of economic centralization that arises when private enterprises grow to large size. By contrast, the newer developments occasionally have involved, in a way compatible with republicanism, efforts at internal decentralization of enterprises and experiments with the use of state power to encourage the decentralization of private market structures, for example, through the kind of credit support and technical assistance to small enterprise that was a central part of some nineteenth-century republican programs.

CONCLUSION

To say that a set of doctrines is grounded in ideology is not to say that these doctrines are not worth learning, even to people who find the ideology unattractive. If the doctrines are employed by the dominant actors in important institutions, then anyone who aspires to be a competent practitioner in those institutions needs to master them. At the least, however, aspirants should try to avoid confusing the power that doctrine derives from its congruence to historical and political contingency with its plausibility as a portrayal of a desirable social order. Moreover, both doctrinal and political structures are susceptible to revision and sometimes to far-reaching reconstruction. The recovery of the republican tradition, the revival of institutional economics, and the wave of innovations in business practice suggest that this may be an auspicious time for such a reconstruction of business law doctrine.

NOTES

1. Bayless Manning, "The Shareholder's Appraisal Remedy—An Essay for Frank Coker," 72 *Yale Law Journal* 223, 245, n. 37 (1962).

2. A good discussion of the contract analogy that recognizes the potential of contract rhetoric to absorb the full range of mainstream opinions on corporate issues is John C. Coffee, Jr., "No Exit?: Opting Out, The Contractual Theory of the Corporation, and the Special Case of Remedies," 53 *Brooklyn Law Review* 919, 931–53 (1988).
3. The classic critiques are John Dewey, "The Historical Background of Corporate Legal Personality," 35 *Yale Law Journal* 655 (1926), and Thurman Arnold, *The Folklore of Capitalism* (New Haven: Yale University Press, 1937), pp. 185–262. *See also* Morton J. Horwitz, "*Santa Clara* Revisited: The Development of Corporate Theory," 88 *West Virginia Law Review* 173 (1985).
4. First National Bank of Boston v. Bellotti, 435 U.S. 765, 778–83 (1978). At one point, Justice Powell suggests that he might consider disproportionate power of corporations in the electoral process relevant to the First Amendment issue if there were any support by way of evidence or legislative findings that corporations in fact have disproportionate power. *Id.* at 789. To the extent that Powell here escapes the conceptual naïveté discussed in the text, he seems guilty of empirical naïveté.
5. *Id.* at 822–25.
6. Cited *supra* note 3, p. 246.
7. The takeover literature is enormous. For an enthusiastic view of the takeover as an accountability mechanism, see Frank Easterbrook and Daniel Fischel, "The Proper Role of a Target's Management in Responding to a Tender Offer," 94 *Harvard Law Review* 1161 (1981). For reservations, see John C. Coffee, Jr., "Regulating the Market for Corporate Control: A Critical Assessment of the Tender Offer's Role in Corporate Governance," 84 *Colorado Law Review* 1145 (1984); Andrei Schleifer and Lawrence Summers, "Breach of Trust in Hostile Takeovers," in *Corporate Takeovers: Causes and Consequences*, ed. A. Auerbach (Chicago: University of Chicago Press, 1988); Reinier Kraakman, "Taking Discounts Seriously: The Implications of Discounted Share Prices As an Acquisition Motive," 88 *Colorado Law Review* 891 (1988).
8. For an impressive critique of corporation doctrine from this perspective, *see* Gerald Frug, "The Ideology of Bureaucracy in American Law," 97 *Harvard Law Review* 1276 (1984).
9. *See* J. Willard Hurst, *The Legitimacy of the Business Corporation in the Law of the United States* (Charlottesville: University of Virginia Press, 1970), pp. 13–57; Lawrence Friedman, A *History of American Law* (New York: Simon and Schuster, 1973), pp. 166–78, 446–59. Hurst's discussion reflects a tendency to associate the republican critique of the corporation with the early-nineteenth-century practice of "special" incorporation in which corporate status was typically legislatively bestowed as a special privilege that carried explicit monopoly or quasi-governmental powers and responsibilities. From this perspective, the persistence of hostility to the corporation after the advent of "general" incorporation processes that made a streamlined

package of corporate attributes routinely available seems obtuse or anachronistic. The remarks in the text are intended to rebut this impression by suggesting that the republicans had a plausible critique of general incorporation.

10. *See* Drew McCoy, *The Elusive Republic: Political Economy in Jeffersonian America* (Chapel Hill: University of North Carolina Press, 1980); Sean Wilentz, *Chants Democratic: New York City and the Rise of the American Working Class 1788–1850* (New York: Oxford University Press, 1984); Eric Foner, *Reconstruction: America's Unfinished Revolution 1863–1866* (New York: Harper and Row, 1988); Lawrence Goodwyn, *Democratic Promise: The Populist Moment in America* (New York: Oxford University Press, 1978); George S. Kealey and Bryan D. Palmer, *Dreaming of What Might Be: The Knights of Labor in Ontario 1880–1900* (Cambridge: Cambridge University Press, 1982).

11. William Klein, *Business Organization and Finance* (Mineola: Foundation Press, 1980); Robert Hamilton, *Fundamentals of Modern Business* (Boston: Little, Brown, 1988).

12. But see the recent efforts of Ronald Gilson and Robert Mnookin. *E.g.*, "Sharing Among the Human Capitalists: An Economic Inquiry Into the Corporate Law Firm and How Partners Split Profits," 37 *Stanford Law Review* 313 (1985); *see also* William H. Simon, "Babbitt v. Brandeis: The Decline of the Professional Vision," 37 *Stanford Law Review* 565 (1985).

13. For some forthcoming pioneering efforts to broaden the focus of corporate doctrine to acknowledge conventionally excluded constituencies, *see* John Coffee, "Unstable Coalitions: Corporate Governance as a Multiplayer Game," 78 *Georgetown Law Journal* — (1990); Henry Hansmann, "When Does Worker Ownership Work?," 99 *Yale Law Journal* — (1990). And for an interesting effort to integrate corporate materials into a treatment of labor and employment law, see Robert Rabin, Eileen Silverstein, and George Schatzki, *Labor and Employment Law* (St. Paul, Minn.: West, 1988).

14. But see the recent effort at invigoration by Gerald Frug, *Local Government Law* (St. Paul, Minn.: West, 1988).

15. *E.g.*, contrast Oliver Williamson, *The Economic Institutions of Capitalism* (New York: Free Press, 1985) with Louis Putterman, "On Some Recent Explanations of Why Capital Hires Labor," 22 *Economic Inquiry* 171 (1984).

Contemporary republicans must deal with the fact that in the one area in which republicanism has remained influential in this century—agriculture—its rhetoric has been used to rationalize policies that seem to pervert its political goals. Whether this fact suggests defects in the republican programs or simply a failure to implement them faithfully is a matter of controversy. *See* Grant McConnell, *The Decline of Agrarian Democracy* (Cambridge: Harvard University Press, 1953).

16. *See* Daniel Fischel and John Langbein, "ERISA's Fundamental Contradiction: The Exclusive Benefit Rule," 55 *University of Chicago Law Review*

1105 (1988); Joseph Blasi, *Employee Ownership—Revolution or Ripoff?* (Cambridge: Ballinger, 1988).

17. In this and the following few paragraphs, I draw on the large recent literature on industrial structure and policy, especially on Michael Piore and Charles Sabel, *The Second Industrial Divide: Possibilities for Prosperity* (New York: Free Press, 1984), which links industrial policy issues to republican political ideals. Roberto Mangabeira Unger's *False Necessity* (Cambridge: Cambridge University Press, 1988) situates the industrial policy issues in the context of a broad theory of radical democracy.

18. *See* Katherine Stone, "Labor and the Corporate Structure: Changing Conceptions and Emerging Possibilities," 55 *University of Chicago Law Review* 73 (1988).

19. *See* David Osborne, *Laboratories of Democracy* (Cambridge: Harvard Businss School Press, 1988).

20. Albert Hirschman, *Exit, Voice and Loyalty* (Cambridge: Harvard University Press, 1970).

21. *See* Williamson, *supra* note 15.

III

PROGRESSIVE
APPROACHES
TO THE LAW

20 ROBERT W. GORDON

NEW DEVELOPMENTS IN LEGAL THEORY

THE current preoccupations of many left-wing writers on law may seem at best baffling or at worst pointlessly academic and obscure. At every meeting of the Conference on Critical Legal Studies, one can sense these barriers of puzzlement or irritation being raised between political allies who see themselves for the occasion mainly as "theorists" or "practitioners." It is not—not at all—that the "practitioners" are against theory. They are hungry for theory that would help make sense of their practices; that would order them meaningfully into larger patterns of historical change or structures of social action; that would help resolve the perpetual dilemma of whether it is or is not a contradiction in terms to be a "radical lawyer," whether one is inevitably corrupted by the medium in which one works, whether one's victories are in the long run defeats or one's defeats victories; or that would suggest what tactics, in the boundless ocean of meanness and constraint that surrounds us, to try next. But what they get back from some "theorists" is not that kind of theory—indeed, to some extent, it is a rejection of that kind of theory—but rather essays with names like "The Structure of Blackstone's *Commentaries*" and "Reification in Legal Reasoning," and even "The Importance of Normative Decision-making: The Limitations of Legal Economics as a Basis for Liberal Jurisprudence As Illustrated by the Regulation of Vacation Home Development,"[1] very technical and seemingly far off the point of any common commitment. My hope here is not to try to explicate or even summarize this body of work, which is dense and difficult and often inaccessible, but rather to suggest why the people who do this work are going about it as they are, how we could think that it might be a useful way of acting on our political commitments.

As one way of showing how someone could have come to adopt this kind of theoretical project, I will try to describe the intellectual biography of such a person. This will be a composite biography, partly imaginary and partly autobiographical. It will not tell the story of any particular person involved in the critical legal studies movement; nor could it, because we have come from so many different starting points—some of us law teachers with humanist intellectual concerns and liberal (civil rights and antiwar) political involvements in the 1960s and 1970s; others radical activists of the 1960s who identified with neo-Marxist versions of socialist theory or feminism or both; still others primarily practitioners, many of whom are associated with the National Lawyers Guild and who work in collective law practices, legal-services offices, or a variety of other progressive jobs. Yet for all the diversity in background of this collection of people, and the perpetual, sharp conflicts over issues of method within it, there is an amazing amount of convergence in the work of this group, which suggests that there may be some common features to our common disenchantment with liberal legalism.

So, imagine someone who first started thinking seriously about law as a student in law school in the late 1960s. There, he or she would have been struck by the amazing contrast between the preoccupations of the curriculum and the world outside. When a law student now mentions "the real world," she usually means the world of law practice; but in 1968, of course, "reality" was the incredible political chaos outside. The contrast with the orthodox agenda of legal education was probably one of many factors that broke up the authority of the old curriculum along with that of the teachers who expounded it, in a way from which they have never quite recovered.

Basically, the teachers taught us to do two things: doctrinal analysis and policy analysis. Doctrinal analysis was (as I now recognize) a kind of toned-down legal realism: we learned how to take apart the *formal* arguments for the outcome of a case and to find the underlying layer of justifications that would *really* explain the case, a layer of "principles" and "purposes" behind the rules. Policy analysis was a kind of quickie utilitarian method for use in close cases—it was supposed to enable us to argue for outcomes that could efficiently serve social policies somehow inhering in the legal system. The policies were derived either by appeal to an assumed general consensus of values (personal security, economic growth), or to an assumed (and assumed to be good) trend of historical development (such as from protecting producers to protecting consumers). Sometimes there would be competing policies, representing conflicting "interests"; here the function of policy analysis was to provide an on-the-spot rapid-fire "balancing" of interests.

A really "smart" lawyer who was adept at all these techniques would be able to discover—by the use of legal reasoning alone—socially optimal solutions for virtually all legal problems. The image of the ideal lawyer was that of the technocrat with mildly reformist-liberal sympathies—half hotshot, half benevolent country squire. Smart corporate lawyer-technicians on one side would be counterbalanced by smart government lawyer-technicians on the other. Moreover, the corporate types, trained to see deeper purposes, policies, and historical trends underlying the rules, would advise their corporate clients to play by the deep-level rules in their own long-term interests, and would engage in law-reform efforts in their spare time to keep the rules consistent with principles and up-to-date with changing conditions.

Outside politics must have made it easier for law students of the late 1960s and early 1970s than it had been for those who had graduated just before then to see what was wrong with this vision of law as neutrally benevolent technique. The appeal to a deep social consensus was hardly a winner in a society apparently splintering every day between blacks and whites, hawks and doves, men and women, hippies and straights, parents and children. The appeal to the underlying march of historical progress was in trouble for the same reason. The vision of law as a technocratic policy science administered by a disinterested elite was tarnished, to say the least, for anyone who watched the "best and the brightest" direct and justify the war in Vietnam. The fluent optimistic jargon of policy science in the middle of such unspeakable slaughter and suffering seemed not only absurdly remote from any real world of experience but literally insane.

Under these conditions young lawyers became desperate for a more plausible and less compromised view of the social uses of law; and many of us found it in the emerging vocation of the liberal but antiestablishment, activist reform lawyer, who would deploy the techniques of the system against the system, work for good, substantive rule change, more open and representative procedures, more responsive bureaucracies, and, in general, who would try to make effective and real the law's formal promises of equal justice.

The focus here is not on the concrete achievements of lawyers who adopted this vocation (though personally I think those achievements substantial), but on how actually doing this work may have contributed to their intellectual development. The greatest contribution was probably an education in all the myriad ways in which the system was not a set of neutral techniques available to anyone who could seize control of its levers and pulleys but a game heavily loaded in favor of the wealthy and powerful. Procedure was so expensive and slow that one's side could be exhausted in a single engagement with an enemy who could fight dozens. One was likely to obtain the most favorable rule outcomes just where enforcement of them seemed most hopeless. And even the doctrinal victories peaked all too early: just as a promising line of rules opened up, it would be qualified before it became truly threatening (e.g., antidiscrimination doctrine became quagmired at sanctioning intentional state action against individuals, not quite reaching systemic private action against groups; equal protection doctrine flirted briefly with remedies for wealth inequalities, then scurried into retreat).[2]

At this point, the felt need for a theory that would help explain what was going on became acute; and the kind of theory that seemed called for was one that connected what happened in the legal system to a wider political-economic context. Here orthodox legal thought had almost nothing to offer because even though liberal lawyers had learned from the legal realists that all law was social policy, their working methods kept technical (narrowly legal) issues at the forefront of legal analysis; the conventions of scholarship dictated that if social context were to be discussed at all, it had to be done casually and in passing. Liberal activist lawyers in the process of radical disillusionment had to reach back to the sources of social and political theory, which law school had pushed out of focus. When they did, it was like discovering that what had happened to them was something they had known about all along but had partially suppressed.

The main kinds of commonsense explanations available to them were what are sometimes called instrumental theories of the relationship between law and society.[3] In the *liberal* version, law is a response to social "demands." These demands are frequently those of specific interest groups that want some advantage from the state; law represents the compromise bargains of multiple conflicting interest groups. Other times the demands are more generally expressed as those of the functional "needs" of "the society" or "the economy"; e.g., "the market" needs stable frameworks for rational calculation, which the legal system responds to with contract enforcement, security devices, recording of land titles, etc. In the *orthodox Marxist* version of instrumentalism, of course, bourgeois law is a product not of just any group's demands but specifically those of the capitalist ruling class. In both versions, a "hard" world of economic actions (or "material base") determines what happens in the "soft" world of legal rules and processes (as part of the ideological "superstructure"). Also common to both versions is a deep logic theory of historical change. In the liberal version, this is usually: feudalism→mercantilism→industrial capitalism→organized capitalism→modern welfare capitalism; in the Marxist version, much the same with slightly different terms. Both versions assume that legal systems go through different stages that are necessary functions of the prevailing economic organization. Liberals, for example, explained nineteenth-century tort rules that put all the risks of accidents or product defects on workers and consumers either as functional to that stage of industrial development (because infant industries needed to keep their costs down) or as the result of a temporary (and soon remedied) imbalance of political power in favor of capitalists; the instrumentalist Marxists said much more straightforwardly that capitalists just imposed these costs on workers.

If one had to choose between these theories—both purposely depicted here in their crudest form and *not at all* meant to represent the best that either liberals or Marxists have to offer—the Marxist version would have considerably more explanatory bite, since the liberal-pluralist notion that any interest group could capture the system and make it play the right tunes seems to contradict historical experience as well as the practical experience of the recently embittered lawyers. The liberal versions do not really explain why masses of people passively suffer atrocious treatment from the system, sometimes for decades, without effectively organizing to fight it, or why it seems to function so as to reinforce class, racial, and sexual inequalities: it seems to have a built-in tilt toward reproduction of existing class relations.

Nonetheless, anyone who thought about it would begin to see a great many problems with crude instrumentalist theory. The capitalists did not seem to win all the time through state policy and law: workers had been granted rights to organize and bargain collectively out of it, blacks had received the abolition of slavery and some affirmative government action promoting their rights, radicals had been granted some rights to teach and write, the poor had received some welfare entitlements, etc. Obviously, all this could be rerationalized as serving the long-term interests of the capitalist ruling class, but that would take considerable refinements of the theory. Some writers spoke of the strategy of "corporate liberalism"—the ruling class promotes government social-welfare programs and regulation of business in order to prevent political (through popular risings) and economic (through chaotic competition) destabilization of the social order. Other writers, borrowing from European neo-Marxist sources, began to speak of law as a means of "legitimating" class society: in order to be bearable to those who suffer most from it, law must be perceived to be approximately just, so the ruling class cannot win all the time. Still others, extending the point, saw the "legitimacy" of capitalist society as importantly inhering in (among a number of other factors, such as a certain degree of social mobility, social security for everyone, and apparently meritocratic criteria for determining people's shares of income and wealth) the legal system's promises to protect rights of freedom and security for everyone in the society equally—promises that must sometimes be made good.[4] So, since the legal system must at least appear universal, it must operate to some extent independently (or with "relative autonomy," as the saying goes) from concrete economic interests or social classes. And this need for legitimacy is what makes it possible for other classes to use the system against itself, to try to entrap it and force it to make good on its utopian promises. Such promises may therefore become rallying points for organization, so that the state and law become not merely instruments of class domination but "arenas of class struggle."[5]

Once leftist lawyers became accustomed to thinking this way, a whole new set of problems and questions opened up. One was that given this view of the matter, hard-won struggles to achieve new legal rights for the oppressed began to look like ambiguous victories. The official legal establishment had been compelled to recognize claims on its utopian promises. But these real gains may have deepened the legitimacy of the system as a whole; the labor movement secured the vitally important legal rights to organize and strike, at the cost of fitting into a framework of legal regulation that certified the legitimacy of management's making most of the important decisions about conditions of work.[6]

In any case, once one begins to focus closely on problems such as these, one begins to pay much more attention to what instrumentalists think of as the "soft" or "superstructural" aspects of the legal system. If what is important about law is that it functions to "legitimate" the existing order, one starts to ask *how* it does that. And for the purposes of this project, one does not look only at the undeniably numerous, specific ways in which the legal system functions to screw poor people—though it is always important to do that too, to point it out as often and as powerfully as possible—but also at all the ways in which the system seems at first glance basically uncontroversial, neutral, acceptable. This is Antonio Gramsci's notion of "hegemony," *i.e.*, that the most effective kind of domination takes place when both the dominant and dominated classes believe that the existing order, with perhaps some marginal changes, is satisfactory, or at least represents the most that anyone could expect, because things pretty much have to be the way they are.[7] So Gramsci says, and the "critical" American lawyers who have accepted his concept agree, that one must look closely at these belief systems, these deeply held assumptions about politics, economics, hierarchy, work, leisure, and the nature of reality, which are profoundly paralysis-inducing because they make it so hard for people (including the ruling classes themselves) even to *imagine* that life could be different and better. It's not that ideology drugs the masses into thinking that their rulers and bosses are ideal, that life is fair and that everyone deserves his fate. Most ordinary people may well think that the system plays with a stacked deck and that the deal they got is a lousy one. Yet an ideology can still be "hegemonic" if its practical effect is to foreclose imagination of *alternative* orders. Workers may not much care for authoritarian rule at the workplace. Even so they may not press for economic democracy, because they have bought the arguments that it would lower efficiency, leaving a smaller pie for everyone; or that they are not really competent to run the shop; or that it would be an alien order, some kind of "communism." The existing order may inflict terrible wounds on health and personality and family life and self-respect, and still be tolerated as "the system we have, with all its faults."

Law, like religion and television images, is one of these clusters of belief—and it ties in with a lot of other nonlegal but similar clusters—that convince people that all the many hierarchical relations in which they live and work are natural and necessary. A small business is staffed with people who carry around in their heads mixed clusters of this kind: "I can tell these people what to do and fire them if they're not *very* polite to me and quick to do it, because (a) I own the business; (b) they have no right to anything but the minimum wage; (c) I went to college and they didn't; (d) they would not work as hard or as efficiently if I didn't keep after them; a business can't run efficiently without a strong top-down command structure; (e) if they don't like it they can leave," etc.—and the employees, though with less smugness and enthusiasm, believe it as well. Take the ownership claim: the employees are not likely to think they can challenge that because to do so would jeopardize their sense of the rights of ownership, which they themselves exercise in other aspects of life ("I own this house, so I can tell my brother-in-law to get the hell out of it"); they are locked into a belief cluster that abstracts and generalizes the ownership claim.

Now, the point of the work that some of the "critical" lawyers are doing[8] is to try to describe—to make maps of—some of these interlocking systems of belief. Drawing here on the work of such "structuralist" writers as Lévi-Strauss and Piaget, they claim that legal ideas can be seen to be organized into structures, *i.e.*, complex cultural codes. The way human beings experience the world is by collectively building and maintaining systems of shared meanings that make it possible for us to interpret one another's words and actions.

"Law" is just one among many such systems of meaning that people construct in order to deal with one of the most threatening aspects of social existence: the danger posed by other people, whose cooperation is indispensable to us (we cannot even have an individual identity without them to help define it socially), but who may kill us or enslave us. It seems essential to have a system to sort out positive interactions (contracts, taxation to pay for public goods) from negative ones (crimes, torts, illegal searches, unconstitutional seizure of property). In the West, legal belief-structures, together with economic and political ones, have been constructed to accomplish this sorting out. The systems, of course, have been built by elites who have thought they had some stake in rationalizing their dominant power positions, so they have tended to define rights in such a way as to reinforce existing hierarchies of wealth and privilege.

Even more important, such system building has the effect of making the social world as it is come to seem natural and inevitable. Though the structures are built, piece by interlocking piece, with human intentions, people come to "externalize" them, to attribute to them existence and control over and above human choice; and, moreover, to believe that these structures must be the way they are. Recall the example given earlier of the person who works in a small business for the "owner" of the business. It is true that the owner's position is backed up by the ultimate threat of force—if she does not like the way people behave on her property, she can summon armed helpers from the state to eject them—but she also has on her side the powerful ideological magic of a structure that gives her the "rights" of an "employer" and "owner," and the worker the "duties" of an "employee" and "invitee" on the "owner's property." The worker feels he cannot challenge the owner's right to eject him from her property if she does not like the way he behaves, in part because he feels helpless against the force she can invoke, but also because in part he accepts her claim as legitimate: he respects "individual rights of ownership" because the powers such rights confer seem necessary to his own power and freedom; limitations on an "owner's" rights would threaten him as well. But the analogy he makes is possible only because of his acquiescence in a belief structure—liberal legalism—that abstracts particular relationships between real people (this man and the woman he "works for"; this man and the brother-in-law he wants to eject from his house) into relations between entirely abstract categories of "individuals" playing the abstract social roles of "owner," "employee," etc. This process of allowing the structures we ourselves have built to mediate relations among us so as to make us see ourselves as performing abstract roles in a play that is produced by no human agency is what is usually called (following Marx and such modern writers as Sartre and Lukács) reification.[9] It is a way people have of manufacturing necessity: they build structures, then act as if (and genuinely come to believe that) the structures they have built are determined by history, human nature, economic law.

Perhaps a promising tactic, therefore, of trying to struggle against being demobilized by our own conventional beliefs is to try to use the ordinary rational tools of intellectual inquiry to expose belief structures that claim that things as they are must necessarily be the way they are. There are many varieties of this sort of critical exercise, whose point is to unfreeze the world as it appears to common sense as a bunch of more or less objectively determined social relations and to make it appear as (we believe) it really is: people acting, imagining, rationalizing, justifying.

One way of accomplishing this is to show that the belief structures that rule our lives are not found in nature but are historically contingent; they have not always existed in their present form. (Elizabeth Mensch's essay in this volume summarizes the history of various forms of American legal thought over the last two hundred years.) This discovery is extraordinarily liberating, not (at least not usually) because there is anything so wonderful about the belief structures of the past, but because uncovering those structures makes us see how arbitrary our categories for dividing up experience are, how nonexhaustive of human potentiality. Another useful exercise is just simple empirical disproof of the claim of necessity. When it is asserted that strict, predictable rules of private property and free contract are necessary to protect the functioning of the market, maintain production incentives, etc., it can be shown that the actual rules are not at all what they are claimed to be, that they can be applied quite differently in quite different circumstances, sometimes "paternalistically," sometimes strictly, sometimes forcing parties to share gains and losses with each other, and sometimes not at all.[10] Or it may be asserted that certain hierarchical ways of organizing are necessary for efficient realization of economies of scale. One can use historical (nineteenth-century worker-organized steel production) or comparative (Japanese, for instance) examples to demonstrate that "efficient" production can occur under all sorts of conditions.[11] Or one can try to show that even at the level of theory, the claim of necessity is, on its own terms, incoherent or contradictory; this approach is currently being practiced on the various forms of "legal economics" that claim that certain regimes of legal rules are "efficient."[12] One can bring similar critiques to bear on claims that things must be the way they are because of some long-term logic of historical change ("modernization," "what is, after all, an inevitable consequence of social life in industrialized societies," "the price of living in a modern pluralistic society," "an inevitable consequence of the declining rate of profit under monopoly capitalism," etc.). It turns out that these theories of development cannot be applied to the concrete histories of particular societies without being so qualified, refined, or partially repudiated that they lose all their force as determining theories—at best, they are only helpful insights or ways of organizing thinking about the world.

If we start to look at the world this way—no longer as some determined set of "economic conditions" or "social forces" that are pushing us around but rather as in the process of continuous creation by human beings, who are constantly reproducing the world they know because they (falsely) believe they have no choice—we will obviously bring a very different approach to the debate over whether legal change can ever effect real ("social and economic") change, or whether law is wholly dependent on the real, "hard" world of production. For if social reality consists of reified structures, "law" and "the economy" are *both* belief systems that people have externalized and allowed to rule their lives. Moreover, if the critiques of legal belief structures are accurate—that even in their theoretically ideal forms they are contradictory and incoherent, and that in practical application they depart constantly from the ideal in wildly varying fashion—it follows that no particular regime of legal principles *could* be functionally necessary to maintain any particular economic order. Similarly, no given economic order can be thought of as requiring for its maintenance any particular bunch of legal rules, except of course those that may be part of the *definition* of that economic order, as "private property" of some sort is to most people's definition of capitalism.

So—if one were to adopt this approach—one would no longer be inclined to look for explanations of how the world works in theories of large-scale social forces such as "industrialization" or "monopoly capitalism," which suggest that the course of social change is objectively determined by processes and structures out of the reach of human agency. It may be that the place to look for insight into how social life is constructed is somewhere quite different—in the smallest, most routine, most ordinary interactions of daily life in which some human beings dominate others and they acquiesce in such domination. It may be, as Foucault's work suggests,[13] that the whole legitimating power of a legal system is built up out of such myriad tiny instances.

I do not want to give the impression that everyone in the critical legal studies movement has adopted the approaches I have just described. On the contrary, these approaches are hotly debated. Some of those who most fiercely dispute the validity of these approaches do so in part on political grounds. I will mention a few of these criticisms and briefly respond to them.

One criticism is that the view that law and the economy as we know them are structures inside people's heads is a form of "idealism"; it assumes that the world can be changed merely by *thinking* about it differently. This charge is, I think, both true and not true. It is true in that the belief it criticizes is indeed that among the main constraints upon making social life more bearable are these terrible, constricting limits on imagination; and that these structures are as obdurate as they are because they are collectively constructed and maintained—we *have* to use them to think about the world at all, because the world makes no sense apart from our systems of shared meanings. But the charge is not true if it means to imply that we believe that all constraints on human action are imaginary, alienated ideas of "false necessity." Obviously there are many constraints on human social activity—scarcities of desired things, finite resources of bodies and minds, production possibilities of existing and perhaps all future technologies, perhaps even ineradicable propensities for evil—that any society will have to face. What is false is to think that these constraints dictate that we are limited to some specific set of social arrangements that we are already familiar with, in history or in our own time; that the human race can live only within its real constraints in a few specific ways (e.g., that it *must* choose between liberal capitalism and state socialist dictatorship).

There are other constraints of a different kind: entrenched power and privilege, which are not easily surrendered; customary inertia; fear even among the dispossessed that any change will leave them with less than they have; terror of the unknown. Obviously it takes more than reimagining the world to overcome these constraints: it takes the courage and cunning to organize with others and struggle against circumstances. But reimagination, getting to the point of seeing that change is possible, is a necessary first step.

People don't revolt because their situation is bad; they can suffer in silence for centuries. They revolt when their situation comes to seem *unjust* and *alterable*. A tiny example from very recent history: Until a few years ago, a working woman had to accept her employer's sexual advances as something she had invited by her dress and manner, or as an inevitable occupational risk, given natural male aggression. Feminists got together and reinterpreted this kind of interaction as "sexual harassment," something both culpable and avoidable; then by engaging in politics got it defined as a legal harm with a legal remedy. That doesn't always help the victims much, because legal rights are hard to vindicate. But the process has switched many people's (including employers') views of the conduct from "It's only natural; that's life," to "He's a creep; that's unacceptable."

Other critics worry that the critique that "rights" lack any objective substance or reality, that they are merely shared practices that people adopt and then reify, may be dangerous to the interests of subordinated groups. Such groups have wrung whatever concessions they have from the dominant society by asserting that they have—that they almost physically *possess*—"rights" that are as real as chairs and tables, that the "rule of law, not of men" requires that their rights be recognized and protected as a kind of property. If "rights" are reanalyzed as conventional and contingent, subject to shifting political winds, won't that leave minorities completely unprotected? I would respond this way: It's certainly true that the language of "rights" has been a powerful mobilizer of insurgency and resistance, has exerted a powerful appeal upon influencial outsiders (as for example the southern black civil rights movement appealed to northern whites in the 1950s and 60s), and has thus delivered powerful leverage for negotiating with people in authority. But the rhetoric of rights can be dangerously double-edged, as the black civil rights movement has also discovered. Floor entitlements can be turned into ceilings (you've got your rights, but that's all you'll get). Formal rights without practical enforceable content are easily substituted for real benefits. Anyway, the powerful can always assert counter-rights (to vested property, to differential treatment according to "merit," to association with one's own kind) to the rights of the disadvantaged. The fact is that "rights" are just shorthand symbols for social practices that people collectively value and maintain. The right to be free of illegal searches and seizures is a bunch of rules governing police conduct, enforced by agencies outside the police bureaucracy. It should be possible to value, and fight for, the substantive practices that the rights only symbolically represent without mystifying and falsely objectifying the symbols themselves.

The notion that there are no objective laws of social change is in one way profoundly depressing. Those who have come to believe it have had to abandon the most comforting hopes of socialism: that history was on its side, and that history could be accelerated through a scientific understanding of social laws. It no longer seems plausible to think that organization of the working class or capture of the state apparatus will magically bring about the conditions within which people could begin to realize the utopian possibilities of social life. Such strategies have led to valuable if modest improvements in social life, as well as to stagnation, co-optation by the existing structures, and nightmare regimes of state terror. Of course, this does not mean that people should stop trying to organize the working class or to influence the exercise of state power; it means only that they have to do so pragmatically and experimentally, with full knowledge that there are no deeper logics of historical necessity that can guarantee that what we do now will be justified later. Yet, if the real enemy is us—*all* of us, the structures we carry around in our heads, the limits on our imagination—where can we even begin? Things seem to change in history when people break out of their accustomed ways of responding to domination, by acting as if the constraints on their improving their lives were not real and that they could change things; and sometimes they can, though not always in the way they had hoped or intended; but they never knew they could change them at all until they tried.

NOTES

1. Duncan Kennedy, "The Structure of Blackstone's *Commentaries*," 28 *Buffalo Law Review* 205 (1979); Peter Gabel, "Reification in Legal Reasoning," in *Research in Law and Sociology*, ed. Stephen Spitzer (Greenwich, Conn.: JAI Press, 1980), 3: 25–51; Thomas C. Heller, "The Importance of Normative Decision-Making: The Limitations of Legal Economics as a Basis for Liberal Jurisprudence as Illustrated by the Regulation of Vacation Home Development," 1976 *Wisconsin Law Review* 385 (1976).
2. *See* Alan D. Freeman, "Legitimizing Racial Discrimination Through Anti-Discrimination Law: A Critical Review of Supreme Court Doctrine," 62 *Minnesota Law Review* 1049 (1978); Derrick A. Bell, "Bakke, Minority Admissions, and the Usual Price of Racial Remedies," 67 *California Law Review* 3 (1979).
3. Some classic instrumentalist texts are David B. Truman, *The Governmental Process: Political Interests and Public Opinion* (New York: Alfred A. Knopf, 1951); and Ralph Miliband, *The State in Capitalist Society* (New York: Basic Books, 1969).
4. *See* Edward P. Thompson, "The Rule of Law," *Whigs and Hunters* (New York: Pantheon Books, 1975); Douglas Hay et al., *Albion's Fatal Tree: Crime and Society in Eighteenth-Century England* (New York: Pantheon Books,

1975); and Mark V. Tushnet, "A Marxist Analysis of American Law," 1 *Marxist Perspectives* 96 (1978).

5. *See* Thompson, *supra* note 4; David M. Trubek, "Complexity and Contradiction in the Legal Order: Balbus and the Challenge of Critical Social Thought About Law," 11 *Law & Society Review* 527 (1977).

6. *See* Karl Klare, chapter 3, *supra*.

7. *See* Antonio Gramsci, *Selections from the Prison Notebooks*, ed. and trans. Quinton Hoare and Geoffrey Nowell-Smith (New York: International Publishers, 1971), pp. 195–96, 246–47.

8. *See, e.g.*, Kennedy, *supra* note 1; Isaac D. Balbus, "Commodity Form and Legal Form: An Essay on the Relative Autonomy of the Law," 11 *Law & Society Review* 571 (1977); Thomas C. Heller, "Is the Charitable Exemption from Property Taxes an Easy Case? General Concerns About Legal Economics and Jurisprudence," *Essays on the Law and Economics of Local Governments*, ed. Daniel Rubinfeld (Washington, D.C.: Urban Institute, 1979), pp. 183–251; Al Katz, "Studies in Boundary Theory: Three Essays in Adjudication and Politics," 28 *Buffalo Law Review* 383 (1979); Roberto Mangabeira Unger, *Knowledge and Politics* (New York: The Free Press, 1975).

9. *See generally*, Gabel, *supra* note 1.

10. *See, e.g.*, Duncan Kennedy, "Form and Substance in Private Law Adjudication," 89 *Harvard Law Review* 1685 (1976); Karl Klare, "Contracts, Jurisprudence and the First-Year Casebook," 54 *New York University Law Review* 876 (1979). *Cf.* James B. Atleson, "Work Group Behavior and Wildcat Strikes: The Causes and Functions of Industrial Civil Disobedience," 34 *Ohio State Law Journal* 750 (1973).

11. *See, e.g.*, Katherine W. Stone, "The Origin of Job Structures in the Steel Industry," 6 *Review of Radical Political Economy* 61 (1974).

12. *See, e.g.*, Mark Kelman, "Choice and Utility," 1979 *Wisconsin Law Review* 769 (1979); Kelman, "Consumption Theory, Production Theory and Ideology in the Coase Theorem," 52 *Southern California Law Review* 669 (1979); Thomas C. Heller, *supra* notes 1 and 8; Morton J. Horwitz, "Law and Economics: Science or Politics?" 8 *Hofstra Law Review* 905 (1980); Duncan Kennedy and Frank I. Michelman, "Are Property and Contract Efficient?" 8 *Hofstra Law Review* 711 (1980).

13. *See, especially*, Michel Foucault, *Discipline and Punish: The Birth of the Prison*, trans. Alan Sheridan (New York: Pantheon Books, 1977).

21 VICTOR RABINOWITZ

THE RADICAL
TRADITION IN THE LAW

ON June 27, 1905, the founding convention of the Industrial Workers of the World (IWW) met in Chicago, pursuant to a call urging the creation of "one big industrial union" to be "founded on the class struggle." The Credentials Committee reported the attendance of nearly two hundred delegates—socialists, anarchists, members of industrial trade unions, and a handful of representatives from craft unions. The committee recommended the seating of the delegates and also recommended the seating, as a fraternal delegate, of a lawyer from New York. A long and bitter debate followed. Lillian Forberg, speaking against the recommendation to seat the lawyer, said:

> This is the first convention, to my knowledge, that has ever been called to organize the working class into an organization by which they can fight the capitalist class. The only thing that an attorney ever did in this world was to support the capitalist class. The only way in which attorneys at law ever express their friendship to the working class is by fighting for injunctions before the courts of law against the working class. I think it is a well-known fact that no attorney of law could be anything else but a parasite. We are here to fight the whole parasitical class and to organize the working class.[1]

The convention resolved not to seat the lawyer, after refusing to permit him to address the convention.

The New York lawyer was Louis B. Boudin. His exclusion by the IWW convention did not put an end to either his political or his legal career. He became a part of the leadership of the Socialist party and, during World War I, was prominent in the left wing of the party, which opposed U.S. participation in the war effort. He was the author of *The Theoretical System of Karl Marx*, a book highly regarded in Marxist circles. After the formation of the CIO, he represented many of the new unions in their early and most militant struggles. He similarly acted for scores of radicals brought up on criminal charges or faced with deportation, and he participated in the formation of the National Lawyers Guild. In his time Louis Boudin was one of the most active, and perhaps the most learned, of the radical lawyers in this country.

The debate over the role of the law (and the lawyer) in the class struggle has not abated since 1905, and the nature and significance of the legal system continue to be the subject of extensive discussion. In 1971 a collection of essays by radical lawyers in the United States, edited by Robert Lefcourt, was published under the title *Law Against the People.*[2] The editor, in his preface, quoted Herbert Marcuse:

> . . . there is no (enforceable) law other than that which serves the status quo, and . . . those who refuse such services are *eo ipso* outside the realm of law even before they come into actual conflict with the law.

The Law, in this view, while pretending to be a benign, neutral force dispensing justice, equality, and due process, actually is but a fraudulent cover-up for the force through which The State rules.

More recently, Critical Legal Studies, which has generally made a very positive progressive contribution to legal scholarship, has generated some writings that indict the law from a different perspective, for its indeterminacy and lack of coherence. These writings, criticized most poignantly by the late Edward Sparer,[3] sometimes repudiate the rule of law and lapse into nihilism and hopelessness.

These approaches encourage cynicism about our legal structure and give up the battle that both the mass of the people and a handful of lawyers have carried on for centuries—a battle for progressive, socially desirable laws and against retrogressive laws—by failing to distinguish between them or even to admit that such differentiation can exist.

This paper is written with a few assumptions in mind, which should be set down. No society of even moderate complexity, whether it be feudal, capitalist, or socialist, can exist without law. All systems of law are constructed to protect the state and its economic base. Conduct that seriously threatens the survival of the state or that would effectuate a basic change in the economic system is, *ipso facto*, "illegal." Those in whose interests the state exists will necessarily make laws to protect that state, and a government that will tolerate effective seditious conduct is almost beyond our imagination.

Having said this, there are several points to be made.

The law sets up standards and rules by which the state agrees to exercise its power and which, by definition, set limits on that exercise. These standards and limits are, of course, self-imposed, but in the long run every state finds it necessary to impose some restrictions upon itself because no structured society can exist for long if state power is lawless and completely arbitrary. Most states find it desirable to act by these standards. Thus, over the past two hundred years in the United States, there has grown up a body of law, some of it statutory, some common law, and some judge-made, that curbs the state's conduct. Similar development has inevitably taken place in every organized society, capitalist, socialist, or somewhere in between. The state relinquishes a part of its power to act, except in conformity with certain rules.

Whether those rules give adequate protection to the people will vary greatly in different situations, but the existence of rules provides some protection against totally arbitrary state action. To the degree that state power is exercised in an arbitrary manner, the state itself becomes unstable and subject to the constant threat of revolutionary violence. When that happens for any considerable period of time, one of the inevitable demands of the people is for a change in the law which will put further checks on the authority of the state. This has been happening for centuries.

In a modern state, the law does more than establish standards by which the state promises to conduct its business. In such a state there is a working class sufficiently well educated and sufficiently articulate not only to carry on the role required of it in a capitalist society but also, in the long run, to demand certain action by the state. Capitalist law (and even precapitalist law in the English common-law tradition), under great pressure from the mass of the people, has, from the earliest days, promised to those masses equality of treatment, justice, fair play, due process, and other abstract idealizations. In this country, the law even promises freedom of speech, press, religion, and assembly, freedom from unreasonable search and seizure, and all of those other good things set forth in the Bill of Rights.

It is true that these promises are often broken, perhaps more often than not, and it may take decades to enforce them effectively. It is also true that many of those who made the promises in the first place never intended that they should be kept. Governments seldom deliver on such promises of equality, justice, and freedom. But the promises are made; and the fact is that very large numbers of the people accept, believe in, and rely on these abstract principles. Often they demand that the promises be kept; they may even be willing to march and riot in the streets, and sit down in factories and churches to enforce the promises. Belief in and devotion to these principles are not confined to the working class; many members of the middle class, including, in our country, even some members of Congress and some judges, believe in these promises or are unwilling to repudiate them.

For example, the trade-union movement of this country in the 1930s and

1940s, the civil rights movement of the 1950s and 1960s, and the antiwar movement of the 1960s and 1970s would not have been possible had we not had a deep tradition of respect for freedom of speech and assembly. It is a mistake to minimize the significance of that tradition in our history. This and related traditions are deeply embedded in the consciousness of most of the American people even though these traditions are frequently frustrated in practice; and much progress has been made because these rights have been assumed by most of us.

For who can deny that progress has been made? Certainly not one who has read Mayhew or Dickens or even Stephen's *History of the Criminal Law*.

A century and a half ago, poor people spent years in custody because they could not pay their debts; in England, many were transported to the other side of the world for such "offenses." Today there are no debtors' prisons in the United States or England, and transportation is no longer acceptable. Less than two centuries ago, trade unions were deemed unlawful conspiracies in the United States; in the past half-century, unions have been given recognition, approval, and encouragement by the state. The factory and housing conditions that characterized the growth of the industrial revolution in England and the United States have largely been ameliorated by the passage of housing, factory, and child-labor laws; the conditions under which men, women, and children customarily worked in Birmingham, England, and Lowell, Massachusetts, would not be tolerated today in any advanced capitalist state.

Censorship of written material has been relaxed; only a few decades ago, Joyce's *Ulysses* could not be imported into the United States or transported through the mails. The situation today is quite different. Less than two centuries ago, there were five hundred crimes punishable by death in England, and public executions were commonplace; today, there is no capital punishment in England. In this country, executions averaged almost one every other day in the 1930s; the number of executions in the United States since 1972, at present writing, has averaged less than ten a year. In an ever-increasing number of states and cities, laws protecting the rights of homosexuals have been enacted. And, of course, the greatest progress of all has been made with respect to the rights of minorities and women in our society.

The catalog could be extended at length. Let us take but a quick look at some of the major developments in our constitutional law in the recent past.

In *Gideon* v. *Wainwright*,[4] the Supreme Court held that all persons charged with serious crimes are entitled to a lawyer and that the court must appoint one where the defendant is indigent. In *Miranda* v. *State of Arizona*,[5] the Court held that persons in police custody must be warned of their constitutional rights and advised of their right to get legal counsel. In *Mapp* v. *Ohio*,[6] the Court held that evidence illegally seized by the police from the defendant may not be used in criminal proceedings against him. In *Furman* v. *Georgia*,[7] the Supreme Court in effect held unconstitutional the capital punishment laws in forty-one of the states. These and many other decisions provided a much greater measure of protection to individuals charged with crimes, but they have no discernible effect one way or another on the continued survival of capitalism.

In *Griswold* v. *Connecticut*,[8] the Court held that a statute prohibiting the use of contraceptives was unconstitutional, and in fact now the sale and use of contraceptives are now both legal and commonplace. In *Roe* v. *Wade*,[9] the Court struck down statutes, effective in twenty-eight states, severely limiting or prohibiting abortions. All of these changes in the law have been in the direction of those very qualities of justice, equality, and fair play which some hold to be irrelevant to the legal system. That view simply denies the reality and importance of these changes.

Nor will it do to point out that *Furman, Mapp, Miranda* and especially *Roe* have been under attack by the Reagan and Bush judges, and that many of the rights won in the civil rights movement of the sixties are in danger of being lost, at least in part. *Roe*, in particular, is likely to be the subject of a continuing struggle to be fought in every state for the next decade or two. The history of the laws governing abortion is set forth in summary in Justice Blackmun's decision, and it is clear that the pendulum between laws permitting abortion and those prohibiting it has swung widely for over two thousand years. It may be that *Roe* represents three steps forward and we may be forced two steps back, but it seems unlikely that we will revert to the situation in 1950 where all but Alabama and the District of Columbia banned abortion "however and whenever performed, unless done to save or preserve the life of the mother."[10]

The current struggle over the *Roe* decision is instructive. Unlike previous times in our history, we have a militant feminist movement which is fighting to establish the law permitting free choice by women. They do not see the law as the instrument of the ruling class, but as an opportunity for greater freedom. It may safely be predicted that this fight will be a successful one in many if not most parts of the country.[11]

It will hardly be productive of success to advise the participants in this struggle that the law is a fraud and serves only the capitalist class. On the contrary, it is the low-income segments of our population who have the most to gain in this battle over changes in the law.

Progress in the assertion and development of human rights has always been slow, and we must not fall into the trap of viewing the history of humankind as if it extended over a mere span of a few decades. It is also true that now, as in Jefferson's day, eternal vigilance is the price of liberty, and many of the gains that have been made are constantly threatened and will continue to be threatened under a capitalist, socialist, or any other kind of economic system. Failure to exercise that vigilance exacts a heavy price, a price we are called upon to pay.

Of course, changes in the law have not transformed our capitalist system; they have not abolished poverty, nor have they eliminated economic classes in our society. But the law was never intended to perform those tasks and, if our earlier assumptions are true, cannot be understood as having so promised. Those changes can be brought about only by political, perhaps even by extralegal or illegal means.

None of this should be understood as suggesting that the law gives adequate protection to the working men and women. This can never be so as long as there are inequalities in wealth and power, and such inequalities will always exist under capitalism. In some respects the law has not significantly improved much in two or three centuries. The election laws are, generally speaking, still rigged to frustrate the democratic process and are helpful principally to the wealthy; the tax laws still impose the heaviest burden on the working class; and the laws relating to real property still leave a tenant with little power. These conditions provide more battles for the progressive lawyer to fight. Unlike Alexander the Great, we still have more worlds to conquer.

It is often argued that these legal reforms and the legal system itself have the effect of preserving the capitalist system and serve to postpone basic change as well. To some extent this is true. Certainly the unemployment insurance and Social Security laws, the extension of suffrage to blacks in the South, and even child-labor laws were required to bring the industrial revolution to fruition; and objectively they strengthen, not weaken, capitalism. Had these reforms not occurred, economic and social conditions would be much worse than they are; but who would advocate their repeal to bring the revolution closer? This argument puts progressives in the untenable position of advocating misery and assumes that misery will lead to progressive change.

Moreover, while capitalism was strengthened by many of these measures, it does not follow that the "ruling class" permitted such reforms in order to preserve the economic system. The contrary is true. The New Deal measures were adopted during the thirties in the context of powerful working-class movements demanding substantial progressive changes. These demands and movements were fought tooth and nail by the capitalist class, to whom President Franklin Roosevelt was the devil incarnate; Roosevelt reciprocated with his attacks on the "economic royalists." Who was responsible for those laws is a complex question and beyond the scope of this paper, but there is no evidence that those laws were merely bones thrown by the leaders of capitalism to the working class to pacify it, or that they were the result of prescient and sagacious planning by United States Steel, General Motors, Chase National Bank et al.

Even more important, most of the changes discussed above have little to do with the preservation of the capitalist system or, for that matter, with the preservation of any economic system except to the extent that they meet the needs of the people and to that extent strengthen the state, which is what the law is supposed to do. They are certainly not merely devices of the ruling class intended to serve only the ruling class.

There is no discernible connection between the preservation of capitalism and the legalization of contraception, the legalization of abortion, the abolition of capital punishment, the effective abolition of censorship over "obscene" literature, the strengthening of the laws against search and seizure and the protection of the rights of people charged with crime. The *Roe* v. *Wade* controversy has its basic roots in religion and conflicting views as to ethics and morality. Capitalism will not be strengthened or weakened by the result of that battle. The lawyers fighting to maintain the pro-choice position are not mere lackeys serving the ruling class, but are, on the contrary, aiding in the preservation and extension of human liberty.

It is noteworthy that many of these recent changes in our law are judge-made and not required by any legislative action. Some of these changes purport to be required by ambiguous language in our Constitution, requirements that were not discovered until about two hundred years after the Constitution was adopted. In fact, the judges who wrote those opinions were "interpreting" a Constitution which they perceived to be a flexible document to meet a current social need. They were moved in some cases under popular pressure and in some cases by what Chief Justice Warren called "the evolving standards of decency that mark the progress of a maturing society."[12]

In recent years, a new and important issue has arisen, not only in our country, but all over the world: respect for and protection of our global environment. The development of a body of law to protect the environment should be high on the agenda of progressive lawyers because here, if anywhere, it is clear that such laws are not for the protection of any class in society but for the protection and indeed survival of all of us. The problems which will face us in this area, I believe, are exceptionally difficult and without clear principles to guide us. Freedoms which have been regarded by most Americans as essential to a decent existence (such as driving an automobile) may have to be curtailed. A system involving some collective control over many of our activities, heretofore regarded as basic liberties, may be required if we are to survive. It is important that this system not be constructed in a manner which deprives persons of low income of the comforts of life while giving the wealthy the freedom to destroy life. We are only at the beginning of this new phase of the development of our law, but certainly there is enough to be done which is not in the service of capitalism.

I suggest that the law develops a dynamic and a life of its own which is independent of capitalism or any other system of economic relationships. It grows out of the pressure of the people for a better, more rational, and more bearable existence, and out of changes in the moral and ethical systems of a society that require changes in the law even when there is no economic reason or popular demand therefore. Even the most conservative judges can be moved, on some occasions, by the horrors of capital punishment, by the fearful consequences of laws against abortion, and by the terrors of police abuse; even conservative state legislators suffer physical discomfort at having to breathe the air of Los Angeles and New York.

Any capitalist legal system undoubtedly crystallizes class relations and masks injustice created by those relations. But what is the alternative? The exercise of naked, arbitrary power without even the forms of law can hardly constitute an improvement. English historian and disarmament activist Edward P. Thompson has made this point most eloquently:

> [T]he notion of the regulation and reconciliation of conflicts through the rule of law—and the elaboration of rules and procedures which, on occasion, made some approximate approach towards the ideal—seems to me a cultural achievement of universal significance. I do not lay any claim as to the abstract, extra-historical impartiality of these rules. In a context of gross class inequalities, the equity of the law must always be in some part sham. . . . I am insisting only upon the obvious point, which some modern Marxists have overlooked, that there is a difference between arbitrary power and the rule of law. We ought to expose the shams and inequities which may be concealed beneath this law. But the rule of law itself, the imposing of effective inhibitions upon power and the defence of the citizen from power's all-intrusive claims, seems to me to be an unqualified human good. To deny or belittle this good is, in this dangerous century when the resources and pretentions of power continue to enlarge, a desperate error of intellectual abstraction. More than this, it is a self-fulfilling error, which encourages us to give up the struggle against bad laws and class-bound procedures, and to disarm ourselves before power. It is to throw away a whole inheritance of struggle *about* law, and within the forms of law, whose continuity can never be fractured without bringing men and women into immediate danger. . . .
>
> . . . It is true that in history the law can be seen to mediate and to

legitimize existent class relations. Its forms and procedures may crystallize those relations and mask ulterior injustice. But this mediation, through the forms of law, is something quite distinct from the exercise of unmediated force. The forms and rhetoric of law acquire a distinct identity which may, on occasion, inhibit power and afford some protection to the powerless. Only to the degree that this is seen to be so can law be of service in its other aspect, as ideology. [13]

Shall we proclaim that the law is a fraud; or should we as progressives interested in creating a better world use the law as a vehicle through which we seek to compel the state to keep the promises it makes—the promises contained in the Constitution and in the Fourth of July orations? When the law fails to keep these promises, is it not our duty to promote a confrontation between the people and the state to compel the latter to move toward the dream of a better world we share with all others?

There is certainly enough to be done. We can do our best to keep activists out of jail and on the streets. We can seek to extend to their ultimate limit the rights of free speech, due process, freedom from unreasonable searches, and similar rights, to make more possible major changes in our economic system. We can expose police abuse and protect the right of privacy, both in political and personal affairs. We can, as lawyers and legal workers, join with rank-and-file trade-union groups in the struggle for the establishment of democracy in the trade unions. We can use our talents to protect the rights of women to an abortion or the rights of gays to a job. We can use our imaginations to devise new methods to attack the environmental problems, which are worldwide in their scope. Many of us have legislative skills that can be put to good service.

And most important of all, we can join with other radical lawyers in developing a modern Marxist theory of the role of the law and the radical lawyer in our society. The office of such a theory will be to point a direction for such lawyers. It will help us to distinguish between reforms that carry the seeds of oppression and developments that truly represent an improvement in the lot of humankind. Such, we understand, are the tasks undertaken by this volume of essays.

NOTES

1. *Proceedings of the First Convention of the Industrial Workers of the World* (New York: New York Labor News Co., 1905), pp. 26, 67–70.

2. R. Lefcourt, ed., *Law Against the People* (New York: Random House, 1971).
3. Edward Sparer, "Fundamental Human Rights, Legal Entitlements, and the Social Struggle: A Friendly Critique of the Critical Legal Studies Movement," 36 *Stanford Law Review* 508 (1984).
4. 372 U.S. 335 (1963).
5. 384 U.S. 436 (1966).
6. 367 U.S. 643 (1961).
7. 408 U.S. 238 (1972).
8. 381 U.S. 479 (1965).
9. 410 U.S. 113 (1973).
10. Roe v. Wade, supra note 9, at p. 139.
11. On July 5, 1989, Mario Cuomo, the Catholic governor of New York announced that he would resist any effort to restrict abortions in New York, in apparent recognition of the fact that reelection would require such a position, despite the powerful presence of the Catholic Church in the state.
12. Trop v. Dulles, 356 U.S. 86 at 101. *See also* Weems v. U.S., 217 U.S. 349.
13. Edward P. Thompson, *Whigs and Hunters* (New York: Pantheon Books, 1975), pp. 265–66.

22 MARK KELMAN

A CRITIQUE OF CONSERVATIVE LEGAL THOUGHT

THERE is an undeniable similarity between two distinct strands of right-wing academic legal thought that emerged as major forces in the law schools in the seventies and the judicial and administrative behavior of the Reagan-era appointees. Of course, the translation from any academic discourse to daily legal practice is rarely smooth or straightforward. It is surely questionable, moreover, whether there is a *causal* nexus between abstract elite ideology and real world political behavior. But particular adherents of both "law and economics" and "libertarianism" have gained prominence as both federal judges and administrative policy advisers (e.g., Posner, Easterbrook, Winter, Bork, Williams, Anderson). More significantly, it is difficult to understand the prevailing conservative political/legal climate without understanding these distinct ideologies.

Libertarians and conservative legal economists frequently advocate parallel institutional programs. Both tend to oppose redistributive taxation and income support programs, favor deregulating the workplace and consumer sales, oppose expansive judicial activity limiting the enforcement of substantively unfair contracts and frequently legitimate monopolies that the American legal system has long not tolerated. Their underlying normative positions, though, are quite distinct in ways that deserve attention.

Legal economists have had vastly more influence on law in part because their concrete policy program better matches the prevailing political mood of the New Right. Since the libertarians favor deregulation of behavior that the religious right clearly wants to see proscribed (e.g., consensual homosexuality), libertarianism as ideology is unacceptable to a significant portion of the Reagan/Bush coalition. But the legal economists have also had a greater impact on the legal culture because their framework is far more compatible with mainstream modern legal thought than is libertarianism.

LIBERTARIANISM[1]

Libertarians start with the supposition that individuals possess certain natural rights, which the state is created simply to protect. Collective bodies do not really *select* an appropriate entitlement scheme, a set of claims people can insist the state enforce. Instead, they simply ratify a natural, conceptually preexisting scheme of entitlements. The scheme of entitlements that is ostensibly simply "recognized" is supposedly the only one compatible with the observation that persons are fundamentally separate, that their interests may diverge, and that each can justly choose to treat his own concerns as paramount.

While libertarians understand that people are altruistic, at least on some occasions toward some other people, altruistic behavior must be a choice, not a duty. To mandate that a person share his resources with another is to treat the "owner" as a means rather than an end, to fail to recognize his separateness and importance as an individual. Not only must the state refrain from mandating duties to share, it must permit all self-seeking activity that is not harmful to others. Thus, the regime must be one of "free contract" (without mandatory terms, without bars on the subject matter of contracts) at least so long as the contract affects only the contracting parties themselves. At the same time, the state is bound to regulate harm causing, which is thought to violate the victim's natural rights. While people must be free to bargain away the right to insist that their "boundaries" be respected against invasion, any invasion (trespass, use of force, or threat) that is not consented to must either be prohibited or give rise to a claim for compensation.

The basic libertarian picture of acceptable social process is seemingly simple. It is thought to be obvious that people "own" their own labor and can therefore withhold that labor unless they find it in their self-interest to use, most typically because others pay them to do so. The labor contract must be "free" in the limited sense that none of its explicit terms are set by the state. People then own the proceeds they have earned through the sale of their labor and can spend those proceeds as they see fit (and as they choose to spend, so they will enrich particular others who satisfy their demands). In the process of either consuming or producing, people may do as they please so long as they don't cross boundaries, don't use force against others, or invade the property that others have justly acquired.

Libertarians generally also rely heavily on the notion that the social order ought to be allowed to emerge "spontaneously," that "collectivists" wrongly imagine they can impose a unitary vision on a world that is too pluralistic, complex, and intractable to be governed by deliberate decisions. Thus, for instance, the prominent libertarian philosopher Robert Nozick, who was quite influential among legal libertarians, argues that "liberty" will upset any desired pattern of resource distribution. Assume, he says, that one starts with one's favorite distributive scheme (e.g., absolute income equality) but allows people to use the resources one has allotted them as they wish. Won't some soon have more than others because others are willing to pay them to perform particular services for them? In a parallel fashion, free markets are touted in part because they give people the sort of information about product scarcity and consumer tastes that enables them to make decisions (how much to invest, what products to market) which a collective planner could make only if she had access to an unattainable mountain of data.

Many people on the political left react with instantaneous hostility and skepticism toward libertarians because of what is thought to be their primitive and unrefined individualism. Libertarians, in this view, posit that people are and should be separate from others; libertarianism is a system that assumes (descriptively) that people are atomistic and selfish and builds a system that is normatively appealing only to the extent that this is true. Feminist legal critics have further sharpened this attack. They have noted that while men may generally perceive themselves as foundationally separate, women's basic experience is one of foundational connection.

Libertarians tend to reject this characterization of their position, though. Descriptively, they say (some) people may well be (somewhat or tremendously) connected to (a few or many) other people. Levels of altruism, though, like all other personality traits, differ among different people. The degree to which altruism manifests itself in the social world will simply be a function of how much altruism turns out to be present in people. Libertarians further note that nothing in the order they advocate precludes spontaneous expressions of altruism. However, a more collectivist order premised on the mistaken belief either that central authorities can know how altruistic everyone is or mold people to be identically altruistic does not allow for the expression of real sociability or altruism but merely uses force to take from some who'd choose not to be truly altruistic, to share voluntarily.

While the libertarians are probably right to reject as caricatured the notion that they assume everyone is egocentric, they do indeed posit that we can imagine some set of authentic individual desires antedating and independent of the existence of a community. If, instead, individual preferences are sensitive to cultural forms which are themselves in part a product of self-conscious collective decisions, the libertarian image of the presocial individual cannot survive.

Libertarianism has had little impact on American legal culture. Even its leading exponent, Richard Epstein, has recently admitted he uses libertarian "natural rights" language largely because of its rhetorical appeal, rather than its content. The general rejection of libertarianism in legal academic life is less a function of its strong individualism—which it basically shares with more mainstream legal beliefs—than its primitive antipositivism.

The notion that the state simply reaffirms some preexisting set of rights is antithetical to the most basic positivist insights that dominate modern legal thought, the insight that legal regimes create a framework of rules, that law derives from sovereign power. Many reject completely amoral positivist relativism, the belief that all laws are equally legitimate if equally the product of a viable sovereign's command. However, most just as firmly reject the idea that individuals possess meaningful rights unless collective bodies choose to recognize them. The basic legal libertarian starting point—that people naturally "own" the fruits of their labor—can hardly survive as an *axiom* in this environment. Modern legal thought is thoroughgoingly consequentialist in orientation; when we evaluate the legitimacy of a claim, we look to see what impact its acceptance will have. As a result, all reasonably sophisticated lawyers educated in the consequentialist/positivist style will inevitably ask "why?" when any claim of right is proffered. The question is *not* what abstracted rights individuals *might* claim. Presumably, to the degree they're selfish, or at least morally entitled to be selfish, they'll claim everything they can. The relevant legal question is which of their claims the state ought to back up, when the collectivity ought to use or threaten force to restrain others who make competing claims. If X wants to hang on to the "fruits of her labor" and Y to consume them, the collective must ultimately mediate the dispute. Perhaps there are reasons X should prevail (e.g., to encourage the production of goods) and perhaps there are reasons Y should (she's needier and we believe the impact on X's production decisions will be minimal). But each must *ground* her claim, appeal to others to validate her claim, in terms of consequences of interest to others.

The problem resurfaces in the libertarian efforts to defend the necessity of adopting a particular contract regime or a particular set of inviolable boundaries between persons. We must inevitably debate when "free" contract meets the ends ordinarily ascribed to contracts made under ideal conditions.

The more prone we are to believe mutually satisfying deals are less likely to be made when parties are underinformed, the more likely we are to decide to expand the domain of contracts that are voidable as fraudulently induced. Similarly, if we believe that parties adjust as best as they can to illegitimate and unnecessary backdrop pressures, we must expand the domain of contracts voidable for duress. We all readily recognize that the decision to "agree" to give money to someone who will physically beat you if you don't might be the best accommodation to an illegitimately constrained choice situation. But until legal/political pressure from the feminist community sensitized the legal system in the late seventies to the powerlessness that women status subordinates justifiably felt in the face of sexual demands from supervisors or teachers, the woman's "decision" to "agree" to have sex with a demanding hierarchical superior was treated as voluntary and presumptively beneficent.

It will always remain a collective political judgment whether "agreements" made in situations in which pressures are less uncontroversably illegitimate, but nonetheless problematic, are to be respected. The issues are often visible in routine casebook contract law. Do we enforce contracts made by people in a variety of emergency situations (to borrow money, to pay high fees for rescue)? Do we permit renegotiation of the once-settled contract price when a contractor's failure to complete a project will dramatically inconvenience a party who planned on completion? But these sorts of issues are also at least potentially present in a far wider array of situations. For instance, one can imagine asking whether we should enforce long-term contracts workers make during periods of atypical dependency (e.g., high unemployment) when pressures later slacken, even though that is not now formally dubbed a duress issue in our legal system.

Similarly, mandatory terms may be the terms that we are reasonably certain would have been bargained for in a more ideal contractual setting. Unable to establish the setting, we impose the terms. For example, we might impose a requirement against unjust discharge that we may believe would have been negotiated if workers were better able to anticipate the risks of capricious discharge and/or if employers could negotiate terms limiting their discretion to fire without facing a problem of "adverse selection." (Adverse selection in insurance settings results when those who wish to purchase insurance are atypically likely to suffer the untoward event that is insured against; in this setting, employers may be unable to "price" a term limiting discretion to fire, fearing that those who want it are most likely to be troublesome employees.) Finally, we may feel a class of contracts is so frequently exploitative, and it is so difficult to recognize exceptions to the generalization, that we ban contracts on the suspect subject matter entirely (e.g., warranty waivers, irrevocable contracts to allow another to adopt an as-yet unborn child).

Similarly, within the dominant positivistic framework, the notion that we can decide when a party has illegitimately invaded another's property depends on convincing decision makers (again, with a consequentialist defense rather than an assertion) that the "invader" ought to be responsible for the costs and frictions caused by social interaction. Whatever one ultimately thinks of the legitimacy of water pollution, it is hard to imagine why the claims of those who want to use pure water to swim or fish in have automatic, undefended precedence over those who want to use the water to allow them to produce manufactured goods more cheaply, just because the polluter physically "invades" property or destabilizes some prior state. Whether the legal system declares that tall buildings illegitimately block light or whether the privilege to build however one wants on one's own property is sacrosanct is answered not by reference to abstractions about "rights," but by reference to the relative consequences of each alternative decision.

The secondary claim that only the libertarian system permits spontaneity also seems legally naive. Nozick's claim that "liberty upsets patterns" (that any desired distribution of resources will be upset so long as people are permitted to use the resources they were supposedly entitled to when the first distribution was made) seems true only if the collectivity distributes *income* rather than a structure of entitlements. But if one's initial distributive decision is that one distributes entitlements in such a way that people who contract with others to labor for them must share a certain proportion of the proceeds of these contracts with a redistributing collectivity, through an income or wage tax, then the range of distributions of income we ultimately see will be more patterned and limited than Nozick implies. More generally, spontaneous adjustment will occur against many distinct entitlement backgrounds. The allocation of resources may be *different* if, for instance, parties have extensive obligations to share information about products they deal in than if they don't, but each allocation will emerge spontaneously, given any starting set of rules.

Libertarians have tended to defend their worldview rather formalistically. By and large, they've been reluctant to appeal to the beneficent consequences they may actually believe will occur in a libertarian regime. Instead, they've relied heavily on the assertion that libertarian principles are, in a sense, harshly dictated by reason. There is an almost reluctant admission, for instance, that if private charity proves inadequate to deal with poverty, that that's just a sad but unavoidable side effect of the compelling need to preserve a coherent entitlement structure. But the pretense that we have no choice but to accept libertarian entitlements unless we "disregard the individual" simply doesn't wash even for those generally committed to individualism. What mainstream modern legal thinkers teach us is that all entitlement decisions are made when there are *clashes* between persons desiring to use the same resource. The resolution of the clash is done by collective deliberative bodies, and is done for reasons. The failure to accept this most basic mainstream insight ultimately marginalizes and trivializes the legal libertarians.

LAW AND ECONOMICS[2]

Legal economists are not nearly so readily marginalized as libertarians. They are decidedly consequentialist in orientation, and they even engage the same "legal process" concerns that have long bedeviled mainstreamers (the question of whether a decision should be made by a court or legislature, a private or public entity).

In a sense, the legal economists have taken antinaturalism even further than traditional lawyers. In the view of legal economists, no claim to an entitlement has any moral, abstract, or transhistorical basis. People simply want things and their desires are morally contentless. Entitlements, then, should simply be assigned in such a way that those who want them the most intensely wind up with them. Assault is illegitimate *not* because it is wrong but because assault victims would (as a matter of descriptive fact) value not being battered more highly than assaulters would value assaulting. If we permit assault, we will simply require wasteful and needless transactions in which victims buy off would-be attackers to waive their entitlement to hit. Worse, if the transactions are too costly to arrange, assaults will occur that would not have occurred had those who prefer not to be attacked had the opportunity to buy off those who'd assault them.

Entitlement claims may then be justified in two distinct ways: First, the assignment can be defended as necessary to ensure that a "resource" (e.g., including one's body to follow the assault example) is used in the fashion that is most highly "valued" (in the limited sense that those with money would pay the most to see it used that certain way). Second, the assignment may be justified in "distributive" terms (to enrich the parties favored by the assignment). Here, though, the legal economists reengage the typical mainstream Legal Process academics concerned above all with the allocation of decision-making authority. It is the job of the courts, say the economists, to ensure that resources wind up used by those who value them most highly; it is the job of legislatures to make distributive judgments.

This view is generally supplemented by a rhetorical strategy which surreptitiously minimizes distributive concerns in three ways. First, these concerns are treated as issues about which nothing rational can be said, treated as issues on which one can express only groundless passions. Second, and more important, legal economists frequently emphasize the purported high costs of efforts to redistribute. In concrete terms, conservative legal economists inevitably seem to feel that in the not-so-long run, redistributive efforts will harm the purported beneficiaries, either by dramatically dampening aggregate production or by creating perverse incentives that lead the poor to dependency rather than longer-term economic self-sufficiency and prosperity.

Third, growingly influential "public choice" theorists claim that a legislature's distributive decisions will rarely be principled and public-minded.[3] Legislation, in this view, is produced in a typical market of rational egotists. Legislators are producers, seeking to hold onto their jobs, voters are consumers. Genuine public legislation though will rarely attract the attention of voters since its benefits are so dispersed; each beneficiary will attempt, instead, to "free-ride" on the efforts of others, but the others will abstain for the same reason. Only small, narrow groups of self-interested people will care enough about issues in their domain to organize. Since the general public that they illegitimately plunder will remain unorganized and unconcerned, legislators will cater to the narrow self-interested groups. This emerging theory is influential not only in academic life, as a counter to the sentimentalization of the legislature by traditional Legal Process scholars, but among conservative judges who want to be more activist in overturning legislative regulation.

The legal economists seem less readily dismissed as outside the mainstream tradition than do the libertarians, in substantial part because they do not so obviously rely on unsupported "naturalistic" authority and because they (at least at first blush) appear to allow some domain for collective political judgments. In fact, though, their undefended "naturalism" is simply a bit better hidden than the libertarians.

The question of whether resources are in fact used as people prefer them to be under a certain allocation of resources depends both on how we initially allocate entitlements and how we measure preferences. Generally speaking, legal economists consider that a resource is efficiently allocated so long as it could not be reallocated to another party without harming at least some party, i.e., so long as the compensation that winners from a change would offer the losers is inadequate to get them to accept the change. But there are two related problems. First, both an entitlement and its opposite may well each appear efficient, in this sense, depending on what the "starting point" is: "winners" from a proposed change might be unable to bribe "losers" to waive their initial entitlement, but had that same group of "losers" never had that entitlement to begin with, they might well have been unable to bribe the other group to waive the very opposite entitlement. (Native Americans entitled to maintain sacred grounds might resist bribes to reallocate their land to Anglo developers; yet if the Native Americans must outbid the developers for the land, pay them enough to keep it in its religiously sacred state, they might be unable to.) Second, the fact that people may be unable either to pay much to make a certain use (or even to resist large bribes to waive the right to insist on that use unless compensated) does not really mean that they don't value the use highly; the legal economists' focus on wealth-dependent valuation of resources is simply biased, without consequentialist explanation, toward those with market power.

Moreover, the notion that people's manifest market preferences should be taken as reflective of their deepest understanding of their long-term self-interest is problematic. Legal systems must often cope with situations in which people are expressly ambivalent. They express one desire at one point in time, conflicting ones at others, as well as desires about which tastes they hope they will sustain ("I wish I wouldn't want to smoke," "I wish I were less materialistic"). Legal economists, though, wish away ambivalence, posit that we always deal with a single stable chooser whose hypothesized "will" should govern.

Perhaps more significantly, even where people are not expressly ambivalent, we must understand that any set of preferences people have emerges in a particular cultural context. At times, "tastes" may be responsive to rather narrow, focused stimuli. We may come to want products we see advertised for instance. Men may well become more aggressive toward women when exposed to pornography. But our broader pattern of desires is surely framed by the larger social context, by what is valued by our subculture, what is generally available and what is not, even where it would be harder to identify the particular source of a particular desire. Activities have social meanings over which we had little control (it means different things to take up golf, hang gliding, drag racing). It means different things for men and for women to work late when there are young kids at home. Legal controversies quite frequently arise over what context is most appropriate, over the preferences it is ultimately desirable to nurture. Laws mandating the integration of public accommodations not only resolved a clash of desires between white bigots and people of color. They were premised in part on the idea that at least some forms of bigoted tastes would diminish over time as whites became accustomed to the presence of nonwhites in once-segregated situations. It is simply question begging to attempt to establish the context people most prefer if one of the main points of creating contexts is to influence the formation of those very preferences.

Feminist scholars, in particular, have emphasized yet another reason to be suspicious of a normative scheme that relies wholly on preference satisfaction, beyond recognizing the problems of ambivalence and the need to look carefully at the social context in which preferences are formed.[4] Relatively disempowered people, as women frequently are in relationship to men, may be unable to form truly self-promoting preferences. The most ready, and dramatic examples, are of women in long-term battering relationships. Their ostensible "desires" may simply be to do whatever will accommodate the batterer's wishes, hoping, often vainly, that if they are able to anticipate each conceivable whim, that they can avoid being victimized. More generally, if men frequently expropriate women's sexuality, women may come to conceive of themselves as sexually giving, not because sexual compliance serves their underlying subjective ends, but because it preserves at least the illusion of self-possession and control to give something before someone else has the opportunity to take it. In either case, to satisfy the woman's ostensible "desire" is not to satisfy *her*, but to accommodate, ultimately, to the men to whom *she* is accommodating.

Still, the legal economists' vision of efficiency has had real impact, despite its limitations. Administrative agencies are asked to assess the costs and benefits of regulations in terms that precisely parallel the technique legal economists use in assessing common law entitlements. Safety regulations are subjected to calculations that compare the value of saved lives with the cost of compliance. Benefits are measured in terms of how much beneficiaries of a program would willingly pay for the program, given their initial access to resources and given the assumption that their preferences are static and exogenous to political decisions.

The legal economists, then, have been influential in establishing a general analytical posture to take toward legal decisions. One treats all legal controversies as simple technical controversies about ensuring efficient resource use. But they have been equally influential in developing a particular complacent view of the economic institutions of laissez-faire capitalism that both reflects and has fortified the general right-wing political revival.

Essentially, legal economists describe all ostensibly conflictual economic relationships as harmonious. They assume that while people may well be motivated by selfish ends, the core legal institutions of capitalism (competitive markets, private property, tort law) ensure that in the pursuit of selfishness, only mutually optimal arrangements will be sustained.

This is quite visible in the paeans to competitive markets. Though the seller may be uninterested in the buyer as a person, may even *want* to exploit him, he will be unable to sell his product unless he offers a product of a particular quality at the lowest possible cost of production, since some other (equally selfish) seller will find it in his interest to undersell the first seller so long as prices remain above production costs. Every imaginable combination of product quality and price will be offered at the cost of production. Consumers may voluntarily sacrifice quality for cheaper price (e.g., accept a product with a higher risk of malfunction) but bad quality will never be *imposed* upon them since if they are willing to pay for the higher production costs of a better product, they will be able to get one.

While private property norms are seemingly focused on protecting the rights of the owner to exclude, for her own ends, they too are thought ultimately to meet universal goals in the economists' picture. Legal economists have argued (or at times simply assumed) that so long as people are basically thought of as selfish maximizers, private property arrangements will most effectively maximize the availability of valued goods by (*a*) ensuring adequate work incentives; (*b*) ensuring that property is held by users who value it most highly; (*c*) minimizing the wasteful expenditures people would engage in to protect their capacity to consume goods unless the state precluded invasion; (d) minimizing the sort of uncertainty which is itself disvalued by people; and, finally, (e) giving people adequate information about all the costs and benefits of their activities.

Moreover, so long as wrongdoers must compensate those that they harm, selfish calculators will do only that damage that is not socially justified. Even if fully selfish, a person will take a precaution so long as the expected tort damage judgment she must pay exceeds the cost of taking the precaution. If the precaution is indeed more costly than the expected damages from not taking it, it would be unwise to avoid harms. A tort system, in the legal economists' view, transforms a selfish to a selfless actor. The tortfeasor acts as she would were she herself the tort victim, with the victim's precise "tastes" about damages. While her activities could be said in a sense to harm her, they must, on balance, simultaneously help her more; a person may ruin her flower garden by barbecuing, but only if she enjoys the grill more than the gardenias.

This tendency to retranslate the ostensibly conflictual relationships in a capitalist economy into harmonious relationships is pronounced not just in the descriptions of the basic core private law areas (contracts, property, and tort). Workplaces, which progressives have long seen as battlefields over work pace and discipline, are transformed by the "transaction cost economists" who've been influential, particularly in analyzing corporate law, into conflictless mutual cooperatives. "Managers" are just technocratic problem solvers who might just as well be hired by the workers to supervise themselves. They must simply solve certain universal problems that face an organization which assigns people tasks to do in a group, without being capable of observing perfectly how well each has contributed to the group's output. "Managers" attempt to "monitor" workers so that they don't "shirk," given the impossibility of establishing compensation schemes that fully eliminate the possibility that a worker's selfish interests will diverge from the group's goal.

Each of the efforts to argue that capitalist legal and social institutions (the market, private property, the tort system, the firm) have overcome problems of antagonism, that each has ensured that unbridled selfishness is harnessed for mutual benefit, are far less internally rigorous and convincing than the legal economists would have us believe.

One can tautologically define a competitive market as one in which all goods are available at their lowest cost of production, but all actual markets will depart significantly from the ideal. As soon as at least some subgroup of consumers faces psychic or physical costs in "shopping around" (and in every case, shopping around poses at least some time costs), it is possible that it is a potentially sensible strategy for a selfish seller to at least try to identify subgroups of buyers who will pay more for a good than it costs to produce rather than shop around. Even in the absence of glaring market imperfections—and consumer misinformation and monopoly are hardly uncommon—it is simply not the case that we can ever guarantee the strong form of discipline on selfishness that competitive market advocates claim. An employee's particular job is never completely fungible with another "like" job. Not only is she apt to be more productive in a familiar setting, having learned plant-specific skills, than she'd be in a new one, but moving invariably necessitates rupturing existing social ties at work and may require moving or restructuring one's ongoing support network. In this context, there is no impersonal market mechanism that will set a single price for a certain sort of job with given characteristics. And when there is a range of possible outcomes, there is always room for "bargaining." Where there is room for bargaining, there is room for exploitation, for the "stronger" party to gain a disproportionate share of the gains from trade.

The efficiency case for private property is dramatically overstated as well. First, the work incentive effects of legally enforced sharing schemes (like a progressive income tax) are indeterminate both theoretically and empirically. People may produce more, not less, when they must share what they produce with others, in part because they have some "target" of how much selfish consumption they aspire to which requires harder work to meet if they have sharing obligations.

Second, it is implausible that goods will invariably most readily be transferred to those who value them more under any particular legal regime. At times, private ownership of a right by a certain party or parties may preclude its narrowly defined efficient use; at other times, collective ownership may unduly tie up property, make it factually inalienable. For instance, if private property owners could enjoin airlines from trespassing through "their" airspace, flights might be impossible to arrange, even though the fliers value the airspace far more than the "owners" disvalue the invasion.

Third, even if one defines "waste" as narrowly as most of the private property advocates do (e.g., solely as spending on preventing theft, spending on protecting ownership claims), it's not at all clear that the "waste" in an inegalitarian private property regime (on police, courts, etc.) won't exceed the waste in a more egalitarian regime in which the risk of "theft" might decline. More dramatically, private property advocates simply ignore the massive waste associated with inegalitarian, consumerist regimes: enormous advertising and marketing expenses and/or an infrastructure developed in substantial part to isolate the more privileged from the impoverished (suburbanization, taxicabs).

Fourth, the claim that private property reduces "uncertainty" is likewise unconvincing. Every sort of property regime generates its own sort of uncertainties for different people who are favored or disfavored by the regime's rules. Whenever one recognizes the right of a private owner to use her property just as she wishes or exclude at whim, one inevitably subjects those who are harmed by free exercise or desire access to the property to the uncertainty inherent in depending on the owner's discretion. One can't be sure it's worthwhile buying fishing equipment if the nearby factory can kill all the fish with uncontrolled emissions. Would-be pickets cannot rely on reaching the public with their message if owners of public gathering places can exclude them whenever their speech is unwanted. Similarly, while those whose earnings are subject to ever-changing rates of taxation may indeed feel they're more sure what command they'll have over resources in a private property regime, those dependent on the whim of private charity in a private property regime might feel more secure in a regime with greater sharing obligations.

Finally, it is simply not the case that a private property regime gives "correct" information on the "true" social costs and benefits of our activities. It simply gives us one particular set of information. If, to continue an earlier example, Native Americans don't own once-sacred grounds, destroying them will be seen as costless to other actors. It doesn't make it "truly" or "naturally" costless, in fact. Similarly, a private corporate owner of a toxic waste disposal site would, if selfishly rational, discount the harms it imposes on distant generations by the probability it will have disappeared as an entity before claimants appear. The hypothetical selfish calculator who balances the costs of a safer disposal system against the damage judgments it must pay for failing to take precautions will recognize that it will never pay if there is no "it" around. Imagine that the corporation knows that if solvent in the year 2050, it will owe an additional ten million dollars of damages from not taking a precaution but also knows there is a 50 percent chance it will have become bankrupt. It will treat the future loss as an expected loss of only five million dollars in that year. A public entity, even one that chose to balance the costs of safer disposal against the harms less safe techniques will impose, will make a *different* calculation, but one which is no less "true" or "natural."

The notion that people will be restrained by tort rules in such a way that they impose only those harms on others that they'd willingly impose on themselves is also highly suspect for a number of reasons. Perhaps most significantly, solely "economically rational" people will impose unwarranted harms (or risks) on others whenever it is difficult to prove causation. The toxic waste disposer may not willingly subject himself to a particular risk or cancer. To the extent, though, that he will not be found liable to someone else unless one can connect that particular plaintiff's cancer to the waste, the selfish tortfeasor will simply ignore the risk he imposes. In addition, if both parties in an interactive harm situation could take steps that would minimize harm net of the costs of preventing harm, as is usually the case, no simple legal rules will ordinarily motivate two selfish actors each to adopt the most cooperatively beneficial strategies.

Finally, the picture of the harmonious workplace, in which people adopt disciplinary institutions to solve certain universal problems of maximizing group production is hard to square with the intense opposition of organized workers to speedups or to distinctions in work style between worker-run and employer-owned firms.

AN EXEMPLARY CASE: SAFETY REGULATIONS

While it would obviously not be possible either to explore the range of issues legal economists have addressed nor even to detail the arguments in any single case with fully adequate care, it might well be helpful to review and critique the basic approach economists typically take to at least one significant legal issue.

Take, for instance, the case of mandatory safety regulations in the workplace. In the first instance, most economists will be skeptical of the utility of even the best-designed regulations. Given the presumptive beneficence of private ordering in competitive markets, most economists will believe that safety levels are set at optimal levels in the absence of regulation. To the extent that a particular job is riskier than an otherwise identical job, it will command a "wage premium" compensating the worker for her exposure to the hazard. Risk reduction, like any other good, will ultimately be "sold" on the market at its cheapest production cost. A competitive employer will be able to pay lower wages if he reduces on-the-job risks and will reduce risks until the marginal costs of reducing risk further exceed the marginal wages saved through the risk reduction (the implicit amount workers "pay" for safety). Regulations will hurt workers, their purported beneficiaries, to the extent they mandate costlier safety precautions than workers would willingly pay for.

This picture of the market in safety is too cheery even for many mainstream economists, who will typically question one (though not all) aspects of the rosy story. Workers, they concede, may be inadequately informed about distinctions in the riskiness of jobs to evaluate properly whether they are adequately compensated for objective risks. Moreover, some economists believe even adequately informed workers will subjectively underestimate risks, so that paternalistic interference with preferences are legitimate. Few, though, question the basic implicit picture of employment that is posited in which risks are imposed on workers who select jobs from a "menu" of more-and-less risky and more-and-less remunerative jobs, and are exposed only to those risks they knew in advance (perhaps imperfectly) would exist on the job. The idea that shifts in safety levels may be imposed on workers already on a particular job, who would inexorably face dislocation costs if they tried to flee to an optimally "safer" setting, is generally simply whisked away.

Given the possibility that markets may "malfunction" because of misinformation, regulation is a plausible solution for economists. However, the regulation is justified only if the costs of compliance are less than the benefits would be. To value the benefits of increased safety, economists typically look back at the market in risk whose failure justified the regulation in the first instance. The basic procedure, roughly, works as follows: If workers who take an incremental risk of dying of 1 in 1,000 receive a $500 lifetime wage premium, the value of a life is said to be $500,000. There are serious problems even if one accepts the moral validity of explicitly trading lives for other material goods, particularly when one is valuing someone else's life against material goods he may not consume. There are likewise problems even beyond those inherent in assuming that there is a functioning market in risk or that a typical life should be "valued" by reference to the preferences of those who would generally presumably be most willing to take risks, those who take these jobs. We still must recognize that a worker might refuse an offer to waive an entitlement to safety for a sum of money she'd not be able to offer to obtain a safer workplace and that her "taste" for safety is framed in particular social settings, with particular suppositions about how effectively she'll be able to control risks more generally and particular suppositions about what incremental wages will mean to her. Cost-benefit analysis in the regulatory setting depends just as much on the legitimacy of the underlying entitlement structure and on the legitimacy of the setting in which preferences are framed as it does in evaluating other legal entitlements.

Finally, economists will tend to believe that safety regulations should be enforced solely through fines, which should simply reflect the loss thought to follow from violation, adjusted upward to account for the low probability of detection. An entity which feels it can make more money violating the regulation and paying the fine than it can by complying *should* violate the regulation in this view; there is an *optimal* level of violation of all norms (including traditional criminal norms). The notion that a killer's willingness to "pay the murder tariff" justifies his crime is a morally peculiar one. We may well reasonably expect full compliance with regulations designed to protect significant interests (like the interest in safety and health) though we know we set penalties too low to discourage selfishly amoral people from violating.

CONCLUSION

Despite the technical deficiencies in the legal economists' unflinchingly cheery view of the harmonizing impact of legal institutions, their basic message both resonates with and helps re-create the conservative American celebration. We are a society, in this view, free from exploitation. If there is suffering, it is irremediable, for prevailing institutions ensure that we have minimized it, that we have harnessed each of our efforts to best serve others and squelched our capacity to take advantage of others. It is this complex message of complacency which progressives must come to understand and to refute. Ultimately, of course, we overcome it only preliminarily through critique. The real response to complacency is a political practice that diminishes the suffering that the conservative legal academics have called immutable.

NOTES

1. The richest general work on libertarianism is Robert Nozick, *Anarchy, State and Utopia* (New York: Basic Books, 1974). Also helpful, particularly in developing themes of spontaneous ordering, is Friedrich Hayek, *The Constitution of Liberty* (Chicago: University of Chicago Press, 1960). Within the legal academy, the most important libertarian commentator is Richard Epstein. His views on basic rights are best expressed in *Takings* (Cambridge: Harvard University Press, 1985). His views on free contract are best developed in "In Defense of the Contract at Will," 51 *University of Chicago Law Review* 947 (1984) and his views on torts are best developed in "A Theory of Strict Liability," 2 *Journal of Legal Studies* 151 (1973).

    For some critiques, *see* M. Kelman, "Taking *Takings* Seriously: An Essay for Centrists," 74 *California Law Review* 1829 (1986); Thomas Grey, "The Malthusian Constitution," 41 *University of Miami Law Review* 21 (1986).

2. One can see most of the main conservative themes in law and economics in Richard Posner's *Economic Analysis of Law*, 3d ed. (Boston: Little, Brown, 1986). Posner's normative structure and his views of appropriate legal process are revealed in more detail in "The Ethical and Political Basis of the Efficiency Norm," 8 *Hofstra Law Review* 489 (1980). For a fuller response to the legal economists claims, *see* M. Kelman, *A Guide to Critical Legal Studies* (Cambridge: Harvard University Press, 1987), chaps. 4 and 5.

3. William Eskridge, "Politics without Romance: Implications of Public Choice Theory for Statutory Interpretation," 74 *Virginia Law Review* 275 (1988) and Jonathan Macey, "Transaction Costs and the Normative Elements of the Public Choice Model: An Application to Constitutional Theory," provide two good, sympathetic lawyers' summaries of the public choice literature. A

critique can be found in M. Kelman, "On Democracy-Bashing: A Skeptical Look at the Theoretical and 'Empirical' Practice of the Public Choice Movement," 74 *Virginia Law Review* 199 (1988).
4. *See,* for instance, Robin West, "The Difference in Women's Hedonic Lives," 3 *Wisconsin Women's Law Journal* 81 (1987).

23 FRANCES OLSEN

THE SEX OF LAW

SINCE the rise of classical liberal thought, and perhaps since the time of Plato, most of us have structured our thinking around a complex series of dualisms, or opposing pairs: rational/irrational; active/passive; thought/feeling; reason/emotion; culture/nature; power/sensitivity; objective/subjective; abstract/contextualized; principled/personalized. These dualistic pairs divide things into contrasting spheres or polar opposites.[1]

This system of dualisms has three characteristics that are important to this discussion. First, the dualisms are sexualized. One-half of each dualism is considered masculine, the other half feminine. Second, the terms of the dualism are not equal, but are thought to constitute a hierarchy. In each pair, the term identified as "masculine" is privileged as superior, while the other is considered negative, corrupt, or inferior. And third, law is identified with the "male" side of the dualisms.

SEXUALIZATION

The division between male and female has been crucial to this dualistic system of thought. Men have identified themselves with one side of the dualisms: rational, active, thought, reason, culture, power, objective, abstract, principled. They have projected the other side upon women: irrational, passive, feeling, emotion, nature, sensitivity, subjective, contextualized, personalized.

The sexual identification of the dualisms has both a descriptive and a normative element. Sometimes it is said that men are rational, active, and so forth, and other times it will be said that men should be rational, active, and so forth. Similarly, the claim about women is sometimes considered to be descriptive; women simply are irrational, passive, and so forth. A lot of people used to believe that this was an inevitable, immutable fact about women—that women were unable to become rational, active, and so forth.

Another version of this chapter will be published as "Feminism and Critical Legal Theory: An American Perspective," 18 *International Journal of the Sociology of Law* — (1990).

Another kind of claim is that women should be irrational, passive, and so forth, or at least that they should *not* become rational, active, and so forth—either because it is important that women remain different from men, or because irrational, passive, and so forth, are good traits *as applied to women*.

HIERARCHIZATION

The system of dualisms is hierarchized. The dualisms do not just divide the world between two terms; the two terms are arranged in a hierarchical order. Just as men have traditionally dominated and defined women, one side of the dualism dominates and defines the other. Irrational is considered the absence of rational; passive is the failure of active; thought is more important than feeling; reason takes precedence over emotion.

This hierarchy has been somewhat obscured by a complex and often insincere glorification of women and the feminine. However much men have oppressed and exploited women in the real world, they have also placed women on a pedestal and treasured them in a fantasy world. And just as men simultaneously exalt and degrade women, so, too, do they simultaneously exalt and degrade the concepts on the "feminine" side of the dualisms. Nature, for example, is glorified as something awesome, a worthy subject of conquest by male heroes, while it is simultaneously degraded as inert matter to be exploited and shaped to men's purposes. Irrational subjectivity and sensitivity are similarly treasured and denigrated at the same time. However much they might romanticize the womanly virtues, most people still believe that rational is better than irrational, objectivity is better than subjectivity, and being abstract and principled is better than being contextualized and personalized. It is more complicated than this, however, because no one would really want to *eliminate* irrational, passive, and so forth, from the world altogether. But men usually want to distance *themselves* from these traits; they want women to be irrational, passive, and so forth. To women, this glorification of the "feminine" side of the dualisms seems insincere.

LAW AS MALE

Law is identified with the hierarchically superior, "masculine" sides of the dualisms. "Justice" may be depicted as a woman, but, according to the dominant ideology, law is male, not female. Law is supposed to be rational, objective, abstract, and principled, as men claim they are; it is not supposed to be irrational, subjective, contextualized, or personalized, as men claim women are.

The social, political, and intellectual practices that constitute "law" were for many years carried on almost exclusively by men. Given that women were long excluded from the practice of law, it is not surprising that the traits associated with women are not greatly valued in law. Moreover, in a kind of vicious cycle, law is considered rational and objective in part because it is highly valued, and it is highly valued in part because it is considered rational and objective.

The most interesting and promising challenges to this dominant system of thought are those made by feminists. Feminist critiques of law bear a close analogy to feminist critiques of male dominance in general and the several conflicting attitudes that various feminists have taken toward law can best be understood when viewed in this broader context.

FEMINIST STRATEGIES

Feminist strategies for attacking the dominant dualistic system of thought fall into three broad categories. The first category consists of strategies that oppose the sexualization of the dualisms and struggle to identify women with the favored side, with rational, active, and so forth. Strategies in the second category reject the hierarchy men have established between the two sides of the dualisms. This second category accepts the identification of women with irrational, passive, and so forth, but proclaims the value of these traits; they are as good as or better than rational, active, and so forth. The third category rejects both the sexualization and the hierarchization of the dualisms. Strategies in this third category question and disrupt the differences asserted between men and women, and they deny the hierarchy of rational, active, and so forth, over irrational, passive, and so forth. Rational and irrational, active and passive, and so forth, are not polar opposites, and they do not and cannot divide the world into contrasting spheres.

REJECT SEXUALIZATION

Strategies that reject the sexualization of the dualisms are like the dominant ideology in that they accept the hierarchy of rational over irrational, of active over passive, and so forth. They differ from the dominant ideology in that they reject the normative claim that women should be irrational, passive, and so forth, and for the most part they reject the descriptive assertion that women are irrational, passive, and so forth. They most strongly reject the idea that women cannot help but be irrational, passive, and so forth.

This strategy is illustrated by an essay written in 1851 by Harriet Taylor Mill. She disputed the assertion that women were naturally or universally inferior to men and argued that each individual should be free to develop his or her own abilities to their fullest, "to prove his or her capacities . . . by trial." According to Mills, "[t]he proper sphere for all human beings is the largest and highest which they are able to attain to."[2]

Harriet Taylor Mill rejected the sexualization of the dualisms but accepted the hierarchy. She used "rational" as an honorific and "irrational" as a term of derision, and argued that "reason and principle," not "sentimentalities," offered the strongest support for women's emancipation. She denied that women were inherently irrational, passive, and so forth, but believed that women's education and situation in life tended to make them so. This was both "an injustice to the individual and a detriment to society." To deny women the opportunity to develop to their fullest potential is an effective way to prevent them from being rational, active, and so forth. "[T]he qualities which are not permitted to be exercised shall not exist." Harriet Taylor Mill dismissed as "nonsensical" the efforts of some feminists to challenge the hierarchy of rational over irrational, active over passive, and so forth. "What is wanted for women is equal rights, equal admission to all social privileges; not a position apart, a sort of sentimental priesthood."[3]

This attitude toward women's equality is widely held today. Many feminists and most liberals believe that sex roles should be a matter of individual choice. When individuals act rationally and reasonably, they should be treated accordingly. If women or men choose to be irrational, passive, and so forth, they cannot expect to be treated as well. Moreover, if women do not want to bear and raise children, they should not have to do so; and if men want to nurture children they should be free to make that choice.

There is more to this category than simple sex blindness. One claim is that women have been trained to be irrational and passive and that this training should be reversed. Affirmative action for women, a departure from sex blindness, may be justified and supported as a method to counteract years of teaching women to be irrational, passive, and so forth. A different claim is that women already are rational, active, and so forth, but are not recognized to be. Affirmative action may still be justified and supported as a technique for counteracting prejudiced, inaccurate views that women are irrational, passive, and so forth. The point of these strategies is not that gender must be ignored, but that women are or should become rational, active, and so forth.[4]

Under these strategies, equal treatment for women is the eventual goal. Equal treatment for women is also considered to be the current norm, and gender-conscious policies are seen as a limited departure from this norm— an exception that may be justified in order to counteract and correct inequality. The result of these gender-conscious policies, according to their advocates, should be to secure to women the same power and prestige that men have, and to let women be, and be recognized to be, as rational, active, and so forth, as men are (which, of course, is less than men like to claim they are).

REJECT HIERARCHIZATION

The second set of strategies rejects the hierarchy but accepts the sexualization. These strategies are like the dominant ideology in that they accept in general the proposition that men and women are different—that men are rational, active, and so forth, and women irrational, passive, and so forth. Also they tend to choose alternative adjectives that are a bit less value-laden, or value-laden in the opposite direction: rationalistic/spontaneous, aggressive/receptive, and so forth.

During the nineteenth and early twentieth centuries, a major focus of the women's movement was the exclusion of women from the public arena and the denial to women of equal opportunities. These concerns were addressed primarily by strategies in the first category, strategies that rejected the sexualization of the dualisms, rather than by strategies in the second category, strategies that rejected the hierarchy. The main exception to this was the movement for social purity and other moral reforms.

For the most part, moral reform movements led by feminists rejected the hierarchization of the dualisms and accepted their sexualization. The reformers argued that women were morally superior to men and thus had a special mission to improve society. Many of these reformers hoped that men would adopt more of the womanly virtues—especially sexual restraint—but they basically accepted the dualisms, accepted women's identification with irrational, passive, and so forth, and were generally resigned to men not changing much. Their chief focus was not on transforming men or abolishing the dualisms, but on forcing a reevaluation of irrational, passive, and so forth.[5]

Charlotte Perkins Gilman, an early feminist who was strongly critical of many of the character traits actually prevalent among turn-of-the-century women, nevertheless wrote an eloquent endorsement of the devalued side of the dualisms. The novel, *Herland* describes a feminist utopia established in a geographically isolated setting after all the men have killed themselves off in war. Gilman passed quickly over the expediency of an implausible miraculous shift to asexual reproduction, in order to get to a description of how an all-female society might function. Although Gilman's women are stronger and more capable than the standard stereotype of the day would have allowed, and although there are some other androgynous overtones to the novel, the main message of the book is a disruption and partial reversal of the hierarchy of rational over irrational, active over passive, and so forth.[6]

A group of modern feminists has continued this disruption and partial reversal of hierarchy. Talk of "women's psychology," "women's imagination," and women's "common language" has become popular.[7] The distinction between the strategy of rejecting the hierarchy while accepting the sexualization of the dualisms, on one hand, and, on the other hand, the strategy of androgyny—rejecting the entire dualistic structure—has begun to break down.

To focus on women's experience and on women's culture, psychology, imagination, or language can be an effective way to recover what has been excluded or obscured by dominant culture; but it can also entail an acceptance of the sexualization of the dualisms. To reverse or invert the hierarchy between rational and irrational, active and passive, and so forth, could simply reinforce the dualisms and ultimately maintain dominant values. Alternatively, such a reversal will occasionally seem to be the most effective way to subvert the dualisms.[8] Moreover, an author may intend for her writing to serve one strategy and readers may use it to serve another. Although some authors articulate clear support for the maintenance of sex roles,[9] in other cases the disruption of the hierarchy within the dualisms may or may not be intended to disrupt the sexualization of the dualisms and the dualisms themselves. When this is the intention, I would classify the strategy in the third category—androgyny.

ANDROGYNY

It is possible to attack both the sexualization and the hierarchy at the same time. Men are not more rational, objective, and principled than women, nor is it particularly admirable to be rational, objective, and principled, at least as the dominant male supremacist ideology has defined the terms. A number of feminists have tried over the years to adopt such a critical stance toward the dual claims of male dominance. A rejection of both the sexualization of the dualisms and the hierarchy established between the two sides of the dualisms is often accompanied by a rejection of the dualisms altogether and a disruption of conventional sex roles.

During the second half of the nineteenth century there was significant support for moderating sex-role expectations for men and women. William Leach, in his study of nineteenth-century feminism, asserts "[a]ll feminists believed that only strong, independent, but also tender men and women, who combined in their natures the best virtues of both sexes, could make good marital partners and parents." Only "symmetrically developed men and women" were considered "whole human beings."[10]

The rebirth of the women's movement has brought these ideas back into popular discourse. Some feminists argue that women are and must be both rational and irrational, objective and subjective, abstract and contextualized, and principled and personalized. Recently, feminists influenced by postmodernism, and especially by such movements as deconstruction, have begun to question the basic dichotomies themselves. This strategy challenges the border between the two terms in each of the dualisms, problematizes the straightforward opposition between them, and denies their separateness. It is rational to be irrational and objectivity is necessarily subjective.[11]

FEMINIST CRITIQUES OF LAW

Feminist criticisms of law fall into three broad categories, corresponding to the categories of feminist strategies for attacking male domination in general. The dominant ideology maintains that law is rational, objective, abstract, and principled and that rational is better than irrational, objective better than subjective, and so forth. The first category consists of those critiques that attack the claim that law is rational, objective, abstract, and principled, while agreeing that rational, objective, and so forth, is better than irrational, subjective, and so forth. These feminists argue that law should be rational, objective, and principled and struggle to improve the lot of women by trying to make law live up to its claims and actually be rational, objective, and principled. Criticisms in the second category accept that law is rational, objective, and principled but reject the hierarchization of the dualisms. Feminists holding this view characterize law as male and patriarchal, and thus ideologically oppressive to women. The third category of criticisms rejects both the characterization of law as rational, objective, abstract, and principled and the hierarchization of rational over irrational, objective over subjective, and so forth. Law is not and cannot be rational, objective, abstract, and principled. Once again, according to these feminists, rational and irrational, active and passive, and so forth, are not polar opposites, and they do not and cannot divide the world into contrasting spheres.

LEGAL REFORMIST

The first category of criticisms questions the accuracy of the assertion that law is rational, objective, and principled. It accepts the notion that law should be rational, objective, and principled, but points out the ways law fails to live up to this aspiration when it deals with women. In particular, reformist feminists condemn laws that deny women rights—or otherwise harm women—as irrational, subjective, and unprincipled. This has been the single most important feminist legal strategy and is the theoretical underpinning of the entire women's rights movement in law. It includes a broad range of arguments for reform, from a demand for sex blindness to the argument that to be "truly neutral" the law must take account of women's current subordination and devise rules carefully tailored to rectify and overcome this unfair inequality. Each of these arguments identifies a different aspect of law to condemn for failing to be rational, objective, and principled.

Denial of Formal Equality. For many years feminists have complained that law draws irrational distinctions between men and women. These critics have argued that law should instead really be rational and objective, by which they mean it should treat women the same way it treats men. This argument has often been successful, and courts have overturned laws preferring male to female executors, discharging parents' obligation to support daughters at a younger age than sons, and prescribing different legal drinking ages for males and females.[12]

Feminists have also argued successfully that laws should forbid employers, schools, and other important private actors from discriminating against women. These laws have been shaped and extended in part by feminist insistence that the law accord formal legal equality of treatment to men and women—that law really become rational, objective, and principled.

Denial of Substantive Equality. To achieve a substantive equality of outcome, it may be necessary for the law to take account of existing differences among people and consequently to deny formal legal equality. Thus, in some cases there will be a conflict between feminists seeking formal equality for women—"equal treatment"—and those seeking substantive equality, sometimes through "special treatment." This "equal treatment" versus "special treatment" debate takes place *within* this same broad category of legal criticism. Both sides agree that the law should be rational, objective, and principled; they just disagree about what particular outcome these traits require in a given case. Feminists urging "special treatment" claim to favor a truly neutral result and debunk certain instances of formal equality as "pseudo-neutrality."[13]

Operating on an Assimilationist or "Male" Model. Another basis for feminist charges that law is not truly rational, objective, and principled is that equality is at present judged by comparing women to men. To state a claim, a woman usually has to show that she was treated worse than a man would have been. This means that sex discrimination law operates on an assimilationist or male model.[14] Sex discrimination law serves only to allow those women who choose to act as men do to receive the rewards men receive—that is, it facilitates the first feminist strategy, the strategy that denies the sexualization of the dualisms. When the law chooses to support this feminist strategy instead of another one, it is not being rational and objective. Antidiscrimination law could require, for example, that jobs be structured so that workers can devote significant periods of time to child care without prejudice to their incomes or careers, or it could require comparable worth, that all jobs—and let us include care for one's own child—be rewarded in accordance with the skill and responsibility they entail.[15]

Exclusion of Law from the Domestic Sphere. Feminists point out that "law has been conspicuously absent from the [domestic] sphere"[16] and that this has contributed to women's subordination. On a practical level, it leaves wives without a remedy against domination by their husbands; and on an ideological level, it "devalues women and their functions." The important activities of our society are regulated by law; and when law maintains a hands-off posture, it implies "women simply are not sufficiently important to merit legal regulation." The insulation of the women's sphere conveys an important message: "In our society law is for business and other important things. The fact that the law in general has so little bearing on women's day-to-day concerns reflects and underscores their insignificance." Thus, once again law has failed truly to be rational, objective, abstract, and principled.

A distinction should be made between this description of part of the ideology and the more complicated picture of ideas and reality. The history of laissez-faire policies toward domestic life is considerably more complex than this description suggests. Laws have regulated family life, directly and indirectly, for centuries. Laws have also long reinforced the dichotomy between the "private" home and the "public" market, and they have done so in ways that have been peculiarly destructive to women.[17]

LAW AS PATRIARCHY

The second category of feminist criticisms of law accepts the descriptive claim that law is rational, objective, abstract, and principled but rejects the hierarchy of rational over irrational, objective over subjective, and so forth. These feminists identify law as part of the structure of male domination; they characterize rational, objective, and so forth, as patriarchal and condemn law for being therefore ideologically oppressive to women. The legal system is said to have a "pervasive maleness." "The whole structure of law—its hierarchical organization; its combative, adversarial format; and its undeviating bias in favor of rationality over all other values—defines it as a fundamentally patriarchal institution."[18]

Janet Rifkin has asserted that law is "a paradigm of maleness," and "the ultimate symbol of masculine authority in patriarchal society."[19] Catharine MacKinnon agrees that law is male. Objectivity is a male norm as well as law's image of itself. Law therefore "not only reflects a society in which men rule women; it rules in a male way."[20]

This conception of law leads to a less than sanguine view of legal reform. MacKinnon writes that "law will most reinforce existing distributions of power when it most closely adheres to its own highest ideal of fairness." Diane Polan warns that to the extent women articulate their grievances in terms of "equal rights" and "equal opportunities" and confine their struggle to litigation and lobbying they are giving tacit approval to the basic social order and "giving up the battle" for more radical challenges to society. Litigation and other forms of lawmaking can be effective, Polan argues, only when "they are undertaken in the context of broader economic, social, and cultural changes." Rifkin goes further. She argues that litigation "cannot lead to social changes, because in upholding and relying on the paradigm of law, the paradigm of patriarchy is upheld and reinforced." To eliminate patriarchy "the male power paradigm of law" must be "challenged and transformed."

CRITICAL LEGAL THEORY

The third category of feminist criticisms of law rejects the hierarchy of rational over irrational, objective over subjective, and so forth, and denies that law is or could be rational, objective, abstract, and principled. The feminists who endorse this third category, feminist critical legal theory, agree in part and disagree in part with the first two categories of criticism.

These feminists do not belittle the benefits obtained by the legal reform feminists in the name of women's rights, but remain unconvinced by their claims about the role of abstract legal theory in obtaining these benefits. Legal reasoning and legal battles are not sharply distinguishable from moral and political reasoning and moral and political battles.

Similarly, critical legal theory feminists agree with the "law as patriarchy" feminists that law is often ideologically oppressive to women. They disagree, however, that law is male; law has no essence or immutable nature. Law is a form of human activity, a practice carried on by people. The people who carry on this activity are predominantly men, and many of them make claims about what they are doing that are just not true and could not be true. While it is true that law has been dominated by men, the traits associated with women have been only obscured, not eliminated. Law is not male. Law is not rational, objective, abstract, and principled. It is as irrational, subjective, concrete, and contextualized as it is rational, objective, abstract, and principled.

Law is not all one side of the dualisms. Law is not now and could not, consistent with what we believe, become principled, rational, and objective.

The claim that law is principled is based on the belief that law consists of a few rules or principles and that these general rules provide a principled basis for deciding individual cases. But instead of this, law is actually made up of an agglomeration of lots of specific rules and some very general standards.

The rules are too specific, definite, and contextualized to count as principles. The existence of these rules is what gives law the degree of predictability that it has—but the rules are too detailed and each rule covers too few cases to make the law *principled*. For example, there is at present a rule that states may use gender-based statutory rape laws to try to reduce the incidence of teenage pregnancy, and there is another rule that age of majority for purposes of terminating parental support may not be gender-based. In *Michael M.* v. *Sonoma County*,[21] the Supreme Court let stand a gender-based statutory rape law that the California Supreme Court said was intended to reduce the incidence of teenage pregnancy. In *Stanton* v. *Stanton*,[22] the Supreme Court struck down a Utah law that required a parent to support his son until age twenty-one but allowed him to stop supporting his daughter at age eighteen. My point is not that these two rules conflict or that the cases cannot be reconciled with one another. Rather, each of these two rules applies in too few circumstances to provide any principled answer to the question of when states may use gender-based laws.

The standards, on the other hand, are too vague and indeterminate to decide cases. In each interesting disputed case, you can find at least two different broad, general standards that could seem to apply to the case and that would lead to different results. For example, the standard of noninterference in the family will often support one outcome, while the standard of protecting children will support the opposite outcome. Just as rules apply to too few cases, standards apply to too many. The legal system fluctuates between being based on rules and being based on standards, but its aspiration to be principled is not achieved. Law is no more abstract and principled than it is personalized and contextualized.

Nor is law rational. The efforts by feminists to work out a rational elaboration of equal rights of human beings in order to achieve rights for women has not worked and it will not work. The classic conflicts between equality of opportunity and equality of result, between natural rights and positive rights, and between rights-as-a-guarantee-of-security and rights-as-a-guarantee-of-freedom, render rights analysis incapable of settling any meaningful conflict.[23] More specifically, if one outcome will protect the plaintiff's right to freedom of action, the opposite outcome will often protect the defendant's right to security. If one outcome will protect a woman's right to formal equality of treatment, her right to substantive equality of result may seem to require a different outcome. This is why, for example, feminists found themselves on opposite sides of the *California Federal* v. *Guerra*[24] case. Some feminists argued that formal equality requires that the law treat pregnancy just like any other temporary disability, while other feminists maintained that substantive equality requires that women be able to give birth to children without losing their jobs—even if no other temporary absence from work is excused. Therefore, some feminists argued that women should insist on formal equality and reject any form of special maternity leave; while other feminists argued that working women need adequate maternity leave, even if no similar leaves of absence are given to men or other people who are not pregnant. Law does not provide a *rational* basis for choosing which right to recognize and protect in any particular case. Rights analysis cannot settle these conflicts but merely restates them in a new—at most somewhat obscured—form.

Finally, law is not objective. The idea that law is objective is refuted by the gradual recognition that *policy* issues appear everywhere. Every time a choice is made, every legal decision that is not obvious and uncontroversial, is a decision based on policy—which cannot be objective. Thus, it is simply a mistake to say that law is or could become rational, principled, and objective. Law is not all one side of the dualisms.

Sometimes dominant legal theory recognizes that law is not principled, rational, and objective. The dominant ideology does recognize the so-called female traits—indeed it celebrates them—but only on the periphery, or in their own "separate sphere." For example, family law may be subjective, contextual, and personalized, but commercial law is thought to be principled, rational, and objective. Similarly, the core doctrines of law are thought to be principled, rational, and objective, although there may be minor exceptions and subdoctrines that permit some influence of the subjective, contextual, and personalized. It is important for feminists to correct these misperceptions, to dissolve the ghettos of law, and to show that you cannot exclude the personalized, irrational, and subjective from any part of the law.

One way that dominant ideology makes law seem principled, rational, and objective is by banishing to the periphery of law those fields believed to be tainted by unruly, discretionary standards—fields such as family law, trust law, and the law of fiduciary obligation in general. The core subjects or the important fields of law are said to remain principled, rational, and objective. We can show, however, that although banished, family law, trusts, and fiduciary obligations continue to influence the rest of law—including those fields that were supposed to be the bastion of the so-called male principles of law. For example, the ideology of the marketplace depends upon the ideology of the family, and commercial law can be understood adequately only by recognizing the interrelationship between it and family law.[25]

Another technique by which the dominant ideology tries to make the law seem principled, rational, and objective is by separating each field between, on one hand, a set of basic rules, or a "male" core that is principled, rational, and objective and, on the other hand, a periphery of exceptions that can contain irrational and subjective elements. For example, contract law is frequently conceptualized as a set of rational, consistent, individualistic rules, softened by somewhat subjective, variable, "altruistic" exceptions, such as promissory estoppel. The basic core of contract law remains principled, rational, and objective. Feminists can disrupt this by showing that the conflict between the individualistic "rule" and the altruistic "exception" reappears with every doctrine. Every doctrine is a choice or compromise of sorts between the individualistic and altruistic impulses. This feminist analysis also problematizes what should be considered the rule and what the exception. It is not possible to separate any field of law into a core and a periphery and the traits associated with women cannot be excluded from law.[26]

CONCLUSION

As I have said, the feminist strategies for attacking legal theory are analogous to feminist strategies for attacking male dominance in general. The "reject sexualization" position resonates with the "legal reformist" position, the "reject hierarchization" with the "law as patriarchy" and the "androgyny" with "critical legal theory." But I do not want to claim that the relationship is anything more than this—an analogy or a resonance. The sets of categories are not identical, and no strategy from one set requires or entails any strategy from the other set.

First there is no necessary relationship between a person's attitude toward the sexualization of the dualisms in general and her attitude toward the identification of law with rational, objective, and principled. Moreover, someone could accept the hierarchization for some purposes—for example, could believe that it is better for law to be rational, objective, and principled—but still reject the hierarchization in general. Some feminists embrace androgyny, but still claim that law is patriarchal. Similarly, one can support feminist critical legal theory and still believe either that women are inherently or morally superior to men, the second feminist strategy, or that women should strive to act rational, active, and so forth, the first feminist strategy.

My support for androgyny would not require me to support critical legal theory or vice versa, but both are related to my values and vision of the universe and both inform my political activity. Nothing in either theory will provide easy answers to concrete questions—such as "Would women really benefit from more state regulation of the family?" or "Could revised statutory rape laws protect young females without oppressing and demeaning them?" What I do hope is that by improving the theories upon which we operate we can understand better what is at stake in questions like these. I hope that by recognizing the impossibility of easy, logical answers we can free ourselves to think about the questions in a more constructive and imaginative manner. Law cannot be successfully separated from politics, morals, and the rest of human activities, but is an integral part of the web of social life.

NOTES

1. See Hélène Cixous, "Sorties," in New French Feminisms, ed. E. Marks and I. Courtivron (New York: Schocken Books, 1981), pp. 90, 90–91; J. Derrida, Dissemination, trans. B. Johnson (Chicago: The University of Chicago Press, 1981); C. Christ, Diving Deep and Surfacing (Boston: Beacon Press, 1980), p. 25; J. Clegg, The Structure of Plato's Philosophy (Lewisberg, Pa.: Bucknell University Press, 1977), pp. 18, 100–1, 188–91; F. Olsen, "The Family and the Market: A Study of Ideology and Legal Reform," 96 Harvard Law Review 1497, 1570–76 (1983); G. Frug, "The City as a Legal Concept," 93 Harvard Law Review 1057, 1057 (1980).
2. See H. T. Mill, "Enfranchisement of Women," in J. S. Mill and H. T. Mill, Essays on Sex Equality, ed. A. Rossi (Chicago: University of Chicago Press, 1970), pp. 89, 100–1; M. Wollstonecraft, A Vindication of the Rights of Woman (London: J. Johnson, 1792), pp. 49–92.
3. H. T. Mill, supra note 2, at 101, 120; M. Wollstonecraft, supra note 2.
4. See Olsen, supra note 1, at 1549–50.
5. See Barbara Easton, "Feminism and the Contemporary Family," in A Heritage of Her Own, ed. N. Cott and E. Pleck (New York: Simon & Schuster, 1979), pp. 555, 556, 557; N. Cott and E. Pleck, Introduction to id. at 11; K. Melder, Beginnings of Sisterhood (New York: Schocken Books, 1977), p. 53; Judith Walkowitz, "The Politics of Prostitution," Signs: Journal of Women in Culture and Society, vol. 6 (1980), reprinted in Women: Sex and Sexuality, ed. C. Stimpson and E. Person (New York: Simon & Schuster, 1980), p. 145.
6. See C. Gilman, Herland (New York: Pantheon Books, 1979).
7. See C. Gilligan, In a Different Voice (Cambridge, Mass.: Harvard University Press, 1982); P. Spacks, The Female Imagination (New York: Knopf, 1975); A. Rich, "Origins and History of Consciousness," in The Dream of a Common Language: Poems, 1974–1977 (New York: Norton, 1978), p. 7.
8. See Drucilla Cornell and Adam Thurschwell, "Femininity, Negativity, Intersubjectivity," in Seyla Benhabib and Drucilla Cornell, Feminism as Critique (Minneapolis: University of Minnesota Press, 1987); C. Christ, supra note 1, at 26, 130.
9. See, e.g., Elshtain, "Against Androgyny," Telos 47 (1981), p. 5.
10. W. Leach, True Love and Perfect Union (New York: Basic Books, 1980), p. 32.
11. See Olsen, supra note 1, at 1577–78; C. Heilbrun, Toward a Recognition of Androgyny (New York: Harper & Row, 1973); E. Cook, Psychological Androgyny (New York: Pergamon Press, 1985); W. O'Flaherty, Women, Androgynes, and Other Mythical Beasts (Chicago: The University of Chicago Press, 1980).
12. See Reed v. Reed, 404 U.S. 71 (1971); Stanton v. Stanton, 421 U.S. 7 (1975); Craig v. Boren, 429 U.S. 190 (1976).

13. *See* F. Olsen, "From False Paternalism to False Equality: Judical Assaults on Feminist Community, Illinois 1869–1895," 84 *Michigan Law Review* 1518, 1518–20, 1541 (1986).

14. *See* C. MacKinnon, *Sexual Harassment of Working Women: A Case of Sex Discrimination* (New Haven, Conn.: Yale University Press, 1979), pp. 144–46.

15. *See* M. J. Frug, "Securing Job Equality for Women: Labor Market Hostility to Working Mothers," 59 *Boston University Law Review* 55 (1979).

16. *See* Taub and Schneider, "Women's Subordination and the Role of Law," in this volume; Kathryn Powers, "Sex, Segregation, and the Ambivalent Directions of Sex Discrimination Law," 1979 *Wisconsin Law Review* 55 (1979).

17. *See* F. Olsen, *supra* note 1, at 1501–7; F. Olsen, "The Myth of State Intervention in the Family," 18 *University of Michigan Journal of Law Reform* 835 (1985).

18. D. Polan, "Toward a Theory of Law and Patriarchy," in *The Politics of Law*, 1st ed., ed. D. Kairys (New York: Pantheon Books, 1982), pp. 294, 300, 302.

19. J. Rifkin, "Toward a Theory of Law and Patriarchy," 3 *Harvard Women's Law Journal* 83, 84, 87, 88, 92 (1980).

20. *See* C. MacKinnon, "Feminism, Marxism, Method and the State: Toward Feminist Jurisprudence," *Signs: Journal of Women in Culture and Society*, vol. 8 (1983), pp. 635, 645.

21. 450 U.S. 464 (1981).

22. 421 U.S. 7 (1975).

23. F. Olsen, "Statutory Rape: A Feminist Critique of Rights Analysis," 63 *Texas Law Review* 391 (1984); *See* J. Singer, "The Legal Rights Debate in Analytical Jurisprudence from Bentham to Hohfeld," 1982 *Wisconsin Law Review* 975 (1982); D. Kennedy, "The Structure of Blackstone's Commentaries," 28 *Buffalo Law Review* 205 (1979); O. W. Holmes, "Privilege, Malice, and Intent," 8 *Harvard Law Review* 1 (1894).

24. 107 S.Ct. 683 (1987).

25. *See* Olsen, *supra* note 1; *see also* D. Kennedy, "The Political Significance of the Structure of the Law School Curriculum," 14 *Seton Hall Law Review* 1 (1983); D. Kennedy, "The Rise and Fall of Classical Legal Thought" (unpublished manuscript, 1975).

26. *See* M. J. Frug, "Rereading Contracts: A Feminist Analysis of a Contracts Casebook," 34 *American University Law Review* 1065 (1985); C. Dalton, "An Essay in the Deconstruction of Contract Doctrine," 94 *Yale Law Journal* 997 (1985); D. Kennedy, "Form and Substance in Private Law Adjudication," 89 *Harvard Law Review* 1685 (1976); R. Unger, "The Critical Legal Studies Movement," 96 *Harvard Law Review* 561, 618–48 (1983).

24 CORNEL WEST

THE ROLE OF LAW IN PROGRESSIVE POLITICS

WHAT is the role and function of the law in contemporary progressive politics? Are legal institutions crucial terrain on which significant social change can take place? If so, how? In which way? What are progressive lawyers to do if they are to remain relatively true to their moral convictions and political goals?

In this essay I shall attempt to respond to these urgent questions. This response will try to carve out a vital democratic left space between the Scylla of upbeat liberalism that harbors excessive hopes for the law and the Charybdis of downbeat leftism that promotes exorbitant doubts about the law. My argument rests upon three basic claims. First, the fundamental forms of social misery in American society can be neither adequately addressed nor substantially transformed within the context of existing legal apparatuses. Yet serious and committed work within this circumscribed context remains indispensable if progressive politics is to have any future at all. Second, this crucial work cannot but be primarily defensive unless significant extraparliamentary social motion or movements bring power and pressure to bear on the prevailing status quo. Such social motion and movements presuppose either grassroots citizens' participation in credible progressive projects or rebellious acts of desperation that threaten the social order. Third, the difficult task of progressive legal practitioners is to link their defensive work within the legal system to possible social motion and movements that attempt to fundamentally transform American society.

Any argument regarding the role of law in progressive politics must begin with two sobering historical facts about the American past and present. First, American society is disproportionately shaped by the outlooks, interests, and aims of the business community—especially that of big business. The sheer power of corporate capital is extraordinary. This power makes it difficult to even imagine what a free and democratic society would look like (or how it would operate) if there were publicly accountable mechanisms that alleviated the vast disparities in resources, wealth, and income owing in part to the vast influence of big business on the U.S. government and its legal institutions. This is why those who focus on forms of social misery—like the ill-fed, ill-clad, and ill-housed—must think in epochal, not apocalyptic, terms.

The second brute fact about the American past and present is that this society is a *chronically* racist, sexist, homophobic, and jingoistic one. The complex and tortuous quest for American identity from 1776 to our own time has produced a culture in which people define themselves physically, socially, sexually, and politically in terms of race, gender, sexual orientation, and "anti-American" activities. One unique feature of the country among other modern nations—with the embarrassing exceptions of South Africa and Hitler's Germany—is that race has served as the linchpin in regulating this national quest for identity. A detailed genealogy of American legal discourse about citizenship and rights—as initiated by the late Robert Cover of Yale—bears out this inescapable reality. The historical articulation of the experiential weight of African slavery and Jim Crowism to forms of U.S. patriarchy, homophobia, and anti-American (usually Communist and socialist) repression and/or surveillance yields a profoundly conservative culture.

The irony of this cultural conservatism is that it tries to preserve a highly dynamic corporate-driven economy, a stable election-centered democracy, and a precious liberties-guarding rule of law. This irony constitutes the distinctive hybridity of American liberalism (in its classical and revisionist versions) and the debilitating dilemma of American radicalism (in its movements for racial, class, and/or sexual equality). In other words, American liberalism diffuses the claims of American radicals by pointing to long-standing democratic and libertarian practices, despite historic racist, sexist, class, and homophobic constraints. Hence, any feasible American radicalism seems to be but an extension of American liberalism. Needless to say, the sacred cow of American liberalism—namely, economic growth achieved by *corporate* priorities—is neither examined nor interrogated. And those that do are relegated to the margins of the political culture.

My first claim rests upon the assumption that the extension of American liberalism in response to movements for racial, class, and sexual equality is desirable yet insufficient. This is so because the extension of American liberalism leaves relatively untouched the fundamental reality that undergirds the forms of social misery: *the maldistribution of resources, wealth, and power in American society.* Yet the extension of American liberalism in regard to race, labor, women, gays, lesbians, and nature *appears* radical on the American ideological spectrum principally because it goes against the deeply entrenched cultural conservatism in the country. In fact, this extension—as seen for example in the 1930s and 1960s—takes place by means of insurgent social motion and movements convincing political and legal elites to enact legislation or judicial decrees over against and imposed on the majority of the population. In short, the very extension of American liberalism has hardly ever been popular among the masses of American people primarily owing to a pervasive cultural conservatism.

The law has played a crucial role in those periods in which liberalism has been extended precisely because of the power of judicial review and an elected body of officials responding to social movements—not because cultural conservatism has been significantly weeded out. The effects of these laws and policies have over time attenuated some of the more crude and overt expressions of cultural conservatism—yet the more subtle expressions permeate the culture. The existing legal apparatuses cannot adequately address or substantially transform the plight of the racially and sexually skewed ill-fed, ill-clad, or ill-housed not only because of the marginalizing of perspectives that highlight the need for a redistribution of resources, wealth, and power, but also because of the perception that the extension of American liberalism is the most radical option feasible within American political culture.

Is this perception true? Is it the case that all workable radical alternatives must presuppose economic growth achieved by corporate priorities? These questions are especially acute given the collapse of social Keynesianism in the mid 1970s—that "magic" Fordist formula of mass production undergirded by mass consumption alongside government provisions to those with no access to resources that sustained economic growth in the postwar period. The conservative project of supply-side economics and military Keynesianism of the eighties yielded not simply a larger gap between the haves and have-nots, but also a debt-financed public sphere and a more corporate-dominated economy—in the name of "free enterprise."

If the extension of American liberalism is the only feasible radical option within American political culture, then the defensive role of progressive lawyers becomes even more important. Their work constitutes one of the few buffers against cultural conservatism that recasts the law more in its own racist, sexist, antilabor, and homophobic image. Furthermore, the work within the existing legal system helps keep alive a memory of the social traces left by past progressive movements of resistance—a memory requisite for future movements. This defensive work, though possibly radical in intent, is *liberal* practice in that it proceeds from within the legal system in order to preserve the effects of former victories threatened by the conservative offensive. Yet this same defensive work has tremendous radical potential—

especially within the context of vital oppositional activity against the status quo. This is why the distinction between liberal and radical legal practice is not sharp and rigid; rather it is fluid and contingent due to the ever-changing larger social situation. Needless to say, the crucial role of this kind of legal practice—be it to defend the rights of activists, secure permits to march, or dramatize an injustice with a class suit—is indispensable for progressive politics. Yet in "cold" moments in American society—when cultural conservatism and big business fuse with power and potency—radical lawyers have little option other than defensive work. This work is often demoralizing, yet it serves as an important link to past victories and a basis for the next wave of radical action.

In our present period, radical legal practice takes two main forms: theoretical critiques of liberal paradigms in the academy that foster subcultures of radical students and professors or participation in radical organizations that engage in extraparliamentary social motion. It is no accident that the first form consists of a pedagogical reform movement within elite institutions of the legal academy. This critical legal studies (CLS) movement is symptomatic of a pessimism regarding feasible radical options in American political culture and a distance between radical legal critiques and radical legal action vis-à-vis the courts. This sense of political impotence and gulf between radical professors of law and radical lawyers results not because CLS consists of insular bourgeois theorists with little grasp of political reality. In fact, their understanding of this reality is often acute. Yet some of the CLS "trashing" of liberalism at the level of theory spills over to liberal legal practice. This spillover is myopic—for it "trashes" the only feasible progressive practice for radical lawyers vis-à-vis the courts. This myopia becomes downright dangerous and irresponsible when aimed at civil rights lawyers for whom the very effort to extend American liberalism may lead to injury or death in conservative America.

Is there any way out of this impasse? Can progressive legal practice be more than defensive? My second claim holds that there are but two ways out. In situations of sparse resources along with degraded self-images and depoliticized sensibilities, one avenue for poor people is existential rebellion and anarchic expression. The capacity to produce social chaos is the last resort of desperate people. It results from a tragic quest for recognition and for survival. The civic terrorism that haunts our city streets and the criminality that frightens us is, in part, poor people's response to political neglect and social invisibility. Like most behavior in U.S. society, it is directly linked to market activity—the buying and selling of commodities. In this case, the commodities tend to be drugs, alcohol, and bodies (especially women's bodies). These tragic forms of expression have yet to take on an explicitly political

character—yet they may in the near future. If and when they do, the prevailing powers will be forced to make *political* responses—not simply legal
ones that lead to prison overcrowding.

One major challenge for progressive politics is to find a way of channeling
the talent and energy of poor people into forms of social motion that can
have impact on the powers that rule. This second way out of the impasse is
the creation of citizens' organized participation in credible progressive projects. Yet American political culture mitigates against this. The status quo
lives and thrives on the perennial radical dilemma of disbelief: it is hard for
ordinary citizens to believe their actions can make a difference in a society
whose resources, wealth, and power are disproportionately held by the big
business community.

The best project progressive politics offered in the eighties was the courageous and exciting presidential campaigns of the charismatic spokesperson
seeking acceptance and respect within the Democratic party: the prophetic
witness of the Reverend Jesse Jackson. Yet his two campaigns reveal the
weakness of American progressive politics: the obsession with televisual visibility alongside little grass-roots organizing beyond elections and the inability
to generate social motion outside electoral politics. In Jackson's case, it also
discloses the refusal to promote democratic practices within one's own organization. Jackson has had a significant and, for the most part, salutary
effect on American progressive politics. The major contribution of his efforts
are that it is the first serious attempt since Martin Luther King, Jr.'s Poor
Peoples' Campaign to constitute a multiracial coalition to raise the issue of
the maldistribution of resources, wealth, and power. Yet, unlike King, Jackson's attempt to highlight this crucial issue is often downplayed or jettisoned
by his quest for entry into the elite groupings of the centrist Democratic
party. Social motion and movements in America tend to be neither rooted
in nor sustained by campaigns for electoral office—no matter how charismatic
the leader.

There can be no substantive progressive politics beyond the extension of
American liberalism without social motion or movements. And despite the
symbolic and cathartic electoral victories of liberal women and people of
color, all remain thoroughly shackled by corporate priorities in the economy
and debt-ridden administrations. Under such conditions, the plight of the
ill-fed, ill-clad, and ill-housed tends to get worse.

With the lethargic electoral system nearly exhausted of progressive potential—though never to be ignored owing to possible conservative politicians
eager for more power—we must look toward civil society, especially to mass
media, universities, religious and political groupings, and trade unions. Despite the decline of popular mobilization and political participation, and the
decrease of unionized workers and politicized citizens, there is a vital and

vibrant culture industry, religious life, student activism, and labor stirrings. In the midst of a market-driven culture of consumption—with its spectatorial passivity, evasive banality, and modes of therapeutic release—there is an increasing sense of social concern and political engagement. These inchoate progressive sentiments are in search of an effective mode of organized expression. Until we create some channels our progressive practice will remain primarily defensive.

How do we go about creating these channels of resistance and contestation to corporate power? What positive messages do we have to offer? What programs can we put forward? This brings me to the third claim regarding the role of law in progressive politics. In a society that suffers more and more from historical amnesia—principally due to the dynamic, past-effacing activities of market forces—lawyers have close contact with the concrete traces and residues of the struggles and battles of the past. This is, in part, what Alexis de Tocqueville had in mind when he called the legal elites America's only aristocracy. Needless to say, he understood continuity with the past in terms of social stability. I revise his formulation to connect continuity with the memory of the effects of progressive victories of the past inscribed in the law of a society whose link with the past is tenuous and whose present is saturated with flashing images, consumer and hedonistic sensibilities, and quick information (much of it disinformation dispensed by unreliable corporate cartels).

The role of progressive lawyers is not only to engage in crucial defensive practices—liberal practice vis-à-vis the courts—but also to preserve, recast, and build on the traces and residues of past conflicts coded in laws. This latter activity is guided by a deep historical sensibility that not only deconstructs the contradictory character of past and present legal decisions or demystifies the power relations operative in such decisions; it also concocts empowering and enabling narratives that cast light on how these decisions constitute the kind of society in which we live and how people resist and try to transform it. Progressive lawyers can be politically engaged narrators who tell analytically illuminating stories about how the law has impeded or impelled struggles for justice and freedom. Like rap artists of the best sort, progressive lawyers can reach out to a demoralized citizenry to energize them with insights about the historical origins and present causes of social misery in light of visions, analyses, and practices to change the world. Lawyers can perform this role more easily than others due to the prestige and authority of the law in American society. Progressive lawyers can seize this opportunity to highlight the internal contradictions and the blatant hypocrisy of much of the law in the name of the very ideals—fairness, protection, formal equality—heralded by the legal system. This kind of progressive legal practice, narrative in character and radical in content, can give visibility and legitimacy to issues neglected by and embarrassing to conservative administrations as well as expose and educate citizens regarding the operations of economic and political powers vis-à-vis the courts. In this regard, historical consciousness and incisive narratives yield immanent critiques, disclose the moral lapses, and highlight the structural constraints of the law while empowering victims to transform society.

Without this kind of historical consciousness and analytical storytelling, it is difficult to create channels for resistance and challenge to corporate power. In addition, there must be an accent on the moral character of the leaders and followers in the past and present who cared, sacrificed, and risked for the struggle for justice and freedom. Progressive lawyers must highlight the *ethical* motivations of those who initiated and promoted the legal victories that further struggles for racial, sexual, and class equality within the limiting perimeters of American law.

The critical legal studies movement is significant primarily because it introduces for the first time in legal discourse a profoundly historicist approach and theoretical orientation that highlights *simultaneously* the brutal realities of class exploitation, racial subordination, patriarchal domination, homophobic marginalization, and ecological abuse in the American past and present. By historicist approach, I mean a candid recognition that the law is deeply reflective of—though not thoroughly determined by—the political and ideological conflicts in American society. By theoretical orientation, I mean a serious encounter with social theories that accent the structural dynamics—of the economy, state, and culture—that shape and are shaped by the law.

Legal formalism, legal positivism, and even legal realism have remained relatively silent about the brutal realities of the American past and present. This silence helped American liberalism remain for the most part captive to cultural conservatism. It also limited radical alternatives in legal studies to extensions of American liberalism. The grand breakthrough of CLS is to expose the intellectual *blinders* of American liberal legal scholarship and to link these *blinders* to the actual blood that has flowed owing to the realities hidden. CLS calls attention to the human costs paid by those who suffer owing to the institutional arrangements sanctioned by liberal law in the name of formal equality and liberty.

Yet CLS cannot be more than a progressive movement within a slice of the professional managerial strata in American society without connections to other social motions in American society. Academic left subcultures have a crucial role to play, yet they do not get us beyond the impasse.

It may well be that American culture does not possess the democratic and libertarian resources to bring about racial, sexual, and class equality. Its cultural conservatism and big business influences may impose insurmountable constraints for such a radical project. Lest we forget, there are roughly three reactionaries (KKK, John Bircherites, etc.) for every leftist in America. Yet it is precisely this kind of cynical—or realistic?—outlook that often confines radicalism to extensions of American liberalism. How does one combat or cope with such an outlook?

There is no definitive or decisive answer to this question. The enabling and empowering response that avoids illusions is to sustain one's hope for social change by keeping alive the memory of past and present efforts and victories and to remain engaged in such struggles owing principally to the *moral* substance of these efforts. As Nietzsche noted (with different aims in mind), subversive memory and other-regarding morality are the principal weapons for the wretched of the earth and those who fight to enhance their plight. This memory and morality in the United States consists of recurring cycles of collective insurgency and violent repression, social upsurge and establishmentarian containment. The American left is weak and feeble during periods of social stability owing to the powers of big business and cultural conservatism; it surfaces in the form of social movements (usually led by charismatic spokespersons) to contest this stability due to their *moral* message that borrows from the nation's collective self-definition (as democratic and free) and to cleavages within big business and culturally conservative groups. The social movements do not and cannot last long; they indeed change the prevailing status quo, but rarely fundamentally rearrange the corporate priorities of American society. In this regard, American radicalism is more than an extension of American liberalism when it constitutes a serious and concrete threat to big business (usually in the call for substantial redistribution of resources, wealth, and power). Yet this threat, though significant, is short-lived owing to repression and incorporation. After such social movements, American radicalism is relegated to a defensive posture, that is, trying to preserve its victories by defending extensions of American liberalism.

If this crude historical scenario has merit, the major role of the law in progressive politics is threefold. First, past victories of social movements encoded in the law must be preserved in order to keep alive the memory of the past, struggle in the present, and hope for the future. Second, this preservation, though liberal in practice, is radical in purpose in that it yearns for new social motion and movements that can threaten the new social stability of big business and cultural conservatism long enough to enact and enforce more progressive laws before repression and incorporation set in. In this regard, radical American legal practice is a kind of Burkean project turned on its head. It fosters tradition not for social stability, but to facilitate threats to the social order; it acknowledges inescapable change not to ensure organic reform but to prepare for probable setbacks and defeats of social movements. Third, the new memories and victories inscribed in new laws are kept alive by the defensive work of progressive lawyers in order to help lay the groundwork for the next upsurge of social motion and movements.

The interplay between the work of progressive lawyers and social change is crucial. In some cases, it is a matter of life or death for charismatic leaders or courageous followers. In other instances, it is a question of serving as the major buffer between the unprincipled deployment of naked state power and "principled" use of the courts against social movements. Such a buffer may prolong these movements and increase their progressive impact on society and culture. The *moral* character of these movements is important precisely because it may make repressive attackers less popular and will more than likely help sustain the memory of the movement more easily. One of the reasons the civil rights movement led by Martin Luther King, Jr., is remembered—more than, say, other equally worthy ones like the CIO-led unionization movement or the feminist movement—is that its *moral* vision was central to its identity and accented by its major spokesperson. Needless to say, this vision appealed to the very ideals that define the national identity of many who opposed the movement.

How do progressive lawyers articulate ideals that may subvert and transform the prevailing practices legitimated by limited liberal versions of these ideals? Progressive legal practice must put forward interpretations of the precious ideal of democracy that call into question the unregulated and unaccountable power of big business; it also must set forth notions of the precious ideal of liberty that lay bare the authoritarian attitudes of cultural conservatism. This two-prong ideological strategy should consist of an unrelenting defense of substantive democracy (in a decentralized, nonstatist fashion) and all-inclusive liberty (as best articulated in the Bill of Rights). This defense is utopian in that it tries to keep alive the possibility of social movements; it is realistic in that it acknowledges the necessity of liberal legal practices for radical lawyers to preserve the gains after social movements have been crushed and/or absorbed.

The possibility of social movements in the 1990s looms large. Eastern Europe has put the spirit of revolution—the quest for substantive democracy and all-inclusive liberty—back on the political agenda. Courageous Chinese students erected a goddess of democracy not to imitate the Statue of Liberty but to put it alongside the statue. The end of colonial rule in Namibia, negotiations in South Africa, electoral activity in Brazil, the reemergence of some semblance of democracy in Chile and free elections in Nicaragua (a country wrecked primarily by an illegal U.S.–sponsored war waged on military and economic fronts)—all partake of this spirit of revolution.

Even in the popular music of the United States during this period of economic decline and cultural decay, a progressive concern for the ill-fed, ill-clad, and ill-housed has surfaced. With solid yet insular academic left subcultures, eager yet sober black, brown, Asian, and red lefts, a battered yet determined labor movement (especially organized public-sector workers), beleaguered yet bold feminist and womanist progressives, scarred though proud gay and lesbian lefts, and the growing number of green and gray activists, united social motion and movements are in the making. What is needed is neither a vanguard party nor purist ideology, but rather a coming-together to pursue the common goals of radical democratic and libertarian projects that overlap. Jesse Jackson's rainbow politics has enlivened the idea of this coming-together. Now it must be enacted—especially locally and regionally—not simply within electoral politics. Democratic leadership of and by ordinary citizens in extraparliamentary modes must flower and flourish. The social stability of the conservative administrations must be bombarded and shaken by democratic demands and libertarian protections. The profits and investments of big businesses should be scrutinized for public accountability and civic responsibility. The xenophobia and jingoism of cultural conservatives have to be morally rejected and judicially checked. A new world is in the making. Let us not allow the lethargy of American politics, the predominance of big business, and the pervasiveness of cultural conservatism to blunt the contributions we can make. Especially if some of us choose the law as the vocational terrain for progressive politics.

THE CONTRIBUTORS

Richard L. Abel is professor of law at UCLA. He is the author of *American Lawyers* and *The Politics of Informal Justice* and president of the Law and Society Association.

Regina Austin is professor of law at the University of Pennsylvania.

W. Haywood Burns is dean of the law school and professor of law at the City University of New York. He is a former president of the National Conference of Black Lawyers and the National Lawyers Guild.

Rhonda Copelon is professor of law at the City University of New York. She is vice president of the Center for Constitutional Rights and has litigated major cases involving reproductive and sexual rights.

Kimberle Crenshaw is professor of law at UCLA. She has written and organized conferences on critical race theory.

Elliott Currie is research associate at the Institute for Study of Social Change at the University of California, Berkeley. He has authored numerous articles and two books, *Confronting Crime* and *America's Problems*.

Sharon Dietrich is a staff attorney representing low-income clients in employment-related cases with Community Legal Services, Philadelphia. The ideas presented in her chapter are hers and her co-author's and do not represent the position of Community Legal Services or the Legal Services Corporation.

Jay M. Feinman is professor of law at Rutgers University, Camden. He has published numerous articles on critical legal studies.

Alan Freeman is professor of law at the State University of New York, Buffalo. He has written extensively on civil rights law and is cosecretary of the Conference on Critical Legal Studies.

Peter Gabel is president and professor of law at the New Collge of California. He is associate editor of *Tikkun* magazine.

Robert W. Gordon is professor of law at Stanford University. He is the author of a forthcoming book, *Lawyers of the Republic,* and many articles on critical legal studies, legal history, and contract law.

Morton J. Horwitz is Charles Warren Professor of American Legal History at Harvard University. He is the author of *The Transformation of American Law, 1780–1860.*

David Kairys is a partner with Kairys & Rudovsky and adjunct professor of sociology at the University of Pennsylvania. He is one of the nation's leading civil rights attorneys and has authored numerous articles on civil rights, civil liberties, and legal theory. In the fall of 1990, he will be professor of law at Temple University.

Mark Kelman is professor of law at Stanford University. He is the author of *A Guide to Critical Legal Studies.*

Duncan Kennedy is professor of law at Harvard University.

Karl E. Klare is professor of law at Northeastern University. He has written numerous articles and practiced in the area of labor law.

Jules Lobel is professor of law at the University of Pittsburgh and a co-operating attorney at the Center for Constitutional Rights. He edited and co-authored *A Less Than Perfect Union: Alternative Perspectives on the Constitution.*

Elizabeth Mensch is professor of law at the State University of New York, Buffalo. She has written extensively on American legal history and is cosecretary of the Conference on Critical Legal Studies.

Frances Olsen is professor of law at UCLA. She is the author and co-author, respectively, of two forthcoming books, *Feminist Jurisprudence* and *Family Law: Legal Concepts and Changing Human Relationships.*

Victor Rabinowitz is a senior partner with Rabinowitz, Boudin, Standard, Krinsky & Lieberman. He is a former president and founding member of the National Lawyers Guild.

Rand E. Rosenblatt is professor of law at Rutgers University, Camden. He is co-author of *American Health Law* and served as special consultant to the court in the Agent Orange settlement case.

David Rudovsky is a partner with Kairys & Rudovsky and senior fellow at the University of Pennsylvania Law School. He is co-author of *Police Misconduct: Law and Litigation.*

Elizabeth M. Schneider is professor of law at Brooklyn Law School.

William H. Simon is professor of law at Stanford University. He has published numerous articles on social welfare and legal ethics.

Nadine Taub is professor of law and director of the Women's Rights Litigation Clinic at Rutgers University, Newark. She is co-author of *The Law of Sex Discrimination* and *Reproductive Laws for the 1990s.*

Mark Tushnet is professor of law at Georgetown University. He is the author of numerous articles and two books, *Red, White, and Blue: A Critical Analysis of Constitutional Law* and *The American Law of Slavery.*

Cornel West is professor of religion and director of the African-American Studies Program at Princeton University. His latest book is *The American Evasion of Philosophy.* He is an honorary chair of Democratic Socialists of America.